Survey of Financial Accounting

Survey of Financial Accounting

GARY L. SCHUGART
University of Houston

JAMES J. BENJAMIN
Texas A&M University

ARTHUR J. FRANCIA
University of Houston

ROBERT H. STRAWSER
Texas A&M University

1993

Dame Publications, Inc.
Houston, TX

© DAME PUBLICATIONS, INC.–1993

All rights reserved. No part of this publication may be reproduced, stored in a retrieval system, or transmitted, in any form or by any means, electronic, mechanical, photocopying, recording, or otherwise, without the prior written permission of the publisher.

ISBN 0-87393-210-2
Library of Congress Catalog Card No. 93-72294

Printed in the United States of America.

Preface

This unique textbook has been prepared for use in an introductory or survey course in accounting. It is ideal for use in a one or a two term first course (depending on the material selected and the depth of coverage desired) at either the undergraduate or graduate level. The text has been written to provide a broad overview of all aspects of accounting from the basic concepts, through the accounting information system to financial statements and special reports, emphasizing the interpretation of these statements and reports. It stresses the analysis of financial accounting data. Fourteen comprehensive chapters have been prepared to permit maximum flexibility in topic selection without any loss of continuity or instructional benefit. The text presents a balanced perspective of practice and theory emphasizing decision making using accounting information. A direct, straightforward approach achieves completeness of coverage using simple but accurate terms, examples and illustrations. SURVEY OF FINANCIAL ACCOUNTING is a usable text geared to the understanding of basic concepts, principles and practices. This unique text emphasizes financial statement understanding and analysis, and decision making using financial information. A wealth of end-of-chapter materials (Summary, Key Definitions, Questions, and Problems) are available to reinforce understanding. A descriptive outline of the text and its contents follows:

1. Introduces the basic accounting concepts and discusses the basic financial statements, including the balance sheet, income statement, and statement of cash flows.

2. Discusses the basic financial statements and introduces the accounting equation.

3. Traces and explains the process of recording transactions, end of period adjustments and the preparation of financial statements.

4. Illustrates the operational differences among companies with special emphasis on the differences between retailing and service organizations and considers the alternative methods for accounting for inventories.

5. Discusses the procedures used for recording, allocating and disposing of long-term assets and the accounting for intangibles and natural resources, including oil and gas accounting. MACRS procedures for computing depreciation for tax purposes are discussed.

6. Considers the issues related to the accounting for firms organized as sole proprietorships and partnerships.

7. Discusses the issues related to the formation of a corporation, the issuance of capital stock and considers matters related to the retained earnings and dividends of a corporation.

8. Discusses the accounting procedures which are used to record and control cash, accounts and notes receivable and current liabilities.

9. Discusses the accounting for bonds payable and investments in corporate securities and explains and illustrates the preparation and use of consolidated financial statements.

10. Discusses and illustrates the basic techniques of analyzing and using the information presented in financial statements.

11. Explains and illustrates the procedures employed in preparing the statement of cash flows.

12. Presents a general discussion of the federal income tax. Explanation and illustration of both interperiod and intraperiod tax allocation are included.

13. Discusses the accounting for foreign currency transactions and foreign currency translation, as well as efforts to achieve uniform international accounting standards.

14. Presents a discussion of disclosures for pensions, other postretirement benefits, leases, segment reporting, interim reporting, management's discussion and analysis, and the auditor's report.

We are indebted to many students and colleagues for their assistance, comments, and constructive criticisms which assisted in making this text a reality. A necessary ingredient in the writing of any textbook is the environment in which the effort took place. Our special thanks go to John M. Ivancevich of the University of Houston, A. Benton Cocanougher, William H. Mobley, William V. Muse and the late John E. Pearson of Texas A&M University for providing us with encouragement in our efforts and with environments in which this book could be created.

We appreciate the permissions received from the American Institute of Certified Public Accountants and the Institute of Management Accountants for allowing us to use selected problem materials from past Uniform CPA

Examinations and CMA Examinations, respectively. Of course, the authors are responsible for any shortcomings of this text.

August, 1993

Gary L. Schugart
James J. Benjamin
Arthur J. Francia
Robert H. Strawser

Contents

0 Prologue xv

Annual Report of PepsiCo, Inc. xxvi

1 Accounting:
An Introduction 1-1

INTRODUCTION. ACCOUNTING AS A PROCESS OF COMMUNICATION. ACCOUNTING VS. BOOKKEEPING. FINANCIAL ACCOUNTING AND MANAGERIAL ACCOUNTING. OBJECTIVES OF FINANCIAL REPORTING. QUALITATIVE CHARACTERISTICS OF ACCOUNTING INFORMATION. Pervasive Constraint. User-Specific Qualities. Ingredients of Primary Qualities. Secondary and Interactive Qualities. Threshold for Recognition. OTHER BASIC ACCOUNTING PRINCIPLES, UNDERLYING ASSUMPTIONS AND CONCEPTS. Entity Assumption. Going-Concern Concept. Monetary Unit Assumption. Stable Dollar Assumption. Time Period Assumption. Historical Cost Concept. Matching Concept. Revenue Realization. Conservatism. Full Disclosure Concept. ELEMENTS OF FINANCIAL STATEMENTS OF BUSINESS ENTERPRISES. Elements. RECOGNITION AND MEASUREMENT IN FINANCIAL STATEMENTS OF BUSINESS ENTERPRISES. The Role of Financial Statements. Recognition and Measurement. DEVELOPING GENERALLY ACCEPTED ACCOUNTING PRINCIPLES. INFLUENCES ON ACCOUNTING PRINCIPLES. American Institute of Certified Public Accountants. The Committee on Accounting Procedure. The Accounting Principles Board. Financial Accounting Standards Board. Securities and Exchange Commission. Internal Revenue Service. Institute of Management Accountants. Governmental Accounting Standards Board. Cost Accounting Standards Board. American Accounting Association. Congress. THE ACCOUNTING STANDARD–SETTING PROCESS. International Aspects. OPPORTUNITIES IN ACCOUNTING. SUMMARY. KEY DEFINITIONS. QUESTIONS.

2 Transaction Analysis:
The Accounting Process 2-1

INTRODUCTION. THE BALANCE SHEET. BALANCE SHEET CLASSIFICATIONS. Assets. Liabilities. Owner's Equity. USES AND LIMITATIONS OF THE BALANCE SHEET. THE INCOME STATEMENT. INCOME STATEMENT CLASSIFICATIONS. THE STATEMENT OF CASH FLOWS. THE FINANCIAL ACCOUNTING PROCESS. Transaction Analysis. The Statement of Cash Flows. STATEMENT OF CAPITAL. SUMMARY. KEY DEFINITIONS. QUESTIONS. EXERCISES. PROBLEMS.

3 The Recording Process 3-1

INTRODUCTION. THE ACCOUNT. THE ACCOUNTING CYCLE. AN ILLUSTRATION. General Journal Entries. Posting. Trial Balance. Adjusting Entries. Posting the Adjusting Entries. Trial Balance After Adjustment. Closing Entries. After-Closing Trial Balance. Financial Statements. ADJUSTING ENTRIES. Prepaid Expenses. Accrued Expenses. Depreciation. Unearned Revenues. Accrued Revenues. COMPARATIVE STATEMENTS. DISCLOSURE TECHNIQUES. AUDITOR'S REPORT. SUMMARY. KEY DEFINITIONS. **APPENDIX:** INTRODUCTION. MODEL OF A FINANCIAL ACCOUNTING SYSTEM. The Chart of Accounts. Coding the Chart of Accounts. The General Journal and General Ledger. Subsidiary Ledgers. Special Journals. An Example—Special Journals and Subsidiary Ledgers. Proving the Control Accounts. Internal Accounting Control. Ethical Issues in Accounting. The Audit Trail. AUTOMATED ACCOUNTING SYSTEMS. Computer Hardware. Computer Software. SUMMARY. QUESTIONS. EXERCISES. PROBLEMS.

4 Merchandising Transactions and Inventories 4-1

INTRODUCTION. ACCOUNTING FOR MERCHANDISING OPERATIONS. Accounting for Cost of Goods Sold. Cost of Merchandise Purchased. Sales of Merchandise. Determination of Cost of Goods Sold and Net Income. OBJECTIVE OF INVENTORY ACCOUNTING. INVENTORY COSTS. PERIODIC AND PERPETUAL INVENTORIES. INVENTORY LOSSES. BASIS OF ACCOUNTING. PURCHASE DISCOUNTS. FREIGHT-IN, RETURNS, AND ALLOWANCES. INVENTORY COST FLOW METHODS. Average-Cost Method. First-In, First-Out (FIFO) Method. Last-In, First-Out (LIFO) Method. Differences in Methods. LOWER-OF-COST-OR-MARKET. GROSS PROFIT METHOD. RETAIL INVENTORY METHOD. SUMMARY. KEY DEFINITIONS. QUESTIONS. EXERCISES. PROBLEMS.

5 Long-Term Assets 5-1

INTRODUCTION. CONTROL OVER TANGIBLE LONG-TERM ASSETS. TYPES OF PLANT AND EQUIPMENT. ACCOUNTING FOR TANGIBLE FIXED ASSETS. DEPRECIATION. ELEMENTS AFFECTING THE DETERMINATION OF PERIODIC DEPRECIATION. Useful Life. Salvage Value. Depreciation Methods. RECORDING LONG-TERM ASSETS. Assets Acquired During the Period. Interest Costs. Disclosure in the Financial Statements. COSTS INCURRED AFTER ACQUISITION. DISPOSALS OF PLANT AND EQUIPMENT. TRADE-INS. PLANT AND EQUIPMENT IN THE FINANCIAL STATEMENTS. NATURAL RESOURCES. Depletion Base and Amortization. Accounting for Oil and Gas Producers. INTANGIBLE ASSETS. Disclosure of Intangibles. SUMMARY. KEY DEFINITIONS. QUESTIONS. EXERCISES. PROBLEMS.

6 Unincorporated Business Organizations 6-1

INTRODUCTION. THE SOLE PROPRIETORSHIP. Accounting for a Proprietorship. THE PARTNERSHIP. Characteristics of a Partnership. Evaluation of the Partnership Form of Organization. Accounting for a Partnership. Formation of a Partnership. Division of Profits and Losses. Partnership Financial Statements. Admission of a Partner. Withdrawal of a Partner. LIQUIDATION OF THE PARTNERSHIP. SUMMARY. KEY DEFINITIONS. QUESTIONS. EXERCISES. PROBLEMS.

7 The Corporation: Capital Stock, Earnings, and Dividends 7-1

INTRODUCTION. CHARACTERISTICS OF THE CORPORATION. FORMING A CORPORATION. CAPITAL OF A CORPORATION. NATURE OF CAPITAL STOCK. RIGHTS OF STOCKHOLDERS. STOCK ISSUANCE COSTS. PAR VALUE AND NO-PAR VALUE. ISSUANCE OF PAR VALUE STOCK. ISSUANCE OF STOCK FOR NONCASH ASSETS. ISSUANCE OF NO-PAR STOCK. SUBSCRIPTIONS FOR CAPITAL STOCK. STOCKHOLDERS' EQUITY IN THE BALANCE SHEET. RETAINED EARNINGS. NATURE OF EARNINGS. EXTRAORDINARY ITEMS. DISCONTINUED OPERATIONS. PRIOR-PERIOD ADJUSTMENTS. ACCOUNTING CHANGES. EARNINGS PER SHARE. DIVIDENDS. Important Dates Related to Dividends. Cash Dividends. Stock Dividends. STOCK SPLITS. TREASURY STOCK. RETAINED EARNINGS. Appropriation of Retained Earnings. Statement of Retained Earnings. BOOK VALUE PER SHARE OF COMMON STOCK. SUMMARY. KEY DEFINITIONS. QUESTIONS. EXERCISES. PROBLEMS.

8 Cash Receivables, and Current Liabilities 8-1

INTRODUCTION. CASH RECEIPTS. CASH DISBURSEMENTS. THE BANK RECONCILIATION STATEMENT. PETTY CASH FUNDS. RECEIVABLES. CLASSIFICATION OF RECEIVABLES AND PAYABLES. CONTROL OVER RECEIVABLES. ACCOUNTS RECEIVABLE. UNCOLLECTIBLE RECEIVABLES. Bad Debts as a Percentage of Sales. Bad Debts as a Percentage of Receivables. Balance Sheet Presentation. Writing-Off an Uncollectible Account. CURRENT LIABILITIES. Liabilities. NOTES RECEIVABLE AND PAYABLE. Issuance of the Note. Accrual of Interest. Payment of the Note. Dishonored Note. Notes Issued at a Discount. Discounting Notes Receivable. STATEMENT PRESENTATION OF RECEIVABLES. PAYROLL ACCOUNTING. SUMMARY. KEY DEFINITIONS. QUESTIONS. EXERCISES. PROBLEMS.

9 Long-Term Liabilities Investments, and Consolidated Financial Statements 9-1

INTRODUCTION. BOND OBLIGATIONS. CLASSES OF BONDS. Issuance of Bonds. Bonds Issued at Face Value. Issuance Between Interest Dates. Issuance of Bonds at a Discount. Issuance of Bonds at a Premium. Convertible Bonds. RETIREMENT OF BONDS. BOND SINKING FUND. RESTRICTION ON DIVIDENDS. BALANCE SHEET PRESENTATION. INVESTMENTS IN CORPORATE SECURITIES. INVESTMENTS IN BONDS. Amortization of Premium. Amortization of Discount. Sale of Bonds. INVESTMENTS IN STOCK. Temporary Investments. Control Over Investments. Accounting for Acquisition of Temporary Investments. Valuation of Temporary Investments. Long-Term Investments in Stock. DISCLOSURES ON FAIR VALUE. CONSOLIDATED FINANCIAL STATEMENTS. Consolidated Balance Sheet at Date of Acquisition. Consolidated Balance Sheet after the Date of Acquisition. OTHER RECIPROCAL ACCOUNTS. POOLING OF INTERESTS. USEFULNESS OF CONSOLIDATED STATEMENTS. CONSOLIDATED INCOME STATEMENT. MINORITY INTEREST. PROFIT ON INTERCOMPANY SALES. SUMMARY. KEY DEFINITIONS. QUESTIONS. EXERCISES. PROBLEMS. **APPENDIX A—Interest and Present Value Concepts.** INTRODUCTION. INTEREST. PRESENT VALUES OF A FUTURE SUM. COMPOUND INTEREST AND PRESENT VALUE ON A SERIES OF EQUAL PAYMENTS. APPLICATION OF PRESENT VALUE CONCEPTS TO BONDS PAYABLE. ACCOUNTING FOR PREMIUM OR DISCOUNT ON BONDS—THE INTEREST METHOD. Bonds Sold at a Premium. Bonds Sold at a Discount. Table A-1: Present Value of $1.00. Table A-2: Present Value of Annuity of $1.00 Per Period. EXERCISES. **APPENDIX B—Mark to Market—FASB Statement No. 115.** FASB STATEMENT NO. 115. Held to Maturity. Trading Securities. Securities Available for Sale. EXERCISES.

10 Financial Statement Analysis 10-1

INTRODUCTION. COMPARATIVE FINANCIAL STATEMENTS. BASIC ANALYTICAL PROCEDURES. Horizontal Analysis. Vertical Analysis. Common-Size Statements. RATIO ANALYSIS. Comparison with Standards. ANALYSIS FOR COMMON STOCKHOLDERS. Rate of Return on Total Assets. Rate of Return on Common Stockholders' Equity. Earnings Per Share of Common Stock. Price-Earnings Ratio on Common Stock. Debt-to-Equity Ratio. ANALYSIS FOR LONG-TERM CREDITORS. ANALYSIS FOR SHORT-TERM CREDITORS. Current Ratio. Acid-Test or Quick Ratio. Analysis of Accounts Receivable. Analysis of Inventories. INTERPRETATION OF ANALYSES. SUMMARY. KEY DEFINITIONS. QUESTIONS. EXERCISES. PROBLEMS.

11 The Statement of Cash Flows 11-1

INTRODUCTION. IMPORTANCE OF CASH FLOWS. A BRIEF HISTORY. ALL FINANCIAL RESOURCES CONCEPT. THE STATEMENT OF CASH FLOWS. Cash from Operations. Preparation of the Statement of Cash Flows. Change in Cash. Changes in Noncash Accounts. The Statement of Cash Flows. Worksheet Approach. Additional Problems in the Analysis of the Statement of Cash Flows. SUMMARY. KEY DEFINITIONS. QUESTIONS. EXERCISES. PROBLEMS.

12 Income Tax Considerations 12-1

INTRODUCTION. THE FEDERAL INCOME TAX. CLASSES OF TAXPAYERS. INDIVIDUAL FEDERAL INCOME TAX. CORPORATE INCOME TAX. DIFFERENCES BETWEEN ACCOUNTING INCOME AND TAXABLE INCOME. Interperiod Tax Allocation. Allocation of Income Tax Within a Period. INCOME TAXES AND MANAGEMENT DECISIONS. SUMMARY. KEY DEFINITIONS. QUESTIONS. EXERCISES. PROBLEMS. **Appendix**

13 International Accounting 13-1

INTRODUCTION. FOREIGN CURRENCY TRANSACTIONS. Spot and Forward Exchange Markets. Import-Export Transactions. Imports Single Time Period. Imports-Multiple Time Periods. Exports. Hedging. FOREIGN CURRENCY TRANSLATION. Basic Illustration of Translation. UNIFORMITY OF ACCOUNTING PRINCIPLES. Differences in Accounting Standards. Standard-Setting Bodies. SUMMARY. KEY DEFINITIONS. QUESTIONS. EXERCISES. PROBLEMS.

14 Accounting for Pensions, Postretirement Benefits, and Leases and Analysis of Other Disclosures 14-1

INTRODUCTION. PART I: PENSIONS, POSTRETIREMENT BENEFITS, AND LEASES. PENSIONS AND OTHER POSTRETIREMENT BENEFITS. Pensions. Other Postretirement Benefits. LEASES. PART II: ANALYSIS OF OTHER DISCLOSURES. FOOTNOTE DISCLOSURE. Significant Accounting Policies. Changes in Accounting Principle. Contingencies. Description of Liabilities Outstanding–Credit Agreements. Information Regarding Stockholder's Equity. Long-Term Commitments. Subsequent Events. Other Useful Disclosure. THE AUDITOR'S REPORT AS AN INFORMATION DISCLOSURE. Scope of the Audit. The Opinion. INTERIM REPORTING. REPORTING FOR SEGMENTS OF A BUSINESS. Problems in Providing Segment Data. Disadvantages to the Reporting Company. Determining Reportable Industry Segments. Foreign Operations and Export Sales. Usefulness of Segment Data. MANAGEMENT'S DISCUSSION AND ANALYSIS. SUMMARY. KEY DEFINITIONS. QUESTIONS. EXERCISES.

Prologue

INTRODUCTION

One of your friends, Bill Kilmer, has been paying for his college education by working at various construction jobs on a part-time basis while going to school. Just before the end of the spring semester, Bill decided to form his own small business, Kilmer Contractors. He began the business by investing his small savings and obtaining a loan from his parents for the balance of the funds needed to start the business. Bill was quite pleased with his initial month's operations. He painted several houses with the help of two classmates who worked with him on a part-time basis. In addition, the prospects for additional future work seemed to be excellent. Bill was able to repay some of the money he borrowed from his parents and was also able to withdraw enough money from the business to pay his tuition for the forthcoming summer school.

Bill decided to go to the local bank and apply for a loan. He planned to use the proceeds from the bank loan to repay the balance of the loan from his parents and also to maintain sufficient cash to continue and, hopefully, even expand his operations over the summer months. He felt he would be able to devote more time to his business this summer since he planned to take only a single course during the summer session.

The loan officer at the bank asked Bill to complete an application form and after a brief discussion of the business, its operations and its future prospects he asked Bill to prepare financial statements for Kilmer Contractors.

MAY 19X1

Sun	Mon	Tue	Wed	Thu	Fri	Sat
			1 began business with savings of $500	**2** borrowed $5,000 from Mom + Dad	**3**	**4**	**5** bought an old truck $3,000
6	**7**	**8**	**9**	**10** cabinet - agreed to paint 3 received $3 package	**11**	**12** took $60 to paint provisions for	**13**
	14	**15** repaid to Mom + Dad $1,000	**16**	**17** painted - finished received $700	**18**	**19** painted - finished received $900 cash	**20**
	21	**22**	**23**	**24**	**25** paid employees $1,500	**26**	**27**
	28	**29**	**30**	**31** painted 3 (houses) silo (see again)			

Bank Statement

Billy Kilmer
919 Park Lane
Bryan, Texas 77802

CUSTOMER NUMBER	
02020769 00	
STATEMENT PERIOD	
FROM	TO
05/01/x1	05/31/x1
PAGE NUMBER	1
ENCLOSURES	

ACCOUNT NUMBER	TOTAL DEBITS		TOTAL CREDITS		FEE	CLOSING BALANCE
PREVIOUS BALANCE	NO.	AMOUNT	NO.	AMOUNT		
.00	4	7,100.00	4	9,500.00	.00	2,400.00

* * * * * *   CHECKING ACCOUNT ACTIVITY   * * * * * * * * * * *

```
                            PREVIOUS BALANCE--                    .00

--------------------------------DEPOSITS--------------------------------
DATE           NUMBER         AMOUNT
05/01          001              500.00
05/02          002            5,000.00
05/10          003            3,300.00
05/17          004              700.00

--------------------------------CHECKS---------------------------------
DATE           NUMBER         AMOUNT
05/05          001            3,000.00
05/12          002              600.00
05/15          003            2,000.00
05/25          004            1,500.00

-----------------------------DAILY BALANCE-----------------------------
DATE           BALANCE
05/01            500.00
05/02          5,500.00
05/05          2,500.00
05/10          5,800.00
05/12          5,200.00
05/15          3,200.00
05/17          3,900.00
05/25          2,400.00
```

While Bill had no formal recordkeeping system, he had recorded all of the activities of Kilmer Contractors in a diary-calendar. Using this source and his bank statement for the month of May he prepared the following financial statement for the loan officer.

Kilmer Contractors
Financial Statement
May, 19x1

Cash received	$9,500
Cash paid out	7,100
Cash balance	$2,400

Bill left the statement and his application with the loan officer's secretary. He was told that he would receive a response the next day.

The loan officer called Bill, as promised, but stated that he would need additional (and more detailed) information about Kilmer Contractors and its operations before he could make a decision on the loan.

Bill took copies of his calendar-diary and his May bank statement to the loan officer, hoping that this would satisfy the loan officer's request for more detailed information.

After reviewing the additional information provided by Bill and making a few quick calculations, the loan officer told Bill that he could not approve a loan to Bill (and Kilmer Contractors). He explained that the results of operations for May simply did not justify the loan request.

Bill was both upset and confused. He had been confident that the loan would be approved by the bank. After all, he had asked for a loan of only $3,000 and Kilmer Contractors had "made" a total of $2,400 in cash during May. At that rate, and given its future prospects, he felt the company would easily make at least 12 times $2,400 or $28,800 in its first year.

Knowing that you plan to major in business administration, Bill comes to you for your advice and help. He outlines his company's success to date and recounts for you his disappointing experience with the loan officer. Bill also provides you with a copy of both his calendar-diary and his bank statement for the month of May.

You want to help your friend Bill. Unfortunately, as you explained to him, you have not yet taken any course work in business, much less in accounting.

After talking further with Bill, reviewing the information that he provided to you and talking briefly with the loan officer at the bank, you decide that what is needed is to assemble the information in a format that will show, in detail, both the current status of the company, Kilmer Contractors, and a history of its operations to date. But, where to begin?

DETAILS OF CASH RECEIPTS AND DISBURSEMENTS

As a starting point, it was decided to examine the details underlying the "Financial Statement" for May 19x1, prepared by Bill Kilmer and previously submitted to the loan officer. This statement, along with the diary-calendar and the bank statement for the month of May 19X1, was used to obtain the details of the cash receipts and payments for May 19X1 for Kilmer Contractors. The analysis is presented below.

Cash received:		
Bill Kilmer's investment on May 1		$ 500
Loan from Mr. and Mrs. Kilmer on May 2		5,000
Received from customers:		
Agreed to paint 3 houses on May 10	$3,300	
Painted house on May 17	700	4,000
Total cash received in May		$9,500
Cash payments:		
For supplies on May 5		$3,000
To owner on May 12		600
To repay loan on May 15		2,000
To employees on May 25		1,500
Total cash disbursements		$7,100
Excess of cash received		
over cash payments		$2,400

TENTATIVE INCOME STATEMENT

A careful review of the cash receipts and disbursements of Kilmer Contractors indicated that several items probably should be excluded from the statement which was intended to show the history of the company's operations to date. These items, with a brief explanation of the reason(s) for excluding them, follow:

Receipts:

1. Bill Kilmer's investment on May 1 of $500—since this was money "put up" by the owner to start the business (hopefully a one-time item) rather than money earned by Kilmer Contractors during the month of May, it is inappropriate to include this item in the income statement.

2. Loan from Mr. and Mrs. Kilmer on May 2 of $5,000—because this is an interest-free loan (again, hopefully a one-time item) rather than money earned by the business during May, it is inappropriate to include this item in the statement.

Payments:

1. Payment to owner on May 12 of $600—since this is a withdrawal made by the owner to pay a non-business item (summer school tuition) rather than an expense of the business for May, it is inappropriate to include this item in the statement.

2. Payment on loan on May 15 of $2,000—because this is a partial repayment of the loan to the business made by Mr. and Mrs. Kilmer rather than an expense of the business for May, it is inappropriate to include this item in the statement. (Recall that Mr. and Mrs. Kilmer made an interest-free loan to Kilmer Contractors of $5,000 on May 2).

After excluding the above items, the tentative income statement was as follows:

Kilmer Contractors
Tentative Income Statement
For the Month of May, 19x1

Received from customers		$4,000
Paid for supplies	$3,000	
Paid to employees	1,500	
Total expenses		4,500
Loss for May		($ 500)

REVISED INCOME STATEMENT

Needless to say, Bill Kilmer was less than pleased with the statement shown above, since it indicates that Kilmer Contractors had experienced a loss of $500 for its May 19X1 operations. Examining this statement, along with the diary-calendar and the bank statement for May, suggested that several modifications of the tentative income statement should be made to more accurately depict the operations of Kilmer Contractors for May 19X1. These modifications, along with an explanation of the reason(s) for them, are as follows:

Receipts:

1. Decrease receipts from customers by $2,200 (2/3 x $3,300) since this represents the portion of the $3,300 total payment made on May 10 by a customer which Kilmer has not earned. The customer paid $3,300 for Kilmer to paint three houses. As of May 31, only one of the three houses has been painted. Kilmer "owes" these services to his customer, he has not yet "earned" this $2,200. He has earned $1,100 for the one house he painted during May.

2. Increase receipts from customers by $900 since this represents the amount that Kilmer earned (although not yet received in cash from the customer) on May 19 when he painted a house. He feels certain that he will receive payment in June.

After these modifications, the revenue (a term substituted for receipts in the statement because not all items earned had been received in cash) from customers was as follows:

1.	May 17–amount received from customer for painting house	$ 700
2.	May 19–amount to be received from customer for painting house	900
3.	May 31–one-third of the $3,300 advance payment for painting 3 houses made by the customer on May 10. One of the 3 houses was painted on May 31	1,100
	Revenue from customers	$2,700

Note that the $2,700 revenue from customers includes only amounts that had actually been earned by Kilmer Contractors by painting houses during the month of May. The $700 from the house painted on May 17 was received on that date. The $900 from the house painted on May 19 was earned even though the customer had not yet paid Kilmer for the work. The $1,100 from the house painted on May 31 was one-third of the $3,300 advance payment made by a customer on May 10. It was decided to focus on amounts *earned* during the month of May 19X1 by Kilmer Contractors in preparing the revised income statement rather than cash receipts for May since Kilmer Contractors had been paid before (1/3 of $3,300 or $1,100), at the time of ($700), and after ($900) the time the work was actually done. Revenues, then, are the amounts *earned* but not necessarily received in cash by the business during May

A similar analysis was made of Kilmer's cash payments.

Payments:

1. Decrease the amount paid for supplies from $3,000 to $1,000 since the $3,000 payment made on May 5 included the cost of supplies which were unused and still on hand at May 31. The cost of these unused supplies was estimated to be $2,000.

After this adjustment, the expenses (a term substituted in the statement for payments because not all payments made in cash had been used up as of May 31) were as follows:

1.	May 5—one-third of the $3,000 payment for painting supplies representing the portion of the supplies actually used during May (approximately $2,000 of unused supplies were estimated to be on hand at May 31)	$1,000
2.	May 25—amount paid to employees for all of their work in May	1,500
	Expenses for May	$2,500

The $2,500 in expenses for May included only items that were actually used during May (supplies used of $1,000, and $1,500 in salaries earned by employees). The timing of the payment of cash for expenses was not considered to be important for purposes of determining income for the month. (As an aside, it was noted that if an expense had been incurred but not paid—for example a bill for May expenses paid in cash during June—it would be included in the determination of income for May). The critical factor is when the item is incurred (used or consumed), not when the cash is paid out.

The revised statement that presents the revenues earned, expenses incurred, and resulting net income (excess of revenues over expenses) for Kilmer Contractors for the month of May 19X1 was as follows:

Kilmer Contractors
Income Statement
For the Month Ending May 31, 19x1

Revenues from painting services		$2,700
Supplies used	$1,000	
Salaries	1,500	
Total expenses		2,500
Income for May		$ 200

STATEMENT OF FINANCIAL POSITION

Satisfied that the above "income statement" provides an adequate history of the operating results of the company for the month of May, 19x1, the focus turned to the current status of Kilmer Contractors. Basic questions to be answered seemed to be: (1) what does the company own; and, (2) what does it owe?

The analysis of Kilmer Contractors' current position at May 31, 19x1, proved to be much easier than the analysis of its operations for May, 19x1.

Owned by the company:

1. Cash of $2,400—this was the amount shown in both Kilmer Contractors' checkbook and on the bank statement for May. (Bill had previously checked all deposits made in May and checks written in May to the bank statement and all of these items had been recorded by the bank during May).

2. The $900 owed to Kilmer Contractors by the customer who had his house painted on May 19.

3. The $2,000 cost of unused supplies which were on hand at May 31, 19X1.

Owed by the company:

1. The $3,000 balance owed to Mr. and Mrs. Kilmer for the loan that they made to Kilmer Contractors on May 2, 19X1. (The original amount of the loan was $5,000.) A payment of $2,000 was made to the Kilmers by Kilmer Contractors on May 15, reducing the balance to $3,000.

2. After some thought, it was decided to list the $2,200 advance payment for painting two houses as an amount owed. On May 10, a customer paid $3,300 to Kilmer for painting three houses at some future date. Kilmer was able to paint one of the houses in May and planned to paint the other two during the summer. Although Kilmer Contractors did not "owe" the $2,200 in the sense that it had to pay the customer $2,200 in cash, it did "owe" a debt to the customer in the context that it had an obligation to paint two houses at a future date and had already received payment in advance for this work.

Using the available information and the above analysis, the following statement was constructed.

Kilmer Contractors
May 31, 19x1

Owns:		Owes:	
Cash in bank	$2,400	Advance payment from customer	$2,200
Payment due from customer	900	Loan from Mr. and Mrs. Kilmer	3,000
Supplies on hand	2,000	Total owed	$5,200
Total owned	$5,300		

Reviewing the above statement, it appeared that since the company *owned* resources of $5,300 and *owed* obligations totaling $5,200, Kilmer Contractors was presently "worth" $100 ($5,300 less $5,200). This amount seemed to be rather low, so it was decided to carefully examine the details of Bill Kilmer's investment in Kilmer Contractors.

OWNER'S INVESTMENT

After a review of the analyses outlined above, the diary-calendar and the bank statement for May, it was concluded that Bill Kilmer's investment or ownership of Kilmer Contractors was affected by three transactions or events.

1. The original investment of $500 made on May 1 to begin the business and open its bank account.

2. The withdrawal of $600 made by Bill on May 12 to pay his summer school tuition.

3. The $200 income earned by the business in May. (See the income statement for details of the company's revenues and expenses).

Using these three transactions, the following statement of owner's investment was prepared.

Kilmer Contractors
Statement of Owner's Investment
May 31, 19x1

Original investment	$500
Add: Income for May	200
Deduct: Owner's withdrawal	(600)
Owner's investment at May 31	$100

It seemed logical that Kilmer's original investment should be increased by the company's income for May (since Bill is the sole owner) and decreased by his withdrawal because he took these funds from the business for his personal use.

REVISED STATEMENT OF FINANCIAL POSITION

At this point, it was noted that the investment by Bill Kilmer was exactly equal to the "worth" of the company, as previously determined. It was decided to incorporate this relationship in the statement of financial position.

Kilmer Contractors
Statement of Financial Position
May 31, 19x1

Owned:			Owed:			
Cash in bank	$2,400		Advance payment by customer	$2,200		
Payment due from customer	900		Loan from Mr. and Mrs. Kilmer	3,000	$5,200	
Supplies on hand	2,000		Owner's investment		100	
	$5,300				$5,300	

Based on the available information and the analysis reported above, it was decided to submit the following financial report for Kilmer Contractors to the loan officer.

Kilmer Contractors
Statement of Financial Position
May 31, 19x1

Owned:		Owed:		
Cash	$2,400	Advances from customer	$2,200	
Due from customer	900	Loan from Kilmers	3,000	$5,200
Supplies	2,000	Owner's investment		100
	$5,300			$5,300

Kilmer Contractors
Income Statement
For the Month Ending May 31, 19x1

Revenue from painting services		$2,700
Supplies used	$1,000	
Salaries	1,500	2,500
Income for May		$ 200

Kilmer Contractors
Statement of Owner's Investment
May 31, 19x1

Original investment	$500
Add: Income for May	200
Deduct: Owner's withdrawal	(600)
Owner's investment At May 31	$100

Kilmer Contractors
Income Statement
For the Month Ending May 31, 19x1

Revenue from painting services		$2,700
Supplies used	$1,000	
Salaries	1,500	2,500
Income for May		$ 200

Kilmer Contractors
Statement of Owner's Investment
May 31, 19x1

Original investment	$500
Add: Income for May	200
Deduct: Owner's withdrawal	(600)
Owner's investment At May 31	$100

Kilmer Contractors
Statement of Cash Receipts and Payments
For the Month Ending May 31, 19x1

Cash received:	
From customers	$4,000
From loan	5,000
From owner	500
Total cash received	$9,500
Cash payments:	
For supplies	$3,000
To employees	1,500
To repay loan	2,000
To owner	600
Total cash payments	$7,100
Increase in cash	$2,400

TO THE STUDENT: The example used in this Prologue is repeated in Chapter 2 where each individual transaction is analyzed in terms of its effect(s) on the financial statements. In Chapter 3, the same example is again used and each individual transaction is analyzed, recorded and processed as it would be done in an accounting information system. Needless to say, you will become very familiar with the operations of Kilmer Contractors and, hopefully, with the preparation of financial statements and the processing of accounting information.

Annual Report for PepsiCo, Inc.

Financial Highlights
(dollars in millions except per share amounts)

	Fifty-two Weeks Ended December 26, 1992	December 28, 1991	Percent Change
Net sales	$21,970	19,292	+14
Beverages	$ 7,606	6,915	+10
Snack Foods	$ 6,132	5,250	+17
Restaurants	$ 8,232	7,127	+16
Segment operating profits	$ 2,502	2,196	+14*
Beverages	$ 799	863	− 7*
Snack Foods	$ 985	757	+30*
Restaurants	$ 719	576	+25*
Income before cumulative effect of accounting changes	$ 1,302	1,080	+21
Per Share	$ 1.61	1.35	+19*
Cumulative effect of accounting changes	$ (927)	—	—
Per Share	$ (1.15)	—	—
Net income	$ 374	1,080	−65*
Per Share	$ 0.46	1.35	−66*
Cash dividends declared—Per Share	$ 0.51	0.46	+11
Net cash provided by continuing operations	$ 2,712	2,430	+12
Purchases of property, plant and equipment for cash	$ 1,550	1,458	+ 6
Cash dividends paid	$ 396	343	+15
Acquisitions and investments in affiliates for cash	$ 1,210	641	
Return on average shareholders' equity	% 23.9	20.7	

*These comparisons are affected by unusual items, including restructuring charges in both 1992 and 1991 and the impact on 1992 results of adopting new accounting rules for retiree health benefits and income taxes. See "Business Segments" on page 28 for detail of unusual items.

Return on average shareholders' equity was calculated using income before cumulative effect of accounting changes.

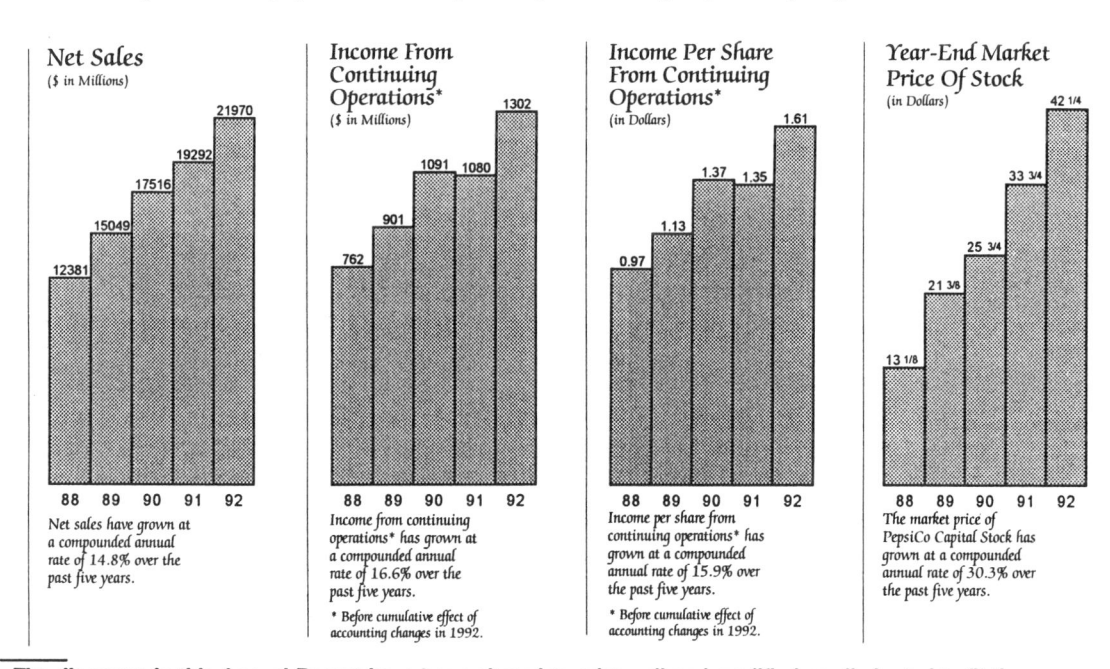

Net Sales ($ in Millions)
Year	Value
88	12381
89	15049
90	17516
91	19292
92	21970

Net sales have grown at a compounded annual rate of 14.8% over the past five years.

Income From Continuing Operations* ($ in Millions)
Year	Value
88	762
89	901
90	1091
91	1080
92	1302

Income from continuing operations* has grown at a compounded annual rate of 16.6% over the past five years.

* Before cumulative effect of accounting changes in 1992.

Income Per Share From Continuing Operations* (in Dollars)
Year	Value
88	0.97
89	1.13
90	1.37
91	1.35
92	1.61

Income per share from continuing operations* has grown at a compounded annual rate of 15.9% over the past five years.

* Before cumulative effect of accounting changes in 1992.

Year-End Market Price Of Stock (in Dollars)
Year	Value
88	13 1/8
89	21 3/8
90	25 3/4
91	33 3/4
92	42 1/4

The market price of PepsiCo Capital Stock has grown at a compounded annual rate of 30.3% over the past five years.

The diagrams in this Annual Report have been altered to print well and modified or eliminated to fit the page.

Dear Friends:

When a big, successful corporation like PepsiCo is really humming, we respond to consumers like a great dancer reacts to music.

We're alert to each note. Our steps are fluid and powerful. We might not be as pretty as "Swan Lake," but to me we have a beauty all our own.

Unfortunately, it isn't always that way. Success has a tendency to slow you down and make you timid. Then, if the marketplace suddenly changes, you might find yourself dancing to yesterday's hit tune.

That's why flexibility is such a central part of PepsiCo's management philosophy. We're not big on layers of management—too slow. We resist centralization—too confining. Local managers have a remarkable amount of authority and power—because they're the ones closest to our customers.

That vision, at the core of PepsiCo, has generated outstanding results for 27 years. Earnings have grown an average 15% a year and our performance has actually accelerated as we've grown bigger.

This year's annual report puts PepsiCo's "flexible" management philosophy at center stage, because it's really what keeps us on our toes. More later, but first a review of 1992.

1992 in Review

We had an excellent year. Sales and ongoing operating profits climbed sharply. But because we adopted some required noncash accounting changes and took some one-time restructuring charges, the reported earnings disguise some great results.

Some highlights:

- Excluding these unusual items, net income rose 21% to $1.4 billion and earnings per share increased 20% to $1.80.
- Sales reached $22 billion, an increase of 14%.
- Dividends per share increased 11% to $0.51, marking our 21st consecutive year of dividend growth.
- The price of a share of PepsiCo stock increased 25%, far exceeding the S&P Industrials' growth of 3%.
- All our lines of business achieved double-digit sales growth, with beverages up 10%, snack foods up 17% and restaurants up 16%.
- All our lines of business achieved strong ongoing profit growth, with beverages up 12%, snack foods up 19% and restaurants up 19%.
- Cash from operations increased 12% to a record $2.7 billion.

Most important, during 1992 we continued to reshape our core businesses, dancing to the ever-changing tune of the marketplace. This reshaping gives us a jump on the future, which is, of course, the whole point of the "flexible corporation."

Further into this report, in the operating review section, we describe some of what we achieved in 1992 and our overall strategy. I also provide some perspective on future opportunity.

Here, I'd like to discuss the vision that motivates our actions.

The Philosophy of the Flexible Corporation

Maybe some corporations have succeeded over the years without changing much, but I doubt if they sell consumer products. The marketplace just won't let you stand still.

As a category leader, we have to dance as fast as we can, always developing new ideas to keep the consumer interested. At the same time, because we don't have a monopoly on imagination, we must respond to new ideas from our competitors. Who would have thought that clear soft drinks would become hot in the 1990s? I certainly didn't, but consumers did.

All of which says consumer products companies have to constantly fight rigidity and inertia, two natural by-products of size and success.

In our battle to beat the dark side of bigness, PepsiCo works to create a highly charged corporate atmosphere that's motivating and, at the same time, nonthreatening. You can't punish people for making mistakes and still expect them to be innovative. You've got to be supportive and encourage them to learn from mistakes.

At our best, we've been able to cultivate a kind of free flowing, flexible management style that can really get things done. The right controls remain, but without thousands of hidebound rules, battalions of supervisors and mountains of paperwork. Instead, we've tried to dispense large doses of personal responsibility to everyone in the organization.

When we get it right, we flourish. The atmosphere keeps us fast, flexible and consumer focused.

How are we doing? Well, we measure our "flexibility quotient" on three levels: Our skill at adjusting broad corporate strategy to meet new business conditions, the adaptability of our operating divisions to marketplace changes and, most important, the willingness of employees to really stretch to satisfy their customers.

Here are some examples:

Bending in New Directions

PepsiCo made an important and far-reaching adjustment in our corporate strategy in the mid-1980s. Up until then, almost all of our profits came from the U.S.—all very solid, safe and reassuring. But with one exception: potential for growth. Because only 5% of the world's population lives in the U.S., we thought it was just too small a base from which to grow.

We began to expand internationally. Since that time, we've invested over $5 billion in our international businesses. Today, about 20% of our operating profits come from outside the U.S. and our investments give us a strong base for far greater growth in the coming decades.

For us, global expansion has been a big jump forward.

Adjusting the Operating Divisions

At the division operating level, we did much more.

As the 1980s began to fade, we noticed subtle shifts in the marketplace. There were distant rumblings. It wasn't that consumers wanted less quality. They just wanted to pay less money. They also wanted much more service and plenty of exciting new products.

Though sales and profits were booming, we thought it time to take new steps. Every single operating division took it upon itself to confront this new challenge. In some cases, we needed to restructure. In all cases, basic assumptions were held up to the light, re-evaluated and redefined.

The most publicized example was Taco Bell. Back in 1988, Taco Bell had a significant market insight. They saw high prices driving consumers out of

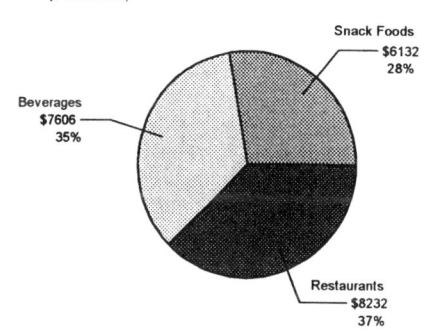

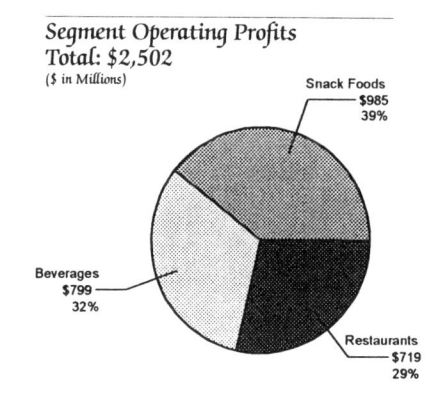

Net Sales
Total: $21,970
($ in Millions)

- Snack Foods — $6132 — 28%
- Beverages — $7606 — 35%
- Restaurants — $8232 — 37%

Segment Operating Profits
Total: $2,502
($ in Millions)

- Snack Foods — $985 — 39%
- Beverages — $799 — 32%
- Restaurants — $719 — 29%

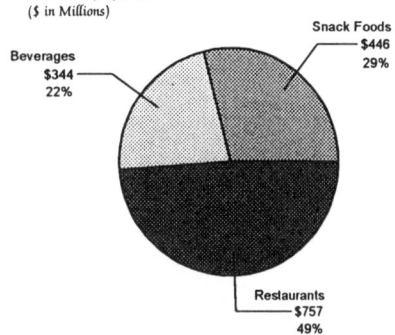

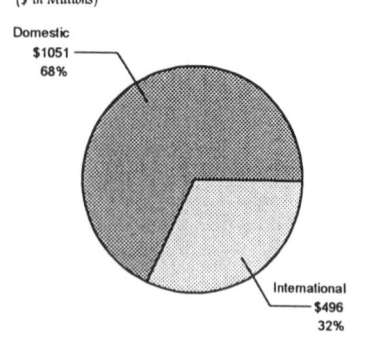

quick service restaurants. A family of four could easily spend more than $20 for lunch at some quick service restaurants. Hardly a good deal.

Taco Bell had a powerful one word answer: "Value." That meant radically reduced prices coupled with *higher* quality and *improved* service. To produce this triple play, Taco Bell totally reorganized its business.

Out went management layers; in came empowered restaurant managers. Taco Bell developed new technology to improve efficiency and slash costs. Performance standards were raised and operations streamlined.

The rest is history. Taco Bell changed the direction of the quick service restaurant business and doubled its system sales in just four years.

PepsiCo's other operating divisions danced to a similar tune.

At Frito-Lay and Pepsi-Cola we reorganized, targeting improved customer service, lower costs and increased operating efficiency. Frito-Lay totally revised the quality standards for its major products, improving taste, texture and appearance. Pepsi-Cola is turning itself "Right Side Up" to better serve customers.

KFC also made big changes. Faced with older restaurants, a narrow product line and an outdated reputation, KFC began to introduce new snackable items and other products. Service was improved and its image upgraded substantially.

Pizza Hut, starting in the mid-1980s, changed its business mission, going from a pizza restaurant operation to a "pizza distribution company." In the years since, they've "pizza-ized" much of America, expanding through delivery, carry-out and kiosks.

It's all called *flexibility*. Being able to move with grace, poise and confidence. And the results can be downright breathtaking. Over the past five years, each of our three lines of business more than doubled ongoing profits.

In sum, flexibility is not just a phrase or catchword. It's a true business building strategy that vastly increases competitiveness and makes us grow.

Flexibility on a Human Scale

Even though PepsiCo has demonstrated great flexibility in both market and organizational strategy, the real test is up close and personal, where it counts. The question: Do PepsiCo employees live the philosophy of flexibility in day-to-day business transactions? Here's our answer.

A while back, one of our KFC managers in Manhattan, Rudy Edghill, received a call from a customer complaining that his carry-out order was wrong. He ordered one thing—but arrived home with something else.

When the complaint came in, Rudy could have shrugged his shoulders and apologized. But that's not Rudy. He jumped into a taxi, raced through Manhattan streets and personally handed the correct order to the customer.

All corporations dream about this kind of initiative, but seldom get it. The reason: Too many controls and too much supervision stifle the people on the scene. They feel restricted, intimidated or bored. Fortunately for us, Rudy trusted his supervisor enough—and his company—to know he wouldn't be second-guessed.

To me, that's the very definition of a flexible corporation.

Incidentally, the KFC customer called back the next day and ordered 75 additional meals for a party that weekend. Flexibility has its rewards.

What It Takes

At PepsiCo, two strong beacons of light guide our day-to-day activities and encourage corporate flexibility. First is a very strong commitment to business results. Second is a high level of corporate and personal integrity.

Segment Capital Spending
Total: $1,547
($ in Millions)

- Snack Foods $446 — 29%
- Beverages $344 — 22%
- Restaurants $757 — 49%

Segment Capital Spending
Total: $1,547
($ in Millions)

- Domestic $1051 — 68%
- International $496 — 32%

Commitment to results is pretty obvious. You can't have much success without excellent individual performance by lots of people. But it's integrity that really makes the difference.

Independent actions, no matter how good, are only effective if they are choreographed into something powerful. That requires teamwork and selflessness, both unattainable without an exceptional degree of integrity throughout the organization.

We mean more than basic honesty, important as that is. We mean things such as candor and openness, even collegiality. We mean a deep-seated sense of confidence and a unity of purpose with your fellow workers, your boss, your division president—everyone. You trust in your colleagues, you trust in your company, and you trust in your collective ability to win the future.

That's how you get a flexible corporation. And, it's to that which PepsiCo aspires.

A Word of Appreciation

Of course, it's always people who get you where you want to go. In that regard, I want to thank our more than 370,000 employees, our franchisees, our business partners and our suppliers. I also want to thank the people who make it all possible—those customers and consumers who buy our products.

A special thanks goes to one of PepsiCo's most "flexible" long-time executives, Board Member Michael Jordan, who retired this year. He will be greatly missed.

Joining our Board is P. Roy Vagelos, M.D., chairman of the board, president and chief executive officer of Merck & Co., Inc. Pretty flexible himself, Roy's been a great help already and we welcome him with open arms.

On a very sad note, just prior to publication of this report, Bob Enright, our vice president of taxes, died in a tragic accident. Bob made an enormous contribution to PepsiCo. He was an extraordinary business leader and a great friend.

A final thought to our shareholders: Martha Graham once said that "nothing is more revealing than movement." True enough, even with corporations. We think movement—gracefully and artfully directed—will reveal growing prosperity for our investors. Last year was great and 1993 should be, too. One thing about flexibility: It allows us to bend over backwards on your behalf.

Wayne Calloway
Wayne Calloway
Chairman of the Board and Chief Executive Officer

Return on Average Shareholders' Equity*
(Percent)

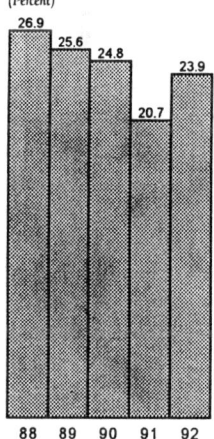

88	89	90	91	92
26.9	25.6	24.8	20.7	23.9

*Based upon income from continuing operations (before cumulative effect of accounting changes in 1992).

Beverages

Pepsi-Cola North America
Pepsi-Cola International

A Well-Positioned Past

Back at the turn of the century, when soft drinks were a novelty, our consumers were satisfied with one soft drink—Pepsi-Cola—and one way of buying it—at the soda fountain.

As our consumers changed and wanted more variety, we added new channels of distribution, more packages and soft drinks: Diet Pepsi, Mountain Dew, Caffeine Free Pepsi, Caffeine Free Diet Pepsi, Slice and Mug brands.

Along the way, we expanded into international markets and began distributing 7UP and Mirinda brands outside the U.S.

Aided by lifestyle changes, better-tasting diet products and the "cola wars," the U.S. soft drink industry grew.

By 1991, soft drinks were a $47 billion retail business in the U.S., but growth had begun to slow down. U.S. consumers were increasingly seeking variety in soft drinks. And a new category of beverages containing natural ingredients, without preservatives—a category that's become known as "new age" beverages—was emerging.

Outside the U.S., the situation was very different. Most people were just beginning to enjoy soft drinks, so providing convenient packaging and increasing distribution were key challenges.

An Adaptable Present

Faced with these challenges, we recognized we had to do several things to ensure continued growth. In the U.S., we had to improve customer focus while increasing efficiency, and we had to respond to the broadening "new age" beverage market.

Outside the U.S., we had to invest in the business to increase the kinds of packaging we offered and to accelerate distribution of our products.

Here are some highlights of what we did to pursue these strategies in 1992 and some of our achievements.
- U.S. sales were up 6%, and profits, excluding unusual items, were up 10%.
- International sales and profits, excluding unusual items, were up 22%.
- Worldwide retail sales of our beverage products reached nearly $28 billion.
- International volume was up 7%, including double-digit growth in key markets such as Mexico, Saudi Arabia and Argentina. We also achieved double-digit growth in important emerging markets such as Pakistan, India, China and Poland.
- In the U.S., we're reshaping our organization to be "Right Side Up," so that the entire company is dedicated to meeting customer needs. The new organization eliminates layers of supervision, creates more efficient work processes and enables us to serve customers better.
- In the U.S., the brand Diet Pepsi campaign—"You've Got The Right One Baby, Uh Huh!"—helped convince consumers to buy Diet Pepsi. Video Storyboards named Ray Charles, the campaign's star singer, the most persuasive celebrity spokesperson.
- Pepsi launched its "Gotta Have It" campaign for brand Pepsi. During the summer, 40 million "Gotta Have It" cards were distributed in the U.S. They provided cardholders with discounts on a range of consumer products.
- In the U.S., we introduced "Get Vertical," our new advertising for brand Mountain Dew. The first network television commercial for brand Diet Mountain Dew—"Do Diet Dew"—was aired. Combined Mountain Dew brands volume climbed 8%.
- We formed a partnership with Thomas J. Lipton Co., owner of the number one tea trademark in the U.S. In May, we introduced Lipton ready-to-drink teas in unsweetened and sweetened versions. In September, we launched two flavors: raspberry and peach.
- We entered an agreement to distribute single-serve bottles and cans of Ocean Spray products in the U.S. Ocean Spray is the number

($ In Millions)	Domestic	International	Total
Sales	$5,485	$2,121	$7,606
% Change	+6	+22	+10
Profits	$ 687	$ 112	$ 799
% Change	−8*	−4*	−7*

*These comparisons are affected by unusual items. See page 28.

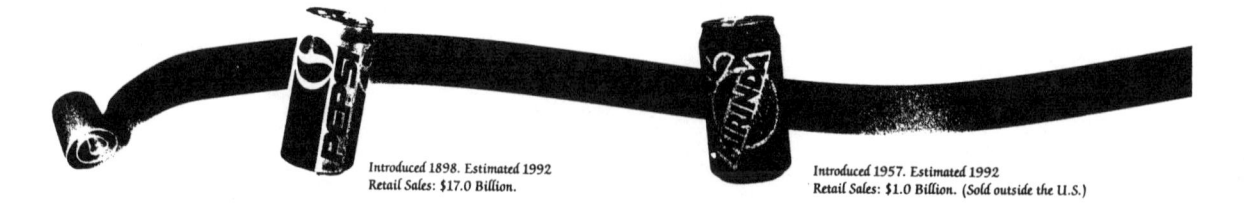

Introduced 1898. Estimated 1992 Retail Sales: $17.0 Billion.

Introduced 1957. Estimated 1992 Retail Sales: $1.0 Billion. (Sold outside the U.S.)

Beverages Net Sales
% Of Total Net Sales
($ in Millions)

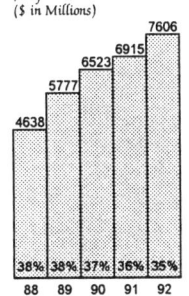

Year	Value	%
88	4638	38%
89	5777	38%
90	6523	37%
91	6915	36%
92	7606	35%

Beverages Operating Profits
% Of Total Segment Operating Profits
($ in Millions)

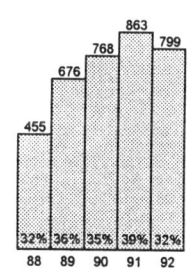

Year	Value	%
88	455	32%
89	676	36%
90	768	35%
91	863	39%
92	799	32%

Beverages Capital Spending
% Of Total Segment Capital Spending
($ in Millions)

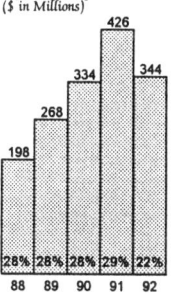

Year	Value	%
88	198	28%
89	268	28%
90	334	28%
91	426	29%
92	344	22%

one non-refrigerated juice trademark in supermarkets.
• We expanded distribution of our All Sport isotonic sports drink to a quarter of the U.S.
• In the U.S., we increased sales of our H2Oh! sparkling water and began distributing Avalon, a still water.
• We introduced brand Crystal Pepsi, a unique-tasting clear cola with 100% natural flavors, no caffeine and no preservatives, in the U.S. Crystal Pepsi was named one of the best new products of 1992 by Time magazine.
• Outside the U.S. and Canada, we continued to build our reputation among the world's youth by featuring pop singing star Michael Jackson in our advertising and sponsoring his worldwide concert tour.
• We introduced Diet Pepsi in eight additional countries. Diet Pepsi is now available in about 75 countries and territories.
• We formed a joint venture with Eastman Chemical and two local companies in the Republic of Belarus, in the Commonwealth of Independent States, to produce plastic for beverage bottles. Light, convenient bottles make it easier to carry our products home.
• We introduced our plastic returnable bottle (PRB) in Austria, Finland and Sweden. This unbreakable, environmentally sound bottle is now in 12 countries and is generating double-digit volume gains almost everywhere it's been introduced.
• We entered a new vending partnership with PepsiCo Foods International and Mars Confections in Europe.
• We strengthened our international business via acquisitions totaling about half a billion dollars during 1992. We entered into new joint ventures in Mexico, Japan, Australia and Cambodia.
• In early fiscal 1993, in Spain, we acquired Kas S.A., owner of several of that country's most popular fruit-flavored beverage brands. We also bought out our joint venture partner, Knörr Elorza S.A., which manufactures and distributes Pepsi-Cola and Kas products.
• We entered the Israeli market through a franchise agreement with Tempo Beer Industries, one of that country's largest beverage producers. We quickly captured more than 15% of the market.
• Early in 1993, we began testing a breakthrough product called Pepsi Max in two international markets. Our new brand has a unique blend of sweeteners (not yet approved for use in the U.S.) that delivers maximum cola taste in a no-sugar product. Developed exclusively for the international market, we expect Pepsi Max to appeal to consumers who want the full taste of regular cola without the sugar.

A Flexible Future...
A Chairman's View:

As you can see, we're doing a lot that's new in pursuit of continuous, accelerated growth.

To me, we've effectively accomplished two big things over the past

Introduced 1964. Estimated 1992 Retail Sales: $4.3 Billion.

Acquired 1964. Estimated 1992 Retail Sales: $2.4 Billion.

Introduced 1984. Estimated 1992 Retail Sales: $600 Million.

couple of years: we've expanded the scope of our domestic beverage business and we've created a strong base for accelerated international growth. That gives me great confidence that we can continue to grow our beverage business for decades to come.

Think of it this way: There are some 5.3 billion thirsty people in the world. In the U.S., each person drinks about 183 gallons of liquids per year. If international consumers drank liquids at the U.S. rate, and we provided just 3% of their needs, our beverage system would be four times as big as it is today.

We're aiming a lot higher than that.

We expect our move in the U.S. from a traditional carbonated soft drink company to a total beverage company, along with international expansion, to provide strong growth in 1993.

Management's Analysis

(See "Management's Analysis — Overview" on page 26 and "Business Segments" on page 28.)

1992 vs. 1991

Worldwide net sales increased 10% to $7.6 billion. Domestic sales rose $314 million (6%) to $5.5 billion. Excluding acquisitions of franchised bottling operations, domestic sales grew $134 million (3%). This growth was driven by higher packaged product and fountain syrup pricing to retailers and higher concentrate pricing to franchised bottlers.

International sales rose $377 million (22%) to $2.1 billion. Excluding acquisitions of franchised bottling operations, principally in Canada, sales grew $186 million (11%). This growth reflected concentrate price increases, led by Latin America, and the combined impact of volume gains and higher pricing in existing bottling operations. About $30 million of the sales increase came from growth in concentrate shipments. The favorable translation impact of a weaker U.S. dollar contributed about $25 million to the sales gain.

Beverage retail sales volume is measured in system bottler case sales (case sales), consisting of sales by company-owned and franchised bottlers to retailers of packaged products and fountain syrup. Domestic case sales increased 1% over 1991, driven by gains in the Mountain Dew brands and the new brand Crystal Pepsi and Lipton tea products, partially offset by a decline in brand Pepsi. Case sales of fountain syrup grew at a faster rate than packaged products. International case sales rose 7%, due to growth in almost all key markets, with a double-digit increase in Mexico, the largest market in case sales, partially offset by declines in Brazil and Canada. Emerging markets in Asia and Eastern Europe also aided case sales growth.

Worldwide operating profits declined 7% to $799 million. Excluding $167.4 million in 1992 unusual items, profits were up 12%. The unusual items were comprised of $145 million in restructuring charges ($115.4 million for domestic and $29.6 million for international) and $22.4 million in incremental expenses due to adopting new accounting rules. The domestic charge relates to an organizational restructuring designed to improve customer focus by realigning resources consistent with Pepsi-Cola's "Right Side Up" operating philosophy and to a redesign

U.S. Consumption in Pepsi-Cola's Beverage Categories
Pepsi-Cola Share

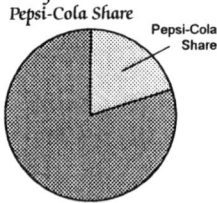

Pepsi-Cola's beverage categories, including soft drinks, tea, bottled water and juices, accounted for about 40% of all beverages consumed. Pepsi-Cola products were about 20% of these combined categories.

U.S. Soft Drink Industry Retail Sales
Pepsi-Cola Share

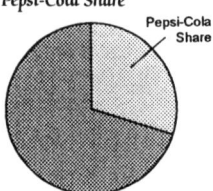

U.S. retail sales of soft drinks exceeded $47 billion. Pepsi-Cola brands account for nearly one-third of the industry.

Beverages

Acquired 1986. Estimated 1992 Retail Sales: $151 Million.

Acquired 1986. Estimated 1992 Retail Sales (Diet and Regular): $1.8 Billion. (PepsiCo owns brand 7UP outside the U.S.)

U.S. Soft Drink Consumption
(Gallons Per Capita)

U.S. soft drink consumption reached 48 gallons per person.

U.S. Soft Drink Industry Case Sales Growth in Supermarkets vs. Pepsi-Cola System Growth 1992

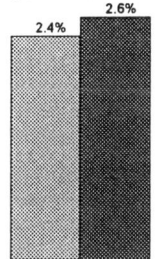

Industry: 2.4%
Pepsi-Cola: 2.6%

Pepsi-Cola's carbonated soft drink volume in U.S. supermarkets grew faster than the industry.

of key administrative and business processes. The organizational restructuring was completed in 1992 and the redesign of core processes is currently underway. Implementation of the redesigned processes is expected to begin in 1994. The charge includes provisions for costs associated with redeployed and displaced employees, the redesign of core processes and office closures. The international restructuring charge includes $18.5 million to streamline a newly acquired Spanish franchised bottling operation, which was formerly a joint venture. The remaining $11.1 million represents costs associated with streamlining the worldwide field management organization. These restructuring actions, when fully implemented, are expected to result in annual domestic and international savings approximating $105 million and $14 million, respectively, providing additional resources to reinvest in the businesses and strengthen Pepsi-Cola's worldwide competitive position. The new accounting rules for retiree health benefits and income taxes resulted in incremental expenses of $16.1 million (almost all domestic) and $6.3 million (all domestic), respectively. Total 1993 expense for retiree health benefits is projected to be approximately $12 million less than the total 1992 expense due to the impact of recent plan amendments described in Note 11.

Worldwide profits included amortization of intangible assets (principally domestic) of $138 million in 1992 and $118 million in 1991. This increase reflects the impact of the new income tax accounting rules and acquisitions.

Domestic profits declined 8% to $686 million. Excluding the 1992 unusual items, profits grew $78 million (10%). This growth was driven by higher prices that exceeded cost increases. The higher costs reflected growth in operating and administrative expenses, partially offset by lower ingredient and packaging costs. Acquisitions added $11 million to profit growth. The domestic profit margin, excluding the 1992 unusual items, grew one-half point to 15.0%.

International profits decreased 4% to $112 million. Excluding the 1992 unusual items, profits increased $25 million (22%). Higher concentrate shipments added about $20 million and acquisitions contributed $8 million to profit growth. The net impact of concentrate price increases that exceeded higher operating expenses, led by Latin America, also contributed to the increase. Profits fell in bottling operations in Canada, reflecting declines in industry sales and intense competitive activity. Profits included gains on sales of assets of $3.1 million in 1992 and $5.7 million in 1991. The international profit margin, excluding the 1992 unusual items, was unchanged at 6.7%.

In 1992, Pepsi-Cola entered into a new, lower cost, long-term supply agreement for NutraSweet brand aspartame sweetener with its current supplier. The new agreement begins in 1993. Because of the dynamics of the highly competitive beverage industry, management cannot reasonably predict the effects, if any, of the new agreement on future operating profits of the segment.

Recent Introductions

1991 vs. 1990

Worldwide net sales increased 6% to $6.9 billion. Domestic sales rose $137 million (3%) to $5.2 billion. The domestic advance reflected acquisitions of franchised bottlers, which contributed $122 million, and higher concentrate pricing that was partially offset by lower prices to retailers in bottling operations.

International sales grew $255 million (17%) to $1.7 billion. Of this increase, acquisitions of franchised bottlers, principally in Canada, contributed $76 million and volume growth provided about $65 million, led by higher concentrate shipments to Latin America and Canada and finished product sales to franchisees in Japan. The balance of the growth was primarily due to higher prices led by Latin America.

Domestic case sales were about even compared to 1990, but rose 2% excluding the impact of the Burger King fountain business lost to a competitor in 1990. This performance was driven by gains in the Mountain Dew and Diet Pepsi brands, partially offset by a decline in brand Pepsi. International case sales increased 6%, but rose 8% excluding the impact of the halt in August 1990 of concentrate shipments to franchised bottlers in Iraq. This performance was driven by double-digit growth in Latin America led by Argentina. Case sales growth was aided by emerging markets such as India and China.

Worldwide operating profits advanced 12% to $863 million. Excluding 1990 unusual charges of $10.5 million for receivables exposures related to highly leveraged domestic retail customers, profits were up 11%.

Worldwide profits included amortization of intangible assets (principally domestic) of $118 million in 1991 and $111 million in 1990.

Domestic profits rose 11% to $746 million. Excluding the 1990 unusual charges, profits grew $62 million (9%). Acquisitions of franchised bottlers provided $7 million of this increase. The balance of the profit growth reflected higher concentrate prices and lower ingredient costs, partially offset by higher marketing costs and lower prices in bottling operations. The domestic profit margin, excluding the 1990 unusual charges, grew almost one point to 14.4%.

International profits increased $23 million (25%) to $117 million. This performance reflected about $15 million from higher concentrate shipments and $5.7 million in gains on asset sales, consisting of the sale to a third party of certain notes receivable previously written-off and the sale of an unused concentrate plant. Price increases were largely offset by higher operating and marketing expenses led by Latin America. The international profit margin increased by almost one-half point to 6.7%.

International Soft Drink Industry Case Sales
Pepsi-Cola and 7UP Share

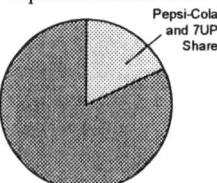

Pepsi-Cola and 7UP brands are available in 155 countries and territories outside the U.S. and account for nearly 18% of the international soft drink industry.

International Soft Drink Consumption vs. U.S. Consumption
(Gallons Per Capita)

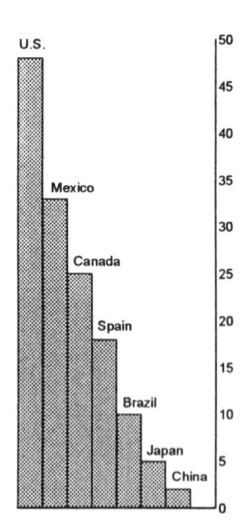

Annual per capita consumption of soft drinks around the world is low compared to U.S. rates.

Snack Foods

Frito-Lay, Inc.
PepsiCo Foods International

A Well-Positioned Past

For as long as most people can remember, Frito-Lay has been the biggest snack chip company in the U.S. The company started about 60 years ago with two brands—Fritos corn chips and Lay's potato chips. Chee·tos brand cheese flavored snacks came next and then Doritos tortilla chips, our biggest brand in the U.S. By the end of the 1980s, we had eight of the 10 largest-selling snack chip brands in the U.S.

Very early on, we realized that there was great opportunity to replicate Frito-Lay's success worldwide. By 1966, we were in six markets outside the U.S. and in some, like Mexico, we had enormous success. In the 1980s, we decided to commit major resources to international snacks and we embarked on an aggressive acquisition program. By 1991, our snack foods were available in 23 countries.

While PepsiCo's success with snack foods was extraordinary, we faced a number of challenges as we entered the 1990s. In the U.S., the market was becoming more competitive, in terms of both price and product quality.

Worldwide, we saw tremendous opportunity to enter new markets, but we also needed to integrate some large acquisitions, just as recessions hit key international markets.

An Adaptable Present

The strategies we are using to meet these challenges are multifaceted.

First, to meet the increased competition, we reorganized our domestic business in 1991 to streamline it and focus more on our customers. Then, we improved the quality of our potato chip brands, and we marketed them more aggressively than ever before.

Overseas, we began building our business through acquisitions and by entering into business partnerships that would provide greater distribution of our products as well as develop new products. At the same time, we began restructuring some of our existing operations.

In 1992, we took many actions in support of these strategies, and we achieved excellent results. Here are some highlights and some of our achievements.

- U.S. sales were up 6%. Profits, excluding unusual items, were up 13%.
- Driven by acquisitions, international sales and profits, excluding unusual items, were up 44%.
- Worldwide retail sales of our snack brands reached nearly $11 billion. U.S. retail sales reached nearly $5.6 billion. International system retail sales exceeded $5.0 billion.
- U.S. snack chip pound volume was up 7%. International systemwide snack chip kilo volume was up 2%.
- In the U.S., we added 11,000 accounts and more than 460 routes. Our marketing activities resulted in some 14,000 additional supermarket displays and 12 additional miles of shelf space.
- We significantly improved the quality of our leading potato chip brands, Lay's and Ruffles, making them tastier, crispier and crunchier.
- Frito-Lay staged "Doritos Day," where in 24 hours over 13,000 Frito-Lay employee volunteers distributed more than five million samples and free coupons for new Nacho Cheesier Doritos brand tortilla chips in 11,000 retail outlets.
- We introduced two new varieties of Doritos brand tortilla chips, two new sizes of Tostitos brand tortilla chips and a new flavor of Sunchips brand multigrain snacks.
- We expanded our distribution through non-traditional channels. For example, in the U.S., Sunchips brand multigrain snacks and Rold Gold brand pretzels are now served to travelers flying on American Airlines.
- We paved the way for major growth in Europe. PepsiCo Foods International (PFI) formed a joint venture with General Mills, Inc. The new company, Snack Ventures Europe, is the continent's largest snack chip company. It combines our snack businesses in Spain, Portugal

($ In Millions)	Domestic	International	Total
Sales	$3,950	$2,182	$6,132
% Change	+6	+44	+17
Profits	$ 776	$ 209	$ 985
% Change	+26*	+49*	+30*

*These comparisons are affected by unusual items. See page 28.

Fritos — Introduced 1932. Estimated 1992 Retail Sales: $604 Million.

Lay's — Introduced 1938. Estimated 1992 Retail Sales: $966 Million.

Snack Foods Net Sales
% Of Total Net Sales
($ in Millions)

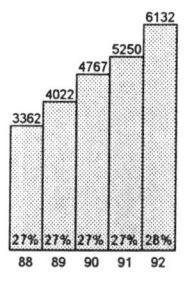

88	89	90	91	92
3362	4022	4767	5250	6132
27%	27%	27%	27%	28%

Snack Foods Operating Profits
% Of Total Segment Operating Profits
($ in Millions)

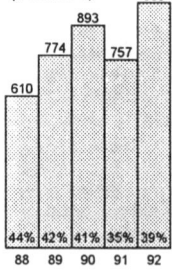

88	89	90	91	92
610	774	893	757	985
44%	42%	41%	35%	39%

Snack Foods Capital Spending
% Of Total Segment Capital Spending
($ in Millions)

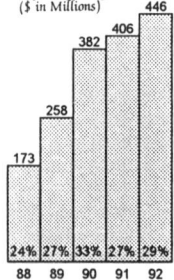

88	89	90	91	92
173	258	382	406	446
24%	27%	33%	27%	29%

and Greece with the snack businesses of General Mills in France, Belgium and the Netherlands. The new venture will develop new products, as well as market existing PFI and General Mills brands.
- In Canada, we bought out our joint venture partner in Hostess Frito-Lay, Canada's number one snack chip company.
- In Mexico, we now have a controlling interest in our Gamesa cookie business.
- We launched 34 snack chip products in international markets. This included everything from our global brands such as Ruffles brand potato chips in Poland to specialty products like Fonzies brand corn snacks in Chile.
- We continued to build our international cookie and confectionery businesses. Today, these snacks account for about one-fourth of international system retail sales.

A Flexible Future...
A Chairman's View:

I see an extraordinary future for our snack food business. Frito-Lay's ability to continue to improve its products and come out with new products shows me we have great momentum.

Overseas, we're currently bucking some rough economies, but we're factoring that into our plans and working to be the low cost competitor.

Most important, we now have a structure in place that allows us to really build the business in our key international countries. For example, we're consolidating our Smiths and Walkers businesses in the United Kingdom and we're improving efficiency at Gamesa in Mexico.

Our snack food products are now available in 27 countries. But that's only about one-sixth of the countries where our beverages are available, so you can be sure we'll be increasing our presence throughout the world.

I see snacks continuing to grow in 1993 and for years to come.

Management's Analysis

(See "Management's Analysis — Overview" on page 26 and "Business Segments" on page 28.)

1992 vs. 1991

Worldwide net sales rose 17% to $6.1 billion. Domestic sales grew $213 million (6%) to $4.0 billion. The domestic increase was driven by volume growth, which contributed about $265 million, partially offset by the impact of lower gross prices and an unfavorable package size mix shift. Promotional price allowances, which declined from last year's level, are reported as marketing expenses and therefore do not reduce reported sales. International sales rose $670 million (44%) to $2.2 billion. Comparisons are affected by acquisition activity that included buying out PepsiCo's joint venture partners at Hostess Frito-Lay (Canada) and Arnott's (Australia) and securing controlling interests in the Gamesa (Mexico) and Wedel (Poland) sweet snack businesses, as well as the absence of results of a small business to be disposed (collectively, "net acquisitions"). Excluding the impact of net acquisitions, international sales grew $75 million (5%). This growth was driven by higher prices, partially offset by an estimated $15 million impact of lower volumes.

Total domestic pound sales advanced 7%, led by Lay's and Ruffles brands potato chips, Tostitos brand tortilla chips and Sunchips brand multigrain snacks. These increases were partially offset by a decline in Santitas and Doritos brands tortilla chips, Fritos brand corn chips and Chee·tos brand cheese flavored snacks. The relative performances of potato and corn products in 1992 were due partly to a weather-related potato crop shortage last year.

Total international snack chip kilo volume, excluding net acquisitions, decreased 1% led by a double-digit decline in Brazil and reflecting a small decline in the U.K. offset by a small increase in Mexico. This volume performance includes only operations consolidated for at least one year. Due to the recent significant changes in the ownership of PepsiCo's snack chip businesses, including the Canada and Australia joint venture buy-outs and the contribution of PepsiCo's previously consolidated businesses in Spain, Portugal and Greece to the new joint venture with General Mills, Inc., this traditional volume measure has become less meaningful. Systemwide volume performance, which includes volume for both consolidated and joint venture businesses operated for at least one year, will be an important measure going forward. For 1992, systemwide snack chip volume grew 2% led by double-digit growth in Canada.

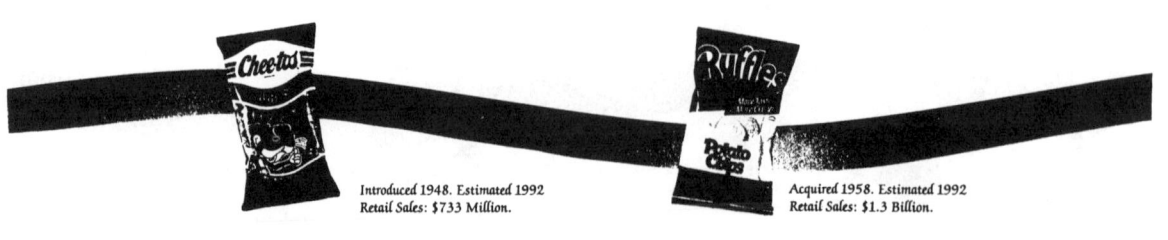

Cheetos
Introduced 1948. Estimated 1992 Retail Sales: $733 Million.

Ruffles
Acquired 1958. Estimated 1992 Retail Sales: $1.3 Billion.

Snack Foods

Worldwide operating profits increased 30% to $1.0 billion. Excluding unusual items in both 1992 and 1991, profits increased 19%. Unusual items in 1992 totaled $71.1 million, comprised of $40.3 million in international charges for restructuring actions, the largest component of which is for consolidating and streamlining the Smiths and Walkers businesses in the U.K., and $30.8 million in incremental expenses due to adopting the new accounting rules for retiree health benefits ($28.2 million, almost all domestic) and income taxes ($2.6 million, all international). The restructuring actions, when fully implemented, are expected to result in annual savings of about $35 million, providing additional resources for reinvestment in the businesses to strengthen competitive positions. Total 1993 expense for retiree health benefits is projected to be approximately $24 million less than the total 1992 expense due to the impact of recent plan amendments described in Note 11. Unusual charges in 1991 totaled $127 million, comprised of $91.4 million and $35.6 million for restructuring actions designed primarily to streamline operations of the domestic and international snack food businesses, respectively.

Worldwide profits included amortization of intangible assets (almost all international) of $41 million in 1992 and $36 million in 1991, with the increase due to acquisitions.

Domestic profits rose 26% to $776 million. Excluding the 1992 and 1991 unusual items, profits increased $96 million (13%). Volume growth contributed about $160 million to profits. Raw material savings, reflecting lower costs for potatoes, packaging and cooking oils, and lower administrative expenses resulting from the 1991 restructuring actions also aided profit growth. The favorable comparison for potato costs, which are at the lowest level in the past five years, reflects the 1991 cost increase resulting from a weather-related crop shortage. These benefits were partially offset by higher operating expenses and other manufacturing costs, including costs associated with improving potato chip quality. An unfavorable sales mix shift as well as lower net prices, reflecting lower gross prices that exceeded the impact of a lower level of promotional price allowances, also hampered profit growth. The domestic profit margin, excluding the 1992 and 1991 unusual items, rose nearly one and one-half points to 20.3%.

International profits increased 49% to $209 million. Excluding the net acquisitions, which contributed $52 million to profits, and the 1992 and 1991 unusual items, profits increased $25 million (14%). This growth reflected price increases that exceeded higher operating costs, partially offset by an estimated $10 million impact of lower volumes. Double-digit profit growth in Mexico and the U.K. was partially offset by a decline in Brazil, due primarily to lower volumes. Profit growth in Mexico primarily reflected price increases that exceeded higher costs. In the U.K., the combined benefit of price increases and the 1992 cost savings from the restructuring actions announced last year was offset by higher product costs and the impact of lower volumes. As a result, the profit growth was driven by lower pension expense

U.S. Snack Food Industry Retail Sales Frito-Lay Share

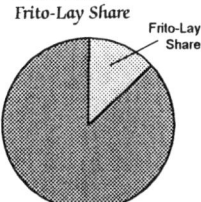

U.S. retail sales of snack foods, such as chips, candy, cookies, nuts and other items, totaled more than $44 billion. Frito-Lay's share was $5.6 billion, about 13%.

U.S. Snack Chip Industry Retail Sales Frito-Lay Share

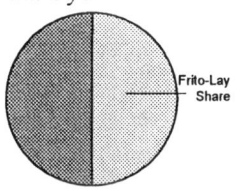

U.S. retail sales of snack chips reached more than $10 billion. Frito-Lay's share was about half.

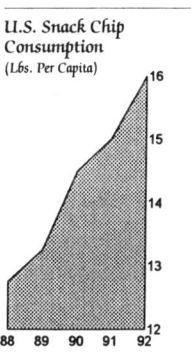

U.S. Snack Chip Consumption (Lbs. Per Capita)

U.S. snack chip consumption climbed to 16 pounds per person.

Acquired 1961. Estimated 1992 Retail Sales: $122 Million.

Introduced 1966. Estimated 1992 Retail Sales: $1.2 Billion.

Introduced 1981. Estimated 1992 Retail Sales: $357 Million.

U.S. Snack Chip Industry Pound Sales Growth in Supermarkets vs. Frito-Lay Growth 1992

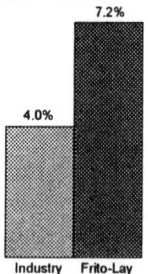

Industry: 4.0%
Frito-Lay: 7.2%

Pound sales of Frito-Lay snack chip products in U.S. supermarkets grew 7.2%, compared with snack chip industry growth of 4.0%.

PFI System Wholesale Sales 1992

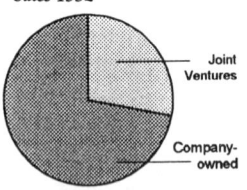

Joint Ventures / Company-owned

Company-owned operations represented 72% and joint ventures represented 28% of PFI system wholesale sales of $3.9 billion, assuming all 1992 acquisition and joint venture activity took place at the beginning of the year. PFI joint venture ownership is principally 50% or more.

International Snack Chip Industry Retail Sales PFI System Share

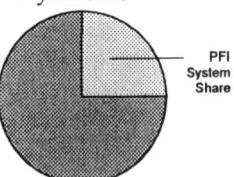

PFI System Share

International retail sales of snack chips totaled about $14 billion. Products of the PFI system represented about $3.5 billion, or 25%.

representing the catch-up effect arising from the final settlement of pension assets related to the 1989 acquisition of the U.K. operations. The international profit margin, excluding the 1992 and 1991 unusual items, was unchanged at 11.6%.

1991 vs. 1990

Worldwide net sales rose 10% to $5.3 billion. Domestic sales grew $266 million (8%) to $3.7 billion, with volume growth, aided by more competitive promotional price allowance programs, contributing about $255 million of the increase. The remaining growth was principally due to price increases that were partially offset by an unfavorable package size and product mix shift. Promotional price allowances, which increased over last year's level, are reported as marketing expenses and therefore do not reduce reported sales. International sales advanced $217 million (17%) to $1.5 billion, with volume gains contributing about $100 million of the increase and the balance of the growth due principally to price increases in Mexico.

Total domestic pound sales advanced 7%, led by the new Sunchips brand multigrain snacks product, Tostitos brand tortilla chips, Lay's brand potato chips and Chee·tos brand cheese flavored snacks. These increases were partially offset by a decline in Ruffles brand potato chips. International snack chip kilo growth was 6%, driven by a double-digit advance in Mexico, while volume in the U.K. was about even with 1990. The volume performance in the U.K. reflected the introduction of Frito-Lay's brands, principally Ruffles brand potato chips, offset by declines in other brands. Growth in smaller markets was led by Brazil.

Worldwide operating profits decreased 15% to $757 million. Excluding unusual charges in both 1991 and 1990, profits declined 2%. Unusual charges in 1991 totaled $127 million, comprised of $91.4 million and $35.6 million for restructuring actions designed primarily to streamline operations of the domestic and international snack food businesses, respectively. Approximately $64 million of the domestic charge related to administrative workforce reorganizations and reductions, and the balance related to product line and production capacity reductions. The international charge included $23.6 million related to productivity initiatives in the U.K., including facility closures and streamlining of selling and administrative processes. These actions, when fully implemented, were expected to result in annual domestic and international savings approximating $100 million and $15 million, respectively, providing additional resources for reinvestment in the businesses to strengthen competitive positions. The international charge also included $12 million related to the probable disposition of a small business. Unusual charges in 1990 totaled $10.6 million for receivables exposures related to highly leveraged domestic retail customers.

Worldwide profits included amortization of intangible assets (almost all international) of $36 million in 1991 and $37 million in 1990.

Domestic profits declined 16% to $617 million. Excluding the 1991 and 1990 unusual charges, profits decreased $35 million (5%).

Santitas — Introduced 1986. Estimated 1992 Retail Sales: $124 Million.

Walkers — Acquired 1989. Estimated 1992 Retail Sales: $378 Million. (Sold outside the U.S.)

Sun Chips — Introduced 1991. Estimated 1992 Retail Sales: $192 Million.

Snack Foods

Volume growth contributed about $145 million to profits. This benefit was more than offset by higher selling and manufacturing expenses, lower net prices (reflecting increased promotional price allowances) and an unfavorable mix shift to lower profit packages and products. Higher manufacturing expenses reflected potato cost increases that were largely due to a weather-related potato crop shortage in the second quarter of 1991. Frito-Lay hedges the costs of a portion of its corn and cooking oil purchases through commodities futures contracts, but there is no futures market for potatoes. The domestic profit margin, excluding the 1991 and 1990 unusual charges, fell two and one-half points to 18.9%.

International profits decreased 13% to $140 million. Excluding the 1991 unusual charges, profits increased $15 million (10%). Volume growth contributed about $65 million to profits. This benefit was partially offset by higher manufacturing and other operating expenses that exceeded price increases. An unfavorable translation impact of a stronger U.S. dollar depressed profits by about $3 million. The profit advance reflected double-digit growth in Mexico that was partially offset by a decline in the U.K. Profits were also aided by growth in Brazil. The profit performance in Mexico was due to volume growth, partially offset by manufacturing and operating cost increases that exceeded higher prices. These cost increases reflected higher commodity costs, principally potatoes, and increased costs associated with new manufacturing plants completed in early 1991. The U.K. profit decline was due principally to higher operating expenses, partially offset by price increases and improved manufacturing productivity. An unfavorable translation impact also contributed to the U.K. profit decline. Profit growth in Brazil was driven by higher volumes. The international profit margin, excluding the 1991 unusual charges, declined nearly one point to 11.6%.

Recent Introductions

(Sold outside the U.S.)

Restaurants

Pizza Hut
Taco Bell
KFC

A Well-Positioned Past

PepsiCo was created in 1965 by the merger of Pepsi-Cola and Frito-Lay. For the next decade, soft drinks and snack foods drove our growth. By the mid-1970s, we were seeking a third growth business that would respond to PepsiCo's skills in marketing and operations.

We focused on the restaurant business and purchased Pizza Hut in 1977 and Taco Bell in 1978. Both of these chains had huge potential. In 1986, PepsiCo acquired Kentucky Fried Chicken, another promising chain. With KFC, we had more units than any other restaurant system in the world.

As we approached the 1990s, our restaurant system faced a number of challenges. We had to respond to more mobile consumers, always on the run. We had to keep costs down as families began to seek greater value. Plus, we had to create new products that excited consumers and responded to their demand for variety.

An Adaptable Present

Our chains began aggressively addressing these challenges as far back as the mid-1980s. At Pizza Hut we began delivery. Taco Bell introduced its value menu. And KFC set about updating its image.

As we entered the 1990s, we continued to adapt our system to the changing market. Pizza Hut and Taco Bell began expanding distribution by selling their products from kiosks. KFC changed its logo from Kentucky Fried Chicken to "KFC" and introduced convenient snack products like Hot Wings pieces.

In 1992, we built on this success. Here are some of our achievements.

- U.S. company-owned restaurant sales were up 14%. Profits, excluding unusual items, grew 17%.
- International company-owned restaurant sales were up 29%. Profits were up 25%.
- Worldwide system sales of Pizza Hut, Taco Bell and KFC products reached $15.7 billion.
- The PepsiCo worldwide restaurant system reached 22,336 units. We added an average of nearly four units every day.
- Average system sales at PepsiCo's U.S. restaurants grew or remained stable, even while we were opening more restaurants and selling our products in more places.
- Pizza Hut opened in five new international markets, Taco Bell in four and KFC in two. We're now in 84 countries and territories outside the U.S.
- PepsiCo acquired an equity position in Carts of Colorado, Inc., the leading manufacturer of mobile merchandising carts. Mobile carts let us sell our products more readily at airports, sports stadiums, fairs and similar places.
- PepsiCo purchased an equity interest in California Pizza Kitchen, Inc., a chain of casual, full-service restaurants that offers specialty wood-fired pizzas, pastas, salads and desserts.
- Pizza Hut U.S. system delivery operations generated nearly $1.5 billion in sales. In 1993, we'll be testing delivery of full meals.

($ In Millions)	Domestic	International	Total
Sales	$7,115	$1,117	$8,232
% Change	+14	+29	+16
Profits	$ 598	$ 121	$ 719
% Change	+25*	+25	+25*

	Pizza Hut	Taco Bell	KFC
Sales	$3,604	$2,460	$2,169
% Change	+11	+21	+18
Profits	$ 335	$ 214	$ 169
% Change	+7*	+19*	+110*
System sales	$5,700	$3,300	$6,700
% Change	+8%	+18%	+8%

*These comparisons are affected by unusual items. See page 28.

Pizza Hut Acquired 1977. Estimated 1992
System Retail Sales: $5.7 Billion.

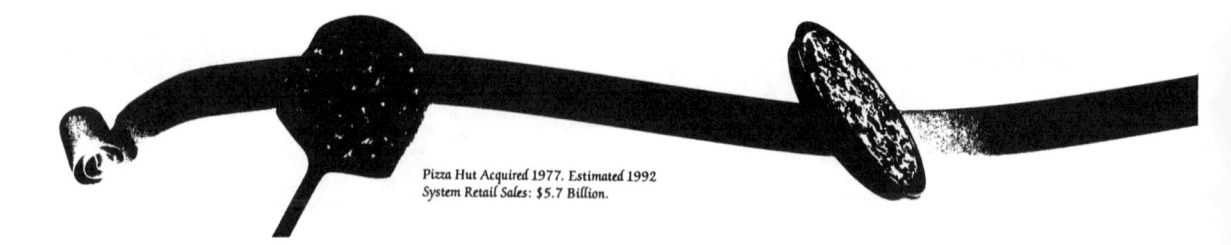

Annual Report for PepsiCo, Inc. **xliii**

Restaurants Net Sales
% Of Total Net Sales
($ In Millions)

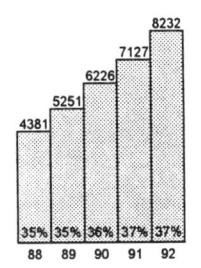

88	89	90	91	92
4381	5251	6226	7127	8232
35%	35%	36%	37%	37%

Restaurants Operating Profits
% Of Total Segment Operating Profits
($ In Millions)

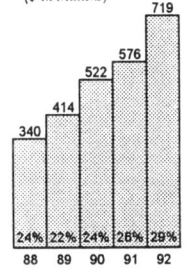

88	89	90	91	92
340	414	522	576	719
24%	22%	24%	26%	29%

Restaurants Capital Spending
% Of Total Segment Capital Spending
($ In Millions)

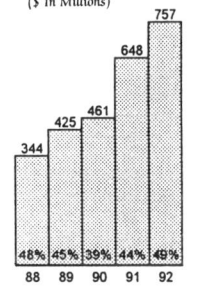

88	89	90	91	92
344	425	461	648	757
48%	45%	39%	44%	49%

- In the U.S., Pizza Hut began testing Fastinos, a fast food pizza and pasta concept with a drive-thru window. With the help of new cooking technology, pizzas are ready in about 90 seconds.
- We added a lunch buffet in 2,100 U.S. company-owned Pizza Hut units, increasing our dine-in sales.
- Taco Bell's commitment to value pricing brought more customers into the restaurants, increasing same store sales by 6%.
- Taco Bell brought its Mexican-style food to Mexico, with the opening of our first kiosk in Mexico City. Since then we've opened two additional kiosks there.
- Taco Bell expanded testing of Hot 'n Now, a double drive-thru hamburger chain, offering fast service and low prices. We purchased Hot 'n Now at the end of 1990.
- KFC improved U.S. operations, raising customer satisfaction and lowering costs. We continued to upgrade KFC units, with more than three-fourths of the U.S. system units refurbished since 1989.
- KFC introduced new limited time menu items to build sales in the U.S. These products include Oriental Wings, Popcorn Chicken and Honey BBQ Chicken, each of which increased sales when offered.
- KFC offered a new, rotisserie chicken in three U.S. test markets. In Australia, we tested Tenderbake chicken. Tenderbake performed so well, we will introduce it to consumers across Australia in 1993.
- KFC introduced its All You Can Eat Buffet in 675 U.S. system restaurants, increasing sales. We plan to have the buffet in about 2,000 units by the end of 1993.
- PFS, our foodservice distribution company that supplies our restaurants with everything required to run a restaurant, added more than 1,200 restaurants to its routes. New operations in Australia and Mexico will serve these key markets. PFS now serves nearly 14,000 worldwide company-owned and franchised restaurants.
- PFS expanded its services to other PepsiCo divisions. For example, PFS provided Pepsi-Cola International with promotional items for pop singer Michael Jackson's international tour.
- PFS added a service to maintain the restaurant equipment it distributes.

A Flexible Future... A Chairman's View:

The U.S. quick service restaurant business is increasingly competitive. But there's still enormous demand for variety, convenience and value. In 1970, quick service sales were about 14% of all foodservice industry sales. Now they're about 30% — that gives us more room to grow.

The key is maintaining a sharp focus on the consumer. For example, people are busier today than ever, so they want prepared foods that are convenient and reasonably priced. We're giving them better value and putting our products in more convenient places.

Consider our potential this way: The typical U.S. consumer eats about 16 meals prepared away from home in a month, with one of those meals purchased at our restaurant chains. If we were to increase that number so each of our three chains served one of those meals, we would add about $20 billion to our system retail sales.

Add to that the burgeoning international market and you can understand why we see great potential.

For 1993, we expect worldwide unit growth, new products and distribution methods, and our "value" commitment to drive strong growth.

Management's Analysis

(See "Management's Analysis — Overview" on page 26 and "Business Segments" on page 28.)

1992 vs. 1991

Worldwide net sales rose $1.1 billion (16%) to $8.2 billion. This advance was driven by additional units (units constructed and acquired from franchisees, net of units closed and sold), which contributed $936 million. Higher net prices and volume growth also aided the sales gain. Domestic sales grew 14% to $7.1 billion and international sales were up 29% to $1.1 billion.

Worldwide operating profits grew 25% to $719 million. Profits in 1992 were reduced by $15.4 million due to adopting the new accounting rules for retiree health benefits ($6.1 million, all domestic) and income taxes ($7.9 million for domestic and $1.4 million for international). Profits in 1991 included $43 million in KFC unusual charges described below. Excluding these 1992 and 1991 unusual items, worldwide profits rose $115 million (19%), driven by $108 million from

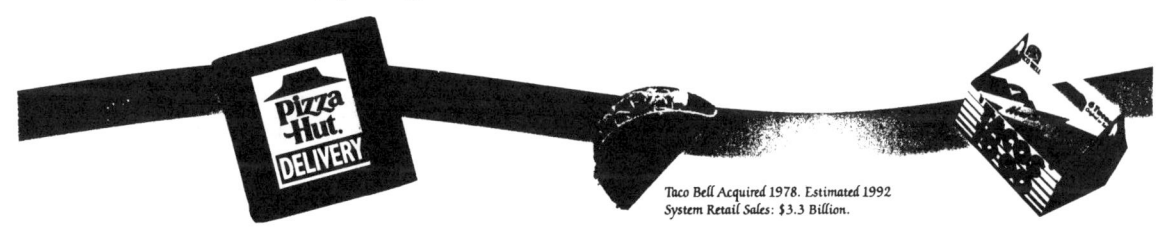

Taco Bell Acquired 1978. Estimated 1992 System Retail Sales: $3.3 Billion.

Restaurants

additional units. Higher franchise royalty revenues were offset by increased operating costs that exceeded higher net prices. Domestic profits grew 17%, excluding the unusual items, and international profits rose 25%.

Pizza Hut's worldwide sales increased $345 million (11%) to $3.6 billion. The domestic operations represent the major portion of worldwide Pizza Hut. Additional units, led by delivery units, contributed $343 million to the worldwide sales increase. The benefit of higher net prices, which reflected a lower level of price promotions in the first half of 1992, was offset by an estimated $95 million impact of lower volumes. Worldwide profits grew 7% to $335 million. Excluding the unfavorable $7.3 million impact (almost all domestic) of the 1992 accounting rule changes, profits rose $28 million (9%). This growth was driven by additional units, which contributed $31 million. An estimated $40 million impact of lower volumes was largely offset by higher net prices that exceeded increased food (including cheese) and other operating costs as well as increased franchise royalty revenues. The profit performance also reflected total domestic field and headquarters administrative expenses that were about even with last year.

Comparable sales for domestic company-owned units (same store sales) were even with 1991 though volumes declined. This performance reflected slowing growth in delivery operations offset by declines in carry-out sales. Although dine-in same store sales were about even, trends are improving due to the introduction of the all-you-can-eat pizza and salad lunch buffet. At year-end 1992, the buffets were in approximately 2,100 units or about 75% of domestic company-owned dine-in units.

Pizza Hut's international sales posted strong double-digit growth led by additional delivery units in Canada and Australia and dine-in units in Puerto Rico. Double-digit profit growth reflected the additional units and higher franchise royalty revenues. Volume declines resulted in slightly lower profits in Australia, the largest sales market.

Pizza Hut's worldwide profits included amortization of intangible assets (principally domestic) of $33 million in 1992 and $26 million in 1991, with the increase reflecting acquisitions of franchisees and the impact of the new income tax accounting rules. The worldwide profit margin, excluding the impact of the accounting rule changes, was about even at 9.5%.

Taco Bell's worldwide sales rose $422 million (21%) to $2.5 billion. The domestic operations represent substantially all of worldwide Taco Bell. Additional units contributed $248 million to the worldwide sales advance and volume gains provided about $150 million. Worldwide profits grew 19% to $214 million. Excluding the unfavorable $2.9 million impact (all domestic) of the 1992 accounting rule changes, profits rose $37 million (20%). Of this increase, volume growth contributed about $40 million and additional units provided $32 million. These benefits, as well as higher franchise royalty revenues, were partially offset by higher labor and other store operating costs and increased headquarters administrative expenses for the development of new systems and

U.S. Foodservice Industry Retail Sales PepsiCo Share

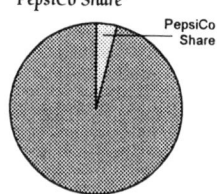

PepsiCo U.S. restaurant system sales represented over 4% of the total $255 billion foodservice industry.

U.S. Quick Service Restaurant Retail Sales PepsiCo Share

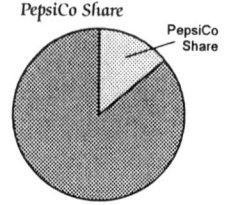

PepsiCo U.S. restaurant system sales of $10.9 billion represented more than 14% of $76 billion quick service restaurant sales.

KFC Acquired 1986. Estimated 1992 System Retail Sales: $6.7 Billion.

Annual Report for PepsiCo, Inc. **xlv**

U.S. Quick Service Restaurant Sales
($ In Billions)

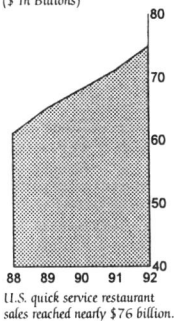

U.S. quick service restaurant sales reached nearly $76 billion.

U.S. Quick Service Restaurant Sales Growth vs. PepsiCo System Growth 1992

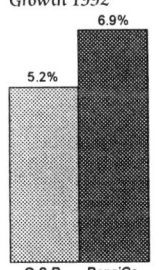

Q.S.R. 5.2%
PepsiCo 6.9%

PepsiCo U.S. restaurant system sales grew 6.9%, compared with quick service restaurant sales growth of 5.2%.

concepts, including costs to support the Hot 'n Now concept. Same store sales grew 6% due to volume growth. Taco Bell's profits included amortization of domestic intangible assets of $16 million in 1992 and $11 million in 1991, with the increase reflecting acquisitions of franchisees and the impact of the new income tax accounting rules.

Taco Bell's international operations posted double-digit sales growth and a small profit compared to a small loss in 1991. This performance was led by volume growth in Canada. The worldwide profit margin, excluding the impact of the accounting rule changes, was even at 8.8%.

KFC's worldwide sales rose $338 million (18%) to $2.2 billion. This increase was driven by additional units, which contributed $345 million. Sales growth was depressed by the unfavorable translation impact of a weaker U.S. dollar late in the year of $22 million. KFC's international sales represented about 30% of KFC's worldwide sales in both 1992 and 1991.

KFC's worldwide profits rose 110% to $169 million. Profits in 1992 were reduced by $5.2 million in incremental expenses ($3.9 million for domestic and $1.3 million for international) resulting from the accounting rule changes. Profits in 1991 included restructuring charges to streamline operations of $32.8 million in domestic and $1.2 million in international and a $9 million domestic charge related to a delay in the U.S. roll-out of Skinfree Crispy chicken. Excluding these 1992 and 1991 unusual items, KFC's worldwide profits rose $51 million (41%), driven by additional units which contributed $46 million. KFC's international profits represented about 50% of KFC's worldwide profits in 1992 and 55% in 1991.

Double-digit growth in KFC's domestic sales was driven by additional units. A significant increase in domestic profits reflected the additional units, a sales mix shift to higher margin products such as Popcorn Chicken, lower headquarters administrative expenses resulting from restructuring actions announced last year and implemented early in 1992, as well as the impact of higher volumes. These benefits were partially offset by a higher level of price promotions. Same store sales were even with 1991 though volumes were up slightly.

Double-digit sales growth in KFC's international operations was driven by additional units, particularly in Canada and Australia. Sales growth was depressed by the unfavorable translation impact noted above. International profits grew at a double-digit rate due to higher franchise royalty revenues and growth in Canada and Mexico. Profits declined in Australia, the largest sales market, reflecting lower volumes and an unfavorable translation impact.

KFC's worldwide profits included amortization of intangible assets of $38 million in 1992 and $17 million in 1991, with the increase reflecting acquisitions of domestic and international franchisees and the impact of the new income tax accounting rules. The worldwide profit margin, excluding the impact of the accounting rule changes and the 1991 unusual charges, increased over one point to 8.0% due to improved domestic results.

1991 vs. 1990

Worldwide net sales rose $901 million (14%) to $7.1 billion. This advance reflected $695 million from additional units and about $280 million from volume growth. These increases were partially offset by lower net prices at Pizza Hut and Taco Bell. Domestic sales grew 13% to $6.3 billion and international sales were up 27% to $869 million.

Worldwide operating profits grew 10% to $576 million. Profits in 1991 included $43 million in KFC unusual charges described below. Profits in 1990 included unusual charges of $17.6 million to close underperforming units at all three chains and $10.4 million at Pizza Hut to consolidate domestic field operations and relocate international headquarters. Excluding the 1991 and 1990 unusual charges, worldwide profits rose $68 million (12%). This advance reflected about $120 million from volume growth and $70 million from additional units, with lower domestic food costs and higher franchise royalty revenues also contributing to the profit growth. These benefits were partially offset by the lower net prices and higher operating expenses. Excluding the unusual charges, domestic and international profits were up 10% and 25%, respectively.

Pizza Hut's worldwide sales increased $308 million (10%) to $3.3 billion. Of this advance, $292 million came from additional units and volume growth contributed about $85 million. These increases were partially offset by lower net prices, due to a higher level of restaurant price promotions, and lower wholesale prices for food products sold to franchisees. Worldwide profits grew 28% to $315 million. Excluding the 1990 unusual charges, profits rose $49 million (19%), reflecting $32 million from additional units and about $30 million from volume growth. These benefits were partially offset by the net impact of the lower net prices, higher labor costs, favorable food costs (principally cheese) and higher franchise royalty revenues. Due partly to benefits of the 1990 reorganization, total domestic field and headquarters administrative expenses were about even with last year. Same store sales advanced 1% though volume growth was higher. Strong same store sales and profit growth in both delivery units and dine-in units with delivery were partially offset by declines in other dine-in units.

Pizza Hut's international sales and profits posted double-digit growth. The sales increase was driven by additional units in Germany and Canada and volume growth in Australia delivery operations. Profit growth was led by higher franchise royalty revenues and advances in Australia and Canada.

Pizza Hut's worldwide profits included amortization of intangible assets (principally domestic) of $26 million in 1991 and $20 million in 1990, with the increase reflecting acquisitions of franchisees. The worldwide profit margin, excluding the 1990 unusual charges, grew over one-half point to 9.7%.

Taco Bell's worldwide sales rose $293 million (17%) to $2.0 billion. Volume growth contributed about $180 million to the sales advance and additional units provided $151 million. Partially offsetting these benefits were lower value-oriented menu prices in restaurants and lower wholesale prices for food products sold to franchisees. Worldwide profits grew 21% to $181 million. Excluding the unusual charge in 1990, profits rose $27 million (18%). Of this increase, volume growth contributed about $80 million and additional units provided $15 million. Higher franchise royalty revenues also aided profits. Partially offsetting these benefits were the lower prices and higher store operating costs, as well as increased headquarters administrative expenses that included strategic spending for field operations management hiring and training, new retail distribution concepts and advanced computer systems for stores. The impact of lower food costs was offset by the increased use of more costly pre-prepared ingredients, which has improved labor efficiency. Same store sales grew 5% though volume growth was higher. Taco Bell's profits included amortization of domestic intangible assets of $11 million in 1991 and $8 million in 1990. On a small base, Taco Bell's international operations posted double-digit sales growth, reflecting volume gains in Canada, while losses were about even with 1990. The worldwide profit margin, excluding the 1990 unusual charge, was even at 8.9%.

KFC's worldwide sales rose $300 million (20%) to $1.8 billion. Additional units contributed $252 million of the increase and about $15 million came from international volume gains. Higher net prices also aided growth. KFC's international sales represented about 30% of KFC's worldwide sales in both 1991 and 1990.

U.S. Pizza Restaurant Segment
Pizza Hut Share

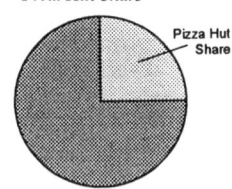

With U.S. system sales of $4.3 billion, or more than 25% of the segment, Pizza Hut led the $16.4 billion pizza restaurant category.

U.S. Mexican-Style Restaurant Segment
Taco Bell Share

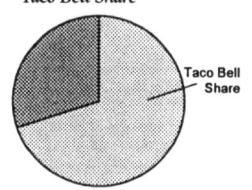

With U.S. system sales of $3.2 billion, or about 70% of the segment, Taco Bell led the $4.6 billion Mexican-style restaurant category.

U.S. Chicken Restaurant Segment
KFC Share

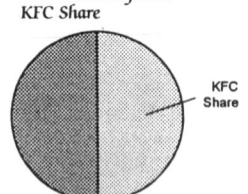

With U.S. system sales of $3.4 billion, or about half the segment, KFC led the $7.0 billion chicken restaurant category.

Recent Introductions

Restaurant Unit Growth

Number of System Units Worldwide (Year-end 1987-1992)

Year	Pizza Hut	Taco Bell	KFC	Total
1987	6,210	2,738	7,522	16,470
1988	6,662	2,930	7,761	17,353
1989	7,502	3,125	7,948	18,575
1990	8,220	3,349	8,187	19,756
1991	8,837	3,670	8,480	20,987
1992	9,454	4,153	8,729	22,336
Five-year Compounded Annual Growth Rate				
	8.8%	8.7%	3.0%	6.3%

Number of System Units Worldwide (Year-end 1992)

	Pizza Hut	Taco Bell	KFC	Total
United States				
Company	4,301	2,498	1,994	8,793
Franchised	2,905	1,446	3,074	7,425
Licensed	402	134	21	557
Total U.S.	7,608	4,078	5,089	16,775
International				
Company	539	51	726	1,316
Joint Venture	370	–	474	844
Franchised/Licensed	937	24	2,440	3,401
Total International	1,846	75	3,640	5,561
Total Worldwide	9,454	4,153	8,729	22,336

Unit totals include 477 kiosks (primarily Pizza Hut) and 293 other special concepts. Taco Bell U.S. unit count includes Hot 'n Now: 99 company and 38 franchised. U.S. count does not include 29 California Pizza Kitchen, Inc. units.

Restaurant Sales Growth
(Compounded annual growth rates)

Average Domestic System Sales Per Unit (Thousands)*

	1987	1988	1989	1990	1991	1992	5-Year % Growth
PH	$490	$520	$570	$607	$613	$612	4.5
TB	.579	589	686	771	814	866	8.4
KFC	558	597	607	650	675	684	4.2

*Excludes sales from kiosks and other special concepts.

Worldwide System Sales 1987-1992 (Billions)

	1987	1988	1989	1990	1991	1992	5-Year % Growth
PH	$2.9	$3.4	$4.1	$4.9	$5.3	$5.7	14.5
TB	1.5	1.6	2.1	2.4	2.8	3.3	17.1
KFC	4.1	5.0	5.4	5.8	6.2	6.7	10.3
Total	$8.5	$10.0	$11.6	$13.1	$14.3	$15.7	13.1

Worldwide System Sales 1992 (Billions)

	Pizza Hut	Taco Bell	KFC	Total
Domestic	$4.3	$3.2	$3.4	$10.9
International	1.4	.1	3.3	4.8
Total	$5.7	$3.3	$6.7	$15.7

KFC's worldwide profits fell 37% to $81 million. Profits in 1991 included a $34 million unusual charge primarily for a restructuring of domestic processes to improve overall productivity and customer service. The charge included costs for the intended elimination of certain positions, relocation of personnel and closing of offices. These actions, when fully implemented, were expected to result in annual savings approximating $25 million, providing additional resources for reinvestment in the business to strengthen competitive positions. Profits in 1991 also included a $9 million domestic unusual charge associated with a delay of the U.S. roll-out of Skinfree Crispy. The charge included payments to suppliers for unrecovered start-up costs and unused capacity costs due to lower 1991 production levels. Improvements in the product's quality and profitability were achieved, and the U.S. roll-out was completed in 1992.

Excluding the 1991 and 1990 unusual charges, KFC's worldwide profits fell $8 million (6%). The lower profits reflected higher store operating costs, due largely to higher domestic product costs, as well as increased field and headquarters administrative expenses. These factors were partially offset by contributions from additional units of $23 million, higher net prices, international volume growth and increased franchise royalty revenues. KFC's international profits represented about 55% of KFC's worldwide profits in 1991 and 45% in 1990.

Double-digit growth in KFC's domestic sales was primarily due to additional units and a reduced level of price promotions. Profits declined reflecting the higher cost of the pre-prepared Skinfree Crispy chicken product and increased store operating costs and administrative expenses, partially offset by the reduced level of price promotions and additional units. Same store sales were about even with 1990 though volume declined.

KFC's international sales and profits posted double-digit growth, driven by additional units in Canada and Australia, higher volumes led by Mexico and growth in franchise royalty revenues. Partially offsetting these profit advances were higher store operating costs and administrative expenses that exceeded increased prices.

KFC's worldwide profits included amortization of intangible assets of $17 million in 1991 and $12 million in 1990, with the increase reflecting acquisitions of domestic and international franchisees. The worldwide profit margin, excluding the 1991 and 1990 unusual charges, fell nearly two points to 6.7% primarily due to lower domestic profits.

Management's Analysis — Overview

To facilitate understanding of PepsiCo's financial results, the various components of "Management's Analysis" are presented near the pertinent data. In addition to this overview discussion, separate analyses of the results of operations, financial condition and cash flows appear on pages 31, 33 and 35, respectively. The analysis of each industry segment's net sales and operating profit performance begins on pages 9, 14 and 20.

PepsiCo's principal objective is to increase the value of its shareholders' investment through integrated operating, investing and financing strategies that seek to maximize cash flows. These strategies are continually fine-tuned to address the opportunities and risks of the global marketplace.

Marketplace Actions

PepsiCo's domestic and international businesses operate in markets that are highly competitive and subject to local economic influences such as inflation, commodity price fluctuations and governmental actions. In the U.S., for example, new economic policies targeted at reducing the federal budget deficit may result in higher taxes. Additionally, many of PepsiCo's markets continue to be affected by recessionary pressures. PepsiCo's operating and investing strategies are designed to mitigate these factors through aggressive actions on several fronts including: (a) enhancing the appeal and value of its products through brand promotion, product innovation, quality improvement and prudent pricing actions, (b) providing better service to customers, (c) increasing worldwide availability of its products, (d) acquiring businesses and forming alliances to increase market presence and utilize resources more efficiently and (e) containing costs through more efficient and effective purchasing, manufacturing, distribution and administrative processes.

Restructurings

Restructuring actions, such as those taken in all three industry segments within the last two years and which may be taken in future years, reflect PepsiCo's willingness to change in anticipation of marketplace trends. These actions are intended to realign resources for more effective and efficient execution of operating strategies. The resulting cost savings help fund activities to enhance PepsiCo's competitive positions throughout the world. For example, restructurings in PepsiCo's beverage and international snack food segments, announced in 1992 and now underway, resulted in charges totaling $193.5 million ($128.5 million after-tax or $0.16 per share). When completed, these actions are expected to generate annual cost savings of approximately $160 million pretax. These savings relate primarily to headcount reductions. See "Business Segments" on page 28 for detail of restructuring charges and other unusual items over the last three years.

Cost of Capital

The cost of capital is a key measure in setting PepsiCo's investing and financing strategies. The cost of capital is a weighting of cost of debt and cost of equity, with the latter representing a measure of expected return to investors in PepsiCo's stock. PepsiCo seeks investments that generate cash returns in excess of its cost of capital, which is currently estimated to be approximately 11%. Financial leverage, which refers to the management of the debt and equity structure, is utilized by PepsiCo to optimize the overall cost of capital, considering the favorable tax treatment of debt. Prudent use of leverage, combined with PepsiCo's strong cash generating capability, provides the flexibility to continue to invest in the business without significantly affecting PepsiCo's overall cost of debt. PepsiCo's strong financial condition provides continued access to capital markets throughout the world.

Currency Exchange Effects

In 1992, international businesses represented 19% of PepsiCo's total segment operating profits, excluding unusual items. Operating in international markets involves risks associated with volatility of currency exchange rates. When appropriate, PepsiCo engages in hedging activities to minimize cash flow transaction exposures. In implementing financing strategies, transaction exposures related to debt are considered along with interest rates to measure effective financing costs. PepsiCo believes its translation exposure related to net income is not material because of its diversified mix of international businesses. For PepsiCo's key international operations, located in Australia, Canada, Japan, Mexico, Spain and the United Kingdom (U.K.), the translation effects of exchange rate movements on net income in recent years have been largely offsetting. As its international operations continue to expand, PepsiCo intends to closely monitor its currency risks and take prudent actions when appropriate to minimize exposures. Net foreign exchange pretax losses included in the Consolidated Statement of Income totaled $17.4 million, $7.8 million and $9.5 million in 1992, 1991 and 1990, respectively. These amounts consist of the effects of remeasurement into U.S. dollars of the net assets of businesses in hyperinflationary countries and net transaction gains and losses.

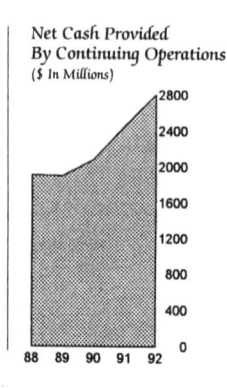

Net Cash Provided By Continuing Operations
($ In Millions)

Accounting Changes

PepsiCo's 1992 financial statements were significantly impacted by the early adoption of two new required Statements of Financial Accounting Standards, "Employers' Accounting for Postretirement Benefits Other Than Pensions" (SFAS 106) and "Accounting for Income Taxes" (SFAS 109). The cumulative effect of adopting SFAS 106, a $575.3 million charge ($356.7 million after-tax or $0.44 per share), represents estimated future retirement benefit costs related to services provided by employees prior to 1992. The adoption of SFAS 106 resulted in incremental expense related to 1992 of $52.1 million ($32.3 million after-tax or $0.04 per share). Because of recent amendments to PepsiCo's retiree benefits plans, the related expense for 1993 is expected to decline by $40 million. See Note 11 for additional details regarding the adoption of SFAS 106.

The cumulative effect of adopting SFAS 109, a $570.7 million charge ($0.71 per share), primarily represents the recognition of deferred tax liabilities related to identifiable intangible assets, principally acquired trademarks and reacquired franchise rights, included in PepsiCo's balance sheet as of the end of 1991. The adoption of SFAS 109 resulted in incremental pretax expense related to 1992 of $20.7 million, but reduced the provision for income taxes by $33.7 million, resulting in a $13.0 million increase in net income ($0.02 per share). The impact on 1993 net income should be roughly the same as 1992 assuming no change in enacted tax rates or other unusual events. The adoption of SFAS 109 reduced PepsiCo's effective income tax rate primarily because tax benefit is recognized for financial accounting purposes for all amortization of identifiable intangibles, regardless of deductibility for tax purposes. See Note 14 for additional details regarding the adoption of SFAS 109.

The adoption of SFAS 106 and SFAS 109 has no impact on PepsiCo's cash flows. The adoption of SFAS 106 resulted in the recognition of a previously existing liability that will be paid in the future. The adoption of SFAS 109 resulted in the recognition of tax liabilities that would be paid in the unlikely event the related identifiable intangible assets were sold.

Late in 1992, the Financial Accounting Standards Board issued new rules for postemployment benefits other than to retirees. (See Note 13.)

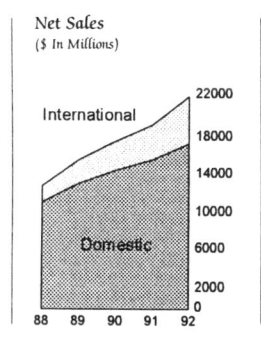

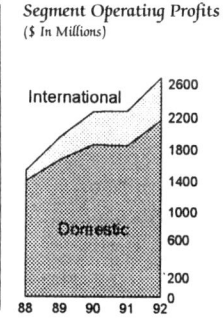

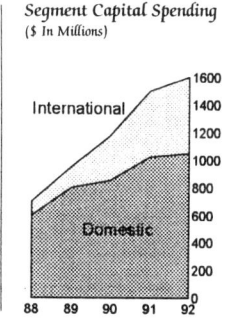

Business Segments

This information constitutes Notes 2 and 3 to the Consolidated Financial Statements. (dollars in millions except per share amounts)

PepsiCo operates on a worldwide basis within three industry segments: beverages, snack foods and restaurants. The beverage segment markets Pepsi, Diet Pepsi, Mountain Dew and other brands worldwide and 7UP outside the U.S. The segment manufactures concentrates sold to franchised bottlers worldwide and operates bottling plants located principally in the U.S. and Canada. The snack food segment manufactures and markets snack chips worldwide, with Frito-Lay representing the domestic business. The international snack food business includes major operations in Mexico, the U.K. and Canada. The restaurant segment includes operations of the worldwide Pizza Hut, Taco Bell and KFC chains. PFS, PepsiCo's restaurant distribution operation, supplies principally domestic company-owned and franchised restaurants. Included in the net sales and operating profits for each chain are the franchisee operations of PFS. "Interest and Other Corporate Expenses, net" includes interest expense, interest income, equity in net income of affiliates, foreign exchange gains and losses and other corporate items that are not allocated to the business segments. "Corporate Assets" consists principally of short-term investments held outside the U.S. and investments in affiliates.

To improve comparability, the 1991 and 1990 net sales and operating profits for international snack foods have been restated to exclude the results of certain previously consolidated businesses, which were contributed to the new Snack Ventures Europe (SVE) joint venture with General Mills, Inc., and equity in net income of affiliates has been restated to include 100% of the net income of these businesses. (See Note 1.) The restatement reduced net sales for 1991 and 1990 by $315.7 and $287.2, operating profits by $30.9 and $41.8 and net corporate expenses by $20.3 and $28.2, respectively.

PepsiCo has invested in about 50 joint ventures, principally international and all within PepsiCo's three industry segments, in which it exercises significant influence but not control. Equity in net income of these affiliates, which includes the two unusual charges noted below, was $40.1, $32.2 and $30.1 in 1992, 1991 and 1990, respectively. International snack food affiliates, which represented the largest component of equity in net income of affiliates, contributed $23.2, $20.5 and $26.9 in 1992, 1991 and 1990, respectively. Dividends received from affiliates totaled $29.6, $32.6 and $17.8 in 1992, 1991 and 1990, respectively.

PepsiCo's investments in affiliates totaled $905 at year-end 1992 and $1.1 billion at both year-end 1991 and 1990. The decline in 1992 primarily reflected the consolidation of two international snack food affiliates, due to securing a controlling interest in the Gamesa cookie joint venture (Mexico) and buying out PepsiCo's joint venture partner in Hostess Frito-Lay (Canada). This activity was partially offset by a $96 investment in a domestic mid-scale gourmet pizza business and the investment in the SVE joint venture with a carrying value of $87. (See Note 5.) Other significant investments in affiliates at year-end 1992 included $216 in a domestic franchised bottler and $129 in the KFC Japan joint venture. The level of both of these investments has not changed materially over the last three years.

Net Unusual Charges and Impact of Accounting Changes

Net Unusual Charges

Profits for the years presented in the tabular data on page 29 include several restructuring and other unusual charges and a nonoperating gain, resulting in a 1992 total charge of $193.5 ($128.5 after-tax or $0.16 per share), a 1991 total charge of $170.0 ($119.8 after-tax or $0.15 per share) and a 1990 net credit of $35.2 ($4.2 charge after-tax or $0.01 per share).

Beverages: 1992 includes $145.0 in charges consisting of $115.4 to reorganize and streamline domestic operations, and $29.6 to streamline a recently acquired franchised bottling business in Spain and other international field operations. 1990 includes $10.5 in charges for domestic trade receivables exposures.

Snack Foods: 1992 includes a $40.3 charge principally to consolidate the Smiths and Walkers businesses in the U.K. 1991 includes $127.0 in charges consisting of $91.4 to streamline domestic operations, $23.6 to streamline operations in the U.K. and $12.0 to dispose of a small international business. 1990 includes $10.6 in charges for domestic trade receivables exposures.

Restaurants: 1991 includes $43.0 in charges at KFC consisting of $34.0 ($1.2 for international) to streamline operations and $9.0 related to a delay in the U.S. roll-out of a new product. 1990 includes a $17.6 charge for closures of underperforming units as follows: $9.0 at Pizza Hut, $4.0 at Taco Bell and $4.6 ($0.6 for international) at KFC. 1990 also includes Pizza Hut charges of $8.0 to consolidate domestic field operations and $2.4 to relocate international headquarters.

Corporate: 1992 includes an $8.2 charge to streamline operations of the SVE joint venture. 1990 includes a $118.2 gain from an initial public stock offering by PepsiCo's KFC joint venture in Japan, an $18.0 charge for accelerated contributions to the PepsiCo Foundation and a $15.9 charge to reduce the carrying value of a Pizza Hut international joint venture investment.

Impact of Accounting Changes

In addition to the cumulative effect impacts, the adoption of SFAS 106 and SFAS 109 affected 1992 profits presented in the tabular data on page 29. SFAS 106 reduced profits by $52.1 ($32.3 after-tax or $0.04 per share), decreasing beverage, snack food and restaurant profits by $16.1, $28.2 and $6.1 (almost all domestic), respectively, and increasing corporate expenses by $1.7. SFAS 109 reduced profits by $20.7 ($13.0 credit after-tax or $0.02 per share), decreasing beverage, snack food and restaurant profits by $6.3, $2.6 and $9.3, respectively, and increasing corporate expenses by $2.5. (See Notes 11 and 14.)

Industry Segments:		Net Sales			Operating Profits			Identifiable Assets[a]		
		1992	1991	1990	1992	1991	1990	1992	1991	1990
Beverages:	Domestic	$ 5,485.2	$ 5,171.5	$ 5,034.5	$ 686.3	$ 746.2	$ 673.8			
	International	2,120.4	1,743.7	1,488.5	112.3	117.1	93.8			
		7,605.6	6,915.2	6,523.0	798.6	863.3	767.6	$ 7,857.5	$ 6,832.6	$ 6,465.2
Snack Foods:	Domestic	3,950.4	3,737.9	3,471.5	775.5	616.6	732.3			
	International	2,181.7	1,512.2	1,295.3	209.2	140.1	160.3			
		6,132.1	5,250.1	4,766.8	984.7	756.7	892.6	4,628.0	4,114.3	3,892.4
Restaurants:	Domestic	7,115.4	6,258.4	5,540.9	597.8	479.4	447.2			
	International	1,116.9	868.5	684.8	120.7	96.2	75.2			
		8,232.3	7,126.9	6,225.7	718.5	575.6	522.4	5,097.1	4,254.2	3,448.9
Total:	Domestic	16,551.0	15,167.8	14,046.9	2,059.6	1,842.2	1,853.3			
	International	5,419.0	4,124.4	3,468.6	442.2	353.4	329.3			
		$21,970.0	$19,292.2	$17,515.5	$2,501.8	$2,195.6	$2,182.6	$17,582.6	$15,201.1	$13,806.5
Geographic Areas[b]:										
United States		$16,551.0	$15,167.8	$14,046.9	$2,059.6	$1,842.2	$1,853.3	$11,957.0	$10,777.8	$ 9,980.7
Canada and Mexico		2,214.2	1,434.7	1,089.2	251.0	198.7	164.2	2,395.2	917.3	689.5
Europe		1,349.0	1,170.3	1,057.5	52.6	30.9	66.7	1,948.4	2,367.3	2,255.2
Other		1,855.8	1,519.4	1,321.9	138.6	123.8	98.4	1,282.0	1,138.7	881.1
								17,582.6	15,201.1	13,806.5
Corporate Assets								3,368.6	3,574.0	3,336.9
Total		$21,970.0	$19,292.2	$17,515.5	2,501.8	2,195.6	2,182.6	$20,951.2	$18,775.1	$17,143.4
Interest and Other Corporate Expenses, net					(603.0)	(535.9)	(528.8)			
Income from Continuing Operations Before Income Taxes and Cumulative Effect of Accounting Changes					$1,898.8	$1,659.7	$1,653.8			

Net Sales
($ In Millions)

	Capital Spending[a]			Depreciation and Amortization Expense[a]		
	1992	1991	1990	1992	1991	1990
Beverages	$ 343.7	$ 425.8	$ 334.1	$ 456.9	$393.2	$338.1
Snack Foods	446.2	406.0	381.6	291.7	253.5	232.5
Restaurants	757.2	648.4	460.6	456.2	379.6	306.5
Corporate	18.0	4.1	21.9	10.1	8.2	6.9
	$1,565.1	$1,484.3	$1,198.2	$1,214.9	$1,034.5	$884.0

Results by Restaurant Chain:	Net Sales			Operating Profits		
Pizza Hut	$3,603.5	$3,258.3	$2,949.9	$335.4	$314.5	$245.9
Taco Bell	2,460.0	2,038.1	1,745.5	214.3	180.6	149.6
KFC	2,168.8	1,830.5	1,530.3	168.8	80.5	126.9
	$8,232.3	$7,126.9	$6,225.7	$718.5	$575.6	$522.4

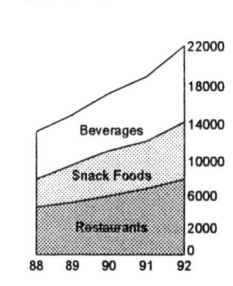

Segment Operating Profits
($ In Millions)

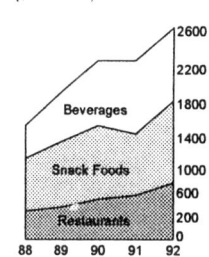

(a) Due to immateriality, identifiable assets, capital spending and depreciation and amortization expense were not restated for certain previously consolidated international snack food businesses contributed to the new SVE joint venture. (See Note 1.)
(b) The results of centralized concentrate manufacturing operations in Puerto Rico and Ireland have been allocated based upon sales to the respective areas.

Consolidated Statement of Income

(in millions except per share amounts)
PepsiCo, Inc. and Subsidiaries
Fifty-two weeks ended December 26, 1992, December 28, 1991 and December 29, 1990

	1992	1991	1990
Net Sales	$21,970.0	$19,292.2	$17,515.5
Costs and Expenses, net			
Cost of sales	10,492.6	9,278.6	8,442.6
Selling, general and administrative expenses	8,840.3	7,693.5	6,842.1
Amortization of intangible assets	265.9	208.3	188.7
Gain on joint venture stock offering	—	—	(118.2)
Interest expense	586.1	613.7	686.0
Interest income	(113.7)	(161.6)	(179.5)
	20,071.2	17,632.5	15,861.7
Income from Continuing Operations Before Income Taxes and Cumulative Effect of Accounting Changes	1,898.8	1,659.7	1,653.8
Provision for Income Taxes	597.1	579.5	563.2
Income from Continuing Operations Before Cumulative Effect of Accounting Changes	1,301.7	1,080.2	1,090.6
Discontinued Operation Charge (net of income tax benefit of $0.3)	—	—	(13.7)
Cumulative Effect of Change in Accounting for Postretirement Benefits Other Than Pensions (net of income tax benefit of $218.6)	(356.7)	—	—
Cumulative Effect of Change in Accounting for Income Taxes	(570.7)	—	—
Net Income	$ 374.3	$ 1,080.2	$ 1,076.9
Income (Charge) Per Share			
Continuing operations before cumulative effect of accounting changes	$ 1.61	$ 1.35	$ 1.37
Discontinued operation	—	—	(0.02)
Cumulative effect of change in accounting for postretirement benefits other than pensions	(0.44)	—	—
Cumulative effect of change in accounting for income taxes	(0.71)	—	—
Net Income Per Share	$ 0.46	$ 1.35	$ 1.35
Average shares outstanding used to calculate income (charge) per share	806.7	802.5	798.7

See accompanying Notes to Consolidated Financial Statements.

Management's Analysis — Results of Operations

(See "Management's Analysis — Overview" on page 26.)

The adoption of new accounting rules for retiree health benefits (SFAS 106) and income taxes (SFAS 109) resulted in cumulative effects of accounting changes that represent the impact of adoption related to years prior to 1992, and also resulted in effects related to 1992 results (see Notes 11 and 14). In addition, income for the years presented included restructuring and other unusual charges (see "Business Segments" on page 28) as well as the gain on joint venture stock offering (see below). These effects, combined with the impacts of SFAS 106 and SFAS 109 related to 1992, are collectively referred to as "the unusual items."

Net Sales rose 14% in 1992, driven by acquisitions of international snack food businesses and domestic and international franchised bottling operations as well as additional restaurant units (constructed and acquired from franchisees). The sales increase also reflects volume gains, driven by domestic snack foods, and higher pricing led by worldwide beverages. Sales rose 10% in 1991, driven by additional restaurant units and volume growth in worldwide snack foods and restaurants. Sales growth was also aided by acquisitions of domestic and international franchised bottling operations and increased international pricing that was partially offset by lower net prices in domestic restaurants. International sales represented 25%, 21% and 20% of total sales in 1992, 1991 and 1990, respectively, reflecting double-digit growth in all three industry segments in 1992 and 1991. The trend of an increasing international component of sales and operating profits is expected to continue.

Cost of sales as a percentage of net sales was 47.8%, 48.1% and 48.2% in 1992, 1991 and 1990, respectively. The 1992 decrease was driven by the beverage segment, reflecting higher worldwide pricing and lower domestic ingredient and packaging costs. In 1991, the impact in beverages of higher concentrate pricing and lower domestic ingredient costs was largely offset in snack foods by a higher rate of manufacturing cost increases than international price advances.

Selling, general and administrative expenses rose 15% in 1992 and 12% in 1991. The unusual items accounted for one point of the growth in both years. The 1992 increase was driven by higher selling and distribution expenses that reflected acquisitions, additional restaurant units and volume growth. The increase also reflected increased marketing expenses due to higher spending in line with business growth as well as acquisitions. In 1991, higher sales volumes, increased marketing expenses and the impact of additional restaurant units led the increase.

Amortization of intangible assets rose 28% in 1992 and 10% in 1991 due primarily to acquisition activity. Of the $58 million increase in 1992, $17 million was due to the adoption of the new income tax accounting rules. (See Note 14.) The per share impact of amortization of intangible assets was $0.24, $0.22 and $0.20 in 1992, 1991 and 1990, respectively. The 1992 increase was mitigated by the incremental tax benefit of $35 million recognized on nondeductible amortization of identifiable intangibles, in accordance with these new accounting rules.

Gain on joint venture stock offering of $118.2 million relates to the 1990 initial public offering of shares of PepsiCo's KFC joint venture in Japan. (See Note 17.)

Interest expense decreased 4% in 1992 and 11% in 1991. The decrease in both years reflected lower average interest rates, partially offset by higher average domestic borrowings related to acquisition activity.

Interest income decreased 30% in 1992 and 10% in 1991. In both years, lower average interest rates were partially offset by higher average short-term investment balances held outside the U.S.

Income from Continuing Operations Before Income Taxes and Cumulative Effect of Accounting Changes ("pretax income") increased 14% in 1992 and was even in 1991. The following discussion excludes the impact of the unusual items. Pretax income increased 18% in 1992 and 13% in 1991, driven by combined segment operating profit growth of 16% in 1992 and 6% in 1991. The change in pretax income also reflected higher net interest expense in 1992 and lower net interest expense in 1991. The 1992 segment operating profit growth, reflecting double-digit growth in all three business segments, was primarily due to volume growth in domestic snack foods, additional restaurant units and international snack food acquisitions. The benefit in international operations of higher prices that exceeded increases in operating costs also aided profit growth. In 1991, the segment operating profit growth was driven by higher volumes and additional restaurant units, partially offset by operating expense increases in excess of higher pricing. International operating profits, which represented 19%, 16% and 15% of combined segment operating profits in 1992, 1991 and 1990, respectively, grew at double-digit rates in all three segments in 1992 and 1991. The growth in international profits in 1992 reflected snack food acquisitions, higher prices that exceeded cost increases and additional restaurant units. The increase in 1991 represented base business growth.

Provision for Income Taxes as a percentage of pretax income was 31.4%, 34.9% and 34.1% in 1992, 1991 and 1990, respectively. Excluding the impact of the adoption of the new income tax accounting rules in 1992, and the unusual tax effects on the restructuring charge at international snack foods in 1991, the gain on joint venture stock offering and the write-down of an international joint venture, both in 1990, the effective rates were 32.9%, 34.2% and 32.1%, respectively. The decrease in 1992 was due primarily to lower effective rates on higher foreign income as well as the resolution of various audits. The increase in 1991 was due primarily to higher taxes on foreign income.

Income and Income Per Share from Continuing Operations Before Cumulative Effect of Accounting Changes ("income" and "income per share") in 1992 increased 21% to $1.3 billion and 19% to $1.61, respectively, and declined 1% to $1.08 billion and $1.35, respectively, in 1991. Excluding the unusual items, income and income per share rose 21% and 20% in 1992 and grew 10% and 9% in 1991, respectively.

Consolidated Balance Sheet

(in millions except per share amount)
PepsiCo, Inc. and Subsidiaries
December 26, 1992 and December 28, 1991

	1992	1991
ASSETS		
Current Assets		
Cash and cash equivalents	$ 169.9	$ 186.7
Short-term investments, at cost	1,888.5	1,849.3
	2,058.4	2,036.0
Accounts and notes receivable, less allowance: $112.0 in 1992 and $97.5 in 1991	1,588.5	1,481.7
Inventories	768.8	661.5
Prepaid expenses, taxes and other current assets	426.6	386.9
Total Current Assets	4,842.3	4,566.1
Investments in Affiliates and Other Assets	1,707.9	1,681.9
Property, Plant and Equipment, net	7,442.0	6,594.7
Intangible Assets, net	6,959.0	5,932.4
Total Assets	$20,951.2	$18,775.1
LIABILITIES AND SHAREHOLDERS' EQUITY		
Current Liabilities		
Short-term borrowings	$ 706.8	$ 228.2
Accounts payable	1,164.8	1,196.6
Income taxes payable	387.9	492.4
Accrued compensation and benefits	638.9	539.7
Accrued marketing	327.0	333.8
Other current liabilities	1,099.0	931.4
Total Current Liabilities	4,324.4	3,722.1
Long-term Debt	7,964.8	7,806.2
Other Liabilities	1,624.0	631.3
Deferred Income Taxes	1,682.3	1,070.1
Shareholders' Equity		
Capital stock, par value 1 2/3¢ per share: authorized 1,800.0 shares, issued 863.1 shares	14.4	14.4
Capital in excess of par value	667.6	476.6
Retained earnings	5,439.7	5,470.0
Currency translation adjustment	(99.0)	330.3
	6,022.7	6,291.3
Less: Treasury stock, at cost: 64.3 shares in 1992, 74.0 shares in 1991	(667.0)	(745.9)
Total Shareholders' Equity	5,355.7	5,545.4
Total Liabilities and Shareholders' Equity	$20,951.2	$18,775.1

See accompanying Notes to Consolidated Financial Statements.

Management's Analysis — Financial Condition

(See "Management's Analysis — Overview" on page 26.)

Assets increased $2.2 billion or 12% over 1991, reflecting purchases of property, plant and equipment (capital spending), acquisitions, the impact of SFAS 109 and base business growth.

Short-term investments substantially represent high-grade marketable securities portfolios held outside the U.S. The portfolio in Puerto Rico, which totaled $1.5 billion at year-end 1992 and 1991, arises from the strong operating cash flows of the centralized concentrate manufacturing facilities that operate there under a tax incentive grant. The grant provides that the portfolio funds may be remitted to the U.S. without any additional tax. In 1992, PepsiCo remitted $360 million of the portfolio to the U.S. In 1991, $500 million of the portfolio was liquidated, with a portion used to refinance an international investment and the remainder remitted to the U.S. PepsiCo continually reassesses its alternatives to redeploy this and other portfolios held outside the U.S., considering other investment opportunities, tax consequences and overall financing strategies.

Inventories increased $107 million or 16%, primarily reflecting acquisitions of international snack food businesses. The $40 million or 10% increase in prepaid expenses, taxes and other current assets was due principally to higher deferred tax assets.

Capital spending totaled $1.6 billion in 1992 and $1.5 billion in 1991, with the increase driven by new restaurant units, which represented about half of the 1992 and 1991 spending. Declines in 1992 capital spending in worldwide beverages and domestic snack foods were partially offset by an increase in international snack foods.

Intangible assets increased $1.0 billion or 17% over 1991, reflecting a $511 million "gross-up" of reacquired franchise rights under SFAS 109. The increase also reflected acquisition activity, partially offset by amortization and the translation impact of a stronger U.S. dollar on the intangibles in the U.K.

Liabilities rose $2.4 billion or 18% over 1991, reflecting the impacts of SFAS 106 and SFAS 109 and an increase in total debt.

Income taxes payable declined $105 million or 21%, reflecting timing of payments as well as cash tax benefits to be received associated with stock option exercises. Accrued compensation and benefits rose $99 million or 18%, reflecting higher payroll-related accruals and the current portion of the retiree health benefits liability under SFAS 106. The increase in other current liabilities of $168 million or 18% was led by increases in restructuring accruals.

The $637 million or 8% increase in total short-term and long-term debt partially funded investing and other financing activities. PepsiCo's unused credit facilities with lending institutions, which exist largely to support the issuances of short-term borrowings, were $3.5 billion at year-end 1992 and 1991. This amount of short-term borrowings was classified as long-term at year-end 1992 and 1991, reflecting PepsiCo's intent and ability, through the existence of the credit facilities, to refinance these borrowings.

Other liabilities increased $1.0 billion or 157%, including a $610 million retiree health benefits liability under SFAS 106. Deferred income taxes rose $612 million or 57%, primarily reflecting the $571 million SFAS 109 cumulative effect and the $511 million "gross-up" of intangible assets, partially offset by the $219 million deferred tax asset associated with the cumulative effect of adopting SFAS 106.

Financial Leverage refers to the management of the debt and equity structure. PepsiCo measures leverage on a net basis, which takes into account its large short-term investment portfolios held outside the U.S. These portfolios are managed as part of PepsiCo's overall financing strategy and are not required to support day-to-day operations. Therefore, PepsiCo believes its net debt position, which reflects the pro forma remittance of the portfolios (net of related taxes) as a reduction of total debt, is the most meaningful historical cost measure of financial leverage used in its business. PepsiCo's ratio of net debt to net capital employed (defined as net debt, other liabilities, deferred income taxes and shareholders' equity) was 45% at year-end 1992 and 47% at year-end 1991. The decline in the ratio was due to a 15% increase in net capital partially offset by a 9% increase in net debt.

PepsiCo also measures financial leverage on a market value basis. Management believes that market leverage (defined as net debt as a percent of net debt plus the market value of equity, based on the year-end stock price) better measures PepsiCo's financial leverage from the perspective of investors in its securities, as it reflects the portion of the current value of PepsiCo that is financed with debt. Unlike historical cost measures, the market value of equity is based primarily on the expected future cash flows that will both support debt and provide returns to shareholders. The market net debt ratio was 17% at year-end 1992 and 19% at year-end 1991. The decline in the ratio was due to a 25% increase in PepsiCo's stock price, partially offset by the 9% increase in net debt. PepsiCo has established a target range for its market net debt ratio of 20-25%. PepsiCo believes that it can safely exceed this range on a short-term basis to take advantage of strategic acquisition opportunities.

PepsiCo's negative operating working capital position, which principally reflects the cash sales nature of its restaurant operations, effectively provides additional capital for investment. Operating working capital, which excludes short-term investments and short-term borrowings, was a negative $664 million and $777 million at year-end 1992 and 1991, respectively. The decline principally reflects the $105 million decrease in income taxes payable.

Shareholders' Equity declined $190 million or 3% from 1991, primarily due to a $429 million decrease in the currency translation adjustment and $405 million in dividends declared, partially offset by net income of $374 million and a $298 million impact of treasury stock issuances for acquisitions and stock option exercises. The decrease in the currency translation adjustment was principally due to the impact of a stronger U.S. dollar on the translation of the net assets (principally intangible assets) of operations in the U.K.

Based on income from continuing operations before cumulative effect of accounting changes, PepsiCo's return on average shareholders' equity was 23.9% in 1992 and 20.7% in 1991. The return on average shareholders' equity was 24.0% in 1992 and 22.7% in 1991, excluding from both income and shareholders' equity the impact of the 1992 and 1991 unusual charges as well as the cumulative effect and 1992 impact of the accounting changes.

Consolidated Statement of Cash Flows

(in millions)
PepsiCo, Inc. and Subsidiaries
Fifty-two weeks ended December 26, 1992, December 28, 1991 and December 29, 1990

	1992	1991	1990
Cash Flows — Continuing Operations:			
Income from continuing operations before cumulative effect of accounting changes	$1,301.7	$1,080.2	$1,090.6
Adjustments to reconcile income from continuing operations before cumulative effect of accounting changes to net cash provided by continuing operations:			
Depreciation and amortization	1,214.9	1,034.5	884.0
Deferred income taxes	(52.0)	98.0	86.4
Gain on joint venture stock offering	—	—	(118.2)
Other noncash charges and credits, net	315.6	227.2	120.3
Changes in operating working capital, excluding effect of acquisitions:			
Accounts and notes receivable	(45.7)	(55.9)	(124.8)
Inventories	(11.8)	(54.8)	(20.9)
Prepaid expenses, taxes and other current assets	(27.4)	(75.6)	(41.9)
Accounts payable	(102.0)	57.8	25.4
Income taxes payable	(16.9)	(3.4)	136.3
Other current liabilities	135.2	122.3	72.8
Net change in operating working capital	(68.6)	(9.6)	46.9
Net Cash Provided by Continuing Operations	**2,711.6**	**2,430.3**	**2,110.0**
Cash Flows — Investing Activities:			
Acquisitions and investments in affiliates	(1,209.7)	(640.9)	(630.6)
Purchases of property, plant and equipment	(1,549.6)	(1,457.8)	(1,180.1)
Proceeds from sales of property, plant and equipment	89.0	69.6	45.3
Short-term investments, by original maturity:			
More than three months — purchases	(1,174.8)	(1,849.2)	(2,093.2)
More than three months — sales	1,371.8	1,873.2	2,139.4
Three months or less, net	(249.4)	(164.9)	(228.0)
Proceeds from joint venture stock offering	—	—	129.6
Other, net	(30.8)	(105.8)	(119.7)
Net Cash Used for Investing Activities	**(2,753.5)**	**(2,275.8)**	**(1,937.3)**
Cash Flows — Financing Activities:			
Proceeds from issuances of long-term debt	1,092.7	2,799.6	777.3
Payments of long-term debt	(616.3)	(1,348.5)	(298.0)
Short-term borrowings, by original maturity:			
More than three months — proceeds	911.2	2,551.9	4,041.9
More than three months — payments	(2,062.6)	(3,097.4)	(2,647.4)
Three months or less, net	1,075.3	(467.1)	(1,480.7)
Cash dividends paid	(395.5)	(343.2)	(293.9)
Purchases of treasury stock	(32.0)	(195.2)	(147.7)
Proceeds from exercises of stock options	82.8	15.8	9.3
Other, net	(30.9)	(47.0)	(37.9)
Net Cash Provided by (Used for) Financing Activities	**24.7**	**(131.1)**	**(77.1)**
Effect of Exchange Rate Changes on Cash and Cash Equivalents	0.4	(7.5)	(1.0)
Net Increase (Decrease) in Cash and Cash Equivalents	(16.8)	15.9	94.6
Cash and Cash Equivalents — Beginning of Year	186.7	170.8	76.2
Cash and Cash Equivalents — End of Year	$ 169.9	$ 186.7	$ 170.8

See accompanying Notes to Consolidated Financial Statements, including Note 4 — Supplemental Cash Flow Information.

Management's Analysis — Cash Flows

(See "Management's Analysis — Overview" on page 26.)

Cash flow activity in 1992 reflected strong cash flows from continuing operations of $2.7 billion and net proceeds of $400 million from debt issuances and payments. Major funding needs included capital spending of $1.5 billion, acquisition and affiliate investment activity of $1.2 billion and dividends of $396 million.

One of PepsiCo's most significant financial strengths is its internal cash generation capability. In 1992, cash flows generated, after capital spending and acquisitions, in the snack food and beverage segments were partially offset by a cash use in the restaurant segment that reflected funding of additional units, both constructed and acquired from franchisees. Net cash flows from PepsiCo's domestic businesses were partially offset by international uses of cash, reflecting strategies to accelerate growth in international operations. As the chart below illustrates, over the last three years, net cash provided by continuing operations substantially funded capital spending, dividend payments and cash acquisition and affiliate investment activity.

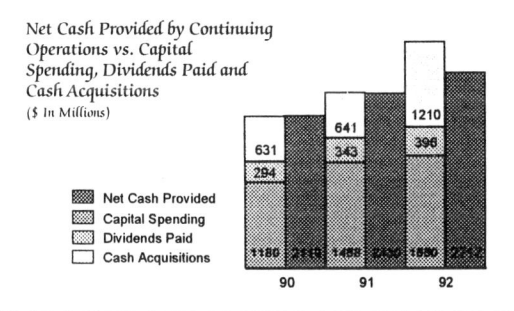

Net Cash Provided by Continuing Operations vs. Capital Spending, Dividends Paid and Cash Acquisitions
($ In Millions)

- Net Cash Provided
- Capital Spending
- Dividends Paid
- Cash Acquisitions

	90	91	92
Net Cash Provided	1180	2119	2742
Capital Spending			1210
	631	641	
		343	396
	294		
	1468	2430	1590

Net Cash Provided by Continuing Operations in 1992 rose $281 million or 12% over 1991, driven by higher income, and in 1991 grew $320 million or 15% over 1990. The increases in depreciation and amortization noncash charges of $180 million in 1992 and $151 million in 1991 reflected capital spending and acquisitions. The 1992 decline of $150 million in the deferred income tax provision was primarily due to the impact of SFAS 106 and SFAS 109, higher restructuring accruals and lower prefunding of employee benefit expenses. The other net noncash charges and credits reflect increased accruals of noncurrent liabilities in 1992 and 1991. The comparison of the 1992 net change in operating working capital to 1991 reflects normal changes in most accounts with the net change, driven by accounts payable, due primarily to timing of year-end payments, partially offset by the impact on prepaid expenses of the lower prefunding of employee benefits. The 1991 to 1990 comparison of operating working capital changes reflects the timing of income tax payments and higher prefunding of employee benefits, partially offset by modest growth in accounts receivable due to slower volume growth in domestic bottling operations as well as the impact of accrued restructuring charges.

Investing Activities over the past three years reflected strategic spending in all three industry segments through acquisitions, investments in affiliates and capital spending. Acquisition and affiliate investment activity in 1992 included cash and noncash (primarily treasury stock issuance) transactions of $1.2 billion and $190 million, respectively, and was led by acquisitions of international and domestic franchised bottling and restaurant operations. About 60% of the acquisitive activity in 1992 represented international transactions compared to 20% in 1991. Significant activity subsequent to year-end 1992 included the buyout of PepsiCo's joint venture partners in a franchised bottling operation in Spain and the related acquisition of their fruit-flavored beverage business for $213 million in cash. High cost local currency debt assumed in the transaction of $114 million will be retired in the first half of 1993. As of February 1993, completed and probable cash and stock acquisitions, including the above transaction, totaled approximately $1 billion. PepsiCo continues to seek opportunities to strengthen its position in its domestic and international industry segments through such strategic acquisitions. Capital spending is expected to increase to approximately $1.7 billion in 1993 from $1.5 billion in 1992. About half of the 1993 amount is targeted for restaurants, led by new units, and the balance is evenly divided between beverages and snack foods, reflecting productive capacity expansion and maintenance. Approximately 30% of the planned 1993 capital spending relates to international businesses, about the same as 1992 and 1991.

Financing Activities resulted in an increase in net cash provided of $156 million over 1991, principally reflecting a decline in purchases of treasury stock and an increase in proceeds from exercises of stock options, partially offset by higher payments of dividends and lower net proceeds from short and long-term debt issuances and payments. Payments of long-term debt in 1991 included retirement of a $300 million nonrecourse obligation.

During 1992, PepsiCo issued $1.7 billion of notes and used the proceeds to refinance short-term borrowings, which partially funded investing and other financing activities. Subsequent to year-end, PepsiCo issued $425 million of notes through February 1993. All of the issuances were under a $3.3 billion shelf registration statement filed with the Securities and Exchange Commission in December 1991. The amount available for future debt issuances under the shelf registration totaled $1.2 billion as of February 1993. As a result of the refinancings and interest rate swap transactions, the amount of variable rate debt increased over last year, representing about half of PepsiCo's debt portfolio at year-end 1992.

Cash dividends declared were a record $405 million in 1992 and $363 million in 1991. PepsiCo targets a dividend payout of approximately one-third of the prior year's income, thus retaining sufficient earnings to provide financial resources for growth opportunities.

Share repurchase decisions are evaluated considering the target capital structure and other investment opportunities. In 1992, PepsiCo repurchased one million shares, all in the first quarter, at a cost of $32 million. Including these repurchases, 21.8 million shares have been purchased under the 45 million share repurchase authority granted by PepsiCo's Board of Directors in 1987.

Consolidated Statement of Shareholders' Equity

(shares in thousands, dollars in millions except per share amounts)
PepsiCo, Inc. and Subsidiaries
Fifty-two weeks ended December 26, 1992, December 28, 1991 and December 29, 1990

	Capital Stock Issued Shares	Capital Stock Issued Amount	Capital Stock Treasury Shares	Capital Stock Treasury Amount	Capital in Excess of Par Value	Retained Earnings	Currency Translation Adjustment	Total
Shareholders' Equity, December 30, 1989	863,083	$14.4	(72,026)	$(491.8)	$323.9	$3,978.4	$66.2	$3,891.1
1990 Net income						1,076.9		1,076.9
Cash dividends declared (per share-$0.38)						(302.3)		(302.3)
Currency translation adjustment							317.0	317.0
Purchases of treasury stock			(6,310)	(147.7)				(147.7)
Shares issued in connection with acquisitions			2,013	16.3	30.1			46.4
Stock option exercises, including tax benefits, and compensation awards			1,072	7.8	9.1			16.9
Other, principally conversion of debentures			557	4.0	1.9			5.9
Shareholders' Equity, December 29, 1990	863,083	$14.4	(74,694)	$(611.4)	$365.0	$4,753.0	$383.2	$4,904.2
1991 Net income						1,080.2		1,080.2
Cash dividends declared (per share-$0.46)						(363.2)		(363.2)
Currency translation adjustment							(52.9)	(52.9)
Purchases of treasury stock			(6,392)	(195.2)				(195.2)
Shares issued in connection with acquisitions			5,613	46.7	95.0			141.7
Stock option exercises, including tax benefits, and compensation awards			1,446	13.6	16.4			30.0
Other, principally conversion of debentures			45	0.4	0.2			0.6
Shareholders' Equity, December 28, 1991	863,083	$14.4	(73,982)	$(745.9)	$476.6	$5,470.0	$330.3	$5,545.4
1992 Net income						374.3		374.3
Cash dividends declared (per share-$0.51)						(404.6)		(404.6)
Currency translation adjustment							(429.3)	(429.3)
Purchases of treasury stock			(1,000)	(32.0)				(32.0)
Shares issued in connection with acquisitions			4,265	44.2	115.3			159.5
Stock option exercises, including tax benefits, and compensation awards			6,333	65.5	75.5			141.0
Other, principally conversion of debentures			107	1.2	0.2			1.4
Shareholders' Equity, December 26, 1992	863,083	$14.4	(64,277)	$(667.0)	$667.6	$5,439.7	$(99.0)	$5,355.7

See accompanying Notes to Consolidated Financial Statements.

Notes to Consolidated Financial Statements

(tabular dollars in millions except per share amounts)

Note 1 — Summary of Significant Accounting Policies

Significant accounting policies are discussed below and, where applicable, in the Notes that follow.

Principles of Consolidation — The financial statements reflect the consolidated accounts of PepsiCo, Inc. and its controlled affiliates. Intercompany accounts and transactions have been eliminated. Investments in affiliates in which PepsiCo exercises significant influence but not control are accounted for by the equity method, and the equity in net income is included in "Selling, general and administrative expenses" in the Consolidated Statement of Income. The Consolidated Statement of Income for 1991 and 1990 has been restated to report under the equity method of accounting the results of previously consolidated snack food businesses in Spain, Portugal and Greece, which were contributed to a joint venture with General Mills, Inc. in late 1992. Although the equity interest and previously consolidated businesses are not significant to PepsiCo's Consolidated Financial Statements, the restatement is intended to improve the comparability of PepsiCo's operating results. The restatement had no effect on income from continuing operations before cumulative effect of accounting changes or net income. The Consolidated Balance Sheet and Statement of Cash Flows were not restated. Certain other reclassifications were made to prior year amounts to conform with the 1992 presentation.

Marketing Costs — Marketing costs are reported in "Selling, general and administrative expenses" in the Consolidated Statement of Income and include costs of advertising, marketing and promotional programs. Promotional discounts are expensed as incurred, and other marketing costs not deferred are charged to expense ratably in relation to sales over the year in which incurred. Marketing costs deferred consist of media and personal service advertising prepayments, materials in inventory and production costs of future media advertising; these assets are expensed in the year used.

Franchise Arrangements — Franchise arrangements with restaurant franchisees generally provide for initial fees and continuing royalty payments to PepsiCo based upon a percentage of sales. The arrangements are intended to assist franchisees through, among other things, product development and marketing programs initiated by PepsiCo for both its company-owned and franchised operations. On a limited basis, franchisees have also entered into leases of restaurant properties leased or owned by PepsiCo (see Note 10). Royalty revenues, initial fees and rental payments from franchisees, which are included in "Net Sales" in the Consolidated Statement of Income, aggregated $344 million, $326 million and $294 million in 1992, 1991 and 1990, respectively. Franchise royalty revenues, which represent the majority of these amounts, are recognized on an accrual basis. PepsiCo also has franchise arrangements with beverage bottlers, which do not provide for royalty payments.

Classification of Restaurant Operating Expenses — Operating expenses incurred at the restaurant unit level consist primarily of food and related packaging costs, labor associated with food preparation and customer service, and overhead expenses. For purposes of the Consolidated Statement of Income, food and packaging costs as well as all labor-related expenses are classified as "Cost of sales," and all other unit level expenses are classified as "Selling, general and administrative expenses."

Cash Equivalents — Cash equivalents represent funds temporarily invested (with original maturities not exceeding three months) as part of PepsiCo's management of day-to-day operating cash receipts and disbursements. All other investment portfolios, primarily held outside the U.S., are classified as short-term investments.

Net Income Per Share — Net income per share is computed by dividing net income by the weighted average number of shares and share equivalents outstanding during each year.

Research and Development Expenses — Research and development expenses, which are expensed as incurred, were $102 million, $99 million and $101 million in 1992, 1991 and 1990, respectively.

Note 2 — Business Segments

Information regarding industry segments and geographic areas of operations is provided on pages 28 and 29.

Note 3 — Net Unusual Charges and Impact of Accounting Changes

Information regarding items affecting comparability, including restructuring actions in both 1992 and 1991 and the 1992 impact of the accounting changes, is provided on page 28. PepsiCo adopted the new Statements of Financial Accounting Standards, "Employers' Accounting for Postretirement Benefits Other Than Pensions" (SFAS 106) and "Accounting for Income Taxes" (SFAS 109), effective December 29, 1991. (See Notes 11 and 14.)

Note 4 — Supplemental Cash Flow Information

	1992	1991	1990
Cash Flow Data			
Interest paid	$574.7	490.1	656.9
Income taxes paid	$519.7	385.9	375.0
Schedule of Noncash Investing and Financing Activities			
Liabilities assumed in connection with acquisitions	$383.8	70.9	126.7
Issuance of treasury stock and debt for acquisitions	$189.5	162.7	105.1
Book value of net assets exchanged for investment in affiliate	$ 86.7	—	—
Additions of capital leases	$ 15.5	26.5	18.1
Issuance of treasury stock for compensation awards and conversion of debentures	$ 2.6	14.7	13.5

Note 5 — Acquisitions and Investments in Affiliates

During 1992, PepsiCo completed a number of acquisitions and affiliate investments in all three industry segments aggregating $1.4 billion, principally for cash. This activity included acquisitions of international (primarily Canada) and domestic franchised bottling operations and a number of domestic and international franchised restaurant operations, the buyout of PepsiCo's joint venture partner in a Canadian snack food business and an equity investment in a domestic mid-scale gourmet pizza business. In addition, PepsiCo exchanged certain previously consolidated snack food businesses in Europe with a net book value of $87 million for a 60% equity interest in a new international snack food joint venture with General Mills, Inc. PepsiCo secured a controlling interest in the Gamesa Mexican cookie business through an exchange of certain non-cookie operations of Gamesa for its joint venture partner's interest.

Significant activity subsequent to December 26, 1992 included the buyout of PepsiCo's joint venture partners in a franchised bottling operation in Spain and the related acquisition of their fruit-flavored beverage business for $213 million in cash.

During 1991, acquisition and affiliate investment activity aggregated $804 million, principally for cash, led by acquisitions of domestic franchised restaurant operations.

During 1990, acquisition and affiliate investment activity aggregated $736 million, principally for cash, and included an equity interest in the Gamesa cookie business as well as acquisitions of franchised bottling and restaurant operations.

The acquisitions have been accounted for by the purchase method; accordingly, their results are included in the Consolidated Financial Statements from their respective dates of acquisition. The aggregate impact of acquisitions was not material to PepsiCo's net sales, net income or net income per share; accordingly, no related pro forma information is provided.

Note 6 — Inventories

Inventories are valued at the lower of cost (computed on the average, first-in, first-out or last-in, first-out methods) or net realizable value. The cost of 44% of 1992 inventories and 49% of 1991 inventories was computed using the last-in, first-out (LIFO) method. The carrying value of total LIFO inventories was lower than the approximate current cost of those inventories by $3.4 million at year-end 1992 and $13.4 million at year-end 1991.

	1992	1991
Raw materials, supplies and in-process	$388.1	$345.3
Finished goods	380.7	316.2
	$768.8	$661.5

PepsiCo hedges certain raw material purchases through commodities futures contracts to reduce its exposure to market price fluctuations. Gains and losses on these contracts are included in the cost of the raw materials.

Note 7 — Property, Plant and Equipment

Property, plant and equipment are stated at cost. Depreciation is calculated principally on a straight-line basis over the estimated useful lives of the assets. Depreciation expense in 1992, 1991 and 1990 was $923 million, $800 million and $686 million, respectively.

	1992	1991
Land	$ 1,010.0	$ 880.1
Buildings and improvements	4,269.5	3,707.1
Capital leases, primarily buildings	330.5	288.2
Machinery and equipment	6,485.2	5,626.3
	12,095.2	10,501.7
Accumulated depreciation	(4,653.2)	(3,907.0)
	$ 7,442.0	$ 6,594.7

Note 8 — Intangible Assets

Identifiable intangible assets arise from the allocation of purchase prices of businesses acquired, and consist principally of reacquired franchise rights and trademarks. Reacquired franchise rights relate to acquisitions of franchised bottling and restaurant operations, and the trademarks principally relate to acquisitions of international snack food operations and the 1986 acquisition of KFC. Values assigned to such identifiable intangibles were based on independent appraisals or internal estimates. Goodwill represents any residual purchase price after allocation to all identifiable net assets.

	1992	1991
Reacquired franchise rights	$ 3,476.9	$ 2,835.6
Trademarks	734.2	764.0
Other identifiable intangibles	159.6	193.3
Goodwill	2,588.3	2,139.5
	$ 6,959.0	$ 5,932.4

Intangible assets are amortized on a straight-line basis over appropriate periods generally ranging from 20 to 40 years. Accumulated amortization was $1.0 billion and $757 million at year-end 1992 and 1991, respectively.

Note 9 — Short-term Borrowings and Long-term Debt

	1992	1991
Short-term Borrowings		
Commercial paper (3.5% and 6.1% weighted average interest rate at year-end 1992 and 1991, respectively)	$ 2,113.6	$ 1,616.7
Current maturities of long-term debt issuances	1,052.6	619.2
Notes (A)	634.5	1,100.0
Other borrowings	406.1	342.3
Amount reclassified to long-term debt (B)	(3,500.0)	(3,450.0)
	$ 706.8	$ 228.2

	1992	1991
Long-term Debt		
Short-term borrowings, reclassified (B)	$3,500.0	$3,450.0
Notes due 1993 through 1999 (6.6% and 7.1% weighted average interest rate at year-end 1992 and 1991, respectively) (A)	4,209.1	3,381.0
Zero coupon notes, $950 million due 1993-2012 (14.4% and 14.1% semi-annual weighted average yield to maturity at year-end 1992 and 1991, respectively)	300.4	365.6
Swiss franc perpetual Foreign Interest Payment bonds (C)	211.4	210.7
European Currency Units 7⅜% notes due 1992 (D)	—	134.2
Pound sterling 9¼% notes due 1993 (D)	91.0	112.5
Swiss franc 5¼% bearer bonds due 1995 (D)	89.1	99.5
Swiss franc 7⅛% notes due 1994 (D)	69.1	74.1
Capital lease obligations (see Note 10)	242.0	213.3
Other, due 1993-2020 (6.8% and 7.7% weighted average interest rate at year-end 1992 and 1991, respectively)	305.3	384.5
	9,017.4	8,425.4
Less current maturities of long-term debt issuances	(1,052.6)	(619.2)
Total long-term debt	$7,964.8	$7,806.2

Long-term debt is carried net of any related discount or premium and unamortized debt issuance costs. The debt agreements include various restrictions, none of which is presently significant to PepsiCo.

The annual maturities of long-term debt through 1997, excluding capital lease obligations and the reclassified short-term borrowings, are: 1993-$1.03 billion, 1994-$1.08 billion, 1995-$803 million, 1996-$835 million and 1997-$312 million.

(A) PepsiCo has entered into interest rate swap agreements to effectively convert $725 million and $865 million of fixed interest rate debt issuances to variable rate debt with a weighted average interest rate of 3.4% and 4.6% at year-end 1992 and 1991, respectively, as well as effectively convert $214 million and $164 million of variable interest rate debt to fixed rate debt with an interest rate of 7.0% and 7.8% at year-end 1992 and 1991, respectively. The differential to be paid or received on interest rate swaps is accrued as interest rates change and is charged or credited to interest expense over the life of the agreements.

(B) At year-end 1992 and 1991, $3.5 billion of short-term borrowings were classified as long-term, reflecting PepsiCo's intent and ability to refinance these borrowings on a long-term basis, through either long-term debt issuances or rollover of existing short-term borrowings. At year-end 1992 and 1991, PepsiCo had revolving credit agreements covering potential borrowings aggregating $3.5 billion, with the current agreements expiring in 1995 through 1998. These unused credit facilities provide the ability to refinance short-term borrowings.

(C) The coupon rate of the Swiss franc 400 million perpetual Foreign Interest Payment bonds issued in 1986 is 7 1/2% through 1996. The interest payments are made in U.S. dollars at a fixed contractual exchange rate. The bonds have no stated maturity date. At the end of each 10-year period after the issuance of the bonds, PepsiCo and the bondholders each have the right to cause redemption of the bonds. If not redeemed, the coupon rate will be adjusted based on the prevailing yield of 10-year U.S. Treasury Securities. The principal of the bonds is denominated in Swiss francs. PepsiCo can, and intends to, limit the ultimate redemption amount to the U.S. dollar proceeds at issuance, which is the basis of the carrying value.

(D) PepsiCo has entered into currency exchange agreements to hedge its foreign currency exposure on these issues of non-U.S. dollar denominated debt. At year-end 1992, the carrying value of this debt aggregated $249 million and the net receivable under related currency exchange agreements aggregated $20 million, resulting in a net effective U.S. dollar liability of $229 million with a weighted average fixed interest rate of 7.2%. At year-end 1991, the aggregate carrying values of the debt and the net receivable under related currency exchange agreements were $420 million and $77 million, respectively, resulting in a net effective U.S. dollar liability of $343 million with a weighted average fixed interest rate of 7.3%. The carrying values of the currency exchange agreements are reflected in the Consolidated Balance Sheet as gross receivables and payables under the appropriate current and noncurrent asset and liability captions. Changes in the carrying value of a currency exchange agreement resulting from exchange rate movements are offset by changes in the carrying value of the related non-U.S. dollar denominated debt, as both values are based on current exchange rates.

In early 1992, PepsiCo effectively fixed the interest rates on $1.1 billion of commercial paper borrowings through several interest rate swap agreements that terminate in February through May of 1993.

Except for these commercial paper swaps, the maturity dates of interest rate swaps and currency exchange agreements correspond with those of the related debt instruments. The counterparties to PepsiCo's interest rate swaps and currency exchange agreements consist of a diversified group of financial institutions. PepsiCo is exposed to credit risk to the extent of nonperformance by these counterparties; however, PepsiCo regularly monitors its positions and the credit ratings of these counterparties and considers the risk of default to be remote. Additionally, due to the frequency of interest payments and receipts, PepsiCo's credit risk related to interest rate swaps is not significant.

Note 10—Leases

PepsiCo has noncancelable commitments under both capital and operating leases, primarily for restaurant units. Certain of these units have been subleased to restaurant franchisees. Commitments on capital and operating leases expire at various dates through 2088 and, in many cases, provide for rent escalations and renewal options.

Most leases require payment of related occupancy costs which include property taxes, maintenance and insurance.

Future minimum commitments and sublease receivables under noncancelable leases are as follows:

	Commitments		Sublease Receivables	
	Capital	Operating	Direct Financing	Operating
1993	$ 48.3	$ 225.9	$ 3.9	$ 8.4
1994	46.5	197.9	3.7	7.9
1995	41.9	177.3	3.5	7.2
1996	35.9	158.0	3.3	6.4
1997	31.3	141.4	3.0	5.4
Later years	211.2	779.6	9.5	24.2
	$415.1	$1,680.1	$26.9	$59.5

At year-end 1992, the present value of minimum payments under capital leases was $242 million, after deducting $1 million for estimated executory costs (taxes, maintenance and insurance) and $172 million representing imputed interest. The present value of minimum receivables under direct financing subleases was $17 million after deducting $10 million of unearned interest income.

Total rental expense and income and the contingent portions of these totals were as follows:

	1992	1991	1990
Total rental expense	$379.0	323.2	272.7
Contingent portion of expense	$ 27.5	22.3	21.4
Total rental income	$ 14.7	13.0	10.5
Contingent portion of income	$ 4.5	4.8	4.9

Contingent rentals are based on sales by restaurants in excess of levels stipulated in the lease agreements.

Note 11—Postretirement Benefits Other Than Pensions

PepsiCo provides postretirement health care and life insurance benefits (postretirement benefits) to eligible retired U.S. employees. Employees who have 10 years of service and attain age 55 while in service with PepsiCo are eligible to participate in the postretirement benefit plans. The plans in effect through 1992 were largely noncontributory and were not funded.

Effective December 29, 1991, PepsiCo adopted Statement of Financial Accounting Standards No. 106 (SFAS 106), "Employers' Accounting for Postretirement Benefits Other Than Pensions." SFAS 106 requires PepsiCo to accrue the cost of postretirement benefits over the years employees provide services to the date of their full eligibility for such benefits. Previously, such costs were expensed as actual claims were incurred. PepsiCo elected to immediately recognize the transition obligation for future benefits to be paid related to past employee services, resulting in a noncash charge of $575.3 million pretax ($356.7 million after-tax or $0.44 per share) that represents the cumulative effect of the change in accounting for years prior to 1992. The expense accrued in 1992 exceeded the amount under the previous accounting method by $52.1 million pretax

($32.3 after-tax or $0.04 per share). PepsiCo's cash flows will be unaffected by this accounting change because PepsiCo intends to continue its current practice of paying the costs of these postretirement benefits as the claims are incurred.

The postretirement benefit expense for 1992 included the following components:

Service cost of benefits earned	$25.5
Interest cost on accumulated postretirement benefit obligation	50.8
Amortization of prior service cost	0.1
Postretirement benefit expense for 1992	$76.4

Health care claims incurred and life insurance premiums paid totaled $24.3 million, $23.9 million and $20.4 million in 1992, 1991 and 1990, respectively.

The 1992 postretirement benefit liability included the following components:

Actuarial present value of postretirement benefit obligations:	
Retirees	$(251.2)
Fully eligible active plan participants	(132.5)
Other active plan participants	(312.1)
Accumulated postretirement benefit obligation	(695.8)
Unrecognized prior service cost	0.5
Unrecognized net loss	58.0
Postretirement benefit liability at year-end 1992	$(637.3)
Included in:	
"Accrued compensation and benefits"	$ (26.9)
"Other Liabilities"	(610.4)
	$(637.3)

The discount rate used to determine the accumulated postretirement benefit obligation was 8.2%. The assumed health care cost trend rate used to measure the accumulated postretirement benefit obligation was 12.5% initially, declining gradually to 5.5% in 2005 and thereafter. A one-percentage-point increase in the assumed health care cost trend rate would have increased the 1992 postretirement benefit expense by $13.3 million and would have increased the 1992 accumulated postretirement benefit obligation by $119.4 million.

Effective in 1993 and 1994, certain features of the plans have been amended. For future retirees, PepsiCo will introduce retiree cost-sharing and will implement programs intended to stem rising costs. Also, PepsiCo has adopted a provision which limits its future obligation to absorb health care cost inflation. These amendments will result in an unrecognized gain of $191 million, which will be amortized on a straight-line basis over the average remaining employee service period of 10 years as a reduction in postretirement benefit expense beginning in 1993. The projected 1993 postretirement benefit expense is approximately $36 million, or about

$40 million less than the 1992 expense. This anticipated net decline is primarily due to the plan amendments, reflecting reductions in service and interest costs as well as the amortization of the unrecognized gain.

Although not yet measured, obligations related to international postretirement benefit plans are not expected to be significant, since these benefits are generally provided through government-sponsored plans.

Note 12 — Pension Plans

PepsiCo sponsors noncontributory defined benefit pension plans covering substantially all full-time domestic employees as well as contributory and noncontributory defined benefit pension plans covering certain international employees. Benefits generally are based on years of service and compensation or stated amounts for each year of service. PepsiCo funds the domestic plans in amounts not less than minimum statutory funding requirements nor more than the maximum amount that can be deducted for federal income tax purposes. International plans are funded in amounts sufficient to comply with local statutory requirements. The plans' assets consist principally of equity securities, government and corporate debt securities and other fixed income obligations. PepsiCo Capital Stock accounted for approximately 20% and 19% of the total market value of the plans' assets for 1992 and 1991, respectively.

Full-time domestic employees not covered by these plans generally are covered by multiemployer plans as part of collective-bargaining agreements. Pension expense for these multiemployer plans was not significant in the aggregate.

For each of the years presented below, the information includes domestic plans and plans in the U.K. Because of 1992 acquisition activity, the information for 1992 also includes plans in Canada. Other international plans are not significant in the aggregate and therefore are not included in the following disclosures.

The net pension expense for company-sponsored plans (the Plans) included the following components:

	1992	1991	1990
Service cost of benefits earned	$ 60.9	$ 46.8	$ 48.1
Interest cost on projected benefit obligation	82.9	69.2	63.3
Return on Plan assets:			
Actual	(97.3)	(224.1)	(27.0)
Deferred gain (loss)	(5.9)	134.2	(55.9)
	(103.2)	(89.9)	(82.9)
Amortization of net transition gain	(19.0)	(19.0)	(19.0)
Pension expense	$ 21.6	$ 7.1	$ 9.5

The following disclosures have been aggregated for all Plans, as the amounts for certain small plans with accumulated benefit obligations exceeding the assets were not significant. Reconciliations of the funded status of the Plans to the prepaid pension liability included in the Consolidated Balance Sheet are as follows:

	1992	1991
Actuarial present value of benefit obligations:		
Vested benefits	$ (853.4)	$ (717.1)
Nonvested benefits	(80.7)	(96.8)
Accumulated benefit obligation	(934.1)	(813.9)
Effect of projected compensation increases	(166.3)	(133.0)
Projected benefit obligation	(1,100.4)	(946.9)
Plan assets at fair value	1,299.2	1,199.3
Plan assets in excess of projected benefit obligation	198.8	252.4
Unrecognized prior service cost	52.2	48.7
Unrecognized net gain	(57.9)	(103.4)
Unrecognized net transition gain	(110.1)	(129.1)
Prepaid pension liability	$ 83.0	$ 68.6
Included in:		
"Investments in Affiliates and Other Assets"	$ 126.1	$ 106.5
"Other current liabilities"	(24.5)	(22.6)
"Other Liabilities"	(18.6)	(15.3)
	$ 83.0	$ 68.6

The assumptions used in computing the information above were as follows:

	1992	1991	1990
Discount rate-pension expense	8.5%	9.5	9.1
Expected long-term rate of return on plan assets	10.1%	10.2	10.2
Discount rate-projected benefit obligation	8.3%	8.6	9.5
Future compensation growth rate	3.3%-7.0%	3.3-7.4	5.0-7.0

The discount rates and rates of return represent weighted averages, reflecting the combined assumptions for the domestic and international plans included as described above.

Note 13 — Postemployment Benefits Other Than to Retirees

In November of 1992, the Financial Accounting Standards Board issued Statement of Financial Accounting Standards No. 112 (SFAS 112), "Employers' Accounting for Postemployment Benefits." SFAS 112, which must be adopted by 1994, requires employers to accrue the cost of postemployment benefits (including salary continuation, severance and disability benefits, job training and counseling and continuation of benefits such as health care and life insurance coverage) to former or inactive employees. PepsiCo accrues some, but not all postemployment benefits. SFAS 112 requires immediate recognition of any obligation upon adoption. PepsiCo has not yet determined the impact of adoption.

Note 14 — Income Taxes

Effective December 29, 1991, PepsiCo adopted Statement of Financial Accounting Standards No. 109 (SFAS 109), "Accounting for Income Taxes." Under SFAS 109, the deferred income tax expense or benefit generally arises from changes in differences between financial reporting and tax bases of all assets and liabilities (with exceptions related to goodwill and investments in foreign businesses), and previously recorded deferred tax assets and liabilities are adjusted upon any changes in enacted tax rates. Differences between financial reporting and tax bases result most frequently from differences in timing of income and expense recognition. Another common source of bases differences is acquisition activity. Tax laws applicable to acquisitions can result in significant differences in values assigned to assets, particularly identifiable intangibles, that are not reflected in tax returns unless the assets are sold. Under the previous accounting rules, Accounting Principles Board Opinion No. 11 (APB 11), the deferred income tax expense or benefit generally arose from changes in bases differences related only to timing, and previously recorded deferred tax assets and liabilities were not adjusted to reflect changes in enacted tax rates.

PepsiCo elected to adopt SFAS 109 on a prospective basis as a change in accounting principle, resulting in a noncash charge of $570.7 million ($0.71 per share) that represents the cumulative effect of the change related to years prior to 1992. The cumulative effect principally represents the recording of deferred tax liabilities related to identifiable intangible assets that have no tax bases. These deferred tax liabilities would be paid only in the unlikely event the related intangible assets were sold in taxable transactions. The cumulative effect impact related to intangible assets was partially offset by a reduction of previously recorded net deferred tax liabilities, principally related to property, plant and equipment, to reflect the impact of lower U.S. tax rates provided by the Tax Reform Act of 1986.

The identifiable intangible assets driving the cumulative effect include acquired trademarks, such as Smiths and Walkers (U.K.), Gamesa (Mexico) and KFC, and reacquired franchise rights arising from nontaxable acquisitions of franchised bottling and restaurant operations. Under previous acquisition accounting rules, the fair values of these nondeductible reacquired franchise rights were reduced by the lost tax benefits in order to determine the financial reporting carrying values. These lost tax benefit amounts, which were determined on a discounted basis, effectively represented deferred tax liabilities. In accordance with SFAS 109, the carrying values of the reacquired franchise rights were "grossed-up" to present the lost tax benefit amounts as deferred tax liabilities, and the related cumulative effect represents an adjustment to increase the liabilities to nominal (i.e., undiscounted) values. With respect to trademark intangibles, amortization of these assets is not deductible in the applicable tax jurisdictions whether acquired in taxable or nontaxable transactions. Therefore, the trademark fair values, which did not include any tax benefits, represented the carrying values, and the cumulative effect related to trademarks represents the recognition of the full amount of related deferred tax liabilities.

Detail of the provision for income taxes on income from continuing operations before cumulative effect of accounting changes:

	1992	1991	1990
Current—Federal	**$413.0**	$315.5	$301.5
Foreign	**170.4**	114.3	112.8
State	**65.7**	51.5	62.3
	649.1	481.3	476.6
Deferred—Federal	**(18.8)**	63.5	66.0
Foreign	**(33.5)**	25.3	12.7
State	**0.3**	9.4	7.9
	(52.0)	98.2	86.6
	$597.1	$579.5	$563.2

The 1992 amounts presented above were calculated in accordance with SFAS 109, and the 1991 and 1990 amounts were calculated in accordance with APB 11. The impact of adopting SFAS 109 related to 1992 was a decrease in pretax income of $20.7 million and a decrease in the deferred provision for income taxes of $33.7 million, resulting in an increase of $13.0 million ($0.02 per share) in income before the cumulative effect. Assuming no changes in enacted tax rates or other unusual events, the impact of SFAS 109 on 1993 results is expected to approximate the 1992 net income benefit. The decrease in pretax income primarily reflects higher amortization expense related to reacquired franchise rights due to the required "gross-up" described above. The decrease in the deferred provision for income taxes related to SFAS 109 is due primarily to the recognition of tax benefits related to amortization of identifiable intangible assets with no tax basis. As these assets are decreased through amortization, the difference between the financial reporting and tax bases also decreases, resulting in a decrease in the related required deferred tax liabilities. In 1992, tax benefits of $57.5 million related to exercises of stock options were allocated directly to capital.

The 1991 and 1990 deferred provisions arose principally from accelerated expense recognition for tax purposes as compared to financial reporting. The 1991 deferred provision included amounts related to depreciation of property, plant and equipment of $56.2 million, amortization of intangibles of $49.0 million and increased prefunding of employee benefits of $23.3 million, partially offset by $41.7 million related to restructuring charges. The 1990 deferred provision included amounts related to amortization of intangibles of $46.0 million and depreciation of property, plant and equipment of $40.6 million.

U.S. and foreign income from continuing operations before income taxes and cumulative effect of accounting changes:

	1992	1991	1990
U.S.	**$1,196.8**	$1,054.3	$ 915.5
Foreign	**702.0**	605.4	738.3
	$1,898.8	$1,659.7	$1,653.8

PepsiCo operates centralized concentrate manufacturing facilities in Puerto Rico and Ireland under long-term tax incentives. The foreign amount in the above table includes approximately 50% (consistent with the allocation for tax purposes) of the income from U.S. sales of concentrate manufactured in Puerto Rico.

Reconciliation of the U.S. federal statutory tax rate to PepsiCo's effective tax rate on income from continuing operations, based on the dollar impact of these major components on the provision for income taxes:

	1992	1991	1990
U.S. federal statutory tax rate	34.0%	34.0%	34.0%
State income tax, net of federal tax benefit	2.3	2.4	1.9
Effect of lower taxes on foreign income (including Puerto Rico and Ireland)	(5.0)	(2.7)	(4.4)
Nondeductible amortization of domestic goodwill (all years) and other intangible assets (1991 and 1990 only)	0.9	1.8	1.6
Tax basis difference related to joint venture stock offering	—	—	1.6
Other, net	(0.8)	(0.6)	(0.6)
Effective tax rate	31.4%	34.9%	34.1%

Detail of the 1992 deferred tax assets and liabilities:

	Deferred Tax Assets	Deferred Tax Liabilities
Current:		
Restructuring accruals	$ 70.6	—
Other, net	154.9	$ 108.6
Current deferred tax asset/liability	$ 225.5	$ 108.6
Noncurrent:		
Postretirement benefits	$ 230.8	—
Net operating loss carryforwards	130.0	—
Deferred state income taxes	63.3	—
Identifiable intangible assets	—	$1,292.2
Property, plant & equipment	—	526.8
Safe harbor leases	—	185.6
Zero coupon notes	—	96.0
Other, net	246.9	124.6
Noncurrent deferred tax asset/liability	$ 671.0	$2,225.2
Total deferred tax asset/liability before valuation allowance	$ 896.5	$2,333.8
Valuation allowance	(181.3)	—
Total deferred tax asset/liability	$ 715.2	$2,333.8
Net deferred tax liability		$1,618.6
Included in:		
"Prepaid expenses, taxes and other current assets"		$ (107.9)
"Other current liabilities"		44.2
"Deferred Income Taxes"		1,682.3
		$1,618.6

The valuation allowance rose by $38.5 million in 1992, which offset higher deferred tax assets related to increased net operating loss carryforwards. The current and noncurrent net operating loss carryforwards, which totaled $138.6 million at year-end 1992, included amounts related to several foreign and state jurisdictions with various expiration dates.

The deferred tax liability for Safe Harbor Leases (the Leases) is related to transactions, which PepsiCo entered into in 1981 and 1982, that decreased income taxes paid by PepsiCo over the initial years of the Leases and are now increasing taxes payable. Additional taxes paid in 1992 related to the Leases totaled $5.2 million, and taxes payable are estimated to be $35.2 million over the next five years. The provision for income taxes is not impacted by the Leases.

Deferred tax liabilities have not been recognized for bases differences related to investments in foreign subsidiaries and joint ventures. These differences, which consist primarily of unremitted earnings intended to be indefinitely reinvested, aggregated approximately $2.4 billion at year-end 1992, exclusive of amounts that if remitted in the future would result in little or no tax under current tax laws and the Puerto Rico tax incentive grant. The comparable amount at year-end 1991 was $1.8 billion. Determination of the amount of unrecognized deferred tax liabilities is not practicable.

Note 15 — Employee Incentive Plans

PepsiCo has established certain employee incentive plans under which stock options are granted. A stock option allows an employee to purchase a share of PepsiCo Capital Stock (Stock) in the future at the fair market value on the date of the grant.

Under the PepsiCo SharePower Stock Option Plan, approved by the Board of Directors and effective in 1989, essentially all employees other than executive officers, part-time and short-service employees may be granted stock options annually. The number of options granted is based on each employee's annual earnings. The options generally become exercisable ratably over five years from the grant date and must be exercised within 10 years of the grant date. SharePower options were granted to approximately 114,000 employees in 1992 and 107,000 employees in 1991.

The shareholder-approved 1987 Long-Term Incentive Plan (the Plan), which has provisions similar to plans in place in prior years, provides incentives to eligible senior and middle management employees. In addition to grants of stock options, which are generally exercisable between 1 and 15 years from the grant date, the Plan allows for grants of performance share units (PSUs) to eligible senior management employees. A PSU is equivalent in value to a share of Stock at the grant date and vests for payment four years from the grant date, contingent upon attainment of prescribed performance goals. PSUs are not directly granted, as certain stock options granted may be surrendered by employees for a specified number of PSUs within 60 days of the option grant date. During 1992, 502,740 stock options were surrendered for 167,580 PSUs. At year-end 1992 and 1991, there were 484,698 and 809,099 outstanding PSUs, respectively.

The Plan also provides for stock appreciation rights (SARs) and incentive stock units (ISUs). SARs were granted prior to 1991 and allowed eligible senior management employees to surrender an exercisable option for a payment representing the difference between the fair market value of Stock on the SAR exercise date and the option exercise price. Unexercised SARs were canceled in 1991 at no cost. Prior to 1989, eligible middle management employees were granted ISUs rather than stock options. ISUs vest for payment at specified dates over a six year period, and each ISU is equivalent in value to a share of Stock at those respective dates. At year-end 1992 and 1991, there were 127,565 and 162,591 outstanding ISUs, respectively.

Grants under the Plan are approved by the Compensation Committee of the Board of Directors (the Committee), which is composed of outside directors. Payment of awards other than stock options is made in cash and/or Stock as approved by the Committee, and amounts expensed for such awards were $11 million, $15 million and $13 million in 1992, 1991 and 1990, respectively. Under the Plan, a maximum of 54 million shares of Stock can be purchased or paid pursuant to grants. There were 22 million and 32 million shares available for future grants at year-end 1992 and 1991, respectively.

1992 and 1991 activity for the stock option plans was as follows (in thousands):

	SharePower	Long-Term Incentive
Outstanding at December 29, 1990	17,227	26,874
Granted	9,249	2,195
Exercised	(325)	(950)
Surrendered for PSUs	—	(50)
Surrendered for SARs	—	(15)
Canceled	(2,350)	(220)
Outstanding at December 28, 1991	23,801	27,834
Granted	8,477	12,653
Exercised	(1,155)	(5,155)
Surrendered for PSUs	—	(503)
Canceled	(2,327)	(1,839)
Outstanding at December 26, 1992	28,796	32,990
Exercisable at December 26, 1992	8,164	10,659
Option prices per share:		
Exercised during 1992	$17.58 to $35.25	$4.11 to $29.88
Exercised during 1991	$17.58 to $29.25	$4.11 to $26.44
Outstanding at year-end 1992	$17.58 to $35.25	$4.11 to $38.75

Note 16 — Discontinued Operation Charge

The discontinued operation charge of $14.0 million ($13.7 after-tax or $0.02 per share) represents additional amounts provided in 1990 for various pending lawsuits and claims relating to a business sold in a prior year. Substantially all of the charge is a capital loss for which PepsiCo has derived no tax benefit.

Note 17 — Joint Venture Stock Offering

In 1990, PepsiCo recorded an unusual gain of $118.2 million ($53.0 after-tax or $0.07 per share) related to an initial public offering (IPO) to Japanese investors by PepsiCo's KFC joint venture in Japan (KFC-J). KFC-J's principal shareholders are Mitsubishi Corporation and PepsiCo. The IPO consisted of 6.5 million shares of stock in KFC-J. Each principal shareholder sold 2.25 million shares, and KFC-J sold an additional two million new shares. PepsiCo's sale of 2.25 million shares generated pretax cash proceeds of $129.6 million.

The gain from the IPO consisted of a $94.3 million gain ($42.3 after-tax) from PepsiCo's sale of the 2.25 million shares and a $23.9 million ($10.7 after-tax) noncash equity gain from the sale of the two million new shares by KFC-J. As a result of these transactions, each principal shareholder's interest declined from 48.7% to 30.5%. The effective tax rate on the gain was 55.2%, reflecting the relatively low U.S. tax basis of PepsiCo's investment in KFC-J compared to its book value, which included nondeductible intangible assets.

Note 18 — Fair Value of Financial Instruments

PepsiCo's financial instruments include cash, cash equivalents, short-term investments, debt, interest rate swap agreements, currency exchange agreements and guarantees. Because of the short maturity of cash equivalents and investments which mature in less than one year, the carrying value approximates fair value. The fair value of investments which mature in more than one year is based upon market quotes. The fair value of debt issuances, interest rate swap agreements and currency exchange agreements is estimated using market quotes, valuation models and calculations based on market rates. The fair value of guarantees is based upon the projected cost to terminate or otherwise settle the obligations with the counterparties. At year-end 1992, the carrying value of all financial instruments approximated fair value.

Note 19 — Contingencies

PepsiCo is subject to various claims and contingencies related to lawsuits, taxes and other matters arising out of the normal course of business. Management believes that the ultimate liability, if any, arising from such claims or contingencies is not likely to have a material adverse effect on PepsiCo's annual results of operations or financial condition. At year-end 1992 and 1991, PepsiCo was contingently liable under guarantees aggregating $200 million and $86 million, respectively. The guarantees are primarily issued to support financial arrangements of certain restaurant and bottling franchisees and PepsiCo joint ventures. PepsiCo manages the risk associated with these guarantees by performing appropriate credit reviews in addition to retaining certain rights as a franchisor or joint venture partner.

Management's Responsibility for Financial Statements

To Our Shareholders:

Management is responsible for the reliability of the consolidated financial statements and related notes, which have been prepared in conformity with generally accepted accounting principles and include amounts based upon our estimates and judgments, as required. The financial statements have been audited and reported on by our independent auditors, KPMG Peat Marwick, who were given free access to all financial records and related data, including minutes of the meetings of the Board of Directors and Committees of the Board. We believe that the representations made to the independent auditors were valid and appropriate.

PepsiCo maintains a system of internal control over financial reporting designed to provide reasonable assurance as to the reliability of the financial statements. The system is supported by formal policies and procedures, including an active Code of Conduct program intended to ensure key employees adhere to the highest standards of personal and professional integrity. PepsiCo's internal audit function monitors and reports on the adequacy of and compliance with the internal control system, and appropriate actions are taken to address control deficiencies and other opportunities for improving the system as they are identified. The Audit Committee of the Board of Directors, which is composed solely of outside directors, provides oversight to the financial reporting process through periodic meetings with our independent auditors, internal auditors and management. Both our independent auditors and internal auditors have free access to the Audit Committee.

Although no cost effective internal control system will preclude all errors and irregularities, we believe our controls provide reasonable assurance that the financial statements are reliable. Late in 1992, the Committee of Sponsoring Organizations of the Treadway Commission issued a report, "Internal Control—Integrated Framework," which defines criteria for effective internal control over financial reporting. These criteria will be considered in assessing our internal control system.

Wayne Calloway
Chairman of the Board and Chief Executive Officer

Robert G. Dettmer
Executive Vice President and Chief Financial Officer

Robert L. Carleton
Senior Vice President and Controller

December 26, 1992

Report of KPMG Peat Marwick, Independent Auditors

Board of Directors and Shareholders
PepsiCo, Inc.

We have audited the accompanying consolidated balance sheet of PepsiCo, Inc. and subsidiaries as of December 26, 1992 and December 28, 1991, and the related consolidated statements of income, shareholders' equity, and cash flows for each of the years in the three-year period ended December 26, 1992, appearing on pages 28, 29, 30, 32, 34 and 36 through 44. These consolidated financial statements are the responsibility of PepsiCo, Inc.'s management. Our responsibility is to express an opinion on these consolidated financial statements based on our audits.

We conducted our audits in accordance with generally accepted auditing standards. Those standards require that we plan and perform the audit to obtain reasonable assurance about whether the financial statements are free of material misstatement. An audit includes examining, on a test basis, evidence supporting the amounts and disclosures in the financial statements. An audit also includes assessing the accounting principles used and significant estimates made by management, as well as evaluating the overall financial statement presentation. We believe that our audits provide a reasonable basis for our opinion.

In our opinion, the consolidated financial statements referred to above present fairly, in all material respects, the financial position of PepsiCo, Inc. and subsidiaries as of December 26, 1992 and December 28, 1991, and the results of its operations and its cash flows for each of the years in the three-year period ended December 26, 1992, in conformity with generally accepted accounting principles.

As discussed in Notes 11 and 14 to the consolidated financial statements, PepsiCo, Inc. adopted the provisions of the Financial Accounting Standards Board's Statements of Financial Accounting Standards No. 106, "Employers' Accounting for Postretirement Benefits Other Than Pensions" and No. 109, "Accounting for Income Taxes" in 1992.

KPMG Peat Marwick
New York, New York
February 2, 1993

Selected Financial Data

(in millions except per share and employee amounts, unaudited) PepsiCo, Inc. and Subsidiaries	Compounded 10-Year 1982-92	Compounded 5-Year 1987-92	Annual 1-Year 1991-92	1992 (a)	1991 (c)
Summary of Operations					
Net Sales	13.4%	14.8%	13.9%	$21,970.0	19,292.2
Cost of sales and operating expenses				19,598.8	17,180.4
Interest expense				586.1	613.7
Interest income				(113.7)	(161.6)
				20,071.2	17,632.5
Income from continuing operations before income taxes and cumulative effect of accounting changes	15.9%	15.0%	14.4%	1,898.8	1,659.7
Provision for income taxes				597.1	579.5
Income from continuing operations before cumulative effect of accounting changes	20.4%	16.6%	20.5%	$ 1,301.7	1,080.2
Cumulative effect of accounting changes				$ (927.4)(b)	—
Net income	5.3%	(8.8)%	(65.3)%	$ 374.3	1,080.2
Per Share Data					
Income from continuing operations before cumulative effect of accounting changes	21.0%	15.9%	19.3%	$ 1.61	1.35
Cumulative effect of accounting changes				$ (1.15)(b)	—
Net income	5.5%	(9.6)%	(65.9)%	$ 0.46	1.35
Cash dividends declared	11.2%	18.0%	10.9%	$ 0.510	0.460
Average shares and equivalents outstanding				806.7	802.5
Cash Flow Data(g)					
Net cash provided by continuing operations	15.2%	15.2%	11.6%	$ 2,711.6	2,430.3
Acquisitions and investments in affiliates for cash				$ 1,209.7	640.9
Purchases of property, plant and equipment for cash	13.2%	15.0%	6.3%	$ 1,549.6	1,457.8
Cash dividends paid	10.7%	18.1%	15.2%	$ 395.5	343.2
Year-End Position					
Total assets	17.9%	18.4%	11.6%	$20,951.2	18,775.1
Long-term debt	25.2%	25.3%	2.0%	$ 7,964.8	7,806.2
Total debt(h)	23.7%	21.9%	7.9%	$ 8,671.6	8,034.4
Shareholders' equity				$ 5,355.7	5,545.4
Per share	13.1%	15.9%	(4.7)%	$ 6.70	7.03
Market price per share	27.4%	30.3%	25.2%	$ 42¼	33¾
Shares outstanding				798.8	789.1
Employees	10.8%	10.6%	10.1%	372,000	338,000
Statistics					
Return on average shareholders' equity (i)				23.9%	20.7
Historical cost net debt ratio (j)				45%	47
Market net debt ratio (k)				17%	19

Certain amounts for 1991–1988 in the Summary of Operations above have been restated. (See Note 1.)
All share and per share amounts reflect three-for-one stock splits in 1990 and 1986.

(a) Includes $193.5 in unusual charges ($128.5 after-tax or $0.16 per share). (See Note on page 28.)
(b) Represents cumulative effect of adopting SFAS 106, "Employers' Accounting for Postretirement Benefits Other Than Pensions," and SFAS 109, "Accounting for Income Taxes." Prior years were not restated for SFAS 106 or SFAS 109. (See Notes 11 and 14.)
(c) Includes $170.0 in unusual charges ($119.8 after-tax or $0.15 per share). (See Note on page 28.)
(d) Fiscal years 1988 and 1983 each consisted of 53 weeks. Normally, fiscal years consist of 52 weeks; however, because the fiscal year ends on the last Saturday in December, a week is added every 5 or 6 years.
(e) Includes a $156.0 unusual charge ($62.0 after-tax or $0.07 per share) related to a program to sell several international bottling operations.
(f) Includes a $79.4 unusual charge ($79.4 after-tax or $0.09 per share) related to a reduction in net assets of certain international bottling operations.
(g) Cash flows from other investing and financing activities, which are not presented, are an integral part of total cash flow activity.
(h) Total debt includes short-term borrowings and long-term debt, which for 1990 through 1987 included a nonrecourse obligation.
(i) The return on average shareholders' equity is calculated using income from continuing operations before cumulative effect of accounting changes.
(j) The historical cost net debt ratio represents net debt, which is total debt reduced by the pro forma remittance of investment portfolios held outside the U.S., as a percent of capital employed (net debt, other liabilities, deferred income taxes and shareholders' equity). For 1990 through 1987, total debt was also reduced by the nonrecourse obligation in the calculation of net debt.
(k) The market net debt ratio represents net debt (see Note j) as a percent of net debt plus the market value of equity, based on the year-end stock price.

Annual Report for PepsiCo, Inc. **lxix**

1990	1989	1988 (d)	1987	1986	1985	1984 (e)	1983 (d)	1982 (f)
17,515.5	15,049.2	12,381.4	11,018.1	9,017.1	7,584.5	7,058.6	6,568.6	6,232.4
15,355.2	13,276.6	11,039.6	9,890.5	8,187.9	6,802.4	6,479.3	5,995.7	5,684.7
686.0	607.9	342.4	294.6	261.4	195.2	204.9	175.0	163.5
(179.5)	(175.3)	(120.5)	(112.6)	(122.7)	(96.4)	(86.1)	(53.6)	(49.1)
15,861.7	13,709.2	11,261.5	10,072.5	8,326.6	6,901.2	6,598.1	6,117.1	5,799.1
1,653.8	1,340.0	1,119.9	945.6	690.5	683.3	460.5	451.5	433.3
563.2	438.6	357.7	340.5	226.7	256.7	180.5	169.5	229.7
1,090.6	901.4	762.2	605.1	463.8	426.6	280.0	282.0	203.6
—	—	—	—	—	—	—	—	—
1,076.9	901.4	762.2	594.8	457.8	543.7	212.5	284.1	224.3
1.37	1.13	0.97	0.77	0.59	0.51	0.33	0.33	0.24
—	—	—	—	—	—	—	—	—
1.35	1.13	0.97	0.76	0.58	0.65	0.25	0.33	0.27
0.383	0.320	0.267	0.223	0.209	0.195	0.185	0.180	0.176
798.7	796.0	790.4	789.3	786.5	842.1	862.4	859.3	854.1
2,110.0	1,885.9	1,894.5	1,334.5	1,212.2	817.3	981.5	670.2	661.5
630.6	3,296.6	1,415.5	371.5	1,679.9	160.0	—	—	130.3
1,180.1	943.8	725.8	770.5	858.5	770.3	555.8	503.4	447.4
293.9	241.9	199.0	172.0	160.4	161.1	154.6	151.3	142.5
17,143.4	15,126.7	11,135.3	9,022.7	8,027.1	5,889.3	4,876.9	4,446.3	4,052.2
5,899.6	6,076.5	2,656.0	2,579.2	2,632.6	1,162.0	668.1	797.8	843.2
7,526.1	6,942.8	4,107.0	3,225.1	2,865.3	1,506.1	948.9	1,073.9	1,033.5
4,904.2	3,891.1	3,161.0	2,508.6	2,059.1	1,837.7	1,853.4	1,794.2	1,650.5
6.22	4.92	4.01	3.21	2.64	2.33	2.19	2.13	1.96
25¼	21⅜	13⅛	11¼	8¾	7⅞	4⅝	4¼	3¼
788.4	791.1	788.4	781.2	781.0	789.4	845.2	842.0	840.4
308,000	266,000	235,000	225,000	214,000	150,000	150,000	154,000	133,000
24.8	25.6	26.9	26.5	23.8	23.1	15.4	16.4	12.7
47	51	37	35	40	24	11	23	30
22	24	20	18	23	12	7	16	20

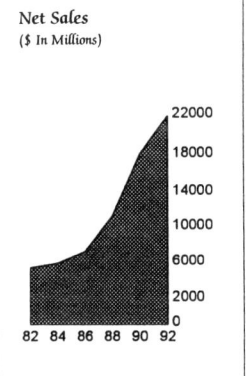

Net Sales
($ In Millions)

Income Per Share From Continuing Operations *
(In Dollars)

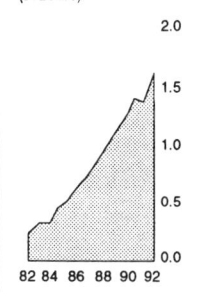

*Before cumulative effect of accounting changes in 1992.

Quarterly Financial Data

(in millions except per share amounts, unaudited)

	First Quarter (12 Weeks) 1992	1991	Second Quarter (12 Weeks) 1992	1991	Third Quarter (12 Weeks) 1992	1991	Fourth Quarter (16 Weeks) 1992	1991	Full Year (52 Weeks) 1992	1991
Net sales	$4,497.3	4,037.8	5,126.4	4,606.1	5,548.3	4,807.1	6,798.0	5,841.2	21,970.0	19,292.2
Gross profit	$2,327.4	2,103.7	2,704.4	2,399.1	2,892.3	2,484.5	3,553.3	3,026.3	11,477.4	10,013.6
Income before income taxes and cumulative effect of accounting changes	$ 349.3	312.5	563.1	486.4	616.0	431.0[b]	370.4[c]	429.8[d]	1,898.8[e]	1,659.7
Provision for income taxes	$ 114.3	107.1	184.3	168.1	193.7	145.6	104.8	158.7	597.1	579.5
Income before cumulative effect of accounting changes	$ 235.0	205.4	378.8	318.3	422.3	285.4	265.6	271.1	1,301.7	1,080.2
Cumulative effect of accounting changes:										
Postretirement Benefits	$ (356.7)[a]	—	—	—	—	—	—	—	(356.7)	—
Income Taxes	$ (570.7)[a]	—	—	—	—	—	—	—	(570.7)	—
Net income (loss)	$ (692.4)	205.4	378.8	318.3	422.3	285.4	265.6	271.1	374.3	1,080.2
Income (charge) per share:										
Income before cumulative effect of accounting changes	$ 0.29	0.26	0.47	0.39	0.53	0.36	0.32	0.34	1.61[e]	1.35
Cumulative effect of accounting changes	$ (1.15)[a]	—	—	—	—	—	—	—	(1.15)	—
Net income (loss) per share	$ (0.86)	0.26	0.47	0.39	0.53	0.36[b]	0.32[c]	0.34[d]	0.46[e]	1.35

The amounts for the first three quarters of 1992 and for all quarters of 1991 have been restated to report under the equity method of accounting certain previously consolidated international snack food businesses contributed to the new Snack Ventures Europe (SVE) joint venture with General Mills, Inc. in late 1992. The restatement had no effect on net income. (See Note 1.)

(a) Represents cumulative effect related to years prior to 1992 of adopting SFAS 106, "Employers' Accounting for Postretirement Benefits Other Than Pensions," and SFAS 109, "Accounting for Income Taxes." (See Notes 11 and 14.)

(b) Includes unusual charges totaling $100.4 ($62.4 after-tax or $0.08 per share) consisting of a $91.4 restructuring charge at domestic snack foods and a KFC charge of $9.0 related to a delay in the U.S. roll-out of a new product.

(c) Includes unusual charges totaling $193.5 ($128.5 after-tax or $0.16 per share) consisting of restructuring charges of $115.4 at domestic beverages, $29.6 at international beverages, $40.3 at international snack foods and $8.2 related to SVE.

(d) Includes unusual charges totaling $69.6 ($57.4 after-tax or $0.07 per share) consisting of restructuring charges of $34.0 at KFC and $35.6 at international snack foods.

(e) Includes the current year effect of adopting SFAS 106, which decreased full-year income before income taxes and cumulative effect of accounting changes by $52.1 ($32.3 after-tax or $0.04 per share), and SFAS 109, which decreased full-year income before income taxes and cumulative effect of accounting changes by $20.7 and the provision for income taxes by $33.7, resulting in an increase in income before cumulative effect of accounting changes of $13.0 ($0.02 per share).

Capital Stock Information

Stock Trading Symbol

PEP

Stock Exchange Listings

The New York Stock Exchange is the principal market for PepsiCo Capital Stock, which is also listed on the Midwest, Basel, Geneva, Zurich, Amsterdam and Tokyo Stock Exchanges.

Shareholders

At year-end 1992, there were approximately 143,000 shareholders of record.

Dividend Policy

Cash dividends are declared quarterly. Quarterly cash dividends have been paid since PepsiCo was formed in 1965, and dividends have increased for 21 consecutive years.

Dividends Declared Per Share
(In Cents)

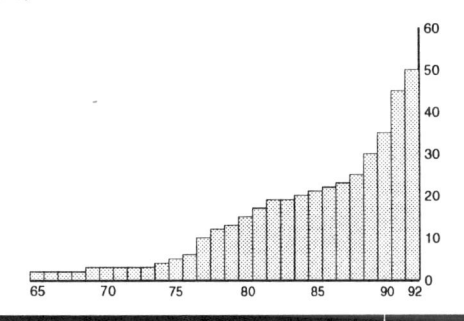

Consistent with PepsiCo's current payout target of approximately one-third of the prior year's income, the 1992 dividends declared represented 38% of 1991 income from continuing operations.

Dividends Declared Per Share (in cents)

Quarter	1992	1991
1	12	10
2	13	12
3	13	12
4	13	12
Total	51	46

Stock Prices

The high, low and closing prices for a share of PepsiCo Capital Stock on the New York Stock Exchange, as reported by The Dow Jones News/Retrieval Service, for each fiscal quarter of 1992 and 1991 were as follows (in dollars):

1992	High	Low	Close
Fourth Quarter	43	36⅛	42¼
Third Quarter	38⅞	34⅛	37⅝
Second Quarter	38¼	32¼	36
First Quarter	35¾	30½	32⅞

1991			
Fourth Quarter	33⅞	27	33¼
Third Quarter	33½	27¾	29⅛
Second Quarter	35⅝	29½	30⅞
First Quarter	35⅛	23½	32⅞

Stock Performance

PepsiCo was formed through the 1965 merger of Pepsi-Cola Company and Frito-Lay, Inc. A $1,000 investment in our stock made in 1965 was worth approximately $64,000 on December 26, 1992, assuming the reinvestment of dividends. This performance represents a compounded annual growth rate of 16%. The chart on the back cover shows growth for the years 1982 to 1992, when the total return to shareholders grew at a compounded annual rate of 30%.

As the chart showing the comparison of monthly market price performance illustrates, the return on PepsiCo Capital Stock compares favorably with the performance of the Standard & Poor's Industrials over the past five years.

The chart showing year-end market price of stock represents the closing price for a share of PepsiCo Capital Stock on the New York Stock Exchange, as reported by the Dow Jones News/Retrieval Service for the end of each fiscal year 1982–1992.

Past performance is not necessarily indicative of future returns on investments in PepsiCo Capital Stock.

Comparison of Monthly Market Price Performance
(Closing Price Indexed at 12/31/87)
— PepsiCo — S&P Industrials

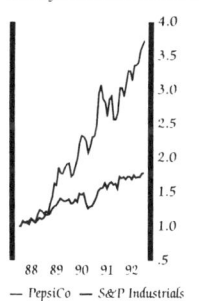

Year-End Market Price Of Stock
(In Dollars)

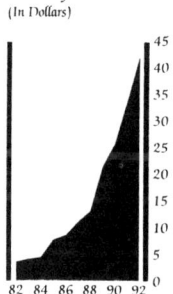

Survey of Financial Accounting

TO THE STUDENT

A *Study Guide*, *Working Papers*, and *Student Solutions Manual* are available through your bookstore. The purpose of the *Study Guide* is to assist you in studying and reviewing the text material and provide you with a means of self-test by the study of the detailed outline and use of the true-false questions, multiple choice questions, matching and completion statements, and exercises included in the guide. These may be used both in your initial study of the chapter material and in your subsequent review. The *Working Papers* have prepared forms and check figures for your problem assignments. The *Student Solutions Manual* has complete solutions for the even numbered problems, check figures for the odd numbered problems, and sample examinations with answers. If the *Study Guide*, *Working Papers*, or *Student Solutions Manual* are not in stock in your bookstore, ask the bookstore manager to order copies for you.

Chapter 1 introduces certain basic accounting concepts. Studying this chapter should enable you to:

1. Describe the basic accounting definition and discuss accounting as a process of communication.

2. Describe the role of the accountant and explain why this role has increased in significance.

3. Compare and contrast accounting and bookkeeping.

4. Contrast financial accounting with managerial accounting and identify the primary users of each.

5. Describe the objectives of financial reporting.

6. Discuss the qualitative characteristics of accounting information.

7. Explain "generally accepted accounting principles" and discuss the major concepts underlying these principles.

8. Define and discuss the elements of financial statements.

9. Explain recognition and measurement in financial statements.

10. Identify the basic financial statements and explain the purpose and use of each.

11. Trace the process of developing generally accepted accounting principles.

12. List and briefly describe certain of the more important influences on accounting principles.

13. Discuss the accounting standard setting process.

14. Discuss the extent and nature of opportunities in accounting.

1

Accounting: An Introduction

INTRODUCTION

Accounting has been described as "... the art of recording, classifying, and summarizing in a significant manner and in terms of money, transactions and events which are, in part at least, of a financial character, and interpreting the results thereof."[1] This definition emphasizes the "... creative skill and ability with which the accountant applies his or her knowledge to a given problem."[2] Another view of the function of accounting, very similar to that reported above, is that "the primary function of accounting is to accumulate and communicate information essential to an understanding of the activities of an enterprise, whether large or small, corporate or non-corporate, profit or non-profit, public or private."[3] The importance of this second definition is the direct relevance of accounting to many and varied types of undertakings, both private and public, and profit and not-for-profit.

Implicit in any definition of accounting is the importance of the accountant's role in the reporting function. In fact, the primary role of the accountant is reporting and communicating information which will aid various users in the financial community in making economic decisions. These users

---

[1] American Institute of Certified Public Accountants, *Accounting Terminology Bulletin No. 1—Review and Resume* (New York: AICPA), 9.

[2] *Ibid.*

[3] *Accounting and Reporting Standards for Corporate Financial Statements* (Columbus, Ohio: American Accounting Association, 1957), 1.

of accounting information include current and potential owners, managers, creditors, and others.

It should be noted however, that "financial reporting is not an end in itself but is intended to provide information that is useful in making business and economic decisions."[4]

In the past, when businesses were less complex than they are today, there were usually only a very limited number of users of accounting information. For example, at the turn of the century, most businesses in the United States were managed and operated by their owners. Since these owners were intimately involved in the day-to-day operations of their businesses, there was little or no need for accounting reports. The owner or decision-maker already had firsthand knowledge of the information he or she required in order to operate the business effectively. Today, however, the situation is quite different. Many organizations have increased in both size and complexity. In many instances, the ownership and the management of a business have been separated. Firms are frequently managed by professional managers for their absentee owners who exercise a minimal amount of formal control over the operations of the business except in the most general sense. These owners often have virtually no involvement in the day-to-day activities of the business. Even professional managers (at all but the most basic levels of authority in the firm) have little *firsthand* involvement in the most fundamental of these activities. Their decisions are, more often than not, made on the basis of reports and summaries which are prepared by their subordinates. It should be noted here that these reports and summaries are prepared using accounting estimates. Too often, managers and other users of financial information may overlook this fact.

Although the above discussion might overstate the case just a bit (the corner pizza parlor may still be owner-operated, but it could well be a franchise operation), the basic point is that most decisions are made on the basis of summary-type reports rather than firsthand information.

What is the role of accounting and the accountant in this process? One observation that has been made is that the task of the accountant is to observe, interpret, summarize, and communicate information in a form which will enable the user of the data to evaluate, control, plan, and even predict performance. It is essential to note the importance of the term "user" in this context. A user could be a manager involved in the evaluation and direction of the continuing operations of the business; a present or a potential stockholder (owner) seeking information for an impending investment decision; a bank officer in the process of reviewing a loan application; a supplier making a decision with regard to a credit application; a federal, state, or local revenue officer evaluating the propriety of a tax return; or

---

[4] *FASB Statement of Financial Accounting Concepts No. 1*, "Objectives of Financial Reporting by Business Enterprises," (Stamford, CT: FASB, 1978), para. 9.

even a citizen attempting to assess the performance of some governmental unit. In each of the circumstances mentioned above, and in countless other situations as well, user needs are met, at least in part, by a report prepared by an accountant on the basis of accounting information.

Not to be overlooked is the impact of accounting on our society. The transfer and distribution of the economic resources of society are often related to the actions of the users described above, taken in response to accounting information. Thus, the failure of accounting information systems to report information on an accurate and timely basis could alter the decisions made by various users and thereby create undesirable economic consequences for society.

ACCOUNTING AS A PROCESS OF COMMUNICATION[5]

Accounting may be regarded as a process of communication in a very real sense. Events occur on a continuing basis which affect the operations of an organization. The accountant acts as an observer-reporter, observing events or transactions as they take place, evaluating the significance of these events, then recording, classifying, and summarizing the events in an accounting report. The user receives the report, analyzes its content, and utilizes the information in making economic decisions. Of course, these decisions made by the user cause new events to take place, again setting the chain in process through another cycle.

Two factors are of major importance in this communication. First, there should be mutual understanding and agreement between the accountant preparing the report and the persons using the report on the basis of its preparation and content. The accountant must know the user's needs and perceptions and prepare the report so that what the user understands the report to express will indeed correspond with what the accountant intended to express in the report. Bedford and Baladouni call this fidelity—the relationship between what is understood by the user of accounting statements and what the accountant intended to express in his or her report.

The second factor is that the accountant's report should show a reliable and relevant relationship to the events it attempts to summarize. The report should, to the degree possible and/or practicable, include and describe all the significant events which did, in fact, take place. In the ideal situation, a user would make the same decision based on the analysis of a report that would have been made if firsthand information obtained on a personal basis was used. Bedford and Baladouni refer to this factor as significance—the relationship between the events which take place and the accounting report which attempts to summarize these events.

---

[5] This discussion is based on Norton M. Bedford and Vahe Baladouni, "A Communication Theory Approach to Accountancy," *The Accounting Review* (October 1962), 650-59.

ACCOUNTING VS. BOOKKEEPING

Often, the distinction between accounting and bookkeeping is not understood. Bookkeeping refers to the actual recording of business transactions. This clerical recordkeeping function may be done manually or electronically with the use of computers. Accounting goes far beyond bookkeeping. The accounting function encompasses the design of the recordkeeping system, the preparation of reports, and the analysis and interpretation of financial and quantitative data. The decision-making involved in the accounting function requires a much greater knowledge and comprehension than the clerical skills which are needed in bookkeeping.

FINANCIAL ACCOUNTING AND MANAGERIAL ACCOUNTING

Although there is considerable overlap between the two, accounting may be thought of as consisting of two basic segments, financial accounting and managerial accounting. The basic difference between these two segments or divisions of accounting lies in their orientation.

Financial accounting is primarily concerned with users who are *external* to the firm and managerial accounting is concerned with *internal* users. Financial accounting attempts to provide external user groups such as current or potential owners, creditors, government agencies, and other interested parties with information concerning the status of the firm and the results of its operations. The objective of financial accounting is to provide these users with the information they require for making decisions.

Managerial accounting attempts to provide the information which is necessary for internal decision-making to those who are charged with this responsibility within the firm. Managerial accounting, unlike financial accounting, is not constrained by the requirements of the standard setting bodies discussed later in this chapter.

This text is concerned with both financial accounting and managerial accounting. Again, it is important to note that the two overlap. For example, the determination of the cost of the products, which are produced by a manufacturing firm, may be regarded as a problem that lies within the domain of managerial accounting; however, it is also a concern of financial accounting because determining the cost of inventory is an important consideration for financial reporting purposes.

OBJECTIVES OF FINANCIAL REPORTING

Financial reporting includes not only the financial statements but also such other forms of communicating financial information as annual reports filed with the Securities and Exchange Commission (SEC), news releases, and management forecasts.

The users of financial information may be divided into internal and external groups. Internal users such as managers and directors can specify the information that they want, can receive additional and more detailed information than is appropriate or necessary for external reports, and can receive information pertaining to planning and controlling operations. External users include owners, lenders, suppliers, potential investors, potential creditors, employees, customers, stockbrokers, financial analysts, taxing authorities, regulatory authorities, trade associations, and teachers. Certain of these external users (e.g., taxing authorities) can specify and obtain both the form and content of the information desired; others lack the authority to prescribe the financial information desired.

Investors and creditors are the most obvious external groups who use financial information and cannot obtain all the information that they may wish to have. Their decisions significantly affect the allocation of resources in the economy. In addition, information which meets the needs of investors and creditors is likely to meet the needs of those other external users who rely on external financial reporting.

A primary objective of financial reporting is to ". . . provide information that is useful to present and potential investors and creditors and other users in making rational investment, credit, and similar decisions."[6] In order to accomplish this goal, it is necessary that the information which is communicated must be understood; it ". . . should be comprehensible to those who have a reasonable understanding of business and economic activities and are willing to study the information with reasonable diligence."[7]

The users of financial information are concerned not only with past and current performance, but also with the future expectations of a business. Recognizing these needs, *the primary focus of financial reporting is on the disclosure of information concerning the earnings of a business*, although information concerning the resources of an enterprise also is emphasized. Consequently, two other important objectives which are stated in FASB Statement of Financial Accounting Concepts No. 1, "Objectives of Financial Reporting by Business Enterprises," are as follows:

> Financial reporting should provide information to help present and potential investors and creditors and other users in assessing the amounts, timing, and uncertainty of prospective cash receipts from dividends or interest and the proceeds from the sale, redemption, or maturity of securities or loans. The prospects for those cash receipts are affected by an enterprise's ability to generate enough cash to meet its obligations when due and its other cash operating needs, to reinvest in operations, and to pay cash dividends and may also be affected by perceptions of investors and creditors generally about that ability, which affect market prices of the enterprise's securities. Thus, financial reporting should provide information to help investors, creditors, and others assess the amounts, timing, and uncertainty of prospective net cash inflows to the related enterprise.[8]

---

[6] *FASB Statement of Financial Accounting Concepts No. 1*, "Objectives of Financial Reporting By Business Enterprises," (Stamford, CT: FASB, 1978), para. 34.
[7] *Ibid.*
[8] *Ibid.*, para. 37.

Financial reporting should provide information about the economic resources of an enterprise, the claims to those resources (obligations of the enterprise to transfer resources to other entities and owners' equity), and the effects of transactions, events, and circumstances that change its resources and claims to those resources.[9]

The board emphasized that accrual accounting is a superior indicator of an enterprise's performance than is accounting on a cash basis. *The measurement of income under the conventions of accrual accounting is intended to provide users with more useful information concerning an enterprise's present and future ability to generate desirable cash flows than is indicated by the income measured on a cash basis. Investors, creditors, and other users of financial information are interested in the current and future cash flows of an enterprise.* Therefore, these users of financial information prefer that information concerning an enterprise's performance be measured on an accrual rather than a cash basis.

QUALITATIVE CHARACTERISTICS OF ACCOUNTING INFORMATION

Pervasive Constraint

In order to be useful, accounting information should possess certain qualitative characteristics.

Benefits and Costs. *In order to justify providing accounting information, the benefits which may be derived from the use of this information must exceed the costs of providing the data.* There are several costs of providing information, including: (1) costs of collecting, processing, and disseminating; (2) costs of auditing; (3) costs associated with dangers of litigation and loss of competitive advantage; and (4) costs to the user for analysis and interpretation. Also, there are benefits to the preparers of the information as well as to the users. These benefits include improved access to capital markets and favorable impact on public relations.

User-Specific Qualities

Understandability. *The information which is provided by financial reporting should be understandable to those who have a reasonable understanding of business and economic activities* and who are willing to study the information with reasonable diligence. Useful information which is difficult to understand should not be excluded. In this context, understandability is the quality which enables users to perceive the significance of information.

Decision Usefulness. The determination as to whether or not information is useful is dependent upon the particular decision to be made, the manner in which the decision is to be made, the other information which already is available, and the ability of the decision-maker to process and use the information. *SFAC No. 2 identifies usefulness for decision-making as the most*

---

[9] *Ibid.*, para. 38.

important quality of accounting information. Usefulness provides the benefits from information to set against the costs of providing the information; without usefulness, there would be no benefits. Decision usefulness may be separated into the qualities of *relevance* and *reliability*, both of which are defined below.

Relevance. *In order to be relevant, accounting information must be capable of making a difference in a particular decision* by helping users to form predictions concerning the outcome of past, current, or future events or to confirm or correct prior expectations. In this context, an "event" is a happening of consequence to an enterprise (for example, receipt of a sales order or a change in the price of a good which is bought or sold), while an "outcome" is the effect or result of a series of events (for example, the amount of last year's profit or the expected profit for the current year). Relevant information does not necessarily mean that a new decision should be made; the information may support the decision which was made previously.

Reliability. *Reliable information is information which is reasonably free from both error and bias and which faithfully represents what it is intended to represent.* To be reliable, accounting information must be verifiable, neutral and possess representational faithfulness.

Reliability and relevance often conflict with one another in the standard setting process. The type of information which is most desired by users of financial accounting information (relevance) is often the most difficult information to obtain in a reliable fashion. Traditionally, standard setters have favored reliability over relevance in those situations in which the two are in conflict.

Ingredients of Primary Qualities

Predictive and Feedback Value. *Accounting information has predictive value when it assists the decision-maker in correctly forecasting the outcome of past or present events.* It possesses feedback value when it assists the decision-maker in either confirming or correcting prior expectations.

Timeliness. *Timeliness means having information available to decision-makers before the information loses its capacity to influence decisions.* Timeliness by itself does not make information relevant. However, information may lose relevance if it is not communicated on a timely basis. Often, a gain in relevance from increased timeliness may involve, for example, a sacrifice of reliability; therefore, trade-offs in the qualitative characteristics of accounting information must be considered by decision-makers.

Verifiability. *Verifiability (sometimes referred to as objectivity) of accounting information means that several measurers are likely to obtain the same measure, so that measurement results may be duplicated independently.* The Certified Public Accountant (CPA) is an independent accountant who examines or audits financial statements and attests to or reports as to whether or not the financial statements "present fairly" the financial position, results of operations and changes in financial position of an entity. In accounting, verification is a primary concern of auditing and the CPA.

Representational Faithfulness. *Representational faithfulness means that there is correspondence or agreement between the accounting numbers and the resources or events that those numbers are supposed to represent.* For example, if a firm reports that its cash account has a balance of $50,000, when the correct balance is actually $35,000, the concept of representational faithfulness is violated. Information that is biased (consistently too high or too low) is not representationally faithful. Bias may arise because the measurement method is not used properly or the measurement method does not represent what it is supposed to represent.

Secondary and Interactive Qualities

Neutrality. *Accounting information should be free from any bias toward or against a predetermined result.* The effect of an accounting rule on the interests of a particular user should not be a major consideration in its selection. The primary concern here is the relevance and reliability that results from the application (or the formulation) of accounting standards.

Comparability. *The significance of information is enhanced greatly when it can be contrasted with similar information concerning other enterprises and with similar information about the same enterprise for some other period or point in time.* Information, especially quantitative information, is most useful when it can be compared with such benchmarks. The purpose of these comparisons is, of course, to detect and explain similarities and differences.

Consistency. The concept of consistency is linked closely to comparability. *Consistency is conformity from one period to another in the use of accounting methods and procedures.*

Accounting principles do not comprise a detailed set of rules and procedures that apply to each and every situation. Rather, they are more in the nature of general guidelines. This is why the accountant may record a particular transaction in alternative ways. Also, different firms may use different accounting methods. Thus, the concept of consistency is essential.

Briefly stated, *the consistency concept requires that once an entity adopts a particular accounting method for its use in recording a certain type of transaction, the enterprise should continue to use that method for all future transactions of the same category.* Note that this concept applies only to the accounting methods used by a particular entity. It does not apply to the methods used by different companies, even though these firms may be engaged in the same line of business or industry.

Consistency, for example, would require that General Motors use the same accounting methods in its reports from one year to the next so that the users of its financial statements are able to make comparisons of the financial position of the company, the results of its operations, and the changes in its financial position between and among years. It would not require, however, that General Motors and Chrysler use the same accounting methods, even though these firms may be somewhat similar in many respects. The financial statements of General Motors and Chrysler may or may not be readily comparable, depending upon the accounting methods which are selected by each of these firms.

Threshold for Recognition

Materiality. *Materiality indicates that the amount involved is sufficiently large to affect or make a difference in a decision. The materiality concept indicates that the accountant should be concerned primarily with those transactions which are of real significance or concern to the users of financial information.* For example, assume that a company acquires a pencil sharpener at a cost of $10. It is expected that this sharpener will be used by the business over a five-year period before it will be replaced. In theory, a portion of the cost of the pencil sharpener should be considered as an expense of each year in which it will be used, because it will be of benefit to the company during each of these years. In practice, however, this would be neither realistic nor practical. The benefits which might be obtained by allocating the cost of the pencil sharpener over the five-year period simply would not be worth the cost that this procedure would involve. This example is, of course, a clear-cut case. A precise definition of what is or is not material is often elusive in particular circumstances.

A general understanding of the basic concept of materiality may be obtained from the following example. Assume that a transaction occurs. It is recorded in accounting report #1 in a manner that is theoretically correct. In alternative accounting report #2, it is recorded in a way that is expedient, but not necessarily correct in terms of accounting theory. If a user of an accounting report would make the same decision irrespective of whether it was based on accounting report #1 (theoretically correct) or accounting report #2 (expedient, but not necessarily theoretically correct), then the item obviously does not affect the decision at hand and is, therefore, clearly immaterial or insignificant in amount. On the other hand, if the user would make a different decision on the basis of accounting report #1 than might be made using accounting report #2, then the item would be considered to be material, because it affected the decision which was made by the user.

Clearly then, decisions as to whether a particular item is or is not material must be made by the accountant and depend on the exercise of professional judgment. Quantitative factors alone are not sufficient to judge the materiality of an item. The nature of the item and the circumstances under which the judgment is to be made must be considered.

OTHER BASIC ACCOUNTING PRINCIPLES, UNDERLYING ASSUMPTIONS, AND CONCEPTS

Entity Assumption

The entity assumption is the basis for the distinction which is made by the accountant between a business and its ownership. In accounting, an organization, often referred to as an entity, is treated as a unit which is separate and distinct from its ownership and is accounted for as such. The affairs and transactions of the owners of a business are not combined or co-mingled with those of their firms. This is true irrespective of the legal form of organization which is used by the business.

There are three basic forms of business enterprises. A *proprietorship* is an enterprise which is owned by a single person who is personally liable for all of the debts of the business. A *partnership* is a business which is owned by two or more persons who share profits or losses according to an agreement, and who are personally liable for all of the debts of the business. A *corporation* is a business which has a legal identity separate from its owners, or stockholders. Therefore, the stockholders are not personally liable for the debts of the corporation.

The entity assumption is a distinction which always is made in accounting, even though the distinction may not be true in a legal sense for businesses which are organized as either single proprietorships or partnerships. In addition, the accounting entity could be a department or a division, or the accounting entity could be a group of companies even though each one is a legal entity.

Going-Concern Concept

The going-concern concept means that it is assumed that an entity will continue its operations for an indefinite future period of time, at least long enough to fulfill its plans and commitments. This assumption is used in accounting unless there is conclusive evidence to the contrary—for example, if a firm is in the process of bankruptcy proceedings.

Monetary Unit Assumption

The monetary unit assumption means that the transactions and events which occur in a business should be recorded in terms of money. As its definition indicates, accounting is ". . . the art of recording, classifying, and summarizing in a significant manner and *in terms of money* . . ."[10] The monetary unit is a useful means to communicate financial results.

Stable-Dollar Assumption

The stable-dollar assumption is closely related to the monetary assumption. *The stable-dollar assumption assumes that all dollars are of equal worth or value, that is, of the same purchasing power.* Thus, the relevant transactions of an entity are recorded and its accounting reports are prepared on the assumption that a dollar is a stable unit of measure. Under the stable-dollar concept, a dollar spent in 1930 is assumed to be equal to a dollar spent in 1975, or a dollar spent today. In other words, any changes that may

---

[10] American Institute of Certified Public Accountants, *Accounting Terminology Bulletin No. 1,* "Review and Resume," (New York: AICPA, 1953), para. 9 (emphasis added).

have occurred in the purchasing power of the dollar due to either inflation or deflation are ignored.

Time Period Assumption

The most accurate determination of an enterprise's performance would be made at the time in which the business ceases to function. However, investors, creditors, and other interested parties need financial information concerning an enterprise on a much more timely basis. *Therefore, financial statements are prepared for such time intervals as a year or a quarter.* Of course, because of estimates and other factors, the resulting information becomes less reliable as the time period is shortened, although the relevance of the information is increased.

Historical Cost Concept

The historical cost concept is the assumption that the original cost (acquisition price) of a resource, and not its current market value or replacement cost, is the basis that normally is used to account for the resources of an entity. This assumption has been justified by accountants on the grounds of its reliability. Its proponents argue that historical cost is a fact, whereas, in many instances, alternative measures such as market values or replacement costs may be somewhat subjective and must be determined each time that the financial statements are prepared. Historical cost also has been justified on the basis of the going-concern concept. An entity is assumed to have an indefinite life, and many (if not most) of its resources are acquired for use rather than for resale. Therefore, there is little need to consider the amount that might be realized if these resources were sold.

Of course, there have been serious objections to the use of historical cost, especially when prices have risen substantially. Under these circumstances, critics believe that the historical cost of an asset has no relation to its "value."

Matching Concept

The *matching concept* is related to the measurement of the earnings or income of an entity. It provides that *expenses that can be associated with revenue should be matched with that revenue when the revenue is realized and recognized during a particular period.* Thus, the matching concept emphasizes a cause-and-effect association in which efforts are matched with accomplishments.

Revenue is recorded in accordance with the realization principle (discussed below), not necessarily as cash is received. For example, assume that an accountant prepares a tax return for her client during the month of March, bills the client for this service in April, and is paid in May. The revenue that is earned by the accountant from the preparation of this tax return is included in income for the month of March, because that is the month in which the accountant performed the work that entitled her to the fee.

Likewise, expenses are recorded as they are incurred, not necessarily as they are paid. The expenses incurred by the accountant in performing her work in March should be recorded in March. When she pays for these expenses is not relevant. From the viewpoint of the client, the cost of having

Revenue Realization

the tax return prepared by the accountant is an expense. This expense should be recorded at the point in time in which it was incurred (in March) rather than when it was actually paid (in May).

Revenue from sales usually is recognized as a component of earnings when it is realized or realizable and earned. A revenue is earned when the "... entity has substantially accomplished what it must do to be entitled to the benefits represented by the revenue."[11] Recognition differs from realization. *Recognition is the process of formally recording an item in the financial statements; realization is the process of converting noncash resources and rights into cash or claims to cash.*[12]

Revenue from sales usually is recognized at the time that both an exchange transaction takes place and the earnings process is complete or virtually complete. Revenue from sales usually is recognized at the time of delivery of the product; revenue from services is recognized when the service has been performed. Recognizing revenue at these times is objective and verifiable, because the sales price provides a measure for the amount of revenue realized.

Revenue which is earned by allowing others to use the enterprise's resources is recognized as time passes (examples of such revenue includes interest and rent). The amount of revenue that is recognized is determined by the amount that is received or is expected to be received.

Cash may be received before production and delivery. Revenue is recognized as the goods are produced and delivered. An example of recognizing revenue in this manner is magazine subscriptions. A publisher may receive payment from subscribers either before or after the subscription period but would recognize income as the magazine is produced and distributed to subscribers.

Conservatism

Conservatism traditionally has meant that accountants who are selecting an alternative from two equally possible ones choose the accounting alternative that is least likely to overstate assets and income. APB Statement No. 4 states:

> Frequently, assets and liabilities are measured in a context of significant uncertainties. Historically, managers, investors, and accountants have generally preferred that possible errors in measurement be in the direction of understatement rather than overstatement of net income and net assets. This has led to the convention of conservatism...[13]

---

[11] *FASB Statement of Financial Accounting Concepts No. 5,* "Recognition," para. 83.
[12] *FASB Statement of Financial Accounting Concepts No. 6,* "Elements," para. 143.
[13] *APB Statement No. 4,* "Basic Concepts and Accounting Principles Underlying Financial Statements of Business Enterprises," (New York: AICPA, 1970), para. 171.

The FASB believes that such a preference not only introduces a bias into financial reporting, but also conflicts with such qualitative characteristics as representational faithfulness, neutrality, and comparability. The board discussed conservatism in its *Statement of Financial Accounting Concepts No. 2* and stated that conservatism in financial reporting "should no longer connote deliberate, consistent understatement of net assets and profits."[14] Continuing, the board stated the following:

> Conservatism is a prudent reaction to uncertainty to try to ensure that uncertainties and risks inherent in business situations are adequately considered. Thus, if two estimates of amounts to be received or paid in the future are about equally likely, conservatism dictates using the less optimistic estimate; however, when two amounts are not equally likely, conservatism does not necessarily dictate using the more pessimistic amount rather than the more likely one. Conservatism no longer requires deferring recognition of income beyond the time that adequate evidence of its existence becomes available or justifies recognizing losses before there is adequate evidence that they have been incurred.[15]

Full-Disclosure Concept

Full-disclosure means that information which is needed by the users of financial statements should be disclosed in an understandable form. The information may be presented in the main body of the financial statements or in the related notes. In addition to the required financial statements, information should be presented on such items as the following:

1. Details pertaining to elements within the financial statements.
2. Summary of accounting policies.
3. The effect of current value on earnings.
4. Management's discussion of the significance of the company's performance and of future prospects.
5. The effect of changes in accounting principles.

Full-disclosure is very important to the efficient operations of the securities market. Efficiency means that security prices react quickly to published financial information.

---

[14] *FASB Statement of Financial Accounting Concepts No. 2,* "Qualitative Characteristics," para. 93.

[15] *Ibid.,* para. 95.

ELEMENTS OF FINANCIAL STATEMENTS OF BUSINESS ENTERPRISES

Elements[16]

Financial statements require certain elements to be reported or disclosed in order to measure the performance and status of an enterprise. Ten inter-related elements of financial statements have been identified and defined.

Assets. Assets are *probable future economic benefits* obtained or controlled by a particular entity as a result of past transactions or events. For example, an acre of land purchased by a company is considered to be an asset, because the company can obtain the future economic benefits, can control others' access to these benefits, and has completed the transaction for the purchase of the land. If access to the land cannot be controlled by the company because the city can use it as a right-of-way or if the transaction has not yet occurred, but will in the future, then the land is not considered to be an asset.

Liabilities. *Liabilities are probable future sacrifices of economic benefits arising from present obligations of a particular entity to transfer assets or provide services to other entities in the future as a result of past transactions or events.* An obligation to pay an account which arose on the credit purchase of inventory or the use of electricity in advance of payment are examples of liabilities. An obligation to pay an executive a bonus in cash is a liability; an obligation to pay an executive a bonus in the company's own stock is not a liability because it does not involve a commitment of assets. An agreement to purchase inventory in the future is not considered to be a liability because no transaction has taken place.

Equity. *Equity is the residual interest in the assets of an entity that remains after deducting its liabilities (i.e., Equity = Assets − Liabilities).* In a business enterprise, the equity is the ownership interest. Equity is the source of distributions to the owners of an enterprise. These distributions are made at the discretion of the owners after any restrictions imposed by law, regulation, or agreements with other entities have been satisfied. Equity is increased by owners' investments and by comprehensive income. The division between liabilities and equity is clear in concept but not always in practice. For example, securities such as convertible bonds and preferred stock have characteristics of both liabilities and equity.

Certain changes in assets and liabilities *do not* produce changes in equity—examples include purchasing inventories for cash, issuing a note payable to settle an account payable, purchasing equipment on account, and repaying bonds payable. Other changes in assets and liabilities *produce* changes in equity—examples include comprehensive income (revenues, expenses, gains and losses) and changes in equity due to investments by owners and distributions to owners. Changes which affect the *composition* of equity but not the *amount* include stock dividends and the conversion of preferred stock into common stock.

---

[16] *FASB Statement of Financial Accounting Concepts No. 6*, "Elements of Financial Statements," (Stamford, CT: FASB, December, 1985).

Investments By Owners. Investments by owners are increases in equity of a particular business enterprise resulting from transfers to the enterprise from other entities of something of value to obtain or increase ownership interests (or equity) in it. Assets are most commonly received as investments by owners, but that which is received may also include services or satisfaction or conversion of liabilities of the enterprise.

Distributions to Owners. Distributions to owners are decreases in equity of a particular business enterprise resulting from transferring assets, rendering services, or incurring liabilities by the enterprise to owners. Distributions to owners decrease ownership interest (or equity) in an enterprise.

Comprehensive Income. *Comprehensive income is the change in equity (net assets) of a business enterprise during a period from transactions and other events and circumstances from non-owner sources.* It includes all changes in equity during a period except those resulting from investments by owners and distributions to owners.

Revenues. *Revenues are inflows or other enhancements of assets of an entity or settlements of its liabilities (or a combination of both) from delivering or producing goods, rendering services, or other activities that constitute the entity's ongoing major or central operations.* For example, a sale of furniture by a furniture manufacturer is considered to be revenue, whereas the sale of one of its short-term investments at a price exceeding its cost is not considered to be revenue.

Expenses. *Expenses are outflows or other consumption or using up of assets or incurrences of liabilities (or a combination of both) from delivering or producing goods, rendering services, or carrying out other activities that constitute the entity's ongoing major or central operations.* For example, the cost of the furniture sold by the furniture manufacturer above is considered to be an expense, whereas the sale of one of its short-term investments at a price less than its cost is not considered to be an expense.

Gains. *Gains are increases in equity (net assets) from peripheral or incidental transactions of an entity and from all other transactions and other events and circumstances affecting the entity during a period except those that result from revenues or investments by owners.* The sale of the short-term investment by the furniture manufacturer at a price exceeding its cost is considered to be a gain.

Losses. *Losses are decreases in equity (net assets) from peripheral or incidental transactions of an entity and from all other transactions and other events and circumstances affecting the entity during a period except those that result from expenses or distributions to owners.* The sale of the short-term investment by the furniture manufacturer at a price less than its cost is considered to be a loss.

RECOGNITION AND MEASUREMENT IN FINANCIAL STATEMENTS OF BUSINESS ENTERPRISES

Since financial statements are the principal means by which financial accounting information is communicated, it is essential to know what information should be incorporated into the financial statements. *SFAC No. 5 identifies this formal incorporation of information as the process of recognition.* For items that meet the criteria for recognition, disclosure by such other means as notes to the financial statements and supplementary information is not a substitute for recognition in the financial statements.

The Role of Financial Statements

According to SFAC No. 5, financial statements should contribute to meeting the objectives of financial reporting both individually and collectively. A complete set of financial statements for a period should include:

1. Financial position at the end of the period.
2. Earnings for the period.
3. Comprehensive income for the period.
4. Cash flows during the period.
5. Investments by and distributions to owners during the period.[17]

Statement of Financial Position. *A statement of financial position (balance sheet) is designed to provide information concerning an entity's assets, liabilities, and equity and their relationship among one another at a moment in time.* It is not designed to present the value of a business enterprise but should assist users in assessing this value.

Statements of Earnings and of Comprehensive Income *Together, these two statements show the degree to which and the ways in which the equity of an entity increased or decreased.* The concept of *earnings is defined as a measure of entity performance based on the extent to which asset inflows (revenues and gains) associated with cash-to-cash cycles substantially completed during the period exceed asset outflows (expenses and losses).* Earnings is similar to net income for a period but, unlike comprehensive income, excludes the effects of certain accounting adjustments of earlier periods that are recognized in the current period—primarily the cumulative effect of a change in accounting principle—as well as changes in net assets attributable to certain types of holding gains and losses.

Statement of Cash Flows. An entity should report its sources of cash receipts and uses of cash payments in a statement of cash flows. Cash flow information should also be provided concerning an entity's operating, financing, and investing activities.

---

[17] *FASB Statement of Financial Accounting Concepts No. 5*, "Recognition and Measurement in Financial Statements of Business Enterprises," (Stamford, CT: FASB, December, 1984), vii.

✓**Statement of Investments By and Distributions to Owners.** This statement is designed to reflect an entity's capital transactions during a period, including the extent and ways to which the equity of the entity was changed from capital transactions with the owners.

Recognition and Measurement

A revenue, expense, gain, or loss item and information about it should meet four criteria subject to the cost-benefit constraint and materiality threshold to be recognized. These are:

1. The item fits one of the definitions of elements in SFAC No. 6 (formerly SFAC No. 3);

2. The item has a relevant attribute measurable with sufficient reliability;

3. The information is relevant; and

4. The information is reliable.

The item can be measured by different attributes (e.g., historical cost, current market value, replacement cost, net realizable value, and present value of future cash flows), depending on the nature of the item and the relevance and reliability of the attribute measured.

SFAC No. 5 provides guidance for the recognition of revenues and gains and of expenses and losses. As a reaction to uncertainty, more stringent requirements are imposed for recognizing revenues and gains than for recognizing expenses and losses.

Recognition of revenues and gains involves the consideration of two factors:

1. Revenues and gains are generally not recognized until realized (assets or services exchanged for cash or claims to cash) or realizable (assets are readily convertible to known amounts of cash or claims to cash).

2. Revenues are not recognized until earned (the entity has substantially accomplished what is needed to be entitled to the benefits); being earned is generally less significant for gains than being realized or realizable.

Recognition of expenses and losses also involves the consideration of two factors:

1. Consumption of economic benefits are recognized by matching the expense with revenues (e.g., cost of the goods sold), by recognizing the expense in the period in which cash is spent or liabilities are incurred (e.g., administrative salaries), and by systematically allocating expenses to the periods during which the related assets are expected to provide benefits (e.g., depreciation).

2. An expense or loss is recognized if an asset no longer has a future economic benefit or if a liability has been incurred without associated economic benefits.

DEVELOPING GENERALLY ACCEPTED ACCOUNTING PRINCIPLES

Generally accepted accounting principles (GAAP) are concerned with the measurement and disclosure of economic activity. GAAP determines the manner in which the accounting process is to be applied in specific situations. *Generally accepted accounting principles have been defined as follows:*

> ... Generally accepted accounting principles incorporate the consensus at a particular time as to which economic resources and obligations should be recorded as assets and liabilities by financial accounting, which changes in assets and liabilities should be recorded, when these changes should be recorded, how the assets and liabilities and changes in them should be measured, what information should be disclosed and how it should be disclosed and which financial statements should be prepared.
>
> Generally accepted accounting principles therefore, is a technical term in financial accounting. Generally accepted accounting principles encompass the conventions, rules, and procedures necessary to define accepted accounting practice at a particular time. The standard of "generally accepted accounting principles" includes not only broad guidelines of general application, but also detailed practices and procedures.
>
> Generally accepted accounting principles are conventional—that is, they become generally accepted by agreement (often tacit agreement) rather than by formal derivation from a set of postulates or basic concepts. The principles have developed on the basis of experience, reason, custom, usage, and, to a significant extent, practical necessity.[18]

INFLUENCES ON ACCOUNTING PRINCIPLES

Accounting principles derive their authority from their general acceptance and use by the accounting profession and the financial community. Some of the more important influences on accounting are described in the paragraphs which follow.

American Institute of Certified Public Accountants

The American Institute of Certified Public Accountants (AICPA) is the primary professional association of certified public accountants (CPAs) in the United States today. For CPAs, it is the accounting profession's equivalent of the American Bar Association (for attorneys) and the American Medical Association (for physicians). The AICPA is responsible for the preparation of the Uniform CPA Examination that is used in all states and which must be completed successfully in order for an individual to become a certified public accountant. For a number of years this organization has

---

[18] *Ibid.*, para. 95.

been involved actively in research, which is intended to improve accounting practices and procedures, through its numerous committees and by the publication of *The Journal of Accountancy*, the most widely read professional publication of the practicing CPA.

Within the last decade, the role of the AICPA has changed. An example of this increased activity is the formation of the Accounting Standards Executive Committee (AcSEC). *AcSEC represents the AICPA in the area of financial accounting and reporting.* It issues Statements of Position (SOP) in response to the pronouncements of other accounting governing bodies. SOPs have the dual purpose of providing guidance where none previously existed and of influencing the standard-setting process. AcSEC also attempts to bridge the gap between the accounting standard setting bodies and practicing accountants with the use of issue papers which identify current financial reporting problems, present alternative treatments, and recommend solutions.

The Committee on Accounting Procedure

The Committee on Accounting Procedure (CAP) was formed by the AICPA in 1939 to establish, review, and evaluate accepted accounting procedures. During the period 1939-1959, the CAP issued fifty-one accounting research bulletins dealing with a variety of accounting practices, problems, and issues. The success of this committee was limited somewhat, because it dealt with specific problems as they arose, rather than establishing an overall framework to deal with these issues, and because the authority of its pronouncements depended solely upon their general acceptance. As the need for additional research into accounting principles intensified, the reasons for the continued existence of the CAP were less evident.

The Accounting Principles Board

In 1959, the AICPA replaced the CAP with the Accounting Principles Board (APB). The APB attempted to establish the basic postulates of accounting as a basis for the formulation of a set of broad accounting principles that would be used to guide the accountant in the specific circumstances of his or her practice. An accounting research division was established simultaneously to assist the board with the research which was necessary to carry out its assigned tasks.

During its fourteen years of existence, the APB issued a total of thirty-one opinions and four statements. *APB Opinions are authoritative pronouncements which established generally accepted accounting principles; APB Statements are designed to increase the understanding of financial reporting.*

The APB's membership ranged from eighteen to twenty-one. Although all of the members belonged to the AICPA and were CPAs, not all were practicing public accountants; some members were selected from industry, government, and the academic community.

The accounting research division issued fifteen research studies during its term of existence. However, the division did not interact with the APB in selecting the topics to analyze, nor did the APB request the division to examine specific accounting problems. This lack of coordination resulted in the board's issuance of opinions on topics for which little or no prior research had been conducted.

Prior to 1964, the enforcement of APB opinions depended primarily on the prestige and influence of the AICPA and the support of the Securities and Exchange Commission, an independent regulatory agency of the Federal government responsible for administering the Federal laws governing the trading of securities. Then the AICPA issued *Rule 203 of the Rules of Conduct of the Code of Professional Ethics. This rule prohibits a member of the AICPA from expressing an opinion that financial statements have been prepared in accordance with generally accepted accounting principles if there is any material departure from the pronouncements of the APB (and now the FASB as well), unless the member can demonstrate that the financial statements otherwise would be misleading due to unusual circumstances.* In addition, all material departures from these pronouncements must be disclosed and the reasons for such departure must be explained in the financial statements.

The APB was criticized for its structure. In addition, the APB's positions on several controversial topics were perceived to be compromises. In 1971, the AICPA established the study group on establishment of accounting principles to examine the organization and operation of the APB and to determine the improvements which were necessary. Its recommendations were accepted and led to the creation of the Financial Accounting Standards Board.

Financial Accounting Standards Board

The Financial Accounting Standards Board (FASB) came into existence in July of 1973 as the successor to the APB. Unlike its predecessor, the APB, *the FASB is an independent board whose membership consists of seven full-time, well-paid, distinguished accountants who are experienced in industry, government, education, and public accounting.* FASB members must sever all ties with former employers or private firms. Like its predecessor, the FASB conducts research in accounting matters using its own full-time technical staff members or commissions outside researchers from the academic and financial communities to work on specific projects of interest to the board.

The research activities of the FASB serve as the basis for an invitation to comment or a discussion memorandum, which is prepared to outline the key issues involved in a particular accounting problem and to invite public comment. After further consideration, the discussion memorandum or invitation to comment is modified and an exposure draft is issued for additional public comment. Depending upon the reaction to the initial exposure draft, the board may issue a new exposure draft for additional comment or, if it is satisfied at this point, may issue its final statement, or may do neither. A 5 to 2 vote of the seven members is required for a statement to be issued. The structure of the FASB and its relationships are depicted in Illustration 1.

The major types of pronouncements which are issued by the FASB are: (1) *statements of financial accounting standards,* which define GAAP; (2) interpretations of financial accounting standards, which modify or extend existing standards and which have the same authority as standards; (3) *statements of financial accounting concepts,* which set forth the fundamental objectives and concepts to be used by the FASB in developing financial accounting standards; and (4) *technical bulletins,* which provide guidance on financial accounting and reporting problems. To date, the FASB has issued over 150 statements, interpretations, and technical bulletins.

Securities and Exchange Commission

The Securities and Exchange Commission (SEC) was established as an independent governmental regulatory agency with the authority to prescribe accounting practices and standards for the financial reporting of firms that offer securities for sale to the public through national (and interstate) securities exchanges, such as the New York Stock Exchange and the American Stock Exchange. The Securities Act of 1933 and the Securities Exchange Act of 1934 require that these companies file registration statements, periodic reports, and audited annual financial statements with the SEC.

The SEC has worked closely with the accounting profession in establishing and improving accounting practices, particularly in the area of financial reporting. The SEC has stated that the standards issued by the FASB are considered to have authoritative support, and that practices which are contrary to the positions taken by the FASB are considered to be lacking in such support.

Internal Revenue Service

Although in most cases the Internal Revenue Service (IRS) influences accounting in an indirect rather than a direct manner, the income tax code and regulations do affect accounting procedures and methods. The effects of income taxes on accounting information will be discussed throughout this text.

Institute of Management Accountants

The Institute of Management Accountants (IMA) is the professional association of accountants who are employed in industry, and as such, is concerned normally with matters which are primarily related to managerial accounting. Of course, many of these issues also have an effect on financial accounting matters as well. Like the AICPA, the IMA sponsors research in accounting and issues periodic reports to its membership.

Governmental Accounting Standards Board

The Governmental Accounting Standards Board (GASB), which was formed in 1984, is an independent organization in the private sector. *The GASB establishes standards for activities and transactions of state and local governmental entities.* The GASB's pronouncements are applicable to such entities and activities as utilities, authorities, hospitals, colleges and univer-

Illustration 1
Structure of the FASB, FASAC, and FAF

Financial Accounting Standards Board (FASB)
7 members

Exclusive authority to set accounting standards and rules of procedure for setting accounting standards
FASB accounting standards are binding on all AICPA members and all accountants practicing before the SEC
Exclusive authority to hire and supervise the FASB staff, and to administer FASB resources

Financial Accounting Standards Advisory Council (FASAC)
32 members

Advises FASB on technical accounting matters
Comments on accounting interpretations issued by FASB

Financial Accounting Foundation (FAF)
9 trustees

Appoints the members of the FASB
Appoints the members of the FASAC
Arranges for the financing of the entire FASB organizational structure, primarily from members of the AICPA and the Financial Executive Institute
Approves the budgets of the FASB and the FASAC
Holds the authority to review and amend the charter and by-laws governing the operation of the FAF, the FASB, and the FASAC

American Accounting Association

Nominates the one FAF trustee with extensive experience as an accounting educator

AICPA Board of Directors

Chairman of the Board is automatically designated as one of the nine FAF trustees
AICPA board exercises exclusive authority to determine suitability and elect all eight of the elected FAF trustees
AICPA board nominates the four FAF trustees who must be practicing CPAs and members of the AICPA

Financial Executives Institute

Nominates one of the two FAF trustees with extensive experience as financial executives

Financial Analysts Federation

Nominates the one FAF trustee with extensive experience as a financial analyst

National Associations of Accountants

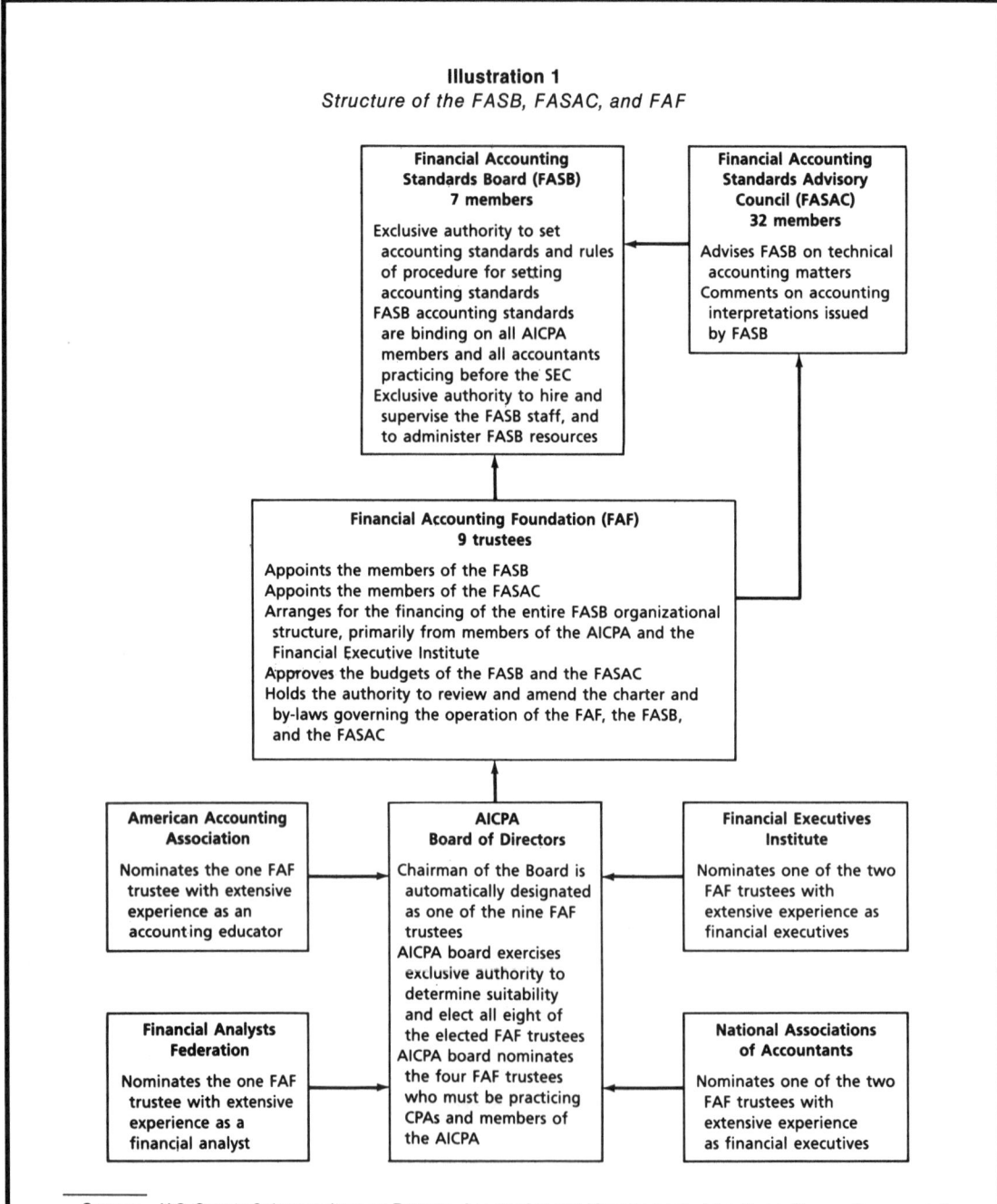

Nominates one of the two FAF trustees with extensive experience as financial executives

Source: U.S. Senate Subcommittee on Reports, Accounting and Management of the Committee on Government Operations. *The Accounting Establishment*, December 1976, 136.

sities, and pension plans. If the GASB has not issued a pronouncement applicable to such entities or activities, the FASB's standards should be used.

Like the FASB, the GASB follows due process procedures to provide for broad public participation at all stages of the standard-setting process. The GASB, like the FASB, issues invitations to comment, discussion memorandums, exposure drafts, statements, interpretations, and technical bulletins.

Cost Accounting Standard Boards

The Cost Accounting Standards Board (CASB) is the managerial accounting equivalent of the FASB. The CASB is charged with establishing uniform cost accounting standards for defense contractors awarded government contracts. The CASB was established in 1971, and the costs of research and investigation into defense contract problems were paid by the U.S. Government. Reports of the board were presented to the Congress of the United States. The CASB ceased to exist in 1980 when Congress failed to fund its operations, but was recently reinstituted.

American Accounting Association

The American Accounting Association (AAA) is concerned primarily with matters relating to accounting education. A sizable portion of its membership consists of accounting faculty of colleges and universities. Like the other professional organizations mentioned above, the AAA sponsors research in accounting and related matters and issues reports from time-to-time.

Congress

Congress also has involved itself directly in the rule-making process. In 1971, the APB adopted a rule concerning the accounting for the investment tax credit. At that time, the SEC stated its support for the APB's position. However, Congress then passed legislation that stated no particular method of accounting for the investment tax credit is required. The APB subsequently rescinded its earlier pronouncement.

The brief descriptions which were included above are intended to provide a general indication of the major thrust and composition of these organizations. In many cases, there is considerable overlap in the objectives and even the membership of these groups. All of these organizations (with the possible exception of Congress) share the common objective of seeking to improve accounting practice and financial reporting on both a national and multi-national basis.

THE ACCOUNTING STANDARD—SETTING PROCESS

A well-accepted view of the accounting standard-setting process asserts that it is essentially a political process involving various user groups each of which is attempting to advance its own self-interests.[19] User groups often react negatively to those proposed standards which are perceived to be dam-

---

[19] Charles Horngren, "The Marketing of Accounting Standards," *Journal of Accountancy* (October, 1973), 61-66.

aging to them and positively to those proposed standards which they perceive to be favorable for them.

User groups are able to politicize the standard-setting process by means of their lobbying efforts with Congress, the SEC, and the President. Since the SEC has both the authority and power to enact accounting standards, the FASB must remain responsive to these user groups or assume the risk of having its standard setting power usurped. Therefore, accounting standards sometimes lack the theoretical background one might expect as greater emphasis is given to the economic consequences of a proposed standard on various user groups.

Some accountants believe that the FASB should not only take accounting theory and the usefulness of accounting information into consideration, but also should support the economic goals of our government. Others believe that if accounting standards are promulgated to achieve macroeconomic objectives, then the confidence in these standards would be destroyed.

Most accounting standards have a definite economic impact. For example, the requirement to expense rather than to capitalize research and development costs has been considered to be a threat to technological progress. The requirement to use the method initially required by the FASB for accounting for the exploration and development costs of oil and gas companies was believed to be injurious to these enterprises.

At the time that the FASB issues a discussion memorandum, invitation to comment, or exposure draft, those companies that would be most affected submit their comments. There are always companies that dislike and oppose a proposed standard, and these companies may appeal to the government to become involved. If a standard is adopted that a company does not feel is beneficial, that company may not follow the standard on the basis of immateriality, or the company may alter its behavior in order to circumvent the effect of the standard. In addition, the company may increase its lobbying efforts in an attempt to have the standard modified or repealed.

International Aspects

Accounting principles and practices vary widely across countries. Accounting practices in certain countries (e.g., the United States and Canada) are prescribed by private organizations (e.g., FASB and the Canadian Institute of Chartered Accountants); accounting practices in other countries (e.g., France) are prescribed by the government.

Some accounting organizations have attempted to standardize practices across national boundaries. Two such organizations are the European Economic Community Commission, which has issued several directives on accounting practices for members of the Common Market, and the International Accounting Standards Committee (IASC), which has issued numerous International Accounting Standards.

Although professional accounting institutes in several countries have conformed their accounting requirements to these International Accounting Standards, the IASC members in many countries (e.g., the AICPA in the

United States) have not been able to ensure that the accounting organizations responsible for prescribing accounting practices in those countries (e.g., the FASB in the United States) issue standards that parallel the requirements stated in the International Accounting Standards. Therefore, in the United States, as well as in many other countries, there are differences between the requirements under the International Accounting Standards and domestic generally accepted accounting principles.

The financial statements of a foreign subsidiary may be included in the consolidated financial statements of a U.S. company. This foreign subsidiary may have prepared its financial statements in conformity with the requirements of the country in which it is located. Such requirements may or may not have been in agreement with the International Accounting Standards, the European Economic Community Commission, or some other multinational organization. Before the financial statements of this foreign subsidiary are included in the consolidated financial statements of the U.S. company, the foreign statements must be prepared in accordance with the generally accepted accounting principles for the United States.

Although a knowledge of accounting requirements in other countries and in multinational organizations is useful to practicing accountants in the United States, an examination of such requirements is beyond the scope of this text. International aspects of accounting are typically covered in advanced accounting courses.

OPPORTUNITIES IN ACCOUNTING

The accounting profession in the United States has achieved a professional status that is comparable to that of both the legal and medical professions. Certified Public Accountants (CPAs) are accountants who have completed educational requirements specified by the state in which they are licensed and who have successfully completed the uniform CPA examination. Accountants are employed in a wide variety of positions; any organization, regardless of its purpose, that requires information to be recorded, processed, and communicated usually needs the services of an accountant.

CPAs, in large and small public accounting firms, render a wide variety of services to their clients on a professional basis, much as do attorneys. The services offered by CPA firms include: auditing—the conducting of examinations and rendering of professional opinions as to the fairness of the presentation of the financial statements of organizations; taxes—tax planning and preparation of local, state, and federal tax returns; SEC work—assisting organizations in filings with the Securities and Exchange Commission; and management services—assisting in the design and installation of accounting systems and, in general, services of an advisory nature that do not fall under any one of the other categories mentioned above.

Many accountants are employed by industry and other profit and not-for-profit organizations. These accountants work in maintaining and improving the information systems of their organizations and are engaged in a wide variety of other tasks and duties.

Accountants also find employment in local, state, and Federal government, ranging from small local municipal agencies to large federal organizations such as the Internal Revenue Service, Securities and Exchange Commission, and the General Accounting Office. It may interest the reader that special agents of the Federal Bureau of Investigation are often either trained attorneys or accountants.

At the turn of the present century there were fewer than 250 certified public accountants in the United States. Today there are more than 150,000 CPAs, and the accounting profession continues to grow at an astonishing rate. An indication that this growth is likely to continue is the increasing demand for accounting graduates reflected in the starting salaries paid to accounting graduates. Along these same lines it is interesting to note that presidents of large U.S. corporations more often have a background in accounting than in any other single functional area. Clearly, there is a future in accounting.

SUMMARY

The accounting profession has grown rapidly in recent years both in terms of the number of accountants demanded and employed and in terms of professional stature. Accounting is basically a process of reporting and communicating financial information to a variety of internal and external users. As more and more decisions are based on information obtained from accounting reports, the communication aspect of accounting is of particular significance.

Financial accounting is concerned primarily with providing financial information to users who are external to the firm. Managerial accounting provides necessary information to those individuals responsible for internal decision-making. Information is typically provided to external users in the form of four basic financial statements: the balance sheet, the income statement, the statement of owners' equity, and the statement of cash flows.

Underlying all accounting practices are certain basic accounting concepts. Once accounting principles based on these concepts are accepted and used by the accounting profession, they become authoritative and are referred to as "generally accepted accounting principles." Many groups influence the acceptance of accounting principles.

Chapter 1 has discussed certain of the basic accounting concepts and definitions that will form a framework for the more detailed explanations included in subsequent chapters.

KEY DEFINITIONS

Accounting Principles Board (APB)—formed in 1959 to replace the Committee on Accounting Procedures (CAP) as the primary agency responsible for establishing, reviewing, and evaluating accounting principles. The APB was replaced in 1973 when criticisms of its structure and positions created the Financial Accounting Standards Board (FASB).

American Accounting Association (AAA)—an accounting organization which is primarily concerned with accounting education and research. Its membership consists of accounting faculty of colleges and universities as well as the practicing accountants.

American Institute of Certified Public Accountants (AICPA)—the primary professional association of Certified Public Accountants (CPAs) in the United States. It is involved in research intended to improve accounting practices and procedures.

Assets—probable future economic benefits obtained or controlled by a particular entity as a result of past transactions or events.

Balance sheet—The balance sheet or statement of financial position is a general purpose financial report which presents the financial position of the firm as of a particular point in time.

Benefits and costs—in order to justify providing accounting information, the benefits which may be derived from the use of this information must exceed the costs of providing the data.

Bias—bias in measurement is the tendency of a measure to fall more often on one side than the other of what it represents instead of being equally likely to fall on either side. Bias in accounting measures means a tendency to be consistently too high or too low.

Bookkeeping—the actual recording of business transactions. It is a clerical function which may be done manually or electronically with the use of computers.

Committee on Accounting Procedure (CAP)—established in 1939 by the AICPA for the role of establishing, reviewing, and evaluating accepted accounting principles. The CAP's successor in this role was the Accounting Principles Board (APB).

Comparability—the quality of information that enables users to identify similarities in and differences between two sets of economic phenomena.

Completeness—the inclusion in reported information of everything material that is necessary for faithful representation of the relevant phenomena.

Comprehensive income—the change in equity (net assets) of a business enterprise during a period from transactions and other events and circumstances from non-owner sources.

Concept of earnings—defined as a measure of entity performance based on the extent to which asset inflows (revenues and gains) associated with cash-to-cash cycles substantially completed during the period exceed asset outflows (expenses and losses).

Conservatism—a prudent reaction to uncertainty to try to ensure that uncertainty and risks inherent in business situations are adequately considered.

Consistency concept—this concept requires that once a firm adopts a particular accounting method for its use in recording a certain type of transaction, it should continue to use that method for all future transactions of the same category.

Corporation—an artificial being which has a legal identity that is separate and distinct from its owners or stockholders.

Cost Accounting Standards Board (CASB)—is the managerial accounting equivalent of the FASB. It is charged with establishing uniform cost accounting standards for defense contractors awarded government contracts.

Elements of financial statements—the elements are the components of the financial statements (e.g., assets, liabilities, revenues, and expenses).

Entity assumption—this assumption is the basis for the distinction which is made between the entity and its owners. The entity is treated as a unit separate and distinct from its ownership and is accounted for as such.

Equity—the residual interest in the assets of an entity that remains after deducting its liabilities (i.e., Equity = Assets − Liabilities).

Expenses—outflows or other consumption or using up of assets or incurrences of liabilities (or a combination of both) from delivering or producing goods, rendering services, or carrying out other activities that constitute the entity's ongoing major or central operations.

Feedback value—the quality of information that enables users to confirm or correct prior expectations.

Fidelity of accounting information—the correspondence between the information the accountant wishes to convey and the user's perception of the meaning of the information the accountant reports. The accountant and the user must have a mutual understanding as to certain basic concepts in order for the communication to be valid.

Financial accounting—the segment of accounting primarily concerned with the needs of users who are external to the firm.

Financial reporting—includes not only the financial statements but also such other forms of communicating financial information as annual reports filed with the SEC, news releases, and management forecasts.

Financial Accounting Standards Board (FASB)—an independent board which conducts research and issues opinions as to the correct treatment and presentation of financial information. Its membership includes accountants from industry, government, education, and public accounting. It is the successor to the Accounting Principles Board of the AICPA.

Full disclosure concept—requires that all information needed by the users of financial statements should be disclosed in an understandable form.

Gains—increases in equity (net assets) from peripheral or incidental transactions of an entity and from all other transactions and other events and circumstances affecting the entity during a period except those that result from revenues or investments by owners.

Going-concern concept—this concept is the assumption made by the accountant that the business will operate indefinitely unless there is evidence to the contrary.

Governmental Accounting Standards Board (GASB)—establishes standards for activities and transactions of state and local governmental entities.

Historical cost concept—the assumption that the original acquisition cost of a resource, not its current market value nor replacement cost, is the basis to be used in accounting for the resources of an entity.

Income statement—a summary of the operations of a firm. It reports the income (or loss) of the company during a specified period of time.

Institute of Management Accountants (IMA)—a professional association of industrial accountants which is concerned primarily with managerial accounting.

Internal Revenue Service (IRS)—a government agency which is charged with the collection of taxes. The income tax code and regulations often affect the procedures and methods of accounting.

Liabilities—probable future sacrifices of economic benefits arising from present obligations of a particular entity to transfer assets or provide services to other entities in the future as a result of past transactions or events.

Losses—decreases in equity (net assets) from peripheral or incidental transactions of an entity and from all other transactions and other events and circumstances affecting the entity during a period except those that result from expenses or distributions to owners.

Managerial accounting—the segment of accounting concerned with the needs of users who are internal to the firm.

Matching concept—requires the accountant to match the revenues earned during the accounting period with the expenses which were incurred to generate these revenues during this period.

Materiality concept—this concept indicates that the accountant should be primarily concerned with those transactions which are of real significance to the users of his or her report. No specific value can be assigned to any transaction to determine materiality, but if the information would affect a financial statement user's decisions, then it is material. It is the magnitude of an omission or misstatement of accounting information that, in the light of surrounding circumstances, makes it probable that the judgment of a reasonable person relying on the information would have been changed or influenced by the omission or misstatement.

Monetary unit assumption—this is the assumption made by the accountant that all transactions of the business can be recorded in terms of dollars.

Neutrality—the absence in reported information of bias intended to attain a predetermined result or to induce a particular mode of behavior.

Objective of financial reporting—a primary objective of financial reporting is to ". . . provide information that is useful to present and potential investors and creditors and other users in making rational investment, credit, and similar decisions. In order to accomplish this goal, it is necessary that the information which is communicated must be understood; it . . . should be comprehensible to those who have a reasonable understanding of business and economic activities and are willing to study the information with reasonable diligence."

Objectives of financial statements—derived from the needs of the users of the financial statements, are the most basic components of the conceptual framework.

Partnership—a business owned by two or more persons who share profits or losses according to an agreement and who are personally liable for all of the debts of the business.

Predictive value—the quality of information that helps users to increase the likelihood of correctly forecasting the outcome of past or present events.

Primary focus of financial reporting—the disclosure of information concerning the earnings of a business.

Proprietorship—a business owned by one person who is individually liable for all of the debts of the business.

Qualitative characteristics of financial statements—the criteria to be used in the selection and evaluation of accounting and reporting policies.

Relevance—the capacity of information to make a difference in a decision by helping users to form predictions about the outcome of past, present, and future events or to confirm or correct prior expectations.

Reliability—the quality of information that assures that information is reasonably free from error and bias and faithfully represents what it purports to represent.

Representational faithfulness—the correspondence or agreement between a measure or description and the phenomenon that it purports to represent (sometimes called validity).

Revenues—inflows or other enhancements of assets of an entity or settlements of its liabilities (or a combination of both) from delivering or producing goods, rendering services, or other activities that constitute the entity's ongoing major or central operations.

Securities and Exchange Commission (SEC)—a government regulatory agency which reviews the financial reporting practices of companies that offer securities for public sale through any national or interstate stock exchange. It works closely with the accounting profession to improve financial accounting practices.

Significance of accounting information—the relationship between the actual transactions of the company and the reports which summarize them. The accounting statements should disclose the events which occurred in a manner such that the user would reach the same decision based on the report that he or she would have made with firsthand information.

Stable dollar assumption—this concept assumes that any fluctuation in the purchasing power of the dollar is not significant. For this reason, changes in the purchasing power of the dollar are not recognized in the accounts.

Statement of cash flows—an entity should report its sources of cash receipts and uses of cash payments in a statement of cash flows.

Statement of changes in owners' equity—summarizes investments made by the owners, additions to equity from earnings, and withdrawals made by owners during the accounting period.

Statement of financial position (balance sheet)—designed to provide information concerning an entity's assets, liabilities, and equity and their relationship among one another at a moment in time.

Statement of investments by and distributions to owners—this statement is designed to reflect an entity's capital transactions during a period, including the extent and ways to which the equity of the entity was changed from capital transactions with the owners.

Statements of earnings and of comprehensive income—these two statements show the degree to which and the ways in which the equity of an entity increased or decreased.

Timeliness—having information available to a decision-maker before it loses its capacity to influence decisions.

Time period assumption—requires the preparation of financial statements at such intervals as a year or a quarter to meet users' needs on a timely basis.

Understandability—the quality of information that enables users to perceive its significance.

Users of accounting information—anyone who will read and analyze the financial statements in order to use the information contained therein to meet his or her own needs.

Verifiability—the ability through consensus among measures to ensure that information represents what it purports to represent or that the chosen method of measurement has been used without error or bias.

QUESTIONS

1. What is the purpose of accounting?

2. Is accounting useful for both profit and not-for-profit businesses? Explain.

3. Has the need for accounting (and accountants) increased in the United States since the turn of the century? Explain.

4. Who are some of the users of financial statements? Do their needs differ? Why?

5. Explain the similarities and differences between managerial accounting and financial accounting.

6. What are the objectives of financial reporting?

7. Define: (a) understandability; (b) decision usefulness; (c) relevance; and (d) reliability.

8. Why is it important that accounting information be timely and verifiable?

9. How does comparability enhance accounting information?

10. Why have accountants adopted the consistency concept?

11. How can the accountant determine whether a particular item is material in amount?

12. Why is the entity assumption necessary in accounting?

13. Discuss the relationship between the monetary unit assumption, the historical cost concept, and the stable dollar assumption. Are these assumptions realistic?

14. Distinguish between revenue recognition and revenue realization.

15. What is meant by full disclosure?

16. Identify and define the elements of financial statements.

17. What are the basic financial statements issued by the typical business? (Briefly describe each statement.)

18. Financial statements are prepared in accordance with "generally accepted accounting principles." What are "generally accepted accounting principles" and how are they determined?

19. What is the role of the Financial Accounting Standards Board in accounting?

20. If you were uncertain as to whether a particular procedure was in accordance with "generally accepted accounting principles," what would you do to find out?

21. What is meant by the term "certified public accountant (CPA)"? How does one become a CPA?

Chapter 2 discusses three of the major financial statements prepared by the accountant. The basic steps in the recording process are traced and explained. Studying this chapter should enable you to:

1. Present and explain the accounting equation.
2. Identify the two basic sources of a firm's assets.
3. Discuss the purpose, format, and major classifications of the balance sheet, income statement, and statement of capital.
4. Analyze transactions as to the effect on the balance sheet and income statement accounts.

2

Transaction Analysis: The Accounting Process

INTRODUCTION

Financial statements are the end product of the financial accounting process. The basic objective of the financial statements of a business is to provide the information which is required by various users for making economic decisions. As was indicated earlier, the basic accounting statements which are included in the accounting reports normally issued to users are the balance sheet, the income statement, the statement of capital, and the statement of cash flows. We will discuss the balance sheet, income statement, statement of capital, and statement of cash flows in this chapter.

THE BALANCE SHEET

The balance sheet, or statement of financial position, is the accounting statement which provides information regarding the financial position of the firm at a particular point in time. It includes information as to the assets, liabilities, and equities of the business as of a given date.

Assets are probable future economic benefits obtained or controlled by a particular entity as a result of past transactions or events.[1] They are the economic resources of the business. An asset is an economic right or a re-

---

[1] *FASB Statement of Financial Accounting Concepts No. 3*, "Elements of Financial Statements of Business Enterprises," (Stamford, CT: FASB, 1980), xi.

source that will be of either present or future benefit to the firm. In general, assets are things of value that are owned by the business. The assets of a business may take various forms. For example, assets include: cash, merchandise held for sale to customers, land, buildings, and equipment. In other words, assets are the resources which are used by the business in its continuing operations.

At any point in time, the total of the assets of a business are, by definition, equal to the total of the sources of these assets. A business obtains its assets from two basic sources: its owners and its creditors. Creditors lend resources to the firm. These debts, referred to as liabilities, must be repaid at some specified future date. Liabilities may be defined as probable future sacrifices of economic benefits arising from present obligations of a particular entity to transfer assets or provide services to other entities in the future as a result of the past transactions or events.[2] Owners invest their personal resources in the firm. Investments by owners are increases in net assets of a particular enterprise resulting from transfers to it from other entities of something of value to obtain or increase ownership interests (or equity) in it. Assets are most commonly received as investments by owners, but that which is received may also include services or satisfaction or conversion of liabilities of the enterprise.[3] In other words, the investments of owners in the firm and any profits retained in the business are its equity (or capital). Equity is the residual interest in the assets of an entity that remains after deducting its liabilities. In a business enterprise, the equity is the ownership interest.[4] Thus, the sources of a firm's assets are its liabilities and owner's equity.

✓ BALANCE SHEET CLASSIFICATIONS

The various classifications included in the balance sheet are intended to assist the user of the statement in acquiring as much information as possible concerning the business. The individual elements of the financial statements are the building blocks with which financial statements are constructed—the classes of items that financial statements comprise. The items included in financial statements represent in words and numbers certain enterprise resources, claims to those resources, and the effects of transactions and other events and circumstances that result in changes in those resources and claims.[5]

It might appear that if a firm desired to provide the user of its statements with the maximum information possible, it could supply him or her with a listing of all transactions which took place during the period so that the user

---

[2] *Ibid.*
[3] *Ibid.*
[4] *Ibid.*
[5] *Ibid.*, xii

could perform his or her own analysis. However, large firms routinely enter into hundreds of thousands or even millions of transactions during any given period. It is therefore highly unlikely that any user would have either sufficient time, the inclination, or the ability to analyze this type of listing. To simplify the analysis of financial statements, firms group similar items in order to reduce the number of classifications which appear on the balance sheet. For example, a chain store may own many buildings of different sizes, at various locations and serving different functions, but instead of listing these assets separately, all buildings will normally be grouped and presented as a single amount on the balance sheet.

Assets

When assets are acquired by a business they are initially recorded at the cost of acquisition or original purchase price. This is true even if the business has paid only a portion of the initial cost in cash at the time of acquisition and owes the remaining balance to the seller of the asset.

Assets will vary somewhat in their characteristics such as their useful life in relationship to the business' operating cycle, physical attributes, and frequency of use. Accountants attempt to describe certain of the relevant characteristics of assets on the balance sheet by the use of general classifications such as current assets, long-term (or fixed) assets, and other assets. Within these broad categories there are also several sub-classifications. The usual ordering of assets on the balance sheet is in terms of liquidity—the order in which the assets would normally be converted into cash or used up.

I. **Current Assets.** Generally, current assets include cash and other assets which are expected to be converted into cash, sold, or used in operations or production during the current accounting period. The accounting period is usually considered to be one year for most businesses. The general sub-classifications of current assets normally found in the balance sheet include cash, marketable securities, accounts receivable, inventories, and prepaid expenses. These individual asset categories are briefly described below.

1. **Cash.** Cash includes all cash which is immediately available for use in the business including cash on hand, in cash registers, and in checking accounts. Cash is discussed in detail in Chapter 7.

2. **Marketable Securities.** Marketable securities are temporary investments in stocks, bonds, and other securities which are readily salable and which management intends to hold only for a relatively short period of time. Marketable securities are discussed in Chapter 8.

3. **Receivables.** The accounts receivable balance represents the amount which is owed to the business by its customers. If a business has a significant amount of receivables from sources other than its normal trade customers, the receivables from customers are normally classified as trade accounts receivable and the amounts owed by others are classified as other accounts receivable.

A balance sheet may also include notes receivable. Notes receivable are the receivables (from customers or others) for which the business has received written documentation of the debtors' intent to pay. Both accounts receivable and notes receivable are discussed in Chapter 7.

4. **Inventories.** Inventories represent the cost of goods or materials which are held for sale to customers in the ordinary course of business, in the process of production for such sale, or to be used in the production of goods or services to be available for sale at some future date. Inventories are described in Chapter 4.

5. **Prepaid Expenses.** Prepaid expenses represent expenditures which were made in either the current or a prior period and which will provide benefits to the firm at some future time. For example, a fire insurance policy which protects the assets of a firm for a three-year period may be purchased during the current year. Although the policy was paid for and a portion of the protection was used during the current year, the firm benefits from the insurance protection in future years as well. Therefore, the portion of the cost of the policy which is applicable to future years would be considered a prepaid expense at the end of the current year.

II. **Fixed Assets.** Fixed or long-term assets are those assets which are acquired for use in the business rather than for resale to customers. They are assets from which the business expects to receive benefits over a number of future accounting periods. Since fixed assets are used in the operations of the firm and benefits are derived from this use or availability, the cost of these assets is considered an expense of those periods which benefit from their use.

The actual classifications which may be included in the balance sheet under the fixed asset caption will, of course, vary depending upon the type of business and the nature of its operations. The accounting for fixed assets is described in Chapter 5.

III. **Other Assets.** The classification, other assets, includes those assets which are not appropriately classified under either the current or the fixed asset categories described above. This classification may include both (tangible) and (intangible) assets. Tangible assets are those that have *physical* substance, such as land held for investment purposes. Intangibles are assets *without* physical substance, such as patents, copyrights, goodwill, etc. This distinction will be discussed in detail in Chapter 5.

Liabilities

Liabilities are debts. They represent claims of creditors against the assets of the business. Creditors have a prior legal claim over the owners of the business. In the event a business is liquidated, creditors will be paid the amounts owed them before any payments are made to owners. Creditors are, of course, concerned with the ability of the business to repay its debts. In certain instances, creditors may earn interest on the amount due them. Normally, a liability has a maturity or due date at which time it must be satisfied.

Liabilities, just as assets, fall into several descriptive categories. The two basic classifications which are usually employed in the balance sheet are current liabilities and long-term liabilities. Both of these general classes may also have sub-classifications.

I. **Current Liabilities.** Current liabilities include those obligations for which settlement is expected to require the use of current assets or the origination of other current liabilities. Examples of current liabilities include accounts payable, notes payable, taxes payable, and unearned revenues. These are described in the following paragraphs.

1. **Accounts Payable.** Accounts payable are claims of vendors who sell goods and services to the company on a credit basis. Accounts payable are usually not evidenced by a formal, written document such as is the case with a note.

2. **Notes Payable.** Notes payable normally arise from borrowing or, on occasion, from purchases, and are evidenced by a written document. Notes payable may or may not be interest bearing. Notes usually have a fixed or determinable due date.

3. **Taxes Payable.** This liability includes any local, state, and federal taxes which are owed by the business at the end of the accounting period but are payable in the next period.

4. **Unearned Revenues.** Unearned revenues are amounts collected from customers for goods which have not been shipped or services which have not yet been performed.

II. **Long-Term Liabilities.** Long-term liabilities generally represent claims which will be paid or satisfied in a future accounting period (or periods). Examples of long-term liabilities are bonds payable and mortgages payable.

Owner's Equity

Owner's equity, also referred to as capital, represents the claims of the owners against the net assets of the firm. Owners normally assume risks which are greater than those of creditors since the return on investment to the owners is usually undefined. In the event of bankruptcy, claims of creditors take priority over those of owners and must be satisfied first. After all creditors have been paid, any assets that remain will then be available to the owners of the firm.

Accounting for owner's equity is influenced by the legal status of the company—the form of its organization. The legal forms of business recognized and used most extensively in the United States are the sole proprietorship, the partnership, and the corporation. There are certain legal differences associated with these types of organizations which will be considered in Chapters 6 and 7. Basically, the owner's equity of a business is normally divided into two major classifications based on the source of the equity: direct investments made by the owner and profits retained in the business. Owner's equity accounts will be discussed in detail in later chapters.

USES AND LIMITATIONS OF THE BALANCE SHEET

Although many accountants and analysts consider the income statement to be the most important of the financial statements, the balance sheet is also a very relevant and useful document. The balance sheet reports the types of assets that are owned by the entity, the various short- and long-term liabilities that are owed, and, in the case of a corporation, the sources of stockholders' equity.

Numerous relationships within the balance sheet and between the balance sheet and the income statement may be observed. A sample of the types of analyses possible is listed below.

1. The ability of a company to pay its current debts as they become due depends primarily upon the relationship between its current assets and its current liabilities.

2. An indication of the risk that is incurred by the common stockholders in being unable to meet the obligations of the firm may be noted from the firm's debt-to-equity ratio.

3. The ability of an enterprise to earn a profit for its common stockholders may be noted by the rate of return on common stockholders' equity.

4. The number of times that accounts receivable were converted into cash during the period may be determined by the accounts receivable turnover.

Comparative balance sheets provide even more information, because favorable or unfavorable trends in factors such as those listed above may be observed and noted.

The balance sheet frequently has been criticized for a number of reasons. Current values are not reflected in most cases (inventories and marketable equity securities may be shown at current value only if current value is less than cost), plant and equipment is presented at its acquisition cost less accumulated depreciation, and inventories are reported at cost (unless lower of cost or market is used and market value is less than cost). Disclosure of the current cost of inventories and plant and equipment is required only as a supplemental disclosure for larger corporations.

A further criticism of the balance sheet is that the values of certain significant items are omitted completely. Examples of omitted items include the quality of the company's management personnel, the location of the enterprise, and the reputation of the firm's products. Some accountants maintain that the balance sheet would be made much more useful by including valuation concepts and additional information not currently reported under the provisions of generally accepted accounting principles.

In spite of the criticisms of its basic nature and content, there is ample evidence that the balance sheet is used frequently by external decision-makers (e.g., investors and creditors) in making investment decisions. Further, it is often maintained that the use of subjective valuations (e.g., current values) would result in both the balance sheet and the income statement becoming distorted and less informative. Clearly, the appropriate methods of measuring or valuing the elements of the balance sheet are a highly controversial accounting issue.

THE INCOME STATEMENT

The income statement or operating statement provides data concerning the results of operations of the firm for a specific period of time, usually a year. The results of the operations of a business are determined by its revenues, expenses, and the resulting net income.

Revenues and expenses are defined as follows:

> *Revenues* are inflows or other enhancements of assets of an entity or settlements of its liabilities (or a combination of both) during a period from delivering or producing goods, rendering services, or other activities that constitute the entity's ongoing major or central operations.[6]
>
> *Expenses* are outflows or other using up of assets or incurrences of liabilities (or a combination of both) during a period from delivering or producing goods, rendering services, or carrying out other activities that constitute the entity's ongoing major or central operations.[7]

Put simply, revenues are the gross increases in assets or gross decreases in liabilities which are recognized and result from the sale of either goods or services. Expenses are gross decreases in assets or gross increases in liabilities that occur as a result of the operations of a business. Net income is the excess of revenues over the related expenses for an accounting period. The revenues, expenses, and the resulting net income for a period are presented in the firm's income statement.

The usual accounting concept of income is based on determining, as objectively as possible, the income earned during a particular accounting period by deducting the expenses which were incurred from the revenues earned. Revenues are the proceeds received from the sale of goods and the rendering of services. Expenses are the costs which are incurred in the process of generating revenues. The accounting concept of income assumes that various rules and principles will be followed. These principles require the accountant to exercise his or her professional judgment in their application since the accounting concept of income measurement stresses the fair determination of income. The reader should note that fair presentation of income does not mean precise presentation. Accounting is an estimating process that requires the accountant to view transactions as objectively as possible in determining both the financial position of a firm and its income for the period.

---

[6] *Ibid.*
[7] *Ibid.*

Since the income statement presents the results of operations for an accounting period, information included in this statement is usually considered to be among the most important data provided by the accountant. This is because profitability is a major concern of those interested in the economic activities of an enterprise.

INCOME STATEMENT CLASSIFICATIONS

As was the case with the balance sheet, classifications which appear in the income statement are intended to be descriptive, functional categories of revenues and expenses. There are many different formats employed for income statements. Variations among industries are substantial and, to compound this problem, variations among firms in the same industry can also be significant. Consequently, the classifications which are used in the income statement will be discussed in detail in later chapters of this text.

THE STATEMENT OF CASH FLOWS

The statement of cash flows explains the causes of changes in cash plus highly liquid marketable securities and provides a summary of the investing and financing activities of an enterprise during a period of time. While the basic purpose of this statement is to provide information concerning the changes in cash plus highly liquid marketable securities, the statement also is useful in appraising other factors such as the firm's financing policies, dividend policies, ability to expand productive capacity, and the ability to satisfy future debt requirements.

Information concerning the amount, sources, and uses of the liquid resources of a business is considered to be of considerable interest and great value to a wide variety of users of financial statements in making economic decisions. While certain information concerning the sources and uses of resources can be derived from comparative balance sheets and income statements, neither of these statements provides complete disclosure of the financing and investing activities of an enterprise over a period of time. An income statement discloses the results of operations for a period of time but does not indicate the amount of resources provided by other activities. Further, reported revenues and expenses may not represent increases or decreases in liquid resources during the period. Comparative balance sheets show net changes in assets and equities but do not indicate the specific causes of these changes. Therefore, while partial information concerning the sources and uses of liquid funds may be obtained from comparative balance sheets and income statements, a complete analysis of the financial activities of a business can be derived only from this third financial statement, the statement of cash flows. This statement is discussed in detail in Chapter 11.

THE FINANCIAL ACCOUNTING PROCESS

As discussed previously, an accounting system must be designed to accumulate data concerning economic events, to process this data, and to summarize the data in periodic financial reports. A basic accounting model is used as the basis for the accounting process. This model may be expressed in equation form as follows:

$$\text{Assets} = \text{Liabilities} + \text{Owners' Equity}$$

The concept expressed in this simple equation underlies the recording process used in accounting, and it also serves as the basis for one of the principal financial statements, the balance sheet (or statement of financial position). In other words, the balance sheet includes a listing of the assets (A) owned by the firm and the sources of or claims to these assets—the liabilities (L) and owners' equity (OE).

$$\frac{\text{Assets} = \text{Sources of Assets}}{A = L + OE}$$

The balance sheet discloses the three major categories included in the above equation—assets, liabilities, and owners' equity—as of a particular point in time.

The economic resources owned and used by the business are referred to as assets. Assets are either of present or future benefit of the firm. *A business obtains its assets from one of two basic sources: its creditors or its owners.* Creditors lend resources to the firm, and the business incurs debts for these loans. These debts, referred to as liabilities, are normally repaid at some specific and agreed-upon future date. Owners invest their personal resources in the firm. These investments and any profits retained in the business are referred to as equities. Thus, the sources of a firm's assets are its liabilities and owners' equity. These liabilities and owners' equity are claims or rights to the assets. At any point in time, the total of the assets of a business are, by definition, equal to the total of the sources of these assets.

The accounting equation also indicates that the owner's equity is equal to the interest of the owners in the net assets (assets − liabilities) of the business. That is, by transposition, the accounting equation may be restated as follows:

$$A - L = OE$$

Transaction Analysis

The accounting process involves the identification of economic events affecting the entity and the recording of the relevant financial information. In effect, the recording process in accounting is used to analyze each transaction or event that takes place during the life of a business and to report the effect that each transaction or event has on the financial position, results of operations, and changes in financial position of the business.

Two types of transactions or events are recognized for financial accounting purposes: (1) exchange transactions between the entity and one or more external parties (e.g., the purchase of an asset); and, *(2) other events that are not represented by exchanges but that have economic impact on the entity* (e.g., an assessment of additional taxes by the Internal Revenue Service) *or that involve the internal conversion or use of resources* (e.g., recording depreciation on assets). The business documents relating to these transactions or events are used as the source of input data in the accounting process. Examples of business documents for external transactions include sales invoices, checks, and purchase orders; internal events are evidenced by such documents as requisitions for the transfer of raw materials to the production process. Once an event or transaction is recorded, the business documents are retained as a means of verifying the accounting records.

The number of transactions that occur in even a small business causes the assets, liabilities, equities, revenues, and expenses to increase and decrease much too frequently to prepare a new set of financial statements each time that a transaction takes place. Consequently, an alternative method of recording information must be used. This recording process, which is basic to every accounting system, is the subject of the following sections of this chapter. The accounting system described is referred to as a *double-entry system* and is applicable to all situations where financial information must be collected and processed. As described in this chapter, this sytem is often maintained by hand in small firms. However, in larger organizations, the system usually will be implemented using mechanical or electronic data-processing equipment. In either circumstance, however, each transaction or event must be recorded in the accounting system, and the basic accounting principles are identical.

In order to illustrate the process of recording transactions and the effect this has on the financial position of a business, we will review the transactions of a small service organization, Kilmer Contractors, during May 19x1, the initial month of its operations.

May 1. Bill Kilmer organized Kilmer Contractors and invested cash of $500 in the business.

This increase in the asset cash and the corresponding increase in the investment by the owner, referred to as capital, would be reflected in the balance sheet as follows:

	Assets	=	Liabilities	+	Owner's Equity
	Cash	=			*Capital*
May 1	$500	=			$500

This transaction is an investment of funds in a business by its owner. The asset, cash, was received by the firm and the owner's equity or capital was increased. Note that the basic accounting equation is in balance.

May 2. Kilmer Contractors borrowed $5,000 from Bill Kilmer's parents.[8]

---

[8] For purposes of illustration, it will be assumed that Kilmer Contractors signed a non-interest bearing note payable to Bill Kilmer's parents.

This increase in both assets (cash) and liabilities (notes payable) would affect the balance sheet as follows:

	Assets	=	Liabilities	+	Owner's Equity
	Cash	=	Note Payable	+	Capital
Balance	$ 500	=			$500
May 2	5,000		$5,000		
	$5,500	=	$5,000	+	$500

This transaction is the receipt of an asset, cash, in exchange for a liability, the promise to pay a creditor at some future time. It reflects the promise of the business to repay $5,000 at a future date in order to have cash on hand and available for use at this time. Again, capital is not affected; what has occurred is an exchange of a promise to pay the liability, notes payable, for the asset cash. The basic accounting equation remains in balance.

> May 5. The company purchased painting supplies, paying the $3,000 purchase price of the supplies in cash.

The increase in supplies and the offsetting decrease in the cash of the business would be reflected in the balance sheet as follows:

	Assets			=	Liabilities	+	Owner's Equity
	Cash	+	Supplies	=	Note Payable	+	Capital
Balance	$5,500			=	$5,000		$500
May 5	(3,000)		$3,000				
	$2,500	+	$3,000	=	$5,000	+	$500

This transaction represents an exchange of one asset for another. The asset, supplies, was increased while the asset, cash, was decreased. Capital was not affected. The equation is still in balance.

> May 10. Kilmer signed a contract whereby he agreed to paint three houses sometime during the next few weeks. The customer paid the fee of $1,100 per house in advance.

This increase in cash and the corresponding increase in liabilities, unearned fees, would be reflected by the business as follows:

	Assets			=	Liabilities			+	Owner's Equity
	Cash	+	Supplies	=	Note Payable	+	Unearned Fees	+	Capital
Balance	$2,500	+	$3,000	=	$5,000			+	$500
May 10	3,300						$3,300		
	$5,800	+	$3,000	=	$5,000	+	$3,300	+	$500

The company has agreed to paint three houses at a future date and has received its fee now, before it has done the work. The receipt of the $3,300 increases cash and the liability, unearned fees, by the same amount. Unearned fees is not a liability in the sense that the company will be required to repay the money. Rather, it represents an obligation on the part of Kilmer Contractors to perform a service at some future date. Capital is not affected by this transaction and the accounting equation, A = L + OE, remains in balance.

> May 12. Bill Kilmer, the owner, withdrew $600 from the business for his personal use.

This decrease in cash and the corresponding decrease in the owner's equity balance would be reflected in the balance sheet as follows:

	Assets			=	Liabilities			+	Owner's Equity
	Cash	+	Supplies	=	Note Payable	+	Unearned Fees	+	Capital
Balance May 12	$5,800 (600)	+	$3,000	=	$5,000	+	$3,300	+	$ 500 (600)
	$5,200	+	$3,000	=	$5,000	+	$3,300	+	($100)

This transaction represents a withdrawal of a portion of the owner's investment from the business. Cash and capital were both decreased by $600. Note also that the balance in the capital account is a minus or negative $100. This is because Kilmer withdrew $600, $100 more than his original investment of $500. The accounting equation is still in balance.

> May 15. Kilmer Contractors repaid $2,000 of the $5,000 it borrowed from Mr. and Mrs. Kilmer.

This decrease of $2,000 in both cash and liabilities would affect the balance sheet as follows:

	Assets			=	Liabilities			+	Owner's Equity
	Cash	+	Supplies	=	Note Payable	+	Unearned Fees	+	Capital
Balance May 15	$ 5,200 (2,000)	+	$3,000	=	$ 5,000 (2,000)	+	$3,300	+	($100)
	$3,200	+	$3,000	=	$3,000	+	$3,300	+	($100)

This transaction is a reduction of both liabilities and assets. The business repaid $2,000 of the $5,000 it owed to Mr. and Mrs. Kilmer. Both cash and the note payable decreased by this amount. Capital is not affected and the accounting equation remains in balance. (Recall that it was assumed this was a non-interest bearing note.)

The transactions of Kilmer Contractors for the first fifteen days of May are summarized below.

Kilmer Contractors
Total Transactions
May 1 to May 15, 19x1

	Assets			=	Liabilities			+	Owner's Equity
	Cash	+	Supplies	=	Note Payable	+	Unearned Fees	+	Capital
May 1	$ 500								$500
May 2	5,000				$5,000				
May 5	(3,000)		$3,000						
May 10	3,300						$3,300		
May 12	(600)								(600)
May 15	(2,000)				(2,000)				
	$3,200	+	$3,000	=	$3,000	+	$3,300	+	($100)

At this point in time, we will prepare a balance sheet for Kilmer Contractors. This balance sheet appears below.

Kilmer Contractors
Balance Sheet
May 15, 19x1

Assets		Liabilities + Owner's Equity	
Cash	$3,200	Note payable	$3,000
Supplies	3,000	Unearned fees	3,300
		Capital	(100)
	$6,200		$6,200

The balance sheet example for Kilmer Contractors was overly simplified for purposes of illustration. An actual balance sheet, such as the one included at the end of the Prologue to this text, includes far more additional account titles and classifications. The reader should note that these classifications are not arbitrary distinctions made by the accountants who prepared the balance sheet. They represent generally followed classifications which are intended to assist the user of the balance sheet in analyzing and interpreting it for his or her use.

The operations of Kilmer Contractors for the first fifteen days of May, 19x1, were analyzed earlier. None of the transactions which occurred during this period were relevant to the income statement since they affected neither the revenues earned nor the expenses incurred by the business. We will now follow the activities for the remainder of May to see how revenue and expense transactions affect *both* the income statement and the balance sheet.

The balance sheet is the starting point for the continuation of our example. Before proceeding, however, certain fundamental relationships should be reexamined. Recall that all assets are obtained from two basic sources, creditors and owners. At this point, we are concerned with the latter, the assets contributed by owners.

Owners may contribute assets either: (1) directly, that is, by the investment of personal resources in the business; or (2) indirectly, by allowing the *income* earned by the firm to remain with the business and not withdrawing it for their personal use. In other words, just as a direct investment made by the owner increases his or her equity, the income earned by the firm also increases both the assets and the owner's equity of the firm. Since income is the excess of revenues over expenses (R − E), the basic accounting equation expressed earlier in the chapter may be expanded and restated for purposes of illustration as follows:

$$\text{Assets} = \text{Liabilities} + \text{Owner's Equity} + \text{Revenue} - \text{Expense}$$

$$A = L + OE + R - E$$

Keep in mind that this restatement is made for purposes of illustration only and does not really change either the substance or the meaning of the equation itself. It merely emphasizes the fact that one way in which the owner's equity of a business may be increased is by income—that is, revenues less expenses. Nothing else is changed. Now let us return to the Kilmer Contractors example.

May 17. Kilmer Contractors painted its first house and billed and collected cash of $700 from the customer.

This transaction was a sale of services for cash. It would affect Kilmer Contractors as follows:

	Assets			=	Liabilities			+	Owner's Equity		
	Cash	+	Supplies	=	Note Payable	+	Unearned Fees	+	Capital	+	Revenue (Expense)
Balance	$3,200	+	$3,000	=	$3,000	+	$3,300	+	($100)		
May 17	700										$700
	$3,900	+	$3,000	=	$3,000	+	$3,300	+	($100)	+	$700

This transaction reflects the fact that the firm has begun to earn revenue. Cash was received and the owner's equity of the business was increased by the amount of the revenue earned, $700. The basic accounting equation is still in balance.

May 19. Kilmer Contractors painted a second house and billed (but did not collect) its fee of $900.

This transaction was a sale of services to a customer on a credit basis. It would affect the business as indicated below:

	Assets					=	Liabilities			+	Owner's Equity		
	Cash	+	Accounts Receivable	+	Supplies	=	Note Payable	+	Unearned Fees	+	Capital	+	Revenue (Expense)
Balance May 19	$3,900			+	$3,000	=	$3,000	+	$3,300	+	($100)	+	$ 700
			$900										900
	$3,900	+	$900	+	$3,000	=	$3,000	+	$3,300	+	($100)	+	$1,600

Again, this transaction records the revenue earned by the firm by painting a customer's house. Unlike the previous transaction, however, cash was not received. The customer was billed for the service and will pay Kilmer Contractors at some future date. Accounts receivable have increased and owner's equity (revenue) has increased by $900, the fee which was charged for painting the house. This transaction illustrates the very important point that revenue is recorded as it is earned, not necessarily as cash is received. This concept reflects the *accrual* basis of accounting, which will be discussed and used throughout the text.

May 25. Kilmer paid his employees salaries of $1,500.

This transaction was the payment of an expense in cash. It would affect Kilmer Contractors as follows:

	Assets					=	Liabilities			+	Owner's Equity		
	Cash	+	Accounts Receivable	+	Supplies	=	Note Payable	+	Unearned Fees	+	Capital	+	Revenue (Expense)
Balance May 25	$ 3,900	+	$900		$3,000	=	$3,000	+	$3,300	+	($100)	+	$1,600
	(1,500)												(1,500)
	$2,400	+	$900	+	$3,000	=	$3,000	+	$3,300	+	($100)	+	$ 100

Expenses of $1,500 were incurred and paid in cash. This transaction reduces both cash and owner's equity. The reduction in owner's equity is due to the fact that an expense has been incurred, thereby reducing income. (Remember that revenues less expenses equals income.) The accounting equation is still in balance.

May 31. Kilmer Contractors painted one of the three houses contracted for on May 10.

By painting one of the three houses, Kilmer Contractors has partially satisfied a non-cash liability by the rendering of services and therefore earned income. This transaction would be reflected as follows:

	Assets			=	Liabilities		+	Owner's Equity	
	Cash	+	Accounts Receivable	+	Supplies	=	Note Payable	+	Unearned Fees	+	Capital	+	Revenue (Expense)
Balance May 31	$2,400	+	$900	+	$3,000	=	$3,000	+	$3,300 (1,100)	+	($100)	+	$ 100 1,100
	$2,400	+	$900	+	$3,000	=	$3,000	+	$2,200	+	($100)	+	$1,200

On May 10, Kilmer signed a contract to paint three houses and received his fee of $1,100 per house in advance. No income was earned at the point the $3,300 in cash was received because no work had been done at that time. Kilmer Contractors had an obligation to paint the three houses at some future date. This represented a liability to perform services, which was previously recorded as unearned fees. Now one of the three houses contracted for has been painted and that portion of the income has been earned. The liability, unearned fees, has been reduced by $1,100 and the income for the current period has been increased by the same amount. These facts require that the statements be adjusted in order to reflect the current status of the contract. Again, this transaction emphasizes the point that income is recorded as it is earned, *not* as cash is received. The accounting equation remains in balance.

May 31. The unused painting supplies on hand at this date had an original cost of $2,000.

The facts of this transaction indicate that an expense has been incurred and should be recorded. It will affect Kilmer Contractors as indicated below:

	Assets			=	Liabilities		+	Owner's Equity	
	Cash	+	Accounts Receivable	+	Supplies	=	Note Payable	+	Unearned Fees	+	Capital	+	Revenue (Expense)
Balance May 31	$2,400	+	$900	+	$3,000 (1,000)	=	$3,000	+	$2,200	+	($100)	+	$1,200 (1,000)
	$2,400	+	$900	+	$2,000	=	$3,000	+	$2,200	+	($100)	+	$ 200

During the month of May, Kilmer Contractors used supplies that had an original cost of $1,000. This amount was determined by subtracting the $2,000 cost of the supplies which were on hand at May 31 from the $3,000 total cost of supplies available for use (that is, the supplies purchased during the month). As in the previous May 31 transaction, an adjustment is required. The asset, supplies, was decreased by $1,000 (the cost of the supplies used) from $3,000 (the total supplies available for use during the month of May) to $2,000 (the cost of supplies on hand at May 31). This transaction reflects the fact that expenses, like revenues, are recorded as they are incurred or used rather than when cash is disbursed. The accounting equation remains in balance.

All of the transactions of Kilmer Contractors for the month of May are summarized as follows:

Kilmer Contractors
All Transactions
For the Month of May, 19x1

	Assets				=	Liabilities			+	Owner's Equity		
	Cash	+	Accounts Receivable	+ Supplies	=	Note Payable	+	Unearned Fees	+	Capital	+	Revenue (Expense)
May 1	$ 500									$500		
May 2	5,000					$5,000						
May 5	(3,000)			$3,000								
May 10	3,300							$3,300				
May 12	(600)									(600)		
May 15	(2,000)					(2,000)						
	$3,200	+	$ 0	+ $3,000	=	$3,000	+	$3,300	+	($100)	+	$ 0
May 17	700											700
May 19			900									900
May 25	(1,500)											(1,500)
May 31								(1,100)				1,100
May 31				(1,000)								(1,000)
	$2,400	+	$900	+ $2,000	=	$3,000	+	$2,200	+	($100)	+	$ 200

We are now in a position to prepare a balance sheet and an income statement for Kilmer Contractors. The balance sheet would be as follows:

Kilmer Contractors
Balance Sheet
May 31, 19x1

Assets		Liabilities and Owner's Equity	
Cash	$2,400	Note payable	$3,000
Accounts receivable	900	Unearned fees	2,200
Supplies	2,000	Capital	100
	$5,300		$5,300

The income statement for the month of May would appear as follows:

Kilmer Contractors
Income Statement
For the Month Ending May 31, 19x1

Revenue			$2,700
Less:	Expenses:		
	Supplies used	$1,000	
	Salaries	1,500	
	Total expenses		2,500
Income			$ 200

The revenues reported in the income statement include $700 earned by painting the house on May 17, $900 earned on May 19 by painting a second house, and $1,100 earned by painting one of the three houses contracted for on May 10 ($700 + $900 + $1,100 = $2,700). The expenses of $2,500 include the salaries of $1,500 paid to Kilmer Contractors' employees on May 25 and the cost of the painting supplies used during the month of May. The cost of the supplies used was determined by subtracting the cost of the supplies on hand at May 31, $2,000, from the $3,000 cost of the supplies which were available for use during the month ($3,000 − $2,000 = $1,000). Again, note that revenues are recorded as they are earned and expenses are recorded as they are incurred, not necessarily as cash is either paid or received. As previously indicated, this practice is referred to as the accrual basis of accounting.

The income for the month is the difference between the total revenues earned ($2,700) and the total of the expenses ($2,500) which were incurred in order to generate these revenues ($2,700 − $2,500 = $200). At the end of the period, this income is added to the owner's capital or equity account.

The Statement of Cash Flows

The statement of cash flows for the month of May for Kilmer Contractors provides a summary of where the company obtained its cash and what it did with its cash. This statement may be prepared by examining the changes (increases and decreases) in the cash account which occurred during May. The statement of cash flows would be as follows:

Kilmer Contractors
Statement of Cash Flows
For the Month Ending May 31, 19x1

Cash flows from operations:			
Receipts from customers[9]			$4,000
Payments to:			
Suppliers		$3,000	
Employees		1,500	4,500
Decrease in cash due to operations			($ 500)
Cash flows from financing activities:			
Receipts from:			
Owner's investment		$ 500	
Borrowing		5,000	
Payments for:			
Repaying loan		(2,000)	
Owner withdrawal		(600)	
Increase in cash due to financing activities			$2,900
Increase in cash			$2,400

---

[9] This includes the $3,300 received on May 10 plus the $700 received on May 17.

STATEMENT OF CAPITAL

Although the company had a decrease in cash due to its operations, it had a net increase in cash because of its financing activities.

At this point, it might be helpful to examine the changes between the balance sheet of May 15 and that of May 31 in order to fully understand the relationship between the income statement and the balance sheet. Balance sheets at May 15 and May 31 are reported in a comparative format as follows:

Kilmer Contractors
Comparative Balance Sheets

	May 15	May 31	Change
Assets			
Cash	$3,200	$2,400	($ 800)
Accounts receivable	0	900	900
Supplies	3,000	2,000	(1,000)
	$6,200	$5,300	($ 900)
Liabilities and Owner's Equity			
Note payable	$3,000	$3,000	$ 0
Unearned fees	3,300	2,200	(1,100)
Capital	(100)	100	200
	$6,200	$5,300	($ 900)

Each change in the comparative balance sheets can be explained by the transactions that affected the particular asset, liability, or the owner's equity (these were summarized previously).

The change in owner's equity is particularly important because it represents the net increase or decrease in the owner's investment in the firm. This change can be explained by the transactions which occurred on May 17, 19, 25, and the two adjustments which were made on May 31. These same transactions are the ones which appear in summarized form in the income statement. In other words, the change in capital or owner's equity which took place during the period May 15 to 31 is due to the earnings of the company. These changes in owner's equity are included in a statement of capital (referred to as a statement of retained earnings for a corporation). The statement of capital reports the details of the equity of the owners in the business. Capital is equal to the direct investments made by the owners plus the earnings of the business and less any withdrawals made by owners.

> Withdrawals or distributions to owners are decreases in net assets of a particular enterprise resulting from transferring assets, rendering services, or incurring liabilities by the enterprise to owners. Distributions to owners decrease ownership interests (or equity) in an enterprise.[10]

---

[10] "Elements of Financial Statements of Business Enterprises," *op.cit.*

Note that the statement of capital for Kilmer Contractors, which covers the entire month of May, includes the investment made by Kilmer on May 1 and the withdrawal made on May 12. In other words, it summarizes all of the transactions which affected owner's equity during the month of May.

A statement of capital for Kilmer Contractors is presented below:

Kilmer Contractors
Statement of Capital
For the Month Ending May 31, 19x1

Capital at May 1, 19x1...............		$ 0
Add: Investment...................	$500	
Income for May...............	200	700
Deduct:		
Withdrawal...................		(600)
Capital at May 31, 19x1..............		$ 100

As indicated above, this statement of capital indicates how and why the owner's equity of Kilmer Contractors changed during the month of May.

The balance sheet, income statement, statement of capital, and statement of cash flows presented above were deliberately kept brief and simple for purposes of illustration. They do, however, illustrate the basic principles and procedures which are followed in the preparation of financial statements. An example of a comprehensive income statement is the income statement for PepsiCo which is presented in the beginning of the text.

SUMMARY

The balance sheet, income statement, statement of capital, and statement of cash flows are the basic accounting statements that provide data to various external users to be used in making economic decisions. These and other financial statements are the end products of the accountant's work. Although companies may vary somewhat in the exact detail and format of the data provided, all companies will include essentially the same type of information in their financial statements.

The balance sheet reflects the financial position of a firm at a particular point in time by providing information regarding the economic resources (assets) of the firm and the sources of these resources (liabilities and owner's equity). The format of the balance sheet reflects the basic accounting equation: Assets = Liabilities + Owner's Equity. By convention, the assets of the firm are generally presented on the balance sheet in the order of their liquidity. The usual subcategories include current assets, fixed assets, and other assets. Similarly, the liabilities (or debts) of the firm are generally subdivided into current and long-term liabilities. The owner's equity section of the balance sheet contains information regarding the direct investment of the owners as well as the income earned by the firm and not withdrawn by the owners.

The income statement is of particular importance to many users of financial statements because it provides information regarding the results of operations of the firm for a specified period of time, usually a year. Only those transactions involving revenues (the proceeds received from the sale of goods and the rendering of services) and expenses (the costs incurred in the process of generating revenues) will be reflected on the income statement. Net income is the excess of revenues over related expenses for an accounting period.

The statement of capital presents a summary of the transactions that affected owner's equity in a given time period. Any change in owner's equity that occurred in that time period will be reflected and explained in the statement of capital.

KEY DEFINITIONS

Accounting equation or dual-aspect concept—the accounting equation may be expressed as follows: *assets = sources of assets* or *assets = liabilities + owner's equity*.

Accounting cycle—the length of the accounting or operating cycle of any company is the period of time required for the company to acquire the basic resources to produce, manufacture goods, receive purchase orders, ship goods, and collect cash from the sale. This cycle depends on many factors and could vary from a short period of time for a company in the grocery industry to a long period of time for a company in the liquor industry.

Accounting period—the longer of one year or one accounting cycle.

Accounts payable—represents the amounts the company owes to its creditors for purchases of goods or services in the ordinary course of business.

Accounts receivable—represents the amounts owed by customers to the company for goods or services which were sold in the ordinary course of business.

Cash—any medium of exchange which is readily accepted and used for transactions. Besides currency or demand deposits, cash usually includes certain negotiable instruments, such as customers' checks.

Current assets—includes cash and other assets which are expected to be converted into cash, sold, or used in operations or production during the current accounting period.

Current liabilities—includes those obligations for which settlement is expected to require the use of current assets or the creation of other current liabilities.

Fixed assets—fixed or long-term assets are those assets which are acquired for use in the continuing operations of a business over a number of accounting periods rather than for resale to customers.

Income statement—a summary of the operations of a firm. It reports the income (or loss) of the company during a specified period of time.

Intangibles—assets without physical substance, such as patents.

Inventory—includes materials which are used in production, goods which are in the process of production, and finished products held for sale to customers.

Investments by owners—increases in net assets of a particular enterprise resulting from transfers to it from other entities of something of value to obtain or increase ownership interests (or equity) in it. Assets are most commonly received as investments by owners, but that which is received may also include services or satisfaction or conversion of liabilities of the enterprise.

Liquidity—normally refers to the order in which assets would be converted into cash or used up.

Long-term liabilities—generally represent claims which will be paid or satisfied in a future accounting period.

Managerial accounting—the segment of accounting concerned with the needs of users who are internal to the firm.

Marketable securities—temporary investments in stocks, bonds, and other securities which are readily salable and which management intends to sell within a relatively short period of time.

Net income—the excess of revenues earned over the related expenses incurred for an accounting period.

Notes payable—normally arise from borrowing and are evidenced by a written document or formal promise to pay.

Owner's equity—also referred to as net worth or capital, represents claims against the assets by the owners of the business. The total owner's equity represents the amount that the owners have invested in the business including any income which may have been retained in the business since its inception.

Owner's withdrawals—distributions to owners are decreases in net assets of a particular enterprise resulting from transferring assets, rendering services, or incurring liabilities by the enterprise to owners. Distributions to owners decrease ownership interests (or equity) in an enterprise. Owner's withdrawals are the removal from the business of cash or other assets by the owners of that business.

Prepaid expenses—represents expenditures which were made in either the current or a prior period and which will provide benefits to the firm at some future time.

Statement of capital—summarizes investments made by the owners, additions to capital from earnings, and withdrawals made by owners during the accounting period.

Statement of cash flows—this statement explains the causes of changes in cash plus highly liquid marketable securities and provides a summary of the investing and financing activities of a company during a period of time.

Tangible assets—those assets that have physical substance.

Transactions—events which occur during the life of a business.

Unearned revenues—amounts collected from customers for goods which have not been shipped or services which have not yet been performed.

QUESTIONS

1. What are the main sources of assets for a company? Why does each source provide assets?

2. A = L + OE expresses what accounting concept? Explain the concept.

3. What is a transaction?

4. What is an asset? Distinguish between current and long-term assets.

5. What is a liability? Distinguish between current and long-term liabilities.

6. Explain the difference between liabilities and owner's equity.

7. What does the balance in the capital account represent?

8. What are some advantages of preparing a balance sheet?

9. What periods of time are covered by the income statement, the statement of capital, and the balance sheet? How is this recorded in the headings of the statements?

10. What is the relationship between the balance sheet and the income statement at the end of the accounting period?

EXERCISES

11. Using these abbreviations, classify each of the following account titles as to what section of the balance sheet they would appear in.

    CA — Current assets
    FA — Fixed assets
    OA — Other assets
    CL — Current liabilities
    LTL — Long-term liabilities
    OE — Owner's equity

    _____ Cash
    _____ Capital
    _____ Note payable
    _____ Prepaid insurance
    _____ Accounts receivable
    _____ Plant and equipment
    _____ Investments
    _____ Patents
    _____ Taxes payable
    _____ Inventory
    _____ Wages payable
    _____ Accounts payable
    _____ Marketable securities
    _____ Land
    _____ Goodwill
    _____ Interest payable

12. Fill in the missing amounts:

	Company Allen	Company Barr
Assets — January 1, 19x1	$120	(d)
Liabilities — January 1, 19x1	80	$ 55
Owner's equity — January 1, 19x1	(a)	95
Assets — December 31, 19x1	130	(e)
Liabilities — December 31, 19x1	(b)	70
Owner's equity — December 31, 19x1	(c)	120
Revenues in 19x1	15	(f)
Expenses in 19x1	19	24

13. Give an example of a transaction which will:

    a. Increase an asset and increase owner's equity.
    b. Increase an asset and increase a liability.
    c. Increase one asset and decrease another asset.
    d. Decrease an asset and decrease owner's equity.
    e. Decrease an asset and decrease a liability.

14. Given the following information, answer the questions below:

Revenue, 19x1	$24,000
Liabilities — December 31, 19x1	25,000
Investments by owner, 19x1	4,000
Withdrawals, 19x1	12,000
Owner's equity — January 1, 19x1	27,000
Owner's equity — December 31, 19x1	35,000

    a. What are the total assets on December 31, 19x1?
    b. What is net income for the year?
    c. What is total expense for 19x1?

    L = 120,000   38,000

15. Fill in the missing figures in the information below:

    EX2M QUESTION

	19x1	19x2	19x3
Assets — January 1	$100,000	$120,000	(f) 147,000
Liabilities — January 1	60,000	(c) 62,000	$72,000
Owner's equity — January 1	(a) 40,000	(d) 58,000	75,000
Withdrawals	20,000	15,000	17,000
Investments by owners	18,000	16,000	0
Owner's equity — December 31	(b) 58,000	(e) 75,000	57,000
Income (Loss)	20,000	16,000	(g) 1,000

16. For each transaction listed below, indicate the effect on the total assets, total liabilities, and owner's equity of the business. Identify the effect of each transaction by using a (+) for an increase, a (−) for a decrease and a (0) for no effect.

		Assets	Liabilities	Owner's Equity
a.	The owner invested cash in the business	( )	( )	( )
b.	Purchased a building for cash	( )	( )	( )
c.	Borrowed cash from the bank	( )	( )	( )
d.	Purchased equipment on credit	( )	( )	( )
e.	Provided a service and collected cash	( )	( )	( )
f.	Paid wages in cash to employees	( )	( )	( )
g.	Paid a bank loan	( )	( )	( )

2 | Transaction Analysis: The Accounting Process **2-25**

17. Classify each of the following items as to whether they would be found on the balance sheet (B), income statement (I), or statement of capital (C).

   Review solution manual

   - **B** Cash
   - **I** Revenue
   - **B** Wages payable
   - **C** Withdrawal
   - **B** Accounts payable
   - **B** Goodwill
   - **B** Unearned fees
   - **I** Salary expense
   - **I** Insurance expense
   - **B** Building
   - **B** Supplies
   - **I** Rental expense
   - **I** Rental income
   - **B** Accounts receivable
   - **B** Bonds payable
   - **B** Prepaid insurance

18. Fill in the missing amounts:

   Lee Company
   Balance Sheet
   June 30, 19x1

Assets		Liabilities and Owner's Equity	
Cash	$ 12,000	Accounts payable	$33,000
Marketable securities	31,000	Taxes payable	(b) – 11,000
Accounts receivable	7,000	Bonds payable	76,000
Inventory	44,000	Total liabilities	$120,000
Buildings	193,000		
Land	75,000	Capital	(c) 242,000
	(a) 362,000		(d) 362,000

19. Longhorn Company had sales revenue of $5,700 for the month of October 19x1. Total expenses incurred during this period were $2,900; including rent for the store of $400; salaries amounting to $900; and the cost of the supplies used of $1,600. Prepare an income statement for October.

20. Fill in the missing amounts:

   Nourallah Company
   Comparative Balance Sheets

	April 30	May 31	Change
ASSETS			
Cash	$13,500	$20,000	(a)
Accounts receivable	7,000	(b)	$3,300
Inventory	(c)	2,700	(5,100)
	(d)	(e)	(f)
LIABILITIES AND OWNER'S EQUITY			
Accounts payable	$14,900	(h)	$ 100
Unearned revenue	(g)	$ 8,000	8,000
Capital	(i)	(j)	(k)
	(d)	(e)	(f)

PROBLEMS

21. Certain transactions of the Ricketts Company for September 19x1 are shown below in equation form. Give a short explanation of the probable nature of each transaction.

		Cash	+	Accounts Receivable	+	Supplies	+	Equipment	=	Accounts Payable	+	Capital
Beginning Balance		$10,000	+	$5,000	+	$3,000	+	$12,000	=	$10,000	+	$20,000
(a)								+ 8,000		+ 8,000		
(b)		+ 1,000										+ 1,000
(c)		− 3,000								− 3,000		
(d)		+ 2,000		− 2,000								
(e)		− 4,000						+ 4,000				
(f)		− 3,000										− 3,000
Ending Balance		$ 3,000	+	$3,000	+	$7,000	+	$20,000	=	$15,000	+	$18,000

Assets = Liabilities + Owner's Equity

22. Certain transactions of the Kreuger Company for the month of October are shown below in equation form. Provide a description of the probable nature of each transaction.

	Cash	+	Accounts Receivable	+	Supplies	+	Equipment	=	Accounts Payable	+	Wages Payable	+	Capital	+	Revenue (Expense)
Beginning Balance	$ 8,000	+	$ 9,000	+	$3,000	+	$ 8,000	=	$7,000	+	$1,000	+	$20,000	+	$ 0
(a)			+ 6,000												+ 6,000
(b)	− 2,000												− 2,000		
(c)					+ 2,000				+ 2,000						
(d)	− 5,000						+ 5,000								
(e)	+ 10,000		− 10,000												
(f)	− 4,000								− 4,000						
(g)					− 3,000										− 3,000
(h)											+ 2,000				− 2,000
Ending Balance	$ 7,000	+	$ 5,000	+	$2,000	+	$13,000	=	$5,000	+	$3,000	+	$18,000	+	$1,000

Assets = Liabilities + Owner's Equity

23. Dave Karwin opened a roofing business on June 1 and during the month of June completed the following transactions.

June 1 Dave Karwin formed the Karwin Roofing Service with an initial investment of $15,000.
3 The company purchased roofing shingles, paying the $4,000 purchase price in cash.
7 Karwin received $3,500 as advance payment on a contract to roof two houses during the month of July.
12 Karwin Roofing Service borrowed $3,000 from the Sharpstown State Bank.
June 15 Dave Karwin withdrew $2,500 from the business for personal use.
30 Karwin Roofing Service made its first payment of $1,000 on the $3,000 loan from Sharpstown State Bank.

Indicate the effects of the transactions on the equation provided below.

Assets	=	Liabilities	+	Owner's Equity
Cash + Roofing Supplies	=	Notes Payable + Unearned Fees	+	Karwin, Capital

24. The following transactions occurred during the initial month of operations of Kingsbery Automotive Service.

Sept. 3 The owner contributed $15,000 cash.
9 Auto parts purchased on account, $5,000.
12 Paid rent for the first month, $2,500.
18 Repaired cars for a $2,200 fee and billed the customers.
20 Auto parts used, $1,150.
26 Collected $850 on customers' accounts.
29 Paid $1,000 to creditors.

a. Indicate the effects of these transactions on the equation provided below.

Assets	=	Liabilities	+	Owner's Equity
Cash + Auto Parts + Accounts Receivable	=	Accounts Payable	+	Kingsbery, Capital + Revenue (Expense)

b. Prepare a balance sheet and an income statement at the end of the month.

25. Sam Jones opened an auto repair business on January 1, 19x1. At the end of 19x1, Jones Auto Repair had the following balances of assets, liabilities, and owner's equity:

Accounts payable	$ 5,000
Accounts receivable	20,000
Building	30,000
Capital	?
Cash	10,000
Land	12,000
Notes payable	12,000
Prepaid insurance	5,000
Supplies	8,000
Unearned fees	16,000
Wages payable	2,000

Required:

Determine the amount in the capital account at year-end and prepare a balance sheet at December 31, 19x1.

26. Below is a balance sheet for Rich Exterminator Company at October 31, 19x1.

Rich Exterminator Company
Balance Sheet
October 31, 19x1

Assets		Liabilities and Owner's Equity	
Cash	$7,500	Note payable	$2,200
Supplies	2,000	Unearned fees	300
		Capital	7,000
	$9,500		$9,500

The unearned fees are the result of receiving in advance a $100 fee for each of three jobs to be performed in the future.

During the month of November, the following transactions occurred.

Nov. 2 Rich Company exterminated a house and billed and collected $100 cash from the customer.
  7 Rich Company exterminated a house and billed but did not collect its fee of $150.
 11 Rich paid his employees salaries of $200.
 17 Rich Company exterminated two of the three houses contracted for in October.
 30 The unused supplies on hand at this date had an original cost of $1,500.

Required:

a. Prepare an income statement for Rich Exterminator Company for the month of November.
b. Prepare a balance sheet at November 30, 19x1.

27. Given the following information, prepare an income statement, a statement of capital and a balance sheet for Pate Company on December 31, 19x1.

Prepaid insurance	$ 500	Wages payable	$ 1,550
Cash	16,600	Goodwill	2,000
Accounts payable	8,800	Equipment	7,900
Unearned revenue	3,840	Salary expense	15,000
Utility expense	750	Rent expense	3,200
Withdrawals	3,000	Office furniture	4,000
Accounts receivable	8,160	Marketable securities	1,200
Revenues	25,000	Capital, January 1, 19x1	17,860
Building	20,000	Bonds payable	20,000
Supplies expense	2,600	Capital, December 31, 19x1	26,310
Supplies	140		

28. The following information was taken from the books of the Dawson Company on December 31, 19x1:

Withdrawal	$ 3,000	Revenue	$60,000
Insurance expense	2,400	Prepaid rent	18,000
Cash	28,000	Wages expense	13,400
Utilities expense	1,900	Supplies expense	1,500
Rent expense	10,200		

Required:

Prepare an income statement for 19x1.

29. Prepare a balance sheet for the Kang Company as of June 30, 19x1.

Kang Company
Balance Sheet
January 1, 19x1

Assets		Liabilities and Owner's Equity	
Cash	$13,000	Accounts payable	$20,000
Accounts receivable	49,000	Salaries payable	9,000
Inventory	1,000	Capital	34,000
	$63,000		$63,000

Transactions which occurred between January 1, 19x1 and June 30, 19x1 were:

a. Accounts receivable of $19,000 was collected in cash.
b. Accounts payable increased by $10,000 due to a purchase of inventory.
c. Salaries payable of $9,000 were paid in cash.

30. Prepare a statement of capital for the Hoffmans Company as of October 31, 19x1, given the following information:

a. On March 27, 19x1, Anne Hoffmans invested $20,000 in the business.
b. Anne Hoffmans invested an additional $57,000 on June 26, 19x1.
c. The capital balance as of January 1, 19x1 was $79,000.
d. The owner withdrew $13,000 on March 8, 19x1.
e. The net income for the period from January 1, 19x1 until October 31, 19x1 was $44,000.

31. The effects on the accounting equation of The Hartford Company are shown on the next page. Write a short explanation of the probable nature of each of the transactions.

32. John King began operating a tax return preparation service on January 1. During the month of January, the following transactions were completed.

Jan. 2 The owner invested $10,000 cash in the business.
     4 The business acquired $3,000 of supplies on account.
     5 Rent of $500 was paid for an office building.
   11 Prepared tax returns on credit for a $3,000 fee.
   15 Salaries of $1,000 were paid to employees.
   25 Collected $1,500 on customer accounts.
   30 Cash of $1,000 was paid to creditors.
   31 Supplies of $1,000 were used.

Required:

a. Show the effects of these transactions on the equation provided below.

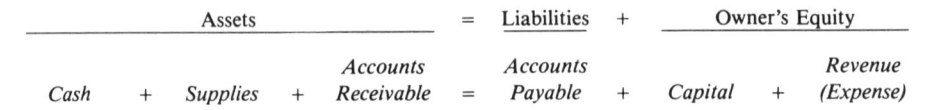

Assets	=	Liabilities	+	Owner's Equity
Cash + Supplies + Accounts Receivable	=	Accounts Payable	+	Capital + Revenue (Expense)

b. Prepare an income statement for the month of January.
c. Prepare a balance sheet as of January 31.

2 | Transaction Analysis: The Accounting Process   2-31

	ASSETS					LIABILITIES			OWNER'S EQUITY	
	Cash	Accounts Receivable	Land	Supplies	Prepaid Insurance	Accounts Payable	Unearned Fees	Wages Payable	Capital	Revenue (Expense)
Beginning Balance	$4,320	$9,370	$19,780	$470	$1,400	$5,460	$1,500	$1,320	$27,060	0
(a)					− 400					− 400
(b)				− 290						− 290
(c)							− 300			+ 300
(d)								+ 1,200		− 1,200
(e)	+ 4,000	− 4,000								
(f)	− 3,000					− 3,000				
(g)	+ 2,000									+ 2,000
Ending Balance	$7,320	$5,370	$19,780	$180	$1,000	$2,460	$1,200	$2,520	$27,060	$ 410

33. The following information was taken from the records of J.S. Wylie and Company as of July 31, 19x1. Prepare the balance sheet at that date.

Wages payable..................................	$ 5,000
Cash	2,345
Land	30,000
Prepaid rent....................................	300
Accounts payable..............................	1,470
Capital	?
Inventory	5,990
Equipment	15,200
Buildings	33,450
Accounts receivable............................	1,350
Patents (just purchased)........................	7,000
Mortgage payable (due January 31, 19x9)............	40,000
Marketable securities............................	1,035
Estimated taxes payable.........................	3,000
Unearned revenue..............................	750

Refer to the Annual Report included in the front of the text.

34. What was the income for the most recent year?

35. Did the most recent year's income increase or decrease from the prior year?

36. Were the increases/decreases in income because of a change in revenue, a change in expenses, or both?

37. What was the largest expense in the most recent year?

38. Which expense increased the most during the most recent year? What expense decreased the most?

39. Which current asset is the largest at the end of the most recent year?

40. Comparing the two most recent years presented, what was the change in long-term debt? What factors might have caused these changes?

41. What is the largest asset amount in the balance sheet at the end of the most recent year?

42. Comparing the two most recent years presented, how much did total stockholders' equity increase/decrease?

43. Comparing the two years presented, did cash dividends paid increase or decrease for stockholders?

Chapter 3 traces and explains the basic steps in the recording process. Studying this chapter should enable you to:

1. Explain what an account is and how it is used in the recording process.
2. Discuss the use of debits and credits and how they affect asset, liability, and owner's equity accounts.
3. List the basic steps in the recording process.
4. Describe a trial balance and identify the types of errors it will (and will not) detect.
5. Explain the use of adjusting entries.
6. Discuss the purpose and illustrate the process of closing the temporary accounts.
7. Identify when revenues and expenses are recognized in an accrual system of accounting.
8. List the five common types of adjusting entries and give examples of each.

3

The Recording Process

INTRODUCTION

Because the number of transactions which occur in even a small business causing its assets, liabilities, equities, revenues, and expenses to increase and decrease occur much too frequently to prepare a new set of financial statements each time a transaction takes place, an alternative method of recording information must be employed. The description of this recording process, which is basic to every accounting system, is the subject matter of this chapter. The accounting system described, referred to as the "double-entry" system, is applicable to all situations in which financial information must be collected and processed. In small firms, the system may be maintained by hand, just as described in this chapter, while in larger organizations it will usually be implemented using mechanical or electronic data processing equipment. In any situation, however, the basic principles involved are the same.

THE ACCOUNT

For purposes of reporting and analysis, the transactions of an entity are summarized or grouped in individual accounts. An account is simply a place or means of summarizing all of the transactions that affect a particular asset, liability, equity, revenue, or expense item. The accounting system of a firm includes an individual account for each type or classification of individual asset, liability, owner's equity, revenue, and expense. The increase or decrease in each of these items will be recorded in its own account using "debits" and "credits." At this point, we cannot overemphasize the fact that the words "debit" and "credit" are simply terms used to identify *left* and *right* sides of an account, respectively, and have absolutely no other meaning in their accounting usage. (The reader who accepts this statement as a fact and keeps it in mind will save himself or herself untold grief and will greatly enhance his or her understanding of the recording process.) For purposes of discussion, a typical account may be illustrated as follows:

```
         (Account Title)
     (debit side) | (credit side)
```

This form of presentation is often referred to as a T-account.

It was indicated earlier that the "double-entry" method is used in accounting in order to record transactions. To understand the double-entry method, a simple rule must be kept in mind: for every transaction recorded, the total dollar amount of the debits must be equal to the total dollar amount of the credits. Since we already know that assets must be equal to liabilities plus owners' equity, the following rules of "debit" and "credit" may be established and used in recording the transactions of an entity:

```
     Assets              Liabilities          Owner's Equity
 debit  | credit       debit  | credit       debit  | credit
  (+)   |  (−)          (−)   |  (+)          (−)   |  (+)
```

Because of the equation:

$$\text{Assets} = \text{Liabilities} + \text{Owner's Equity}$$

and the rule:

$$\text{Total Debits} = \text{Total Credits}$$

the procedures (or rules) for recording increases and decreases in the accounts logically follow:

> To increase an *asset*, debit the account.
> To decrease an *asset*, credit the account.
>
> To increase a *liability* or *owner's equity*, credit the account.
> To decrease a *liability* or *owner's equity*, debit the account.

Since revenues and expenses increase and decrease owner's equity, respectively, the rules of debit and credit for owner's equity apply to revenue and expense accounts. Because revenues increase owner's equity, the rule for recording increases or decreases in this account is the same as that for owner's equity:

To increase *revenue*, credit the account.
To decrease *revenue*, debit the account.

On the other hand, since expenses decrease owner's equity, the rule for recording expenses is opposite of that for owner's equity:

To increase an *expense*, debit the account.
To decrease an *expense*, credit the account.

Consequently, the above model may be expanded as follows:

Permanent Accounts			Temporary Accounts		
Assets =	Liabilities +	Owners' Equity	+ Revenues −	Expenses −	Withdrawals
Debit (+) | Credit (−)	Debit (−) | Credit (+)	Debit (−) | Credit (+)	Debit (−) | Credit (+)	Debit (+) | Credit (−)	Debit (+) | Credit (−)

The balance in an account at any point in time is equal to the difference between the total debits and the total credits recorded in that account. The revenue, expense, and withdrawal accounts are often referred to as *temporary (or nominal) accounts*, because they ultimately result in or represent changes in owners' equity that occur during an accounting period. *All of the temporary accounts are closed to owners' equity at the end of the accounting period.* The asset, liability, and owners' equity accounts are called *permanent (or real)* accounts, because the balances in these accounts at the end of one accounting period appear in the balance sheet and are carried forward to the subsequent period.

In order to illustrate the operation of these rules, assume that a firm obtains a $2,000 cash loan from its bank. This transaction would increase the firm's cash, an asset, by $2,000 and also increase its loans payable, a liability, by the same amount. In order to record this transaction, the firm would debit (increase) its cash account for $2,000 and, at the same time, credit (increase) its loans payable account for $2,000. This transaction would be summarized in the accounts of the firm as follows:

Cash		Loans Payable	
2,000			2,000

Note that the total of the debits (in this instance a debit to the cash account of $2,000) is equal to the total of the credits (a credit to the liability account, loans payable for the same amount). In addition, accounting equation, A = L + OE remains in balance since the assets and liabilities were both increased by $2,000 (owner's equity was not affected).

When the firm repays its loan to the bank, the payment of $2,000 would decrease the firm's asset, cash, by $2,000 and decrease its liability, loans payable, by the same amount. This transaction would be recorded in the accounts by a debit (decrease) to loans payable of $2,000 and a credit (decrease) to cash of $2,000. The effects of the two transactions, the loan and its repayment, are recorded in the accounts as follows:

	Cash				Loans Payable		
(1)	2,000	(2)	2,000	(2)	2,000	(1)	2,000

(1) Borrow $2,000 from bank.
(2) Repay $2,000 to bank.

Again the total debits are equal to the total credits and the accounting equation remains in balance.

It is often useful to consider, analyze, and record the transactions of a business as they occur. The simplest example of this process is the use of the general journal entry which could be used to record the two transactions explained above as follows:

	Debit	Credit
Cash..........................	2,000	
Loans payable		2,000
Loans payable	2,000	
Cash.......................		2,000

A general journal entry, usually referred to as a journal entry, is a simple means of recording the transactions of a firm in terms of debits and credits. *The journal entry represents the initial input of economic data into the accounting system.* As illustrated above, the format for each journal entry is to write the title of the account to be debited and the amount of the debit on the first line, then indent and write the title of the account to be credited and the amount of the credit on the second line. This is simply a matter of convention.

For purposes of illustration, transactions will be recorded initially in general journal form and then transferred to the individual T-accounts (as illustrated in the foregoing). This latter process is referred to as "posting," transferring information from the general journal to the ledger (the book of entry which contains all the accounts of the firm). The same data which were used in Chapter 2 in order to illustrate the preparation of financial statements for Kilmer Contractors will be employed again in this example.

THE ACCOUNTING CYCLE

The steps involved in collecting, processing, and reporting financial information are referred to as the accounting cycle. The key elements of the accounting cycle are as follows:

1. The preparation of general journal entries.
2. Posting these general journal entries to the ledger.
3. The preparation of a trial balance before adjustment.
4. The preparation of adjusting journal entries.
5. Posting these adjusting entries to the ledger.
6. The preparation of the adjusted trial balance.
7. The preparation of closing entries.
8. Posting these closing entries to the ledger.
9. The preparation of the after-closing trial balance.
10. The preparation of the financial statements.

AN ILLUSTRATION

To illustrate the recording process described above, we will again follow the activities of Kilmer Contractors, the small painting contractor described in Chapter 2, through May, the initial month of its operations.

General Journal Entries

The transactions of Kilmer Contractors which occurred during the month of May 19x1, would be recorded as follows:

> May 1. Bill Kilmer organized Kilmer Contractors and invested cash of $500 in the business.

This transaction is an investment of funds in a business by its owner. Cash held by the firm and the owner's equity account, capital, were both increased. It would be recorded as follows:

```
Cash..........................   500
    Bill Kilmer, Capital ...............       500
```

Cash		Capital	
5/1 500		5/1	500

As indicated above, the increase in the asset cash would be recorded by a debit to the cash account and the corresponding increase in the investment by the owner would be recorded by a credit to the capital account. This entry illustrates the rule that increases in assets are recorded by debits and increases in equities are recorded by credits. Note that the basic accounting equation, A = L + OE, is in balance and the total debits are equal to the total credits. These rules will hold true for each of the transactions of the business as they are recorded.

> May 2. Kilmer Contractors borrowed $5,000 from Bill Kilmer's parents.[1]

This transaction is the receipt of an asset, cash, in exchange for a liability, the promise to pay a creditor at some future date. It reflects the promise of the business to repay $5,000 at a future date in order to have cash on hand and available for use at this time. It would be recorded by the following entry:

```
Cash............................  5,000
    Note payable....................          5,000
```

Cash		Note Payable	
5/1 500			5/2 5,000
5/2 5,000			

The increase in the asset cash is recorded by a debit to the cash account and the increase in the liability, note payable, is recorded by a credit to the note payable account. This transaction illustrates the rule that increases in assets are recorded by debits and increases in liabilities are recorded by credits.

> May 5. The company purchased painting supplies, paying the $3,000 purchase price in cash.

This transaction represents an exchange of one asset for another. The asset supplies was increased while the asset cash was decreased. It would be recorded as follows:

```
Supplies .........................  3,000
    Cash............................          3,000
```

Cash			Supplies	
5/1 500	5/5 3,000		5/5 3,000	
5/2 5,000				

The increase in the asset supplies would be recorded by a debit to the supplies account while the cash outlay would be recorded by a credit to the cash account. This entry follows the rule that increases in assets are recorded by debits while decreases in assets are recorded by credits.

---

[1] For purposes of illustration, it was assumed that Kilmer Contractors signed a non-interest bearing note payable to Bill Kilmer's parents.

May 10. Kilmer signed a contract whereby he agreed to paint three houses sometime during the next few weeks. The customer paid Kilmer the fee of $1,100 per house in advance.

The company has agreed to paint three houses at a future date and has received its fee now, before it has done the work. The receipt of the $3,300 increases cash and the liability, unearned fees, by the same amount. Unearned fees are not a liability in the sense that the company will be required to repay the money. Rather, this account represents an obligation on the part of Kilmer Contractors to render a service by painting three houses at some future date. This transaction would be recorded by the following entry:

Cash.............................. 3,300
    Unearned fees 3,300

Cash				Unearned Fees		
5/1	500	5/5	3,000		5/10	3,300
5/2	5,000					
5/10	3,300					

The increase in the asset cash would be recorded by a debit to the cash account while the increase in the liability, unearned fees, would be recorded by a credit to the unearned fees account. Again, this entry illustrates the rule that increases in assets are recorded by debits and increases in liabilities are recorded by credits.

May 12. Bill Kilmer, the owner, withdrew $600 from the business for his own personal use.

This transaction is a withdrawal of a portion of the owner's investment from the business. Cash and capital were both decreased by $600. It would be recorded as follows:

Withdrawals 600
    Cash............................ 600

Cash				Withdrawals	
5/1	500	5/5	3,000	5/12	600
5/2	5,000	5/12	600		
5/10	3,300				

The withdrawal of $600 in cash from the business by the owner would be recorded by a debit to the withdrawals account and a credit to the cash account. This entry illustrates the rule that decreases in equity accounts are recorded by debits and decreases in asset accounts are recorded by credits.

May 15. Kilmer Contractors repaid $2,000 of the $5,000 it borrowed from Mr. and Mrs. Kilmer.

This transaction is a reduction of both liabilities and assets. The business repaid $2,000 of the $5,000 it owed to the Kilmers. Both cash and the note payable decreased by this amount. (Recall that it was assumed that this note was not interest bearing.) The following entry would be made:

```
Note payable ....................... 2,000
     Cash ............................         2,000
```

Cash				Note Payable			
5/1	500	5/5	3,000	5/15	2,000	5/2	5,000
5/2	5,000	5/12	600				
5/10	3,300	5/15	2,000				

The repayment of $2,000 to the Kilmers would be recorded by a debit to the liability account, note payable, and a credit to the asset account, cash. This entry illustrates the rule that decreases in liabilities are recorded by debits while decreases in assets are recorded by credits.

May 17. Kilmer Contractors painted its first house and billed and collected a fee of $700 from the customer.

This transaction indicates that the firm has begun to earn revenue. It is a sale of services for cash. Cash was received and the owner's equity of the business was increased by the amount of the revenue earned. It would be recorded by the following entry.

```
Cash ............................. 700
     Painting fees ..................        700
```

Cash				Painting Fees	
5/1	500	5/5	3,000	5/17	700
5/2	5,000	5/12	600		
5/10	3,300	5/15	2,000		
5/17	700				

The sale of services for cash would be recorded by a debit to the cash account and a credit to the revenue account, painting fees. This entry illustrates the rule that increases in assets are recorded by debits and increases in revenues are recorded by credits.

May 19. Kilmer Contractors painted a second house and billed (but did not collect) its fee of $900.

Again, this transaction records the revenue earned by the firm in painting a customer's house. Unlike the previous transaction, however, cash was not received. The customer was billed for the service rendered and will pay Kilmer Contractors at some future date. An asset, accounts receivable, has increased and owner's equity (revenue) has increased by $900, the fee charged for painting the house. This transaction illustrates the very important point that revenue is recorded as it is earned, not necessarily as cash is received. This concept reflects the *accrual* basis of accounting. The transaction would be recorded by the following entry:

```
Accounts receivable . . . . . . . . . . . . . . . . . . .   900
    Painting fees . . . . . . . . . . . . . . . . . . . . . . .          900
```

Accounts Receivable		Painting Fees	
5/19 900		5/17	700
		5/19	900

This sale of services to a customer on a credit basis would be recorded by a debit to the asset, accounts receivable, and a credit to the revenue account, painting fees. Again, this transaction illustrates the rule that increases in assets are recorded by debits and increases in revenues are recorded by credits.

May 25. Kilmer paid salaries of $1,500 to his employees.

Expenses of $1,500 were incurred and paid in cash. This transaction reduces both the cash balance and owner's equity. The reduction in owner's equity is due to the fact that an expense has been incurred, thereby reducing income. (Remember that revenues less expenses equals income.) The transactions would be recorded by the following entry:

```
Salaries . . . . . . . . . . . . . . . . . . . . . . . . . . . . .   1,500
    Cash . . . . . . . . . . . . . . . . . . . . . . . . . . . . .            1,500
```

Cash				Salaries	
5/1	500	5/5	3,000	5/25 1,500	
5/2	5,000	5/12	600		
5/10	3,300	5/15	2,000		
5/17	700	5/25	1,500		

The payment of salaries to employees would be recorded by a debit to the expense account, salaries, and a credit to the asset account, cash. This entry illustrates the rule that increases in expenses are recorded by debits and decreases in assets are recorded by credits.

Posting

The second step in the recording process would be to post each of the journal entries to the appropriate ledger accounts. Posting is the process of transferring the individual debits and credits of each entry to the appropriate account or accounts in the ledger. This step enables the accountant to summarize and group the transactions which occurred according to the individual accounts which they affect. For each transaction, the debit amount in the journal entry is posted by entering it on the debit side of the appropriate ledger account and each credit amount in the entry is posted by entering it on the credit side of the appropriate ledger account. This process was illustrated in the previous section on general journal entries. Recall that the initial transaction of Kilmer Contractors was as follows:

May 1. Bill Kilmer organized Kilmer Contractors and invested cash of $500 in the business.

This transaction was recorded by the following general journal entry:

```
Cash .............................  500
    Bill Kilmer, Capital ...............      500
```

It would be posted to the ledger as follows:

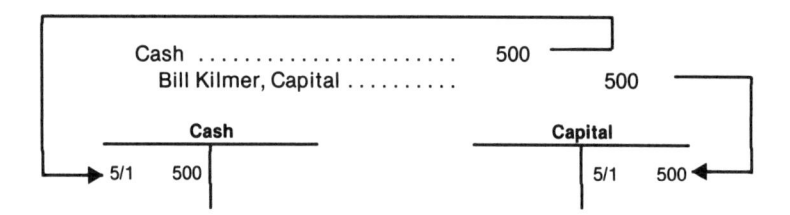

```
        Cash .......................  500
            Bill Kilmer, Capital ..........      500

            Cash                          Capital
    5/1   500                        5/1   500
```

The debit to cash of $500 in the journal entry is posted to the debit side of the cash account in the general ledger and the credit to capital of $500 is posted to the credit side of the capital account in the general ledger. The date in the ledger accounts provides a reference back to the original source of the posting, the general journal. Usually, a page reference will also be provided by each entry in the journal and each account in the general ledger in order to facilitate the cross-referencing of transactions.

Each of the transactions of Kilmer Contractors would be posted in this manner. In our example, the transactions journalized in the previous section are posted to the T-accounts included below. The dates of the transactions appear by each amount and are included for reference purposes.

	Cash				Accounts Receivable		Supplies	
5/1	500	5/5	3,000	5/19	900	5/2	3,000	
5/2	5,000	5/12	600					
5/10	3,300	5/15	2,000					
5/17	700	5/25	1,500					
	2,400				900		3,000	

	Note Payable				Unearned Fees		Capital	
5/15	2,000	5/2	5,000			5/10	3,300	5/1	500
			3,000				3,300		500

	Withdrawals			Painting Fees	
5/12	600			5/17	700
				5/19	900
	600				1,600

	Salaries	
5/25	1,500	
	1,500	

Trial Balance

After all of the transactions which were initially recorded in the general journal have been posted to the general ledger, the next step in the accounting process would be to prepare a trial balance. A trial balance is simply a listing of all of the accounts included in the general ledger along with the balance, debit or credit, of each account. The purpose of a trial balance is simply to prove the equality of the debits and credits and to "catch" or detect any obvious errors which may have occurred in either the recording or the posting process. The reader should note, however, that even if the total of the debits in the trial balance is equal to the total of the credits, this only proves that the accounts are "in balance;" it does not indicate that errors have not been made. (For example, a posting could have been made to the wrong account or a transaction may not have been posted at all.)

The trial balance of Kilmer Contractors at May 31, 19x1, before adjustments would be as follows:

Kilmer Contractors
Trial Balance Before Adjustment
May 31, 19x1

	Debit	Credit
Cash	$2,400	
Accounts receivable	900	
Supplies	3,000	
Note payable		$3,000
Unearned fees		3,300
Capital		500
Withdrawals	600	
Painting fees		1,600
Salaries	1,500	
Total	$8,400	$8,400

Adjusting Entries

As previously indicated, the accrual basis of accounting requires that revenues be recorded as they are earned and expenses be recorded as they are incurred. This procedure is followed without regard to either the receipt or disbursement of cash. At the end of any period, then, there will usually be transactions which are still in the process of completion or which have occurred but have not yet been recorded. These transactions require adjusting entries so that all revenues and expenses (and related assets and liabilities) are stated properly at the end of the period. In the case of Kilmer Contractors, adjustments are required for: (1) the revenue which was earned by painting one of the three houses contracted for on May 10, and (2) the painting supplies which were used during the month of May. These adjustments, referred to as adjusting entries, would be recorded in the accounts by the general journal entries presented below.

May 31. Kilmer Contractors painted one of the three houses contracted for on May 10.

This adjustment records the partial satisfaction of a non-cash liability by the rendering of services (that is, painting one of the three houses) and the earning of income. It would be recorded by the following journal entry:

Unearned fees	1,100	
Painting fees		1,100

Unearned Fees		Painting Fees	
5/31 1,100 | 5/10 3,300		5/17 700	
		5/19 900	
		5/31 1,100	

Recall that on May 10 Kilmer signed a contract whereby he agreed to paint three houses at a future date and received his fee of $1,100 per house in advance. No income was earned at the point the contract was signed and the cash received, because no work had been done at that time. Kilmer Contractors had an obligation to paint the three houses at a future date. This was a liability to perform services, which was reflected as unearned fees. Now, at the end of May, one of the three houses contracted for has been painted and that portion of the income has been earned. The liability, unearned fees, has been reduced by $1,100 and the income for May has been increased by the same amount. These facts require that the financial statements be adjusted in order to reflect the current status of the contract. Again, this transaction emphasizes the fact that income is recorded as it is earned, *not* as cash is received.

The decrease of $1,100 in the liability, unearned fees, would be recorded by a debit to the unearned fees account and the increase in the revenue, painting fees, would be recorded by a credit to the painting fees account. This adjusting entry illustrates the rule that decreases in liabilities are recorded by debits and increases in revenues are recorded by credits.

May 31. The unused painting supplies on hand at this date had an original cost of $2,000.

The facts of this transaction indicate that an expense has been incurred during the month which has not yet been recorded in the accounts. The following adjusting entry would be required at May 31:

```
Supplies used ....................... 1,000
    Supplies ......................         1,000
```

Supplies Used		Supplies	
5/31 1,000		5/2 3,000	5/31 1,000

During May, Kilmer Contractors used supplies that had an original cost of $1,000. This amount was determined by subtracting the $2,000 cost of the supplies which were still on hand at May 31 from the $3,000 total cost of supplies that were available for use (that is, the supplies purchased during the month). As in the previous May 31 transaction, an adjusting entry was required. The asset, supplies, was decreased by $1,000 (the cost of the supplies used), from $3,000 (the total supplies available for use during the month of May) to $2,000 (the cost of supplies still on hand at May 31). This transaction reflects the fact that expenses are recorded when incurred or used rather than when cash is disbursed.

The increase in the supplies used expense would be recorded by a debit to the supplies used account. The decrease in the asset, supplies, would be recorded by a credit to the supplies account. This adjusting entry illustrates the rule that increases in expenses are recorded by debits and decreases in assets are recorded by credits.

Posting the Adjusting Entries

After these two journal entries have been made, all of the transactions of Kilmer Contractors which occurred during the month of May have been recorded in the accounts.

The adjusting entries would then be posted to the ledger in the same manner as were the regular journal entries. This has been done below. Again, the dates of the transactions are included for the use of the reader for purposes of reference. (Note that the two adjusting entries are dated May 31.)

Cash			
5/1	500	5/5	3,000
5/2	5,000	5/12	600
5/10	3,300	5/15	2,000
5/17	700	5/25	1,500
	2,400		

Accounts Receivable	
5/19 900	
900	

Supplies			
5/5	3,000	5/31	1,000
	2,000		

Note Payable			
5/15	2,000	5/5	5,000
			3,000

Unearned Fees			
5/31	1,100	5/10	3,300
			2,200

Capital			
		5/1	500
			500

Withdrawals	
5/12 600	
600	

Painting Fees			
		5/17	700
		5/19	900
		5/31	1,100
			2,700

Salaries	
5/25 1,500	
1,500	

Supplies Used	
5/31 1,000	
1,000	

Trial Balance After Adjustment

The next step in the recording process would be the preparation of a trial balance *after* adjustment. This trial balance is simply the trial balance which was prepared after the adjusting entries were made and posted to the general ledger. The trial balance after adjustment for Kilmer Contractors is presented below.

Kilmer Contractors
Trial Balance After Adjustment
May 31, 19x1

	Debit	Credit
Cash	$2,400	
Accounts receivable	900	
Supplies	2,000	
Note payable		$3,000
Unearned fees		2,200
Capital		500
Withdrawals	600	
Painting fees		2,700
Salaries	1,500	
Supplies used	1,000	
Total	$8,400	$8,400

Again, the only difference between the trial balance after adjustment and the trial balance before adjustment presented previously is the inclusion of the effect of the adjusting entries which were made.

Closing Entries

The purpose of closing entries is to close out the temporary accounts (revenues, expenses, and withdrawals) into the owners' equity (capital) account. This process is facilitated by the introduction of a temporary account created solely for the closing process. This account is known as the *income summary account* and is used to collect or summarize all of the revenues and expenses of the firm in a single account which is then, in turn, closed to the capital account (or the retained earnings account for a corporation).

The purpose of the closing process is to systematically reduce all of the balances in the temporary accounts to a zero balance at the end of the accounting period. Each temporary income statement account with a debit balance is credited for an amount that will result in a zero balance in the account, and the total of these accounts is debited to income summary. Similarly, all of the temporary income statement accounts with a credit balance are debited for an amount that yields a zero balance, and the total of these debits is credited to income summary. This means that at the beginning of the next period all revenues, expenses, and drawing accounts will have a zero balance so that these accounts can again be used in order to record the results of operations of that period.

The closing process is accomplished by the preparation of journal entries known as closing entries. These entries are recorded in the general journal and posted to the ledger in the same manner as all other transactions are processed.

We will now illustrate the closing process for Kilmer Contractors. The journal entries which are required to close out the revenue and expense accounts would be made at the end of the month of May, the accounting period used in this illustration. Referring back to the trial balance after adjustment for Kilmer Contractors, the temporary accounts were as follows:

	Balance Debit	Balance Credit
Withdrawals	$ 600	
Painting fees		$2,700
Salaries	1,500	
Supplies used	1,000	

The entry to close out the revenue account would be:

May 31. Painting fees 2,700
          Income summary 2,700

```
        Painting Fees                  Income Summary
              5/17    700                  5/31  2,700
              5/19    900
              5/31  1,100
   5/31  2,700       2,700
                        0
```

Revenue accounts have credit balances. Therefore, the entry which is required in order to close out the balance in a revenue account consists of a debit to the revenue account for the total revenue for the period and a credit to the income summary account for the same amount. This entry closes out (i.e., brings the account balance to zero) the revenue account and transfers the total for the period to the credit side of the income summary account.

In our illustration, the painting fees account is now closed and has a zero balance, and the $2,700 revenue from painting fees has been transferred to the credit side of the income summary account.

The two expense accounts would be closed out by the following entry:

May 31. Income summary 2,500
          Salaries 1,500
          Supplies used 1,000

```
    Salaries              Supplies Used            Income Summary
5/25  1,500           5/31  1,000              5/31  2,500 | 5/31  2,700
      1,500 | 5/31  1,500      1,000 | 5/31  1,000
          0                        0
```

Expense accounts have debit balances. Therefore, the entry which is required in order to close out the balance in an expense account credits the expense account for the total expense for the period and debits the income summary account for this amount. This closing entry reduces the expense account balance to zero and transfers the total expenses for the period to the debit side of the income summary account.

Both the salaries and the supplies used expense accounts are now closed out and the total of these two accounts ($1,500 + $1,000 = $2,500) which is the total expense for the period has been transferred to the debit side of the income summary account.

The balance in the income summary account ($2,700 − $2,500 = $200) is then transferred to Kilmer's capital account by the following closing entry:

```
May 31.   Income summary ....................   200
              Capital ...........................        200
```

Income Summary				Capital		
5/31	2,500	5/31	2,700		5/1	500
5/31	200		200		5/31	200
			0			

As indicated above, all revenue and expense accounts are closed to the income summary account. Therefore, the credit side of the income summary account will include the total revenue for the period while the debit side of the account will include the total expenses. The account balance will be the income or loss of the business for the period. If the total of the credits (revenues) in the income summary account exceeds the total of the debits (expenses), revenues are greater than expenses and the difference is the income for the period. On the other hand, if the total of the credits (revenues) is less than the total of the debits (expenses), expenses exceed revenues and the difference is the loss for the period. In either case, the balance in the income summary account after all of the revenue and expense accounts have been closed is transferred to the capital account.

In the Kilmer Contractors example, the balance in the income summary account, a credit of $200 (revenues of $2,700 less expenses of $2,500), was closed out and the income for the period was transferred to the capital account.

As a final step in the closing process, the balance in any drawing or withdrawals account is closed out to owner's equity. In the Kilmer Contractors illustration, this step would be to close the balance in the withdrawals account directly to capital.

```
May 31.   Capital .............................   600
              Withdrawals ......................        600
```

Withdrawals				Capital		
5/12	600			5/31	600	5/1 500
		600	5/31 600			5/31 200
		0				

Withdrawals made by the owner do not pass through the income summary account since they are not an expense of the period and therefore do not enter into the determination of income. Withdrawal or drawing accounts have debit balances. Therefore, the closing entry which is required to close withdrawals credits the withdrawal account and debits the capital account for the drawings made by the owner during the period.

In the Kilmer Contractors example, the withdrawals of $600 are closed out and transferred to the capital account as a reduction of the end-of-period capital balance.

The closing process can be depicted graphically as follows:

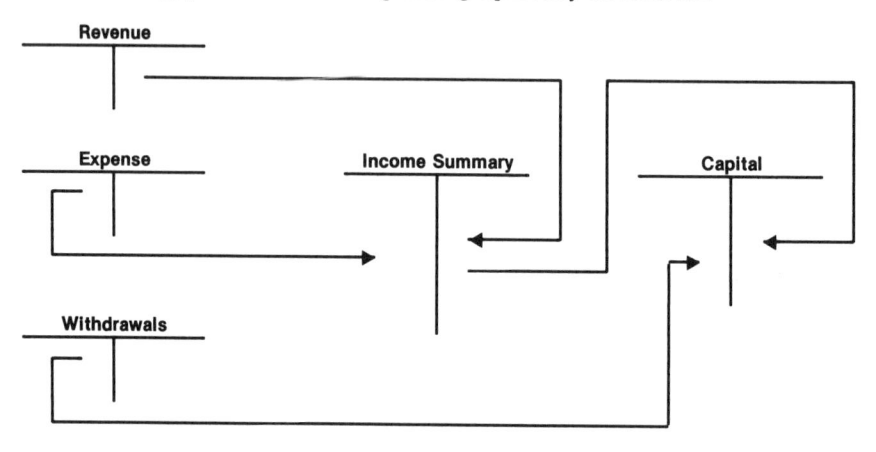

In terms of the specific accounts which were used in the Kilmer Contractors illustration, the closing process is shown below, after all of the closing entries are posted to the accounts.

After-Closing Trial Balance

After all of the temporary accounts have been closed out, a trial balance, referred to as an after-closing trial balance, may be prepared as a test of the equality of the total debits and credits. The after-closing trial balance of Kilmer Contractors is presented below. Since all of the temporary accounts have been closed out, the after-closing trial balance includes only the permanent or balance sheet accounts.

Kilmer Contractors
After-Closing Trial Balance
May 31, 19x1

	Debit	Credit
Cash	$2,400	
Accounts receivable	900	
Supplies	2,000	
Note payable		$3,000
Unearned fees		2,200
Capital		100
Total	$5,300	$5,300

```
                Painting Fees
        (c)   2,700  |  2,700
                     |      0

          Salaries                    Income Summary
        1,500  (c)  1,500    (c)   2,500  (c)   2,700
            0                (c)     200          200
                                       0

         Supplies Used                    Capital
        1,000  (c)  1,000    (c)     600          500
            0                        (c)          200
                                                  100

          Withdrawals
          600  (c)   600
            0
```

(c) Designates closing entry.

Financial Statements

After all of the adjusting and closing entries have been prepared and made and the posting process has been completed, the general ledger account balances will be up-to-date as of the end of the period. The information regarding the assets, liabilities, capital, revenues, and expenses included in the general ledger will be used as a basis for preparing the financial statements.

Asset, liability, and capital balances as of the end of the period will be taken from the general ledger accounts and used to prepare the balance sheet or statement of financial position. As previously indicated, the after-closing trial balance may be used to check the accuracy of the balance sheet since it includes all permanent accounts which appear in the balance sheet.

The revenues and expenses for the period will also be taken from the general ledger and used to prepare the income statement. The trial balance after adjustment and the detailed amounts which are included in the income summary account may be used as a check on the accuracy of the income statement since both of these sources include the details of the revenues and expenses for the period.

The statement of cash flows is prepared by examining the details of the cash account in the general ledger. The statement of capital will also be prepared using the capital account from the general ledger as a source. The financial statements for Kilmer Contractors for the month of May are below.

Kilmer Contractors
Balance Sheet
May 31, 19x1

Assets		Liabilities and Owners' Equity	
Cash	$2,400	Note payable	$3,000
Accounts receivable	900	Unearned fees	2,200
Supplies	2,000	Capital	100
	$5,300		$5,300

Kilmer Contractors
Income Statement
For the Month Ending May 31, 19x1

Revenue from painting services		$2,700
Supplies used	$1,000	
Salaries	1,500	
Total expenses		2,500
Income		$ 200

Kilmer Contractors
Statement of Cash Flows
For the Month Ending May 31, 19x1

Cash flows from operations:		
Receipts from customers		$ 4,000
Payments to:		
Suppliers	$ 3,000	
Employees	1,500	4,500
Decrease in cash due to operations		($ 500)
Cash flows from financing activities:		
Receipts from:		
Owner's investment	$ 500	
Borrowing	5,000	
Payments for:		
Repaying loan	(2,000)	
Owner withdrawal	(600)	
Increase in cash due to financing activities		$ 2,900
Increase in cash		$ 2,400

Kilmer Contractors
Statement of Capital
For the Month Ending May 31, 19x1

Capital at May 1, 19x1		$ 0
Add: Investment	$500	
Income for May	200	700
Deduct: Withdrawal		(600)
Capital at May 31, 19x1		$100

At this time, several points should be noted by the reader in review. First, the general journal entries were prepared as the transactions occurred. These entries represent a chronological record of the transactions of the company which took place during the month of May. These journal entries were then posted to the ledger accounts. At the end of the month, a trial balance was prepared and the transactions and the status of the company at that point in time were reviewed. All adjustments which were necessary to bring the accounts up-to-date were made.

The next step in the process was the preparation of a trial balance after adjustment. Again, it is important to note that any trial balance only proves the equality of the totals of the debits and the credits; it gives no other assurance as to the absence of errors.

Entries were then prepared to "close-out" all temporary accounts, the revenues, expenses, and withdrawals for the period. These are the only accounts closed. The permanent accounts, assets, liabilities, and capital, which appear in the balance sheet, are not closed out. The closing entries summarize the balances of the revenue and expense accounts in an income summary account.[2] The balance in the withdrawals account is then closed out to the capital account. The closing entries were then posted to the ledger and the after-closing trial balance. Then the financial statements were prepared.

ADJUSTING ENTRIES

As previously indicated, the accrual basis of accounting requires that all revenues be recorded as they are earned and that expenses be recorded as they are incurred. That is, there is a proper matching of revenues and expenses only if the income statement for the period includes all of the revenues and expenses which are applicable to the accounting period without regard to the timing of either the receipt or the disbursement of cash. At the end of any accounting period, then, there will usually be certain transactions which are still in the process of completion or which have occurred but which have not been recorded in the accounts. These transactions require adjusting entries to record revenues and expenses and to allocate them to the proper period or periods. In the case of Kilmer Contractors, adjustments were required to record for the revenue which was earned by painting one of the two houses for which payment had been received in advance and to record the cost of the painting supplies which were used during the month of May. In general, the types of transactions which require end-of-period adjusting entries fall into the following groups:

1. Allocation of prepaid expenses to the proper periods.

2. Recognition of unrecorded (accrued) expenses.

---

[2] The reader will note that the income summary is, in fact, a duplication of the income statement itself. That is, the credits to the summary are the revenues for the period and the debits are the expenses for the period. The difference, or balancing figure, is, of course, the income (or loss) for the period.

3. Allocation of a portion of the recorded cost of a fixed asset to the accounting periods which benefit from its use (depreciation).

4. Allocation of recorded revenue to the proper periods.

5. Recognition of unrecorded (accrued) revenues.

The remainder of this chapter will discuss these types of adjusting journal entries. In order to illustrate the different types of adjusting entries, the trial balance before adjustment of Brown Company as of December 31, 19x1, will be used. This trial balance appears in Illustration 3.

Prepaid Expenses

Certain goods and services, such as insurance, rent, and supplies, are purchased prior to their use by the business. If these goods have been used or the services have expired during the accounting period, these costs should be classified as expenses. However, the portion of the goods which is unused or the services which have not expired should be included in the balance sheet and classified as an asset. These assets are referred to as prepaid expenses. A prepaid expense will be reclassified as an expense in a subsequent accounting period (or periods) as it is used or as it expires. Adjusting entries are necessary in order to allocate the cost of each item between the asset account and the expense account.

Illustration 3
Brown Company
Trial Balance Before Adjustment
December 31, 19x1

	Debit	Credit
Cash	$ 2,760	
Accounts receivable	4,000	
Supplies	3,000	
Office furniture	3,600	
Accumulated depreciation—office furniture		$ 360
Accounts payable		2,000
Unearned rent		3,000
Capital		5,000
Withdrawals	1,000	
Service revenues		20,000
Rent expense	9,000	
Salaries	6,000	
Other expense	1,000	
	$30,360	$30,360

To illustrate, assume that Brown Company purchased supplies at a cost of $3,000 on June 30. This transaction was recorded by the following journal entry:

  Supplies 3,000
   Cash   3,000

This entry indicates that an asset has been acquired by the company. Supplies will be carried in the accounts as an asset until they are used, at which time they will become an expense and be reclassified as such. Note that the trial balance before adjustment reflects the $3,000 balance in the supplies account as an asset.

At the end of December, the supplies which were still on hand had a cost of $2,000. Subtracting the cost of the supplies on hand at December 31 ($2,000, as indicated above) from the cost of the supplies which were available for use during the year ($3,000 of supplies purchased on June 30) indicates that it is necessary to record the difference of $1,000, the cost of the supplies used during the year, as an expense. This would be accomplished by means of the following entry:

  Supplies used 1,000
   Supplies   1,000

Alternatively, a prepaid expense may be initially recorded as an expense. For example, Brown Company could have recorded the purchase of the supplies on June 30 with the following journal entry:

  Supplies used 3,000
   Cash   3,000

Since only $1,000 of the supplies were actually used and should be considered as an expense, the following entry would be necessary at the end of the accounting period in order to reclassify the $2,000 of supplies which were still on hand as an asset.

  Supplies 2,000
   Supplies used   2,000

Note that this alternative method results in identical balances at the end of the period in both the supplies acccount ($2,000) and the supplies used account ($1,000). Thus, either method is acceptable as long as the appropriate adjusting entries are made at the end of the period.

In some instances, companies will purchase supplies or prepay expenses which will be entirely used or consumed prior to the preparation of financial statements. In these instances, the amounts paid may be charged directly to expense when the outlay is made, simply as a matter of convenience. For example, assume that Brown Company pays the monthly rent on its office space in advance on the first day of each month. This outlay could be recorded on December 1 as follows:

    Prepaid rent 750
     Cash   750

If the transaction is recorded in this manner, the following adjusting entry would be required at the end of December in order to reclassify the outlay as an expense:

    Rent expense 750
     Prepaid rent   750

Alternatively, it might be expedient to record the expenditure as follows, since the rent is paid and the benefit is received during the month:

    Rent expense 750
     Cash   750

Assuming that Brown Company recorded the transaction in this manner, an adjusting entry would not be required at the end of the month since the expense has been fully incurred and the "prepayment" has been fully used by December 31.

Accrued Expenses At the end of an accounting period there are usually expenses which have been incurred but which have not been paid because payment is not due until a subsequent period. Many expenses, such as wages and salaries or interest on loans, may be incurred during a period but not recorded in the accounts because they have not been paid. These expenses are referred to as accrued expenses. Adjusting entries are necessary at the end of an accounting period in order to record all accrued expenses. For example, assume that Brown Company placed a newspaper advertisement which appeared during the month of December, but was not billed for the ad until some time in January. Since Brown Company did not pay for the advertisement during December, this amount does not appear on the trial balance before adjustment. Therefore, the following adjusted entry would be required at the end of December:

    Advertising expense 75
     Accounts payable   75

This adjusting entry records the expense which was incurred but not paid during December and the corresponding liability which exists at the end of the month.

When the bill is received in January and is paid, the payment would be recorded by the following journal entry:

  Accounts payable 75
   Cash   75

This entry records the fact that the liability has been satisfied (and assets reduced) by the cash payment. The timing of the recognition of the expense is not determined by the date of the payment; the expense was recorded during the previous month when it was incurred.

Depreciation

Businesses normally acquire assets which are used in their operations over a number of years. Buildings and equipment are examples of this type of asset. A business may purchase equipment and use it for a number of years. For example, assume that Brown Company acquired office furniture on January 1, 19x0, and expects to use this furniture for ten years before it will be replaced. Assuming that the cost of this furniture was $3,600, the purchase would have been recorded as follows:

  Office furniture 3,600
   Cash   3,600

The office furniture is an asset of the business and is recorded as such. Its cost should be charged to expense over the period that it is used, in this case ten years. The process of allocating the cost of an asset to expense over its useful life is referred to as depreciation. Depreciation is the systematic allocation of the cost of an asset to the periods which benefit from its use. The primary difference between allocating the cost of a fixed asset to expense (i.e., depreciation) and the allocation of the cost of a prepaid item, such as supplies or insurance, to expense is that it is normally much more difficult to measure the portion of the cost of a fixed asset which has been used during an accounting period. Therefore, the allocation of the cost of a fixed asset to expense during an accounting period is only an *estimate* of the part of the usefulness of the asset which has expired or been used during the year. Since the cost of the furniture was $3,600 and the expected useful life of this asset was ten years or 120 months, depreciation in the amount of $360 ($3,600 ÷ 10) should be recorded annually. Assuming that Brown Company did not make monthly entries to record the depreciation, the adjusting entry which should be made on December 31, 19x0 and 19x1 in order to record depreciation expense would be as follows:

  Depreciation expense 360
   Accumulated depreciation   360

The debit to depreciation expense records the portion of the cost of the asset which is recorded as an expense of the year. The credit is to accumulated depreciation, a contra account which would appear as an offset or deduction from the related asset account in the balance sheet. As the title accumulated depreciation implies, the depreciation taken over the useful life of the asset is accumulated in this account. Usually a reduction in an asset account is recorded with a credit made directly to the account. However, a contra account is used for fixed assets in order to provide additional information concerning the asset—that is, both the original cost and the depreciation expense which has been taken to-date may be recorded and reported in the balance sheet. The asset and the related accumulated depreciation account would appear in the balance sheet as follows at the end of 19x1:

```
Office furniture........................ $3,600
Less:   Accumulated depreciation.........   720    $2,880
```

A more complete discussion of the procedures which are involved in determining depreciation expense is presented in Chapter 5.

Unearned Revenues

Revenue which is collected before a business actually performs a service or delivers goods to a customer is referred to as unearned revenue. Since cash is received prior to the performance of the service or delivery of the goods, the amount received represents a liability to the firm. Unearned revenues are not a liability in the sense that the company will be required to repay the money. Rather, they represent an obligation of the company to perform a service or deliver goods at some future date (i.e., revenues that have been received but not earned). Examples of unearned revenues include rent collected in advance and subscription fees received prior to delivery of a magazine or newspaper.

To illustrate, assume that Brown Company subleased a portion of its office space to Smith for a rental of $3,000 per year. Terms of the lease agreement specify that Smith will pay the yearly rental in advance on July 1. The entry to record the receipt of the $3,000 advance payment on July 1, 19x1 would be as follows:

```
Cash ............................ 3,000
    Unearned rent ....................        3,000
```

Note that the trial balance before adjustment includes the $3,000 balance in the unearned rent account. Since no service had been performed at the time the cash was received, the entire amount was initially recorded in a liability account, unearned rent. Since rent is earned over the twelve month period that Brown Company provides office space to Smith, exactly one-half of the service will be rendered during the period July 1 to December 31, 19x1. Thus $1,500 (½ × $3,000) of the rent has been earned and would be recorded by the following adjusting entry on December 31:

```
Unearned rent ..................... 1,500
    Rental income ...................        1,500
```

The liability account, unearned rent, has been reduced by $1,500 and revenue for the period has been increased by this amount. The remaining balance in the unearned rent account represents an obligation to provide office space to Smith during the first six months of 19x2. This adjusting entry made on December 31 emphasizes the fact that income is recorded as it is earned, not as cash is received.

Accrued Revenues

Accrued revenues are revenues that have been earned but not recorded in the accounts during an accounting period because cash has not yet been received. As such, accrued revenues are the opposite, so to speak, of unearned revenues. Therefore, adjusting entries are necessary in order to record any revenue which has been earned but not recorded in the accounts as of the end of the accounting period. To illustrate, assume that Brown Company entered into an agreement with the Fooler Brush Company on December 1, 19x1. Brown Company agreed to display a line of brushes at their offices in return for a commission of 10 percent on any sales made by Fooler if the initial contact with the customer was made by Brown Company. The commissions are payable on a quarterly basis. Assume that Brown Company earned commissions of $100 during the month of December. The following adjusted journal entry would be made on December 31:

```
Commissions receivable  ............     100
    Commissions earned  .............            100
```

This entry increases the assets (commissions receivable) of Brown Company by the $100 due from Fooler Brush Company and records the revenue which has been earned to-date by providing the agreed-upon service. When payment is received from the Fooler Brush Company, the following journal entry would be made:

```
Cash  ............................     100
    Commissions receivable  ...........           100
```

It is important to note that this second entry simply records the fact that one asset, cash, was received in exchange for another, commissions receivable; revenues were not affected. The revenues were recorded at the time the service was performed, which was when they were earned by Brown Company.

COMPARATIVE STATEMENTS

Comparative statements, as opposed to statements of a single period, increase the usefulness of financial statements. *Comparative statements allow the user to learn about the trends affecting the financial position, operating results, and changes in financial position of an enterprise.* Comparative balance sheets for a company are presented before Chapter 1 of this text.

In addition to comparative financial statements, many companies present a *financial review* for an extended period of time (e.g., 10 years). *Items that are reported in these financial reviews include revenues, cost of goods sold, interest expense, income taxes, net income, extraordinary items, earnings per share, dividends, current assets, total assets, stockholders' equity, shares of stock outstanding, and average stock prices.* The specific items that are included in the financial review vary from company-to-company.

DISCLOSURE TECHNIQUES

Footnotes to the financial statements and supporting schedules are used to increase the information that is available in the financial statements. Frequently, the information that is included on the balance sheet is very brief, and more complete explanations are presented in the footnotes and supporting schedules. *Parenthetical notations are used to clarify or cross reference items included on the face of the balance sheet.*

Amost all large companies round the amounts presented in the financial statements to the nearest dollar amounts or larger amounts such as the nearest thousand dollars.

Although the specific format that is used in the balance sheet varies somewhat among companies, *there are three basic formats that generally are used: the report form; the account form; and the financial position form.* The report form lists the assets first, followed by the liabilities and then the stockholders' equity. The account form differs from the report form in that the assets are listed on the left-hand side of the statement and the liabilities and stockholders' equity accounts are listed on the right-hand side. The financial position form lists the current assets first, and follows by deducting the current liabilities to derive the working capital. The noncurrent assets then are added and the noncurrent liabilities are deducted in order to obtain the residual stockholders' equity amount.

AUDITOR'S REPORT

Since many users rely on the fairness and accuracy of financial statements, independent examinations by CPAs have evolved and have become common practice. *The certified public accountant (auditor) examines the accounting records, supporting documents, physical properties, and financial statements to decide whether the financial statements and the accompanying notes have been prepared in accordance with generally accepted accounting principles, and whether or not they present fairly the financial position, results of operations, and changes in financial position.* The auditor then gives the company an unqualified opinion, a qualified opinion, an adverse opinion, or a disclaimer of opinion, depending upon his or her findings.

SUMMARY

Transactions that affect the financial statements of a firm occur much too frequently to permit a revision of the statements after each transaction takes place. Therefore, firms use various "accounting systems" that record and accumulate the essence of these transactions. This allows the accountant to use the summarized data provided by the accounting system to prepare financial statements at designated points in time. The most commonly used accounting system, and the one discussed in this chapter, is the "double-entry" system.

The basic element of the double-entry system, as well as other systems, is the account. An account is simply a place or means of collecting and summarizing all of the transactions that affect a particular asset, liability, or owners' equity account. Each account is increased or decreased by use of debits (left-side entries) and credits (right-side entries). A debit entry increases assets and expenses, but decreases liabilities, owners' equity, and revenue accounts. Conversely, a credit entry increases liabilities, owners' equity, and revenues, but decreases assets and expenses.

The actual recording process involves a number of separate but related steps. The initial step is the preparation of the general journal entries at the time the transactions take place. These general journal entries are then posted to the individual accounts in the ledger. After these two steps are completed, the accountant prepares a trial balance before adjustment. This trial balance is simply a listing of each account and the corresponding debit or credit balance in the account. This listing will only detect the most obvious errors and does not guarantee that other errors have not been made.

The next step in the recording process is the preparation of adjusting entries. These entries are necessary to adjust the accounts so that the final balances will reflect the proper updated balances as of the end of the accounting period. The adjusting entries are then posted to the appropriate ledger accounts and a trial balance after adjustment is prepared.

The next phase in the recording process is the preparation of closing entries. These entries are required to close the temporary accounts (revenues, expenses, and withdrawals) so that these accounts can be used to accumulate similar data for the next accounting period. To accomplish this, all revenues and expenses are closed to the income summary account. The income summary account and the withdrawal account are then closed to the capital account. Once the closing entries are prepared and entered into the general journal, they are then posted to the ledger accounts and an after-closing trial balance is prepared.

The final step is the actual preparation of the financial statements. As indicated in previous chapters, the primary financial statements prepared by the accountant are the balance sheet, income statement, statement of cash flows, and statement of capital.

KEY DEFINITIONS

Account—a place or means of summarizing all of the transactions that affect a particular asset, liability, equity, revenue, or expense item.

Accrual basis of accounting—the process of recording revenues in the period in which they are earned and recording expenses in the period in which they are incurred.

Accrued expenses—expenses, such as wages and salaries or interest on loans, which have been incurred during a period but not yet recorded in the accounts because they have not yet been paid.

Accrued revenues—revenues which have been earned but not yet recorded in the accounts during the accounting period because cash has not yet been received.

Accumulated depreciation—contra account which appears as an offset or deduction from the related asset account in the balance sheet. The depreciation taken over the useful life of the asset is accumulated in this account.

Adjusted trial balance—prepared by combining the trial balance before adjustments with the related adjusting entries.

Adjusting entries—at the end of any accounting period there will usually be certain transactions which are still in the process of completion or which have occurred but which have not yet been recorded in the accounts. These transactions require adjusting entries in order to record revenues and expenses and to allocate them to the proper period.

Closing entries—the purpose of closing entries is to close out or transfer the balances in the temporary accounts (revenues, expenses, and withdrawals) into the capital account.

Contra account—an account which is offset against or deducted from another account in the financial statements.

Credit—the term used to identify the right-hand side of an account. A credit decreases an asset and increases a liability, equity, or revenue account.

Debit—the term used to describe the left-hand side of an account. By debiting an asset or expense account, the account is increased and by debiting a liability or equity account, the account is decreased.

Depreciation—the systematic allocation of the cost of an asset to the periods which benefit from its use.

Double-entry method—this method requires that for every transaction recorded, the total dollar amount of debits must be equal to the total dollar amount of the credits.

General journal entry—a means of recording the transactions of a firm chronologically in terms of debits and credits.

General ledger—a compilation of all the accounts of a firm and their balances.

Posting—posting to ledger accounts is the process of transferring the information from the general journal to the individual accounts of the general ledger. This enables the accountant to review and summarize all changes in the accounts.

Prepaid expenses—certain goods and services, such as insurance, rent, and supplies, are often paid for prior to their use by the business. The portion of the goods which has not been used up or the services which have not expired should be included in the balance sheet and classified as an asset.

Trial balance—a listing of all the accounts in the general ledger. If the accounts are "in balance," the total of the accounts with debit balances will equal the total of those with credit balances. The trial balance only indicates that the accounts are in balance. It does not prove that errors have not been made in the recording process.

Unearned revenues—revenues which are collected before a business actually performs a service or delivers goods to a customer.

Appendix

INTRODUCTION   A primary function of accounting is to accumulate the information which is required by decision-makers and communicate this data to them. The accounting system used for communicating information consists of business documents (such as invoices or checks) and records the procedures that are used in recording transactions and preparing reports. A financial accounting system must communicate data to users in such a way that the operating performance and current financial position of a company is reported in a manner that is both meaningful and useful. All pertinent information which is required for decision-making and planning and control purposes must be made available to the user on a timely basis. There are also certain other basic housekeeping functions that the system should accomplish. For example, detailed information must be made available in order to identify the specific accounts receivable balance of each customer, detailed information regarding payroll and deductions is required in order to pay employees and satisfy government regulations, and inventory balances must be available on a current basis for purposes of inventory planning and control. The accounting system of an organization should be designed to handle all of the many facets of accounting and the system must operate in a manner which is efficient, effective, accurate, and timely.

MODEL OF A FINANCIAL ACCOUNTING SYSTEM

A model of a basic financial accounting system is presented in tabular form and in the form of a diagram below. The financial accounting system shown in these illustrations indicates the procedures which are followed during the accounting cycle. Presentation of the system in these illustrations is intended to provide a comprehensive picture or overview of the information flows that are required in a typical organization. Note that this example is a summarization of the steps in the recording process which was discussed in Chapters 3 and 4. The next illustration diagrams the same general data flows in a financial accounting system. Certain features, which will be discussed in this chapter, have been added to the system which provide for more efficient means of processing the accounting data.

The basic components of the system are as follows:

1. A chart of accounts.
2. A coding system.
3. A general journal.
4. A general ledger.
5. Subsidiary ledgers.
6. Special journals.
7. Internal control.
8. An audit trail.

These components of the financial accounting system are discussed in the following paragraphs.

The Chart of Accounts

A chart of accounts is a listing of all of the accounts that an organization may use in its accounting system. The scope of the chart of accounts and the ability to adapt new account titles to the existing listing is a very important factor to be considered in the process of designing and installing an accounting system. The design of the chart of accounts will affect the manner in which accounting information will be accumulated, summarized, and used by the organization.

At a minimum, the chart of accounts should include all of the accounts that appear on the balance sheet, income statement, and statement of capital or retained earnings. In most cases, however, limiting the chart to only these accounts would be inadequate since management often requires information which is more detailed than that which is included in the basic financial statements. This detailed information is required in order to manage the day-to-day operations of the business. Also, external users such as governmental agencies frequently require information not included in the financial statements, often in detailed and specified formats. In addition to the basic functional classifications, management normally requires:

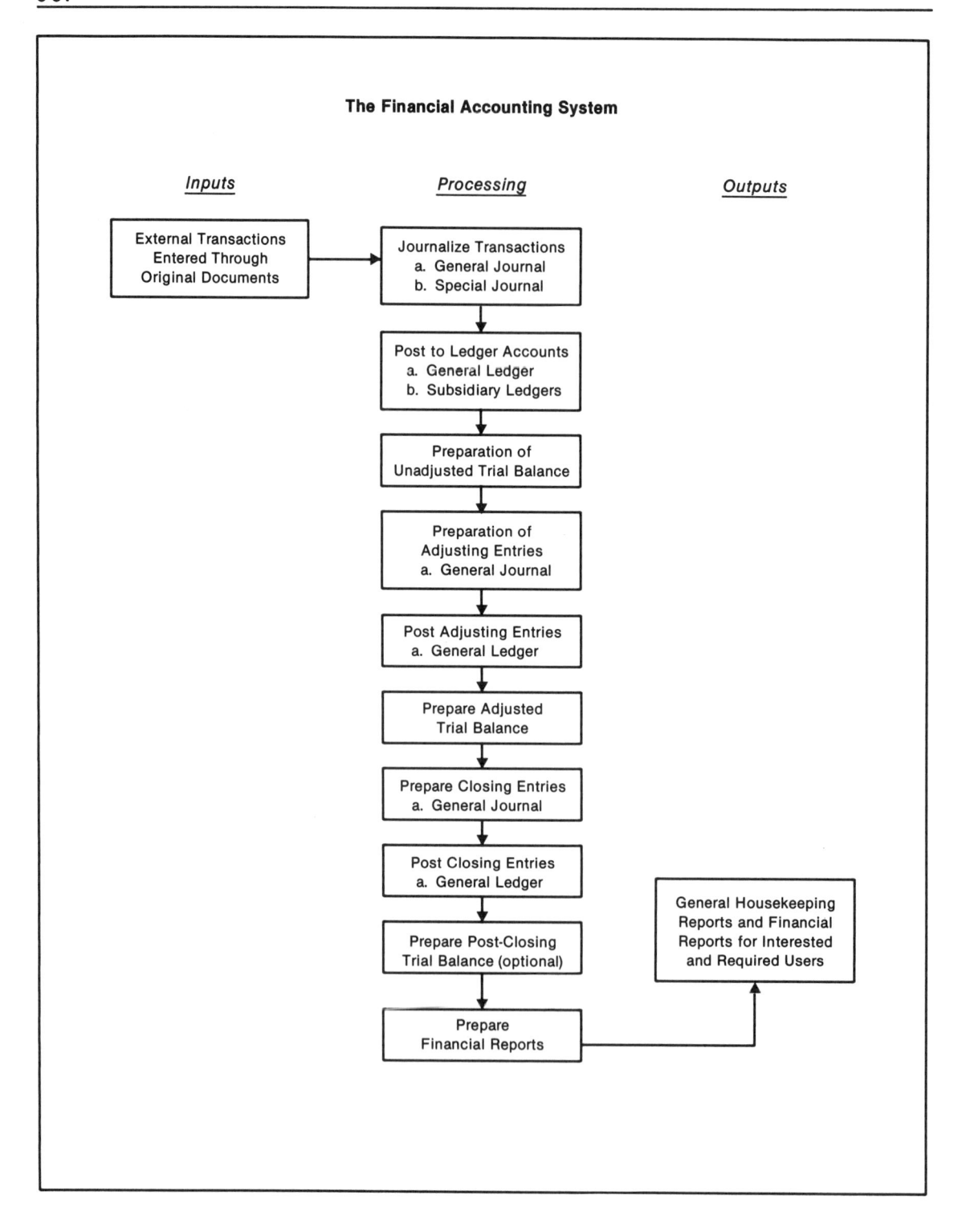

The Financial Accounting System

Inputs

- External Transactions Entered Through Original Documents

Processing

- Journalize Transactions
  a. General Journal
  b. Special Journal
- Post to Ledger Accounts
  a. General Ledger
  b. Subsidiary Ledgers
- Preparation of Unadjusted Trial Balance
- Preparation of Adjusting Entries
  a. General Journal
- Post Adjusting Entries
  a. General Ledger
- Prepare Adjusted Trial Balance
- Prepare Closing Entries
  a. General Journal
- Post Closing Entries
  a. General Ledger
- Prepare Post-Closing Trial Balance (optional)
- Prepare Financial Reports

Outputs

- General Housekeeping Reports and Financial Reports for Interested and Required Users

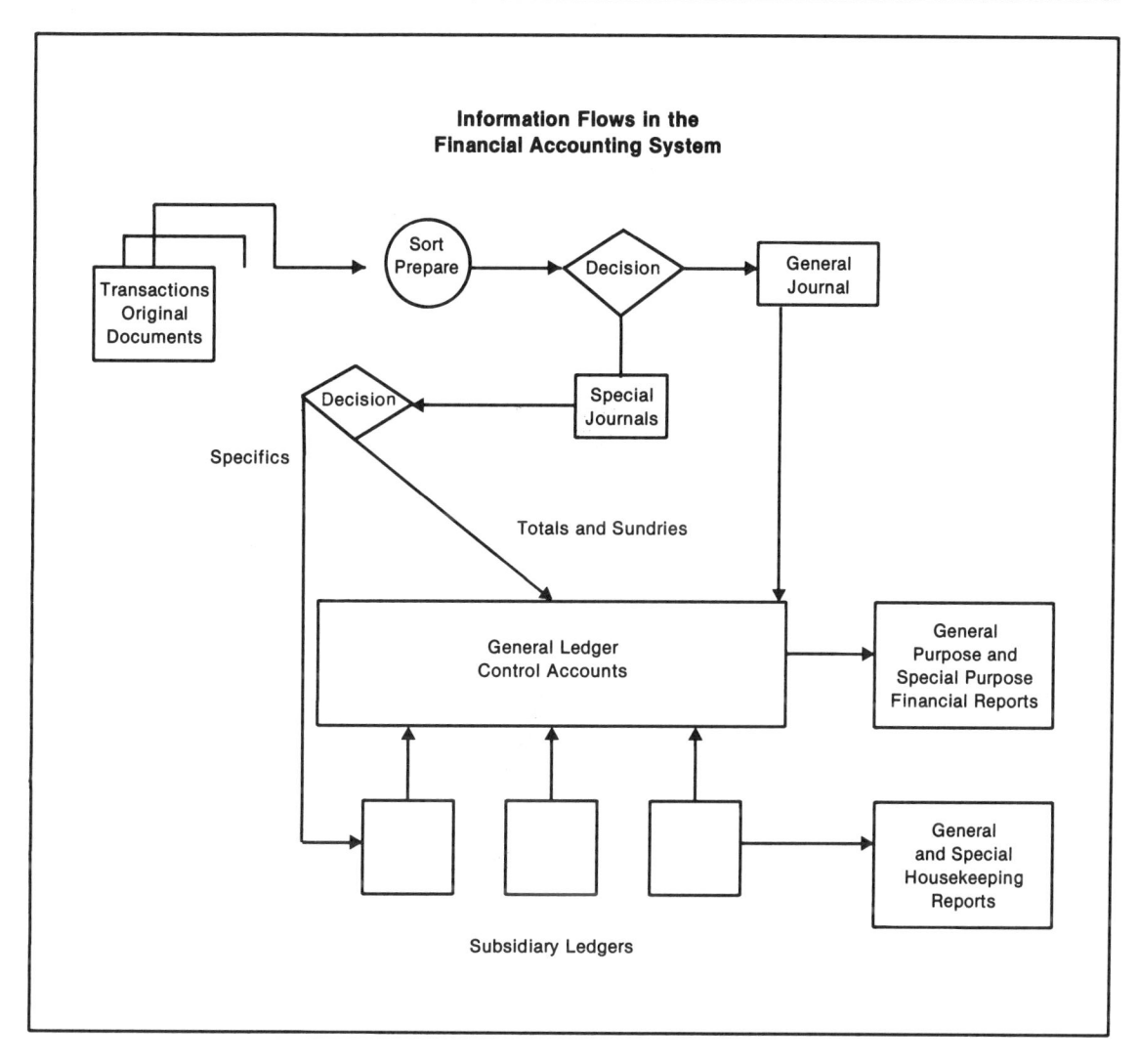

Information Flows in the Financial Accounting System

```
Transactions          Sort
Original    ───────▶  Prepare  ──────▶  Decision  ──────▶  General
Documents                                                   Journal

                              Special
              Decision  ◀──── Journals
          Specifics │
                    │     Totals and Sundries
                    ▼         │
                ┌─────────────────────────┐         General
                │   General Ledger        │ ──────▶ Purpose and
                │   Control Accounts      │         Special Purpose
                └─────────────────────────┘         Financial Reports
                    ▲    ▲    ▲
                  ┌──┐ ┌──┐ ┌──┐                    General
                  │  │ │  │ │  │ ─────────────────▶ and Special
                  └──┘ └──┘ └──┘                    Housekeeping
                                                    Reports
                  Subsidiary Ledgers
```

1. Accounting information which is based on cost behavior patterns for purposes of planning and control.
2. Accounting information which is based on areas of responsibility for purposes of performance measurement and control. For example, information regarding divisions or geographical regions may be used in order to measure the performance of these segments.

Many of the accounts used by the organization will be utilized for multiple purposes in the management and operations of the business. For example, production cost data is required in the process of inventory valuation, but it is also necessary for evaluating the performance of the specific departments which are involved in the production process.

Coding the Chart of Accounts

In order to facilitate the use of data and to provide a unique identity for each account, the chart of accounts is normally coded numerically. A normal pattern of arrangement and coding of the chart of accounts is in the format and the order of the financial statements and the accounts included in these statements. A simplified example of the broad categories of accounts which might be included in a typical chart of accounts is presented below:

1000-1999	Asset accounts
2000-2999	Liability accounts
3000-3999	Owner's equity accounts
4000-4999	Revenue accounts
5000-5999	Manufacturing cost accounts
6000-6999	Distribution expense accounts
7000-7999	Administrative expense accounts
8000-8999	Other income accounts
9000-9999	Other expense accounts

To illustrate the usefulness of coding and the means of identifying specific items using numerical codes, a code for asset accounts will be expanded and explained. The first digit in the code may be used to identify the general account classification. Any search of the accounts is then limited to one thousand possible accounts in that category. The second digit could be used to identify an asset's location; that is, for example, whether the asset is located at the home office or at a division. The third digit could be used to identify the classification of the asset; that is, whether the asset is a current asset, a long-term asset, an intangible asset, etc. The fourth digit might be used to identify the specific asset itself.

Obviously, in a large organization the coding structure may be very complex. In order to deal with the complexity of the coding structure, a code dictionary, identifying the specific account and its code, is often employed. In situations where automated equipment with sensing or scanning capability is used, numerical characters are usually considered necessary for reasons of both economy and efficiency.

The General Journal and General Ledger

Until this point, the mechanics of recording and handling transactions described in this text has been limited to the general journal and the general ledger. As previously indicated, each transaction is recorded in the general journal chronologically, and then the debits and credits from the general journal are posted individually to the appropriate accounts in the general ledger.

In the accounting procedures illustrated to this point, the general journal was used as the book of original entry while the general ledger served as the book of final entry. Financial statements were usually prepared from an adjusted trial balance or worksheet. The mechanics of this system would make it almost impossible for all but the smallest business to operate effectively or, at least, efficiently. This type of system is simply unable to process large volumes of transactions on a timely basis, primarily because no effective division of labor is possible since each and every journal entry must be written out on an individual basis.

In addition, this system might not provide the detailed information necessary to operate business efficiently. For example, the system previously described did not always identify the specific individual who purchased goods on account. Likewise, it did not provide information as to the identity of individual creditors. Division of labor and necessary detail may be accomplished in this basic system by the addition and use of special journals and subsidiary ledgers in addition to the general journal and general ledger.

Subsidiary Ledgers

Subsidiary ledgers are supplemental detailed records which provide underlying support for the amounts recorded in control accounts included in the general ledger. An example of a subsidiary ledger is the accounts receivable subsidiary ledger. An individual record must be maintained on a current basis for every customer for purposes of control, billing, and for handling any inquiries.

The use of individual customer records eliminates the problem of including large numbers of detailed accounts receivable accounts in the general ledger. There are also many other obvious advantages to the use of subsidiary ledgers other than the accumulation of necessary detail. Subsidiary ledgers permit a division of duties among employees by allowing a number of different individuals to assist in the preparation of the records. In addition, personnel with less experience may be used to post to subsidiary ledgers. Also, an error in a trial balance may be localized in a subsidiary ledger, thus reducing the effort necessary to locate the error.

Subsidiary ledgers are necessary to permit the classification of a large group of accounts under a single control account in the general ledger. The subsidiary ledgers found in most systems include: accounts receivable, accounts payable, inventories, employee pay records, property records, and the stockholders' register.

When a company maintains a subsidiary ledger, the corresponding general ledger account is referred to as a control account. If no recording errors are made, the total of the balances in a subsidiary ledger should be equal to the total in the corresponding control account which is included in the general ledger.

Special Journals

The initial step in the flow of information through the financial accounting system is identifying the transactions that will be processed. One means of reducing the amount of individual recording and posting is to separate the transactions into groups that have common elements and to provide special journals for recording the transactions in each group. A decision is then made as to whether the transaction falls into a class that should be entered in a special journal or is an infrequently occurring transaction that should be entered directly in the general journal. A special journal is useful in those instances where there is a large volume of transactions which result in debits and credits to the same accounts. For such transactions, the recording process is facilitated by entering the amounts in the columns of a special journal and posting the totals periodically to the general ledger. The types of transactions which normally occur with sufficient frequency to justify the use of special journals include receipts of cash, disbursements of cash, sales of merchandise on credit, and the purchase of merchandise on account. Of course, transactions not recorded in any of the special journals are recorded in the general journal. That is, every transaction must be recorded in some type of journal, and the effects of all transactions are still posted, either individually or by cumulative totals, to the ledger.

The accounts receivable example which was employed to illustrate the use of subsidiary ledgers is also applicable to special journals. When goods are sold on account, the sale is made and should be recorded at that time. The relevant aspects of credit sales from a data gathering standpoint include: identity of the customer; amount of the sale; nature of any credit terms;[1] date of the sale; and, for any future inquiries, the invoice number. This is repetitive data which will be accumulated for each and every sale.

Special journals permit a division of labor, allow the use of less experienced personnel, employ preprinted account columns or summaries which reduce the incidence of error, and allow special transactions of like kind to be easily analyzed since the original data was accumulated by category rather than on an individual basis.

If a specific type of transaction occurs frequently in the business, a special journal should be designed and used for these transactions. As previously indicated, the types of special journals most frequently used by a business normally include: sales, cash receipts, cash disbursements, and purchases.

An Example—Special Journals and Subsidiary Ledgers

Before considering the following example, the reader should review the two examples given to make certain that the general steps included and the information flows illustrated are understood.

The credit sales and cash collections for the Yello Brewery for January illustrates the interrelationships of special journals, subsidiary ledgers, and the general ledger.

---

[1] Credit terms include the time allowed for payment and any discounts allowed. Payment required within thirty days would be shown by the notation n/30 indicating that the full amount is due in thirty days.

Jan.	2	Sold 200 cases at $4 per case to Harry the Hat's Bar & Grill (on account)—Invoice #101.
	5	Sold fifty cases at $4 per case to Big Brother's Place (on account)—Invoice #102.
	7	Received a check from Harry the Hat's Bar & Grill for $800.
	11	Sold 200 cases at $4 per case to Harry the Hat's Bar & Grill (on account)—Invoice #103.
	13	Sold ten cases at $4.50 per case to the Bachelor's Club (on account)—Invoice #104.
	15	Sold twenty cases at $4.10 per case to Dink's Place (on account)—Invoice #105.
	25	Received a check from Big Brother's Place for $200.
	31	Received a check from the Bachelor's Club for $45.
	31	Received a dividend check of $50 on marketable securities.

Sales Journal. The transactions for the Yello Brewery are journalized and posted in the special journals, subsidiary ledgers, and general ledger in Illustration 1.

Note that each individual credit sale is recorded in the sales journal. Any merchandise sold for cash would be recorded directly in the cash receipts journal. The amount of each credit sale is posted daily to the individual customer account in the accounts receivable subsidiary ledger. This procedure assures that each customer's account will be kept up-to-date for purposes of responding to inquiries from customers and for making decisions regarding future extensions of credit to individual customers. The check mark (✓) in the sales journal indicates that the posting to the subsidiary ledger has been made. Then, at the end of the month, the total of the sales journal column ($1,927) is debited to accounts receivable control and credited to sales revenue in the general ledger.

Cash Receipts Journal. Similarly, a cash receipts journal is used to record all transactions involving the receipt of cash. The cash receipts journal must include several columns for recording transactions since the source of the receipts may differ. For example, note that the cash receipts journal in Illustration 1 includes credit columns for collections on accounts receivable, sales of merchandise for cash, and all other (sundry) transactions. Thus, a receipt of cash is recorded by entering the amount received in the debit column for cash and in the appropriate column to record the credit.

As in the case of the sales journal, the individual credits in the accounts receivable credit column are posted daily to the customer accounts in the accounts receivable subsidiary ledger. The check mark (✓) in the cash receipts journal indicates that the posting has been made to the subsidiary ledger.

The various sales of merchandise in the business which are made for cash are typically recorded in total by the means of an entry in the cash receipts journal made at the end of the day. This entry is recorded in the cash debit column and the sales credit column of the journal. Cash received from sources other than collections of receivables on cash sales are recorded in the sundry credit column.

Illustration 1
Special Journals and Subsidiary Ledgers

Sales Journal

Date	Invoice No.	Terms	Customer Account	✓	Dr. A/R and Cr. Sales
1-2	101	N/30	Harry the Hat's	✓	←800
1-5	102	N/30	Big Brother's Place	✓	←200
1-11	103	N/30	Harry the Hat's	✓	←800
1-11	104	N/30	Bachelor's Club	✓	← 45
1-15	105	N/30	Dink's Place	✓	← 82
				✓	1,927

Column totals posted monthly to General Ledger

Individual Transactions posted daily to Subsidiary Ledger

Cash Receipts Journal

Date	Account Credited	✓	Dr. Cash	Cr. A/R	Cr. Sales	Cr. Sundry
1-7	Harry the Hat's	✓	800	800		
1-25	Big Brother's Place	✓	200	200		
1-31	Bachelor's Club	✓	45	45		
1-31	Dividend Inc.	✓	50			50
1-31	Balances	✓	1,095	1,045		50

Individual Transactions posted daily to Subsidiary Ledger

Column totals posted monthly to General Ledger

Sundry Accts. posted to General Ledger as convenient

Accounts Receivable Subsidiary Ledger

Acct. #1401   Bachelor's Club
79 Main St.
Normal 200 Cases   Minco

Date	Ref.	Debit	Credit	Bal.
1-11	S.J.	45		45
1-31	C.R.		45	-0-

Acct. #1402   Big Brother's Place
1984 Watch Lane
Normal 60 Cases   Sardina

Date	Ref.	Debit	Credit	Bal.
1-5	S.J.	200		200
1-25	C.R.		200	-0-

Acct. #1403   Dink's Place
22 Top Plaza
Normal 60 Cases   Bryantown

Date	Ref.	Debit	Credit	Bal.
1-15	S.J.	82		82

Acct. #1404   Harry the Hat's
12 Tower Bldg.
Normal 200 Cases   Locusttown

Date	Ref.	Debit	Credit	Bal.
1-2	S.J.	800		800
1-7	C.R.		800	-0-
1-11	S.J.	800		800

General Ledger Accounts

Acct. #1000   Cash

Date	Ref.	Debit	Credit	Bal.
1-1				1000
1-31	C.R.	1095		2095

Acct. #1400   Accounts Rec.–Control

Date	Ref.	Debit	Credit	Bal.
1-1				800
1-31	S.J.	1927		2727
1-31	C.R.		1045	1682

Acct. #4000   Sales Revenue

Date	Ref.	Debit	Credit	Bal.
1-31	S.J.		1927	1927

Acct. #8000   Dividend Income

Date	Ref.	Debit	Credit	Bal.
1-31	C.R.		50	50

At the end of the month, the column totals in the cash receipts journal are posted to the appropriate general ledger accounts. Prior to this posting, it is necessary to prove that the total of the debit columns is equal to the total of the credit columns. After the totals in the cash receipts journal have been checked, the total in the cash column is posted as a debit to the cash account and the total of the accounts receivable column is posted as a credit to the accounts receivable control account. Similarly, the total of the credits in the column for cash sales would be posted to the sales account in the general ledger. The individual items in the sundry account column are posted separately to the appropriate general ledger accounts.

Cash Disbursements Journal. A cash disbursements journal may be used to record all expenditures of cash made by the business. Normally, a journal of this type will include individual credit columns for cash and the purchase discounts and a sundry or other credit column. The total of the credits to cash and to purchase discounts would be posted directly to these accounts on a monthly basis while the amounts included in the other credit column would be posted to the individual accounts at any time that it is convenient to do so. Debit columns are normally included for accounts frequently affected by cash disbursements such as purchases and accounts payable. The totals of these account columns are posted directly to the purchases and accounts payable control accounts on a monthly basis. The individual debits in the accounts payable debit column must be posted daily to the accounts payable subsidiary ledger. There will be a sundry or other debit column where debits to accounts other than purchases and accounts payable may be recorded. These entries would be posted to the appropriate general ledger accounts as it is convenient to do so.

The mechanics of the cash disbursements journal are almost identical to those of the cash receipts journal. Like any other special journal, the cash disbursements journal should be designed in a manner that meets the specific requirements of its user. It should include debit and credit columns for the accounts most often affected by the payment of cash. The columns suggested above are typical of those included in the cash disbursements journals of many businesses, but others may be required in particular circumstances. An example of a cash disbursements journal is included on the following page.

Payroll Journal. A payroll journal is a specialized form of a cash disbursements journal. As its name implies, it is used exclusively to record the payment of salaries and wages to employees. A payroll journal will normally include credit columns for cash, federal income taxes withheld, state income taxes withheld, social security taxes withheld (employees' share), and other deductions such as union dues, employee hospitalization, etc. A debit column will be included for payroll expense, gross salaries, and the employer's share of social security taxes and federal and state unemployment taxes. Summary entries are made to record total payroll expense, payment of the salaries and wages, and the incurring of the liabilities related to the pay-

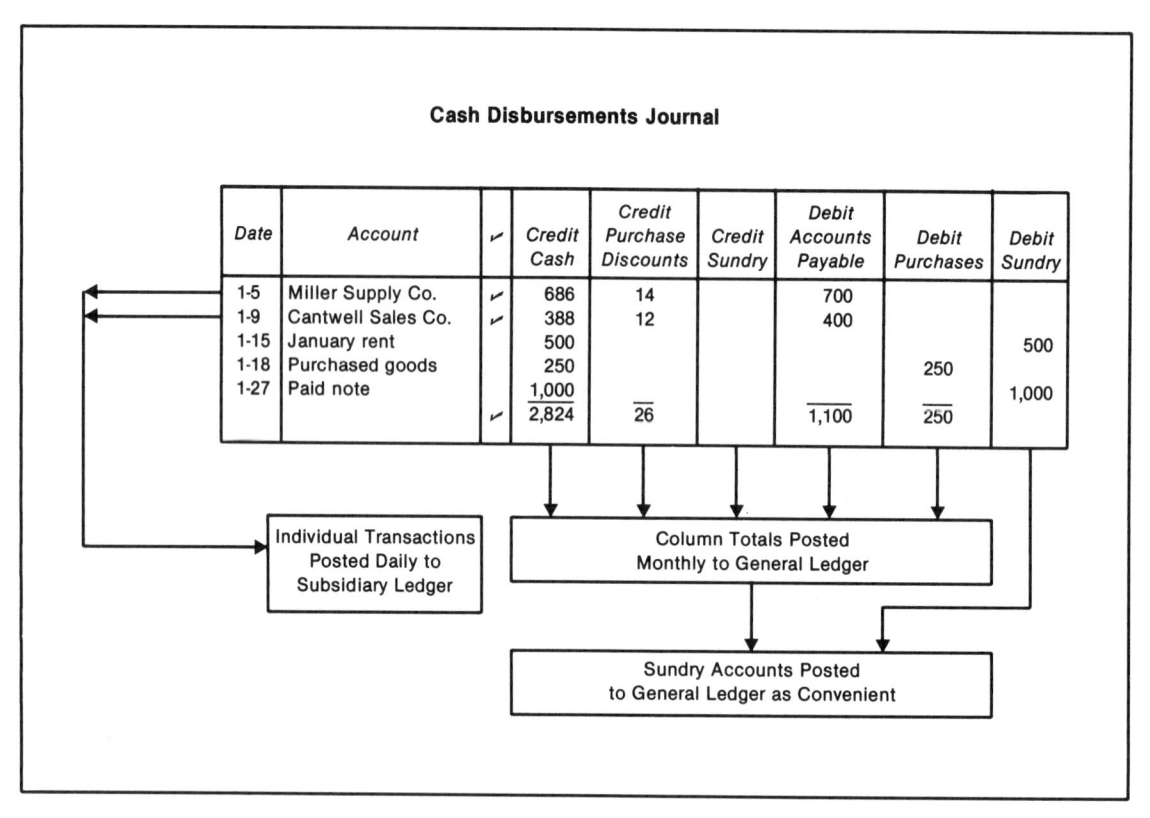

Cash Disbursements Journal

Date	Account	✓	Credit Cash	Credit Purchase Discounts	Credit Sundry	Debit Accounts Payable	Debit Purchases	Debit Sundry
1-5	Miller Supply Co.	✓	686	14		700		
1-9	Cantwell Sales Co.	✓	388	12		400		
1-15	January rent		500					500
1-18	Purchased goods		250				250	
1-27	Paid note		1,000					1,000
		✓	2,824	26		1,100	250	

Individual Transactions Posted Daily to Subsidiary Ledger

Column Totals Posted Monthly to General Ledger

Sundry Accounts Posted to General Ledger as Convenient

roll. Information for individual employees is posted to the separate payroll records maintained for each employee. These records are, in effect, subsidiary records for payroll from which various reports and tax returns are prepared and filed.

Purchases Journal. A purchases journal is very similar to the sales journal. Credit purchases are entered in the journal, with a notation made of such information as the date of purchase, the name of the vendor, date of the invoice, terms of the purchase, and the purchase amount. As individual purchases are made, they are recorded in the accounts payable subsidiary ledger which would include a separate account for each of the suppliers of the business. Periodically, the total amount of the purchases is posted as a debit to the purchases account and a credit to the accounts payable control account. At this time, the balance in the control account should be equal to the total of the balances in the accounts payable subsidiary ledger. This information included in the accounts payable subsidiary ledger is used for making decisions regarding future purchases from particular suppliers, for checking prices, for testing the accuracy of billings made by suppliers, etc.

An example of a purchases journal is shown below. This journal includes an entry for each credit purchase of merchandise made during the month.

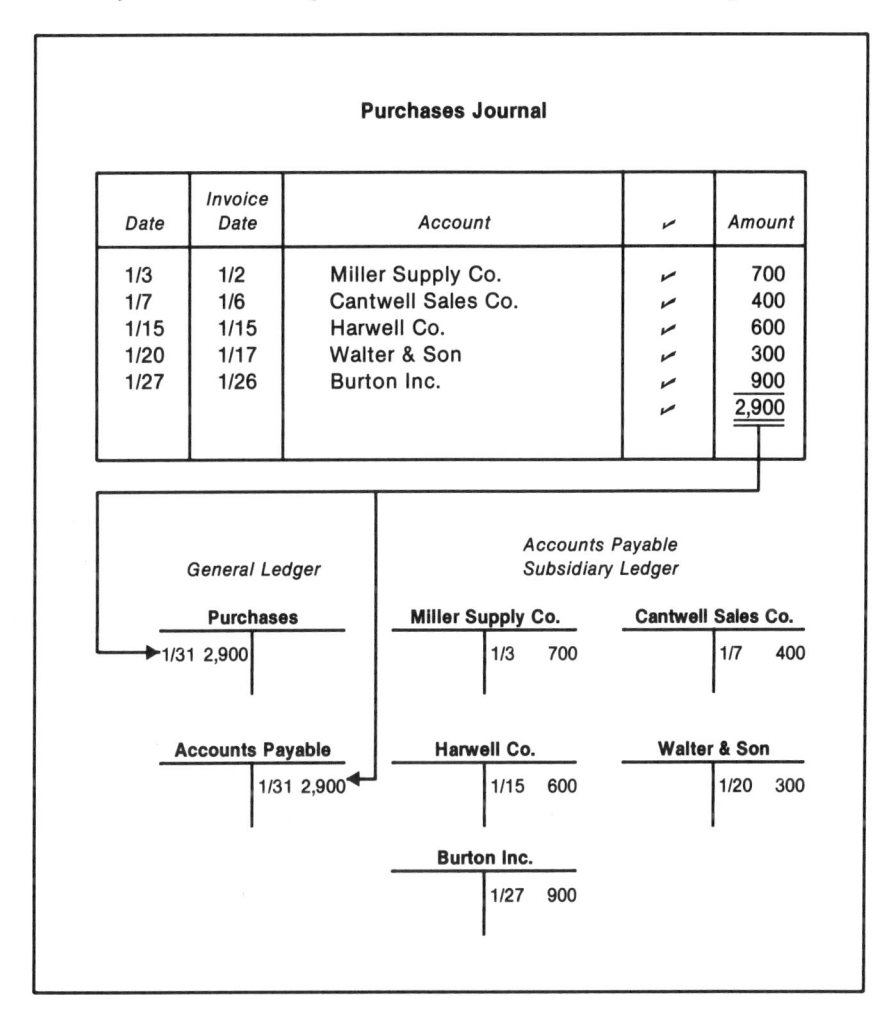

Purchases Journal

Date	Invoice Date	Account	✓	Amount
1/3	1/2	Miller Supply Co.	✓	700
1/7	1/6	Cantwell Sales Co.	✓	400
1/15	1/15	Harwell Co.	✓	600
1/20	1/17	Walter & Son	✓	300
1/27	1/26	Burton Inc.	✓	900
			✓	2,900

General Ledger

Purchases
1/31 2,900

Accounts Payable
1/31 2,900

Accounts Payable Subsidiary Ledger

Miller Supply Co.
1/3 700

Harwell Co.
1/15 600

Burton Inc.
1/27 900

Cantwell Sales Co.
1/7 400

Walter & Son
1/20 300

Form of Special Journals. There is no specified format for special journals nor is there any limit as to the number of types of special journals and subsidiary ledgers that are necessary. As mentioned previously, special journals and subsidiary ledgers should be designed so as to meet the individual needs of the particular company that will use them.

The check marks found in the special journals are made for purposes of control. The bookkeeper will check the transactions as he or she posts them to the appropriate ledger accounts.

Proving the Control Accounts

After all posting is completed for a period, the general ledger control accounts should be checked (often referred to as proved) against the balances in the corresponding subsidiary ledger accounts. This proof is usually made by preparing a schedule of the individual balances in the subsidiary ledger. The total of the individual balances must be equal to the balance in the corresponding control account; otherwise, an error has occurred in the accounting process.

Internal Accounting Control

Certain accounting controls are necessary within a business to safeguard the assets from waste, fraud, and inefficiency and to ensure the accuracy and reliability of the accounting data. Ideally, the system of internal control should provide assurance regarding the dependability of the accounting data relied upon in making business decisions. Generally, these accounting controls include a specified system of authorization and approval of transactions, separation of the recordkeeping and reporting functions from the duties concerned with asset custody and operations, physical control over assets, and internal auditing.

A subdivision of responsibility in a financial accounting system is necessary to provide adequate checks on the work of company personnel. When one transaction is handled from beginning to end by a single individual and that person makes an error, the mistake will probably be carried through in the mechanics of recording the transaction and will be very difficult to locate. On the other hand, if different aspects of a transaction are processed by different people, each acting on an independent basis, an error will be much more readily identifiable. Many of the errors that would have affected the accounts will never occur because the mistake may be identified and corrected on a timely basis.

A division of responsibility among employees is also necessary for control purposes. In a properly designed accounting system that has adequate division of duties, fraud and embezzlement should be very difficult and require the collusion of two or more people. However, even in a properly designed system, the possibility of errors and embezzlement cannot be completely eliminated.

The division of duties should, of course, be logically based on the desired purposes of the system. For example, the person who maintains the subsidiary ledger of accounts receivable should not have access to cash. This will prevent him or her from being able to manipulate the accounts receivable and retain the cash. Likewise, a single individual should not be given the responsibility of both approving purchases and then signing the checks that are used to pay for them. Payments made to nonexistent companies for fictitious purchases would be difficult to prevent if one person is able to approve both the purchase and the payment.

The goals of an effective system of accounting controls and the elements of such a system can be summarized as follows:

Goals:
1. Safeguard assets.
2. Ensure an efficient accounting system with reliable financial statements.

Subgoals:
1. Ensure that transactions are carried out according to management's policies.
2. Ensure that transactions are recorded as needed so that:
    a. Financial statements are prepared according to GAAP.
    b. Specific employees are held accountable for assets.
3. Ensure that only authorized individuals have access to assets.
4. Ensure accounting records agree with actual existing assets under company's control.

Emphasis on Transactions:
1. Ensure that transactions are properly authorized.
2. Ensure that transactions are properly executed.
3. Ensure that transactions are properly recorded.
4. Ensure that employees are accountable for assets acquired in transactions.

General Principles:
1. Competent and responsible employees.
2. Separation of duties.
3. Rotation of duties.
4. Rules for control of assets.
5. Well-designed source documents.
6. Internal auditing.

A system of internal control is frequently justified because it assists the business in the detection of errors and the prevention of embezzlement. Another major benefit of a system of internal control is that it provides an atmosphere and system which are deterrents to inefficient utilization of the company's resources, fraudulent conversion of assets, and inefficient and inaccurate handling of the company's accounts. Independent auditors also rely upon the system of internal controls in determining the extent and nature of their audit work. Many firms also have internal audit departments. The internal auditors are normally involved in evaluating and maximizing the effectiveness of the internal control system.

Ethical Issues in Accounting

Unfortunately, there are always inherent limitations in any system of internal control. One source of these limitations is human abilities, carelessness, fatigue, errors in judgment, misunderstanding of instructions, etc. Another source relates to the integrity of managers. Internal controls are only as effective as the integrity and competence of the individuals who develop, administer, and monitor these controls. Integrity must be based upon appropriate ethical values and it must be initiated by the senior management of a company and permeate the entire organization.

Serious questions have been raised concerning the activities and accountability of publicly-owned corporations as a result of unexpected failures and disclosures of questionable and illegal activities by management. Many believe that the emphasis on short-term results in our society—particularly as evidenced by the focus on reported income—is one of the greatest threats to ethical behavior in business. In a recent annual report of a large corporation, the chief executive officer wrote that "as long as investors—including supposedly sophisticated institutions—place fancy valuations on reported 'earnings' that march steadily upward, you can be sure that some managers and promoters will exploit GAAP (generally accepted accounting principles) to produce such numbers, no matter what the truth may be."

Deceptive financial reporting clearly decreases the value of financial reports to decision-makers. Such deception may be a result of either fraud or questionable, but not explicitly illegal, activities. Fraud represents an intentional manipulation of the financial data for the benefit of the perpetrator. Most fraudulent reporting practices cause an overstatement of assets and/or understatement of liabilities with a resulting positive effect on current income. Examples of fraudulent practices include recording transactions without substance (e.g., creating fictitious sales), failing to disclose information (e.g., concealing a significant decline in value of certain assets), or falsifying records or documents (e.g., changing invoice amounts to understate the amount of recorded expense).

A more frequent problem of deceptive reporting involves legal but unethical or questionable practices. Unfortunately, no precise definition has been developed to adequately differentiate between acceptable and unacceptable practices. Some of the practices which have been cited as questionable include:

1. Choosing the most liberal accounting method allowable under generally accepted accounting principles.

2. Changing accounting methods to increase reported income.

3. Timing the amounts of expenses or significant write-downs of assets (e.g., writing down assets in the fourth quarter or postponing write-downs until later periods.)

4. Changing judgments or estimates to manipulate reported income.

The primary cost of deceptive financial reporting is the suboptimal decisions made by those rely upon such information. Financial resources of the economy are not allocated effectively to the most deserving entities. Investors and lending institutions suffer losses as reported results depart from economic reality and disclosures of these abuses undermine both the integrity and the reliability of the entire corporate financial reporting process. Clearly, the ethical environment in business is critical to the well-being of our society.

There are obviously a number of factors which encourage fraudulent and questionable financial reporting practices. However, it is clear that there are also factors within the organization which influence the likelihood of such practices. Commonly, organizations evaluate and reward managerial performance on the basis of short-term results (e.g., income, sales). As salaries, bonuses, and even holding one's job are tied to short-term results, managers are often motivated to respond with fraudulent or questionable financial reporting practices. Moreover, lack of clear communication within the organization also contributes to questionable practices. In many instances, the mangers involved in questionable behavior either did not know what they were doing was wrong or inappropriately assumed that they were acting in the best interests of the organization.

In order to overcome the problems of conflicting incentives and misinformation, top management of a company must both provide ethical guidance by clearly written regulations. They must supply leadership and act as role models to communicate the message that the regulations are important. A National Commission on Fraudulent Reporting (1987) recommended that companies develop and implement codes of conduct. A documented code of conduct provides all employees with a common foundation in implementing the firm's ethical policies. To be effective, a code of conduct must be supported by top management, monitored continuously, and vigorously enforced. The internal audit function should incorporate reviews to assure compliance with the corporate goals and provide for corrective action for any deviations from the code.

The Audit Trail

An audit trail is the traceability factor that is built into an accounting system. It permits a person, normally an independent certified public accountant (referred to as an auditor), to follow the processing of a specific transaction from the beginning of the system described to the final output of the system. This procedure should also be reversible; that is, the final output of the system should be traceable back to the original source documentation that represents the transactions which caused the final output. An audit trail provides a path that can be followed in order to verify the accuracy with which transactions were handled as well as their legitimacy. The audit trail relies on a good system of internal control and documentation of transactions.

A flowchart of the purchase, receipt, payment, and use of office supplies for the Brown Grass Seed Company is presented on the following page. This flowchart describes both the internal control and audit trail for these types of transactions. Note that only three sets of forms are used: a purchase requisition, the invoice prepared by purchasing (which is the first of a series of invoices in this case), and the bill of lading and the invoice received from the vendor. Multiple copies of these documents are used by the business for internal control purposes. The entire transaction may be traced from the financial statements to any point in the accounting system.

Brown Grass Seed Company
Purchase Order Flows

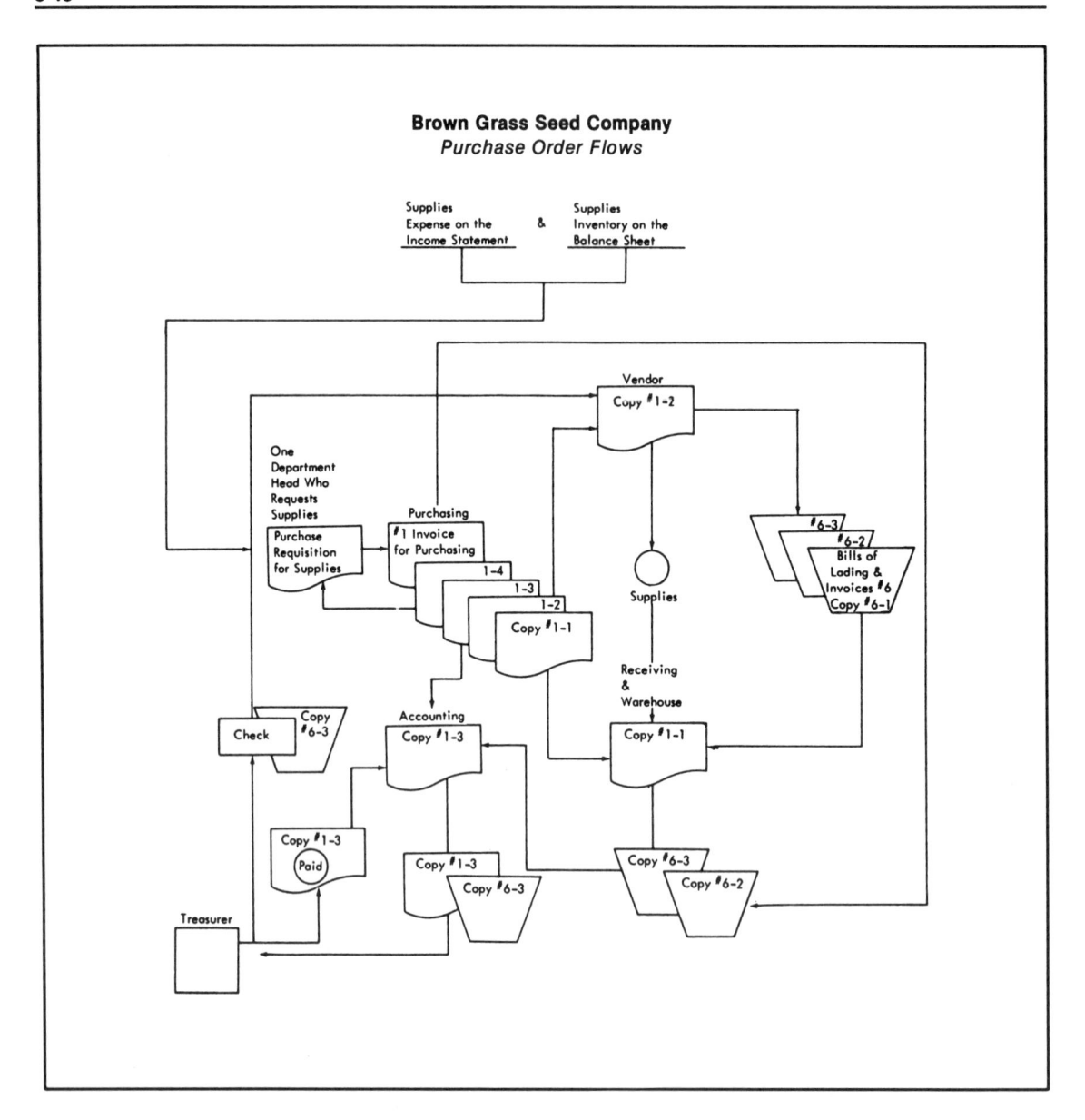

AUTOMATED ACCOUNTING SYSTEMS

The introduction of a computer system into the accounting function does not alter the data flow, but instead parallels the manual processing system. The computer system simply performs many functions that would be performed by people in a manual system. Any automated system will, however, affect the form of transaction documentation and other factors such as:

1. Methods of establishing source documents.
2. Methods of transmitting data.
3. Techniques of data preparation.
4. Amount of data handled.
5. Speed and accuracy.
6. Processing of the data.
7. Methods of data storage.
8. Methods of information retrieval.
9. Number of accounting reports used.
10. Types of controls necessary for adequate internal control.

The objective of any accounting information system (whether manual or automated) is to produce the financial information required by internal and external users. The basic components of any computer system are the "hardware" and appropriate "software."

Computer Hardware

Computer hardware is the equipment used to process the accounting information. Hardware can change from the very sophisticated and expensive system which possesses tremendous computing capability to the relatively simple and inexpensive system such as a personal computer which costs less than $2,000. In general, the equipment can be classified into three categories: mainframe computers, minicomputers, and microcomputers.

Mainframe computers are large-scale systems that would be used when a large volume of data needs to be processed rapidly. Minicomputers are much cheaper and less powerful. Minicomputers provide the computing capacity needed by many small to medium size companies which need the capability to process many transactions but do not necessarily need the power and efficiency of a mainframe computer.

A microcomputer is a system which is smaller than a minicomputer and could be used by a small business that does not have a large number of transactions to process. In many business firms, microcomputers are widely used in conjunction with mainframe or minicomputer systems. Selected data can be transferred between mainframe computers and microcomputers. Some tasks are better suited for microcomputers applications, such as spreadsheet analysis or word processing applications.

Computer Software

Computer software are the instructions that are developed to make the hardware perform the functions that are necessary to process transactions. The software controls the computer activities by instructing the hardware, in a step-by-step program, to perform a specific function. For example, in a payroll program (software) all the deductions from each person's paycheck (such as taxes and other payroll deductions) would have to be programmed and "read" into or made available to the computer. When each employee's hours and pay rate are entered, the program could calculate payroll deductions and, with the proper hardware, print the employees' checks. When a program is written to handle a specific application such as payroll or order handling or inventory, the programs for that application are usually called a software package. Software packages are available from most computer vendors to perform the usual accounting functions. In addition, a company can have a program "tailored" or written to their specifications when they have unique processing and/or control requirements.

SUMMARY

A financial accounting system must communicate economic information efficiently, effectively, accurately, and on a timely basis. Basic components of the system include: (1) a chart of accounts, (2) a coding system, (3) a general journal, (4) a general ledger, (5) special journals, (6) subsidiary ledgers, (7) a system of internal control, and (8) an audit trail.

A chart of accounts is a listing of all the accounts that may be used by a company. The basic design of the chart of accounts determines how accounting information will be accumulated, summarized, and used. A coding system is necessary for the chart of accounts to provide a unique identity for each account included in the chart of accounts. A general journal is used to record those transactions which occur on an infrequent basis. A general ledger contains the control accounts for the system. Special journals will be used for recording transactions which occur frequently. Subsidiary ledgers are supplemental detailed records which provide underlying support for the control accounts included in the general ledger. An effective system of internal control serves as a deterrent to the inefficient utilization of a company's resources; it discourages the fraudulent conversion of assets and the inefficient and inaccurate handling of a company's accounts. An audit trail is necessary to allow traceability of transactions after the fact.

The use of automated equipment in the financial accounting system does not alter the data flows in the system per se; but the equipment may cause significant changes in: (1) the source documents, (2) methods of transmitting data, (3) techniques of data preparation, (4) amount of data handled, (5) speed and accuracy, (6) processing of data, (7) methods of data storage, (8) methods of information retrieval, (9) the number of accounting reports used, and (10) the types of controls necessary for adequate internal control.

KEY DEFINITIONS

Audit trail—the traceable sequence of steps through which a transaction is processed from the beginning of the accounting system to the final output. The procedures and documentation should be clear so as to provide traceability from the output back to the original documents.

Cash disbursements journal—a special journal which may be used to record all expenditures of cash made by the business.

Cash receipts journal—a special journal which may be used to record all transactions involving the receipt of cash.

Chart of accounts—the list of all accounts that a company will use in conducting its business. It includes all accounts used in the preparation of the balance sheet, income statement, and statement of capital, and in addition, all accounts that management needs for planning and control purposes. The design of the chart of accounts will determine how the information will be gathered, summarized, and used in its accounting system.

Coding—the process of assigning a system of numbers to the various accounts included in the chart of accounts.

Coding dictionary—identifies an account with its coding number to simplify use of the coding system and the accounts.

Control account—a general ledger account which is supported by detailed information included in subsidiary accounts.

Internal control—comprises the plan of organization and all of the coordinate methods and measures adopted within a business to safeguard its assets, check the accuracy and reliability of its accounting data, promote operational efficiency, and encourage adherence to prescribed managerial policies.

Payroll journal—a specialized form of a cash disbursements journal used exclusively to record the payment of salaries and wages to employees.

Purchases journal—a special journal which may be used to record credit purchases.

Sales journal—a special journal which may be used to record credit sales.

Special journals—designed to record the type of transactions where there is a large volume of transactions that occur on a frequent basis. Special journals are often used for accounts receivable, accounts payable, and cash receipts and disbursements.

Subsidiary ledgers—a supplementary record which provides underlying support for control accounts which are included in the general ledger. A subsidiary ledger will include more detail than the related general ledger account, and the total of all subsidiary accounts will equal the balance of the applicable control account.

QUESTIONS

1. What is the purpose of the double-entry system of recording business transactions?

2. Explain the terms "debit" and "credit." What effect does each of these have on asset and liability accounts?

3. What is the general rule of the double-entry system?

4. Describe a general journal entry.

5. What is a T-account?

6. What is "posting"?

7. What is the purpose of a trial balance?

8. What concept of accounting requires adjusting entries? Explain.

9. What type of accounts do closing entries affect? Why are these accounts closed?

10. How is the adjusted trial balance prepared?

11. Which accounts are closed at the end of the period?

12. Are prepaid expenses reclassified as expenses in future periods? Why?

13. How is revenue which is collected before a business actually performs a service classified in the financial statements?

14. Explain the accrual basis of accounting.

EXERCISES

15. The first nine transactions of a newly formed business, Smart Company, appear in the T-accounts below. For each set of debits and credits, explain the nature of the transaction. Each entry is designated by the small letters to the left of the amount.

Cash		Accounts Receivable		Equipment
(a) 10,000	(c) 2,000	(d) 6,000	(g) 2,000	(b) 3,000
(g) 2,000	(e) 4,000			
(i) 2,500	(f) 1,000			
	(h) 1,500			

Accounts Payable		Unearned Fees
(f) 1,000	(b) 3,000	(i) 2,500

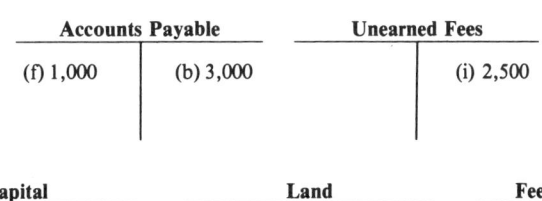

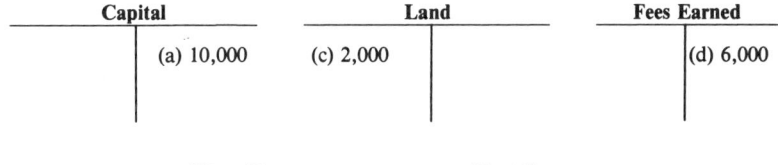

Capital		Land		Fees Earned
	(a) 10,000	(c) 2,000		(d) 6,000

Wage Expense		Rent Expense
(e) 4,000		(h) 1,500

16. Assume that the ledger accounts given in Exercise 15 are for the Smart Company as of December 31, 19x1. Prepare a trial balance for Smart Company as of that date.

17. Prepare the closing entries, the income statement for 19x1 and the balance sheet as of December 31, 19x1, for the Smart Company assuming the data given in Exercise 15.

18. Bob Feller opened a driving range and the following transactions took place in July, 19x1:

July 1   The owner invested $10,000 cash in the business.
     5   Purchased fixed assets for $5,000; made a cash down payment of $2,000 and signed a 60 day note for the balance.
     10 The total revenue for the month was $1,500; $1,200 in cash was collected and the balance was owed on account by customers.
     15 The total expenses for the month were $1,100; $900 was paid in cash and the balance was owed on account.
     25 The owner withdrew $100 in cash.

Required:

Prepare the journal entries to record these transactions and enter the debits and credits in T-accounts.

19. After recording and posting the transactions from Exercise 18, prepare a trial balance for Feller Company as of July 31, 19x1.

20. Given the following T-accounts, prepare the closing entries for the White Company for the month of August, 19x0.

Cash		Accounts Receivable		Supplies	
B.B. 20,000	1,100 (2)	B.B. 4,000	2,000 (1)	B.B. 800	1,000 (8)
(1) 2,000	5,000 (4)	(6) 7,000		(2) 1,100	
(3) 35,000	2,800 (5)				
	14,000 (9)				
	900 (10)				
	500 (11)				
32,700		9,000		900	

Note Payable		Unearned Fees		Capital	
(5) 2,800	2,800 B.B.	(7) 30,000	7,000 B.B.		15,000 B.B.
			35,000 (3)		
			12,000		15,000

Withdrawals		Fees Earned		Supplies Used	
(4) 5,000			7,000 (6)	(8) 1,000	
			30,000 (7)		
5,000			37,000	1,000	

Salaries		Utilities		Property Taxes	
(9) 14,000		(10) 900		(11) 500	
14,000		900		500	

21. Using the information in Exercise 20, prepare an After-Closing Trial Balance for White Company.

22. From the information given in Exercise 20, prepare a balance sheet, income statement, and statement of capital for White Company.

23. Prepare the journal entries for the Wicks Company for the month of December.

Dec. 1 Office supplies were purchased on credit for $5,000.
     3 A new machine was purchased for $15,000 cash.
     4 Revenues of $7,500 were received in advance of services being rendered.
     7 Services were performed on credit for $400.
     9 The bank loaned Wicks Company $10,000.
    12 Ivan Ingot invested $25,000 in the company.
    16 The $400 credit extended for services performed was collected.
    18 A remittance was sent for the office supplies.
    19 Services were performed for one-half of the revenues received in advance.
    21 Ivan Ingot withdrew $3,000 from the company.
    24 Performed services and collected amount due of $600 in cash.
    27 Repaid one-fourth of the bank loan.
    30 Salaries of $2,500 were paid to employees.

24. Post each journal entry in Exercise 23 to the appropriate ledger account and prepare closing entries.

25. Boyd Company purchased a two-year insurance policy on June 30 for $900 and recorded the transaction with a debit to the Prepaid Insurance account. Give the adjusting journal entry necessary to record the insurance that has expired as of December 31.

26. Below are the 19x1 adjusting entries for Branson Shoe Repairs.

a.	Supplies expense..	275	
	Supplies		275
b.	Rent expense..	500	
	Prepaid rent..		500
c.	Interest receivable...	150	
	Interest income...		150
d.	Wage expense...	75	
	Wages payable...		75
e.	Repair fees..	25	
	Unearned fees..		25
f.	Fees receivable..	33	
	Repair fees...		33

Give a possible explanation for each of the above adjusting entries.

27. Gardner Company leases a building to a client at a rental of $2,400 per year on June 1, 19x1. Give the required December 31, 19x1, adjusting entry on the books of Gardner Company under each of the following assumptions.

   a. The rent is paid in advance on June 1, 19x1, and is recorded by crediting Unearned Rent.
   b. The rent is paid in advance on June 1, 19x1, and is recorded by crediting Rental Income.
   c. The rent for the period of June 1, 19x1, to May 31, 19x2, is to be paid on May 30, 19x2.

28. Prepare the adjusting entries required at December 31, 19x1, in each of the following cases:

   a. Herman Company was assessed property taxes of $350 for 19x1. The taxes were due April 15, 19x2.
   b. Norton Company's payroll was $6,000 per month and wages were paid on the 15th of the following month. The company closes its books on December 31.
   c. Frazier Company has $3,000 of savings bonds. Interest receivable on these bonds was $180 at December 31.
   d. Foreman Company owns a building costing $30,000. $1,000 of the cost is to be allocated to expense in 19x1.

29. The income statement for 19x2 for the Lang Company reflected wage expense of $80,000. The year-end balances in the wages payable account were $10,000 at December 31, 19x1, and $12,000 at December 31, 19x2. Determine the amount of cash paid for salaries during 19x2.

30. Yestramski, Inc. signed a contract on June 30, 19x1 to rent a building for three years. The total contract price of $9,000 was paid on June 30, 19x1. Give the journal entry to record payment and the adjusting entries made on December 31, 19x1 and 19x2.

31. On March 30, 19x1 the Dandridge Company purchased a truck for $8,000 cash. The company planned an annual depreciation of $2,000. Give the journal entries to record the purchase of the truck and depreciation on December 31, 19x1 and December 31, 19x2.

32. Henderson Incorporated purchased $7,800 of office supplies on August 1. On December 31, it was determined that 35 percent of these supplies had been used. Prepare the journal entries for the initial purchase and the later adjustment. Prepare one set of entries assuming supplies are initially recorded as an asset and another assuming they are recorded as an expense.

33. The Kupchak Company is adjusting its accounts as of December 31. Make the adjusting entries for the following accounts:

   a. Depreciation on equipment is $2,000 for the year.
   b. Two years' rent was paid on January 1. The amount paid ($36,000) was debited to prepaid rent.
   c. Unpaid salaries as of December 31 were $9,000.
   d. Interest not yet received on an investment was $1,700.
   e. Unearned revenues were reduced by $4,500.

34. Below are two partial trial balances for the Bing Company, one before and the other after closing entries have been posted to the accounts as of December 31, 19x1. You are required to reconstruct the closing entries for December 31, 19x1.

	Before Closing	After Closing
Rent expense	$ 500	$ 0
Accounts receivable	2,200	2,200
Capital	350	2,600
Withdrawals	425	0
Fees for services	4,543	0
Income summary	0	0
Accounts payable	1,350	1,350
Insurance expense	110	0
Salaries expense	1,200	0
Prepaid insurance	25	25
Supplies used	58	0

PROBLEMS

35. Presented below are the transactions of the Home Finder Realty Company for the month of May, 19x1.

   May 1 The owner invested $20,000 cash in the business.
   3 Purchased office equipment for $1,800 on account.
   5 Purchased a car for $3,000, giving $1,000 in cash and a note payable of $2,000.
   10 Purchased $500 of office supplies on account.
   15 Paid $300 office rent for the month of May.
   16 Paid for office supplies purchased on May 10.
   18 Received a bill for $200 for radio advertising.
   20 Earned and collected $1,500 commission for the sale of a house.
   21 Paid bill for advertising that was received on May 18.
   23 Earned but did not collect an $800 commission.
   25 Paid salaries of $400.
   27 Received payment in full from customer of May 23.
   29 Paid the telephone bill, $50.

Required:

Prepare the general journal entries that would be required to record the above transactions.

36. On September 1, 19x1 Mark Walls, a bookkeeper, organized a bookkeeping service business. The following events occurred during September.

Sept. 1 Walls withdrew $10,000 from his personal savings and invested this amount in the business.
  2 Paid September rent of $250.
  4 Purchased office furniture for $2,000 on account.
  6 Received and paid a bill for $200 for advertising in the local newspaper.
  9 Received cash of $1,400 as payment for services to customers.
  15 Paid the $300 salary of a part-time secretary.
  17 Paid for office furniture purchased on account.
  18 Purchased $150 of office supplies on account.
  20 Received a utilities bill for $75.
  21 Completed $600 of services on credit for customers.
  23 Collected $200 of receivables for credit services provided.
  27 Walls withdrew $600 from the business.

Required:

1. Prepare the general journal entries to record the above transactions.
2. Post the above journal entries to T-accounts.
3. Prepare a trial balance as of the end of September.
4. Prepare closing entries.

37. The following transactions involving the Mantle Company occurred during the month of July, 19x1:

July 1 Mantle organized the company, contributing $1,000 as an initial investment.
  3 Purchased office supplies paying $100 in cash.
  6 Performed services for his first customer and collected $500 in cash.
  9 Performed services for another customer and agreed to accept his payment of $700 later in the month.
  13 Contracted to perform certain services for a third customer and received the full payment of $1,000 in advance.
  18 Received the payment from the customer for whom services were performed on July 9.
  24 Paid the following operating items:

  Salaries for July.......................... $250
  Office rent for July and August............ 300
  Other July expense......................   75

(Mantle will prepare financial statements at the end of July.)
  31 Noted that exactly one-fourth of the services contracted for on the thirteenth by a customer had been performed. Counted the office supplies on hand and ascertained that supplies with an original cost of $65 were still on hand.

Required:

1. Record the above transactions with general journal entries.
2. Post the journal entries by entering debits and credits in T-accounts.
3. Prepare a trial balance as of July 31, 19x1.
4. Prepare closing entries.

38. Below is the trial balance of the Nittany Lion Company as of October 31, 19x1.

Cash	$10,000	
Accounts receivable	4,000	
Notes receivable	2,500	
Supplies	1,000	
Accounts payable		$ 4,500
Note payable		3,000
Unearned revenue		1,500
Capital		7,500
Withdrawals	500	
Revenues		3,000
Expenses	1,500	
	$19,500	$19,500

Required:

1. Prepare the entries which are necessary to close the accounts as of October 31, 19x1.
2. Prepare the following statements:

   a. Balance sheet
   b. Income statement
   c. Statement of capital

39. Certain data relating to River Corporation are presented below:

Trial balance data as of June 30, 19x1.

Advertising expense	$ 75
Capital	3,195
Cash	895
Commissions earned	1,900
Commissions receivable	950
Interest earned	5
Land	2,000
Mercantile Company bonds	1,000
Notes payable	700
Office rent	80
Salaries expense	800

Adjusted trial balance data as of June 30, 19x1.

Accrued interest receivable	5
Accrued interest payable	7
Accrued rent receivable	55
Accrued salaries payable	100
Advertising expense	75
Capital	3,195
Cash	895
Commissions earned	1,960
Commissions receivable	1,010
Interest earned	10
Interest expense	7
Land	2,000
Mercantile Company bonds	1,000
Notes payable	700
Office rent	80
Rent earned	55
Salaries expense	900

Required:

Compare the unadjusted and adjusted account balances and prepare the adjusting journal entries made by River Corporation as of June 30, 19x1. Also prepare the closing entries as of June 30, 19x1. (No withdrawals were made during the period ending June 30, 19x1.)

40. The following information has been developed by the bookkeeper of the Sneed Company. It relates to the company's operations for 19x1.

Cash receipts		
From customers..............................	$46,100	
Cash disbursements		
For expenses................................	10,600	
Account balances as of December 31	*19x0*	*19x1*
Accounts receivable from customers, (all collectible).	$10,400	$9,600
Accrued expenses payable......................	1,900	1,600

Required:

Prepare the company's income statement for the year ended December 31, 19x1.

41. On June 30, 19x1, the Repertory Theater Co. was organized. On that date the owners invested $25,000 in cash and the company manager signed a 10-year lease on a building. The lease called for a monthly rental of $4,000. The first payment under the lease was made immediately; all future rentals were to be paid on the last day of each month. The theater capacity was 800 seats which were to be sold for $3 at each performance. A 3-year comprehensive insurance policy was paid for on July 1, 19x1, at a cost of $600.

The theater opened on August 1, 19x1. There were 8 performances each week (each evening Monday through Saturday and matinees on Wednesday and Saturday). Through December 31, 19x1, there had been exactly 22 full weeks of performances. The player companies who were engaged to perform received 40 percent of the gate with settlement to be made after each Saturday evening performance for the 8 performances of the week then ending. At the beginning of the 19th week of business a smash hit opened. This show played to capacity crowds and was sold out through the first 7 weeks of 19x2.

A refreshment counter in the lobby dispensed soft drinks, candy, etc., and proved to be most lucrative. This was the only source of revenue other than ticket sales. Refreshments with an invoice cost of $19,000 had been purchased during 19x1. The inventory of refreshments on hand at December 31, 19x1, had an invoice price of $2,200. All purchases had been paid for except one made on December 27, 19x1, at a cost of $1,200.

Prior to the opening of the smash hit, the theater enjoyed good success, averaging exactly 75 percent of capacity of all performances. All receipts during the year had been deposited intact and deposit slips showed a total of $517,400 deposited through December 31, 19x1.

Salaries for ushers, ticket-takers, the manager, and other employees were paid after each Friday evening performance for work done through that performance. These salaries averaged $900 per week. Advertising had been run in local newspapers and $2,900 had been paid for as of December 31, 19x1. The bill for ads run during the last week of 19x1 had not been received by

December 31, but based upon knowledge of the rates it was estimated that it would be $150. Utilities bills through December 31 totaled $2,700 and had been paid.

There were no liabilities at December 31, 19x1, other than those which have been specifically mentioned or alluded to above. No additional investments by the owners had been made and no withdrawals were made.

Required:

1. A statement of financial position as of December 31, 19x1.
2. An income statement for the six months ended December 31, 19x1.

42. Following are given the *total debits* and *total credits* for the year (which include beginning-of-the-year balances) in certain accounts of the Ace Company, *after the closing entries have been posted to the accounts* as of December 31, 19x1.

	Debits	Credits
Advertising expense	$ 210	$ 210
Salaries expense	700	700
Telephone expense	48	48
Prepaid insurance	90	15
Insurance expense	15	15
Fees earned	1,880	1,880
Drawings	600	600
Income summary	1,880	1,880
Accounts receivable	2,330	2,330
Capital	600	19,257

Required:

Reconstruct the December 31, 19x1, *closing entries* (in general journal form).

43. Given the following T-accounts, prepare the following items for the Cowens Company for the month of January, 19x1:

a. Closing entries
b. After-closing trial balance
c. Balance sheet
d. Income statement
e. Statement of capital

Cash		Accounts Receivable	
25,000	(1) 3,500	11,710	(2) 4,700
(2) 4,700	(3) 2,300	(7) 1,000	
(4) 12,000	(5) 9,000	8,010	
	(6) 1,000		
25,900			

Note Payable		Supplies	
(1) 3,500	3,800	1,090	
	300	(3) 2,300	(8) 1,900
		1,490	

Unearned Fees		Fees Earned	
(9) 7,000	4,000		(7) 1,000
	(4) 12,000		(9) 7,000
	9,000		8,000

Capital		Withdrawals	
	30,000	(6) 1,000	
	30,000	1,000	

Salaries		Supplies Used	
(5) 9,000		(8) 1,900	
9,000		1,900	

44. Given the following data for the Havlicek Company for March, 19x1, prepare the following items:

a. Adjusting entries
b. Closing entries
c. Income statements
d. Statement of capital
e. Balance sheet

Havlicek Company
Trial Balance Before Adjustment
March 31, 19x1

	Debit	Credit
Cash	$57,000	
Accounts receivable	4,500	
Supplies	2,000	
Note payable		$ 7,000
Unearned fees		20,000
Capital		33,000
Withdrawals	2,000	
Earned fees		12,000
Salaries	6,500	
	$72,000	$72,000

Additional data:

1. Supplies on hand at the end of March were $1,500.
2. Unearned fees decreased by $10,000 in March.

45. Presented below are the transactions of the Goodson Realty Company for the month of June, 19x1.

June 2 The owner invested $15,000 cash in the business.
     5 Purchased office furniture for $1,500 cash.
     7 Paid $300 in cash for June rent.
     9 Office supplies of $200 were purchased on account.
    10 Received and paid a bill for $300 for advertising in a local newspaper during June.
    13 Paid wages of $200 in cash for the month of June.
    15 Received a cash advance of $500 from a customer for services to be rendered during July.
    16 Sold a house and collected $800 commission.
    17 Sold a house and will collect the $600 commission in July.
    21 The owner withdrew $500 from the business.
    23 Received and paid the June telephone bill for $100.
    25 Paid for office supplies purchased on June 9.
    27 Paid the utilities bill for the month, $35.

Required:

Prepare the general journal entries necessary to record the above transactions.

46. On August 1, 19x1, Bill King began operating a bicycle repair shop. The transactions of the business during the month of August were as follows:

Aug. 2 King began the business by investing $15,000 in cash and repair equipment with a fair value of $2,000.
     4 Purchased land for $4,000 cash.
     7 Purchased a building for $20,000. The terms of the purchase required a cash payment of $5,000 and the issuance of a note payable for $15,000.
    11 Purchased supplies on account in the amount of $700.
    13 Completed repair work for customers and collected $700 cash.
    15 Paid the $400 salary of an employee.
    17 Completed repair work of $500 on credit.
    19 Paid for supplies purchased on account.
    21 Withdrew $300 from the business to be used for personal expenses.
    25 Received $500 cash for repair work previously completed.
    27 Paid a $50 utility bill.
    30 Made first payment of $1,000 on the note payable.

Required:

1. Prepare the general journal entries to record each of the above transactions.
2. Post the above journal entries to T-accounts.
3. Prepare a trial balance as of the end of August.
4. Prepare closing entries.

47. Below is given certain data relating to the operations of Maxwell Company for the year ended December 31, 19x1.

Trial balance data as of December 31, 19x1:

	Before Adjustment	After Adjustment
Advertising expense..................	$ 210	$ 210
Salaries expense.....................	700	750
Accrued salaries payable.............	0	50
Telephone expense...................	48	58
Accrued telephone expenses payable.....	54	64
Capital............................	19,350	19,350
Land..............................	5,600	5,600
Cash..............................	365	365
Prepaid insurance...................	90	55
Fees earned........................	1,880	1,960
Insurance expense...................	30	65
Unearned fees......................	175	95
Withdrawals.......................	600	600
Accounts receivable.................	2,330	2,330

Required:

Prepare adjusting entries as of December 31, 19x1 by comparing the above data. Also, prepare the closing entries as of December 31, 19x1.

48. The Maryland Wholesale Company has kept no formal books of accounts. The owner has, however, made up a statement of assets and liabilities at the end of each year. For 19x1 and 19x2, a portion of this statement appears as follows, as of December 31:

	19x1	19x2
Cash...........................	$3,000	$ 5,000
Accounts receivable...............	7,000	5,000
Accounts payable for expenses......	8,000	10,000

An analysis of the checkbook for 19x2 shows (1) deposits of all amounts received from customers totaling $50,000 and (2) cash payments to creditors for expenses amounting to $33,000.

Required:

Prepare the company's income statement for the year ended December 31, 19x2.

49. On January 1, 19x1, the Rowe Realty Company began operations. On that date, Rowe executed a contract for the purchase of five apartment buildings costing $30,000 each. Rowe paid $40,000 of the total purchase price and gave a mortgage note payable for the balance. This note was to be paid in equal installments of $10,000 due each December 31. In addition to the $10,000 principal payment, Rowe must also pay interest of $1,000 each year on December 31.

Additional information:

1. Each apartment building consisted of 24 apartments, each apartment renting for $150 a month including all utilities. During the year, every apartment was rented for the full 12 months, and all rent had been collected to date. Cash receipts were immediately deposited in a checking account when collected, and all cash disbursements were made by check.
2. Salaries for the year consisted of $200 per week for maintenance and $10,000 per year for the apartment manager. Utilities expense paid by Rowe Realty amounted to an average of $500 per month for six months out of the year and $700 for the other six months. Property taxes paid were $6,000. Other expenses paid were $3,500.
3. All expenses have been paid to date and there have been no additional investments or withdrawals made by Rowe.

Required:

1. An income statement for the year ended December 31, 19x1.
2. A balance sheet as of December 31, 19x1.

50. The following information for adjustments was available at December 31, the end of the accounting period. Prepare the necessary adjusting entry for each item of information.

a. Annual office rent of $1,200 was paid on July 1, when the lease was signed. This amount was recorded as prepaid rent.
b. The office supplies account had a $100 balance at the beginning of the year and $600 of office supplies were purchased during the year. An inventory of unused supplies at the end of the year indicated that $150 of supplies were still on hand.
c. Wages earned by employees during December but not yet paid amounted to $700 on December 31.
d. The company subleased part of its office space at a rental of $50 per month. The tenant occupied the space on September 1 and paid six months rent in advance. This amount paid was credited to the unearned rent account.
e. Equipment was purchased on January 1 for $5,000. The useful life was estimated to be ten years with no salvage value.
f. Services provided for clients which were not chargeable until January amounted to $800. No entries had yet been made to record these earned revenues.

51. From the information given below concerning the College Inn Ski Resort, prepare the adjusting entries required at December 31, 19x1.

a. Accrued property taxes at December 31, 19x1, were $500.
b. Accrued wages payable at December 31, 19x1, were $2,400.
c. Interest receivable on United States government bonds owned at December 31, 19x1, was $75.
d. A tractor had been obtained on October 31 from Equipment Rentals, Inc., at a daily rate of $4. No rental payment had yet been made. Continued use of the tractor was expected through the month of January.
e. A portion of the land owned by the resort had been leased to a riding stable at a yearly rental of $3,600. One year's rent was collected in advance at the date of the lease (November 1) and credited to Unearned Rental Revenue.
f. Another portion of the land owned had also been rented on October 1 to a service station operator at an annual rate of $1,200. No rent had as yet been collected from this tenant.
g. On December 31, the College Inn Ski Resort signed an agreement to lease a truck from Gray Drive Ur-Self Company for the next calendar year at a rate of 10 cents for each mile of use. The Resort estimates that they will drive this truck for about 1,000 miles per month.
h. On September 1, the Company purchased a three-year fire insurance policy for $360. At the time the policy was acquired, the Company debited insurance expense and credited cash.

52. Below is given the September 30, 19x1, trial balance *before* adjustment of the Cavilier Company.

Cavilier Company
Trial Balance
September 30, 19x1

Cash	$ 2,700	
Supplies	1,250	
Prepaid rent	1,800	
Land	10,000	
Accounts payable		$ 3,500
Fees received in advance		2,500
Capital		7,250
Drawings	500	
Commissions earned		5,800
Fees earned		2,200
Wages and salaries expense	4,000	
Utilities expense	550	
Miscellaneous expense	450	
	$21,250	$21,250

Other data:

1. Supplies on hand at the end of September totaled $750.
2. In accordance with the terms of the lease, the annual rental of $1,800 was paid in advance on April 1, 19x1.
3. Wages and salaries earned by employees but unpaid at September 30, 19x1, amounted to $450.
4. Of the balance in the Fees Received in Advance account, $1,500 had not been earned as of September 30, 19x1.
5. On September 1, 19x1, Cavilier Company rented certain equipment to the Alpha Fraternity under the following terms: $50 per month payable on the first day of each month following the start of the rental arrangement.

Required:

Prepare all journal entries necessary to: (1) adjust the accounts and (2) close the books as of September 30, 19x1.

53. Given below is the trial balance before adjustment and the adjusted trial balance for Doak Company at December 31, 19x1.

Doak Company
Trial Balance and Adjusted Trial Balance
December 31, 19x1

	Trial Balance		Adjusted Trial Balance	
Cash	$ 3,000		$ 3,000	
Accounts receivable	2,500		2,500	
Rent receivable	0		200	
Prepaid insurance	1,000		600	
Supplies	1,200		400	
Office furniture	3,000		3,000	
Accumulated depreciation—office furniture		$ 900		$ 1,200
Land	7,000		7,000	
Accounts payable		1,500		1,500
Notes payable		2,000		2,000
Interest payable		0		100
Unearned fees		800		300
Wages payable		0		600
Withdrawals	500		500	
Capital		9,000		9,000
Service fees		10,000		10,500
Rental income		600		800
Wage expense	6,000		6,600	
Insurance expense	0		400	
Depreciation expense	0		300	
Interest expense	100		200	
Supplies expense	0		800	
Other expenses	500		500	
	$24,800	$24,800	$26,000	$26,000

Prepare the adjusting journal entries made by Doak Company on December 31, 19x1. Prepare the closing entries as of December 31, 19x1.

54. Below is the trial balance for the Martin Company:

Martin Company
Trial Balance
December 31, 19x1

Cash	$ 800	
Notes receivable	2,500	
Prepaid insurance	750	
Land	21,000	
Service revenue received in advance		$ 3,500
Mortgage payable		5,000
Capital		14,700
Commissions earned		9,000
Salaries expense	6,500	
Miscellaneous expense	650	
	$32,200	$32,200

Data for adjustments:

a. Accrued salaries at December 31, 19x1, were $220.
b. Accrued interest on the mortgage at December 31, 19x1, was $250.
c. At year-end, one-half of the service revenue received in advance had been earned.
d. Insurance expense for 19x1 was $375.
e. Accrued interest on the notes receivable at December 31, 19x1, was $20.

Required:

1. Prepare the adjusting and closing journal entries for Martin Company at December 31, 19x1.
2. Prepare an income statement for the year and the balance sheet as of December 31, 19x1.

55. As chief accountant for Ford Company, it is your job to prepare end-of-period financial statements for the firm. You had an assistant prepare the following unadjusted trial balance from the books of the company.

Ford Company
Trial Balance
December 31, 19x1

Cash	$ 1,100	
Accounts receivable	800	
Prepaid insurance	900	
Office furniture	4,000	
Accumulated depreciation—		
office furniture		$ 400
Land	8,000	
Accounts payable		900
Unearned revenues		1,500
Note payable		2,500
Capital		9,600
Withdrawals	400	
Service revenues		4,100
Rent expense	600	
Salaries expense	1,000	
Supplies expense	2,000	
Other expenses	200	
	$19,000	$19,000

The following information was also gathered from the books of the Ford Company:

a. The company paid $900 for a three-year insurance policy on June 30, 19x1.
b. The office furniture was purchased January 1, 19x0, and is expected to have a 10-year life and no salvage value. Depreciation for 19x1 has not been recorded.
c. The unearned revenues account was created when Ford Company was paid $1,500 for services to be rendered. One-third of these services were rendered on December 1, 19x1.
d. Interest of $20 has accrued on the note payable at December 31.
e. Ford Company paid $600 on August 1 as annual rent for its warehouse. This amount was debited to rent expense.
f. $100 of salaries have been earned by employees but not yet paid or recorded on the books.
g. Supplies on hand at December 31 had a cost of $500.

Required:

1. Prepare the adjusting and closing entries for Ford Company at December 31, 19x1.
2. Prepare the company's balance sheet, income statement, and statement of capital.

56. Given below is a trial balance before adjustment for Unseld Company.

Unseld Company
Trial Balance Before Adjustment
December 31, 19x3

Cash	$ 2,500	
Accounts receivable	1,600	
Notes receivable	2,100	
Office furniture	3,000	
Accumulated depreciation—office furniture		$ 300
Accounts payable		1,800
Unearned fees		425
Capital		5,900
Withdrawals	360	
Service fees		2,050
Rent income		350
Supplies expense	800	
Insurance expense	115	
Wage expense	350	
	$10,825	$10,825

On December 31, the accountant for Unseld Company found several items which he thought needed adjustment in the preparation of the worksheet. Below are listed these items which may or may not need adjustment.

a. The office furniture which was purchased on January 1, 19x1 is being depreciated over a 20-year life with no salvage value.
b. Wages for the last week of the year amounted to $50 which would not be paid until January 6, 19x4.
c. Unearned fees worth $200 will be earned as of December 31, and the rest will be earned in January.
d. Insurance of $100 was unexpired as of December 31.
e. Supplies worth $500 were on hand at the end of the year.
f. Accrued interest on notes receivable amounts to 6 percent of the ending notes receivable balance.
g. Rental income earned but not yet received included $200 for the month of November and $100 for December.

Required:

Prepare the adjusting and closing journal entries as of December 31, 19x3 for Unseld Company.

57. Given below is a trial balance before adjustment for Holmes Company.

Adjusting Entries

	Dr.	Cr.
(a) Interest receivable	20	
Interest income		20
(b) Supplies	250	
Supplies expense		250
(c) Prepaid insurance	600	
Insurance expense		600
(d) Depreciation expense—office furniture	200	
Accumulated depreciation—office furniture		200
(e) Unearned fees	200	
Service fees		200
(f) Rent income	100	
Unearned rent		100

Closing Entries

	Dr.	Cr.
(1) Service fees	2,200	
Rent income	200	
Interest income	20	
Income Summary		2,420
(2) Income Summary	2,350	
Supplies expense		1,250
Insurance expense		300
Wage expense		600
Depreciation expense		200
(3) Income Summary	70	
Capital		70
(4) Capital	400	
Withdrawals		400

58. The trial balance of the Aggie Company as of September 30, 19x1, was as follows:

Aggie Company
Trial Balance
September 30, 19x1

Cash...................................	$ 6,000	
Supplies................................	500	
Prepaid rent...........................	900	
Land...................................	8,500	
Accounts payable......................		$ 4,000
Unearned revenues.....................		1,050
Capital................................		10,000
Withdrawals...........................	1,000	
Commissions earned...................		10,100
Salaries expense.......................	7,500	
Miscellaneous expense.................	750	
	$25,150	$25,150

Other financial data:

a. The cost of supplies on hand at the end of September was $100.
b. In accordance with the terms of its lease, the company paid its annual rent of $900 on September 1.
c. Salaries earned by employees but not paid as of September 30, 19x1 totaled $500.
d. Of the balance in the unearned revenues account, $450 had not been earned as of September 30, 19x1.
e. Included in the miscellaneous expense account was the cost of a fire insurance policy purchased on August 31, 19x1, at a cost of $180. The policy expires on August 31, 19x3.

Required:

Prepare adjusting journal entries for the above data. Prepare closing entries.

59. Below is given a trial balance before and after adjustment for Bonham Company at December 31, 19x1.

Bonham Company
Trial Balance Before Adjustment
December 31, 19x1

Cash	$ 800	
Accounts receivable	1,100	
Prepaid insurance	600	
Supplies	2,250	
Office furniture	2,500	
Accumulated depreciation— office furniture		$ 500
Land	4,000	
Accounts payable		700
Unearned fees		750
Note payable		2,000
Capital		5,450
Withdrawals	150	
Service fees		3,750
Rent income		200
Salaries expense	1,200	
Other expenses	750	
	$13,350	$13,350

Bonham Company
Trial Balance After Adjustment
December 31, 19x1

Cash	$ 800	
Accounts receivable	1,100	
Rent receivable	200	
Prepaid insurance	300	
Supplies	750	
Office furniture	2,500	
Accumulated depreciation— office furniture		$ 1,000
Land	4,000	
Accounts payable		775
Interest payable		20
Unearned fees		500
Unearned rent		50
Note payable		2,000
Capital		5,450
Withdrawals	150	
Service fees		4,000
Rent income		350
Salaries expense	1,200	
Advertising expense	75	
Insurance expense	300	
Depreciation expense	500	
Interest expense	20	
Supplies expense	1,500	
Other expenses	750	
	$14,145	$14,145

Required:

Prepare the adjusting entries for Bonham Company for 19x1. Also, prepare closing entries.

Refer to the Annual Report included in the front of the text.

60. Which account *does not* appear in the financial statements, but *is* used in the closing process?

61. Using a T-account, show how retained earnings changed from the previous year to the current year.

62. Using the totals from net cash provided by continuing operations, net cash used for investing activities, net cash provided by financing activities, and effect of exchange rate changes, show in T-account form how cash and cash equivalents decreased from $186.7 million at the end of 1991 to $169.9 million at the end of 1992.

63. From the information presented in the income statement, create the Income Summary account and show how it was closed out.

64. Did accrued expenses increase or decrease in the most recent year?

Chapter 4 discusses the accounting for a company that sells a product and the alternative methods of accounting for inventory. Studying this chapter should enable you to:

1. Illustrate the accounting for a retailing firm.
2. Discuss the components of inventory cost, including purchase discounts, freight-in, returns, and allowances.
3. Distinguish between periodic and perpetual inventory methods.
4. Explain the concept of cost allocation.
5. Distinguish between product and period costs.
6. Describe basic inventory control procedures.
7. Discuss the objective of inventory accounting.
8. Identify the primary cost basis used in accounting for inventories and describe the elements of this cost.
9. Discuss inventory cost flow methods and the basic assumption each makes.
10. Explain the concept of lower of cost or market as it relates to inventories.
11. Apply the retail and gross profit methods of estimating inventory costs.

4

Merchandising Transactions and Inventories

INTRODUCTION　　The preceding chapters have illustrated the basic steps of the complete accounting cycle for Kilmer Contractors, a firm rendering personal services. The income of a service business is equal to the excess of its revenues (i.e., its fees, commissions, etc.) earned for the services it provides over the expenses which were incurred by the company in rendering these services. Service companies, such as travel agencies, hotels and airlines, are responsible for a significant dollar volume of business in our economy. However, the majority of businesses in the United States are engaged in selling products. Businesses which earn revenues by selling products may be either merchandising firms or manufacturing companies. Merchandising companies, both wholesalers and retailers, acquire merchandise in ready-to-sell condition, whereas manufacturing companies acquire input materials and produce a product for sale. In contrast to a service type business, the net income of a merchandising or manufacturing company results when the revenues earned from selling products exceed the total of the cost of goods sold and the operating expenses.

While many of the accounting concepts discussed previously are also applicable to product oriented companies, there are certain additional techniques required to account for the purchase and sale of products.

ACCOUNTING FOR MERCHANDISING OPERATIONS

Accounting for Cost of Goods Sold

The cost of merchandise sold during the period is included in the income statement as an expense referred to as the cost of goods sold. The merchandise which was available for sale but which was not sold during the period is referred to as inventory on hand at the end of the year. The cost of this inventory is included in the balance sheet as an asset.

There are two general methods of recordkeeping which are used in accounting for inventories: the periodic and the perpetual inventory methods. The basic difference between these two methods is in the timing of the recording of the cost of goods sold for the period.

Under the periodic method, the cost of goods sold is determined at the end of the period by making a physical count of the goods on hand and subtracting the cost of the goods which are still on hand from the total cost of goods which were available for sale. Using the perpetual method, an entry recording the cost of goods sold is usually made at the time of the sale. A physical inventory is still taken, either at the end of the year or periodically during the year, and the inventory amounts on the books are then adjusted, if necessary, in order to reflect the cost of the actual goods which are on hand. The perpetual inventory method is most appropriate for a business which has only a limited number of sales each day. In such a case, it would not be difficult to determine the cost of each item sold and to record the specific cost of goods sold expense at the time of the sales transaction. However, in a business with a high volume of sales and/or a variety of merchandise items, it may not be practical to record the cost of each item sold at the time the sale is made. Instead, the periodic method could be used by taking a physical count of goods on hand at the end of the period to determine the cost of goods sold. To illustrate the application of accounting for merchandising operations, assume that Kilmer Contractors decided to expand its decorating operations by selling carpet to its customers in addition to its painting activities. Recall that its balance sheet at May 31, 19x1, was as follows:

Kilmer Contractors
Balance Sheet
May 31, 19x1

Assets		Liabilities and Owner's Equity	
Cash	$2,400	Note payable	$3,000
Accounts receivable	900	Unearned fees	2,200
Supplies	2,000	Capital	100
	$5,300		$5,300

Cost of Merchandise Purchased

The cost of items purchased for resale is debited to a purchases account. This purchases account is used to accumulate the cost of all merchandise acquired for resale during an accounting period. To illustrate, assume that on June 1, the company purchased 1,000 square yards of carpet, paying $5 per yard in cash. The journal entry to record the purchase of this carpet would be as follows:

> Purchases 5,000
> Cash 5,000

This transaction represents an exchange of one asset for another (i.e., cash for inventory). The debit to the purchases account records the acquisition of the carpet, and the credit to cash indicates the cash expenditure. Because the carpet has not been sold, its cost is considered an asset and not reclassified as an expense until the period the carpet is sold. Under the periodic inventory system, the purchases account accumulates the total cost of merchandise purchased during the period. Therefore, the balance in the purchases account during the period does not normally indicate whether the goods purchased during the period are still on hand or were sold.

Sales of Merchandise

When a business sells merchandise to its customers, it either receives immediate payment in cash or acquires a receivable from its customer which will be collected in cash at a future date. In this illustration, assume that during the month of June, Kilmer sold 800 square yards of this carpet at a selling price of $9 per yard. These sales would be recorded as follows, assuming that they were made for cash:

> Cash 7,200
> Sales 7,200

This transaction was a sale of a product for cash. The debit to the cash account records the increase in cash, and the credit to sales records the total amount of revenue generated from the sale of the carpet. If this sale had been made on a credit basis, the entry would have been a debit to accounts receivable and a credit to sales.

Determination of Cost of Goods Sold and Net Income

To continue our illustration, we will assume that the only expense (other than the cost of the carpet itself) incurred by Kilmer Contractors during the month of June was the payment of salaries to the crew which was hired to install carpet. This outlay of $1,500 would be recorded as follows:

> Salaries expense.................... 1,500
> Cash 1,500

This journal entry reflects the fact that period expenses of $1,500 were incurred and paid in cash. This cost is a period cost since it cannot be associated with the purchase or manufacture of a product and since the benefits were obtained by the firm from this outlay (that is, installation of the carpet sold) during the current accounting period.

The next step in the recording process would be to post the journal entries to appropriate ledger accounts in order to summarize the transactions which have occurred. This process would be identical to that described in Chapter 2 and will not be repeated here.

After the posting process is completed, the trial balance would appear as follows:

Kilmer Contractors
Trial Balance Before Adjustment
June 30, 19x1

Cash	$ 3,100	
Accounts receivable	900	
Supplies	2,000	
Note payable		$ 3,000
Unearned fees		2,200
Capital		100
Sales		7,200
Purchases	5,000	
Salaries expense	1,500	
	$12,500	$12,500

At the end of the accounting period, the balance accumulated in the purchases account represents the total cost of the merchandise purchased during the period. An adjusting journal entry would now be required to determine the product cost for the month. Note that the balance in the purchases account is $5,000, representing the cost of the 1,000 square yards of carpet which were purchased during the month of June. It is necessary to allocate this balance to record the cost of carpet which was still on hand as of June 30 and the cost of the carpet which was sold during the month of June. The cost of the items still on hand at the end of the period represents an asset referred to as *inventory*. The cost of the items sold during the period is an expense called *cost of goods sold*. The adjusting entry necessary to record the cost of the 800 square yards of carpet sold during June and the cost of the 200 square yards of carpet still on hand at June 30, 19x1, would be as follows:

Inventory	1,000	
Cost of goods sold	4,000	
Purchases		5,000

The debit to cost of goods sold records the cost of the carpet which was sold during June (800 yards × $5) and the debit to inventory records the cost of the carpet still on hand at June 30 (200 yards × $5). Since the purchases account is closed out, it has a zero balance at the beginning of the next accounting period, July 1. The balance in the inventory account at June 30 is also the inventory at the beginning of the next period. Thus, the cost of goods available for sale during the next accounting period will include the beginning inventory plus any purchases made during July. Note that cost of goods available for sale is divided into two components at the end of the period—the cost of goods sold and the inventory on hand. This is done by means of an adjusting entry which would then be posted to the ledger accounts. The next step in the recording process would be the preparation of a trial balance *after* adjustment. This trial balance is presented below:

Kilmer Contractors
Trial Balance After Adjustment
June 30, 19x1

Cash	$ 3,100	
Accounts receivable	900	
Supplies	2,000	
Inventory	1,000	
Note payable		$ 3,000
Unearned fees		2,200
Capital		100
Sales		7,200
Salaries expense	1,500	
Cost of goods sold	4,000	
	$12,500	$12,500

Again, the only difference between the trial balance above and the one presented previously is the inclusion of the effect of the adjusting entry which was made to record the cost of goods sold for June.

The next step in the recording process would be to prepare closing entries. The journal entries required to close out the revenue and expense accounts of Kilmer Contractors are as follows:

Sales	7,200	
Income summary		7,200
Income summary	5,500	
Salaries expense		1,500
Cost of goods sold		4,000

The balance in the income summary account is then transferred to Kilmer's capital account by the following entry:

Income summary	1,700	
Capital		1,700

The closing entries would then be posted to the general ledger. The reader should note that the closing entries for a retailing concern are almost identical to those for a service organization.

4-6

After the closing entries have been made and posted to the ledger, the financial statements would then be prepared as follows:

Kilmer Contractors
Balance Sheet
June 30, 19x1

Assets		Liabilities and Owner's Equity	
Cash	$3,100	Note payable	$3,000
Accounts receivable	900	Unearned fees	2,200
Supplies	2,000	Capital	1,800
Inventory	1,000		
	$7,000		$7,000

Kilmer Contractors
Income Statement
For the Month Ending June 30, 19x1

Sales		$7,200
Less: Cost of goods sold:		
Beginning inventory	$ 0	
Purchases	5,000	
Goods available for sale	$5,000	
Ending inventory	1,000	4,000
Gross profit		$3,200
Salaries		1,500
Income		$1,700

Kilmer Contractors
Statement of Cash Flows
For the Month Ending June 30, 19x1

Cash flows from operations:		
Cash receipts:		
From customers		$7,200
Cash payments:		
To suppliers	$5,000	
To employees	1,500	
		6,500
Increase in cash		$ 700

Kilmer Contractors
Statement of Capital
For the Month Ending June 30, 19x1

Capital at June 1, 19x1	$ 100
Add: Income for the month of June	1,700
Capital at June 30, 19x1	$1,800

Note that the difference between the balance sheet for a service business and that of a retailing firm is that the latter includes inventory as an asset. The primary difference between the financial statements of the two types of organizations is in the income statement. The income statement for a service business (see Chapter 2) usually includes a revenue account for each major source of revenue followed by a grouping of expenses which are deducted, in total, from the total revenues for the period in order to determine income. The income statement for a retailing firm includes two major segments or sections. The revenue from the sale of goods is shown first. The determination of the cost of the goods sold (product cost) is then made and is deducted from sales in order to disclose the gross profit from sales for the period (sales less cost of goods sold). The other expenses (period costs) are then subtracted from the gross profit figure in order to determine the net income for the period.

OBJECTIVE OF INVENTORY ACCOUNTING

The objective of inventory accounting is two-fold. First, it is concerned with valuation of the asset inventory. Valuation of the asset account is important because the funds invested by a firm in its inventories are usually quite significant; the inventory of a business is often the largest of its current assets. Second, and at least of equal importance, is the proper determination of net income of the business for the period by matching the appropriate costs (the cost of the inventory sold) against the related revenue (the revenue received from the sale of the inventory). In other words, the matching process requires that costs be assigned: (1) to those goods which were sold during the period, and (2) to those goods which are still on hand and available for sale at the end of a period. It should be noted that this is really a single process; the procedures which are employed in the valuation of inventories also simultaneously determine the cost of goods sold. In order to illustrate this general process, consider the following activities of Art's Wholesalers for the month of June:

1. Purchased one hundred cases of Coca-Cola at a cost of $3 per case.

2. Sold eighty cases of Coca-Cola at a price of $5 per case.

3. Selling expenses for June totalled $25.

4. On June 1, Art had ten cases of Coke which had also cost him $3 per case on hand. At June 30, Art's inventory consisted of thirty cases of Coke.

If Art were to prepare an income statement for the month of June, it would appear as follows:

Art's Wholesalers
Income Statement
For the Month of June

Sales (80 cases @ $5)		$400
Less: Cost of goods sold:		
Beginning inventory,		
June 1 (10 cases @ $3)	$ 30	
Add: Purchases (100 cases @ $3) ...	300	
Goods available for sale	$330	
Deduct: Ending inventory,		
June 30 (30 cases @ $3) ..	90	
Cost of goods sold		240
Gross profit from sales......................		$160
Selling expenses...........................		25
Income		$135

Several points should be noted from the analysis of the above income statement. The total inventory of Coke which was available for sale, identified in the income statement as the *goods available for sale*, was accumulated by combining the cost of goods which were on hand at the start of the period (*beginning inventory*) with the cost of Coke purchased during the period (*purchases*).

Goods available for sale was then divided into its two components: (1) the cost of Coke which was still on hand and available for sale at the close of the period (*ending inventory*), and (2) the cost of Coke which was sold during the period (*cost of goods sold*). *Cost of goods sold* was subtracted from the sales revenue for the period (*sales*) in order to determine *gross profit from sales*. Note that the gross profit from sales is determined and presented before the other costs and expenses incurred during the period are considered. The next step in the preparation of the income statement is the deduction of these expenses, in this example *selling expenses*, in order to arrive at the income for the period.

Of course, the example used above was very simple for purposes of illustration. All Coke was assumed to be acquired at a single price and no discounts, returns, or losses were encountered. Our purpose was to illustrate the general concepts of inventory accounting; we will now consider some of the detailed procedures which are normally involved in this process.

INVENTORY COSTS

Inventory values should reflect all costs that are required in order to obtain merchandise (retailer or wholesaler) in the desired condition and location. If any costs of obtaining inventory (in addition to the purchase price) are not included as product costs and instead are considered to be costs of the period, inventory values on the balance sheet would be understated and expenses on the income statement would be overstated. When these goods are sold in a later period, expenses on the income statement of that period would be understated.

All indirect costs that were incurred by the business in obtaining and placing the goods in a marketable condition should be included as a part of inventory cost if it is possible and practical to identify these costs with inventory purchases. Examples of these costs would include such items as sales taxes, duties, freight-in, and insurance. The cost of merchandise is also reduced by any discounts, returns, and allowances.

PERIODIC AND PERPETUAL INVENTORIES

The quantities of inventories on hand may be determined by means of either a *periodic inventory system* or a *perpetual system*. Determining inventory quantities is necessary for preparing financial statements, making managerial decisions, and controlling inventory. The basic difference between the periodic and perpetual methods is in the timing of the determination of the inventory quantities.

The periodic method is based on a physical count (or weight or measurement) of the goods that remain on hand at the close of each accounting period. Values are assigned to these quantities to determine the inventory valuation, and *the cost of goods sold is computed by subtracting the ending inventory value from the cost of goods that were available for sale during the period (beginning inventory plus purchases).* The purchases account is debited at the time that goods are purchased. The inventory account is adjusted by crediting the beginning inventory and debiting the income summary and by debiting the ending inventory and crediting the income summary in the closing process at the end of the accounting period. This method of accounting for inventory quantities is relatively simple and accurate as of the end of the period. However, the periodic method does not provide the up-to-date summary of inventory quantities that is often essential for effective managerial control over inventories.

The perpetual inventory method provides a continuous summary of the quantities on hand by recording all receipts and withdrawals of each inventory item as these occur. Individual records are maintained for each type of inventory item. These records may be maintained in terms of quantities only or in both quantities and dollars. If the record is in terms of quantities only, the accounting entries used under the perpetual system are generally identical to those that are employed under the periodic method. With a perpetual system on a quantity basis, a "running count" of each class or category of inventory item may be maintained, either manually or by the use of electronic data processing equipment, in order to provide information with regard to the quantity of a particular inventory item on hand at any particular point in time. On the other hand, if the perpetual records are maintained in terms of both quantities and dollars, ledger accounts for each type of inventory are debited for increases (e.g., purchases) and credited for withdrawals (e.g., sales). Under this procedure, *the valuation of both inven-*

tory and the cost of goods sold to date are available immediately from the accounting records on a current basis.

When either type of perpetual inventory system is used, a physical count of the goods on hand should be made at least once during each period in order to verify the accuracy of the inventory records. Some companies use various statistical sampling techniques that often make a complete physical count unnecessary.

If perpetual records are kept for both quantities and dollars, variations between the book records and the actual quantities determined by a physical count should be recognized. To correct the inventory records, the inventory account is debited or credited for any difference, with the offsetting debit or credit made to an inventory adjustment or to a gain or loss account. If an inventory adjustment account is used, the balance usually is closed out to cost of goods sold at the end of the period.

The basic difference between the perpetual and periodic methods is illustrated by the following example:

1. Purchased ten cases of beer @ $3 per case (assume that the firm had no inventory at the beginning of the period).

Perpetual			*Periodic*		
Inventory	30		Purchases	30	
Cash		30	Cash		30

2. Sold seven cases of beer for $5 per case.

Perpetual			*Periodic*		
Cash	35		Cash	35	
Sales		35	Sales		35
Cost of goods sold	21				
Inventory		21			

3. Ending inventory is two cases of beer.

Perpetual			*Periodic*		
Loss	3		Cost of goods sold	24	
Inventory		3	Inventory	6	
			Purchases		30

An analysis of the entries presented above indicates that using the perpetual system the cost of goods sold is $21 and a loss of $3 is shown for the missing case of beer (10 cases purchased − 7 cases sold − 2 cases in the ending inventory indicates that 1 case was "missing"). Using the periodic method, the $3 cost of the missing case would be included in the cost of goods sold since the cost of goods sold under this method was determined by subtracting the $6 cost of ending inventory from goods available for sale of $30 and assuming that the difference represented inventory that was sold.

This is a disadvantage of the periodic method, because the cost of sales under this method will include not only the cost of the goods actually sold, but also the cost of any merchandise lost or stolen as well. More effective control over inventories may be established by using the perpetual method, either on a dollar or a quantity basis.

INVENTORY LOSSES

Under a periodic inventory system, it is assumed that all cost of goods available for sale during the period are either sold or are on hand at the end of the period. Based upon this assumption, the cost of any merchandise lost through shrinkage, spoilage, or theft by shoplifting, etc., is automatically included in cost of goods sold for the period. To illustrate, assume that a firm purchased ten cases of Coke at $3 per case during a period, and the firm had no inventory at the beginning of the period. Further assume that the business sold seven cases of Coke during the period, and that one case of Coke was stolen by shoplifters. Thus, the ending inventory, as determined by a physical count, would be two cases of Coke. Under the periodic method, the following entry would be made at the end of the period.

```
    Cost of goods sold......................  24
    Inventory...............................   6
         Purchases..........................        30
```

In this circumstance, the $3 cost of the stolen merchandise is included in cost of goods sold because the cost of goods sold was determined by subtracting the ending inventory ($6) from the cost of goods available ($30). If the theft had not occurred, the ending inventory would have been $3 greater. In reality, the cost of goods sold was $21 and the cost of goods stolen was $3.

More effective control over inventories and inventory losses may be established by using the perpetual inventory method which was discussed earlier. However, because the perpetual method is impractical for many types of businesses, a means of estimating inventory losses have been developed. This estimation technique is discussed later in this chapter.

The above procedures describe periodic and perpetual systems in terms of dollar amounts. Either of these inventory systems can also be maintained on a quantity basis. For example, with a perpetual system on a quantity basis, a "running count" of each class or category of inventory item may be maintained, either manually or by the use of electronic data processing equipment, in order to provide information with regard to the quantity of a particular inventory item on hand at any particular point in time.

BASIS OF ACCOUNTING

Historical cost is the primary basis used in accounting for inventories. This cost includes not only the price of the asset itself, but also any direct or indirect outlays which were made or incurred in order to bring the inventory to the firm's location in the desired form and condition. For example, shipping costs would be considered a part of the cost of the inventory if they were paid by the purchaser.

PURCHASE DISCOUNTS

Sellers of goods frequently offer discounts to their customers to recognize quantity purchases and to encourage prompt payment for goods sold on account. Quantity discounts, often referred to as trade discounts, usually represent an adjustment of a catalog or list price which is made to arrive at the selling price of merchandise to a particular customer. For this reason, trade discounts are not usually reflected in the accounts. For example, assume that the distributor offered Coke at a list price of $4 per case and allowed Art's Wholesalers a trade discount of 25 percent. From an accounting viewpoint, Art would determine the cost to be employed in his accounts as follows:

List price per case	$4
Less: Trade discount (25% of $4)	1
Cost per case	$3

Art would use the $3 figure as his cost; the $4 list price and the $1 discount would not appear anywhere in the accounts.

Discounts which are offered to encourage the prompt payment of purchases made on a credit basis are another matter. These discounts usually are reflected in the accounts. Such discounts, often referred to as purchase discounts, are usually stated in terms such as 2/10; n/30. This notation means that a 2 percent discount is offered to the customer if his or her account is settled within ten days of the date of sale, the full amount is due at the end of the thirty day period. Two methods may be used in accounting for these discounts, the *net* method and the *gross* method. In order to illustrate these two methods, we will return to the transactions of Art's Wholesalers for the month of June and record the purchase of the one hundred cases of Coke at $3 per case in Art's books and in the distributor's accounts using both the net and gross methods. We will assume that the terms offered were 2/10; n/30.

Note that the seller of merchandise normally records the sale at the gross amount. One reason for this procedure lies in the fact that the seller has no control over whether or not the purchaser will make payment during or after the discount period. If payment is made by the purchaser during the discount period, the difference between the cash payment and the amount of the receivable (which was set up for the gross amount of the sale) is recorded by the seller as a *sales discount*. Of course, if payment is made after

Transaction	Coca-Cola Distributor	Art's Net Method	Art's Gross Method

Sale of one hundred cases of Coca-Cola; terms: 2/10; n/30.	Accounts receivable 300
	    Sales 300
		Purchases 294
		    Accounts payable 294
			Purchases 300
			    Accounts payable 300

Payment made *during* the discount period.	Cash 294
	Sales discounts 6
	    Accounts receivable .. 300
		Accounts payable 294
		    Cash 294
			Accounts payable 300
			    Cash 294
			    Purchase discount 6

Payment made *after* the discount period.	Cash 300
	    Accounts receivable .. 300
		Accounts payable 294
		Discount lost 6
		    Cash 300
			Accounts payable 300
			    Cash 300

the expiration of the discount period there is no problem since the purchaser will be required to pay the gross amount in full. If this is the case, the seller will simply debit cash and credit accounts receivable for the amount of cash received.

In the purchaser's accounts, the sales price *less* the purchase discount will be recorded at the time of the purchase if the net method is used. If payment for the goods is made during the discount period, there is no problem. The purchaser will simply debit accounts payable and credit cash for the amount paid. On the other hand, if payment is made after the discount period has passed, the purchaser will be required to pay the full or gross price. Since the payable was originally recorded at the net amount, the entry for payment will require a debit to accounts payable for the net amount and a credit to cash for the amount paid (gross price); the difference between the gross and the net price will be debited to a *discounts lost* account. Discounts lost is considered to be an expense of the period and is included as such in the income statement.

Under the gross method of recording purchases, the initial entry will be for the buyer to debit purchases and credit accounts payable for the full (gross) price. If payment is made during the discount period, the entry will consist of a debit to accounts payable for the original amount recorded as a liability (gross price), a credit to cash for the amount actually paid (net price), and the difference will be credited to a purchase discounts account. Purchase discounts is reported as a deduction from the purchases made during the period. If the payment is made after the discount period has passed or expired, the entry will simply consist of a debit to accounts payable and a credit to cash for the full or gross price.

Note that the difference between the two methods lies in the information which is provided by each. The net method provides information as to the discounts which were lost but gives no data as to those which were taken. The gross method indicates the amount of discounts taken but gives no information as to the discounts which were lost. Because of the significance[1] of discounts lost to the business, the authors feel that information regarding the discounts not taken is critical and for this reason believe that the net method should be used by purchasers. We feel that any discounts lost are, in fact, interest costs and should be disclosed as such and not included as a part of the cost of inventories.

FREIGHT-IN, RETURNS, AND ALLOWANCES

The purchase of merchandise often involves payment of shipping costs necessary to bring the goods to the purchaser's place of business. The cost of the merchandise logically includes these transportation costs.

---

[1] Failure to take a discount when the terms are 2/10; n/30 represents an interest cost in excess of 36 percent per annum. ($294 × R × $20/360$ = $6; solving for R, the interest rate is 36.7%.)

Frequently purchasers of goods will also find it necessary to return goods to their suppliers because the goods are damaged or unacceptable. In other instances, such goods will be retained by the purchaser and the supplier will allow him or her an adjustment of the purchase price, known as an allowance. To illustrate these occurrences, we will assume the following facts:

1. Art ordered one hundred cases of Coke, fifty cases of Pepsi, and fifty cases of Dr. Pepper, all at a price of $3 per case. The terms were F.O.B. shipping point,[2] 2/10; n/30, and Art uses the net method for recording purchases. Art pays the freight of $10.
2. Art's distributor ships him one hundred cases of Coke, fifty cases of Pepsi, and, by mistake, fifty cases of Orange Crush instead of the Dr. Pepper.
3. Art returns fifty cases of the Coke, agrees to keep the Orange Crush in lieu of the Dr. Pepper since the distributor gave him a $5 allowance, and pays the balance in full within the discount period.

The entries to record these transactions would be as follows:

Art			Distributor		
Purchases	588		Accounts receivable	600	
Freight-in	10		Sales		600
Accounts payable		588			
Cash		10			
Accounts payable	588		Cash	436	
Purchase returns		147	Sales returns	150	
Purchase allowance		5	Sales allowance	5	
Cash		436	Sales discount	9	
			Accounts receivable		600

Art debits purchases and credits accounts payable for the net amount of the purchase ($600 less 2% of $600 or a net amount of $588). He debits freight-in and credits cash for the $10 freight charge that he paid in cash, since according to the terms of the purchase (F.O.B. shipping point) this is his responsibility. The seller, using the gross method, simply debits accounts receivable and credits sales for the full price of the sale (200 cases @ $3).

At the time payment is made, Art would debit accounts payable for the amount of the liability originally recorded (net price). He would credit purchase returns for the net cost of the fifty cases of Coke that he returned to

---

[2] The initials F.O.B. stand for free on board. F.O.B. shipping point means that the seller pays the costs *to* the shipping point only; the buyer pays the cost of transit *from* the shipping point to the destination. Alternatively, F.O.B. destination terms would require the seller to pay all shipping costs.

the seller (50 cases @ $3 or $150, less 2% of $150, or a net of $147) and credit purchase allowances for the $5 adjustment made to Art for keeping the Orange Crush, rather than the Dr. Pepper that he ordered. The credit to cash would be for the net cash paid ($588 less the $147 return, less the $5 allowance, or a net amount of $436).

When the seller receives Art's payment, he would debit cash for the $436 received, debit sales returns for $150 (the 50 cases of Coke returned @ $3), debit sales allowance for the $5 adjustment, and debit sales discounts for $9 (150 cases @ $3 or $450 multiplied by 2%). The distributor would credit accounts receivable for the amount he originally recorded, the gross amount of $600.

The partial income statement presented below is an example of how these items can be disclosed in the statements.

The reader should note that the account purchase discounts does not appear in the statements since we assumed that Art is using the net method of recording purchases. If the gross method were used, purchases would be included at their gross rather than net amount and purchase discounts would appear along with purchase returns and purchase allowances as a deduction in arriving at the net purchases for the period. Discounts lost would not appear in the statements when using the gross method.

Art's Wholesalers
Partial Income Statement
For the Year Ending December 31, 19x1

Sales				$102,800
Less: Sales returns			$ 500	
Sales allowances			300	
Sales discounts			2,000	2,800
Net sales				$100,000
Less: Cost of goods sold:				
Beginning inventory			$10,000	
Purchases		$70,000		
Less: Purchase returns	$1,000			
Purchase allowances	100	1,100		
Net purchases		$68,900		
Add: Freight-in		600	69,500	
Goods available for sale			$79,500	
Ending inventory			15,500	
Cost of goods sold				64,000
Gross profit on sales				$ 36,000
Discounts lost		$ 100		
All other expenses		20,000		20,100
Income				$ 15,900

INVENTORY COST FLOW METHODS

Once the quantities of goods on hand at the end of the period and the quantity of goods sold during the period are determined, the next step is to decide how costs should be allocated between cost of goods sold and ending inventory. If all purchases of inventory were made at the same unit price, this allocation does not create any problems. However, if the inventory items were acquired at different unit costs, it is necessary to determine which costs should be assigned to each inventory item. One method of determining the cost of the inventory on hand would be to maintain records of the exact cost of each item sold during the period and each item on hand at the end of the period. In many cases, this specific identification procedure would require excessive recordkeeping costs, while in other instances it would be impossible to do so. In addition to practical considerations, specific identification also presents a potential problem, because this method allows for the potential manipulation of reported income. When identical units are acquired or produced at different unit costs, management may manipulate cost of goods sold and net income by selecting either a higher or lower priced item at the time a good is sold. Consequently, some systematic method for assigning costs to inventory is usually necessary both for practical reasons and for obtaining a more objective inventory valuation and income determination.

The cost flow methods are based on assumptions that are made regarding the assumed flow of inventory costs. Cost flow refers to both the inflow of costs when goods are purchased or manufactured and the outflow of costs when the goods are sold. The cost flow assumptions are systematic procedures that determine the order in which unit costs are assigned to cost of goods sold and inventory. Using alternative cost flow assumptions has generated considerable controversy regarding inventory accounting, because the use of different methods may result in substantial variations in net income and inventory valuations in the financial statements.

There are a number of cost flow methods that are acceptable for financial accounting purposes. Each of the acceptable cost flow methods is based on the cost principle; they differ only in terms of the costs that are assigned to cost of goods sold and those that are assigned to inventory.

There are three commonly used methods in costing inventories (excluding the specific identification method discussed above) and, therefore, determining cost of goods sold for the period: *the average-cost method; the first-in, first-out (FIFO) method; and the last-in, first-out (LIFO) method. These methods employ assumptions regarding the flow of inventory costs, not the actual physical flow of goods.* Accordingly, the order in which costs are assigned to cost of goods sold does not have to be consistent with the physical order in which the goods are sold. The major objective in selecting a cost-flow method should be to choose the one that most clearly reflects periodic income under the circumstances.

The application of these methods result in a different amount of ending inventory and cost of goods sold for each period because they are based upon different arbitrary assumptions as to the flow of costs of merchandise through the business. These methods are assumptions regarding the flow of inventory *costs* and not about the actual *physical* flow of goods. The following data relating to a special brand of foreign beer, again taken from the inventory records of Art's Wholesalers, will be used to illustrate these methods:

January 1:	Beginning inventory (100 cases @ $2)	$200
February 7:	Purchase (150 cases @ $3)	450
March 25:	Purchase (200 cases @ $4)	800
October 6:	Purchase (150 cases @ $5)	750
November 10:	Purchase (100 cases @ $6)	600

Thus, the goods available for sale during the year were 700 cases at a total cost of $2,800. Art's records indicate that 500 cases were sold during the year. The accounting problem is in assigning or allocating the $2,800 cost of goods available for sale between the ending inventory and the cost of goods sold. The valuation of the ending inventory (and therefore, the determination of the cost of goods sold) under each of the alternative methods of inventory valuation is illustrated in the paragraphs which follow.

Average-Cost Method

Using the periodic system, the average-cost method (often called the weighted-average cost method) assigns costs to inventory and to cost of goods sold based on the weighted-average cost of all the items that were available for sale during the period. A weighted-average unit cost is computed at the end of the period by dividing the total cost of the beginning inventory plus the purchases by the total number of units included in the inventory. The weighted-average cost is multiplied by the number of units sold to derive the cost of goods sold and is also applied to the units on hand to determine the valuation of the ending inventory. Thus, a feature of the average method is the assignment of cost on an equal unit basis to both the ending inventory and cost of goods sold.

In the example stated above, the average cost would be calculated as follows:

January 1:	Inventory (100 cases @ $2)	$ 200
February 7:	Purchase (150 cases @ $3)	450
March 25:	Purchase (200 cases @ $4)	800
October 6:	Purchase (150 cases @ $5)	750
November 10:	Purchase (100 cases @ $6)	600
	Total 700 cases	$2,800

The total cost of the goods available for sale ($2,800) would be divided by the number of cases (700) and the result of $4 would be the average cost of the inventory. This average cost figure would be used both in valuing the ending inventory (200 × $4 = $800) and in determining the cost of goods sold for the period (500 × $4 = $2,000).

First-In, First-Out (FIFO) Method

The FIFO method assumes that the cost of the first item acquired or produced is the cost of the first item used or sold. Its use is advantageous because it assigns a current cost to inventories on the balance sheet and is relatively easy to apply. In many cases, the assumption is also consistent with the actual flow of goods. (FIFO inventories are priced by using the actual invoice costs or production costs for the latest quantities purchased or produced which are still on hand). It is a good method to use in those instances where the inventory turnover is rapid or where changes in the composition of the inventory are frequent since the costs associated with the oldest inventory are always transferred to cost of goods sold first.

The major advantage of FIFO is that it assigns a relatively current cost to inventories included on the balance sheet, because the ending inventory is composed of the most recent purchases. In many cases, this assumption is also consistent with the actual flow of goods. FIFO is a good method to use when the inventory turnover is rapid or when the composition of the inventory changes frequently, because the costs associated with the oldest inventory are transferred to cost of goods sold first.

The primary disadvantage of the FIFO method is that it fails to match the most recent costs with current revenues. If prices are rising, matching the oldest unit costs with current revenues may result in an overstatement of net income in terms of current dollars.

The FIFO inventory and the related cost of goods sold for Art's Wholesalers would be calculated as follows:

FIFO Cost of Goods Sold
The First 500 Units

January 1:	Inventory (100 cases @ $2)	$ 200
February 7:	Purchase (150 cases @ $3)	450
March 25:	Purchase (200 cases @ $4)	800
October 6:	Purchase (50 cases @ $5)	250
	FIFO cost of goods sold	$1,700

FIFO Ending Inventory
The Last 200 Units

October 6:	Purchase (100 cases @ $5)	$ 500
November 10:	Purchase (100 cases @ $6)	600
	FIFO cost of ending inventory	$1,100

Last-In, First-Out (LIFO) Method

The last-in, first-out (LIFO) method assumes that the cost of the last item received or produced is the cost of the first item used or sold. A principal advantage of the LIFO method is that it matches current costs more nearly with current revenues. Another advantage of LIFO is the fact that in periods of price increases, net income computed using LIFO is less than the amount that would result from using FIFO or the average-cost method. Therefore, it reduces federal income taxes. Providing that prices do not decline below the prices of the year in which LIFO was adopted, the method results in a postponement of income taxes. Unlike many other instances where alternative accounting procedures exist, federal income tax laws require the use of the LIFO inventory method for financial reporting purposes whenever it is used for income tax purposes.

Its disadvantages are that it gives a "noncurrent" value to inventories in the balance sheet and it reduces reported income in periods of rising prices.

When there is an increase in the quantity of inventory, the year-end LIFO inventory consist of the prior year-end inventory plus the earliest additions at cost in the current year. The cost of the LIFO inventory and the related cost of goods sold would be calculated as follows:

LIFO Ending Inventory
The First 200 Units

January 1:	Inventory (100 cases @ $2).................	$ 200
February 7:	Purchase (100 cases @ $3).................	300
	LIFO cost of ending inventory	$ 500

LIFO Cost of Goods Sold
The Last 500 Units

February 7:	Purchase (50 cases @ $3).................	$ 150
March 25:	Purchase (200 cases @ $4).................	800
October 6:	Purchase (150 cases @ $5).................	750
November 10:	Purchase (100 cases @ $6).................	600
	LIFO cost of goods sold	$2,300

Conceptually, the LIFO inventory method may be described as a series of cost layers. Under the periodic basis, an increase in inventory quantities during a period results in an ending inventory that consists of the beginning inventory layer plus a purchase layer that is added at the cost of the earliest acquisitions made during the period. If inventory quantities decrease during any period, the cost of the most recently added layers and some or all of the beginning inventory layer would be allocated to the cost of goods sold. If the inventory quantity increases in the next period, a new layer is added at the cost at which the purchases were made during that period.

Once all or part of a layer is removed from the inventory and added to the cost of goods sold, the cost of that layer is never restored to the inventory. Thus, if the inventory subsequently increases, a new layer is added from the acquisitions of the current year.

Differences in Methods

The effect of the differences in the three methods which we described above are illustrated by the following summary.

	Average	FIFO	LIFO
Sales (500 cases @ $10)	$5,000	$5,000	$5,000
Less: Cost of goods sold:			
Beginning inventory (100 cases)	$ 200	$ 200	$ 200
Purchases (600 cases)	2,600	2,600	2,600
Goods available for sale (700 cases)	$2,800	$2,800	$2,800
Ending inventory (200 cases)	800	1,100	500
Cost of goods sold (500 cases)	$2,000	$1,700	$2,300
Gross profit on sales	$3,000	$3,300	$2,700

The total cost of goods available for sale ($2,800) was allocated either to cost of goods sold or ending inventory in every case. The sales, beginning inventory, and purchases included in the example are identical irrespective of the inventory method chosen. An inventory method is only used to cost the ending inventory and determine the cost of goods sold. It does not necessarily reflect the actual physical flow of goods. That is, a bakery could use the LIFO method for accounting purposes although obviously the physical flow would be FIFO—who wants a ten-year-old cake!

It should be obvious that *the alternative choices of inventory valuation methods may have a substantial impact on both the financial statements and income taxes.* Therefore, management must consider the effects on the reported data and on cash flows in selecting or changing an inventory method. Although a firm may select any one of several acceptable methods, the consistency principle requires that a firm use the same method over time.

Many businesses use different inventory valuation methods for various components of their inventories. The inventory methods a company uses must be disclosed in the financial statements.

LOWER-OF-COST-OR-MARKET

As previously indicated, the primary basis for accounting for inventories is cost. Therefore, if the value of the item increases or decreases prior to its sale, no record of this fact is normally entered in the books. However, an exception to this rule may occur when the market price, which is defined as the current replacement cost of the goods, is less than their historical cost. In this case, the inventory may be carried at its replacement cost. In other words, inventories may be carried at the lower of their cost or their market value. If the market price for a firm's inventory falls below its original cost, an entry is made recognizing the difference between cost and market as a loss and reducing the carrying value of the inventory to market. The reduced figure becomes the new "cost" of the inventory for accounting purposes. However, if the market price exceeds the original cost, no entry is made in the accounts. The recognition of losses but not gains prior to sale is based on the principle of conservatism. To illustrate the lower-of-cost-or-market method, assume the same facts as presented previously—that a firm had 700 cases of beer available for sale and that this beer had been purchased at an average price of $4 per case. Sales for the period were 500 cases at a selling price of $10 per case. If the business used the "average" inventory method, the gross profit on sales would be calculated as follows:

Sales (500 cases @ $10)		$5,000
Less: Cost of goods sold:		
Beginning inventory (100 cases)	$ 200	
Purchases (600 cases)	2,600	
Goods available for sale (700 cases)	$2,800	
Ending inventory (200 cases)	800	
Cost of goods sold		$2,000
Gross profit on sales		$3,000

If the replacement cost of the ending inventory had declined to $750 as of the end of the period, the ending inventory might be written down from its original cost of $800 to its current replacement cost of $750 by the following entry:

Loss on inventory decline	50	
Inventory		50

The effect of the write-down of inventory would be to reduce income for the period by $50 by recognizing the reduction in the replacement cost of the inventory below its original cost. In subsequent periods, inventory would be carried at a "cost" of $750 in the balance sheet and this amount would be used in determining the cost of goods sold when the inventory was sold. The lower of cost or market method may be applied: (1) to each individual type of inventory item, (2) to major classes of inventory, or (3) to the inventory as a whole. Although the application of lower-of-cost-or-market valuation is optional, once the method is adopted it should be followed consistently from year-to-year.

The lower-of-cost-or-market rule may be viewed as an extension of the convention of conservatism. Although this rule yields a conservative balance sheet and income statement in the period of the write-down, it provides a *greater net income in subsequent periods* that would be determined using the cost basis. Consequently, this procedure has been critcized for allowing the manipulation of income, because an excessive write-down in one period could result in excessive income in a subsequent period.

The procedure also has been criticized because of its *apparent inconsistency in the treatment of anticipated losses and anticipated gains*. Market decreases are recognized in the period in which the decrease in utility occurs, but market increases are not recognized until the period in which goods are sold. The only logical explanation for this discrepancy is that the conservatism convention is more important than treating market decreases and increases alike.

GROSS PROFIT METHOD

In many instances, such as in the case of the preparation of interim financial statements, it may be desirable simply to estimate the amount of the ending inventory rather than go to the time and trouble of taking a physical inventory. One method which is often used in estimating inventories is the gross profit method. The gross profit method frequently is used to verify the inventory valuation determined through normal procedures or to determine the inventory value in the absence of a physical count. *The primary uses of the gross profit method include: (1) to estimate inventories for interim statement purposes (e.g., quarterly financial statements), (2) to test the reasonableness of inventory values determined by physical count or perpetual inventory records, and (3) to estimate the value of inventory destroyed or lost by a casualty or other causes.* The gross profit method *is not a generally acceptable method* that is appropriate for annual financial reporting purposes, because it is an estimating procedure. Therefore, even if the method is used for estimating inventory values, a physical inventory count should be made at least once a year.

This method assumes that the relationship between sales, the cost of goods sold, and gross profit will remain relatively constant from one accounting period to the next. This relationship is normally based upon actual amounts from the preceding year, adjusted for any changes which occurred in the current year. To illustrate, consider the following example for Art's Wholesalers for the month of January, 19x1.

Sales.	$10,500
Sales returns	500
Purchases	5,500
Purchase returns	100
Purchase allowances	50
Freight	150
Inventory, January 1, 19x1	15,500

In addition to the data summarized above, information concerning the gross profit percentage (gross profit of $36,000 divided by net sales of

$100,000 or 36%)[3] and the inventory at the beginning of the year ($15,500) was obtained from the 19x0 income statement. This information would be used to estimate the cost of the ending inventory on hand at January 31, 19x1, as follows:

1. Determine the cost of goods available for sale to date, using the ledger accounts.

2. Estimate the cost of goods sold by multiplying the net sales by the estimated costs of goods sold percentage (100% minus the estimated gross profit rate).

3. Subtract the estimated cost of goods sold from the cost of goods available for sale to determine the estimated inventory on hand.

The calculation of the estimated inventory at January 31, 19x1, for Art's Wholesalers is as follows:

Beginning inventory			$15,500
Purchases		$ 5,500	
Less: Purchase returns	$100		
Purchase allowances	50	150	
Net purchases		$ 5,350	
Freight-in		150	5,500
Goods available for sale			$21,000
Less: Estimated cost of goods sold			
Sales		$10,500	
Less: Sales returns		500	
Net sales		$10,000	
Multiply by the cost of goods sold percentage (100% − 36%)		× 64%	
Estimated cost of goods sold			6,400
Estimated cost of January 31, 19x1, inventory			$14,600

The reader should keep in mind that the gross profit method is a method of *estimating* inventories, not *costing* inventories. The gross profit method can be used in order to estimate inventories for interim statement purposes; to test the accuracy of inventories determined by physical count; and to estimate inventory destroyed by fire, lost by theft, etc.

---

[3] Information from the 19x0 income statement was as follows:

Sales	$100,000	(100%)
Cost of goods sold	64,000	(64%)
Gross profit on sales	$ 36,000	(36%)

RETAIL INVENTORY METHOD

The retail inventory method is commonly used by retail businesses to simplify their accounting for inventories. An advantage of the use of this method is that the physical inventory is computed on the basis of selling prices, which are readily available. The physical inventory at selling prices is then converted to its estimated cost by applying the average ratio of costs to selling prices of goods that were on hand during the period. Thus, it is an averaging method which assumes that the cost of merchandise on hand at any time bears the same relationship to total retail prices as the total cost of all goods handled during the period bears to original selling prices. In using this method, when sales are subtracted from goods available for sale at retail selling prices, the result is the estimated ending inventory at retail prices. Then, this amount is multiplied by the average ratio of cost to selling prices to give an estimate of ending inventory at cost. Its principal advantages are: it provides a clerically feasible means of determining inventories on hand; it provides a measure of control over inventories and a means of computing the cost of merchandise sold at any time, even though the store handles a large number of items and has a very high volume of sales transactions; it simplifies the taking and pricing of physical inventories; it provides information for a monthly determination of gross profit for each department and store; and it helps control inventory by disclosing shortages which may indicate either thefts or sales made at unauthorized prices.

As goods are purchased, information regarding the goods is accumulated on both a cost and a selling price basis. The determination of the estimated cost of inventory using the retail method is illustrated with the following example:

	Cost	Selling Price
Beginning inventory	$ 1,500	$ 2,000
Add: Purchases	10,000	18,000
Freight	500	
	$12,000	$20,000
Deduct: Sales		16,000
Ending inventory (at retail)		$ 4,000

Cost percentage: $\dfrac{\$12{,}000}{\$20{,}000} = 60\%$

Ending inventory (at cost): $\$4{,}000 \times 60\% = \underline{\$2{,}400}$

SUMMARY

This chapter has discussed certain of the operational differences in companies, with special emphasis placed on the differences in retailing and service organizations.

For accounting purposes, inventories include all goods which are held for sale to customers, those in the process of being produced for sale, and those to be used in the production of goods for sale. The objective of inventory accounting is to provide a proper valuation of inventory, both for balance sheet reporting purposes and for the proper determination of income.

Inventories are normally accounted for at historical cost, with any savings due to trade and purchase discounts and expenses due to freight charges considered in the determination of historical cost. In addition, inventory costs must be adjusted for any returns or allowances on inventory items. When the market price falls below cost, inventories may be written down to their current replacement cost using the lower of cost or market concept.

The periodic and perpetual inventory methods are the two general methods of determining inventory amounts. The perpetual method requires recording the cost of goods sold as inventory items are sold. The periodic method involves making a physical count of goods on hand and subtracting this amount from the total goods available for sale to determine the cost of goods sold. Each inventory system can be maintained on either a dollar or unit basis or both.

Two basic general classifications of cost used for purposes of income determination are product costs and period costs. A product cost is a cost which can be directly identified with the purchase or manufacture of goods that are available for sale. A period cost, which is usually associated with the passage of time, is recognized on the income statement as an expense of the period in which it is incurred.

Where inventory items are purchased at different prices, certain assumptions regarding cost flows must be made to allocate costs between cost of goods sold and ending inventory. The average cost method assumes that all units should carry the same cost. The first-in, first-out (FIFO) method assumes that the cost of the first item acquired or produced is the cost of the first item used or sold. The last-in, first-out (LIFO) method assumes that the cost of the last item received or produced is the cost of the first item used or sold. Currently, the FIFO method results in balance sheet valuations that reflect current cost more appropriately than LIFO, but the LIFO method results in a better matching of current costs with current revenues.

For a variety of reasons, firms may wish to estimate ending inventory amounts instead of taking an actual physical count. Two methods for such estimation are the retail method and the gross profit method. Neither of these should be considered costing methods; they are basically methods of estimating cost.

KEY DEFINITIONS

Average cost inventory method—a method based on the theory that one unit cannot be distinguished from another. The average cost is computed by dividing the total cost of the beginning inventory plus purchases by the total number of units.

Beginning inventory—includes the goods which are on hand and available for sale at the beginning of the period.

Cost of goods sold—the cost of the inventory sold during the period. Beginning inventory plus purchases minus the ending inventory equals the cost of goods sold.

Cost of inventory—the price of the inventory itself plus all direct and indirect outlays incurred in order to bring it to the firm's location in the desired form.

Cost percentage—the percentage obtained from the ratio of the goods available for sale at cost to the goods available for sale at selling price. This percentage is used in the retail method in order to calculate the estimated cost of the ending inventory.

Discounts lost—an account used under the net method of recording purchases to record the amount of the discounts which were not taken.

Ending inventory—goods which are still on hand and available for sale at the end of the period.

Expenses—outflows or other using up of assets or incurrences of liabilities (or a combination of both) during a period from delivering or producing goods, rendering services, or carrying out other activities that constitute the entity's ongoing major or central operations.

F.O.B.—means "free on board."

F.O.B. destination—would require the seller to pay all shipping costs.

F.O.B. shipping point—means that the seller pays the costs to the shipping point only. The buyer pays the cost of transit from the shipping point to the destination.

Finished goods inventory—includes completed goods which are held for resale.

First-in, first-out (FIFO)—an inventory method which assumes that the cost of the first item acquired or produced is the cost of the first item used or sold.

Freight-in—the shipping costs incurred for goods purchased.

Goods available for sale—includes the beginning inventory plus the net purchases for the period.

Gross method—a method of recording purchases (sales) whereby purchases (sales) are recorded at the gross price.

Gross profit from sales—the difference between the revenue from sales and the cost of the goods sold.

Gross profit method—this is a method which estimates the cost of the ending inventory by assuming that the relationship between sales, cost of goods sold, and gross profit remains constant.

Gross profit percentage—the gross profit or gross margin (sales minus cost of goods sold) divided by sales.

Inventories—includes those assets which are acquired and/or produced for sale in the continuing operations of a business.

Last-in, first-out (LIFO)—an inventory method which assumes that the cost of the last item received or produced is the cost of the first item used or sold.

Lower-of-cost-or-market—a method of pricing inventory whereby the original cost or the market value, whichever is lower, is used to value inventory for financial statement purposes.

Net method—a method of recording purchases whereby purchases are recorded at the net price—that is, the gross price less the purchase discount.

Period cost—a cost which cannot be directly identified with the production of a specific product or products. It is usually more closely associated with the passage of time.

Periodic inventories—under the periodic method, the cost of goods sold is determined at the end of the period by making a physical count of the goods on hand and subtracting the cost of the goods which are still on hand from the total cost of goods available for sale. This inventory system may also be maintained on a quantity basis.

Perpetual inventories—under the perpetual method, an entry recording the cost of goods sold is usually made at the time a sale is made. This inventory system may also be maintained on a quantity basis.

Product cost—a cost which is directly associated with the production or purchase of goods that are available for sale.

Purchases—includes all inventory acquired by purchase during the period.

Purchase allowances—an adjustment of the purchase price allowed the buyer by the seller. See sales allowances.

Purchase discounts—discounts which are offered to encourage the prompt payment of purchases made on account. Purchase discounts are reflected in the accounts. It is also an account used under the gross method to record purchase discounts taken. See sales discounts.

Purchase returns—the account used by the buyer to record the cost of goods returned to the seller. See sales returns.

Retail method—this is a method of estimating inventories which assumes that the cost of merchandise on hand at any time bears the same relationship to total retail prices as the total cost of all goods handled during the period bears to the original selling prices.

Revenues—inflows or other enhancements of assets of an entity or settlements of its liabilities (or a combination of both) during a period from delivering or producing goods, rendering services, or other activities that constitute the entity's ongoing major or central operations.

Sales allowances—adjustments of the purchase price allowed the buyer by the seller. See purchase allowances.

Sales discount—this is a discount offered by the seller to the purchaser. See purchase discounts.

Sales returns—the account used by the seller to record the goods returned by the buyer. See purchase returns.

Trade discount—a quantity discount that represents an adjustment of a catalog or list price which is made in order to arrive at the selling price to a particular customer. Trade discounts are not reflected in the accounts.

QUESTIONS

1. What are the major differences between the income statements of a service organization and that of a retailer?

2. Why do businesses offer discounts and how are they recorded in the accounts?

3. Explain how the gross price method and the net price method each provide an evaluation of management. Which method is preferred?

4. Explain F.O.B. shipping point and F.O.B. destination. What effect do these have on the valuation of inventory?

5. What are two methods of inventory recordkeeping? Describe these methods.

6. How is the cost of goods sold figure arrived at under the periodic inventory method?

7. How does the perpetual inventory method act as a control?

8. Why should a company have accounting control over its inventory?

9. What are "goods available for sale"?

10. Explain the term "cost" with respect to accounting for inventories.

11. Briefly discuss three inventory cost flow methods.

12. Give examples of some kinds of inventories in which average cost, Fifo, and Lifo would actually match the flow of goods.

13. What problems of valuation occur with Fifo? With Lifo?

14. What is the main advantage of Lifo?

15. Explain the exception to the general cost rule for inventories.

16. What are some reasons why a company would want to estimate its inventory?

17. What is the basic assumption of the retail method of estimating inventory? What are some advantages of this method?

18. What is the gross profit method? When is it especially useful?

EXERCISES

19. Using the following information, calculate the total sales for the period.

Inventory purchases	$ 50,200
Beginning inventory	10,350
Wage expense	9,300
Rent expense	1,500
Interest expense	700
Ending inventory	9,350
Net income	12,000

20. The following balances were taken from the accounts of Norris Company. Using this information, calculate the amount of the beginning inventory.

Sales	$510,000
Ending inventory	84,000
Purchases	300,000
Net income	162,000
Other expenses	108,000

21. Fill in the blanks:

Beginning inventory	$ 20,000
Purchases	(a)
Ending inventory	22,000
Cost of goods sold	54,000
Expenses	(d)
Net income	(c)
Beginning owners' equity	200,000
Owners' additional investments	12,000
Owners' withdrawals	8,000
Ending owners' equity	230,000
Gross margin	(b)
Net sales	108,000

22. Determine and fill in the missing amounts in the following situations. Each column of figures is a separate situation.

	A	B	C	D
Sales	$100,000	$100,000	$200,000	120,000
Beginning inventory	10,000	15,000	30,000	$15,000
Purchases	60,000	70,000	100,000	75,000
Ending inventory	20,000	10,000	20,000	10,000
Cost of goods sold	50,000	75,000	110,000	80,000
Gross profit	50,000	25,000	90,000	40,000
Expenses	30,000	15,000	60,000	25,000
Net income	20,000	10,000	30,000	15,000

23. Prepare journal entries to record the following transactions under both a perpetual and a periodic inventory system.

   a. Purchased 15 dozen apples @ $2 per dozen (assume that the firm had a beginning inventory of 3 dozen apples which were purchased at $2 per dozen).
   b. Sold 14 dozen apples @ $3 per dozen.
   c. Counted the remaining apples and discovered that 3 dozen were on hand.

24. Scott ordered 50 cases of Swan soap, 90 cases of Sweet Breath mouthwash, 70 cases of Brush-It toothpaste, and 40 cases of Talc deodorant. Each case cost $15 regardless of the item. Carbo Distributor, the seller, extended credit terms of 2/10; n/30; however, Scott must pay the freight of $50. Carbo made an error in shipping the merchandise. Instead of the Swan soap, they shipped Rose soap. Scott agreed to keep this soap in return for a $20 allowance. Scott also returned 30 cases of Sweet Breath. Scott uses the net method for recording the purchases, and pays the balance within the discount period.

   Required:

   1. Make the journal entries for Scott.
   2. Make the journal entries for Carbo.

25. Given below are the pertinent data for Griswold's Bookkeeping Services for August.

   a. Purchased 100 cartons of ledger tablets @ $5 per carton during August.
   b. Sold 90 cartons of tablets at $7.50 per carton during the month.
   c. Incurred selling expenses of $35 during August.
   d. On August 1, Griswold had 15 cartons of tablets on hand which had cost $5 per carton.

   From the above information, prepare an income statment for Griswold's Services for the month of August.

26. Determine the missing figures in each of the following independent cases.

	Sales	Beginning Inventory	Ending Inventory	Gross Profit	Expenses	Net Income	Purchases	Cost of Goods Sold
1.	$1,000	$300	a	b	$100	c	$500	$600
2.	a	100	$200	$400	b	$200	700	c
3.	800	a	150	100	100	b	400	c

27. Grasso, Inc. began its operations on January 1, 19x1. It purchased goods for resale during the month as follows:

   January 3 .... 3 units @ $3
   January 11 .... 2 units @ $4
   January 20 .... 3 units @ $5
   January 30 .... 2 units @ $6

Sales for the month totaled 6 units. The selling price per unit was $10. A count of the units as of January 31, 19x1, shows four (4) units on hand.

Required:

The inventory at January 31, 19x1 would be carried at the following amounts (for each method listed below):

   Fifo.................................... _____
   Lifo.................................... _____
   Weighted Average...................... _____

All computations should be shown.

28. On December 31, 19x1, the end of its first year of operations, the management of the Busby Company is trying to decide whether to use the Fifo or Lifo method of measuring inventory. It determines that the Lifo method would produce the lower asset amount.

Required:

 1. Which method would produce the higher cost of goods sold?
 2. Which method would produce the higher net income for 19x1?
 3. Which method would produce the higher cost of goods available for sale for 19x1?
 4. In what direction do you think prices have been moving during the year?

29. The following information was available from the records of a merchandising company at the end of an accounting period.

	At Cost	At Retail
Beginning inventory...............	$10,000	$ 20,000
Net purchases.....................	69,000	100,000
Freight-in	1,000	(n/a)
Sales	(n/a)	90,000

Required:

Estimate the cost of the ending merchandise inventory using the retail inventory method.

30. Bando Company determines its ending inventory by taking a physical inventory at the end of each accounting period. On June 15, the merchandise inventory was completely destroyed by a fire. In the past, the normal gross profit rate was 20 percent. The following data were salvaged from the accounting records:

```
Inventory, January 1......................... $ 20,000
Purchases, January 1 to June 15..............   90,000
Sales, January 1 to June 15..................  100,000
```

Required:

Estimate the cost of the merchandise destroyed by the fire.

31. For the month of March, Lynn Distributors had the following transactions:

```
Sales....................................  $ 50,000
Sales returns............................     6,000
Purchases................................    24,000
Purchase returns.........................       900
Purchase allowances......................       200
Freight..................................       575
```

Inventory at the beginning of March was $32,700. This amount, as well as the gross profit percentage of 34 percent, was obtained from the February financial statements.

Required:

Use the gross profit method to estimate the ending inventory for March.

32. For each of the following five inventory cases, give the necessary journal entry to reflect the lower of cost or market rule.

	1	2	3	4	5
Cost........................	900	750	400	1,000	620
Market (replacement cost)....	950	600	300	1,200	590

PROBLEMS

33. The following transactions took place during October, 19x1. Prepare the journal entries to record these transactions.

Oct. 1 Purchased merchandise from supplier A on account, $5,000.
　　 2 Merchandise was sold on account to R.P. Jones for $1,000.
　　 3 A $1,500 credit sale was made to J.R. Lowry.
　　 6 Purchased merchandise from supplier B on account, $3,000.
　　 9 Received payment from R.P. Jones.
　　15 Sales on account of $2,000 and $2,500 were made to K.L. Putnam and A.R. Hardy, respectively.
　　17 Paid supplier A in full.
　　18 Received payment from J.R. Lowry.
　　23 Sold merchandise on account to M.S. Fletcher for $2,500.
　　24 Received payment of half of K.L. Putnam's account.
　　25 Paid supplier B half of the amount owed to him.
　　26 Received full payment from A.R. Hardy.
　　30 Received balance of payment from K.L. Putnam.
　　31 Paid supplier B the balance of the account.

34. A trial balance of the Sport Shop at the end of the first year of its operations is:

Sport Shop
Trial Balance
December 31, 19x1

Cash	$ 7,000	
Accounts receivable	9,000	
Supplies	3,000	
Inventory, January 1	0	
Accounts payable		$ 1,000
Notes payable		4,000
Capital		15,000
Sales		20,000
Purchases	15,000	
Wage expense	4,000	
Other expense	2,000	
	$40,000	$40,000

The inventory on hand at December 31, 19x1 was determined to be $3,000.

Required:

Prepare the income statement for the year ended December 31, 19x1.

35. Paul Peach opened a small office supply store on January 1, 19x1. The following trial balance was taken from the ledger at the end of the first year of operation.

Peach Office Supply
Trial Balance
December 31, 19x1

Cash	$ 3,500	
Accounts receivable	13,500	
Inventory	0	
Prepaid insurance	1,000	
Equipment	20,000	
Accounts payable		$ 5,000
Unearned revenue		15,000
Peach, capital		13,000
Sales		75,000
Purchases	40,000	
Wage expense	10,000	
Rent expense	12,000	
Other expense	8,000	
	$108,000	$108,000

A physical count taken on December 31, 19x1, showed merchandise on hand in the amount of $7,000. Other information available on December 31 included the following:

a. The equipment was purchased on January 1, 19x1, and had an estimated useful life of 10 years and no salvage value.
b. The amount of insurance that expired during the year was $400.
c. Certain customers paid in advance for regular deliveries of supplies. The amounts collected were credited to Unearned Revenue. As of December 31, $5,000 of the supplies purchased had been delivered.
d. Accrued wages payable amounted to $500.

Required:

1. Prepare the necessary adjusting journal entries at December 31, 19x1.
2. Prepare the entries required to close the books.
3. Prepare an income statement for the year ended December 31, 19x1.

36. The following transactions took place between Flintstone's Friendly Fish Market and Barney's Beanery during June of 19x1.

June 1 Barney buys the following items from Flintstone:

  10 cases of Charlie the Tuna Fish @ $10 per case
  1 Fishing submarine @ $2,000,000

Terms of the sale are 2/10; n/30. The purchase was made on account.

  9 Barney notifies Flintstone that the shipment included eight cases as ordered, one case of horse meat, and one case of caviar. The submarine was O.K. Barney proposes that he keep the caviar and deduct 50¢ from the net amount which would otherwise be due. He plans to return the horse meat. Flintstone agrees and Barney mails him a check for the net amount after making the agreed-on deductions.

  15 Barney pays for the submarine.

Required:

1. Record the above transactions on Flintstone's books assuming that he records sales using the gross method.
2. Record the above transactions on Barney's books assuming he uses:

  a. The net method of recording purchases.
  b. The gross method of recording purchases.

37. Prepare the necessary journal entries for the Doyle Company for the following transactions. Make one set of entries assuming a perpetual inventory system, then make another assuming a periodic inventory system. In each case, assume inventory is determined on a Fifo basis.

    Jan. 1 Purchased 7 stoves at $300 each (assume no beginning inventory).
              3 Sold 2 stoves for $380 each.
              7 Sold 3 stoves for $370 each.
           11 Purchased 11 stoves at $260 each.
           19 Sold 1 stove for $370.
           23 Sold 3 stoves for $350.
           28 Purchased 5 stoves at $310 each.
           31 Ending inventory was 14 stoves.

38. Peterson Company sells a single product. The company began 19x1 with 20 units of the product on hand with a cost of $4 each. During 19x1 Peterson made the following purchases:

    February 3, 19x1..........................10 units @ $5
    April 16, 19x1.............................25 units @ $6
    October 6, 19x1..........................10 units @ $7
    December 7, 19x1........................10 units @ $8

During the year, 50 units of the product were sold. The periodic inventory method is used.

Required:

Compute the ending inventory balance and the cost of goods sold under each of the following methods:

1. Fifo.
2. Lifo.
3. Weighted Average.

39. Dente Company began business on January 1, 19x1. Purchases of merchandise for resale during 19x1 were as follows:

January 1......................	300 units @ $3.00	$ 900.00
February 7....................	600 units @ $3.50	2,100.00
March 25.....................	400 units @ $3.00	1,200.00
October 6.....................	800 units @ $2.50	2,000.00
November 10.................	300 units @ $2.50	750.00
November 16.................	300 units @ $2.25	675.00
	2,700 units	$7,625.00

A total of 2,200 units were sold during 19x1.

Required:

1. Compute the ending inventory at December 31, 19x1, under each of the following methods: (1) Fifo; (2) Lifo; (3) Average.
2. Considering the information given above and your computations for Dente Company, answer the following:

   a. Would the net income for 19x1 have been greater if the company had used (a) Fifo or (b) Lifo in computing its inventory?
   b. Assume that the market cost of the merchandise sold by Dente Company was $2.15 per unit at December 31, 19x1. Assuming the Fifo method of inventory valuation, what would the *total* carrying value of the inventory be if the lower of cost or market method is used?
   c. Give the journal entry necessary to reduce the inventory to market in (b) above.

40. On February 1, 19x1, the Sporting Goods Department of the Most Store had an inventory of $11,000 at retail selling price; the cost of this merchandise was $8,000.
During the three months ended April 30, purchases of $18,000 were made for that department and were marked to sell for $25,000. Freight-in on this merchandise was $1,000. Sales for the period amounted to $25,000. Sales returns and allowances were $900.
The physical inventory at retail amounted to $2,500.

Required:

Estimate the cost of theft or shrinkage.

41. The McDermott Company had a fire on June 30, 19x2, which completely destroyed its inventory. No physical inventory count had been taken since December 31, 19x1. The company's books showed the following balances at the date of the fire:

Sales		$180,000
Sales returns and allowances.............	$ 1,400	
Inventory, December 31, 19x1.............	40,000	
Purchases.............................	130,000	
Purchases returns and allowances..........		2,000
Transportation-in	1,600	
Selling expenses........................	50,000	
Administrative expenses..................	30,000	

4-38

Assume that the company's records show that in prior years it made a gross profit of approximately 25 percent of net sales, and there is no indication that this percentage cannot be considered to have continued during the first six months of this year.

Required:

Determine the cost of inventory destroyed by fire on June 30, 19x2.

42. A condensed income statement for the year ended December 31, 19x1 for Murcer Products shows the following:

Sales	$80,000
Cost of goods sold	50,000
Gross profit on sales	$30,000
Expenses	20,000
Net income	$10,000

An investigation of the records discloses the following errors in summarizing transactions for 19x1.

a. Ending inventory was overstated by $3,100.
b. Accrued expenses of $400 and prepaid expenses of $900 were not given accounting recognition at the end of 19x1.
c. Sales of $250 were not recorded although the goods were shipped and excluded from the inventory.
d. Purchases of $3,000 were made at the end of 19x1 but were not recorded although the goods were received and included in the ending inventory.

Required:

1. Prepare a corrected income statement for 19x1.
2. Prepare the entries necessary to correct the accounts in 19x1, assuming the books have not been closed.

43. The Yost Company began business on January 1, 19x1. Its reported net losses for the calendar years 19x1 and 19x2 were as follows:

19x1	$95,000 loss
19x2	$40,000 loss

Selected information from its accounting records is presented below:

Purchases of Goods for Resale

Date	Units		Price
February 1, 19x1	10,000	@	$10
May 1, 19x1	10,000	@	12
September 1, 19x1	10,000	@	15
December 1, 19x1	10,000	@	18
January 1, 19x2	10,000	@	20
March 1, 19x2	10,000	@	24
June 1, 19x2	10,000	@	25
November 1, 19x2	10,000	@	26

Sales

19x1	25,000 units
19x2	40,000 units

Other data:

The company uses the last-in, first-out (Lifo) method of inventory valuation.

Required:

1. Using the company's present inventory method (Lifo) compute:

    a. Ending inventory for the calendar years 19x1 and 19x2.
    b. Cost of goods sold for the calendar years 19x1 and 19x2.

2. Determine what the net income or net loss for each year would have been if the company had used the first-in, first-out (Fifo) method of inventory valuation.

44. Selected data for the Vernon Co., is as follows:

	Sales	Purchases
October	$10,000	$ 8,000
November	12,000	8,000
December	13,000	10,000

The inventory on hand at October 1st had a cost of $4,000. Goods are sold at a gross profit of 20 percent on sales.

Required:

Estimate the cost of the inventory on hand at October 31, November 30, and December 31.

Periodic + Perpetual

45. Purchases and sales for the Yastrzemski Company are as follows:

Date		Event	Units	Unit Cost	Total Value
June	1	Balance	300	$1.00	$300.00
	8	Sale	150		
			150		
	15	Purchase	330	2.00	660.00
			480		
	23	Sale	300		
			180		
	29	Purchase	400	2.10	840.00
	30	Balance	580		

Required: (Assume a periodic inventory.)

1. What is ending inventory under Fifo?
2. Determine ending inventory under Lifo.
3. Under Fifo, what is the cost of goods that were sold on June 23?
4. Using the average price, what is ending inventory?
5. Determine gross profit on sales of $4,000 for June, assuming the average, Fifo, and Lifo methods of inventory accounting.

46. Tiant Company began business on January 1, 19x1. During 19x1, it reported a loss of $104,000; during 19x2, it had a loss of $60,000.

    Selected information from its accounting records is presented below.

Purchases of Goods for Resale

Date	Units		Price
January 1, 19x1	10,000	@	$11
April 1, 19x1	10,000	@	13
August 1, 19x1	10,000	@	14
November 1, 19x1	10,000	@	16
February 1, 19x2	10,000	@	17
May 1, 19x2	10,000	@	20
August 1, 19x2	10,000	@	22
October 1, 19x2	10,000	@	23

Sales

19x1	27,000 units
19x2	42,000 units

Other data:

The company uses Lifo in valuing its inventory.

Required:

1. Using the company's present inventory method (Lifo) compute:

    a. Ending inventory for 19x1 and 19x2.
    b. Cost of goods sold for 19x1 and 19x2.

2. Determine what the net income or net loss for each year would have been if the company had used first-in, first-out (Fifo) method of inventory valuation.

Refer to the Annual Report included in the front of the text.

47. What inventory methods are used?

48. Comparing the two years presented, was there an increase or decrease in inventories?

49. What was the average inventory maintained during the most recent year?

50. During the most recent year, what were net sales?

51. Did gross profit increase or decrease in the most recent year?

52. What caused the increase or decrease in gross profit during the most recent year?

53. During the most recent year, what percentage gross profit was earned in relation to sales?

Chapter 5 discusses the accounting procedures used for recording and allocating the cost of plant and equipment, the disposition of plant and equipment, and the accounting for intangible assets and natural resources. Studying this chapter should enable you to:

1. Identify the purpose of, and information included on, a fixed asset ledger card.
2. Recognize the three basic factors that must be considered in recording periodic depreciation.
3. Discuss and apply the depreciation methods discussed in the chapter.
4. Differentiate between capital expenditures and revenue expenditures.
5. Record the disposition of plant and equipment.
6. Discuss the nature of intangible assets and the computation of amortization.
7. Explain the concept of depletion of natural resources.

5

Long-Term Assets

INTRODUCTION The term plant and equipment refers to long-lived tangible assets which are used in the continuing operations of a business over a number of years. They are assets which are aquired for *use* in the firm's operations as contrasted to those assets which are purchased for *resale* to the customers of a business. Examples of plant and equipment include land, buildings, equipment, furniture, and fixtures. Plant and equipment may be regarded as a "bundle" of services that are used over the life of the asset in the process of generating revenue. In accordance with the matching principle, as these services expire through use in generating revenue, a portion of the cost of the asset should be allocated to expense. The costs which are to be allocated to expense in future periods may be considered deferred costs and are shown as assets on the balance sheet. This process of periodically allocating the cost of tangible plant and equipment to expense is referred to as *depreciation*.

In this chapter we will discuss the accounting procedures used to record the acquisition and use of long-lived assets including tangibles and material resources, and those procedures used to determine the depreciation expense for the period.

CONTROL OVER TANGIBLE LONG-TERM ASSETS

A fixed asset ledger card should be prepared and maintained for each individual asset purchased. This card should include all of the pertinent information relating to the asset and its use. This data will enable the management of the firm to establish and maintain control over each individual asset (for example, by providing the basis for taking a physical inventory of all fixed assets owned by the firm). It will also assist in accounting for all transactions relating to plant assets. For example, the fixed asset ledger card will provide the information which is required in order to calculate the periodic depreciation expense for the asset and the data required to adjust the accounts as assets are sold or retired.

Using a ledger card for an automobile as an illustration, the following information should ordinarily be provided:

Asset Ledger Account

Description	Cost	Depreciation	Other Information
Name of asset	Date acquired	Estimated life	Repairs:
Account number	Invoice cost	Estimated salvage	Date
Asset number	Other costs	value	Amount
Manufacturer's serial		Depreciation	Actual life
number		to date	Date on disposal:
Horsepower			Date
Insurance carried			Sales price
Property tax valuation			(if any)
			Gain or loss
			To whom sold

TYPES OF PLANT AND EQUIPMENT

Plant and equipment may be classified into two categories for accounting purposes: land and depreciable assets. Since the assumption is made that land is not used up over time, the cost of land is not subject to depreciation. All other items of plant and equipment are assumed to have a limited useful life, and therefore, the cost of these items is allocated to expense through periodic depreciation charges.

ACCOUNTING FOR TANGIBLE FIXED ASSETS

All costs incurred in acquiring an asset and preparing the asset for productive use are capitalized as the cost of the asset by debiting them to the asset account. The costs include the net invoice price, transportation costs, and installation costs. All costs that are incurred before the asset becomes productive, such as demolition of old buildings on a building site or repairs of or to used equipment acquired for production, is considered to be a cost of the acquired asset. A proper determination of the total cost of a plant asset is important because the cost of an asset (less any salvage value, i.e., the amount the firm can recover when the firm has finished using it) becomes an expense which should be charged against the income of the business during the periods the asset is used by the firm.[1] This process of allocating the cost of an asset to expense is known as depreciation.

Plant assets are normally acquired either by cash purchase or by incurring a liability (or by a combination of a cash down payment and incurring a liability for future payments). If a liability is incurred, the interest cost associated with the liability should be recorded as interest expense and not as a cost of the asset acquired. Plant assets may also be acquired in exchange for other assets owned by the firm. The procedures used in accounting for assets acquired by exchange are discussed in the following chapter.

In certain cases, more than a single asset may be acquired for a lump sum purchase price. Because the assets acquired may have different useful lives (or, in the case of land, an unlimited life), it is necessary to allocate the total purchase price among the assets acquired. Normally, this allocation is based upon the relative appraisal values of the assets involved. For example, assume that a company acquired land, building, and equipment for a total cost of $200,000. Assume that the company making the acquisition determined the following appraisal values for the individual items:

Land	$ 75,000
Building	150,000
Equipment	25,000
Total appraised value	$250,000

The apportionment of the $200,000 purchase price is made on the basis of the relative values of the assets and would be as follows:

Asset	Appraisal Value	Fraction of Total Appraisal Value	Allocation of Cost
Land	$ 75,000	$ 75,000 ÷ $250,000 = .3	$ 60,000
Building	150,000	$150,000 ÷ $250,000 = .6	120,000
Equipment	25,000	$ 25,000 ÷ $250,000 = .1	20,000
	$250,000		$200,000

The cost of an asset includes all expenditures which are necessary to acquire the asset and place it in use. For example, a company buys a delivery truck with a list price of $10,000. The company received a 10 percent reduction in price from the dealer and also a 2 percent cash discount. The company pays a 5 percent sales tax and in addition, purchases a stereo for the truck paying $300 including installation. The cost of the new truck is computed as follows:

---

[1] The cost of land, which is not used up in the generation of revenue, is not allocated to expense. Instead, the original cost of the asset is maintained in the accounts until the asset is disposed of.

List price		$10,000
Less:	10% reduction	1,000
		$ 9,000
Less:	2% cash discount	180
		$ 8,820
Sales taxes		441
Stereo		300
Cost of the truck		$ 9,561

The $9,561 cost is the balance in the asset account and is the basis for computing depreciation. To charge the sales tax and the stereo to the expenses in the year the truck is acquired would overstate expenses for that period and understate expenses for the following periods.

Land. The cost of land includes the purchase price, commissions, any taxes due, and other similar costs. Any cost incurred to grade, level, and demolish old buildings are added to the cost of the land but any proceeds from the sale of scrap reduces the cost. Land is not subject to depreciation and its cost is retained in the land account until it is sold.

Buildings. The cost of constructing a building includes excavation, building materials, labor, and all other costs necessary to place the building in use. Costs, such as interest on borrowed construction funds and real estate taxes, incurred during the construction are also part of the total building cost.

Machinery and Equipment. In addition to the normal costs of acquiring machinery and equipment, such costs as supports, wiring, inspection, and testing are charged to the machinery and equipment account.

DEPRECIATION

As previously indicated, the process of charging the cost of a fixed asset to expense over its useful life is referred to as depreciation. *Depreciation is defined more formally as the systematic and rational allocation of the cost of an asset, less its salvage value (if any), over the periods in which benefits are received from the use of the asset.* Note that this definition indicates only that the allocation of cost should be systematic and rational. A basic problem with this approach is that there is no precise definition of "systematic and rational." The criterion of rationality normally is related to the expected benefits (decline in service potential) of an asset. In this context, depreciation is a process of allocating the cost of an asset, and not a process of asset valuation. Therefore, the accounting definition of depreciation does not consider either a change in market value or a physical change in an asset.

Depreciation accounting is a method of allocation by which an attempt is made to match the cost of an asset against the revenue that has been generated or produced from using the asset. In this cost allocation approach, the depreciation expense for a particular period represents an estimate of the portion of the cost of an asset that is used up or that otherwise expires during that period.

A precise determination of the depreciation expense related to an individual asset for any given period is difficult, because it generally is impossible to predict accurately either the exact useful life of an asset or the decline in service potential that occurs during any specific period. The life of an asset and, therefore, the related depreciation are affected by a combination of factors such as the passage of time, normal wear and tear, physical deterioration, and obsolescence. In addition, even if the useful life of an asset were entirely predictable, it normally would be impossible to determine the distribution of the benefits (service potential) to be received from the use of the asset over time. Although the various techniques that may be employed in determining depreciation may appear to be precise, and from a mathematical viewpoint this is the case, it should be noted that depreciation is always an estimate or approximation because of the estimation of both useful life and salvage value. However, periodic measurement of that portion of the cost of an asset that has been used up or has expired during a period is a necessary element in determining the income for that period.

The basic nature of and the problems involved in depreciation accounting may be illustrated by the use of a simple example. Assume that you decide to purchase a Chevrolet for use as a taxi cab. The cost of the auto is $9,000. You feel that you will be able to earn approximately $12,000 each year in fares, and the estimated operating costs (gas, oil, repairs, insurance, etc.) will be approximately $4,000 per year. You further estimate that the auto will last for four years at which time it will probably have to be replaced. At the end of the four-year period you estimate that your used Chevrolet may be sold for about $1,000. What would your earnings be over the four years if your estimates prove to be accurate? Total income for the four-year period might be calculated as follows:

Your Taxi Company
Income Statement
For Four Years

Revenues ($12,000 per year for 4 years)		$48,000
Operating costs ($4,000 per year for 4 years)	$16,000	
Cost of the taxi ($9,000 cost less $1,000 received from its sale at the end of the four-year period)	8,000	
Total costs.		24,000
Net income.		$24,000

Assume now that you wished to prepare separate income statements for each of the four years. You could do the following:

Your Taxi Company
Income Statements

	For the Year				
	1	2	3	4	Total
Revenues	$12,000	$12,000	$12,000	$12,000	$48,000
Operating costs	$ 4,000	$ 4,000	$ 4,000	$ 4,000	$16,000
Cost of the taxi	9,000	0	0	(1,000)	8,000
	$13,000	$ 4,000	$ 4,000	$ 3,000	$24,000
Net income (loss)	($1,000)	$ 8,000	$ 8,000	$ 9,000	$24,000

*The negative thousand dollars shown as "cost of the taxi" represents the proceeds received from its sale at the end of the fourth year (i.e., its salvage value).

But do these statements really reflect the actual facts of the situation? Is it reasonable to report that your income increased significantly during year two, remained constant during the third year and then increased slightly in year four? Of course not. The total for the four years seems to be reasonable, but the problem lies in attempting to measure the income for *each* individual year. This difficulty arises because you purchased the car and paid for it at the beginning of year one, used it for four years and sold it at the end of the fourth year. In order to measure the income for each year properly, it is necessary to allocate, in a rational and systematic manner, the net cost of owning the auto (i.e., the purchase price of the car less its estimated salvage value) over the periods which benefit from its use.

As previously indicated, the process of amortizing or charging the cost of a fixed asset to expense over the period of its useful life is referred to as depreciation. A more formal definition of depreciation is ". . . the systematic allocation of the cost of an asset, less salvage value (if any) over its estimated useful life."

From a theoretical viewpoint, depreciation expense for a particular period represents an estimate of the portion of the cost of an asset which is used up or which otherwise expires during that period. A precise determination of the depreciation expense related to an individual asset for any given year is difficult because it is almost impossible to accurately predict the exact useful life of an asset. The life of an asset, and therefore its depreciation, is affected by a combination of factors such as the passage of time, normal wear and tear, physical deterioration, and obsolescence. Even though the various techniques which can be employed in determining the depreciation may appear to be precise, and from a mathematical viewpoint they are. It should be noted that because of the estimating of useful life, salvage value, etc., depreciation is always an estimate or approximation. However, periodic measurement of that portion of the cost of an asset which has been used up or has expired during a period is a necessary element in determining the income of the firm for that period. Depreciation accounting is a method of allocation by which an attempt is made to "match" the cost of an asset against the revenue which has been generated or produced from using the asset.

ELEMENTS AFFECTING THE DETERMINATION OF PERIODIC DEPRECIATION

The depreciation process represents the allocation of the costs (less any estimated residual or salvage value) of property, plant, and equipment over the expected useful life of the asset. As discussed previously, the cost of a long-lived asset includes all of the expenditures associated with its acquisition and preparation for use. The additional factors which must be considered in the estimate of periodic depreciation for an asset include:

1. Estimated useful life
2. Estimated salvage (residual) value
3. Methods of allocation.

Useful Life

The useful life of an asset is that period of time during which it is of economic use to the business. The estimation of the useful life of an asset should consider such factors as economic analysis, engineering studies, previous experience with similar assets, and any other available information concerning the characteristics of the asset. However, regardless of the quantity of information available, the determination of the useful life of an asset is a judgment process which requires the prediction of future events.

The period of economic usefulness of an asset to a business is a function of both physical and functional factors. Physical factors include normal wear, deterioration and decay, and damage or destruction. These physical factors limit the economic useful life of an asset by rendering the asset incapable of effectively performing its intended function. Thus, the physical factors limit the maximum potential economic life of the asset.

Functional factors may also cause the useful life of an asset to be less than its physical life. The primary functional factors which may limit the service life of an asset are obsolescence and inadequacy. Obsolescence is caused by changes in technology or changes in demand for the output product or services which cause the asset to be inefficient or uneconomical before the end of its physical life. Inadequacy may result from changes in the size or volume of activity which cause an asset to be economically incapable of handling or processing the required output. In a high technology, growth-oriented economy such as that of the United States, functional factors generally impact significantly upon the determination of the useful life of an asset.

Salvage Value

Salvage value is the estimated realizable value of an asset at the end of its expected life. Depending upon the expectations regarding the disposition of an asset, this amount may be based on such factors as scrap value, second-hand market value, or anticipated trade-in value. The depreciation base used for an asset normally is equal to the difference between the acquisition cost of the asset and its salvage value.

This depreciation base is the amount of the cost of an asset which is allocated to expense over the expected useful life of the asset.

The relationship between salvage value and the cost of an asset varies considerably. In some cases, particularly when the estimated useful life of an asset is significantly less than its physical life, salvage value may be substantial. On the other hand, in certain instances, the estimated residual value of an asset may be so small that the salvage value is assumed to be zero in computing the depreciation base. Of course, the validity of the periodic depreciation expense is dependent upon a reasonably accurate estimate of both the salvage value of an asset and its useful life.

Depreciation Methods

Theoretically, the selection of a depreciation method should be based on the expectations regarding the pattern of decline in the service potential of the asset under consideration. Because both the nature and the characteristics of various assets may vary significantly, alternative depreciation patterns may be justified. Accordingly, there are a number of acceptable depreciation methods which mathematically approximate the possible pattern of use expected from an asset. However, in practice, the criteria for selecting a particular depreciation method are often not determinable. It has been suggested by some that depreciation accounting is used by management as a factor in implementing its financial policy. That is, management may select the method(s) which contribute to the desired financial results that it hopes to achieve over time. The consistency principle does require that once a method has been adopted for a particular type of asset, the firm must continue to use that method over time. Because of the number of alternative methods which are available, the depreciation expense for each period may vary significantly depending upon the method selected. Each of the methods, however, results in the identical total depreciation expense over the useful life of the asset(s).

In recording the periodic depreciation for fixed costs, three basic factors must be considered:

1. The cost of the asset—the invoice cost plus all costs which are necessary to place it in use.
2. The estimated useful life of the asset.
3. The estimated salvage or scrap value of the asset—the amount which will be recovered when the asset is retired.

This section of the chapter will discuss four of the methods which are used in accounting for the use of long-term tangible assets in the operations of businesses: the straight-line method, the declining-balance method, the sum-of-the-years'-digits method, and the accelerated cost recovery system. Each of these methods results in identical total depreciation over the life of a fixed asset—an amount equal to the original cost of the asset or, when appropriate, the original cost less its estimated salvage value. The methods differ, however, in the amount of cost which is allocated to expense during each year of the life of the asset. To illustrate these techniques, the following data will be used:

Type of asset............................	Chevrolet
Date acquired	January 1, 19x1
Cost (including delivery, sales tax, etc.).......	$9,000
Estimated useful life	4 years
Estimated salvage value	$1,000

Straight-Line Depreciation. One of the simplest and most commonly used methods of computing depreciation is the straight-line method. This method considers the passage of time to be the most important single factor or limitation on the useful life of an asset. It assumes that other factors such as wear and tear and obsolescence are somewhat proportional to the elapsed time; this may or may not be the case in fact. The straight-line method allocates the cost of an asset, less its salvage value, to expense equally over its useful life. A formula which may be employed in calculating depreciation using the straight-line method is as follows:

$$\frac{\left(\begin{array}{c}\text{Cost of} \\ \text{the Asset}\end{array} - \begin{array}{c}\text{Estimated} \\ \text{Salvage} \\ \text{Value}\end{array}\right)}{\text{Estimated Useful Life}} = \text{Depreciation for the Period}$$

Substituting the illustrative data presented above in the formula, we obtain the following calculation of depreciation for 19x1:

$$\frac{(\$9,000 - \$1,000)}{4 \text{ years}} = \$2,000 \text{ per year}$$

Since the straight-line method of depreciation allocates an identical dollar amount of depreciation expense to each period, depreciation for the years 19x2, 19x3, and 19x4 (the remaining useful life of the automobile) would also be $2,000 each year.

Accelerated Methods of Depreciation. Business-persons recognize that the benefits obtained from the use of a fixed asset frequently may not be uniform over its useful life. Both the revenue producing ability of an asset and its value may decline at a faster rate during the early years of its life. Also, the costs of repairing and maintaining the asset may increase during the later years of its life. Furthermore, one accelerated depreciation method, Modified Accelerated Cost Recovery System (MACRS) is permitted for income tax purposes and may benefit the taxpayer by postponing or deferring the payment of taxes to a later year. Although a business may use different methods of computing depreciation for accounting and tax purposes, firms often wish to simplify their recordkeeping by using the same method for both purposes. For these reasons, many businesses will adopt MACRS. In general, accelerated methods of calculating depreciation allow the recording of larger amounts of depreciation in the early periods of an asset's life rather than in later years. As indicated above, a business may choose to employ the MACRS method for computing the expense relating to the use of its fixed assets for tax purposes because the increased depreciation charges (which do not require the outlay of cash, since the cash expenditure was made at the time the asset was acquired) reduce taxable income and therefore reduce the amount of income tax currently payable. By postponing or deferring the payment of income taxes from an earlier to a later year of an asset's life, the business has obtained, in effect, an interest-free loan from the taxing authority.[2]

Three commonly-used methods of accelerated depreciation will be illustrated: the double-declining balance method, the sum-of-the-years'-digits method, and MACRS.

The Double-Declining Balance Method. The procedures used in applying the double-declining balance method arbitrarily double the depreciation rate which would be used in calculating depreciation under the straight-line method.[3] This increased rate is then applied to the book value (i.e., the cost of the asset less the total depreciation taken to-date) of the assets. The formula used in calculating double-declining balance depreciation is as follows:

$$[(2 \times \text{Straight-line rate}) \times (\text{Cost} - \text{Depreciation taken in prior periods}) = \text{Depreciation for a period}]$$

Salvage value is ignored in the computation of depreciation under the double-declining balance method with the exception of the final year. In the final year of the asset's life, the formula is ignored and the depreciation taken is simply whatever amount is necessary to reduce the book value of the asset to its salvage value.

Using the same data as in the previous example, the calculation of double-declining balance depreciation may be illustrated as follows:

$$(2 \times 25\%) \times (\$9,000 - \$0) = \$4,500 \text{ depreciation for 19x1}$$

---

[2] See Chapter 12 for a detailed discussion of income tax allocation.

[3] The straight-line rate may be calculated by dividing the useful life of the asset (in years) into 100 percent. For the example used, the straight-line rate would be 100 percent divided by 4 or 25 percent.

The straight-line rate is 25 percent; since the asset has a useful life of four years, one-fourth (or 25%) of the cost is expensed each year using the straight-line method. The doubled rate (2 × 25%) is applied to the full cost of $9,000 since the salvage value is ignored in the initial years of the asset's life and there is, of course, no depreciation from prior years.

The depreciation charge for 19x2 would be calculated as follows:

(2 × 25%) × ($9,000 − $4,500) = $2,250 depreciation for 19x2

The only change from the previous year is that $4,500, the depreciation taken in 19x1, is substituted for $0 in the first calculation.

Depreciation for 19x3 would be:

(2 × 25%) × ($9,000 − $6,750) = $1,125 depreciation for 19x3

Again, the only change in the formula is in the depreciation taken in prior years. The $6,750 amount used in the computation of depreciation for 19x3 is the 19x1 depreciation of $4,500 plus the 19x2 depreciation of $2,250.

The formula would not be used to calculate the depreciation expense for 19x4, since this is the final year of the asset's useful life. Depreciation for 19x4 would be computed as follows:

Cost of the asset...........................		$9,000
Less: Depreciation taken in prior years:		
19x1...........................	$4,500	
19x2...........................	2,250	
19x3...........................	1,125	7,875
Net book value of the asset at January 1, 19x4.......		$1,125
Less: Estimated salvage value................		1,000
Depreciation for 19x4		$ 125

The Sum-of-the-Years'-Digits Method. The use of the sum-of-the-years'-digits method also produces greater charges for depreciation in the early years of an asset's useful life. The life-years of an asset are totalled[4] and utilized as the denominator of a fraction that uses the number of years of life remaining from the beginning of the year (i.e., the years in reverse order) as the numerator. This fraction is then applied to the cost of the asset less its estimated salvage value in order to compute the depreciation for the period.

Again, using the same data as in the previous illustrations, the depreciation expense for each of the four years, 19x1 through 19x4, using the sum-of-the-years'-digits method, would be calculated as follows:

---

[4] The sum of the numbers from one to the estimated life of an asset in years. For example, the life-years of an asset with a three-year estimated life would be 1 + 2 + 3 = 6. [Sum of arithmetic progression of n consecutive numbers $= n\dfrac{(n+1)}{2}$.]

Sum-of-the-years'-digits:

$$1 + 2 + 3 + 4 = 10$$

Depreciation for each period:

19x1: 4/10 × ($9,000 − $1,000) = $3,200
19x2: 3/10 × ($9,000 − $1,000) = $2,400
19x3: 2/10 × ($9,000 − $1,000) = $1,600
19x4: 1/10 × ($9,000 − $1,000) = $ 800

MACRS and ACRS. Effective January 1, 1981, the Accelerated Cost Recovery System (ACRS) was implemented, introducing significant changes in the manner in which depreciation expense is computed for federal income tax purposes. The Tax Reform Act of 1986 made some additional changes and adopted the Modified Accelerated Cost Recovery System (MACRS). While the straight-line, sum-of-the-years'-digits, and double-declining balance methods may still be used for financial accounting and reporting purposes, MACRS methods are the only accelerated methods which may be used for federal income tax purposes.[5] Essentially, MACRS places all depreciable assets into six classes of depreciable personal property or to one of two classes of real property, summarized on the following page.

Although the property classes described above are identified by years, the concept of useful life for the calculation of depreciation expense has been discontinued under the MACRS rules. Rather, depreciation expense for the three-, five-, seven-, and ten-year classes is calculated using double-declining balance depreciation. Depreciation on assets in the fifteen- and twenty-year classes is computed using the 150 percent declining balance method. A switch to a straight-line approach is permitted in the year that the depreciation expense using the straight-line method exceeds MACRS depreciation. The straight-line method must be used for all real estate and under MACRS rules, a taxpayer may elect to use the straight-line method of depreciation rather than MACRS. Also, the taxpayer electing MACRS must use the half-year convention which requires that the taxpayer take one-half year's depreciation expense in the year an asset is acquired and disposed of, regardless of the actual dates. Salvage value may be ignored in calculating depreciation under MACRS.

---

[5] MACRS is used for tangible assets placed in service after 1986. ACRS was used for assets placed in service after 1980 but before 1987. For tangible assets acquired prior to 1981, the depreciation methods that are permissable for tax purposes are: straight-line, double-declining balance, and sum-of-the-years'-digits.

MACRS Property Classifications

MACRS Classes and Methods	Special Rules
Three-year, 200% declining balance	Includes some race horses and road tractors. Excludes cars and light trucks.
Five-year, 200% declining balance	Includes cars and light trucks, heavy general purpose trucks, typewriters, computers, and copiers.
Seven-year, 200% declining balance	Includes office furniture and fixtures, single-purpose agricultural and horticultural structures placed in service before 1989. Includes property never assigned a class life.
Ten-year, 200% declining balance	Includes water transportation equipment, fruit or nut-bearing trees or vines, and single purpose agricultural and horticultural structures placed in service after 1988.
Fifteen-year, 150% declining balance	Includes telephone distribution plants.
Twenty-year, 150% declining balance	Includes farm buildings. Excludes real property with ADR midpoint of twenty-five years or more.
27.5-year, straight-line	Residential rental property.
31.5-year, straight-line	Nonresidential real property.

Using the same data as in the previous examples, the depreciation expense using MACRS would be calculated as follows:

				Annual	Cumulative
19x1:	(2 × 20%) × ($9,000 − 0) × ½	=		$1,800	$1,800
19x2:	(2 × 20%) × ($9,000 − $1,800)	=		2,880	4,680
19x3:	(2 × 20%) × ($9,000 − $4,680)	=		1,728	6,408
19x4:	(2 × 20%) × ($9,000 − $6,408)	=		1,037	7,445
19x5:	(2 × 20%) × ($9,000 − $7,445)	=		622	8,067
19x6:	$9,000 − $8,067	=		833	9,000

Note that only one-half year's depreciation is taken in 19x1, the year of acquisition, because of the half-year convention. The remaining undepreciated cost is charged to depreciation in 19x6, also because of the half-year convention.

As is now apparent, except for MACRS (which ignores salvage value), the *total* amount of depreciation taken for a fixed asset over its useful life will be identical regardless of the method used, although the timing and pattern of the depreciation charges vary widely according to the particular method chosen. The effects of the various methods on the example data are illustrated below:

Year	Straight-Line	Double-Declining Balance	Sum-of-the-Years'-Digits	MACRS
19x1	$2,000	$4,500	$3,200	$1,800
19x2	2,000	2,250	2,400	2,880
19x3	2,000	1,125	1,600	1,728
19x4	2,000	125	800	1,037
19x5	0	0	0	622
19x6	0	0	0	833
Total	$8,000	$8,000	$8,000	$9,000

The differences in the depreciation expense depending on the method chosen are illustrated graphically on the following page.

Because depreciation expense is an important factor which enters into the determination of the income of a firm for a period, the reported income will also vary according to the depreciation method selected. The effect of depreciation on the reported income of the firm is an important factor in the selection of the depreciation method(s) a firm will use. However, *the consistency principle requires that once a method has been adopted for a particular type of asset, the firm must continue to use that method consistently over time.*

RECORDING LONG-TERM ASSETS

Using the Chevrolet acquired by Your Taxi Company as an example, the accounting procedures for recording the acquisition and use of plant assets will be illustrated.

On January 1, 19x1, the acquisition of the automobile would be recorded as follows:

```
Automobile ..........................  9,000
    Cash ...........................          9,000
```

It should be noted that the debit to the asset account was for the total cost of the Chevrolet including delivery charges, sales tax, etc. In this instance, the car was paid for in cash. Had a liability been incurred, it would have been recorded by a credit. The procedures required when an old asset is traded in on a new asset are discussed later in this chapter.

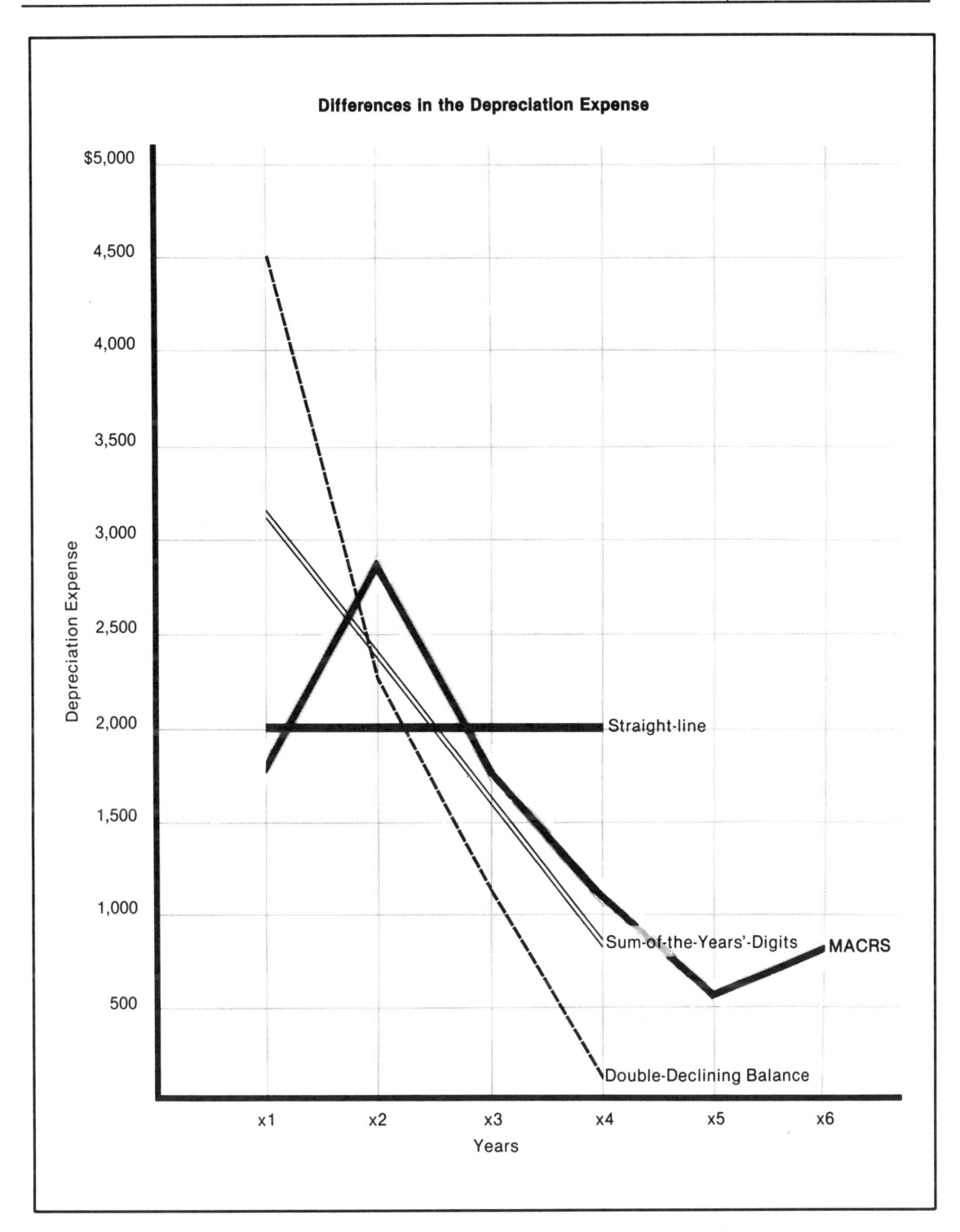

Differences in the Depreciation Expense

At the end of 19x1, it would be necessary to record depreciation on the asset in order to charge to expense the portion of the cost of the asset which had been "used up" during the period. For purposes of illustration, we will assume that the straight-line method of depreciation was used. On December 31, 19x1, depreciation would be recorded in the books of Your Taxi Company by the following entry:

    Depreciation expense 2,000
        Accumulated depreciation   2,000

The debit to depreciation expense records the portion of the cost of the asset which is to be charged as an expense of the period. The credit to the accumulated depreciation account adds the current period's depreciation to that which was taken in prior years (in this case zero since this is the initial year of the asset's useful life); the total of this account indicates the total amount of depreciation taken to-date at any given point in time. The depreciation expense of $2,000 would appear in the income statement along with the other expenses of the period and would be deducted from revenue in the determination of income. Accumulated depreciation would appear as an offset (called a contra account) against the related asset account in the balance sheet as follows:

Current assets........................			$10,000
Automobile	$9,000		
Less: Accumulated depreciation	2,000		7,000
Total assets.........................			$17,000

Since the straight-line method of depreciation was used, the entries which are required in order to record depreciation expense for the years 19x2, 19x3, and 19x4 will be the same as the one which was made on December 31, 19x1, shown above. The automobile and accumulated depreciation accounts would appear as follows:

Automobile		Accumulated Depreciation	
(a) 9,000		(b)	2,000
		(c)	2,000
		(d)	2,000
		(e)	2,000
		(f)	8,000

Key:
(a) Cost of the automobile on January 1, 19x1.
(b) Depreciation for 19x1.
(c) Depreciation for 19x2.
(d) Depreciation for 19x3.
(e) Depreciation for 19x4.
(f) Balance in the account at December 31, 19x5.

Occasionally, plant assets are used for periods of time beyond their originally estimated lives. Since the purpose or objective of depreciation accounting is to allocate the cost of a plant asset to expense over its useful life, no additional depreciation should be recorded for an asset which has already been fully depreciated. The cost of the asset, along with the associated accumulated depreciation should remain in the accounts until the asset is disposed of.

Assets Acquired During the Period

In the example used in the previous section, the automobile was acquired at the beginning of the period. In practice, assets will be acquired throughout the accounting period and this will require that depreciation be recorded for a part of a period in the year of acquisition. For example, the purchase of the automobile on June 1, 19x1, would be recorded as follows:

```
Automobile........................  9,000
    Cash ..........................         9,000
```

At the end of 19x1, it would be necessary to record depreciation on the asset for the seven-month period that it was used during the year (June 1, 19x1 to December 31, 19x1). Again, we will assume the same facts as before (4-year life, $1,000 salvage value) and that the straight-line method of depreciation was used, so the calculation would be as follows:

$$\frac{(\$9,000 - \$1,000)}{4 \text{ years}} = \$2,000 \text{ per year}$$

$$\frac{\$2,000}{12 \text{ months}} = \$166.67 \text{ per month}$$

Depreciation for the period June 1, 19x1 to December 31, 19x1, would be 7 months × $166.67 per month or a total of $1,167 (rounded). At December 31, 19x1, depreciation for the period would be recorded by the following entry:

```
Depreciation expense .................  1,167
    Accumulated depreciation ..........         1,167
```

The entries to record depreciation expense for the years 19x2, 19x3, and 19x4 would each cover a full year and each would be as follows:

```
Depreciation expense .................  2,000
    Accumulated depreciation ..........         2,000
```

In 19x5, depreciation would be recorded for the final five months of the life of the asset (5 months × $166.67 per month or $833) by the following entry:

```
Depreciation expense .................  833
    Accumulated depreciation ..........         833
```

The automobile and accumulated depreciation accounts would appear as follows:

Automobile			Accumulated Depreciation	
(a) 9,000			(b)	1,167
			(c)	2,000
			(d)	2,000
			(e)	2,000
			(f)	833
			(g)	8,000

Key:
- (a) Cost of the automobile on June 1, 19x1.
- (b) Depreciation for 19x1 (7 months).
- (c) Depreciation for 19x2 (12 months).
- (d) Depreciation for 19x3 (12 months).
- (e) Depreciation for 19x4 (12 months).
- (f) Depreciation for 19x5 (5 months).
- (g) Balance in the account at May 31, 19x5.

In the above example, depreciation was calculated from the exact date of acquisition until the end of the useful life of the asset. In practice, as a matter of convenience, a business may establish a procedure whereby it will always take six months' depreciation in the year an asset is acquired and six months' depreciation in the year it is disposed of (see next section) irrespective of the exact dates of acquisition or disposal. Alternatively, a firm might take a full year's depreciation in the year of acquisition and no depreciation in the year of disposal, or vice-versa. The use of procedures such as those described above do not change the entries illustrated and are generally acceptable as long as there is no significant distortion of depreciation expense or income.

Interest Costs

Frequently, firms borrow substantial sums for the purpose of constructing or acquiring property, plant, and equipment. A basic accounting issue which exists with regard to the interest costs relating to these borrowings is whether the interest should be considered an expense of the period or included (capitalized) as a part of the cost of the asset acquired or constructed. The charging of interest to expense has been defended on the grounds that interest represents the cost of financing and is not a cost which should be associated with a specific asset. Capitalizing interest costs, on the other hand, has been justified on the basis that an asset should be charged with all of the costs necessary to place it in its intended use. It may be argued that the interest incurred is as much a cost of acquiring an asset as is the cost of any other resources used or expended.

Until recently, the proper accounting for interest costs had been an unresolved issue. In 1979, however, the FASB issued its *Statement No. 34*, "Capitalization of Interest Costs," which *requires* capitalizing interest as a part of the cost of acquiring *certain* assets. In this pronouncement, the FASB concluded:

On the premise that the historical cost of acquiring an asset should include all costs necessarily incurred to bring it to the condition and location necessary for its intended use, . . . in principle, the cost incurred in financing expenditures for an asset during a required construction or development period is itself a part of the asset's historical acquisition cost.

The assets which qualify for interest capitalization generally are those assets that require a period of time to place them in their intended use. Interest *should be capitalized* for those assets that are: (1) constructed by a company for its own use, (2) constructed for a company by another entity and for which progress payments are made, and (3) constructed as discrete projects (e.g., shipping or real estate developments) intended for sale or lease. Examples of these qualifying assets include those constructed for an entity's own use (e.g., a manufacturing facility) or those intended for sale or lease that are constructed as discrete projects (e.g., ships or real estate projects). Interest should not be capitalized as a part of the cost of inventories that are routinely manufactured or otherwise produced in large quantities on a repetitive basis even if these inventories require lengthy maturation periods, such as is the case with whiskey or tobacco. Interest cost eligible for capitalization is limited to amounts incurred on borrowings and other obligations. *The amount of interest to be capitalized during the construction period is that portion of the incurred interest charges that theoretically could have been avoided by either not borrowing additional funds for the asset or by using the amounts expended on the asset for the retirement of existing debt.* The amount to be capitalized is determined by applying an interest rate to the average amount of accumulated expenditures for the asset during the construction or development period.

Disclosure in the Financial Statements

Because the amount of periodic depreciation depends on the method or methods of depreciation in use, it is necessary that information on the depreciation method(s) be disclosed in the financial statements. Such information is necessary for a meaningful comparison of the depreciation charges of different companies or for prediction of future depreciation charges of a company. Consequently, the Accounting Principles Board in Opinion No. 12 indicated that the following disclosures should be made in the financial statements or accompanying notes:

1. Depreciation expense for the period.
2. Balances of major classes of depreciable assets, by nature or function, at the balance sheet date.

3. Accumulated depreciation, either by major classes of depreciable assets or in total, at the balance sheet date.

4. A general description of the method or methods used in computing depreciation with respect to major classes of depreciable assets.[6]

COSTS INCURRED AFTER ACQUISITION

It is often necessary to make additional expenditures relating to plant assets subsequent to the date of acquisition. These expenditures occur for various reasons, from routine maintenance and repairs to major additions and improvements.

The major accounting issue relating to these expenditures is determining whether they should be charged to expense in the period in which they are incurred or capitalized as an asset. The general rule for handling these costs is that *those expenditures that increase future economic benefits should be capitalized (i.e., be recorded as capital expenditures), whereas those expenditures that simply maintain the existing economic benefits should be expensed (i.e., recorded as revenue expenditures).* An increase in future economic benefits may occur if the expenditure extends the economic life of the asset, increases its productivity, increases the quality, or reduces the cost of the items produced by the asset.

It is important to classify an expenditure properly as either an asset or an expense. If the cost of an asset is classified incorrectly as an expense, then the net income for the current period will be understated and the net income of the future periods, in which the benefits of the expenditures are received, would be overstated due to an understatement of depreciation expense.

Since capital expenditures increase the future economic benefits of an asset, the costs incurred are recorded in an asset account. On the other hand, revenue expenditures benefit only the current operations, and these costs are recorded by debits to expense accounts.

Capital expenditures for existing assets are often classified as additions or improvements. An addition represents an increase in the physical substance of an asset, such as a new wing on a building. Improvements (or replacements) involve the substitution of new parts on an existing asset. Examples of improvements include the installation of elevators in a building or an air conditioner in a delivery truck. If the addition or improvement has the same economic life as the existing asset, the cost should be capitalized directly to the asset account. When the expenditure extends the economic life of the asset, the depreciable life of the asset should be extended accordingly. If the item has a different economic life than the existing asset, the cost should be capitalized in a separate asset account and expensed over the period of expected benefit.

---

[6] *Opinions of the Accounting Principles Board No. 12,* "Omnibus Opinion—1967" (New York: AICPA, 1967), para. 5.

Revenue expenditures are routine and recurring expenditures which are incurred to maintain an asset in operating condition and which do not increase the economic benefits associated with the asset. Examples of typical revenue expenditures are routine maintenance (i.e., oil change and lubrication) and ordinary repairs (i.e., replacing a worn out tire).

Theoretically, if an expenditure increases the economic benefits originally expected from an asset, then the cost should be capitalized. In practice, however, it is often difficult to make a distinction between a capital expenditure and a revenue expenditure. In many companies, arbitrary policies are established for defining capital and revenue expenditures. For example, an expenditure might be capitalized only if it: (1) clearly increases the economic benefits associated with an existing asset, and (2) exceeds a minimum cost (such as $50). The use of a minimum cost for capitalization eliminates the need to recompute depreciation schedules for minor improvements or additions.

To illustrate the accounting for a capital expenditure, assume that in January, 19x5, a company spent $3,000 to recondition an existing delivery truck. The truck had been acquired on January 1, 19x1, for $16,000, and at that time, had an estimated useful life of five years and a salvage value of $1,000. The truck was depreciated using the straight-line method. Therefore, as of December 31, 19x4, the balance in accumulated depreciation was $12,000 [($15,000 ÷ 5) × 4]. The company estimated that the reconditioning process would both significantly improve the gas mileage of the truck and extend the useful life to a total of seven years (with no change in salvage value). The journal entry to record the improvement is:

        Delivery truck........................ 3,000
            Cash.............................   3,000

The new balance in the asset account is $19,000 (the original cost plus the improvement). The remaining book value of $7,000 ($19,000 − $12,000) less the estimated salvage value is divided equally over the three remaining years of the estimated life. Thus, the depreciation expense for 19x5, 19x6, and 19x7 would be recorded as follows:

        Depreciation expense.................. 2,000
            Accumulated depreciation   2,000

Practical considerations often outweigh theoretical considerations, however. Frequently, companies classify capital expenditures as revenue expenditures if these costs are relatively small. For example, a company might adopt a policy of charging the cost of any asset to an expense account if the dollar amount is below a specified limit (e.g., $1,000). This practice saves a company the time and cost of maintaining records for the depreciation of immaterial items. As long as the aggregate cost of these items is not significant, net income is not materially affected.

DISPOSAL OF PLANT AND EQUIPMENT

At some point in time, the cost of continuing to use a particular asset will exceed the benefits derived from its use and it will be to the advantage of the firm to dispose of it. Upon disposal of an asset, the cost of the asset must be removed from the asset account and the accumulated depreciation at the date of disposal also must be removed from the accumulated depreciation account.

For example, assume that after using the Chevrolet as a taxi for four years, it was sold for $1,000, its book value at that time. (Recall that the auto had an original cost of $9,000, an estimated life of four years, and an anticipated salvage value of $1,000.) The entry to record the sale of the Chevrolet would be as follows:

```
Cash .................................  1,000
Accumulated depreciation ...............  8,000
    Automobile..........................         9,000
```

The debit to cash records the amount of cash received while the debit to accumulated depreciation and the credit to automobile remove the automobile and its related accumulated depreciation account from the books of Your Taxi Company. In this example, the estimate of useful life and salvage value were precise. This would occur only infrequently in actual practice.

At the time of the disposal of an asset, if the book value of the asset (cost less accumulated depreciation) is not exactly equal to the amount received from the sale, the difference is a gain or loss on disposal. If the selling price exceeds the book value there is a gain, while if the sales price is less than book value there is a loss. Such gains or losses are included in the income statement.

For example, if the same Chevrolet were sold at the end of the fourth year for $1,100. the entry to record this transaction would be as follows:

```
Cash ....................................  1,100
Accumulated depreciation .................  8,000
    Automobile ...........................        9,000
    Gain .................................          100
```

The only difference between this entry and the preceding entry is that the amount of cash received increased from $1,000 to $1,100. This amount exceeds the book value of the asset (original cost of $9,000 less accumulated depreciation of $8,000 or $1,000) and therefore a gain ($1,100 − $1,000 or $100) is realized. On the other hand, if the car had been sold for $350, a loss would have been incurred. The calculation of the gain and/or loss on the disposal of the automobile in all three cases mentioned above may be summarized as follows:

	A	B	C
Selling price	$1,000	$1,100	$ 350
Cost of automobile $9,000			
Accumulated depreciation (8,000)			
Book value	(1,000)	(1,000)	(1,000)
Gain (loss) on the sale of the automobile	$ 0	$ 100	($650)

The entries for the disposal of the asset under cases A and B have been presented above. The entry for case C, the loss situation, is as follows:

Cash	350	
Accumulated depreciation	8,000	
Loss	650	
Automobile		9,000

Again, the only difference between this entry and the two preceding entries is the amount of cash received, $350. Since the cash received was less than the book value of the automobile ($9,000 less $8,000 or $1,000) a loss equal to the difference ($1,000 less $350 or $650) occurred and should be recorded in the accounts.

In some instances, an asset may be discarded prior to the end of its useful life. For example, assume that the automobile was involved in an accident at the end of its third year of use and was damaged to the extent that repairs were not considered to be feasible. The entry to record the loss from the accident would be as follows:

Loss	3,000	
Accumulated depreciation	6,000*	
Automobile		9,000

*For purposes of the example, it was assumed that the straight-line method of depreciation was used.

Of course, the taxi would probably be insured. If this was the case and $1,000 was received from an insurance policy on the automobile, the entry would be as follows:

Cash	1,000	
Accumulated depreciation	6,000*	
Loss	2,000	
Automobile		9,000

*For purposes of the example, it was assumed that the straight-line method of depreciation had been used.

In any case, cash is debited for the amount received (if any), accumulated depreciation is debited for the depreciation taken to the date of disposal, and the asset is credited for its original cost in order to remove these accounts from the books. A loss (or gain) is recorded for the difference between the book value of the asset and the cash received (if any).

In each of the illustrations included above, it was assumed that the disposal of the asset took place at the end of the period. If the disposal is made during the period, the only difference would be that an entry would be required to record the depreciation for the period from the end of the preceding year up to the date of the disposal. The entry to record the disposal itself would be exactly the same as those illustrated above.

In the above examples, it was assumed that cash was received in the disposition of the asset. In some cases, however, a plant asset may be simply retired from productive service. When this occurs, the asset's cost and accumulated depreciation are removed from the accounts, and any difference is recorded as a loss on retirement.

TRADE-INS

In acquiring assets, a firm will frequently trade in an old asset in purchasing the new asset. In these cases, a trade-in allowance is given on the old asset and the balance of the purchase price is paid in cash or by a combination of cash and debt. The accounting procedures used in recording a trade-in depend on whether the assets exchanged are *similar* (an automobile traded in on another automobile) or *dissimilar* (an automobile traded in on a printing press). When items of property, plant, and equipment are acquired by trading in a *dissimilar* asset, the transaction should be accounted for using the fair market values of the assets involved as the base. Thus, the cost of the acquired asset is the fair market value of the assets given up (old asset and cash) or the fair market value of the asset acquired, if its fair value is is more clearly determinable. Any difference between the fair value of the asset surrendered and the book value of the old asset should be recognized as a gain or a loss on the disposition of the old asset. Caution must be used in determining and recording the fair values of the assets involved, as the quoted list prices of new assets and trade-in allowances are often not good or accurate indicators of actual or true market values. Dealers often establish list prices that are in excess of the actual cash price to allow them to offer inflated trade-in allowances to their customers.

When *similar* assets are exchanged, a loss may be recognized based upon the fair market value of the asset traded in but not a gain. If the terms of the exchange of similar assets indicates that there is a gain, this "gain" is not recognized. Rather, the new asset is recorded at an amount equal to the total of the book value of the old asset traded in and the cash paid. The logic supporting the nonrecognition of gains is that the income of a firm should not be increased by the act of substituting a new productive asset for an old one. The "gain" is recognized in future years because the recorded cost of the new asset will be less than if the gain was recognized in the current period. Thus, depreciation expense will be less in future years (and income greater) because of the reduced recorded cost of the new asset.

Assume that Your Taxi Company traded in its Chevrolet on a new asset on January 1, 19x5. The following data will be used in the example:

List price of the new asset	$10,000
Cost of the Chevrolet (at January 1, 19x1)	9,000
Accumulated depreciation on the Chevrolet (at December 31, 19x4)	8,000
Trade-in allowance	500
Fair market value of the Chevrolet (at January 1, 19x5)	200
Cash difference paid	9,500

The entry to record the acquisition of the new asset would be as follows:

New asset	9,700	
Accumulated depreciation	8,000	
Loss	800	
Automobile		9,000
Cash		9,500

The debit to new asset records the $9,700 "cost" of the new asset as the $9,500 cash paid plus the $200 fair market value of the Chevrolet traded in. The debit to accumulated depreciation of $8,000 and the credit to automobile of $9,000 remove the original cost of the Chevrolet and its related accumulated depreciation from the accounts. The debit to loss of $800 records the loss on the disposal of the Chevrolet and was calculated as follows:

Original cost of the Chevrolet	$9,000
Less: Accumulated depreciation as the date of trade-in	8,000
Book value of the Chevrolet at the date of trade-in	$1,000
Less: Fair market value of the Chevrolet at the date of the trade-in	200
Loss	$ 800

The credit to cash of $9,500 records the cash outlay which was made in order to acquire the new asset.

If, in the above example, the fair market value of the old car was not available, but it was known that the new asset could have been acquired for a cash price of $9,800, this value would have been used in recording the acquisition of the new asset. In this situation, the apparent value of the old asset is $300 ($9,800 − $9,500) even though the trade-in allowance is stated at $500. Thus, the loss on this exchange is $700, the difference between the actual or apparent trade-in value ($300) and the book value ($1,000) of the old asset. The entry required to record this transaction would be as follows:

New asset	9,800	
Accumulated depreciation	8,000	
Loss	700	
Automobile		9,000
Cash		9,500

In the above example, there was a loss on the trade, so the entries would be the same whether the assets were similar or dissimilar.

We will now modify the example as follows:

Trade-in allowance	$1,500
Fair market value of the Chevrolet (at January 1, 19x5)	1,500
Cash difference paid	8,300

These facts indicate a gain on the disposal of the Chevrolet, calculated as follows:

Fair market value of the Chevrolet at the date of the trade-in		$1,500
Original cost of the Chevrolet	$9,000	
Less: Accumulated depreciation as of the date of trade-in	8,000	
Book value of the Chevrolet at the date of the trade-in		1,000
Gain		$ 500

If the assets are dissimilar, the entry to record the acquisition of the new asset would be as follows:

New asset	9,800	
Accumulated depreciation	8,000	
Automobile		9,000
Cash		8,300
Gain		500

If the assets are assumed to be similar, the entry required to record the trade would be as follows:

New asset	9,300	
Accumulated depreciation	8,000	
Automobile		9,000
Cash		8,300

Note that the debit of $9,300 to the new asset is the total of the cash paid and the book value of the asset traded in ($8,300 + $1,000).

In the preceding examples, the trade-in took place at the beginning of the period. If a trade-in is made during the period, depreciation should be recognized on the old asset for the period up to the time of the trade-in, and the entry to record the exchange should recognize the book value of the old asset as of the date of exchange.

In APB, *Opinion No. 29*, "Accounting for Nonmonetary Transactions" (1973), the Accounting Principles Board recognized several exceptions to the general requirement of using market values to determine the gain or loss on the exchange of nonmonetary assets. The circumstances which require exceptions to the general rule include:

1. If market values are not determinable within reasonable limits.
2. If the general rule indicates a gain, and the exchange is:
   a. An exchange of inventory between dealers to facilitate sales to customers other than the parties involved in the exchange.
   b. An exchange of *similar* productive assets not held for sale.
3. If nonmonetary assets are transferred to owners in a spin-off, or other forms of reorganization.

The details of the accounting procedures required to record the other exceptions are beyond the scope of this text.

For federal income tax purposes, a gain or loss is never recognized on the exchange of similar productive assets. Rather, the cost of the new asset is considered to be the book value (cost less accumulated depreciation) of the old asset plus the additional cash paid (or cash and debt incurred) in the exchange.

PLANT AND EQUIPMENT IN THE FINANCIAL STATEMENTS

Plant assets are carried in the balance sheet at their acquisition cost, less any accumulated depreciation. The depreciation on long-term assets is included in the income statement as an expense and is deducted in determining income from operations. Gains or losses on the disposal of long-term assets would appear on the income statement in a special section after income from operations, since they are normally not considered to be a part of the normal operations of the firm.

NATURAL RESOURCES

In addition to plant assets such as property, plant, and equipment described in the earlier sections of this chapter, a firm may also own assets in the form of natural resources. These resources include such items as oil deposits, tracts of timber, and coal deposits. Like the other long-term assets of the firm, the basis for accounting for these resources is primarily cost. As these resources are converted into salable inventory by drilling, cutting, and mining operations, the cost of these operations along with the original cost of the resources themselves are transferred to expense.

The process of writing off or amortizing the cost of these natural resources is generally referred to as depletion. Since the natural resource provides a salable product, the depletion charges are included in inventory costs as production occurs and cost of goods as the natural resource is sold. The primary difference between depreciation and depletion is that depreciation represents the allocation of the cost of a productive asset in relation to the decline in service potential, while depletion represents the allocation of cost of a natural resource in relation to the quantitative physical exhaustion of the resource.

Depletion Base and Amortization

The depletion base of any wasting asset is the total cost of acquiring and developing the property less the estimated residual value of the land after the natural resource has been economically exhausted. The total cost of the natural resource may be classified in three categories: (1) acquisition cost of the property, (2) exploration costs, and (3) development costs.

Generally, depletion for the period is determined on the basis of the relationship between actual production for the period and total estimated production during the economic life of the resource. To apply this approach, the quantity of economically recoverable units of the natural resource must be estimated. Then the total cost of the natural resource less any estimated residual value is divided by the estimated number of recoverable units to obtain a cost per unit of output. This cost per unit is multiplied by the number of units extracted during the period to determine the depletion charge.

To illustrate this process, consider the following example:

1. An oil field is acquired at a cost of $1,000,000. Geological surveys indicate that a total of approximately 400,000 barrels of oil will ultimately be taken from the field.

2. The estimated residual value of the field after the oil has been extracted is approximately $200,000 (net of restoration costs).

3. During the first year of operations, the drilling costs total $125,000. A total of 25,000 barrels of oil are extracted and sold at a price of $10 per barrel.

These transactions would be recorded as follows:

Acquisition of the Field

Oil field	1,000,000	
Cash		1,000,000

Drilling During the First Year

Inventory of oil	125,000	
Cash		125,000
Inventory of oil	50,000	
Accumulated depletion—oil field		50,000

The $125,000 cost of drilling was assumed to be entirely applicable to the oil taken during the year and was therefore assigned to the inventory of oil as a part of its costs. The depletion of $50,000 was calculated as follows:

Cost of the field	$1,000,000
Estimated residual value of the field	200,000
Cost of the 400,000 barrels of oil	$ 800,000
Divide by 400,000 in order to obtain the *cost per barrel*	$ 2
$2 × 25,000 barrels extracted	$ 50,000

The total cost per barrel would be the cost of the oil; that is, the depletion per barrel of $2 plus the drilling cost of $5 per barrel[7], or $7.

Sale of the 25,000 Barrels of Oil

Cash	250,000	
Sales		250,000
Cost of goods sold	175,000	
Inventory of oil		175,000

Frequently, additional development costs may be incurred after the production begins or estimates of recoverable units are revised based on production data. In either case, a revision in the unit depletion charge is necessary. In the revision process, a new rate is determined by dividing the unamortized total cost less the estimated residual value by the estimate of the remaining recoverable units.

The procedures described above are known as cost depletion and are required for accounting and financial reporting purposes. For income tax purposes, independent producers use either depletion based on cost or percentage depletion. Further, if cost depletion is used for tax purposes, the amount of periodic tax depletion need not be equal to the cost depletion determined for financial reporting purposes. It is often advantageous from a tax standpoint to use the percentage depletion method, since depletion calculated by this method frequently exceeds depletion on a cost basis. Furthermore, in many cases it allows the taxpayer to deduct more than the cost of the property over its useful life. The percentage depletion method allows the firm to deduct from revenues a given percentage of gross income depletion without regard to the number of units produced or the cost of the property. In this method, the amount of depletion for tax purposes may exceed the total cost of the natural resource. Percentage depletion is not acceptable for financial accounting purposes.

Accounting for Oil and Gas Producers

Normally the exploration costs of oil and gas companies are substantial. There have been two methods which have long been used by oil and gas companies to account for costs incurred in the exploration, development, and production of crude oil and natural gas—the successful efforts method and the full cost method. The larger oil and gas companies have tended to use the successful efforts method; the smaller companies have tended to use the full cost method.

---

[7] Drilling costs of $125,000 divided by the 25,000 barrels extracted, or $5 per barrel.

Under the successful efforts method, only the costs of successful drilling efforts are capitalized and subsequently charged against the revenue of the producing wells. Costs in connection with nonproducing wells are written off as expenses in the period incurred. Under the full cost method, the costs of both successful and unsuccessful drilling efforts are capitalized and amortized against subsequent petroleum production in the same relatively large cost center (e.g., a country or a continent).

There has been considerable pressure on the accounting profession to eliminate the alternatives available for accounting for exploratory costs in the oil and gas industry. In December, 1977, the FASB issued Statement No. 19, "Financial Accounting and Reporting by Oil and Gas Producers," which essentially required the adoption of a form of the successful efforts method by all oil and gas producers. However, in Accounting Series Release No. 253 issued in August, 1978, the SEC rejected the FASB's attempt to eliminate use of the full cost method, asserting that both cost-based methods were so inadequate that it did not matter which method was employed.

In 1982, the FASB issued Statement No. 69, "Disclosures about Oil and Gas Producing Activities," which superceded the disclosure requirements of all previous FASB statements concerned with oil and gas producing activities. In applying Statement No. 69, companies are required to disclose information about quantities of reserves, capitalized costs, costs incurred, and a standardized measure of discounted cash flows related to proved reserves.

INTANGIBLE ASSETS

From a legal viewpoint, an intangible asset normally is defined as an asset without physical substance, the value of which resides in the rights that its possession confers upon its owner. This definition alone is insufficient to describe the distinguishing characteristics of intangibles for accounting purposes, however. For example, certain items that lack physical substance, such as accounts receivable and prepaid rent, are classified as current assets. Similarly, certain noncurrent assets, such as long-term investments, that lack physical substance are not classified as intangible assets. Thus, the absence of physical existence alone does not indicate that an item should be classified as and accounted for as an intangible asset.

Several characteristics are attributed to intangible assets. Probably the most important of these characteristics is the high degree of uncertainty regarding the future benefits that may be expected to be derived from the asset and the difficulty of associating these benefits with either specific revenues or periods. An additional factor distinguishing intangibles from the many other assets that also lack physical substance is that intangible assets are expected to benefit the firm beyond the current operating cycle of the business, even though intangibles have indeterminate life spans.

Rather than attempting to define the characteristics of intangible assets succinctly, many accountants rely on tradition to classify assets as intangible rather than tangible. *Those assets that typically are classified as intangibles include copyrights, patents, trademarks, trade names, organization costs, franchises, and goodwill.* In certain types of businesses, the value of intangible assets may be greater than the value of the tangible assets.

Individual intangible assets differ in many respects. These assets may be subdivided on the basis of the following characteristics:

1. *Identifiability*—separately identifiable or lacking specific identification.
2. *Manner of acquisition*—acquired singly, in groups, or in business combinations, or developed internally.
3. *Expected period of benefit*—limited by law or contract, related to human or economic factors, or indefinite or indeterminate duration.
4. *Separability from an entire enterprise*—rights transferable without title, salable, or inseparable from the enterprise or a substantial part of it.

A firm may obtain an intangible asset by purchase or by development within the firm. The objectives of accounting for intangible assets are similar to those for tangible assets which were described earlier in the chapter—the cost of the asset is recorded upon acquisition and this cost is allocated to expense over the useful life of the intangible. The cost of an intangible asset includes all expenditures which are incurred in the acquisition of the rights or privileges. The cost of an intangible asset acquired by purchase can usually be measured with little difficulty. The cost of internally developed intangibles is often more difficult to determine. For example, it may be quite difficult to estimate how much of the total research and development cost for a particular period should be allocated to the development of a single patent. For this reason the cost of internally developed patents includes only legal fees. Any other costs incurred in developing the patent are expenses as they are incurred. This treatment is consistent with the handling of research and development costs in general.

The costs of intangible assets are written off to expense over their estimated useful lives in a manner similar to the depreciation of tangible fixed assets. This is referred to as amortization. Amortization is recorded by a debit to amortization expense and a credit to the intangible asset account. Like tangible fixed assets, the cost of intangibles should be amortized over their estimated useful lives. However, according to Accounting Principles Board *Opinion No. 17*, the period of amortization should not exceed a maximum of forty years. The board also concluded that the straight-line method of amortization should be used unless the firm shows evidence that some other systematic method is more appropriate in the circumstances.

To illustrate the accounting for intangible assets, assume that Landry Company purchased a patent from Allen Company for $10,000 on January 1, 19x1. The purchase would be recorded as follows:

Patents	10,000	
Cash		10,000

If the remaining useful or economic life of the patent was ten years, the adjusting entry required to record the amortization of the patent at the end of each year of its useful life would be as follows:

Amortization expense	1,000	
Patents		1,000

Note that the amortization is credited directly to the asset account rather than to an accumulated amortization account as in the case of tangible fixed assets. There appears to be no logical reason for this procedure other than tradition.

Certain intangibles, such as patents, copyrights, and franchises may be identified with a specific right or privilege. The costs of these intangibles when purchased can be measured and amortized or allocated to expense over their useful lives. Other intangibles, however, cannot be specifically identified. This type of intangible is usually referred to as goodwill. The intangible asset goodwill represents the sum of all the special advantages which are not identifiable and which relate to the business as a whole. It encompasses such items as a favorable location, good customer relations, and superior ability of management. The existence of such factors enables the firm to earn an above normal rate of return.

Unlike tangible assets or identifiable intangible assets, goodwill cannot be sold or acquired separately from the business as a whole. Because of the uncertainty involved in estimating the goodwill of a business enterprise, goodwill is normally recorded only when a business is acquired by purchase. In a purchase transaction, goodwill may be measured as the excess of the purchase price of an entity over the sum of the fair values of all its identifiable assets less its liabilities. The source of this excess is the potential of the firm to earn an above average rate of return.

To illlustrate, assume that Richard Smith purchased the Campus Book Store on January 1, 19x1, for $100,000 cash. Further assume that the identifiable assets were determined to have a total fair value of $90,000 at the date of purchase (including inventory, $10,000; equipment, $20,000; building, $140,000; and land, $20,000). The liabilities assumed by the purchaser were accounts payable of $20,000. The $30,000 excess of the purchase price over the value of all the identifiable assets less the liabilities represents the value of the goodwill. The purchase would be recorded as follows:

Inventory	10,000	
Equipment	20,000	
Building	40,000	
Land	20,000	
Goodwill	30,000	
Accounts payable		20,000
Cash		100,000

Once goodwill is recorded in a purchase transaction, it is amortized like all other intangible assets—the recorded cost is allocated to expense over its estimated life with a maximum of forty years.

Many businesses engage in research and development (R&D) activities in order to develop new products or processes, or to improve present products. A problem in accounting for R&D expenditures lies in determining the amount and timing of the future benefits which are associated with such activities. Prior to 1974, there was considerable diversity in the procedures used in accounting for R&D costs. In 1974, however, the FASB issued its *Statement No. 2* which simplified the accounting for R&D expenditures by requiring that most research and development costs should be charged to expense as they are incurred. This treatment eliminated the need to assess the uncertain future benefits associated with R&D costs and to measure the cause and effect relationship of these costs for accounting purposes.

FASB *Statement No. 2* stated that R&D costs include the costs of materials, personnel, purchased intangibles, contract services, and a reasonable allocation of indirect costs which are specifically related to R&D activities and have no alternative future uses. Disclosure should be made in the financial statements of the total R&D costs charged to expense for each period for which an income statement is presented.

Disclosure of Intangibles

Intangible assets normally are reported separately in the balance sheet. In contrast to plant assets, the amortization of intangibles usually is credited directly to the intangible asset account. The financial statements should disclose the method of amortization, the period of amortization, and the amount of amortization expense for the latest period. The example shown below provides a typical disclosure regarding intangible assets.

Disclosure of Intangible Assets

	19x2	19x1
Goodwill and other intangibles:		
Goodwill	$4,618	$4,675
Patents	1,248	1,248
Organization costs	206	206
Other	290	382
Total	$6,362	$6,511
Less: Accumulated amortization	325	166
Goodwill and other intangibles—net	$6,037	$6,345

Goodwill and Other Intangibles:
Goodwill represents the excess of cost over the amount ascribed to the net assets of ongoing businesses purchased. Goodwill arising from acquisitions prior to November 1, 1970, is not being amortized. Capitalized organization costs and goodwill acquired after November 1, 1970, are being amortized on a straight-line basis over a forty-year period.

The cost of internally developed patents is charged to income as incurred. Purchased patents are amortized over their estimated economic lives.

SUMMARY

The resources of a firm which are used in the continuing operations of a business over a number of years are referred to as plant and equipment or fixed assets. Such assets are generally classified as tangible fixed assets if they have physical substance and are depreciable or non-depreciable assets (land).

Control over tangible fixed assets is usually achieved by the use of a ledger card that includes all data related to the asset item. This card will reflect the cost of the item, which includes all expenditures necessary to place the asset in use as well as the actual invoice price.

Since long-term assets benefit a firm over an extended period of time, the cost of the asset must be allocated in some manner to the periods which benefit from its use. This is achieved through the process of depreciation. In the case of most tangible fixed assets, the depreciation process will result in either a uniform charge for each year (under the straight-line depreciation method) or larger charges in the early years of operation (under the accelerated depreciation methods). In either case, the consistency principle requires that the same method of depreciation be used in all periods. Fixed tangible assets are presented on the balance sheet at their acquisition cost along with an offset or deduction for accumulated depreciation.

Costs incurred for existing assets subsequent to acquisition are classified as either capital expenditures or revenue expenditures. Capital expenditures increase the economic benefits of the existing asset and the cost is debited to an asset account. Revenue expenditures are routine expenditures incurred to maintain an asset in operating condition and such costs are debited to expense.

Eventually, the economic usefulness of an item of plant and equipment expires and the asset must be sold, scrapped, retired, or traded-in on a new asset. When an asset is disposed of, the cost of the asset is removed from the asset account and the accumulated depreciation balance is eliminated. When a plant asset is sold, there is a gain or loss equal to the difference between the asset's book value (cost less accumulated depreciation) and its sales price.

When an old asset is traded in on a new asset, the accounting treatment depends upon the nature of the assets involved. If the assets are dissimilar, the cost of the new asset is equal to the fair market value of the old asset plus the cash paid, and a gain or loss on the disposition of the old asset is recognized for the difference between the book value and the fair market value at the date of exchange. If the assets are similar, the accounting treatment is the same as for dissimilar assets if a loss is indicated. However, if the fair market value is greater than the book value of the old asset, no gain is recognized and the new asset is recorded at the book value of the old asset plus the cash paid.

Identifiable intangible assets, which generally involve property rights rather than physical property, are written off in a similar manner referred to as amortization. Goodwill differs from tangible assets and identifiable intangible assets in that it cannot be sold or acquired separate from the business.

Therefore, due to the uncertainty of measuring goodwill, it is only recorded and amortized if purchased with a business already in existence. A similar uncertainty exists in matching expenses incurred by research and development efforts with possible future revenues resulting from these efforts. Therefore, R&D expenditures are considered expenses of the period in which they are incurred.

Allocation of the cost of natural resources is referred to as depletion. For financial accounting purposes, depletion must be calculated on a cost basis over the estimated units to be produced. However, for tax purposes, firms must take the higher of cost depletion or a specified percentage of gross income (referred to as percentage depletion).

KEY DEFINITIONS

Accelerated methods of depreciation—techniques for computing depreciation that assume the rate of depreciation decreases with the passage of time.

Accumulated depreciation—a contra account which appears as an offset or deduction from the related asset account in the balance sheet. The depreciation taken over the useful life of the asset is accumulated in this account.

Book value of an asset—the cost of an asset less accumulated depreciation. The book value of an asset is the remaining undepreciated cost.

Capital expenditures—expenditures which extend the useful life or quality of services provided by plant assets.

Contra account—an account which is offset against or deducted from another account in the financial statements.

Declining balance method—an accelerated method of depreciation that assumes the rate of depreciation to be some multiple of the rate which would have been used in the case of the straight-line method.

Depletion—the process of writing-off or amortizing the cost of natural resources over the periods which benefit from their use.

Depreciation—the systematic allocation of the cost of an asset, less the salvage value (if any), over its estimated useful life.

Fixed asset ledger card—prepared for each individual asset purchased. It includes all of the important information relating to the asset and its use.

Goodwill—may be measured as the excess of the purchase price of an entity over the sum of the fair values of all its identifiable assets less its liabilities.

Intangible fixed asset—one that does not have physical substance, usually a property right.

Modified Accelerated Cost Recovery System (MACRS)—MACRS is an accelerated method of depreciation permitted for federal income tax purposes and may also be used for financial accounting purposes.

Plant and equipment—long-term or fixed assets are those resources of a firm which are used in the continuing operations of a business over a number of years.

Revenue expenditures—expenditures for ordinary maintenance, repairs, and other items necessary for the operation and use of plant and equipment.

Salvage value—the residual amount of a long-term tangible asset that the firm expects to recover at the end of the useful life of the asset.

Straight-line depreciation—this method of depreciation assumes that factors such as wear and tear and obsolescence are somewhat uniform over time. The method allocates the cost of an asset, less its salvage value, to expenses equally over its useful life.

Sum-of-the-years'-digits method—this is an accelerated method of depreciation where the life years of an asset are totalled and utilized as the denominator of a fraction that uses the number of years of life remaining from the beginning of the year as the numerator.

Tangible fixed asset—a long-term asset that has physical substance.

QUESTIONS

1. Which expenditures are included in the total cost of a fixed asset?

2. What is the purpose of depreciation accounting?

3. What factors should be considered when determining periodic depreciation?

4. Explain the equations used in calculating straight-line, double-declining balance, and sum-of-the-years'-digits depreciation.

5. Four basic depreciation methods are straight-line, sum-of-the-years'-digits, double-declining balance and ACRS. In what ways are the four depreciation methods similar? In what ways are they different?

6. What is the purpose of the accumulated depreciation account?

7. What does the balance in the accumulated depreciation account indicate at any given point in time?

8. What is the difference between a capital expenditure and a revenue expenditure?

9. Why is periodic depreciation not recorded for land?

10. What factors must be known to compute depreciation on a plant asset?

11. How is accumulated depreciation reported in the balance sheet?

12. When a plant asset is disposed of for cash, how is the gain or loss on the sale determined?

13. If an old asset is traded in on a dissimilar new asset, how should the cost basis of the new asset be measured?

14. Explain the rules for recognizing gains or losses on the exchange of similar productive assets.

15. Over what period should the cost of an intangible asset be amortized?

16. When should goodwill be recorded in the accounts?

17. Discuss the appropriate accounting treatment of research and development costs.

18. List some possible causes of goodwill.

19. What is the basis for accounting for natural resources? Is this basis the same as that for other long-term assets?

EXERCISES

20. What is depletion? Is it similar to depreciation, and if so, in what way?

21. What is the difference in the accounting for intangible assets and the accounting for tangible assets?

22. A machine was purchased for an invoice price of $10,000, F.O.B. destination. The freight charges were $200. Costs of installation amounted to $500. At what cost should the machine be recorded?

23. Determine which of the following accounts is to be debited for each of the transactions below.

    A. Buildings   F. Machinery
    B. Accumulated Depreciation G. Insurance Expense
    C. Land   H. Freight Expense
    D. Patents   I. General Repairs
    E. Depreciation Expense   J. Legal Fees

    _C_ 1 Purchased land and unusable building.
    _J_ 2 Paid legal fees for above purchase.
    _A_ 3 Constructed new building on site.
    _F_ 4 Purchased machinery for building.
    _H_ 5 Paid freight on machinery.
    _F_ 6 Paid cost of installing machinery.
    _I_ 7 Paid minor repairs on building.
    _E_ 8 Recorded depreciation of equipment.
    _G_ 9 Paid insurance for year on building.
    _D_ 10 Obtained patent from U.S. Patent Office.

24. A machine was installed at a total cost of $8,000, assumed to have an estimated useful life of 5 years and a salvage value of $2,000. Calculate the initial year's depreciation assuming (a) the straight-line method is used, (b) the sum-of-the-years'-digits method is used, (c) the double-declining balance method is used, and (d) ACRS depreciation is used.

25. In each of the following cases, make the journal entry for the initial year of depreciation, assuming the straight-line method is used by Pat Kelly. (Round to the nearest dollar.)

    a. Original cost, $9,000; salvage value, $500; useful life, 4 years; purchased on April 1.
    b. Original cost, $25,000; salvage value, $5,000; useful life, 5 years; purchased on October 1.
    c. Original cost, $16,000; salvage value, $0; useful life, 8 years; purchased on December 1.
    d. Original cost $5,000; salvage value, $1,000; useful life, 2 years; purchased on July 31.
    e. Original cost, $30,000; salvage value, $2,000; useful life, 7 years; purchased on May 31.

26. Smith Company paid $100,000 to acquire land, building, and equipment. At the time of acquisition, appraisal values for the individual assets were determined as: land, $30,000; building, $60,000; and equipment, $30,000. What cost should be allocated to the land, building, and equipment, respectively?

27. Putnam Company purchased a new machine on January 1, 19x1 for a $1,000 down payment and a liability for six monthly payments of $2,000 beginning on February 1, 19x1. The machine could have been purchased for a cash price of $8,600. The company paid delivery and installation costs of $400. Prepare the journal entry to record the acquisition of the machine.

28. Which of the following items are capital expenditures and which are revenue expenditures?

    a. Cost of a major overhaul of a machine.
    b. Routine maintenance of a delivery truck.
    c. Replacement of an oil furnace with a gas furnace.
    d. Replacement of stairs with an escalator.
    e. Annual repainting of the administrative offices.
    f. Lubricating, inspecting, and cleaning factory machinery.
    g. Addition to a new wing on the factory building.

29. A truck with an original cost of $10,000 and accumulated depreciation to date of $8,000 was traded in on a new truck with a list price of $20,000. The dealer allowed a trade-in allowance of $3,000 on the old truck (which was equal to the fair market value). Give the journal entry to record the exchange.

30. Assume the same facts as in Exercise 29, except that the trade-in allowance and the fair market value of the old truck were $1,000. Give the journal entry to record the exchange.

31. A company had a plant asset with an original cost of $15,000 and accumulated depreciation to date of $12,000. Give the journal entry to record the disposition of the asset under the following circumstances:

    a. Sold the asset for $5,000.
    b. Sold the asset for $2,000.
    c. The asset was destroyed by fire; insurance proceeds of $1,500 were received.
    d. Abandoned the asset.

32. The Get Rich Quick Mining Company obtained a uranium mine for $1,350,000 on February 1, 19x1. It is estimated that approximately 335,000 pounds of uranium can be extracted from the mine. The residual value of the property after uranium has been removed is approximately $10,000. In 19x1, 74,000 pounds of uranium were extracted from the mine and in 19x2, 90,000 pounds were extracted. Mining costs were $14,800 for 19x1 and $22,500 for 19x2. The uranium is sold for $10 per pound.

Required:

Record the above transactions on the books of the Mining Company.

33. The Bratton Company purchased a patent for $56,000 on January 1, 19x1. Additional legal costs of $4,000 were incurred in obtaining the patent. The patent was estimated to have a useful life of 10 years. (Its legal life is 17 years.) What will be the patent amortization expense for 19x1?

34. From the following information make the necessary journal entries for the trade-in of an asset by the Singleton Company. Assume that the old and new assets were dissimilar.

List-price of new machine...........................	$20,795
Original cost of old machine........................	18,560
Accumulated depreciation on old machine at trade-in date....................................	10,560
Trade-in allowance................................	2,000
Fair market value of old machine at trade-in date....................................	1,000
Cash difference paid..............................	18,795

35. Al Bumbry bought Billy's Grocery on March 27 for $250,000 cash. On the date of purchase, the following fair values were determined: inventory, $50,000; equipment, $18,000; building, $68,000; land, $45,000; and accounts payable, $7,000. Make the entry required on the date of purchase.

36. For each of the following items owned by Mark Belanger, determine what the gain or loss will be upon the disposition of the asset and make the necessary journal entries.

   a. Original outlay, $7,900; sales price, $1,750; accumulated depreciation, $6,450.
   b. Original outlay, $13,050; sales price, $5,110; accumulated depreciation, $10,250.
   c. Original outlay, $21,400; sales price, $9,790; accumulated depreciation, $8,330.
   d. Original outlay, $91,625; sales price, $40,000; accumulated depreciation, $40,580.
   e. Original outlay, $47,985; sales price, $25,470; accumulated depreciation, $29,645.

PROBLEMS

37. The Carson Carton Company purchased a new cutting machine at an invoice price of $13,000. It paid the seller in time to take advantage of a 3 percent discount. Carson Carton then paid $400 shipping charges and $550 installation costs. However, after the machine was installed, it was discovered that the electrical wiring in the plant was not adequate to carry the additional current needed by the new asset. The company rewired that section of the building at a cost of $875. At what amount should Carson Carton Company value the new cutting machine on its books?

38. Cutler Cutlery Company purchased a large storage cabinet on January 1, 19x1, at a cost of $7,500. It was assigned an estimated useful life of 5 years and a salvage value of $500. Prepare a depreciation schedule for the cabinet under the straight-line, double-declining balance, sum-of-the-years'-digits, and ACRS methods.

39. For each of the depreciation methods listed, complete the following schedule of depreciation over the first two years of the life of a delivery truck costing $8,800 and having a salvage value of $800. The truck has an estimated life of 5 years.

Method	Year	Depreciation Expense	Accumulated Depreciation	Book Value
Straight-line	1	$1600	$1600	$7200
Straight-line	2	1600	3200	5600
Sum-of-the-years'-digits	1	2666.67	2666.67	6133.33
Sum-of-the-years'-digits	2	2133.33	4800	4000
Double-declining balance	1	3520	3520	5280
Double-declining balance	2	2112	5632	3168
MACRS	1			
MACRS	2			

40. During the course of your audit of Confused, Inc. for the year ended December 31, 19x2, you find the following account:

Equipment	
(a) 20,000	(c) 3,400
(b) 14,000	(d) 6,600

Key:
(a) Cost of machine A purchased on January 1, 19x1.
(b) Cost of machine B purchased on January 1, 19x1.
(c) Credit resulting from the recording of depreciation expense for 19x1. (Debit was to "depreciation expense.")
(d) Credit resulting from the recording of the sale of machine B on April 1, 19x2. (Debit was to cash.)

Each machine had an estimated life of ten years with no salvage value anticipated. The company uses the straight-line method of recording depreciation.

Required:

Give all the adjusting and correcting entries (or entry) required on April 1, 19x2.

41. Snowden Manufacturing Company decided to construct a new plant in 19x1 rather than continue to rent its present plant. On January 1, 19x1, the company purchased 10 acres of land with two old buildings standing on it. The old buildings were demolished and construction of the new plant was begun. The company set up a Land and Buildings account to which all expenditures relating to the new plant were charged.

The balance in the Land and Buildings account after completion of the plant was $740,450. Entries in the account during the construction period were:

a.	Cost of land and old buildings (old buildings appraised at $17,000).........................	$137,000
b.	Legal fees involved in securing title to property.............	250
c.	Cost of demolishing old buildings........................	9,500
d.	Surveying costs..	1,200
e.	Price paid for construction of new building................	425,000
f.	Salary paid to Jim Seales, engineer, supervisor of construction of new plant.............................	12,500
g.	Fencing of plant property...............................	3,000
h.	Machinery for new plant................................	113,000
i.	Installation costs of new machinery......................	9,500
j.	Landscaping of grounds................................	6,250
k.	Office equipment......................................	12,000
l.	Payment to architect for designing plans and for services during construction...........................	13,000
m.	Paneling and finishing work done on executive offices...	2,250
	Total Debits..	$744,450
n.	Proceeds from sale of scrap from old buildings.............	4,000
	Total Credit..	$ 4,000
	Balance...	$740,450

Required:

Reclassify the items presently in the Land and Buildings account to the proper general ledger accounts.

42. Blintz, Inc. has followed the practice of depreciating its building on a straight-line basis. The building has an estimated useful life of 20 years and a salvage value of $20,000. The company's depreciation expense for 19x3 was $20,000 on the building. The building was purchased on January 1, 19x1.

Required:

1. The original cost of the building.
2. Depreciation expense for 19x2 assuming:

    a. The company has used the double-declining balance method.
    b. The company has used the sum-of-the-years'-digits method.

43. The Silver Fox Company purchased a parcel of land on which was located a large home and a riding stable on January 7, 19x2, for $87,500. Additional expenditures made at the time of settlement were as follows:

Attorney's fees in connection with the purchase	$ 500
Cost of property transfer taxes	1,000
Real estate taxes for 19x1 (the seller was to repay Silver Fox for these taxes)	2,000
Title insurance	500
Broker's commission	500
Gardening equipment	1,000
	$5,500

Silver Fox had the property appraised by a professional appraiser on the purchase date. His appraisal showed the following valuations:

Land	$ 55,000
Home	45,000
Stable	10,000
Total appraised value of property	$110,000

Extensive remodeling and redecorating was undertaken immediately to ready the property for rental. The following outlays were made during the month of January:

Cost of tearing down the stable	$ 10,000
Cost of removing fourth story of home	35,000
Architect's fee	15,000
Replacement of plumbing	11,000
New electrical wiring	14,000
Landscaping	25,000
Payment of hospital bill of passer-by injured by falling debris	5,000
	$115,000
Less: Sale of materials salvaged from stable	1
	$114,999

Required:

Indicate the accounts which would be charged with the cost of each of the items listed below. If an item is to be allocated to more than one account, simply list each account that would be charged.

In indicating your answers, use the following code:

Land.....................	L	Any expense or loss account......		E
Home.....................	H	Any revenue or gain account.....		R
Stable....................	S	Any other account..............		X
Any other asset account......	A			

Purchase price of $87,500................. ( )
Attorney's fees........................ ( )
Property transfer taxes.................. ( )
Real estate taxes for 19x1................ ( )
Title insurance........................ ( )
Broker's commission.................... ( )
Gardening equipment................... ( )
Cost of tearing down stable............... ( )
Cost of tearing down fourth
   floor of home...................... ( )
Architect's fee........................ ( )
Plumbing............................ ( )
Electrical wiring....................... ( )
Landscaping.......................... ( )
Hospital bill.......................... ( )
Sale of materials salvaged
   from stable........................ ( )

44. On October 30, 19x1, Thomas Brothers, Inc. purchased a used machine for $7,800 from a company in a neighboring state. The machine could not be shipped until November 15 so Thomas Brothers were forced to pay $150 storage costs and $35 insurance fees. After the asset was received and $250 shipping costs had been paid, it was overhauled and installed at a cost of $320, including parts costing $130. On December 21, additional repair work was performed at a cost of $180 in order to put the asset in working condition. At what value should this machine be recorded on the balance sheet on December 31?

45. For each of the depreciation methods listed, complete the following schedule of depreciation over the first two years of the life of a building costing $57,500. The building is expected to have a salvage value of $7,500 at the end of 10 years.

Method	Year	Depreciation Expense	Accumulated Depreciation	Book Value
Straight-line	1	$ _____	$ _____	$ _____
Straight-line	2	_____	_____	_____
Sum-of-the-years'-digits	1	_____	_____	_____
Sum-of-the-years'-digits	2	_____	_____	_____
Double-declining balance	1	_____	_____	_____
Double-declining balance	2	_____	_____	_____
MACRS	1	_____	_____	_____
MACRS	2	_____	_____	_____

46. Crowley Company decided to construct a new plant in order to meet the rising demand for its product. On January 1, 19x1, the company purchased five acres which adjoin their present plant site. The land had an old barn on it and a number of trees which had to be cleared before construction could begin. A Land & Buildings account was charged with all expenditures relating to the new plant. Entries in the account included:

a.	Cost of land...............................	$ 50,000
b.	Survey costs...............................	750
c.	Legal fees involved in securing title to property.....	500
d.	Cost of clearing trees and removing barn..........	1,600
e.	Proceeds from sale of trees for lumber............	(2,000)
f.	Construction costs for new plant.................	375,000
g.	Cost of parking lot at new plant.................	87,000
h.	Machinery for new plant.......................	167,500
i.	Shipping costs for machinery....................	875
j.	Installation cost of machinery...................	980
k.	Office equipment..............................	7,800
l.	Office supplies...............................	690
m.	Raw materials to be used in production of product..	10,750
	Balance......................................	$701,445

Required:

Reclassify the items presently in the Land & Buildings account to the proper general ledger accounts.

47. Anderson Aerospace Company traded in its Boeing 707 for a new Boeing 747 on January 1, 19x5. The following is the pertinent data for the transaction:

Cost of the 707 (at January 1, 19x1).................	$785,000
Accumulated depreciation on the 707 (at December 31, 19x4).........................	300,000
Fair market value of the 707 (at January 1, 19x5)......	325,000
List price of the 747...............................	925,000
Trade-in allowance................................	350,000
Note payable given for difference...................	575,000

Required:

Record the acquisition of the Boeing 747. Discuss the theoretical validity of this accounting treatment.

48. Marshall Furniture Manufacturers purchased a new lathe on January 1, 19x1, for $1,600. It has an estimated salvage value of $100 and an estimated useful life of 3 years. The company uses the sum-of-the-years'-digits depreciation method and maintains records on a calendar year basis. Prepare the journal entries to record the disposal of the lathe under each of the following independent conditions:

   a. Sold for $725 cash on October 1, 19x2.
   b. Destroyed by flood on July 1, 19x3. Insurance proceeds were $200.
   c. Traded in on purchase of new lathe on January 1, 19x2. List price of new lathe was $2,000, market value of old lathe was $1,200, and $700 cash was paid on the transaction.

49. On January 1, 19x1, the Confused Company purchased a new truck for $5,600 paying cash. On May 1, 19x2, the Company purchased a new truck which had a list price of $6,200. They were given a trade-in allowance of $2,000 for the old truck, the balance being paid in cash. On December 1, 19x2, the second truck was completely destroyed by fire. Confused received $3,200 from their insurance company as full settlement for the loss. Truck operating expense for 19x2 totaled $2,200.

You are called in by the company's accountant who states that in preparing the December 31, 19x2, trial balance he noted that the truck account had a balance of $8,800 although the company does not own any trucks. He also tells you that he failed to record depreciation on either truck during 19x2, although the company's accounting manual requires straight-line depreciation, two-year life, and $800 salvage value for all automotive equipment.

You obtain a copy of the company's ledger account "Trucks," which shows the following:

Trucks	
5,600	2,000
6,200	3,200
2,200	
8,800	

Required:

1. Prepare all journal entries regarding the trucks as they *should* have been made originally.
2. Prepare an entry to correct the accounts as of December 31, 19x2. You may assume that the books have not yet been closed for 19x2.

50. During an audit of Lee May Company for the year ended December 31, 19x2, you find the following account:

Machinery	
(a) 42,000	(b) 7,273
(c) 200	(d) 6,545
	(e) 5,600

Key:

(a) Cost of machinery purchased on January 1, 19x0.
(b) Credit to record the depreciation expense for 19x0. (Debit was to Depreciation Expense.)
(c) Cost of minor repairs which will not lengthen the life of the machine.
(d) Credit to record depreciation expense for 19x1. (Debit was to Depreciation Expense.)
(e) Credit to record sale of machinery on March 31, 19x2.

The machinery had an estimated life of ten years with a salvage value of $2,000. The company uses the sum-of-the-years'-digits method of recording depreciation.

Required:

Give all of the adjusting and correcting entries (or entry) required.

51. King Company purchased a truck on January 1, 19x1, at a cost of $4,200. The truck was depreciated using the straight-line method with an estimated useful life of four years and a salvage value of $200. On January 1, 19x3, the truck was traded in on a new truck with a list price of $6,000. The fair market value of the old truck was $1,500 and the truck dealer gave a trade-in allowance of $2,400 on the old truck. King Company gave a note payable for the balance of the purchase price.

Required:

Record the acquisition of the new truck.

52. A truck was purchased on October 1, 19x1, at a cost of $29,400. The expected life of this truck was 4 years with an expected salvage value of $600. The company used the straight-line depreciation method and the accounting records are maintained on a calendar year basis.

Required:

Prepare journal entries to record the disposal of the truck on *May 1, 19x3* under *each* of the following *separate* conditions:

a. Sold for $18,000 cash.
b. Completely destroyed by fire, and the insurance company paid $6,000 as full settlement of the loss.
c. Traded in on the purchase of another truck which had a cash price of $34,000; trade-in allowance granted on the old truck was $20,000 and the balance was paid in cash.

53. Kelly Company acquired a mine for $2,500,000. It was estimated that the land would have a value of $400,000 after completion of the mining operations, and that 1,000,000 tons of ore could be extracted from the mine. During the first year of operations, 100,000 tons of ore were extracted and additional production costs of $200,000 were incurred.

Required:

Prepare the journal entries to record the acquisition of the property and the cost of production for the year.

Refer to the Annual Report included in the front of the text.

54. Comparing the two years, what are the changes in gross and net property, plant and equipment?

55. What caused the difference in the change in net property, plant and equipment and in the change in gross property, plant and equipment mentioned above?

56. What assets are included in property, plant and equipment?

57. Which of these assets is the largest?

58. What is the amount of the depreciation expense in the most recent year?

59. What is the balance in the accumulated depreciation account at the end of the most recent year?

60. Does the difference in the amount of accumulated depreciation from the previous year to the current year equal the amount of depreciation expense in the current year? Why not?

61. What is the amount of the intangible assets at the end of the most recent year?

62. What assets are included in intangible assets?

Chapter 6 discusses the issues related to the accounting for sole proprietorships and partnerships. Studying this chapter should enable you to:

1. Discuss the advantages and disadvantages of the sole proprietorship and partnership forms of business organization.
2. Explain how the owners' equity accounts are affected by investments, withdrawals, and earnings.
3. Identify the purpose of the partnership agreement and the information it normally includes.
4. Summarize the significant characteristics of a partnership.
5. Describe the procedures for recording the formation of a partnership, division of profits and losses, admission and withdrawal of partners, and liquidation of a partnership.

6

Unincorporated Business Organizations

INTRODUCTION

There are three basic types of business organizations: (1) the sole proprietorship, (2) the partnership, and (3) the corporation. This chapter considers the accounting for unincorporated business organizations—sole proprietorships and partnerships. The following two chapters concentrate on the accounting issues related to corporations.

THE SOLE PROPRIETORSHIP

The simplest form of business organization is the sole proprietorship, a business owned by a single individual. In terms of the absolute number of business firms, the sole proprietorship greatly outnumbers all other forms of business organizations in the United States. Because of their size, however, corporations account for the greatest dollar amount of both assets and sales. Sole proprietorships are the dominant form of business organization among smaller firms, particularly among businesses engaged in retail trade and in the rendering of services.

One of the principal advantages of the sole proprietorship is the ease of establishing this type of business. Other than local and possibly state licensing requirements, an owner need only have the necessary capital and begin operations in order to establish his or her firm. Legal contracts are not necessary and the proprietor is not required to comply with provisions of certain regulations or laws which apply to corporations. A proprietor owns, controls, and usually manages the firm's assets and receives the profits (or losses) from its operations. All earnings of the business are taxable to the owner whether he or she withdraws them from the firm or not. A sole proprietorship is not considered to be a separate entity for income tax purposes.

Usually, the primary disadvantage of a sole proprietorship as a form of business organization is its unlimited liability feature. If the assets of the business are insufficient to meet its obligations, a sole proprietor will be required to satisfy business creditors from his or her own personal resources. Other principal disadvantages of the sole proprietorship form of business organization include limitations on the availability of funds to the business and difficulties involved in the transferability of ownership. Funds or resources available to a sole proprietorship are limited to the personal assets of the owner and what he or she is able to borrow. Ownership may be transferred only by selling the entire business or by changing to another form of business organization.

Accounting for a Proprietorship

It is primarily in the accounting for owner's equity that the accounts of an unincorporated business differ significantly from those of a corporation. The owner's equity accounts of a sole proprietorship normally include only a capital account and a drawing account.

The capital account reflects the proprietor's equity in the assets of the business as of a specific point in time. Capital is credited for the investments made by the owner in the business and for the earnings of the period, and it is debited for a net loss during the period.

A separate drawing or withdrawals account may be maintained which is debited for the withdrawals of cash or other business assets made by the owner, or for any payments which are made from business funds in order to satisfy personal debts of the owner. The balance in the drawing account is closed or transferred to the capital account during the preparation of closing entries which are made at the end of the period. As an alternative, the drawing account may be omitted with all changes in the owner's equity recorded directly in the capital account. Either procedure accomplishes the same end result.

THE PARTNERSHIP

A somewhat more complicated form of business organization is the partnership. A major difference between the sole proprietorship and the partnership is that the partnership has more than a single owner. The partnership form of business organization is often used as a means of combining the resources and special skills or talents of two or more persons. In addition, state laws sometimes prevent the incorporation of certain businesses which provide professional services such as certified public accounting firms or associations of physicians. Although only two persons are required to form a partnership, there is no limit as to the number of partners. For example, in some CPA firms there are more than 800 partners.

The Uniform Partnership Act defines a partnership as "an association of two or more persons to carry on, as co-owners, a business for profit." Even though two or more persons may, in fact, operate a business as a partnership without a formal agreement, it is important that a written contract, known as the articles of co-partnership, be drawn up in order to clearly delineate the rights and duties of all partners and thereby avoid possible misunderstandings and disagreements. The partnership agreement serves as the basis for the formation and operation of the partnership. At a minimum, the partnership contract should usually include the following points:

1. Names of all partners.
2. Rights and duties of each partner.
3. Name of the partnership.
4. Nature and location of the business.
5. Effective date and the duration of the agreement.
6. Capital contribution of each partner.
7. Procedures for dividing profits and losses.
8. Any rights or limitations on withdrawals of partners.
9. Accounting period to be used.
10. Provisions for dissolution.
11. Procedures for arbitrating disputes.

Characteristics of a Partnership

The significant characteristics of the partnership form of organization are summarized briefly in the following paragraphs.

Ease of Formation. Partnerships may be formed with little difficulty. As was the case with a sole proprietorship, there are few legal formalities or regulations (aside from local and possibly state licensing requirements) to be complied with.

Mutual Agency. Normally, all partners act as agents of the partnership and as such have the power to enter into contracts in the ordinary course of business. These contracts bind the remaining partners. The concept of mutual agency provides an important reason for the careful selection of partners.

Unlimited Liability. Usually each partner may be held personally liable to partnership creditors for all the debts of the partnership in the event that the partnership assets are insufficient to meet its obligations. If one partner is unable to meet his or her obligations under the partnership agreement, the remaining partners are liable for these debts.

If a new partner is admitted to a partnership, the partnership agreement should indicate whether he or she assumes a liability for debts which were incurred prior to his or her admission into the partnership. When a partner withdraws from a partnership, he or she is not liable for partnership debts incurred *after* his or her withdrawal if proper notice has been given to the public, for example, by a legal notice in a newspaper. He or she is, however, liable for all debts which were incurred prior to his or her withdrawal unless he or she is released from these obligations by the creditors of the partnership.

Since any partner may bind the entire partnership when making contracts in the normal scope of business, a lack of good judgment on the part of a single partner could jeopardize both partnership assets and the personal resources of the individual partners. The mutual agency and unlimited liability features may discourage certain individuals with substantial personal resources from entering into a partnership agreement.

Limited Life. Since a partnership is based on a contract, a partnership is legally ended by the withdrawal, death, incapacity, or bankruptcy of any of its partners. Addition of a new partner also terminates the old partnership. Although the entry of a new partner or the exit of an old partner legally dissolves the partnership, the business may be continued without interruption by the formation of a new partnership. This is done on a continual basis by firms of attorneys, doctors, and CPAs.

Co-Ownership By Partners. Partners are the co-owners of both the assets and the earnings of a partnership. The assets invested by each partner in the partnership are owned by all of the partners collectively. The income or loss of a partnership is divided among the partners according to the terms which are specified in the partnership agreement. If the partnership agreement specifies a method of dividing profits among the partners but is silent as to the division of losses, losses will be shared in the same manner as profits. If the manner of dividing profits or losses is not specified in the partnership agreement, partners will share profits and losses equally.

Evaluation of the Partnership Form of Organization

The primary disadvantages of organizing a business as a partnership include the unlimited liability of the owners, the mutual agency of all partners, and the limited life of the partnership. However, a partnership has certain advantages over both the sole proprietorship and the incorporated forms of business organization. In comparison to a sole proprietorship, a partnership has the advantage of being able to combine the individual skills or talents of partners and of pooling the capital of several individuals, both of which may be required to carry on a successful business. A partnership is much easier to form than a corporation and is subject to much less governmental regulation. In addition, a partnership may provide certain tax advantages. Like the sole proprietorship, the partnership itself is not subject to taxes. Individual partners are, however, required to pay income taxes on their share of the income of the partnership, whether or not these earnings are withdrawn from the business.

Accounting for a Partnership

The accounting for a partnership is very similar to that of a proprietorship except with regard to specific transactions involving the accounting for owner's equity. Since a partnership is owned by two or more persons, a separate capital account must be maintained for each owner and a separate drawing account may also be used for each partner. Further, the net income or loss for a period must be divided among the partners as specified by the terms of the partnership agreement. Additional accounting problems which are unique to partnerships may occur with the formation of a partnership, admission of a partner, withdrawal or death of a partner, and liquidation of a partnership.

Formation of a Partnership

Upon the formation of a partnership, resources invested by the partners are recorded in the accounts. A capital account for each partner is credited for the amount of net assets invested (assets contributed less liabilities assumed by the partnership). Individual asset accounts are debited for the assets contributed and liability accounts are credited for any debts assumed by the partnership.

If the investments made by the partners are entirely in the form of cash, the entry required would be a debit to cash and a credit to the partner's capital account for the amount of cash invested. When noncash assets such as land, equipment, or merchandise are invested, these assets should be recorded at their fair market values as of the date of investment. The valuations assigned to these assets may differ from the cost or book value of the assets on the books of the contributing partner prior to the formation of the partnership. Of course, the amounts recorded by the partnership must be agreed upon by all partners. Amounts agreed upon represent the acquisition cost of the assets to the newly formed partnership. The recording of assets at their current market value as of the date they are contributed to the partnership is necessary in order to provide a fair presentation in the partnership financial statements, and to assure a fair distribution of the property among partners in the event a dissolution of the partnership occurs.

To illustrate the entries which are required at the formation of a partnership, assume that Mantle and Maris, who operate separate sporting good stores as sole proprietorships, agree to form a partnership by combining their two businesses. It is agreed that each partner will contribute $10,000 in cash and all of his individual business assets, and that the partnership will assume the liabilities of each of their separate businesses. Assuming that the partners have agreed upon the amounts at which noncash assets are to be recorded, the following journal entries on the books of the partnership would be necessary in order to record the formation of the M&M Partnership:

Cash	10,000	
Accounts receivable	15,000	
Merchandise inventory	30,000	
Accounts payable		5,000
Mantle, capital		50,000
Cash	10,000	
Merchandise inventory	35,000	
Building	50,000	
Land	15,000	
Notes payable		10,000
Maris, capital		100,000

Division of Profits and Losses

The net income or loss of a partnership is divided among the partners according to the terms or procedures specified in the partnership agreement. As previously indicated, if provisions are made only for dividing profits, any losses are divided in the same manner as profits. In the absence of any provisions for sharing profits and losses in the partnership agreement, the law provides that they must be shared equally among the partners.

The specific method of dividing profits and losses selected in a partnership situation may be designed to recognize and compensate the partners for differences in their investments in the partnership, for differences in their personal services rendered, for special abilities or reputations of individual partners, or for some combination of these and other factors. The following are examples of some of the methods which may be given consideration in the division of partnership profits or losses:

1. A fixed ratio base.
2. A capital ratio base.
3. Interest on capital.
4. Salaries to partners.

The specific method chosen by the partners may incorporate one or more of the methods of dividing partnership profits and losses which are mentioned above and illustrated in the following paragraphs. As a basis for these illustrations, assume that the M&M Partnership had net income of $30,000 for the year ended December 31, 19x1. The following capital accounts reflect the investments made by Mantle and Maris during 19x1.

Mantle, Capital		Maris, Capital	
	1/1x1 50,000		1/1x1 100,000
	7/1x1 20,000		5/1x1 60,000

Fixed Fractional Basis. Partners may agree on any fractional or percentage basis as a means of dividing partnership profits and losses. For example, assume that in order to reflect differences in their initial capital contributions, services provided, and abilities, Mantle and Maris agreed to allocate one-fourth of any profits or losses to Mantle and three-fourths to Maris. Consequently, at the end of 19x1 the $30,000 net income would be allocated $7,500 to Mantle ($\frac{1}{4} \times $30,000) and $22,500 to Maris ($\frac{3}{4} \times $30,000). The division of net income is recorded with a closing entry—the income summary account is closed to each partner's individual capital account according to the terms of the partnership agreement. The entry required in order to divide the net income among the two partners is as follows:

Income summary	30,000	
Mantle, capital		7,500
Maris, capital		22,500

Additional closing entries are also necessary in order to transfer any balances in the partners' drawing accounts to their respective capital accounts.

Capital Ratio. When the invested capital of a partnership is a major factor in the generation of income, net income is often divided on the basis of the relative capital balances of the partners. If a capital ratio is used, the partners must agree whether the beginning capital balances or average capital balances should be used.

For example, the partners may agree to distribute net income on the basis of capital balances at the beginning of the period. Division of the $30,000 net income of the M&M Partnership on the basis of the ratio of the partners' beginning capital balances would be as follows:

Partner	Capital Balance 1/1x1	Fraction of Total Capital	Division of Income
Mantle	$ 50,000	$ 50 ÷ $150 or $\frac{1}{3}$	$10,000
Maris	100,000	$100 ÷ $150 or $\frac{2}{3}$	20,000
Total	$150,000		$30,000

Thus, the income summary account would be closed to the partners' capital accounts at the end of the year by the following journal entry.

Income summary	30,000	
Mantle, capital		10,000
Maris, capital		20,000

In order to reflect any significant changes in the capital accounts which may occur during a period in the division of income, the partners may agree to use the average capital balance ratio as a means of sharing partnership income. The average capital balance for each partner is equal to the weighted average of the different balances in their capital account during a period. In order to compute the weighted average, each balance in a partner's capital account is multiplied by the number of months until the next transaction affected the balance or to the end of the period. The sum of these amounts is divided by twelve in order to yield the partner's average capital balance during the period.

For purposes of illustration we will assume that Mantle's capital balance at the beginning of the year was $50,000 and that Maris's was $100,000. Maris invested an additional $60,000 on May 1 and Mantle invested an additional $20,000 on July 1. The computation of the average capital balance for Mantle and Maris is as follows:

Partner	Date	Balance	×	Time		Total			Weighted Average
Mantle	1/1/x1	$ 50,000	×	6	=	$ 300,000			
	7/1/x1	70,000	×	6	=	420,000			
						$ 720,000	÷ 12 =		$ 60,000
Maris	1/1/x1	$100,000	×	4	=	$ 400,000			
	5/1/x1	160,000	×	8	=	1,280,000			
						$1,680,000	÷ 12 =		$140,000

After the average capital balances have been computed, the division of net income is based on the ratios of average capital per partner to total average capital. In the case of the M&M Partnership, the calculation would be as follows:

Partner	Average Capital	Fraction of Total Average Capital	Division of Income
Mantle	$ 60,000	$ 60 ÷ $200 or 3/10	$ 9,000
Maris	140,000	$140 ÷ $200 or 7/10	21,000
Total	$200,000		$30,000

Interest on Capital. In some instances, only partial recognition may be given to unequal investments made by the partners in determining the division of income. This may be accomplished by allowing some fixed rate of interest on the capital balances and dividing remaining profits on some other basis. As in the use of capital ratios, interest may be based on beginning or on average capital balances during the period.

To illustrate, assume that Mantle and Maris agreed to allow each partner interest at the rate of 8 percent on his beginning capital balance, with any remaining profit to be divided equally. Under this agreement, the $30,000 net income for 19x1 would be divided as follows:

	Mantle	Maris	
Income			$30,000
Interest:			
8% × $ 50,000	$ 4,000		$ 4,000
8% × $100,000		$ 8,000	8,000
			$12,000
Remainder:			$18,000
$18,000 × ½	$ 9,000		$ 9,000
$18,000 × ½		$ 9,000	9,000
Total	$13,000	$17,000	$30,000

Salaries to Partners. As a means of recognizing differences in the value of personal services contributed to the partnership by individual partners, the partnership agreement may provide for "salary" allowances in the division of income. For this purpose, the agreed-upon salaries are used in the allocation of income but need not actually be paid to the partners. The partnership agreement may also allow for withdrawals of cash by the partners described as salaries. These withdrawals are treated like all withdrawals made by partners and debited to the drawing accounts; they are *not* salary expenses similar to those paid to employees. Salary allowances may be used in the division of partnership income whether or not the partners make any cash withdrawals.

To illustrate, assume that Mantle and Maris are allowed annual salaries of $6,000 and $8,000, respectively, with any remaining profits divided equally. The following division of the $30,000 profit for 19x1 would be made:

	Mantle	Maris	Total
Salaries	$ 6,000	$ 8,000	$14,000
Remainder	8,000	8,000	16,000
Total	$14,000	$16,000	$30,000

Salaries and Interest on Capital. Sometimes both the investments of the individual partners and the value of the personal services contributed by each may be quite different. In these situations, partners may agree to take into consideration both salaries and interest on capital investments in determining the division of income. Any remaining profit or loss may then be allocated on any agreed-upon fractional basis.

For example, assume that Mantle and Maris agree on the following division of income:

1. Annual salaries of $6,000 to Mantle and $8,000 to Maris.

2. Eight percent interest on beginning capital balances.

3. Any remainder to be divided equally.

Under this agreement, the $30,000 net income for 19x1 would be divided as follows:

	Mantle	Maris	Total
Salaries (per agreement)	$ 6,000	$ 8,000	$14,000
Interest:			
8% × $ 50,000	4,000		4,000
8% × $100,000		8,000	8,000
Remainder	2,000	2,000	4,000
Total	$12,000	$18,000	$30,000

Allowing salaries or interest on capital is simply a procedure or step in the process of dividing partnership profits. Since partners are owners, their contributions of capital and personal services are made in an attempt to earn profits. Therefore, these amounts are not considered to be expenses and do not reduce the income of the business.

Salaries and/or Interest in Excess of Income. In the previous illustrations, partnership net income exceeded the total salary and interest allowances to the partners, and the balance was divided between the partners according to the agreed-upon percentage. If net income is less than the sum of the allowable salaries and interest, or if there is a net loss for the period, the residual after the deduction of salaries and interest will be negative in amount. This negative amount must then be divided between the partners according to the agreed-upon fractional basis.

To illustrate this situation, assume the same salary and interest allowances as in the previous example. Further, assume that the M&M Partnership had net income of only $20,000 for 19x1. The salary and interest allowances total $10,000 for Mantle and $16,000 for Maris. The total interest and salary allowances of $26,000 exceed the net income of the partnership for the period by $6,000. This excess must be deducted in determining the partners' share of the income as follows:

	Mantle	Maris	Total
Salaries	$ 6,000	$ 8,000	$14,000
Interest	4,000	8,000	12,000
Remainder (divided equally)	(3,000)	(3,000)	(6,000)
Total	$ 7,000	$13,000	$20,000

Partnership Financial Statements

The income statement of a partnership is very similar to that of either a sole proprietorship or a corporation. The statement does not reflect income tax expense, however, because the partnership is not subject to an income tax on its earnings. (Partners are taxed as individuals on their share of the partnership income.) In addition, the allocation of the net income among the partners is often included in the income statement as a final item below the net income figure.

The balance sheet of a partnership differs from that of a sole proprietorship or a corporation primarily in the owner's equity section. The equity section of a partnerhsip reflects the end-of-period capital balances of each individual partner.

A statement disclosing the nature and amount of changes in the partners' capital balances during a period is often prepared for a partnership. For example, the statement of partners' capital for the M&M Partnership might appear as follows:

M&M Partnership
Statement of Partners' Capital
For the Year Ended December 31, 19x1

	Mantle	Maris	Total
Balances, January 1, 19x1............	$50,000	$100,000	$150,000
Add: Additional investments	20,000	60,000	80,000
Net income	15,000	15,000	30,000
Total	$85,000	$175,000	$260,000
Less: Withdrawals	(5,000)	(15,000)	(20,000)
Balances, December 31, 19x1	$80,000	$160,000	$240,000

Thus, the December 31, 19x1, balance sheet for M&M would include capital balances of $80,000 for Mantle and $160,000 for Maris.

Admission of a Partner

Although the admission of a new partner to a partnership legally dissolves the exiting partnership, a new agreement may be created without disruption of business activities. An additional person may be admitted by purchasing an interest directly from one or more of the current partners or by making an investment in the partnership. When a new partner purchases his share of the partnership from a current partner, the payment is made directly to the selling partner(s). Therefore, there is no change in either the total assets or the total capital of the partnership. When a new partner invests in the partnership by contributing assets to the partnership, however, both the total assets and total capital of the partnership are increased.

Purchase of an Interest From Current Partner(s). When a new partner acquires his interest by purchasing all or part of the interest of one or more of the existing partners, the purchase price is paid directly to the selling partner(s). Therefore, the amount paid is not recorded in the partnership records. The only entry which is required in the accounts of the partnership is to transfer the interest sold from the selling partner's capital account(s) to a capital account for the new partner.

For example, assume that Mantle and Maris have capital balances of $80,000 and $160,000, respectively. Mantle agrees to sell one-half of his $80,000 interest in the partnership directly to Berra for $50,000. The entry to record this transaction on the partnership books is as follows:

Mantle, capital	40,000	
Berra, capital		40,000

The effect of this transaction is to transfer one-half of Mantle's current capital balance (½ × $80,000) to the new capital account created for Berra. The total capital of the partnership, $240,000, is not affected by the transaction. The entry which was made was not affected by the amount paid by the incoming partner to the selling partner. The $50,000 payment made by Berra to Mantle reflects a bargained transaction between the two men acting as individuals, and as such, does not affect the assets of the partnership.

Purchase of Interest by Investment in the Partnership. When the incoming partner contributes assets *to* the partnership for his interest, both the assets and the capital of the partnership are increased. To illustrate, again assume that Mantle and Maris are partners in the M&M Partnership with capital accounts of $80,000 and $160,000, respectively. They agree to admit Berra as a new partner with a one-fourth interest in the partnership for an investment of $80,000. The admission of Berra would be recorded by the following journal entry:

Cash	80,000	
Berra, capital		80,000

After the admission of Berra, the total capital of the new partnership is as follows:

Maris, capital	$160,000
Mantle, capital	80,000
Berra, capital	80,000
Total capital	$320,000

Berra's capital balance of $80,000 represents a one-fourth interest in the total partnership capital of $320,000. It does not necessarily follow, however, that the new partner is entitled to a one-fourth share in the division of partnership income. Instead, the division of income or loss must be specified in the new partnership agreement.

Because balances in the asset accounts usually are not equal to their current values, the investment of the new partner may be more or less than the proportion of total assets represented by his agreed-upon capital interest. However, since the agreement concerning the new partner's relative capital interest should be reflected in the capital accounts, adjustments to the capital accounts will be necessary if the amount invested is not equal to the book value of the capital interest acquired. The adjustment required in recording the investment of the new partner is accomplished by using either the bonus method or the goodwill method.

When a new partner invests more than book value for his relative capital interest, a bonus or goodwill may be allocated to the old partners. To illustrate these two different methods, assume that Mantle and Maris, who share profits equally and have capital balances of $80,000 and $160,000, respectively, agree to admit Berra to a one-fourth interest in the new partnership for $120,000.

Bonus to Old Partners. The total net assets of the partnership after the $120,000 investment by Berra will be $360,000 ($240,000 + $120,000). In order to acquire a one-fourth interest in the net assets of the partnership, or $90,000 ($\frac{1}{4} \times $360,000), Berra was required to invest $120,000. The excess of the investment over the amount of capital allocated to Berra may be regarded as a bonus to the old partners. The old partners share the bonus in their agreed-upon profit and loss ratio. Each partner's share of the bonus is credited to his capital account. The entry to record Berra's investment in the partnership (assuming an equal distribution of profits and losses between Mantle and Maris) is:

Cash	120,000	
Berra, capital		90,000
Mantle, capital		15,000
Maris, capital		15,000

Thus, after the investment, Berra has a capital balance of $90,000 which represents one-fourth of the total capital of $360,000.

Goodwill to Old Partners. Alternatively, if the new partner's investment exceeds his relative share of the net assets of the new partnership, it may be assumed that the old partnership had goodwill. The amount of goodwill is determined by the initial investment of the new partner. To illustrate, the $120,000 investment made by Berra represented a one-fourth interest in the partnership. The fact that a one-fourth interest required an investment of $120,000 implies that the business is worth $480,000 ($120,000 ÷ $\frac{1}{4}$). The amount of goodwill is computed as follows:

Investment by Berra for a ¼ interest		$120,000
Implied value of business ($120,000 ÷ ¼)		$480,000
Net asset value exclusive of goodwill:		
Capital of old partners	$240,000	
Investment by Berra	120,000	360,000
Goodwill		$120,000

As was the case with the bonus, the goodwill is divided between the old partners in the same proportion as their profit and loss ratios unless a specific agreement is made to the contrary. The entries which are required in order to record the admission of the new partner (again assuming an equal distribution of profits and losses) are as follows:

Cash	120,000	
Berra, capital		120,000
Goodwill	120,000	
Mantle, capital		60,000
Maris, capital		60,000

The capital balances of the partners after the admission of Berra are as follows:

Mantle, capital	$140,000
Maris, capital	220,000
Berra, capital	120,000
	$480,000

It can be seen that Berra's share of the total capital is the agreed-upon one-fourth interest in the partnership ($120,000 ÷ $480,000).

Note that the choice between the bonus and goodwill methods results in different account balances (but the same relative capital interests). The goodwill method causes the total capital of the partners to be larger by the amount of the goodwill recorded. Thus, the choice between methods results in different financial statements.

When the new partner invests less than the book value of his relative capital interest, a bonus or goodwill may be allocated to the incoming partner. To illustrate, assume that Mantle and Maris agree to admit Berra with a one-fourth interest in the partnership for an investment of only $60,000.

Bonus to New Partner. Based on this method, the excess of the new partner's share of total capital over his investment is allocated as a bonus to the new partner. The amount of the bonus is calculated as follows:

Total capital prior to admission:		
Mantle, capital	$ 80,000	
Maris, capital	160,000	$240,000
Investment by Berra		60,000
Total capital		$300,000
Berra's one-fourth interest		$ 75,000
Investment by Berra		60,000
Bonus to Berra		$ 15,000

The bonus may be treated as a reduction of the old partners' capital accounts on the basis of their profit and loss ratio and as a credit to the new partner's capital. The entry to record the admission of the new partner assuming an equal distribution of profits and losses between Mantle and Maris is:

Cash	60,000	
Mantle, capital	7,500	
Maris, capital	7,500	
Berra, capital		75,000

Goodwill to New Partner. If the new partner's investment is less than his agreed-upon capital interest, the difference may be due to goodwill brought to the partnership by the incoming partner. This goodwill may be attributable to the reputation or special skills of the new partner which might be imparted to increase the earning power of the partnership entity. The goodwill is recorded as an asset with a corresponding credit to the new partner's capital account in order to allow him the agreed-upon capital interest in the partnership. There is no change in the capital accounts of the old partners.

To illustrate, assume that Mantle and Maris had capital balances of $80,000 and $160,000, respectively, prior to the admission of Berra with a one-fourth interest in the partnership. Since the total capital of Mantle and Maris, $240,000, represents a three-fourths interest in the total capital of the partnership after Berra is admitted, the implied value of the partnership is $320,000 ($240,000 ÷ ¾). However, the actual tangible assets of the firm after Berra's investent are $300,000, consisting of net assets of $240,000 prior to the admission of Berra plus the $60,000 investment. Therefore, the implied goodwill is $20,000 ($320,000 − $300,000). The entry required to record the admission of the new partner under the goodwill method is as follows:

Cash	60,000	
Goodwill	20,000	
Berra, capital		80,000

After his admission, Berra has the agreed-upon one-fourth interest in total capital ($80,000 ÷ $320,000).

Withdrawal of a Partner

When one partner withdraws from a partnership, he may dispose of his partnership interest in any one of several ways:

1. Sell his interest to a new partner.

2. Sell his interest to one or more of the remaining partners with the payment coming from the personal resources of the purchasing partner(s).

3. Sell his interest to the partnership with the payment from partnership funds.

In the first two cases, the sale and purchase is made among the partners themselves acting as individuals. Therefore, the accounting treatment is the same as for the admission of a new partner through the purchase of an interest from the existing partners. The journal entry required on the partnership books is simply to transfer the capital account balance by debiting the capital account of the retiring partner and crediting the capital account(s) of the purchase partner(s). There is no effect on either the assets or the total capital of the partnership.

If the withdrawing partner is paid from partnership assets, both the total assets and total capital of the firm are decreased. Because the current value and the recorded book values of the partnership assets probably differ, the withdrawing partner may be paid either more or less than the amount of his capital balance. The difference may be attributable, for example, to the change in value of certain specific assets or alternatively to the existence of goodwill or to a combination of both factors. The change in the asset values or goodwill may be recorded in the accounts and shared by the partners in their profit and loss ratios.

For example, assume that Mantle, Berra, and Maris have capital balances of $100,000, $120,000, and $180,000, respectively, and share profits and losses on a one-fourth, one-fourth, and one-half basis. Further, assume that it is agreed to pay Mantle $120,000 from partnership funds upon his withdrawal from the partnership, and that the fair value of the partnership at that time is $480,000. Assuming that specific assets cannot be identified to account for the increase in value, the entries required in order to record the goodwill and the withdrawal of Mantle are as follows:

Goodwill	80,000	
Mantle, capital		20,000
Berra, capital		20,000
Maris, capital		40,000
Mantle, capital	120,000	
Cash		120,000

Instead of an increase in the value of specific assets or the existence of goodwill, the difference between the payment to the withdrawing partner and his capital balance may be regarded as a bonus paid to the withdrawing partner by the remaining partners. This bonus is charged to the capital accounts of the old partners in the relative profit and loss ratios of the remaining partners. Under this assumption, the withdrawal of Mantle would be recorded as follows:

Mantle, capital	100,000	
Maris, capital	13,333	
Berra, capital	6,667	
Cash		120,000

The $20,000 bonus to the retiring partner was deducted from the remaining partners' capital balances on the basis of their relative profit and loss ratios of two-thirds for Maris (50% ÷ 75%) and one-third for Berra (25% ÷ 75%).

If the payment made to the withdrawing partner is less than his capital balance, the difference may be attributable either to specific assets that have fair values which are less than their recorded book values or to a bonus paid by the retiring partner to the remaining partners in order to retire from the partnership without undergoing a liquidation of the business. Again, the re-valuation of the assets of the partnership or the bonus is divided among the partners according to their profit and loss sharing ratio.

For example, if Mantle agrees to retire for a payment of $85,000, and it is agreed that the assets of the partnership are not overvalued, the entry to record the withdrawal would be as follows:

Mantle, capital	100,000	
Maris, capital		10,000
Berra, capital		5,000
Cash		85,000

Again, Maris and Berra would share the $15,000 difference ($100,000 − $85,000) on the basis of their relative profit and loss ratios of ⅔ and ⅓ (as above).

LIQUIDATION OF THE PARTNERSHIP

When a partnership goes out of business, its assets are sold, its liabilities are paid, and any remaining cash is distributed to the partners. This process is referred to as a liquidation.

As a basis for illustration, assume that Mantle, Maris, and Berra agree to liquidate their partnership. Profits and losses are allocated one-fourth to Mantle, one-fourth to Berra, and one-half to Maris. The balance sheet of the partnership just prior to the liquidation process appeared as follows:

MM&B Partnership
Balance Sheet
As of December 31, 19x1

Cash	$ 20,000	Liabilities	$ 50,000	
Noncash assets	430,000	Mantle, capital	100,000	
		Maris, capital	180,000	
		Berra, capital	120,000	
	$450,000		$450,000	

Assume that all of the noncash assets of the partnership are sold for $330,000, a loss of $100,000 ($430,000 − $330,000).

Any gain or loss on the sale of the partnership assets must be divided among the partners according to their agreed-upon profit and loss ratios before any cash is distributed to the partners. Thus, the $100,000 loss on the sale of the noncash assets of the partnership would be distributed among the partners as follows:

	Total	Mantle	Maris	Berra
Capital balance	$400,000	$100,000	$180,000	$120,000
Distribution of loss	(100,000)	(25,000)	(50,000)	(25,000)
Capital balance after sale	$300,000	$ 75,000	$130,000	$ 95,000

The entries required in order to record the sale of the assets and the distribution of the loss would be as follows:

Cash	330,000	
Loss on sale	100,000	
Noncash assets		430,000
Mantle, capital	25,000	
Maris, capital	50,000	
Berra, capital	25,000	
Loss on sale		100,000

After the noncash assets of the partnership have been sold and the gain or loss has been divided among the partners, the cash will be distributed first to creditors and then to the partners. The amount of cash to be distributed to each partner is reflected in the capital balances after all gains or losses on the sale of noncash assets have been recorded. The balance sheet prior to the distribution of cash appears as follows:

MM&B Partnership
Balance Sheet
January 10, 19x2

Cash	$350,000	Liabilities	$ 50,000	
		Mantle, capital	75,000	
		Maris, capital	130,000	
		Berra, capital	95,000	
	$350,000		$350,000	

The distribution of the cash, first to the creditors of the partnership and then to the partners, is recorded by the following entries:

Liabilities	50,000	
Cash		50,000
Mantle, capital	75,000	
Maris, capital	130,000	
Berra, capital	95,000	
Cash		300,000

In the previous example, the capital account of each partner had a credit balance after the loss on the sale of noncash assets were distributed. In some instances, one or more of the partners may have a debit balance in his capital account as a result of losses on the disposal of the assets. This debit balance is referred to as a capital deficit since the partnership has a legal claim against the partner. If this claim cannot be collected by the partnership, the deficit must be divided among the remaining partners' capital balances according to their profit and loss ratios.

To illustrate, assume that the MM&B Partnership has the same assets and liabilities as in the preceding example. Further assume that the capital balances prior to liquidation are Mantle, $40,000; Maris, $210,000; and Berra, $150,000; and that the noncash assets are sold for $230,000 (a loss of $200,000). The capital accounts after the distribution of the loss would be as follows:

	Total	Mantle	Maris	Berra
Capital balance	$400,000	$40,000	$210,000	$150,000
Loss on sale of noncash assets	(200,000)	(50,000)	(100,000)	(50,000)
Capital balance	$200,000	($10,000)	$110,000	$100,000

After payment of the $50,000 of liabilities, the balance sheet of MM&B Partnership would appear as follows:

MM&B Partnership
Balance Sheet
January 10, 19x2

Cash	$200,000	Mantle, capital	$ (10,000)
		Maris, capital	110,000
		Berra, capital	100,000
	$200,000		$200,000

If Mantle is able to pay his capital deficiency to the partnership, the following entry would be made:

Cash	10,000	
Mantle, capital		10,000

At this point, Mantle would have a zero capital balance and the $210,000 cash on hand would be distributed to Maris and Berra in amounts equal to the balances in their capital accounts.

If the partnership is unable to collect the capital deficiency from Mantle, this loss would be absorbed by the remaining partners. Since the partnership agreement provides that Maris had a one-half share and Berra a one-fourth share of profits and losses, their current interest in profits and losses is Maris's two-thirds (50% ÷ 75%) and Berra's one-third (25% ÷ 75%). The loss should be written off against the capital accounts of the remaining partners as follows:

Maris, capital	6,667	
Berra, capital	3,333	
Mantle, capital		10,000

Accordingly, the distribution of the $200,000 cash would be based on the amount of the partners' capital balances after allowances for the loss on the noncollection of the capital deficiency. These amounts are as follows:

	Mantle	Maris	Berra
Capital balance	($10,000)	$110,000	$100,000
Capital deficiency	10,000	(6,667)	(3,333)
	0	$103,333	$ 96,667

The entry to record the distribution of the cash would be:

Maris, capital	103,333	
Berra, capital	96,667	
Cash		200,000

In the event that any cash is subsequently received from the deficient partner, it would be divided between the remaining partners in their profit and loss sharing ratio, since that is how they shared the deficiency.

SUMMARY

The simplest and most common form of business organization is the sole proprietorship. A single individual owns, controls, and usually manages the firm's assets and receives the profits from its operations. The sole proprietorship is not considered a separate entity for income tax purposes and the owner is taxed on all earnings of the business, whether or not the owner withdraws them. Investments and earnings are generally recorded in the capital account and withdrawals in the drawing account. The drawing account, if used, is then closed to the capital account at the end of the period.

Accounting for the partnership form of business organization is considerably more complex in that more than a single owner is involved. A partnership is an association of two or more persons organized to carry on, as co-owners, a business for profit. The partnership agreement serves as the basis for the formation and operation of the partnership and should include all essential data. Significant characteristics of a partnership include the ease of formation, the applicability of the mutual agency concept, the existence of unlimited liability of each partner and limited life of the enterprise, and the co-ownership of the assets and earnings. The partnership has certain advantages, such as the ability to combine the skills and capital of several individuals, and certain disadvantages, such as unlimited liability of the partners. Of course, these (and other relevant) factors should be evaluated and weighted in each case.

A separate individual capital and drawing account is maintained for each partner. Upon the formation of the partnership, each capital account is credited for that individual's cash contribution or an agreed-upon value of property contributions. At the end of each period, profits or losses are divided among the partners according to the terms of the partnership agreement. When a new partner is admitted to an existing partnership, either by the purchase of an interest from a current partner or by a direct investment in the partnership, the old partners may receive a bonus which is credited to their capital accounts. In addition, if the new partner's investment differs from his or her relative share of the net assets of the new partnership, goodwill may need to be allocated to either the old partners or the new partner. When an existing partner withdraws from the partnership, the exact nature of the necessary entries to record the withdrawal will depend on whether it is accomplished by a sale to a new partner, by a sale to existing partners as individuals, or by a sale to existing partners with payment from partnership funds. When and if the partnership is liquidated, its assets are sold, its liabilities are paid, and any remaining cash is distributed to the partners.

This chapter has discussed the basic accounting procedures applicable to unincorporated business organizations. The next chapter will discuss the accounting for corporations.

KEY DEFINITIONS

Capital account—the capital account of a partnership consists of a separate account for each partner which reflects the investments by the partners plus each partner's share of the earnings or losses from the operations of the business less any withdrawals made by the partners.

Division of profits and losses—the agreement determines the method of dividing partnership profits or losses among the partners. In the absence of such an agreement, the law provides that profits or losses shall be divided equally among the partners.

Drawing account—cash or other assets withdrawn by a partner during the period are reflected in the partner's drawing account. The drawing accounts are closed to the partners' capital accounts at the end of the period.

Interest on capital—this is a method which provides for partners' capital interests as a factor in the distribution of the partnership earnings.

Limited life—a partnership is legally dissolved upon the withdrawal, death, incapacity, or bankruptcy of any of its partners.

Liquidation—the process of terminating a business in which its assets are sold, its liabilities are paid, and any remaining cash or other assets are distributed to its owners.

Mutual agency—each partner may act as an agent of the partnership, with the power to enter into contracts within the scope of the normal business operations.

Partnership—an association of two or more persons to carry on a business under a contractual arrangement.

Partnership agreement—this written contract of partnership sets forth the agreement between the partners as to the conditions for the formation and operation of the partnership.

Salaries to partners—a method which provides for the division of a portion of the partnership income by allocating specified salaries to the partners.

Sole proprietorship—a business owned by one person.

Statement of partners' capital—this statement shows the nature and amount of changes in the partners' capital accounts during a period.

Uniform Partnership Act—this act, which has been adopted in most states, governs the formation, operation, and liquidation of partnerships.

Unlimited liability—each partner is personally liable to the creditors of the partnership in the event that the partnership assets are insufficient to meet its obligations.

QUESTIONS

1. List the three basic types of business organizations.

2. What are the primary advantages of the partnership form of organization?

3. List and describe three important disadvantages of organizing a business as a partnership.

4. Explain the difference between admittance of a new partner to a partnership by making an investment in the partnership and admittance by purchasing an interest from a partner.

5. Smith is a partner in the Smith and Jones Partnership. At the end of the year, Smith's share of the partnership income is $20,000. During the year, Smith had withdrawals of $10,000. What amount of income should be included in Smith's taxable income for the year?

6. Upon the formation of a partnership, at what amount should the investments of noncash assets be recorded? Why is this necessary?

7. What factors are usually considered in determining the method for dividing partnership income?

8. In the absence of a specific agreement, how should the profit or loss of a partnership be allocated among the partners? If there is a specific method for allocating profits in the partnership agreement but no mention of losses, how should a net loss be divided among the partners?

9. Why does the agreement for division of partnership earnings often allow for salaries and interest on partners' capital balances?

10. When a new partner is admitted to a partnership and goodwill or a bonus is attributed to the old partners, how is the goodwill or bonus distributed to the capital accounts?

11. What is the effect of gains or losses resulting from the liquidation of a partnership on the partners' capital balances? How are the gains or losses divided among the partners?

12. After the distribution of a loss on liquidation, assume that one partner has a debit balance in his capital account. If the partner is unable to contribute any personal assets, how is the loss divided among the remaining partners?

EXERCISES

13. Bibby and Rowe formed a partnership on January 1, 19x1. Bibby contributed $75,000 capital while Rowe contributed $50,000 capital. No additions to capital were made during the year. For the year ended December 31, 19x1, the partnership had net income of $25,000. Prepare a schedule showing the division of income in each of the following cases:

a. Partners agree to allocate ⅓ of profits or losses to Rowe and ⅔ to Bibby.
b. Partners agree to distribute net income on the basis of their capital balances in the partnership.
c. Bibby and Rowe agree to allow each partner 8 percent interest on his beginning capital balance and divide the remaining profits equally.

14. Assume that Bibby and Rowe made withdrawals of $5,000 and $7,000, respectively, during 19x1. Give the entries to record the division of income in 13(a) above and the entries to record the closing of the withdrawals account.

15. Assume that Erickson and Goodrich, who have capital balances of $160,000 and $320,000, respectively, and who divide profits equally, agree to admit Hazard to a ¼ interest in the new partnership for $200,000. Make the entry to record Hazard's investment in the partnership under both the bonus method and the goodwill method.

16. Martin is withdrawing from the partnership of Martin, Water, and Osmond. The capital accounts of partnership are as follows: Martin, $10,000; Water, $10,000; and Osmond, $20,000. The partners share profits and losses equally. The partners agree that Martin will be paid $12,000 cash for his interest in the partnership. Give the entries to record the retirement of Martin using the bonus method.

17. The partnership of Jones, Clare, and Jackson is being liquidated on December 31, 19x1. The balances in the capital accounts prior to liquidation of the assets were as follows: Jones, $25,000; Clare, $20,000; and Jackson, $5,000. The partners share profits and losses equally. On December 31, partnership assets with a book value of $60,000 were sold for $39,000, and liabilities of $10,000 were paid.

Required:

How should the remaining $29,000 available cash be distributed if Jackson is unable to pay the amount he owes to the firm?

18. Bob Billy and Thomas Sloan decided to form a partnership. Bob said he would contribute a building which he purchased three years ago for $15,000. The book value of the building now is $10,000. A real estate dealer said the building could be sold presently for $18,000. Thomas said he would contribute land worth $50,000 to the partnership. The land had a mortgage of $35,000 which was to be paid over the next 10 years.

Required:

1. What will be the balance in Bob and Thomas' capital accounts when the partnership is formed?
2. Make entries to record the formation of the partnership.

19. In the Bell and Grubb Partnership, Bell had a capital balance on January 1, 19x1 of $26,000 and Grubb, $32,000. On June 1, Bell made a contribution of $6,000 to the partnership and on October 1, Grubb made a $3,000 contribution. The partners both receive 6 percent interest a year on their average capital balances and also divide net income based on the capital ratio of their average capital balances. If net income for 19x1 is $12,000, calculate each partner's share of the profits.

20. The capital balances for the partners of the Kingston Company as of December 31, 19x1 are as follows: Joe Kingston, $12,000; Bill Kingston, $15,000; and Paul Kingston, $13,000. The following transactions affecting their capital accounts occurred during the year.

   a. Joe and Bill Kingston withdrew $1,000 a month from the business and Paul withdrew $1,500 a month.
   b. Bill and Paul contributed $3,000 and $5,000 to the partnership, respectively.
   c. Net income for the year ending 12/31/x2 is $35,600. The profits are divided in the following manner: Joe, 50 percent; Bill, 20 percent; Paul, 30 percent.

   Required:

   Write a statement of partners' capital for the year December 31, 19x2.

21. Assume that in the Torberg and Haddix Partnership, Torberg has a capital balance of $75,000 and Haddix has a capital balance of $60,000. Make journal entries under each of the following unrelated assumptions.

   a. Haddix sells one-half of his $60,000 interest in the partnership to Carty for $40,000.
   b. Carty is admitted with a one-third interest in the partnership for an investment of $67,500. Total capital is to be $202,500.
   c. Carty is admitted with a one-third interest in the partnership for an investment of $70,500. Bonus is allowed old partners.
   d. Carty is admitted with a one-third interest in the partnership for an investment of $66,000. Bonus to Carty is recognized.

22. Lowenstein, Manning, and Norris have decided to liquidate their partnership. The balance sheet just prior to liquidation appears as follows:

LM&N
Balance Sheet
As of September 30, 19x1

Cash.................	$ 40,000	Liabilities.............	$100,000
Noncash assets.........	860,000	Lowenstein, Capital.....	360,000
		Manning, Capital.......	200,000
		Norris, Capital.........	240,000
	$900,000		$900,000

The noncash assets were sold for $980,000. Make the journal entries to record the gain or loss on the sale of the assets, payment of liabilities, and distribution of remaining cash to the partners. The profits and losses are shared equally.

PROBLEMS

23. Vallely and Patterson form a partnership with Vallely investing capital of $70,000 and Patterson investing capital of $30,000. The partners agree to allow 8 percent interest on each partner's beginning capital balance. Also, due to differences in services rendered, Patterson is to receive a salary of $8,000 while Vallely receives a salary of $4,500. Any remaining profits or losses are to be divided equally. Make a schedule showing the division of partnership net income assuming the partnership earned $16,000 for the first year of its operations.

24. Johnson and Kennedy formed a partnership on January 1, 19x1, with investments of $40,000 each. Kennedy made an additional investment of $20,000 on June 30, 19x1. Given each of the following assumptions, determine the division of partnership net income of $27,000 for the year:

   a. No method for division of income specified in the partnership agreement.
   b. Divided in the ratio of the ending capital balance.
   c. Divided in the ratio of the average capital balances.
   d. Interest at a rate of 10 percent on the ending capital balance and the remainder divided equally.
   e. Salary allowances of $10,000 to Johnson and $5,000 to Kennedy and any remainder divided ⅓ to Johnson and ⅔ to Kennedy.
   f. Interest at a rate of 10 percent on the ending capital balances, salary allowance of $12,000 to Johnson and $8,000 to Kennedy, and any remainder divided equally.

25. Taylor, Smith, and Jones are partners in the TSJ Partnership. The partnership agreement provides for the following procedures for division of income:

   a. Each partner is allowed 5 percent interest on the average capital balance.
   b. Salary allowances of $10,000 to Taylor and $12,000 to Smith.
   c. Remainder divided 50 percent to Taylor, 30 percent to Smith, and 20 percent to Jones.

During the current year, the average capital balances were $60,000, Taylor; $40,000, Smith; and $20,000, Jones.

Calculate the division of income among the partners in each of the following cases:

a. Net income, $38,000.
b. Net income, $18,000.
c. Net loss, $2,000.

26. Able and Baker agree to admit Comer into their partnership with a one-fourth interest. Currently, Able has capital of $20,000 and Baker has capital of $10,000. They share profits and losses equally. Give the journal entries necessary to record the admission of Comer for each of the following investments by Comer:

a. $10,000.
b. $20,000 using the bonus method.
c. $20,000 using the goodwill method.
d. $ 6,000 using the bonus method.
e. $ 6,000 using the goodwill method.

27. Wilkes, Lee, and Curtis have capital balances of $60,000, $80,000, and $100,000, respectively, in their partnership. They share profits on a ¼, ¼, and ½ basis, respectively. Wilkes withdraws from the partnership, and it is agreed that he will be paid $70,000 for his share of the partnership. At the time of Wilkes's withdrawal, the fair value of the partnership is $280,000.

Required:

Make the entries to record the withdrawal of Wilkes under the goodwill and bonus methods.

28. Kemp, Killough, and Kubin agree to liquidate their partnership on January 1, 19x1. The balance sheet of the firm as of that date is as follows:

Cash		$10,000
Accounts receivable		15,000
Inventory		30,000
Equipment	$60,000	
Less: Accumulated depreciation	(30,000)	30,000
Total Assets		$85,000
Accounts payable		$ 5,000
Kemp, capital		40,000
Killough, capital		30,000
Kubin, capital		10,000
Total Liabilities and Capital		$85,000

Profits and losses are distributed 50 percent to Kemp, 30 percent to Killough, and 20 percent to Kubin. On January 1, 19x1, the noncash assets were sold as follows: Accounts Receivable, $10,000; Inventory, $20,000; and Equipment, $15,000.

Required:

Prepare a schedule showing the distribution of cash to the partners upon liquidation.

29. Brown, Gray, and White agree to liquidate their partnership. Prior to beginning the liquidation process, they have cash, $15,000; other assets, $90,000; liabilities, $20,000; and capital balances of $50,000, $25,000, and $10,000, respectively. Profits and losses are divided among the partners in the ratio of 4:4:2, respectively. None of the partners had any personal assets outside of the firm. The realization and liquidation proceeded as follows:

a. $50,000 of other assets were sold for $30,000.
b. The liabilities were paid.
c. The remaining other assets were sold for $10,000.
d. The cash was distributed to the partners.

Required:

Prepare a schedule showing the effects of the liquidation process on the partners' capital accounts and the amounts distributed to the partners upon liquidation.

30. Hawk and Dove formed a partnership on January 1, 19x1, combining their separate businesses that they had operated as sole proprietorships. The account balances of the noncash assets contributed, and their agreed-upon fair values are shown below:

Hawk	*Book Value*	*Fair Value*
Accounts receivable	$20,000	$20,000
Inventory	10,000	15,000
Equipment	20,000	25,000
Accounts payable	10,000	10,000
Dove		
Inventory	5,000	6,000
Building	25,000	32,000
Land	10,000	12,000

In addition, Hawk invested $5,000 in cash and Dove contributed $25,000 in cash. They agreed to share profits and losses equally.

Required:

1. Prepare the journal entries required on the books of the partnership to record the investments in the partnerships on January 1, 19x1.
2. Prepare a balance sheet for the partnership on January 1, 19x1.
3. On December 31, 19x1, the partnership income was calculated as $20,000. Hawk and Dove had $5,000 and $8,000 debit balances, respectively, in their drawing accounts. Prepare the entries to close the Income Summary and Drawing accounts on December 31, 19x1.

31. The Lord & Davis partnership began business on January 1, 19x1, Lord and Davis were to share profits in a 2:1 ratio. Below is a list of transactions affecting the partner's capital accounts which occurred during their first year of business. Journalize these transactions in chronological order, including closing entries.

    a. Initially, Lord contributed a building with a fair market value of $55,000. The building held an unpaid mortgage of $15,000. Davis contributed cash of $35,000.
    b. On February 10, July 16, and November 12, Lord withdrew $7,000 and Davis withdrew $6,500 (i.e., Lord withdrew a total of $21,000 during the year).
    c. On June 15, Lord contributed stock to the partnership worth $25,000.
    d. On September 30, the partnership admitted a new partner, Gagnon, for a one-fourth interest. Gagnon invested $15,000 in cash and his capital balance was to equal $17,000. A bonus was recognized to Gagnon because of his knowledge and expertise in the business.
    e. Net income for the year ended December 31, 19x1 was $96,000. Since Gagnon entered the partnership on September 30, he was to receive one-fourth of his pro rata share of the profits and losses.
    f. Due to severe illness, Davis decided to withdraw from the partnership as of the end of the year. It is agreed upon by the other partners that the assets of the partnership are not overvalued, and that Davis should receive a payment of $40,000 with a bonus recognized to the remaining partners.

32. Below is the trial balance for the A&M Partnership.

A&M
Trial Balance
For the Year Ended December 31, 19x1

	Dr.(Cr.)
Current assets	$307,100
Fixed assets, net	844,180
Current liabilities	(157,000)
8 percent mortgage note payable	(290,000)
Anthony, Capital	(515,000)
Martini, Capital	(150,000)
Anthony, Drawing	24,000
Martini, Drawing	16,000
Sales	(827,000)
Cost of sales	695,000
Administrative expenses	16,900
Other miscellaneous expenses	11,120
Interest expense	11,700
Depreciation expense	13,000

Anthony and Martini share profits and losses in 3:1 ratio. Anthony has a tax rate of 35 percent and Martini has a tax rate of 20 percent.

Required:

1. What is the net income for the A&M Partnership for the year ended December 31, 19x1?
2. After allocation of net income and closing entries, what is the balance in each partner's capital account?
3. What income taxes must be paid by the partnership? The partners? (Disregard any other possible deductions by the partners).

33. On July 1, 19x1, Alford and Billy combined their two potato chip businesses into a partnership. Below are the balances in their accounts at that date:

	Book Value	Fair Market Value
Alford:		
Accounts receivable	$ 30,000	$30,000
Inventory	12,000	9,000
Equipment	45,000	50,000
Accounts payable	18,000	18,000

	Book Value	Fair Market Value
Billy:		
Accounts receivable	$ 22,000	$22,000
Marketable securities	35,000	42,000
Buildings and land	100,000	90,000
Accounts payable	23,000	23,000

The fair-market value has been agreed upon by the two partners on each item. Also, Alford and Billy each contributed $5,000 in cash. During the year, Alford withdrew $20,000 in cash and Billy, $25,000 in cash. The net profit for the year was $65,000.

Required:

Prepare journal entries to record:

1. Initial investment in the partnership on July 1, 19x1.
2. Closing entries as of June 30, 19x2, the end of the partnership's fiscal year along with a statement of Partner's Capital for the year then ended.

34. The 3C's Partnership began operations on July 1, 19x1. Each partner, Coon, Cassidy, and Candon, was to receive a one-third interest in the partnership. The following transactions occurred during the fiscal year which affected their capital accounts:

    a. On July 1, each partner contributed $25,000 in cash to the partnership. In addition to the cash, Coon contributed a building with a fair market value of $33,000 and a book value of $37,000.
    b. Each partner decided to withdraw their yearly salary at different dates. Therefore, Coon withdrew $15,000 on October 1; Cassidy withdrew $13,500 on December 15; and Candon withdrew $14,000 on February 1, 19x2.
    c. On December 30, Cassidy decided he wanted to sell his partnership interest and join the Peace Corps. Candon's brother-in-law, Casey, said he would pay Cassidy $12,000 for his one-third interest. It was decided at this time that Casey would receive Cassidy's share of the profit or loss up to December 30.
    d. On January 31, Candon contributed land to the partnership with a fair market value of $80,000. However, the land still had an outstanding mortgage of $60,000.
    e. On March 19, Casey contributed an additional $15,000 in cash.
    f. The first year ending June 30, 19x2 turned out to be rather unsuccessful, netting a loss of $27,000.
    g. Also on June 30, Coon decided to withdraw from the partnership and join Vista. The remaining partners agreed to pay Coon $36,500, and that the fair value of the partnership at this time is $81,000. The partners could not identify specific assets which had increased in values. Therefore, goodwill was recognized.

    Required:

    Record these transactions in journal form, including closing entries as of June 30, 19x2.

Chapter 7 considers issues relating to the formation of a corporation, the issuance of capital stock, and the retained earnings and dividends of a corporation. Studying this chapter should enable you to:

1. Discuss the steps required to form a corporation and the accounting treatment of any related expenditures incurred in so doing.
2. Distinguish between capital stock authorized, issued, and outstanding.
3. Describe the accounting entries necessary to record issuance of or subscriptions to capital stock.
4. Provide examples of extraordinary items and discuss the two essential characteristics of an extraordinary item.
5. Describe the situation in which prior period adjustments are appropriate.
6. List and give examples of three types of accounting changes.
7. Compute earnings per share and book value per share and explain the significance of each.
8. Recognize the accounting entries required to record the declaration and payment of both cash and stock dividends.
9. Discuss the purpose of and accounting procedures for treasury stock.

7

The Corporation: Capital Stock, Earnings, and Dividends

INTRODUCTION

A corporation is an artificial "legal" person that is both separate and distinct from its owners and, as such, is permitted to engage in any acts which could be performed by a natural person. It may hold property, enter into contracts, and engage in other activities not prohibited by law. The classic definition of a corporation was given by Chief Justice Marshall in 1819 as ". . . an artificial being, invisible, intangible, and existing only in contemplation of the law."

Although there are fewer businesses organized as corporations than as either sole proprietorships or partnerships, corporations are by far the dominant form of business organization in terms of both total assets and dollar value of output of goods and services. Because of the dominance of the corporate form of business organization and the widespread ownership interests in corporations, accounting for corporations is a very important topic.

CHARACTERISTICS OF THE CORPORATION

Because it is a separate legal entity, a corporation has several characteristics which differentiate it from both partnerships and sole proprietorships. The most important of these characteristics are described in the following paragraphs.

Separate Legal Existence. A corporation, unlike both sole proprietorships and partnerships, is a legal entity which is separate and distinct from its owners. Accordingly, a corporate entity may acquire and dispose of property, enter into contracts, and incur liabilities as an individual entity separate from its owners.

Transferable Units of Ownership. Ownership of a corporation is usually evidenced by shares of capital stock. These shares permit the subdivision of ownership into numerous units which may be readily transferred from one person to another without disrupting business operations and without prior approval of the other owners.

Continuity of Life. Status as a separate legal entity provides the corporation with a continuity of life. Unlike a partnership, the life or existence of a corporation is not affected by factors such as the death, incapacity, or withdrawal of an individual owner. A corporation may have a perpetual life or in some instances, its existence may be limited by the terms specified in its charter.

Limited Liability of Owners. As a separate legal entity, a corporation is legally liable for any debts which it incurs. Usually, the creditors of a corporation may not look to the personal property of the corporate stockholders for payment of any debts which are incurred by the corporation. Thus, the maximum loss which may be incurred by an individual stockholder is normally limited to the amount of his or her investment in the capital stock he or she owns. This limited liability feature is a primary advantage of the corporate form of business organization from the viewpoint of the owners. In addition, the absence of stockholder liability and the transferability of ownership usually increase the ability of a corporate entity to raise substantial capital by means of individual investments made by many owners. On the other hand, the limited liability feature may limit the ability of a corporation to obtain funds from creditors in those instances where solvency of the corporate entity may be questionable.

Separation of Ownership and Management. Although a corporation is owned by the individuals who hold its shares of capital stock, their control over the general management of the business is generally limited to their right to elect a board of directors. The board of directors, as representatives of individual owners or stockholders of the corporation, establishes corporate policies and appoints corporate officers who are responsible for the day-to-day management of the business and its operations. Officers of a corporation usually include a president, one or more vice presidents responsible for various functions within the business, a treasurer, a secretary, and a controller. The controller is the officer responsible for the accounting function of the business. A summary organization chart indicating the normal structure of a corporation is presented as follows.

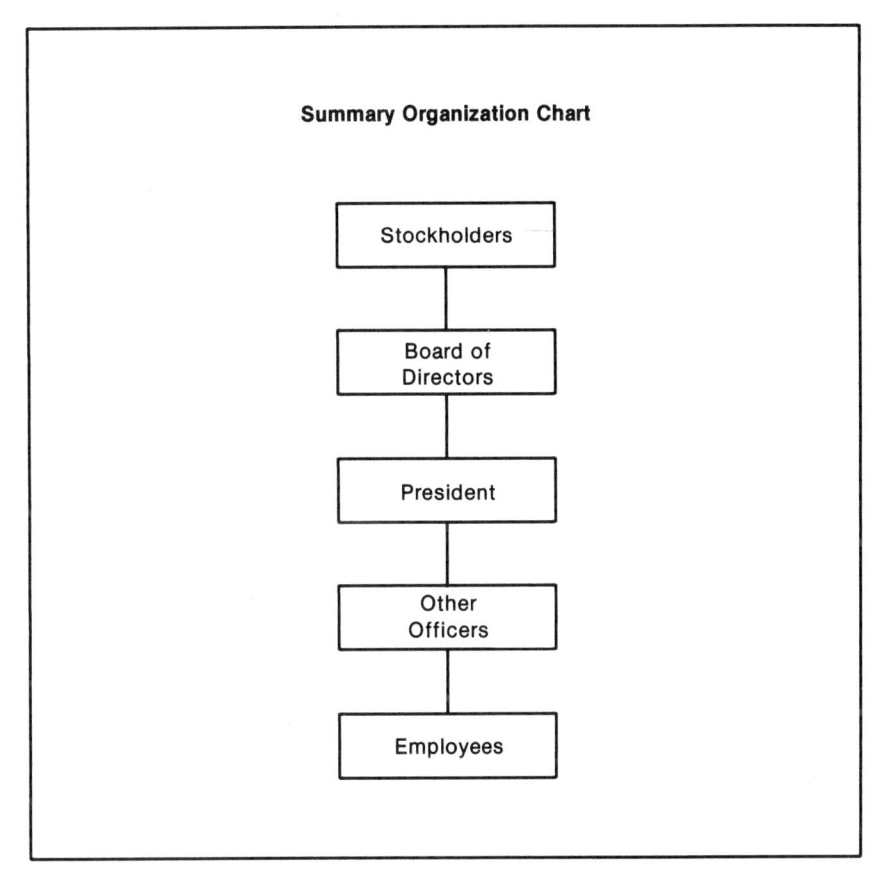

Summary Organization Chart

Stockholders → Board of Directors → President → Other Officers → Employees

Corporate Taxation. As a separate legal entity, corporations are required to file and pay local, state, and federal income taxes on corporate earnings. In addition, when corporate earnings are distributed to shareholders as dividends, these distributions are included in the taxable income of individuals receiving the dividend. Thus, "double taxation" occurs because earnings of a corporation are taxed twice—initially as corporate income and subsequently as dividend income when distributed to stockholders.

Certain businesses may elect to operate as corporations without filing and paying corporate income taxes. In order to qualify for such an election, a corporation must meet certain requirements—for example, it must have only a single class of stock and thirty-five or fewer stockholders. If this election is made, corporate income is taxed directly to the shareholders as it is earned by the corporation, just as would be the case if the business were organized as a partnership.

Government Regulation. Corporations are subject to numerous state and federal regulations and restrictions which are not imposed on either partnerships or sole proprietorships. This occurs primarily because corporations are separate legal entities and shareholders normally have limited liability for actions of the corporation.

FORMING A CORPORATION

A business corporation may be created by obtaining a charter from the state in which the business is to be incorporated. Although requirements for establishing a corporation vary, most states require a minimum of three natural persons to act as incorporators. An application for a corporate charter is usually made by filing articles of incorporation with the appropriate state official. Some of the more important information usually included in the articles of incorporation are:

1. Name of the corporation.
2. Location of its principal offices.
3. Nature of the business to be conducted by the corporation.
4. Identity and addresses of incorporators.
5. A detailed description of the capital stock authorized to be issued.
6. Identify of, and the amounts paid by, the original subscribers for the corporation's capital stock.
7. Names of the initial directors.

If the articles of incorporation are approved, the state issues a corporate charter which includes the general corporation laws of the state as well as any specific provisions of the articles of incorporation. The state usually charges a fee or organization tax for the privilege of incorporation.

Upon approval of the corporate charter, a corporation is authorized to begin its operations. Incorporators are required to hold a meeting in order to elect a board of directors and to adopt a set of bylaws which provide detailed operating regulations for the corporation. Directors of the corporation then elect appropriate corporate officers and authorize the issuance of capital stock certificates to the original stockholders.

Various expenditures such as those for state taxes and charter fees, legal costs, and other organization costs are necessary in order to establish a corporation. These costs are normally accumulated in an intangible asset account referred to as organization costs. Since organization costs are expenditures which are necessary in order to provide for the creation and continued existence of a business, benefits obtained from these costs extend over the entire life of a corporation. Therefore, from a theoretical viewpoint, organization costs should be amortized over the life of the business. However, except when otherwise specified in the corporate charter, the life of a corporation is considered to be indefinite. Consequently, two different methods have evolved for accounting for organization costs. One is to simply charge organization costs to expense in the period incurred. The other alternative is to amortize these costs over a selected reasonable, but somewhat arbitrary, period of time, usually a period not exceeding forty years. Although this alternative is certainly not justified in theory, it is usually acceptable in practice since organization costs are normally immaterial in amount and since this procedure is acceptable for income tax purposes.

CAPITAL OF A CORPORATION

Owners' equity of a corporation is commonly referred to as stockholders' equity and is accounted for in separate classifications according to the source of capital. Two primary sources of equity capital are: (1) contributed capital—amounts invested directly by shareholders, and (2) earned capital—amounts which are provided by profitable operations and retained in the business. A third major source of corporate capital, amounts obtained from creditors through borrowing, is discussed in Chapter 15.

Corporate capital provided by operations of the corporation is referred to as retained earnings. At the end of each period, any income or loss from operations of the corporation is transferred from the income summary account to retained earnings. The dividends account, which is used to record the dividends declared during the period, is also closed out to retained earnings during the closing process. Therefore, the balance in retained earnings at any point in time is equal to the total accumulated earnings of the business (net of any losses) less the total distributions which were paid to the stockholders in the form of dividends since the corporation's inception. If losses and dividends paid to stockholders exceed the cumulative earnings of the corporation, the resulting debit balance in retained earnings is referred to as a deficit. This deficit is deducted from invested capital in order to determine total stockholders' equity of the corporation.

NATURE OF CAPITAL STOCK

The investments made by stockholders in a corporation are represented by shares of ownership referred to as capital stock. Ownership of corporate stock is evidenced by a stock certificate. This certificate usually includes such information as the name of the corporation, rights of the shareholders, and the number of shares owned by each individual shareholder.

The maximum number of shares of stock *authorized* for issuance by the corporation is specified in the corporate charter. *The corporate charter indicates the total number of shares that may be issued by the corporation.* The number of *authorized shares* may be recorded by a memorandum notation and be reported parenthetically in the capital stock account. The number of shares *issued* refers to the total number of shares of stock which have been issued to stockholders since the formation of the corporation. Under certain circumstances, a corporation may reacquire shares of stock which were originally issued to its stockholders. Therefore, the remaining shares held by stockholders are referred to as *outstanding* shares. A current listing of the stockholders who own outstanding shares is maintained by the corporation's registrar or by the firm itself in a stockholders' ledger.

A corporation with a large number of shares outstanding which are traded regularly on an organized stock exchange must assign the function of transferring stocks and maintaining stock records to a stock transfer agent and a registrar. Banks or trust companies usually fulfill these functions for corporations. When a stockholder wishes to sell his or her stock, he or she endorses the stock certificate and forwards it to the transfer agent. The transfer agent cancels the certificate which was sold and prepares a new certificate which he or she sends to the registrar. The registrar records the stock transfer and issues a new stock certificate to the purchaser(s). Independent records maintained by the independent transfer agent and registrar provide additional controls which are intended to decrease the possibility of error or fraud in a corporation's ownership records.

RIGHTS OF STOCKHOLDERS

Many corporations issue only a single class of stock. In this instance, each shareholder possesses identical ownership rights and privileges. For an individual stockholder, these rights are proportionate to the number of shares of stock owned. Among these basic rights are:

1. The right to vote in stockholders' meetings. This includes the right to vote for directors and on decisions requiring stockholder approval as specified by the terms of the corporate charter. A stockholder has one vote for each share of stock that he or she owns. For example, if a stockholder owns 1,000 shares of stock, he or she is entitled to 1,000 votes. If a shareowner does not wish to attend a stockholders' meeting, he or she may assign his or her votes to a specified representative through a proxy statement.

2. The right to share in corporate earnings through dividends declared by the board of directors.

3. The right to maintain a proportionate interest in the ownership of the corporation whenever any additional shares of stock are issued by the corporation. This right, referred to as the preemptive right, provides that each stockholder may purchase a percentage of the number of new shares to be issued which is equal to his or her ownership percentage in the number of shares outstanding prior to the new issuance. To illustrate, assume that Aaron owns 100 (10%) of the 1,000 outstanding shares of stock of Matthews Co. If Matthews Co. decides to issue an additional one hundred shares of stock, Aaron has a right to purchase 10 percent (100 ÷ 1,000), or ten of the new shares issued. Therefore, Aaron will be permitted to maintain his 10 percent interest (110 ÷ 1,100) in the corporation. Thus, by exercising his preemptive right, a stockholder is able

to maintain his or her relative interest or ownership in the corporation. However, a shareholder is not required to exercise his or her preemptive right; he or she may elect to do so at his or her option.

4. The right to a proportionate share in assets upon the liquidation of the corporation. Shareholders, however, are entitled only to those assets which remain after all corporate creditors have been paid in full.

When a corporation issues only a single class of stock, its shares are referred to as common stock and the four basic rights described above apply to all shares issued and outstanding. In certain circumstances, a corporation may issue additional types of capital stock in order to satisfy management objectives and to appeal to investors who may have various investment objectives. These additional classes of stock usually grant certain preferential rights to the holders of these shares. Accordingly, such shares are usually referred to as preferred stock. Ordinarily, preferred stockholders either have no voting rights or only limited voting rights under certain conditions specified by the corporate charter. Preferred stock usually has one or more of the following preferences or privileges:

1. *Dividend Preference.* Stock which is preferred as to dividends entitles its owner to receive a stated dividend *before* any distributions are made to owners of common stock. Dividends on preferred stock are normally limited to a fixed amount per share. However, this dividend preference does not assure the stockholder that he or she will receive a dividend. Thus, if the board of directors of a corporation chooses not to declare a dividend, neither common nor preferred shareholders will receive any distribution from the corporation.

   As an example, assume that a corporation has outstanding 40,000 shares of $20 par, 7 percent preferred stock and 60,000 shares of $5 par common stock. If the board of directors does not declare a dividend, the preferred and common shareholders do not receive any distributions. If the board of directors declares a $60,000 dividend, the preferred stockholders receive $56,000 (40,000 shares multiplied by $20 per share multiplied by .07) and the common stockholders receive the remaining $4,000.

2. *Cumulative Preference.* Cumulative preferred stock provides that if all or part of the required dividend on preferred stock is not paid during a given year, the unpaid dividend accumulates and carries forward to succeeding years. The accumulated amount of unpaid dividends as well as current dividends must be paid before any dividends can be paid on common stock. Unpaid dividends on cumulative preferred stock are referred to as dividends in arrears. To illustrate, assume that a corporation has 10,000 shares of cumulative preferred stock outstanding and a $5 stated dividend per share was not paid in the preceding year. In the

current year, no dividends may be paid on the common stock until preferred dividends of $50,000 ($5 × 10,000) from the preceding year and the dividend of $50,000 for the current year are paid. Dividends in arrears are not considered to be a liability of the corporation until they are declared by the board of directors. However, because this information is important to the users of financial statements, any dividends in arrears on preferred stock should be disclosed, usually by means of a footnote to the balance sheet.

Preferred stock not having cumulative rights is referred to as noncumulative. Dividends omitted in any one year on noncumulative preferred stock do not carry forward. Therefore, dividends may be paid on common stock if preferred stock dividends are paid for the current year. Since a dividend preference is usually one of the most important rights or features of preferred stock, noncumulative preferred stock is normally not considered to be a very desirable investment under most circumstances. Consequently, most preferred stock issues provide for cumulative dividends.

3. *Participating Preference.* Preferred stock is usually entitled to receive a dividend of a specified amount each year. Preferred stock is nonparticipating when preferred stockholders receive only this amount regardless of the dividends paid to common stockholders. In some cases, however, certain types of preferred stock also provide for the possibility of dividends in excess of the normal amount. This preferred stock, referred to as participating, has the right to participate with common stockholders in dividends in excess of a specified amount paid to common shareholders. The preferred stock contract must indicate the extent to which preferred shares will participate with common shares. Fully participating preferred stock is entitled to dividends at an amount which is equal to the excess of the common dividend over the regular amount for preferred. Thus, if the preferred stockholders receive dividends up to their regular rate and the common stockholders receive a like rate, any excess dividends that are declared are divided proportionately between the preferred and common stockholders. The proportionate rate is based on the par value of the stock. If the common stock does not have a par value, then its stated value should be used. If the common stock has neither a par nor a stated value, then the board of directors will be required to assign a value to the common stock for purposes of computing dividend distributions. Partially participating preferred stock is entitled to participate with common stock, but it is limited to a maximum rate or amount. Issues of preferred stock normally do not include participation rights.

To illustrate, assume that a corporation has outstanding 50,000 shares of $25 par, 8 percent fully participating preferred stock and 80,000 shares of $10 par common stock. If the board of directors declares a

$369,000 dividend, the distribution between the preferred and common stockholders would be as follows:

a. The preferred stockholders initially are allocated $100,000 according to the following computation:

$$50,000 \times \$25 \times .08 = \$100,000$$

b. The common stockholders initially are allocated dividends based on a like rate. Therefore, the following computation is used:

$$80,000 \times \$10 \times .08 = \$ 64,000$$

c. The remaining $205,000 (the declared dividend of $369,000 less the amount already allocated, $164,000) is divided in proportion to the relative par values. The computation for the preferred stockholders is as follows:

$$\frac{50,000 \times \$25}{(50,000 \times \$25) + (80,000 \times \$10)} \times \$205,000 = \$125,000$$

The common stockholders are allocated the remaining $80,000 ($205,000 less $125,000).

d. The total distribution is as follows:

$$\text{Preferred}—\$225,000$$
$$\text{Common}—\$144,000$$

Using the same example, we now will assume that the preferred stock is partially participating up to a maximum of 2 percent above its stipulated 8 percent rate. In this case, the remaining $205,000 would be allocated as follows:

$$\text{Preferred}—50,000 \times \$25 \times .02 = \$25,000$$
$$\text{Common}—\$205,000 - \$25,000 = \$180,000$$

4. *Liquidation Preference.* Preferred stock is normally preferred as to assets upon liquidation of the corporation. That is, owners of such preferred stock are entitled to receive the stated liquidation value for their shares before any payments may be made to common stockholders.

5. *Convertible Preferred Stock.* Preferred stock is convertible when it includes a privilege which allows stockholders to exchange their preferred shares to a specified number of common shares of the corporation at the shareholders' option. A conversion privilege allows the owner of preferred stock the option of obtaining common stock on which there is no dividend limitation in exchange for his or her preferred stock.

6. *Callable Preferred Stock.* Preferred stock contracts frequently allow corporations to repurchase outstanding shares from preferred stockholders at a fixed price in excess of the issue price of the stock. When a corporation has this option, the preferred stock is referred to as callable.

STOCK ISSUANCE COSTS

Typically, there are various costs incurred by a corporation in the issuance of capital stock. These costs include administrative and printing costs involved in preparing and issuing the certificates, legal fees, advertising costs, and underwriters' fees.

There are two methods that generally are used in accounting for these issue costs. *One method is to treat these costs as a reduction of the amounts received from the sale of the securities.* Under this method, any costs incidental to the sale are considered to be a reduction of additional paid-in capital. *An alternative method is to view issue costs as an intangible asset, usually referred to as organization costs, which yields a benefit to the corporation over an indefinite future period.* These organization costs are charged to expense over an arbitrary period of time, not to exceed forty years.

PAR VALUE AND NO-PAR VALUE

The par value of a share of capital stock is an arbitrary value established by the corporate charter. It is usually printed on the stock certificate and may be any amount decided upon by the corporation. The par value specified has no relationship whatsoever to the actual market value of the stock. Market value, which is the price at which a share of stock can be bought or sold, is dependent upon factors such as expected earnings and dividends, financial condition of the corporation, and general economic conditions. It is not unusual for a stock with a par value of $5 per share to be traded at a market value of $50, $100, or more.

The primary significance of par value is that it is used in many states in order to establish the corporation's "legal capital." The concept of legal capital was used by state laws to protect corporate creditors from possible dishonest actions of stockholders or corporate directors. In the absence of such a provision, corporate assets could be distributed to stockholders prior to the final liquidation of a corporation. Since stockholders have no liability for corporate debts, creditors would be unable to obtain satisfaction of their claims. Therefore, the concept of legal capital limits the assets that may be distributed to stockholders prior to the liquidation of the corporation and the settlement of its debts. Consequently, dividends cannot be declared by a corporation if such payments would decrease the owners' equity to an amount which is below the specified minimum legal capital—that is, the par value of the outstanding share or, in some instances, par value plus a certain additional amount. Most state laws also provide that if the amount invested by individual stockholders is less than the established par value of the stock purchased, the stockholders may be held liable to the corporation's creditors for any difference between the amount paid and par value in the event the corporation is unable to meet its debts.

Laws requiring that stock have a par value were originally intended to protect the creditors of a corporation by restricting the distribution of a portion of corporate capital. However, the existence of a par value for capital stock has also caused certain problems. In some instances, investors have confused an arbitrary par value with the actual value of the ownership interest in the corporation. Also, if the market value of the stock falls below the par value established by the corporate charter, a potential liability to the investor may prevent the sale of additional[1] shares of stock by the corporation unless or until the corporate charter is amended to change the par value of the stock. Consequently, some states have enacted legislation permitting the issuance of stock without par value, referred to as no-par stock. In these states, the legal capital of the corporation may be the total amount paid for the shares by the stockholders, or a stated value per share may be established by the board of directors.

Occasionally, a corporation may desire to make certain changes in the structure of its contributed capital. Such action requires approval of the corporation's board of directors and also must conform with applicable state laws. Changes in the capital structure of a corporation typically involve either a change in the par or stated value of a class of stock or the replacement of par value stock with no-par stock. The new capital structure is recorded by debiting the existing contributed capital accounts and crediting the appropriate new capital accounts.

ISSUANCE OF PAR VALUE STOCK

The primary significance of par value from an accounting viewpoint is that the capital stock account is credited with the par value of shares issued regardless of the amount received when the stock is sold. For example, if 1,000 shares of $10 par value common stock are sold at par value for cash, the entry would be as follows:

    Cash 10,000
      Common stock   10,000

When stock is sold for more than its par value, the amount received in excess of the par value is recorded as "additional paid-in capital." To illustrate, assume that 1,000 shares of $10 par value common stock were sold for $12 per share. The entry to record the issuance is as follows:

    Cash 12,000
      Common stock   10,000
      Additional paid-in capital in
        excess of par value   2,000

The additional paid-in capital account is added to the capital stock account in reporting the total invested or contributed capital of the corporation. Contributed capital of the corporation in the above example would be

---

[1] This liability applies only to the original issue of stock, not to stock purchased and then resold by investors.

shown in the stockholders' equity section of the balance sheet as shown below:

> Stockholders' Equity:
> Common stock, $10 par value, 5,000
>   shares authorized, 1,000 shares issued
>   and outstanding $10,000
> Additional paid-in capital on common stock   2,000
> Total contributed capital $12,000

If capital stock is issued for an amount less than its par value, the difference is charged or debited to a "discount on capital stock" account. This account would be shown as a deduction from the capital stock account in the balance sheet. Since selling stock at a discount is illegal in many states and usually represents a contingent liability to the creditors of the corporation in the remaining states, it is seldom encountered in practice. The par value of stock will normally be set at an amount which is less than its anticipated selling price, thus avoiding this problem.

ISSUANCE OF STOCK FOR NONCASH ASSETS

Sometimes a corporation may issue shares of its capital stock in exchange for assets such as land, buildings, or equipment. In such a case, the transaction may be recorded at the market value of the shares issued or at the market value of the assets acquired, whichever is a better indicator of market value. The purpose of this approach is to record the transaction either at the amount of cash that could have been received from the sale of the stock or the amount that would have been paid for the property or services in a cash transaction. If the issuance of stock for noncash assets or services represents an arm's-length transaction, these fair values should be approximately equal. Therefore, if the value of only one of the items in the exchange is known or determinable, it is used as the basis for valuing the exchange. The market value of stock may be determined by reference to recent cash purchases and sales of the same class of stock by investors. Often, many shares of a large, publicly held corporation are traded daily through stock exchanges. Alternatively, if the market value of the shares issued cannot be determined, recent cash sales of similar assets or an independent appraisal of the asset may be used in order to record the transaction. Usually, the board of directors is given the responsibility by law for establishing a proper valuation for the issuance of stock for assets other than cash. To illustrate, assume that a corporation acquired land in exchange for 500 shares of its $10 par value common stock. If the stock is traded on an established stock exchange and the current market price was $20, the transaction would be recorded as follows:

> Land 10,000
>   Common stock........................   5,000
>   Additional paid-in capital   5,000

If there is no established market for the stock, the market value of the asset acquired may be used in recording the exchange. For example, if similar acreage had recently sold for $11,000, the entry to record the transaction would be:

Land	11,000	
Common stock........................		5,000
Additional paid-in capital		6,000

ISSUANCE OF NO-PAR STOCK

At one time, all states required that stocks have a specified par value. However, to eliminate problems such as the liability for issuance discount and potential confusion over the meaning of par value, many states now permit the issuance of stock without par value.

The accounting entries which are necessary in order to record the issuance of no-par capital stock depend upon the specific laws of the state in which the shares are sold. Some states require that the entire issue price of no-par stock be regarded as legal capital. In these states, the capital account is credited for the entire amount received when the stock is issued. To illustrate, assume that a corporation issues 1,000 shares of its no-par common stock for $12 per share. This transction would be recorded as follows:

Cash	12,000	
Common stock........................		12,000

Other states allow the corporation to specify a stated value for no-par shares. When a stated value has been established, that amount is credited to capital stock and any excess is credited to additional paid-in capital in excess of stated value. For example, assume that the board of directors established a stated value of $10 per share for its stock. Issuance of 1,000 shares at a price of $12 would be recorded as follows:

Cash	12,000	
Common stock........................		10,000
Additional paid-in capital		2,000

The additional paid-in capital in excess of stated value account is reported as a part of contributed capital in the stockholders' equity section of the balance sheet.

SUBSCRIPTIONS FOR CAPITAL STOCK

In some instances, a corporation may make an agreement with an investor to sell a number of shares of stock to him or her at a stipulated price. If the purchaser agrees to pay for the stock at some future date or with installment payments over a period of time, the sale of stock is referred to as a subscription. Subscriptions are an asset to the corporation since they represent cash or other assets to be received from the investor at some future date. Therefore, an account entitled subscriptions receivable is debited when subscriptions are accepted. Although shares are not actually issued until they are paid for, a corporation accepting stock subscriptions is committed to issue the shares upon receipt of the total specified purchase price. Accordingly, a common stock subscribed account is credited for the par value of the stock subscribed. The difference between the specified subscription price and par value is credited to additional paid-in capital (or discount). For example, assume that a corporation accepts subscriptions for 1,000 shares of its $10 par value common stock at a price of $18 per share. The subscription contract requires payment in two equal installments due in sixty and ninety days. This transaction would be recorded as follows:

Subscriptions receivable	18,000	
Common stock subscribed		10,000
Additional paid-in capital		8,000

When subscribers make payments on their subscriptions, the amount collected by the corporation is credited to the subscriptions receivable account. For example, upon receipt of the first installment of the subscription illustrated above, the following entry would be made:

Cash	9,000	
Subscriptions receivable		9,000

When the subscription price has been collected in full, shares of stock are issued to the investor by the corporation. For example, when the second installment is collected, stock certificates for 1,000 shares of stock will be issued. Collection of the installment payment and issuance of the shares would be recorded as follows:

Cash	9,000	
Subscriptions receivable		9,000
Common stock subscribed	10,000	
Common stock		10,000

During the period in which subscriptions are outstanding, subscriptions receivable from investors may be reported as an asset on the balance sheet and common stock subscribed is shown as a part of contributed capital in the stockholders' equity section of the balance sheet.

STOCKHOLDERS' EQUITY IN THE BALANCE SHEET

The stockholders' equity section of the balance sheet should report adequate information concerning each class of corporate stock outstanding. The balance sheet presentation, classification, and footnote disclosure associated with stockholders' equity should report, at a minimum, the following information:

1. The par or stated value of each class of stock.
2. The rights and priorities of the various classes of stock.
3. The number of shares authorized, issued, and outstanding for each class of stock.
4. The terms and provisions of convertible securities, of stock options, and other arrangements involving the future issuance of stock.
5. The additional paid-in capital associated with each class of stock.

The method of disclosure of capital stock and the amount of detail vary considerably among companies. Presentation of stockholders' equity in the balance sheet might appear as follows:

Stockholders' Equity:

6% preferred stock, $100 par value, 10,000 shares authorized, 6,000 shares issued and outstanding		$ 600,000
Common stock, $10 par value, 100,000 shares authorized, 50,000 shares issued and outstanding		500,000
Common stock subscribed, 1,000 shares		10,000
Additional paid-in capital:		
Common stock issued and subscribed	$130,000	
Preferred stock	60,000	190,000
Total contributed capital		$1,300,000
Retained earnings		450,000
Total stockholders' equity		$1,750,000

RETAINED EARNINGS

The stockholders' equity section of a corporation is divided into two major segments, contributed capital and retained earnings. Retained earnings represent accumulated earnings which were retained in the business. The retained earnings account is increased by the net income of the business and reduced by net losses and distributions to shareholders in the form of dividends. In the end-of-period closing entries, revenue and expense accounts are closed to the income summary account. When revenues exceed expenses, the credit balance which remains in the income summary account is equal to the firm's net income for the period. Conversely, a debit balance in the income summary account indicates a net loss for the accounting period. The balance in the income summary account is closed to retained earnings. Similarly, the debit balance in the dividends account is transferred or closed out as a reduction in retained earnings. This chapter considers the accounting for transactions affecting retained earnings and discusses various issues which are related to both corporate earnings and dividends.

NATURE OF EARNINGS

A primary purpose of reporting corporate earnings is to provide useful information to stockholders, potential investors, creditors, and other interested users of financial statements. The net income or loss of a corporation is determined in basically the same manner as that of a partnership or sole proprietorship.

A major problem of determining and reporting the net income for a period has been the treatment of unusual and nonrecurring transactions that are unrelated to normal operations. *Most accountants generally have agreed that the financial statements should disclose and distinguish clearly between those items considered to be normal and recurring and those considered unusual and nonrecurring.* For many years, the issue was how and where this distinction should be made in the financial statements.

This controversy led to a substantial variation in the handling of and definition of extraordinary items, discontinued operations, accounting changes, and prior-period adjustments both between companies and by the same company over time. Opinions issued by the APB and statements issued by the FASB have dealt with the classification and reporting of unusual items. As a result, there are four major sections of an income statement, although not every income statement will include all or any of the last three sections. These four sections are:

1. Income from continuing operations.
2. Results from discontinued operations.
3. Extraordinary items.
4. Cumulative effects of changes in accounting principles.

Each of these sections should be presented net of income taxes (i.e., both the income or loss and the related tax effect should be shown). In addition, *the earnings per share on common stock should be presented on the income statement.*

EXTRAORDINARY ITEMS

The net income of a corporation, as reported in its income statement, includes earnings from normal operations of the business as well as certain infrequently occurring transactions which are not related to the ordinary activities of the business. As a result of *Opinions No. 9* and *No. 30* of the Accounting Principles Board, transactions which occur infrequently and which do not result from the normal operations of the business, referred to as extraordinary items, are reported as a separate amount in the income statement.

To be classified as an extraordinary item in the income statement, an item must be both unusual in nature and not reasonably expected to recur in the foreseeable future. Determining the degree of abnormality and the probability of recurrence of a particular transaction should take into account the environment in which the business operates. Examples of potential extraordinary items include the effects of major casualties (e.g., an earthquake, if rare in the area, and an expropriation of assets by a foreign government). In addition, the effect of an extraordinary event should be classified separately only if it is considered to be material in amount in relation to income from normal operations. To illustrate, assume that in 19x1 the Dolphin Company had income after taxes from normal operations of $100,000 and a $20,000 gain (net of taxes)[2] which meets the criteria for classification as an extraordinary item. A simplified income statement for the Dolphin Company might appear as follows:

Dolphin Co.
Income Statement
For the Year Ended December 31, 19x1

Net sales	$400,000
Cost of goods sold	100,000
Gross margin	$300,000
Expenses	200,000
Income before extraordinary items	$100,000
Extraordinary gain, net of tax	20,000
Net income	$120,000

As indicated above, special consideration is given to the reporting of gains and losses. The FASB has defined gains and losses as follows:

> Gains are increases in equity (net assets) from peripheral or incidental transactions of an entity and from all other transactions and other events and circumstances affecting the entity during a period except those that result from revenues or investments by owners.
> Losses are decreases in equity (net assets) from peripheral or incidental transactions of an entity and from all other transactions and other events and circumstances affecting the entity during a period except those that result from expenses or distributions to owners.[3]

Certain gains or losses should not be classified as extraordinary items, even if material in amount, because they could be expected to occur in the normal or ordinary operations of the business. For example, a loss resulting from a write-down made to recognize a decline in the value of inventory due to obsolescence should not be reported as an extraordinary item. Such an item should be included in the computation of income before extraordinary items. Other examples of items that would not normally be considered extraordinary items regardless of their amount include:

---

[2] See Chapter 12 for a discussion of the allocation of income tax within a period.

[3] *FASB Statement of Financial Accounting Concepts No. 6*, "Elements of Financial Statements of Business Enterprises," (Stamford, CT: FASB, 1985), 82-83.

1. The write-down or write-off of receivables, inventories, equipment leased to others, or intangible assets.
2. The gains or losses from exchanges or translation of foreign currencies, including those relating to major devaluation or revaluations.
3. The gains or losses on the disposal of a segment of a business.
4. Other gains or losses from the sale or abandonment of property, plant, or equipment used in the business.
5. The effects of a strike.
6. The adjustments or accruals on long-term contracts.

Items which are either unusual in nature or occur infrequently, but do not meet both criteria, should not be classified as extraordinary items. However, if such items are material in amount, they should be separately disclosed by reporting them as separate components in income before extraordinary items or by including a description of the item and its effect as a footnote to the income statement.

DISCONTINUED OPERATIONS

The term "discontinued operations" refers to the operation of any subsidiary, division, or department of a business that has been or will be sold, abandoned, or otherwise disposed of. In APB *Opinion No. 30*, the board concluded that the results of continuing normal operations should be reported separately from discontinued operations. Any gain or loss from the disposal of a segment of a business along with the results of operations of the segment should be reported in a separate section of the income statement. The purpose of reporting on the continuing operations of a business separately from the discontinued operations is that it allows financial statement users to make better judgments about the future earnings prospects of the business. Accordingly, an income statement of a firm that has discontinued operations would appear as follows:

Kingsberry Company
Income Statement
For the Year Ended December 31, 19x1

Sales		$10,000
Less: Cost of goods sold		4,000
Gross profit		$ 6,000
Operating expenses		4,000
Income from continuing operations before income taxes		$ 2,000
Provision for income taxes		800
Income from continuing operations		$ 1,200
Discontinued operations (footnote):		
Income from operations of discontinued division (less taxes of $300)	$500	
Loss on disposal of division (less tax effect of $200)	(300)	200
Net income		$ 1,400

PRIOR-PERIOD ADJUSTMENTS

The provisions of *FASB Statement No. 16* indicate that, with one exception, all items of profit or loss recognized in a given year should be included in the determination of net income for that year. The only exception is corrections of errors in previous financial statements. Errors may result from computational mistakes, omission of data, incorrect application of accounting principles, or the use of unacceptable accounting principles. Corrections of errors of prior-periods are not included in the income statement of the year in which the error is discovered. Instead, these items are shown as direct adjustments to beginning retained earnings.[4] The nature of the error, the effect of its correction on income before extraordinary items and on net income, and the effects of its correction on the related earnings per share amounts should be disclosed in the period in which the error is discovered and corrected. The financial statements of subsequent periods do not have to report the disclosures again.

Errors in financial statements can occur due to mathematical mistakes, mistakes in the application of accounting principles, oversights, or misuses of the facts that existed at the time that the statements were prepared. Examples of these errors would include the following:

1. Computing the percentage incorrectly for the percentage-of-completion method on long-term construction contracts.

2. Failing to make an adjusting entry for wages expense at the end of the accounting period.

3. Using an unrealistic useful life for an asset in computing depreciation.

---
[4] *Statement on Financial Accounting Standards No. 16*, "Prior Period Adjustments" (Stamford, CT: FASB, 1977).

4. Using an accounting principles which is not generally accepted.

5. Using the bank prime interest rate rather than the average Aa corporate bond yield in determining whether convertible securities that were issued after February 28, 1982, are common stock equivalents.

The correction of the error is accomplished by computing the net cumulative effect on all prior-periods and adjusting the beginning balance of retained earnings as well as any other accounts that are affected. Of course, for errors such as (5) above, there would be no net cumulative effect on prior-periods and, therefore, no adjustment made to any accounts.

Errors. Accounting errors may result from mistakes in the application of accounting principles, oversights, misuse of facts, or mistakes in mathematics. To illustrate, assume that the truck acquired on January 1, 19x1, had been incorrectly recorded as an expense rather than as an asset. This error was discovered on December 31, 19x2, at which time it was decided that the asset should have been assigned an estimated useful life of four years and a $400 salvage value. The company uses the straight-line method of depreciation. The entry at December 31, 19x2, to record the correction of the error would be:

Asset	4,000	
Accumulated depreciation		900
Prior period adjustment..............		3,100

This entry records the asset at its costs of $4,000, the accumulated depreciation of $900 that should have been recorded in 19x1, and an adjustment of the prior year's earnings of $3,100 ($4,000 asset expenditure erroneously recorded as an expense less $900 depreciation expense which should have been recorded in 19x1). The prior period adjustment would be a correction of retained earnings and would not appear in the income statement. Depreciation for 19x2 would be recorded in the normal manner:

Depreciation expense	900	
Accumulated depreciation		900

ACCOUNTING CHANGES

Prior to the issuance of *APB Opinion No. 20* on accounting changes, there were various practices and procedures for reporting the effects of accounting changes on financial statements. In *Opinion No. 20*, the board clarified the different types of changes and provided guidelines for the reporting procedures to be employed. Two types of changes may be involved: (1) a change in accounting principle, and (2) a change in accounting estimate.[5] These two types of changes will be illustrated and discussed in the paragraphs that follow.

---

[5] A third type of accounting change, a change in reporting entity, is **not** applicable to this discussion.

Change in Accounting Principle. As previously indicated, the consistency principle requires that the same accounting methods be used from one accounting period to the next. However, as an exception to this principle, a change in accounting methods is allowed if the new method used can be justified as being preferable to the previously used method, and the effects of the change are adequately disclosed in financial statements. Thus, a change in accounting principle results from the adoption of a generally accepted accounting method which differs from the one that was previously used. An example would be a change from the sum-of-the-years'-digits method of depreciation to the straight-line method. For most types of changes in accounting methods, the cumulative effect which the use of the new method would have had on income in all prior periods that the old method was used must be included in the income statement in the year in which the accounting change is made.[6]

To illustrate, assume that a company acquired a truck on January 1, 19x1, at a cost of $4,000. The useful life of the truck was estimated to be four years with a salvage value of $400. At the date of acquisition, the company decided to use the sum-of-the-years'-digits depreciation method. Further assume that the company decided to switch to the straight-line method at the end of 19x3. At the time of the change in methods, the cumulative difference between the old and the new methods of depreciation must be determined. The amount of this difference would be computed as follows:

Year	Sum-of-the Years'-Digits	Straight-Line	Difference to December 31, 19x2
19x1	$1,440	$ 900	$540
19x2	1,080	900	180
	$2,520	$1,800	$720

The $720 difference in depreciation between the two methods would be adjusted during 19x3 as follows:

Accumulated depreciation	720	
Depreciation adjustment, change in accounting principle		720

This entry reduces the balance in the accumulated depreciation account to what it would have been had the straight-line method been used from the time the asset was purchased. The depreciation adjustment would appear in the income statement in the year of the change. After the adjustment is made, the depreciation expense for 19x3 and 19x4 would be recorded at $900 per year on the straight-line method.

---

[6] Certain specfific types of accounting changes are disclosed by revising the financial statements of prior periods to reflect the effects of the use of the new method.

The effect of this change on the current and prior years' income should be explained by a footnote to the financial statements. A change in accounting principle is appropriate only when it can be demonstrated that the new method is preferable.

Change in Accounting Estimate. Changes in the estimates used in accounting may occur as additional information regarding the original estimate is obtained. An example of such a change would be a change in the estimated salvage value or service life of an asset. The procedure used in adjusting for this change is to spread the remaining undepreciated cost of the asset over its remaining useful life. This procedure will allocate the remaining book value of the asset, less the new estimated salvage value, to expense over the revised estimated remaining useful life of the asset.

To illustrate, assume the company in the previous example decided in 19x4 that while the straight-line method should be used, the useful life of the asset should have been six (rather than four) years and the salvage value should have been $100 (instead of $400). The amount of depreciation expense for 19x4 would be computed as follows:

```
Original cost ................................. $4,000
    Less:   Accumulated depreciation
                    to December 31, 19x3 ................  2,700
Book value at December 31, 19x3 ................  1,300
    Less:   Estimated salvage value ................    100
Amount to be depreciated ...................... $1,200
    Divide by:   Estimated remaining useful life ......        3  years
Depreciation per year .......................... $  400
```

At the end of 19x4, 19x5, and 19x6, the following entry would be made to record the depreciation expense:

```
Depreciation expense..................   400
        Accumulated depreciation............          400
```

EARNINGS PER SHARE

An amount referred to as earnings per share is basically the net income of a company per share of common stock outstanding for a given period. Data on earnings per share of a corporation probably receive more attention than any other single item of financial information. Earnings per share ratios are included in annual reports issued by corporations and receive extensive coverage in the financial press and the investment services. Earnings per share is often considered to be an important indicator of the market price of common stock and, in some cases, an indication of expected dividends per share.

Because of the widespread attention given to earnings per share data, it was recognized that such information should be computed on a consistent and meaningful basis by all companies. Accordingly, *Opinion No. 15* of the Accounting Principles Board provided detailed procedures for the computation and presentation of earnings per share figures under different circumstances.[7] Further, the APB concluded that earnings per share data should be disclosed in income statements for all period covered by the statement. If extraordinary items and gains or losses from discontinued operations are included in net income for the period, separate earnings per share figures would normally be provided for: (1) income from continuing operations, (2) discontinued operations, (3) extraordinary items, and (4) net income. This data is usually presented in the income statement following the net income figure.

The computation of earnings per share is relatively simple when the capital structure of the corporation includes only common stock and the number of shares outstanding have not changed during the period. In this case, earnings per share of common stock is computed by dividing net income by the number of shares of common stock outstanding. To illustrate, assume that Dolphin Co. had 40,000 shares of common stock outstanding during 19x1 and earnings as shown below. Its earnings per share information would be computed as follows:

$$\text{Ordinary income} \quad \frac{\$100{,}000}{40{,}000} = \$2.50$$

$$\text{Extraordinary gain} \quad \frac{\$20{,}000}{40{,}000} = \$.50$$

$$\text{Net income} \quad \frac{\$120{,}000}{40{,}000} = \$3.00$$

When there are both common and preferred stock outstanding, the net income must be reduced by the preferred dividend requirements to determine the net income available to common stockholders. If the firm issues or acquires shares of stock during the period, the divisor in the calculation is the average number of shares outstanding during the year. In such circumstances, the earnings per share is computed as follows:

$$\left[\frac{\text{Earnings}}{\text{Per Share}} = \frac{\text{Net Income} - \text{Preferred Dividends}}{\text{Average Number of Common Shares Outstanding}} \right]$$

---

[7] *Opinions of the Accounting Principles Board No. 15*, "Earnings Per Share" (New York: AICPA, 1969).

The capital structures of many corporations include convertible securities, stock options, and other securities which may include rights that can be converted into shares of common stock at the option of the holder. A capital structure is considered to be complex when it includes securities and rights that could potentially decrease earnings per share by increasing the number of common shares outstanding. The existence of a complex capital structure results in significant complications in computations of earnings per share data. Essentially, they involve the calculation of hypothetical earnings per share figures which assume conversion of certain securities into common stock. The details of these considerations, however, are beyond the scope of this text.

DIVIDENDS

Dividends are distributions made by a corporation to its shareholders. Such distributions are paid in proportion to the number of shares owned by each stockholder. Dividends may be in the form of cash, other assets, or shares of the corporation's own stock. Unless otherwise specified, a dividend represents a distribution of cash. Payment of dividends is provided by action of the board of directors. The board has complete control of the type, amount, and timing of any and all dividend payments. However, once dividends are declared, they become a legal liability of the corporation to its stockholders.

In most cases, dividends represent a distribution of accumulated corporate earnings. It is ordinarily illegal to declare dividends in excess of the balance in the retained earnings account. In other words, an ordinary dividend usually may not be paid from any amounts which were invested by stockholders. The existence of a credit balance in the retained earnings account, however, does not necessarily indicate that there is cash available for the payment of dividends. Retained earnings is unrelated to the balance in the cash account because funds obtained from the accumulated income of the business may have been used to increase noncash assets or to decrease liabilities. Thus, a corporation with a large retained earnings balance may be unable to distribute cash dividends to its stockholders. On the other hand, a corporation with a substantial amount of cash may decide to pay little or no dividends to its stockholders so that the cash may be retained and used for other corporate objectives.

Because dividends are important to investors and therefore have an effect on the market price of the stock, most corporation attempt to adhere to a well formulated or established dividend policy. Although the percentage of earnings paid out in dividends varies widely according to the objectives of the firm, most corporations usually attempt to maintain a stable or increasing record of dividend payments.

While ordinary dividends are usually limited to the amount of retained earnings, a corporation may pay a liquidating dividend in order to return to the stockholders a portion of their original investment. Such a dividend is normally paid in conjunction with a permanent reduction in the size of a business or, alternatively, upon liquidation of a firm. Accordingly, such distributions are recorded by reducing capital stock and additional paid-in capital accounts.

Important Dates Related to Dividends

There are three important dates related to dividends:

1. Date of declaration.
2. Date of record.
3. Date of payment.

On the date of declaration, the board of directors of a corporation formally establishes a liability of a specified amount to its stockholders. The dividend and related liability, dividends payable, are recorded at that time. If financial statements are prepared after dividends are declared but before they are paid, dividends payable are classified as a current liability in the balance sheet. Following the declaration date, the corporation prepares a list of the stockholders as of the date of record—these are the stockholders who are entitled to receive the dividends. No entry is required by the corporation on the record date.

A period of time is usually necessary between the record date and the date of payment to allow the corporation sufficient time to identify those stockholders who will receive dividends and to process the dividend checks. An entry is made on the date of payment to record the distribution of cash and to remove the liability for dividends payable.

Cash Dividends

Dividends are usually paid in cash. Such dividends result in a reduction of both the cash and retained earnings of a corporation. Dividends on common stock are usually stated as a specific amount per share, while preferred stock dividends may be stated at either a specific dollar amount or a percentage of the par value per share. For example, a dividend on $100 par value preferred stock might be specified as either $5 or as 5 percent of par value. In either case, dividends paid to each stockholder are in proportion to the number of shares owned.

To illustrate, assume that the Jet Co. has 10,000 shares of common stock and 5,000 shares of 6 percent, $100 par value preferred stock outstanding. Further assume that on December 15 the company declares the preferred dividend and a $5 per share dividend on common stock. The $30,000 preferred dividend (.06 × $100 × 5,000 shares) and the $50,000 common dividend ($5 × 10,000 shares) are payable on January 15 to its stockholders of record on December 20. The entries which are required to record the declaration of the dividend on December 15 and its payment on January 15 are as follows:

Dec.	15	Preferred dividends	30,000	
		Common dividends	50,000	
		Dividends payable		80,000
	20	No entry		
Jan.	15	Dividends payable	80,000	
		Cash		80,000

The dividend accounts are closed to retained earnings during the normal year-end closing process. Assuming that the accounting period for the Jet Co. ends on December 31 the following entry would be made on that date:

Dec.	31	Retained earnings	80,000	
		Preferred dividends		30,000
		Common dividends		50,000

In some instances, the corporation may debit retained earnings directly, rather than a dividend account. In these instances, a closing entry would not be required.

Stock Dividends

A distribution made to stockholders in the form of additional shares of a company's own stock is referred to as a stock dividend. Usually, such a distribution consists of additional common stock given to common stockholders. A stock dividend results in a proportionate increase in the number of shares owned by each stockholder. For example, a 10 percent stock dividend entitles a stockholder to receive one additional share of each ten shares of stock he or she owns.

Since a stock dividend is paid on a pro rata basis, each stockholder retains the identical percentage interest in the firm after the dividend as he or she owned prior to the distribution. For example, assume that a stockholder owned 100 of 1,000 outstanding shares of a corporation. Thus, the stockholder owned 10 percent (100 ÷ 1,000) of the corporation's outstanding stock. Further assume that the corporation declared a 5 percent stock dividend. The stockholder would receive five (.05 × 100) of the fifty (.05 × 1,000) additional shares of stock issued. Consequently, the stockholder's percentage interest in the corporation remains at 10 percent (105 ÷ 1,050) after the stock dividend. A stockholder, however, may benefit from a stock dividend if there is less than a proportionate decrease in the market price of the stock associated with the distribution. In this case the market value of the total shares owned by the stockholder would increase.

Unlike a cash dividend, a stock dividend does not result in a decrease in either the corporation's assets or its total stockholders' equity. If a stock dividend has no effect on either the assets or the equity of the corporation, or in the relative ownership interests of the shareholders, why do corporations distribute such dividends? A primary purpose of issuing stock dividends is to enable the corporation to give its stockholders some evidence of increased retained earnings without actually distributing cash. Thus, although a stock dividend does not affect corporate assets or increase the individual stockholder's relative interest in the corporation, it is perceived to be a distribution of earnings by many shareholders.

Another reason for distributing a stock dividend is to reduce the selling price of the corporation's stock. Because a stock dividend of a sizable amount increases the number of shares outstanding with no change in corporate assets, the market price of the stock normally decreases. A corporation may desire to reduce the market price of its stock so that it will be more readily marketable among investors.

Since a stock dividend increases the number of shares outstanding, many states require an associated increase in the legal capital of the corporation. Therefore, even though such a dividend has no effect on total stockholders' equity, an entry is required in order to transfer a portion of retained earnings to contributed capital if such capitalization is required by the state. This is referred to as "capitalizing" a part of retained earnings. Consequently, the retained earnings "capitalized" is no longer available for distribution to stockholders in the form of cash dividends.

In many states, the minimum amount which must be transferred from retained earnings to contributed capital is an amount equal to the par or stated value of the shares issued. In other states, there is no such requirement. However, because it is generally believed that most shareholders regard a stock dividend as something of value, the American Institute of CPAs has recommended that in certain circumstances an amount equal to the fair market value of the shares to be issued as a stock dividend should be capitalized. This reasoning was explained by the Committee on Accounting Procedure of the AICPA as follows:

> ... many recipients of stock dividends look upon them as distributions of corporate earnings and usually in an amount equivalent to the fair value of the additional shares received. Furthermore, it is presumed that such views of recipients are materially strengthened in those instances, which are by far the most numerous, where the issuances are so small in comparison with the shares previously outstanding that they do not have any apparent effect upon the share market price and, consequently, the market value of the shares previously held remains substantially unchanged.[8]

The committee further suggested that these circumstances exist with the issuance of a small stock dividend. A small stock dividend is defined as an increase of less than 20 percent to 25 percent of the number of shares previously outstanding.

To illustrate the entries for the issuance of a small stock dividend, assume that the stockholders' equity of a corporation on May 1 was as follows:

---

[8] *Accounting Research Bulletin No. 43*, "Restatement and Revision of Accounting Research Bulletins" (New York: AICPA, 1953), Ch. 7, para. 10.

Common stock, $5 par value, 20,000 shares outstanding	$100,000
Additional paid-in capital	20,000
Total contributed capital	$120,000
Retained earnings	80,000
Total stockholders' equity	$200,000

Assume further that on May 2 the company declares a 10 percent stock dividend, or a dividend of 2,000 shares (.10 × 20,000), which is to be distributed on June 1. Assuming that the shares are selling in the market on the declaration date at a price of $20 per share, an amount equal to the fair value of the shares to be issued, or $40,000 (2,000 × $20), would be transferred from retained earnings to the appropriate contributed capital accounts. The capital stock account is credited for the par value of the shares issued and the remainder is added to additional paid-in capital. The following entries would be made to record the declaration and distribution of the stock dividend:

May 2	Retained earnings	40,000	
	Stock dividend distributable		10,000
	Additional paid-in capital		30,000
June 1	Stock dividend distributable	10,000	
	Common stock		10,000

If financial statements are prepared between the date of declaration and the date of distribution of a stock dividend, the stock dividend distributable account should be included in the stockholders' equity section of the balance sheet. It is not classified as a liability because the corporation has no obligation to distribute cash or any other asset.

As previously indicated, the distribution of a stock dividend has no effect on either the assets or the total stockholders' equity of a corporation. In the illustration above, the only effect on the corporation was a transfer of $40,000 from retained earnings to contributed capital. The stockholders' equity after payment of the stock dividend on June 1 would appear as follows:

Common stock, $5 par value, 22,000 shares outstanding	$110,000
Additional paid-in capital	50,000
Total contributed capital	$160,000
Retained earnings	40,000
Total stockholders' equity	$200,000

The committee on accounting procedure further indicated that stock dividends in excess of 20 percent to 25 percent would be expected to materially reduce the market value per share of stock. Accordingly, the committee recommended that if capitalization is required by the state, such stock dividends should be recorded by capitalizing retained earnings only to the extent of the par or stated value of the shares issued. Under these circumstances, the entry to record the stock dividend would be a debit to retained earnings and a credit to capital stock for the par value of the shares issued. Again, there is no effect on the total stockholders' equity of the corporation.

STOCK SPLITS

A corporation may desire to reduce the selling price of its stock in order to facilitate purchases and sales of its shares by investors. Reducing the price of shares to a reasonable amount normally increases the number of investors who are willing to purchase a corporation's stock. This may be accomplished by increasing the number of shares outstanding and decreasing the par or stated value of the stock by a proportionate amount. This procedure is referred to as a stock split.

For example, assume that a corporation has 20,000 shares of $10 par value common stock outstanding with current market price of $200 per share. The company might declare a two-for-one stock split in which each current stockholder receives two new shares with a $5 par value for each share of $10 par stock he or she owned prior to the split. This action would tend to cause the market price to decrease to approximately $100 per share because there would be twice as many shares outstanding after the split with no change in the value of the corporation.

In a stock split there is a significant increase in the number of shares outstanding without a change in total stockholders' equity. A basic difference between a stock split and a stock dividend is the magnitude of the increase in the number of shares outstanding. Also, a stock split never requires any capitalization of retained earnings. Consequently, only a memorandum entry to the common stock account to indicate the change in par value and the new number of shares outstanding is required upon a stock split.

TREASURY STOCK

Corporations often require shares of their own stock from their stockholders. If the corporation does not cancel these shares but instead holds the stock, it is referred to as treasury stock. A corporation may desire to reacquire shares of its stock which have been previously issued in order to have stock available for employee stock purchase plans, for stock options, for bonuses, or for some other legitimate reason. Unissued stock may not be used for these purposes because of the preemptive right of the existing stockholders. Purchases of treasury stock are limited to the amount of retained earnings if the corporation is to maintain its legal capital. This occurs because the purchase of treasury stock results in the distribution of cash to certain stockholders. If assets are distributed to stockholders in excess of the retained earnings, the corporation is returning a portion of the invested capital. Therefore, the purchase of treasury stock reduces the amount available for subsequent distributions to the stockholders.

Although the stock of another corporation is an asset of the firm which owns it, treasury stock is generally not considered to be an asset because a corporation cannot have an ownership interest in itself. Instead, the purchase of a corporation's own shares represents a return of capital to the selling shareholder and, thus, a reduction in the stockholders' equity of the corporation. Consequently, treasury stock is shown as a deduction in the stockholders' equity section of the balance sheet.

There are several different methods for recording treasury stock transactions. However, one approach, referred to as the cost method, is a method commonly used in practice for recording the acquisition of treasury stock. For this reason, the cost method will be discussed in the paragraphs which follow.

When a corporation acquires its own shares, treasury stock is debited for the cost of the shares purchased. Note that neither the par (or stated) value of the stock nor the amount originally received for the shares when they were issued is used to record the acquisition of treasury stock. If treasury shares are subsequently reissued, the difference between the cost of the shares and their selling price does not represent a gain or a loss to the corporation. Instead, the corporation has simply changed the amount of invested capital by acquiring and reissuing treasury shares. Consequently, any difference between the acquisition cost and the resale price of treasury stock is credited to additional paid-in capital if the selling price exceeds cost. If the shares are sold below cost, additional paid-in capital is reduced. If this account is not sufficient to absorb the excess of the cost over the selling price, any remainder may be charged or debited to retained earnings. To illustrate, assume that the stockholders' equity of a corporation appeared as follows on January 1:

Common stock, $10 par value, 10,000 shares authorized, issued, and outstanding	$100,000
Additional paid-in capital	20,000
Total contributed capital	$120,000
Retained earnings	30,000
Total stockholders' equity	$150,000

Further assume that the corporation purchased 300 of its outstanding shares on January 15 at a price of $20 per share. The following entry would be necessary to record the purchase:

Treasury stock	6,000	
Cash		6,000

To illustrate the reissuance of treasury stock, assume that the corporation subsequently sold 100 of the treasury shares on March 15 for $25 per share and another 100 shares on April 15 for $18 per share. The entries to record these transactions are as follows:

Mar. 15	Cash..............................	2,500	
	Treasury stock.....................		2,000
	Additional paid-in capital from treasury stock transactions		500
Apr. 15	Cash..............................	1,800	
	Additional paid-in capital from treasury stock transactions	200	
	Treasury stock.....................		2,000

When the treasury shares were sold, the treasury stock account was credited for the acquisition cost and carrying value of the shares, or $20 per share. Further, note that the $200 excess of cost over the resale price in the April 15 sale was debited to an "additional paid-in capital from treasury stock transactions" account. If the balance in the "additional paid-in capital from treasury stock transactions" account is not sufficient to absorb the difference between cost and resale price, any remaining amount is normally charged against retained earnings.

If a company holds treasury shares at the time financial statements are prepared, any balance in the treasury stock account should be shown as a deduction from total stockholders' equity. In addition, any restriction on the amount of retained earnings available for dividends should be disclosed. Additional paid-in capital from treasury stock transactions is reported in the contributed capital section of stockholders' equity. For example, the stockholders' equity of the corporation on April 15 would appear as follows:

Common stock, $10 par value, 10,000 shares authorized and issued of which 100 shares are in the treasury		$100,000
Additional paid-in capital:		
From stock issuances	$20,000	
From treasury stock transactions	300	20,300
Total contributed capital		$120,300
Retained earnings (of which $2,000 is not available for dividends because of the purchase of treasury stock)............		30,000
Total		$150,300
Less: Treasury stock at cost (100 shares)		2,000
Total stockholders' equity		$148,300

For various reasons, stockholders may donate shares of stock to the corporation. Since there is no cost to the corporation, no entry is required for the receipt of the donated stock. When these shares are resold, the entire proceeds would be credited to the additional paid-in capital from treasury stock transactions account. An alternative treatment is to record donated treasury stock at its fair market value as of the date of donation with a cor-

RETAINED EARNINGS

responding credit to a donated capital account. If this procedure is followed, subsequent entries affecting treasury stock would be recorded in the same manner as if the treasury stock had been purchased.

Retained earnings is that portion of stockholders' equity which results from the total net earnings of the firm less any dividends paid to stockholders since its inception. Accumulated earnings include income from normal operations and discontinued operations, extraordinary gains or losses, and prior-period adjustments. If the accumulated losses, dividend distributions, and transfers to other capital accounts exceed the accumulated earnings since the inception of the business, *the debit balance in the retained earnings account is referred to as a deficit.*

The retained earnings account may be affected by a number of items. Some of these are presented in the T-account shown below.

Retained Earnings

Decreases	*Increases*
1. Net loss	1. Net income
2. Prior-period adjustments	2. Prior-period adjustments
3. Cash and property dividends	
4. Stock dividends	
5. Purchase of treasury stock	
6. Appropriation of retained earnings	

The earnings or losses of the current period transferred to retained earnings include profits or losses from continuing operations, gains or losses from discontinued operations, extraordinary gains and losses, and the cumulative effects of accounting changes. In addition, certain corrections of income related to prior-periods, termed prior-period adjustments, are excluded from the determination of net income for the current period, and, therefore, are debited or credited directly to the retained earnings account.

The balance in the retained earnings account normally represents the maximum amount that may be distributed to the stockholders in the form of dividends. Dividends may be paid in the form of cash, other assets (property dividends), or in shares of the corporation's own stock (stock dividends). Cash or property dividends, once declared, become a liability of the corporation and result in a reduction of retained earnings by an amount equal to the cash to be paid or the fair value of the other assets to be distributed. A stock dividend, on the other hand, is accounted for by transferring a specified amount from retained earnings to contributed capital (the capital stock and additional paid-in capital accounts).

The existence of a credit balance in the retained earnings account does not indicate that there is cash or other assets readily available for the payment of dividends. Rather, retained earnings represents a source of the corporation's equity in the various assets owned and is unrelated to the balance in the cash account or to any other specific account. Thus, a corporation with a credit balance in its retained earnings account may be either unable or unwilling to distribute cash or property dividends to its stockholders.

As explained previously, there are certain circumstances in which retained earnings may be reduced by the acquisition or reissuance of a corporation's own stock. If treasury stock is reissued at an amount below its cost, retained earnings may be debited under the cost method if the paid-in capital accounts are insufficient to absorb the excess of cost over the reissuance price.

A reduction in retained earnings by appropriation is discussed in the following section.

Appropriation of Retained Earnings

In general, the balance in the retained earnings account of a corporation is the amount which is legally available for dividend distribution to stockholders. However, in some cases, the board of directors may restrict the amount of retained earnings that can be used to pay dividends. Such restrictions may be required either by law or by contract, or they may be made at the discretion of the board of directors. For example, retained earnings available for dividends are often legally limited by the cost of any treasury stock held by the company. In addition, contractual agreements with creditors or certain classes of stockholders may also impose limitations on the amount of retained earnings which is available for dividends. On the other hand, the board of directors may desire to voluntarily restrict dividends in order to provide for a future use of the assets represented by accumulated earnings. For example, a firm may wish to retain assets generated from profitable operations for future expansion of the business.

There are several methods which may be used for disclosing such restrictions on the amount of the retained earnings available for distribution to shareholders. The simplest, and probably the most logical method, is to indicate the amount and nature of the restriction by footnote or parenthetical disclosure in the financial statements. However, because many stockholders may not readily understand such disclosures, an alternative is to reclassify a portion of the retained earnings in order to indicate the amount of earnings which is unavailable for dividends. This reclassification, referred to as an appropriation, is accomplished by transferring the desired amount of retained earnings to an appropriation account.

To illustrate an appropriation of retained earnings, assume that the directors of a corporation with retained earnings of $300,000 decide that $100,000 of retained earnings should be restricted for future plant expansion. The following entry is necessary to record this appropriation:

Retained earnings	100,000	
Appropriation for plant expansion		100,000

This appropriation does not affect either the assets or liabilities of the corporation. The appropriation account is not an asset to be used for expansion nor does it guarantee that cash or other assets will actually be available for this purpose. Instead, it merely restricts the assets that may be distributed to shareholders. Further, the appropriation does not change the total retained earnings; it simply divides it into appropriated and unappropriated segments. The retained earnings of the corporation in the example would appear as follows after the appropriation was made:

Retained earnings:	
Appropriated for plant expansion	$100,000
Unappropriated	200,000
Total retained earnings	$300,000

When the purpose for the appropriation ceases to exist, the amount of the appropriated retained earnings account should be transferred back to unappropriated retained earnings. Since an appropriation represents a segregation of retained earnings, no other entry may be made to this account. For example, assume that the corporation in the previous illustration completed the desired expansion of the business. The appropriation would be restored to unappropriated retained earnings by means of the following entry:

Appropriation for plant expansion	100,000	
Retained earnings		100,000

In recent years, the formal appropriation of retained earnings has been recognized as potentially confusing or misleading to the users of financial statements. Consequently, there has been a trend to disclose both voluntary and required restriction of retained earnings in the notes accompanying the financial statements.

Statement of Retained Earnings

Normally, the periodic financial statements issued by a corporation include a statement of retained earnings as well as a balance sheet, income statement, and statement of changes in financial position. The retained earnings statement indicates all changes which have occurred in that account during the period. The format of the statement varies considerably; sometimes the changes in retained earnings are included with income data in a combined statement of income and retained earnings. The general form of the statement is illustrated as follows:

Redskins Company
Statement of Retained Earnings
For the Year Ended December 31, 19x1

Balance at beginning of the year:		
As originally reported		$200,000
Prior period adjustment—correction		
of an error applicable to 19x0		(50,000)
As restated		$150,000
Add: Net income for the year		90,000
		$240,000
Less: Cash dividends:		
$6 per share on preferred	$30,000	
$5 per share on common	50,000	(80,000)
Balance at end of the year		$160,000

BOOK VALUE PER SHARE OF COMMON STOCK

The book value of a share of stock is the amount of stockholders' equity which is applicable to a single share of stock. Since the stockholders' equity is equal to total assets minus total liabilities, book value also represents the net assets per share of stock. Data on book value per share of a corporation's common stock is often included in corporate annual reports and in the financial press.

If a corporation has only common stock outstanding, book value per share is computed by dividing total stockholders' equity by the number of shares outstanding. When a corporation has both preferred and common stock outstanding, the stockholders' equity must be divided between or among the various classes of stock. This allocation depends on the nature of the preferred stock. Generally, if preferred stock is nonparticipating, the equity allocated to the preferred shares is an amount equal to the liquidation or redemption value of the preferred stock plus any cumulative dividends in arrears. To illustrate assume that a corporation has the following stockholders' equity:

5% cumulative preferred stock, $100 par value, 1,000 shares authorized and outstanding (callable at $106)		$100,000
Common stock, $10 par value, 20,000 shares authorized issued, and outstanding		200,000
Additional paid-in capital:		
On preferred stock	$40,000	
On common stock	10,000	50,000
Total contributed capital		$350,000
Retained earnings		56,000
Total stockholders' equity		$406,000

If there are no unpaid dividends on the preferred stock, equity equal to the call price or redemption value of the preferred stock ($106 per share) is allocated to the preferred shares, and the remainder applies to the common stock. Thus, the book value per share of common stock is computed as follows:

Total stockholders' equity	$406,000
Less: Amount allocated to preferred	106,000
Equity to common stock	$300,000

$$\text{Book value per share of common stock} = \frac{\$300,000}{20,000} = \underline{\$15}$$

If there are unpaid preferred dividends, an additional amount equal to the arrearage is allocated to the preferred stock. For example, assume that the preferred stock mentioned in the previous illustration had one year of dividends in arrears. In that situation, the unpaid preferred dividends of $5,000 would also be allocated to the preferred stock, and the book value per share of common stock would be computed as follows:

Total stockholders' equity		$406,000
Less: Amount allocated to preferred:		
Redemption value	$106,000	
Dividends in arrears	5,000	111,000
Equity to common stock		$295,000

$$\text{Book value per share of common stock} = \frac{\$295,000}{20,000} = \underline{\$14.75}$$

Because the market value of the assets may differ from book values based on generally accepted accounting principles, the book value per share does not indicate the amount that would be distributed to the owner of each share of stock if the assets of the corporation were sold and its liabilities were paid. That is, any gains or losses from the disposal of assets or the settlement of liabilities, and any expenses involved in the liquidation process, would affect the shareholders' equity. As noted above, book value per share is not necessarily equal to the market price of the stock. Although book value per share may have some effect on the market price, market price is much more likely to be influenced by factors such as current and expected future earnings, dividend prospects, and general economic conditions. Depending upon the specific circumstances, book value per share may be more or less than market price per share. Therefore, book value data should be used with extreme caution in making decisions concerning the value of a corporation's stock.

SUMMARY

A corporation is a separate legal entity permitted to engage in activities in a manner similar to those performed by a natural person. Other important characteristics of a corporation include the transferability of ownership, continuity of life, limited liability of owners, separation of ownership and management, corporate taxation, and government regulation.

Forming a corporation includes obtaining a state corporate charter, electing a board of directors, adopting bylaws, and issuing capital stock to shareholders. The expenses incurred in this process are referred to as organization costs and are accumulated in an intangible asset account and either retained as an asset indefinitely or amortized over a reasonable but arbitrarily selected period of time.

The two primary sources of the equity capital of a corporation are contributions by shareholders and earnings retained in the business. In exchange for their contributions, the shareholders receive stock certificates and certain basic rights. Common stock usually entitles its owners to vote in stockholders' meetings, to share in corporate earnings through dividends, to maintain a proportionate interest in the firm when additional shares are issued, and to share in the distribution of remaining assets upon liquidation. Preferred stock usually has limited or no voting rights but does have preference in dividend and liquidation distributions. In addition, preferred stock may be cumulative, participating, convertible, and/or callable.

Capital stock may have an arbitrary value established by the corporate charter (referred to as par value) or established by the corporate directors (referred to as stated value). This value generally has no relationship to the selling price of the stock, but a firm may be required to retain a corresponding amount in the business to protect corporate creditors. Upon issuance of stock, the corporation credits the capital stock account for the par or stated value and credits additional paid-in capital for any excess. If the stock has no par or stated value, the entire proceeds of the sale are usually credited to capital stock.

When common stock subscriptions are taken by a corporation, receivables are created and a common stock subscribed account is credited. The actual stock is not issued until the payment is received, at which time common stock subscribed is debited and common stock is credited.

The retained earnings of a corporation reflect the accumulated net income and losses of the firm less all dividend distributions to shareholders. The net income of the firm is usually presented on the income statement in a manner that separates earnings related to the normal operations of the business from other income-related items. Such other items include extraordinary items and discontinued operations. Prior period adjustments are direct adjustments to the beginning balance of retained earnings resulting from error correction and other adjustments stipulated in FASB *Statement No. 16*.

The income statement will also include information regarding the earnings per share of the firm. This amount is basically the net income per share of common stock outstanding for a given period. Where preferred stock or convertible securities are outstanding, certain adjustments must be made to either the net income or number of shares of common stock outstanding to compute the earnings per share of the firm. In addition, if there are extraordinary items or gains or losses from discontinued operations it will be necessary to compute several earnings per share figures.

Certain accounting changes may necessitate an adjustment of the accounting records and/or mention in the corporation's financial statements. Included in this category are changes in accounting principles, changes in accounting estimates, and corrections of errors made in prior periods.

A corporation may distribute a portion or all of its accumulated earnings to the stockholders in the form of ordinary dividends. Additionally, the firm may return a portion of the original investment in the form of a liquidating dividend. The important dates to be noted in relation to a dividend distribution are the dates of declaration, record, and payment. Although dividends are usually paid in cash, the corporation may choose to issue a stock dividend. A stock dividend has no effect on the amount of stockholders' equity, but does require a transfer of an appropriate amount from the retained earnings account to the capital accounts. Stockholders may also be issued additional shares in a stock split. In this case, no capitalization of retained earnings is required although a memorandum is made to indicate the change in the number of shares outstanding and in the par value of the stock.

A firm may wish to purchase its own stock from shareholders and retain the shares for future reissuance or cancellation. The purchase and resale of such stock is referred to as treasury stock transactions. Treasury stock held by a corporation when financial statements are prepared is shown on the balance sheet as a deduction from total stockholders' equity.

In reporting financial position to its stockholders, a firm may wish to indicate that the entire balance of retained earnings is not available for distribution as dividends, because certain amounts have been appropriated for special purposes. This is commonly accomplished by segregating the unappropriated retained earnings from the appropriated amount on the balance sheet. Additional detail regarding the retained earnings account is provided by the statement of retained earnings, which is normally included as one of the periodic financial statements issued by a corporation.

The book value per share of common stock represents the amount of stockholders' equity or net assets applicable to a single share of common stock. If preferred stock is outstanding, an appropriate amount of equity must first be allocated to those shares before computing book value.

KEY DEFINITIONS

Additional paid-in capital—the amount received on the issuance of capital stock in excess of its par or stated value.

Appropriation of retained earnings—the reclassification of a portion of retained earnings by transfer to an appropriation account.

Articles of incorporation—included in the application made to the state for a corporate charter and include information concerning the corporation.

Book value per share—the amount of stockholders' equity (i.e., net assets) applicable to each share of common stock outstanding.

Capital stock—transferable shares of stock which evidence ownership in a corporation.

Capitalization of retained earnings—an amount which is transferred from retained earnings to contributed capital at the time a stock dividend is declared.

Cash dividend—a distribution of cash to stockholders in the form of a dividend.

Change due to accounting errors—may result from errors in the application of accounting principles, oversights, misuse of facts, or mistakes in mathematics.

Change in accounting estimate—occurs as additional information modifying an original estimate is obtained.

Change in accounting principle—results from the adoption of a generally accepted accounting principle which differs from one that was previously used.

Charter—a contract between the state and the corporation which includes the general corporation laws of the state and the specific provisions of the articles of incorporation.

Common stock—stock which has the basic rights of ownership and represents the residual ownership in the corporation.

Continuity of life—status as a separate legal entity gives the corporation a perpetual existence.

Contributed capital—capital invested directly by the shareholders of the corporation.

Controller—an officer who is responsible for the accounting function of the business.

Convertible preferred stock—stock which includes the privilege of allowing the shareholder to exchange preferred shares for a specified number of common shares at his or her option.

Corporation—an association of persons joined together for some common purpose, organized in accordance with state laws as a legal entity, separate, and distinct from its owners.

Cumulative preferred stock—backed by a provision that if all or part of the specified dividend on preferred stock is not paid during a given year, the amount of the unpaid dividends accumulates and must be paid in a subsequent year before any dividends can be paid on common stock.

Date of declaration—the date on which the board of directors formally establishes a liability for a dividend of a specified amount to the stockholders.

Date of payment—the date of payment of a dividend is the date on which the dividends are paid to the stockholders of record.

Date of record—the date of record of a dividend is the date on which the corporation prepares a list of stockholders who are to receive the dividends.

Deficit—a debit balance in the retained earnings account.

Discontinued operations—refers to the operations of any subsidiary, division, or department of a business that has been, or will be sold, abandoned, or disposed of.

Dividends—distributions which are made by a corporation to its shareholders.

Earned capital—includes amounts provided by profitable operations and retained by the business.

Earnings per share—the amount of net income per share of the common stock outstanding during a period.

Extraordinary item—a gain or loss which is both unusual in nature and not reasonably expected to recur in the foreseeable future. As a result of *Opinions No. 9* and *No. 30* of the Accounting Principles Board, these items are reported as separate amounts in the income statement.

Gains—increases in equity (net assets) from peripheral or incidental transactions of an entity and from all other transactions and other events and circumstances affecting the entity during a period except those that result from revenues or investments by owners.

Incorporators—the persons who legally form a corporation.

Legal capital—a limit on the amount of assets that can be distributed to the stockholders of a corporation prior to liquidation and settlement of the corporate debts.

Limited liability—the creditors of the corporation have a claim against the assets of the corporation and not against the personal property of the stockholders.

Losses—decreases in equity (net assets) from peripheral or incidental transactions of an entity and from all other transactions and other events and circumstances affecting the entity during a period except those that result from expenses or distributions to owners.

No-par stock—stock without a par value.

Organization costs—the costs which are necessary to form the corporation.

Par value—an arbitrary value which is established in the corporate charter and printed on the stock certificate. It establishes the legal capital of the corporation in many states.

Participating preferred stock—preferred stock which has the right to participate in some specified manner with common stockholders in dividends in excess of a stipulated amount paid to the common shareholders.

Preferred as to dividends—stock which is preferred as to dividends is entitled to receive a stated dividend each year before any dividend is paid on the common stock.

Preferred stock—a class of stock which has different rights from those associated with common stock.

Prior period adjustment—items of gain or loss which represent material corrections of reported earnings of prior periods and are shown as direct adjustments of retained earnings.

Retained earnings—represents the accumulated earnings of the corporation, increased by net income and reduced by net losses and distributions to shareholders.

Stock dividend—a distribution of additional shares to the stockholders in proportion to their existing holdings.

Stock split—a proportionate increase in the number of shares outstanding, usually intended to effect a decrease in the market value of the stock.

Stock subscriptions—involves an agreement by the corporation to sell a certain number of shares at a specified price to an investor with the payment at some future date(s). Upon full payment, the purchaser gains control of the stock.

Treasury stock—consists of shares of stock which have been previously issued and are reacquired by the corporation but not formally retired.

QUESTIONS

1. What are some of the main advantages of organizing a business as a corporation rather than as a sole proprietorship or partnership?

2. Describe the following characteristics of a corporation:

    a. separate legal entity
    b. limited liability
    c. transferability of ownership interest
    d. continuity of existence

3. Explain the meaning of the term "double taxation" as it applies to a corporation.

4. Explain what is meant by the number of shares of stock authorized, issued, and outstanding.

5. What are four basic rights of a stockholder?

6. Describe the following features which may be applied to an issuance of preferred stock:

    a. cumulative
    b. participating
    c. preferred as to assets
    d. callable
    e. convertible

7. Explain the meaning of par value. Describe the accounting treatment of stock issued for more or less than par value.

8. Distinguish between par value and no-par stock.

9. What is the primary disadvantage of issuing stock for an amount less than par value?

10. What are organization costs? Describe two alternative accounting treatments for such costs.

11. Indicate the nature and balance sheet classification of the subscriptions receivable and common stock subscribed accounts.

12. What information regarding preferred stock should be disclosed in the balance sheet?

13. How should preferred dividends in arrears be reported in the balance sheet?

14. Distinguish between an ordinary item and an extraordinary item on an income statement. How is an extraordinary item presented in the income statement?

15. What is a prior period adjustment? Where is a prior period adjustment shown in the financial statements?

16. Define earnings per share of common stock. Where is this information shown in the financial statements?

17. What is the effect on earnings per share presentation when a company has extraordinary gains or losses?

18. Describe the nature of the following three dates related to dividends: (a) date of declaration, (b) date of record, and (c) date of payment. What is the accounting significance of each of these dates?

19. Distinguish between a cash dividend and a stock dividend.

20. Why does a corporation normally declare (a) a stock dividend and (b) a stock split?

21. Why is a portion of retained earnings capitalized upon the issuance of a stock dividend?

22. What is the difference between a stock dividend and a stock split? How does the accounting for a large stock dividend and a stock split differ?

23. For what purposes might a company purchase shares of its own stock?

24. What is treasury stock? How does it affect the ability of the corporation to pay dividends? How does it differ from authorized but unissued stock?

25. What is the effect on stockholders' equity when treasury stock is reissued for (a) more than the original cost, (b) less than its cost to the corporation?

26. What is the purpose of an appropriation of retained earnings? How does a company provide for and eliminate an appropriation of retained earnings?

27. What is the significance of the book value per share of common stock? Does the book value equal the amount of assets which would be distributed to each share of stock upon liquidation? Explain.

28. How is the book value per share of common stock computed when there is preferred stock outstanding?

7 | The Corporation: Capital Stock, Earnings, and Dividends   7-43

EXERCISES

29. Give the journal entries required to record each of the following stock transactions:

    a. Issuance of 1,000 shares of $10 par value common stock at $14 per share.
    b. Issuance of 100 shares of $100 par value preferred stock for a total of $12,000.
    c. Issuance of 500 shares of no-par common stock for $20 per share.
    d. Issuance of 2,000 shares of $10 par value common stock for land. Recent sales and purchases of the stock have been made at a price of $20 per share. The value of the land is not readily determinable.

30. Make the journal entries necessary to record the issuance of stock in each of the following independent cases.

    a. One hundred shares of $25 par value stock are sold at par for cash.
    b. Eighty shares of $15 par value stock are sold at $17 each for cash.
    c. One thousand shares of no-par capital stock are issued at $14 per share.
    d. Five hundred shares of no-par capital stock with a stated value of $10 per share are sold for $11 per share.

31. Jeffry Company was organized on March 1, 19x1. The authorized capital was 20,000 shares of $50 par value, 6 percent, cumulative preferred stock and 50,000 shares of $10 par value common stock. At the date of organization, all the common stock was issued at $20 per share and 10,000 shares of the preferred stock were sold at par.

    Required:

    Prepare the stockholders' equity section of the balance sheet for Jeffry Co. on March 1, after the issuance of the stock.

32. Niblet Corporation was organized on January 1, 19x1. On that date, the corporation issued 1,000 shares of $100 par value, 6 percent preferred stock and 20,000 shares of $10 par value common stock. During the first five years of its life, the corporation paid the following total dividends to its stockholders.

19x1	$ 0
19x2	6,000
19x3	20,000
19x4	15,000
19x5	18,000

    Determine the total dividends paid to each class of stockholders assuming that the preferred stock is:

    a. cumulative and nonparticipating.
    b. noncumulative and nonparticipating.

33. Loggins Music Stores, Inc. accepted subscriptions for 250 shares of its no-par, $10 stated value capital stock on January 1, 19x1, at a price of $13 per share. On March 1, the firm collected $1,625 as a partial payment on the subscriptions. Then, on April 1, the balance in the subscriptions account was paid and all the shares were issued.

Required:

Prepare the journal entries necessary to record the above transactions on the books of Loggins Music Stores, Inc.

34. Monte Carter owns 300 of the 30,000 outstanding shares of stock in the MNX Company, which allows preemptive rights to all its existing stockholders. If MNX Company decides to issue an additional 6,000 shares of stock, how many of the new shares may Carter purchase? What would be his percent interest in the company?

35. The Drinkwater Corporation, still in its preliminary stages of organization, is trying to decide in which state they should incorporate. They have selected two possible states (fictitious names) in which to incorporate: Atokad and Odaroloc. Atokad requires that the entire issue price of no-par stock be regarded as legal capital. Odaroloc allows the corporation to specify a stated value for no-par shares. If Drinkwater Corporation issues 3,000 shares of no-par capital stock for a price of $40 and a stated value of $35, what would be the entries for this transaction in each of these two states?

36. Gung-Hoe contributed land to the Howdy-Handy Corporation in exchange for 3,600 shares of its $12 par value stock. Journalize this transaction under each of the following assumptions:

    a. For the past 2 weeks, Howdy-Handy's stock has traded for about $33 a share on the American Stock Exchange.
    b. Howdy-Handy's stock is not traded on any stock exchange and therefore has no established market. However, Gung-Hoe did receive an offer from a broker a week ago to buy the land for $130,000.

37. Hoagland, Inc. accepted subscriptions for 3,000 shares of its $20 par value common stock at a price of $21 a share. However, because of the large quantity of stock being issued, Hoagland required the subscriber to pay a downpayment of 20 percent and the remainder in two months.

Required:

Prepare the journal entries to record these transactions assuming the downpayment was made on June 30, 19x1 and the remainder was paid when due.

38. A junior accountant for the Fetters Company is unsure as to how to complete the following stockholders' equity section of the balance sheet.

Stockholders' Equity:

5 percent preferred stock *(1)* par value, 15,000 shares authorized, 9,000 shares issued and outstanding	$ 810,000
Common stock, $20 par value, 200,000 shares authorized, *(2)* shares issued and outstanding	3,000,000
Common stock subscribed, 1,500 shares	*(3)* 30,000
Additional paid-in capital:	
Common stock issued and subscribed	*(4)* 125,000
Preferred stock	80,000
Total Contributed Capital	*(5)*
Retained earnings	*(6)*
Total Stockholders' Equity	$4,099,000

Additional information:

Earnings for the corporation over its life were $18,000 a year. No dividends had ever been paid.

Required:

Complete this stockholders' equity section by filling in the numbers 1-6.

PROBLEMS

39. The Fabian Co. is organized on January 1, 19x1, with authorized stock of 30,000 shares of $5 par value common and 5,000 shares of $100 par value preferred. Give the entries required to record each of the following transactions:

    a. Assets are accepted as payment for 10,000 shares of common stock. The assets are valued as follows: land, $50,000; buildings, $130,000; and equipment, $20,000.
    b. The 5,000 preferred shares are sold at $105 per share.
    c. Subscriptions are received for 5,000 shares of common stock at $25.
    d. A payment of $50,000 is received on the subscribed stock.
    e. Subscriptions receivable of $75,000 are collected and the stock is issued.
    f. The remaining common stock is sold for $30 per share.

40. Consider each of the following independent cases.

    a. Kanoch, Inc. issues 50 shares of $25 par value stock in exchange for land appraised at $1,500. The shares are not actively traded. Record the issuance of the stock on the books of Kanoch, Inc.
    b. Red Rider Stables, Inc. acquired 100 acres of prime grazing land in exchange for 200 shares of no-par capital stock. It was found that a similar

100-acre tract had sold the previous year for $11,000. The company's stock has not been registered with a major exchange but the company's balance sheet reveals a book value of $50 per share. Record the issuance of the stock on the books of Red Rider Stables, Inc.

c. Monzingo Grocers, Inc. obtained a new store site in exchange for 400 shares of its $15 par value capital stock. The store site is in a recently developed area. Ten years ago wooded lots of similar size sold for $8,000. The latest New York Stock Exchange quotation for the stock was $30 per share. Record the issuance of the stock on the books of Monzingo Grocers, Inc.

41. Assume that Ham Farm Supplies, Inc. had income after taxes from normal operations for 19x1 of $200,000. Also, the firm had an extraordinary loss of $40,000 (net of tax). The firm had 25,000 shares of stock outstanding throughout 19x1. Compute the earnings per share figures required by APB *Opinion No. 15*.

42. Make the journal entries necessary to record the declaration and payment of dividends in each of the following situations:

a. Bruin Company has 8,000 shares of common stock and 3,000 shares of 7 percent, $100 par value preferred stock outstanding. On June 15 the company declares a preferred dividend and a $3.50 per share dividend on the common stock. The dividends are payable on July 15 to the stockholders of record on June 30.

b. Wolfpack Company has 10,000 shares of $15 par value common stock outstanding. On May 1, the company declares a 10 percent stock dividend to be distributed on May 15. At the time, the market price of a share is $19.

43. On March 15, the board of directors of Gunsmith Corporation declared a cash dividend of $1 per share to the stockholders of record on March 20. The dividend is payable on April 1. The corporation had 10,000 shares of common stock outstanding.

Required:

Prepare the journal entries required on the date of declaration, the date of record, and the payment date.

44. The Robinson Corporation was organized in 19x0. The company was authorized to issue 5,000 shares of $50 par value common and 1,000 shares of $100 par value, cumulative preferred stock. All of the preferred and 4,000 shares of common were issued at par. The preferred shares were entitled to dividends of 6 percent before any dividends were paid to common. During the first 5 years of its existence, the corporation earned a total of $120,000 and paid dividends of 50 cents per share each year on common stock.

Required:

Prepare *in good form* the stockholders' equity section as of December 31, 19x4.

45. Shown below is the stockholders' equity section of the balance sheet of Falcon Company at December 31, 19x1.

Common stock, 10,000 shares issued and outstanding, $10 par value.....................	$100,000
Additional paid-in capital.......................	50,000
Retained earnings..............................	75,000
Total Stockholders' Equity....................	$225,000

On January 1, 19x2 the company reacquired 500 shares of its stock at $15 per share.

Required:

1. Prepare the entry to record the purchase of the stock.
2. Prepare the entry to record the reissuance of the treasury stock at $18 per share.
3. Prepare the entry to record the reissuance of the stock at $13 per share.

46. Arnold Company had a $100,000 balance in its retained earnings account on January 1, 19x1. On January 2, 19x1, by action of the Board of Directors, $25,000 of retained earnings was appropriated for future plant expansion. The plant expansion was completed on December 31, 19x2, and the appropriation of retained earnings was released.

Required:

1. Give the journal entry necessary to record the appropriation.
2. Give the entry necessary to release the appropriation.

47. The stockholders' equity section of the balance sheet of Park Company on December 31, 19x1, is shown below:

6% preferred stock, $100 par value (callable at $105) 5,000 shares authorized, issued, and outstanding...........................	$ 500,000
Common stock, $5 par value, 60,000 shares, authorized and 50,000 shares issued and outstanding....	250,000
Additional paid-in capital...........................	400,000
Retained earnings..................................	75,000
Total Stockholders' Equity.......................	$1,225,000

Required:

Compute the book value per share of common stock.

48. By using the following code, indicate each transaction's effect on the respective columns.

| + | = increases | 0 | = no effect |
| − | = decreases | ? | = cannot be determined |

The market value of the company's common stock exceeds par value.

		Common Stock	Retained Earnings	Stockholders' Equity	Book Value Per Share of Common Stock
a.	Company declared a cash dividend payable in the next fiscal year to persons holding shares of preferred stock.				
b.	Company received shares of its own common stock, donated by a wealthy shareholder.				
c.	Company purchased shares of its own common stock through a broker at the New York Stock Exchange.				
d.	Company declared and issued a stock dividend on the common stock.				
e.	A cash dividend was declared and paid.				
f.	Retained Earnings were appropriated for plant expansion.				
g.	Treasury shares of common stock were sold at an amount in excess of the purchase price to the corporation.				

49. Jones Co. had the following stock outstanding from January 1, 19x0, to December 31, 19x5.

a. Common stock, $10 par value, 20,000 shares authorized and outstanding.
b. Preferred stock, $100 par value with a $6 stated dividend, 10,000 shares authorized, 5,000 shares issued and outstanding.

During that period, Jones Co. paid the following dividends:

19x0	$ 0
19x1	80,000
19x2	0
19x3	30,000
19x4	70,000
19x5	20,000

Compute the amount of preferred dividends and common stock dividends in each year assuming that:

1. The preferred stock is noncumulative.
2. The preferred stock is cumulative.

50. Smith Corporation was organized on January 1, 19x1, with 100,000 shares of $10 par value common stock and 10,000 shares of $50 par value preferred stock authorized. During 19x1, Smith Corporation had the following stock transactions:

Jan. 1		Issued 5,000 shares of preferred stock for $60 per share.
Jan. 1		Issued 5,000 shares of common stock for $60 per share.
Oct. 1		Accepted subscriptions for 1,000 shares of common stock at a price of $16 per share. Payment is to be made in two equal installments payable in 60 and 120 days.
Nov. 30		Collected the first installment on the subscribed stock but issued no stock at this time.

Required:

1. Prepare the journal entries to record the stock transactions.
2. Prepare the stockholders' equity section of the balance sheet for Smith Corporation as of December 31, 19x1. (Assume that retained earnings are $64,000 on December 31, 19x1.)

51. Akens Co. was organized on January 1, 19x1. A portion of the December 31, 19x2, balance sheet of Akens Co. appeared as follows:

Stockholders' Equity:

6 percent preferred stock, $100 par value, 20,000 shares authorized............		$ 500,000
Preferred stock subscribed.................		100,000
Common stock, $10 par value, 100,000 shares authorized................		400,000
Common stock subscribed.................		50,000
Additional paid-in capital:		
On common stock issued.................	$200,000	
On common stock subscribed.............	50,000	
On preferred stock issued................	25,000	
On preferred stock subscribed............	10,000	285,000
Retained earnings.........................		330,000
Total Stockholders' Equity.............		$1,665,000

Required:

1. How many shares of preferred stock are outstanding?
2. How many shares of common stock are outstanding?
3. How many shares of preferred stock are subscribed?
4. How many shares of common stock are subscribed?
5. What were the average issue prices of the common and the preferred shares outstanding?
6. What were the average subscription prices of the common stock and the preferred stock?
7. What is the total contributed capital of Akens Co.?

52. In examining the accounts of Longhorn Steel Company, you discover the following information pertaining to the stockholders' equity of the company at December 31, 19x1.

    a. 3,000 shares of $100 par value preferred stock issued, 9,000 shares authorized.
    b. The preferred dividend requirement for the year was met by paying dividends of $18,000.
    c. 16,000 shares of $10 par value common stock issued and outstanding.
    d. 20,000 shares of $10 par value common stock authorized.
    e. 2,000 shares of common stock subscribed.
    f. The average issue price of the common stock was $17.
    g. The average issue price of the preferred stock was $106.
    h. The average subscription price of the common stock was $19.
    i. Retained earnings were $219,000.

Required:

Prepare the stockholders' equity section of Longhorn Steel Company's balance sheet at December 31, 19x1.

53. The Babson Corporation began business on January 1, 19x1. During the first year of operations, the following transactions were completed that affected stockholders' equity.

   a. Sold for cash 300,000 shares of capital stock for $13 per share. The charter for the corporation authorized 1,000,000 shares of capital stock.
   b. Sold 5,000 shares of capital stock to the president of the company for $14 per share. Collected 35 percent of the subscription immediately and the balance is due at the end of 11 months.
   c. Exchanged 30,000 shares for a plant site. The seller had recently had an offer to sell the plant site for $380,000 and the site was carried on the seller's books at $420,000.
   d. Collected 25 percent on the subscription contract in (b).

   Required:

   Give entries for the above transactions using each of the following assumptions:

   1. The stock has a par value of $8 per share.
   2. The stock has no par value and no stated value.
   3. The stock has no par value but has a stated value of $10 per share. State any necessary assumptions of your own.

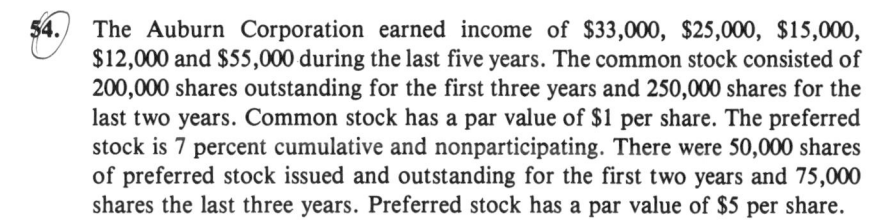

54. The Auburn Corporation earned income of $33,000, $25,000, $15,000, $12,000 and $55,000 during the last five years. The common stock consisted of 200,000 shares outstanding for the first three years and 250,000 shares for the last two years. Common stock has a par value of $1 per share. The preferred stock is 7 percent cumulative and nonparticipating. There were 50,000 shares of preferred stock issued and outstanding for the first two years and 75,000 shares the last three years. Preferred stock has a par value of $5 per share.

   Required:

   Calculate the dividends which each class of stock would receive over each of the last five years assuming (1) the entire net income was distributed each year, and (2) only 80 percent of the reported net income was distributed in the first three years, 90 percent in the last two years.

55. Record the following transactions on the books of the El Paso Corporation.

   a. The El Paso Corporation accepted subscriptions for 2,500 shares of its $15 par value common stock at a price of $23 per share. The subscription contract requires three installments, ½ now, ¼ in 60 days and the remainder in 90 days.
   b. The second installment was made on time.

c. The subscriber didn't pay for the third installment when it became due. It is the policy of the corporation to issue to a forfeiting subscriber the number of shares actually paid for rather than the total number contracted.

56. The Charles Brothers Company has decided to dissolve their partnership on January 1, 19x2, and incorporate their company in order to obtain additional capital. The new company will be called Charles Manufacturing Corporation. There were three brothers in the partnership, Joe, Jim, and Dick. Joe had an adjusted capital balance on December 31, 19x1 of $135,000, Jim's balance was $129,000, and Dick's balance was $141,000. Record the following transactions dealing with the incorporation of the Charles Manufacturing Corporation and prepare the stockholders' equity portion of the balance sheet for the newly-formed company.

   a. 100,000 shares of common stock with a par value of $5 per share were authorized and 20,000 shares were issued to the public for cash at $8 per share on January 1, 19x2.
   b. Each partner received 20,000 shares of stock in exchange for his share of the partnership's total capital. Goodwill was recognized.
   c. Dick Charles also contributed 500 shares of Lakeview Company stock to the corporation in exchange for 300 shares of the new corporation's stock. Dick had purchased the stock several years earlier for $10 a share.

57. Below is the stockholders' equity portion of Corpos Company's balance sheet.

    Stockholders' Equity:

6 percent preferred stock, $200 par value, 25,000 shares authorized............................	$1,000,000
Class A common stock, $12 par value 200,000 shares authorized.................................	1,800,000
Class B common stock, $15 stated value, 150,000 shares authorized...........................	1,500,000
Class B common stock subscribed......................	45,000
Additional paid-in capital:	
Preferred stock issued..............................	210,000
Class A common stock issued......................	865,000
Class B common stock issued.......................	125,000
Class B common stock subscribed..................	12,000
Retained earnings.....................................	216,000
Total Stockholders' Equity......................	$5,773,000

   a. What is the total contributed capital of Corpos Company?
   b. How many shares of preferred stock are outstanding?
   c. How many shares of Class A common stock are outstanding?
   d. How many shares of Class B common stock are outstanding?
   e. How many shares of Class B common stock are subscribed?

f. What are the average prices for which the common stock, Classes A and B, were issued?
g. What is the average subscription price for the Class B common stock subscribed?

58. In order to obtain additional capital and limited liability, the Star Street Partnership decided to dissolve on January 1, 19x1, in order to form the Star Street Corporation. The newly-formed corporation was issued a charter from the state which authorized them to issue 60,000 shares of $8 par value common stock. The adjusted balances in the four partners' capital accounts before incorporation was Ott, $65,000; Sinclair, $45,000; Hanscom, $96,000; and Shute, $21,000. Each partner received one share of the new corporation's stock for every $10 in their capital account. Goodwill was recognized. In addition, 30,000 shares of the corporation's stock was issued to the public for $12 a share. Also, a building with a book value of $58,715 was contributed in exchange for 4,900 shares of capital stock.

Required:

Record the above transactions in journal form and prepare the stockholders' equity portion of the balance sheet for the newly-formed corporation.

59. Certain account balances of the Gobbler Company as of December 31, 19x2, are shown below:

Sales	$1,000,000
Cost of goods sold	500,000
Gain on sale of Meat Packing Division (net of tax)	100,000
Loss from earthquake (net of tax)	50,000
Operating expenses	350,000
Cash dividends:	
Common stock	250,000
Preferred stock	100,000
Correction of an error—prior period (income overstated)	100,000
Taxes on income from normal operations	75,000

The retained earnings balance on December 31, 19x1, was $850,000. The sale of the Division should be treated as a discontinued operation.

Required:

1. Prepare an income statement for 19x2.
2. Prepare a statement of retained earnings for the year ended December 31, 19x2.

60. The income statement for Bonko Company for the year ending December 31, 19x1, is shown below:

Bonko Company
Income Statement
For the Year Ended December 31, 19x1

Sales	$200,000
Cost of goods sold	100,000
Gross profit	$100,000
Operating expenses	80,000
Income before extraordinary items	$ 20,000
Extraordinary gain (net of tax)	10,000
Net income	$ 30,000

Bonko Company had 60,000 shares of common stock outstanding during 19x1.

Required:

Compute earnings per share for 19x1.

61. The stockholders' equity of Billy, Inc. appears as follows on its December 31, 19x1 balance sheet.

Common stock, $9 par value, 25,000 shares outstanding	$225,000
Additional paid-in capital	125,000
Total contributed capital	$350,000
Retained earnings	195,000
Total Stockholders' Equity	$545,000

Required:

Make the journal entries necessary to record the transactions in the following independent cases:

1. Billy, Inc. declares and distributes a 60 percent stock dividend on July 1 when the stock is selling for $30 per share.
2. Billy, Inc. declares a 3-for-1 stock split on July 1 when the market price of its stock is $60 per share.
3. Billy, Inc. declares and distributes a 5 percent stock dividend on July 1 when the market price of the stock is $15 per share.

62. The stockholders' equity section of the Buckeye Company appeared as follows on January 1:

Common stock, $15 par value, 20,000 shares authorized, issued, and outstanding........	$300,000
Additional paid-in capital.......................	75,000
Total contributed capital......................	$375,000
Retained earnings............................	80,000
Total Stockholders' Equity...................	$455,000

On February 1, the company purchased 800 of its outstanding shares at $25 per share. On June 15, the company reissued 500 of these shares at $29 per share. Then, on July 15, the company resold the other 300 shares for $24 per share.

Required:

Prepare the journal entries necessary to record the above transactions on the books of the Buckeye Company. Also, prepare the stockholders' equity section of their balance sheet as of July 15.

63. The stockholders' equity section of the X Corporation as of December 31, 19x1 shows:

6% preferred, cumulative capital stock, $100 par value, 50,000 shares authorized, 20,000 shares issued and outstanding........................		$2,000,000
Common stock, no par, $10 stated value, 400,000 shares authorized, 260,000 shares issued and outstanding.......		2,600,000
Additional paid-in capital:		
On preferred stock.....................	$ 80,000	
On common stock......................	1,560,000	1,640,000
Retained earnings.........................		1,200,000
Total Stockholders' Equity...............		$7,440,000

Note: Dividends on preferred stock are three years in arrears.

Required:

Compute the book value per share of the common stock at December 31, 19x1.

64. The Texan Co. had the following stockholders' equity on January 1, 19x1.

Common stock, $5 par value, 100,000 shares authorized, 50,000 shares issued and outstanding	$250,000
Additional paid-in capital	150,000
Total Contributed Capital	$400,000
Retained earnings	100,000
Total Stockholders' Equity	$500,000

During 19x1, the company had the following transactions related to the stockholders' equity.

Jan.	20	Issued 5,000 shares of stock for $10 per share.
Feb.	15	Purchased 3,000 shares of Texan Co. common stock for $11 per share.
May	10	Declared a $.20 per share cash dividend to the stockholders of record on May 15. The dividend is payable on June 1.
June	1	Paid the cash dividend.
	15	Sold 1,000 shares of treasury stock for $13 per share.
Aug.	15	Sold 1,000 shares of treasury stock for $10 per share.
Sept.	10	Declared a 10 percent stock dividend for the stockholders of record on September 15 to be distributed on October 1. The market price of the stock was $11 per share on September 15.
Oct.	1	Distributed the stock dividend.
Nov.	1	The Board of Directors decided to appropriate $20,000 of retained earnings for future plant expansion.
Dec.	31	Net income for the year was $35,000. The income summary and dividend accounts were closed to retained earnings.

Required:

1. Give the necessary journal entries to record the transactions.
2. Prepare a statement of retained earnings at December 31, 19x1.

65. The stockholders' equity of the National Company at December 31, 19x1, was as follows:

6% noncumulative preferred stock, $100 par value, call price per share $110, authorized 70,000 shares, issued 10,000 shares.............................	$1,000,000
$5 noncumulative preferred stock, $100 par value, call price per share $105, authorized 100,000 shares, issued 5,000 shares.............................	500,000
Common stock, $50 par value, authorized 100,000 shares, issued 40,000 shares, of which 1,000 shares are held in the treasury......................	2,000,000
Additional paid-in capital:	
On 6% preferred stock...........................	100,000
On common stock...............................	255,000
Total Contributed Capital......................	$3,855,000
Retained earnings (of which $60,000, an amount equal to the cost of the treasury stock purchased, is unavailable for dividends)......................	1,500,000
	$5,355,000
Deduct: Cost of treasury stock (1,000 shares)...........	60,000
Total Stockholders' Equity......................	$5,295,000

Note: Preferred dividends for 19x0 and 19x1 have not been paid.

During 19x2, National Company had the following transactions affecting the stockholders' equity:

Jan. 5 Sold 11,000 shares of the common stock at $55 per share.
Feb. 1 Declared a 10 percent stock dividend on the common stock; the market value of the stock on that date was $60 per share.
    28 Paid the stock dividend declared on February 1.
May 1 Purchased 500 shares of the common stock for the treasury at a cost of $65 per share.
    5 Sold all of the treasury stock held for $70 per share.
    9 Stockholders voted to reduce the par value of common stock to $25 per share and increase authorized shares to 200,000. The company issued the additional shares to effect this stock split.
June 30 The Board of Directors declared a $1 per share dividend on common stock and the regular annual dividend on both classes of preferred stock. All dividends are payable on July 20 to shareholders of record as of July 10.

Required:

1. Prepare the necessary journal entries to record the preceding transactions.
2. Prepare the stockholders' equity section of the balance sheet at June 30, 19x2.

66. Below is data relating to the income statement of the Benjamin Corporation:

   a. Sales for the year ended September 30, 19x1 were $850,000. Cost of goods sold were $600,000 and expenses were $260,000.
   b. In addition to the above, certain other revenue and expense items were incurred during the year:

   1. Benjamin Corporation discontinued the operations of a segment of its firm. There was no income from that segment for the current year and the segment was sold at a gain of $30,000.
   2. A write-down of inventory totaling $1,500 was recorded because of a decline in demand for the inventory due to obsolescence.
   3. An earthquake occurred during the year which caused a total loss in corporate property valued at $75,000. Earthquakes are not a usual occurrence in the corporation's geographic area.
   4. The average number of shares of common stock for the year was 80,000. The corporation does not have preferred stock.

   Required:

   Ignoring income taxes:

   1. Calculate the total amount of extraordinary items.
   2. Prepare an income statement in proper form including all appropriate earnings per share calculations.

67. On January 2, 19x0, the White Company purchased a building for $178,000. At that time, it was estimated that the building would have a useful life of 32 years and a salvage value of $18,000. The company decided to use the straight-line depreciation method. Calculate the effect in the financial statements of each of the following unrelated accounting changes and give journal entries to record current depreciation and any other necessary adjusting entries.

   a. On December 31, 19x3, before the depreciation adjustment for the year had been made, it was decided that the building should be depreciated by the sum-of-the-years'-digits method.
   b. On December 31, 19x3, the building was found to have a remaining useful life of only 22 years and a salvage value of $20,000.
   c. Depreciation was inappropriately calculated for three years because the asset was recorded on the books at an original cost of $78,000 (i.e., the building was debited for $78,000 and cash was credited for $78,000).

68. The accountant for the Sloan Manufacturing Corporation has provided you with the following data:

   a. Average common shares outstanding during 19x1, 60,000 shares, par $3; outstanding December 31, 19x1, 70,000 shares.

b. 6 percent cumulative preferred stock outstanding December 31, 19x1, 10,000 shares; redemption value, $120 per share; par value, $100 per share.
c. Cash dividends declared on December 31, 19x1—$420,000 to common stockholders and $60,000 to preferred stockholders. There are no dividends of preferred stock in arrears.
d. Net income for the year was $560,000.
e. Total stockholders' equity as of December 31, 19x1 was $2,600,000.

Required:

1. What is the earnings per share for common stock?
2. What is the dividend declared per share of common stock?
3. What is the dividend declared per share of preferred stock?
4. What is the book value of common stock?

69. The Peterson Company was organized on January 1, 19x0, with 10,000 shares of $10 par value common stock authorized, issued, and outstanding. Journalize the following transactions which took place in 19x4:

Jan. 1 The corporation purchased 100 shares of its common stock for $15 a share.
Feb. 1 The corporation sold the 100 shares purchased on January 1 for a total price of $1,750.
Mar. 1 Mrs. Moneybags, a stockholder, donated 100 shares of the X Corporation's common stock to the corporation.
    5 The corporation sold the 100 donated shares for a total price of $2,500.
Apr. 1 The corporation purchased 100 shares of its own stock for $9 a share.
May 1 The corporation sold the 100 shares purchased on April 1 for a total price of $500.
Dec. 15 A $.50 per share dividend on common stock was declared, to be paid on January 15, 19x5.

70. The Jones Co. was organized on January 1, 19x0, with 20,000 shares of $10 par value common stock and 5,000 shares of $100 par value, 6 percent preferred stock authorized. The balances in the stockholders' equity accounts on December 31, 19x3, were as follows:

Preferred stock	$100,000
Common stock	120,000
Additional paid-in capital:	
On preferred stock	5,000
On common stock	60,000
Retained earnings	$190,000

During 19x4, the company had the following transactions that affected the stockholders' equity:

		Number	Amount
a.	Issuance of common stock....................	5,000	$ 20 per share
b.	Purchase of its own shares of common stock....	4,000	$ 22 per share
c.	Reissuance of treasury stock.................	1,000	$ 24 per share
d.	Issuance of preferred stock..................	1,000	$ 102 per share
e.	Payment of dividend on common stock........		$ .50 per share
f.	Payment of dividend on preferred stock........		$ 6 per share
g.	Appropriation of retained earnings for future plant expansion.....................		$100,000
h.	Net income for the year.....................		$ 60,000
i.	Stock split on common stock with par value reduced to $5 per share...............	2 for 1	

Required:

Prepare the stockholders' equity section of the balance sheet for Jones Co. on December 31, 19x4.

71. On July 1, 19x0, the Morehouse Company purchased two pieces of equipment: a tractor for $11,000 and a truck for $9,000. On that date it was estimated that the tractor would have a life of eight years with a salvage value of $300 and the truck would have a life of ten years with a salvage value of $500. The company decided to use the double-declining balance method to depreciate both assets. Calculate the effect on the financial statements of each of the following unrelated accounting changes. Also, give journal entries to record any necessary adjusting entries and current depreciation expense. The company's fiscal year ends on June 30.

 a. On June 30, 19x3, the company realized the truck only had a remaining life of four years. Salvage value was expected to remain at $500.

 b. On June 30, 19x4, the accountant found an error in the calculation of the tractor's depreciation expense. The bookkeeper had erroneously subtracted out the salvage value in the first year when calculating depreciation on the declining balance method.

 c. On June 30, 19x3, it was decided that the tractor should be depreciated using the straight-line method.

7 | The Corporation: Capital Stock, Earnings, and Dividends

Refer to the Annual Report included in the front of the text.

72. At the end of the most recent year, what is the amount of the total stockholders' equity?

73. At the end of the most recent year, which account represents the largest amount of stockholders' equity?

74. At the end of the most recent year, where is net income reflected in the stockholders' equity section of the balance sheet?

75. Comparing the two most recent years presented, what is the increase/decrease in the capital stock account?

76. How much were the dividends per share in the most recent year?

77. What is the net income per share (EPS) for the most recent year?

78. On which financial statement can the EPS amount be located?

79. In which statement would a prior period adjustment be reflected?

80. What amount of treasury stock was issued during the current year? What amount of treasury stock was purchased?

81. In any year shown, was there an accounting change? If so, what type of change was it and how did it affect net income?

Chapter 8 discusses the accounting procedures used to record and control cash and the procedures used for recording receivables and payables. Studying this chapter should enable you to:

1. Describe the basic procedures for controlling cash receipts and disbursements.
2. Discuss the steps involved in preparing a bank statement reconciliation.
3. Describe the procedures used to control and account for imprest funds.
4. Illustrate the use of control and subsidiary accounts for recording receivables.
5. Discuss the purposes and mechanics of estimating bad debt expense.
6. Make the entries necessary to record the issuance and payment of a note and the related interest on the books of both the borrower and the lender.
7. Describe the process of discounting a note and the effect it has on a firm's accounts.
8. Calculate and prepare the entry to record the payroll taxes levied on an employer.

8

Cash, Receivables, and Current Liabilities

INTRODUCTION Cash includes currency, coins, checks, money orders, and monies on deposit with banks. On the balance sheet, cash is classified as a current asset. Usually, the total of all cash on hand and cash on deposit in multiple bank accounts will be shown as a single amount in the balance sheet.

Almost every transaction of any business organization will eventually result in either the receipt or disbursement of cash. The accounting procedures which enable a business to establish effective control over its cash transactions are among the most important, if not *the* most important, "controls" necessary for the operation of a business. While it is certainly true that cash is no more important than any of the other individual assets of the business, cash is more susceptible to misappropriation or theft because it can easily be concealed and because it is not readily identifiable. It is essential, therefore, that the company institute procedures or controls throughout every phase of its operations in order to safeguard cash from the time of its receipt until the time it is deposited in the company's bank account.

A good system of internal control over cash transactions should provide adequate procedures for protecting both cash receipts and cash disbursements. Such procedures should include the following elements:

8-1

1. Responsibilities for handling cash receipts, making cash payments, and recording cash transactions should be clearly defined.
2. Employees who handle cash transactions should not maintain the accounting records for cash.
3. All cash receipts should be deposited daily in a bank account and all significant cash payments should be made by check.
4. The validity and amount of cash payments should be verified, and different employees should be responsible for approving the disbursement and for signing the check.

The application of these procedures in developing an adequate system of internal control over cash transactions varies from company-to-company depending upon such factors as the size of the company, the number of its employees, its sources of cash, etc. However, the following discussion illustrates typical procedures which may be used effectively in the control of cash receipts and cash disbursements.

CASH RECEIPTS

The effective control of cash transactions begins at the moment cash is received by the business. Among the basic principles to be followed in controlling cash receipts are the following:

1. A complete record of all cash receipts should be prepared as soon as cash is received. This involves the listing of all cash items received by mail (often accomplished by the use of EDP equipment) and the use of devices such as cash registers to record "over-the-counter" sales. The immediate recording of each cash transaction is important because the likelihood of misappropriations of cash receipts occurring is usually greatest before a record of the receipt has been prepared. Once the receipt of cash has been properly recorded, misappropriation or theft is much more difficult to accomplish and conceal.

2. Each day's cash receipts should be deposited intact in the company's bank account as soon as possible. Disbursements should never be made directly from cash receipts; each and every cash item received should be promptly deposited in the bank. All major disbursements should be made by check, while outlays of smaller amounts may be made from controlled petty cash funds (described in a later section of this chapter). Adherence to these procedures will provide the firm with a valuable test of the accuracy of its cash records since every major cash transaction will be recorded twice: by the firm in its accounting records and by the bank. The periodic comparison or reconciliation of the accounting records of the business with those maintained by an independent, external source (the bank) is an important control feature in itself and will be discussed in detail in a later section of this chapter.

3. The employees charged with the responsibility of handling cash receipts should not be involved in making cash disbursements. This is a normal procedure employed by most firms of any size. Insofar as possible, the internal functions of receiving and disbursing cash should be kept separate in order to prevent the possible misappropriation or theft of cash. The employees handling cash receipts should not have access to the other accounting records of the firm for the same reasons.

"Over-the-Counter Sales." The cash proceeds at the time a sale is made should be recorded by means of a cash register. In larger firms, it may be preferable to have all sales recorded by a cashier at a centrally located cash register. One employee may "make the sale" and prepare a prenumbered sales slip which is given to the cashier who then records the sale on the cash register and accepts the customer's payment. Involving two (or more) employees in each sales transaction, rather than permitting a single employee to handle a transaction in its entirety, increases the control over cash. The use of a cash register also provides certain other benefits. Customers will observe that their purchases are recorded at the proper amount (another form of control). You may recall making a purchase where your money was refunded "if a star appears on your receipt" or where your drink was free if the waiter failed to give you a receipt. These are simple, yet effective examples of control procedures which are intended to encourage customers to note whether the sale has been properly recorded at the correct amount. The cash register may also be used as a means of classifying the sources of receipts, such as sales by departments.

At the end of each day, or more often if necessary (for example, at the end of each cashier's shift), the cash in the register should be counted and recorded on a cash register summary or other report by an employee who does not have access to the sales slips. A second employee should total the sales slips and reconcile the total of the sales slips to the cash register total. As previously indicated, all cash received should be deposited intact in the bank and the receipts recorded in the accounting records.

In certain circumstances, it may not be feasible to use prenumbered sales slips. If this is the case and a cash register is used, the above procedures should still be followed to the extent applicable. The major difference will be that the cash in the register will be reconciled to the totals contained in the register rather than to totals obtained from sales slips.

Receipts From Charge Sales. Remittances from customers for sales which were made on account may be received either by mail or by payment in person. In either case, procedures should be employed so that the receipt and the recording of the cash is performed by different employees whenever it is possible and practical to do so. If this separation of duties can be effectively maintained, the misappropriation of cash would require the collusion of two or more employees, thus diminishing the likelihood of the occurrence of any irregularity.

The employee who opens the mail should immediately prepare a listing of all cash items received. Of course this can be done *automatically*, such as by the use of punched cards as remittance forms and EDP equipment. This listing, along with a summary of over-the-counter receipts described previously, may be used to record each day's receipts in the cash receipts summary. Mail remittances are then combined with over-the-counter receipts, and the daily bank deposit is prepared and made. The amount deposited will be equal to the total cash receipts for the day. The employee making the bank deposit should obtain a duplicate deposit slip or other receipt from the bank for subsequent comparison to the cash receipts book.

The advantages of the procedures described above are many. The most important of these benefits may be summarized as follows:

1. The possibility of irregularities with respect to cash transactions are reduced, since any misappropriation will generally require the collusion of two or more employees.

2. The prompt deposit of each day's receipts intact (along with the disbursement procedures described in a later section of this chapter) provides the basis for an independent, external check on the internal records of the firm by reconciliation with bank statements.

3. Frequent deposits of receipts minimizes the idle cash and thereby reduces interest or other carrying charges which might otherwise be incurred by the business.

Several sections of this chapter have discussed the possible misappropriations of cash and outlined certain procedures which are intended to minimize these occurrences. It is obvious that the owners and/or management of any organization are naturally concerned with establishing effective controls that will prevent irregularities, but it may not be as apparent that every employee of the business also has a definite interest in these safeguards. If, for example, cash is misappropriated in an instance where the control procedures are ineffective or not in existence, any employee who might possibly be involved will be under suspicion. Although it may not be possible to identify the guilty person, no employee will be able to prove his or her innocence. Employee morale and efficiency will be adversely affected. An effective system of internal control avoids this situation; responsibilities are well-defined, definite, and fixed. Internal control is often an excellent preventive measure, as it often removes the temptation which might cause an otherwise good employee to succumb.

Cash Over and Short. Regardless of the care exercised in handling cash transactions, employees may make errors which cause cash overages or shortages. These differences will normally be detected when the cash on hand is counted and reconciled to the beginning cash balance plus any inflows of cash less any cash outlays.

Assume, for example, that total "over the counter" cash sales for the day are shown as $1,500 on the cash register while cash on hand after deducting the $100 beginning balance, is counted and found to be $1,505. The following journal entry would be made to record the cash sales for the day:

```
Cash ............................. 1,505
   Sales........................       1,500
   Cash over and short..............      5
```

The cash over and short account is credited for any cash overages and debited for any cash shortages. At the end of the accounting period, the net balance in the cash over and short account is treated as miscellaneous revenues if there is a net credit balance or as a miscellaneous expense if there is a net debit balance.

CASH DISBURSEMENTS

As previously indicated, one of the basic rules of effective internal control over cash transactions is that each day's receipts should be deposited intact in the bank and that all disbursements should be made by check. The functions of handling cash receipts and cash disbursements should be separated or divided among employees to the greatest extent practical. Other procedures which may be used to establish effective control over cash disbursements include the following:

1. All checks should be prenumbered consecutively and should be controlled and accounted for on a regular basis. Checks which are voided or spoiled should be retained and mutilated to prevent any possible unauthorized use.

2. Each disbursement should be supported or evidenced by an invoice and/or voucher which has been properly approved. The procedures which identify that obligations for which checks are prepared are proper obligations and in the appropriate amount are often referred to as a voucher system. The details of a voucher system will be discussed later in this chapter.

3. Invoices and vouchers should be indelibly marked as "paid" or otherwise cancelled in order to prevent duplicate payments.

4. The bank statement and returned checks should be routed to the employee charged with the preparation of the bank reconciliation statement (described as follows). This employee should be someone other than the person who is responsible for making cash disbursements.

THE BANK RECONCILIATION STATEMENT

As indicated earlier, if all receipts are deposited intact in the bank and all major disbursements are made by check, each cash transaction will be recorded twice: by the business in its accounting records, and in the records of the bank. It might seem logical, then, that at any given time the cash balance obtained from the accounting records of the firm should be identical to (i.e., equal to) the balance in the business's checking account at the bank. This is very seldom the case, however. Comparison of the balance shown in the firm's records with the balance shown at the same date by the bank statement usually reveals a difference in the two amounts. One reason for the difference could, of course, be erroneous entries made either by the firm or by the bank. A more frequent cause for the difference is, however, attributable to the difference in the timing of the recording of the transactions by the firm and the bank. If all transactions were recorded simultaneously by the business and by the bank, no differences would result (except in the case of errors), but this is almost never the case. The firm, for example, will write a check and immediately deduct the amount of the expenditure from the cash balance in its checkbook. The bank will not deduct this same disbursement from the firm's account until the check is presented to the bank for payment, perhaps several days later. Until the disbursement is deducted by the bank, the balance in the firm's account at the bank will exceed the firm's cash balance in its checkbook by the amount of the check. Similarly, the bank may levy a service charge against the firm's bank account from time-to-time. The business is usually unaware of the amount of this charge until it receives its monthly statement from the bank. Until the bank statement is received and the service charge is deducted, the balance on the firm's records will exceed the bank statement balance by the amount of the service charge.

The above examples are but two of the many items which may cause a difference between the bank statement balance and the cash balance as shown on the accounting records of the business. Other items which are often reflected in the bank statement but which have not yet been recorded by the depositor include:

1. N.S.F. checks—checks that were received from the depositor's customers and which were deposited in the bank, but for which the bank on which the check was written refuses payment (usually because of insufficient funds in the customer's account).

2. Deductions for bank service changes, printing of checks, safe deposit box rentals, etc.

3. Collections by the bank in acting as a collecting agent for the depositor.

A bank reconciliation is prepared to identify and account for all items which cause a difference between the cash balance as shown on the bank statement and the balance as it appears in the firm's accounting records.

One format of this statement which is often used is such that both the book and bank balances are adjusted to the actual amount of cash which is available to the business. This amount is often referred to as the "adjusted cash balance" or "true cash." This is the amount which should appear on the balance sheet. A typical bank reconciliation statement is presented in Illustration 1.

Illustration 1
Carol's Bakery
Bank Reconciliation Statement
June 30, 19x1

Balance per the bank statement, June 30, 19x1.........	$4,590
Add: Deposit in transit.............................	500
Bank error, check drawn by Carol's Tavern	
charged to the account of Carol's Bakery......	10
Less: Outstanding checks:	
Number 95—$50	
Number 101— 15	
Number 106— 30	
Number 110— 5.........................	(100)
"True" cash balance, June 30, 19x1...................	$5,000
Balance per the books, June 30, 19x1................	$4,000
Add: Note collected by the bank....................	1,000
Error made by the accountant in recording	
check #100.............................	45
Less: Bank charges...............................	(5)
N.S.F. check................................	(40)
"True" cash balance, June 30, 19x1...................	$5,000

The initial step in preparing a bank reconciliation statement is to examine the bank statement and any debit and credit memoranda accompanying it. A debit memorandum is evidence of a deduction made by the bank from a depositor's account which arises from a transaction other than the normal payment of a check by the bank. Likewise, a credit memorandum is an addition to the depositor's account which arises from a transaction other than a normal deposit. These documents should be compared with the firm's accounting records in order to determine whether or not they have been previously (and properly) recorded by the business. If these transactions have not been recorded, they will be included as additions or deductions in the bank reconciliation statement and then recorded at a subsequent time. Examples of these types of reconciling items which were included in Illustration 1 are as follows:

1. The $1,000 addition to the book balance represents the proceeds from a note payable to Carol's Bakery which was collected by the bank and added to Carol's bank account.

2. The bank charges of $5 for the month of June were deducted from Carol's account by the bank.

3. The N.S.F. (Not Sufficient Funds) check of $40 represents a check received from a customer and deposited by Carol. The check was returned unpaid by the customer's bank.

The second step in preparing the reconciliation is to arrange the paid checks returned with the bank statement in numerical sequence. The checks returned by the bank are then compared with the checks issued as listed in the business checkbook or cash disbursements journal. Distinctive *tick marks* or symbols (such as a ✓) may be used in the checkbook in order to indicate those checks which have been returned by the bank. The amount of each check should be compared to the amount listed in the checkbook during this process. The outstanding checks are those which have been issued but not yet returned by the bank.

Checks which were outstanding at the beginning of the month and which cleared the bank during the month may be traced to the bank reconciliation statement prepared at the end of the previous month. Any checks which were outstanding at the beginning of the month and which did not clear the bank will, of course, still be included as outstanding in the current month's reconciliation. In the example, the $100 total of outstanding checks included in the bank reconciliation statement was determined by comparing the cancelled checks returned with the bank statement with the checkbook and the listing of outstanding checks included in the previous month's bank reconciliation.

In our example, examination of the cancelled checks returned with the bank statement disclosed the fact that the bank had deducted a check of Carrol's Tavern in the amount of $10 from the Carol's Bakery account. This item is shown as an addition to the balance per bank in the reconciliation and would be called to the attention of the bank for correction.

The next step in the reconciliation process is to ascertain whether or not there are any deposits in transit. A deposit in transit is a receipt which has been included in the cash balance per books and deposited in the bank (for example, in a night depository or by mail) but which has not yet been processed by the bank and credited to the depositor's account. In the illustration, the total receipts of $500 for June 30th were deposited in the bank's night depository on that date. The bank, however, did not credit the firm's account until the next day, July 1st. The $500 amount is therefore shown as a deposit in transit in the June 30, 19x1, bank reconciliation statement.

An excellent test of the accuracy of the firm's cash receipts records is to reconcile the total receipts for the month (or other period) to the total deposits credited to the bank account in the bank statement. In order to perform this test, the following information would be required:

1. The total deposits which are included in the bank statement for the month of June [including a deposit in transit at the beginning of the month (May 31, 19x1) of $700] $15,000

2. The total cash receipts shown in the firm's accounting records for the month of June (including the receipts of June 30th of $500) 14,800

The receipts, as per the books for the month of June, would be reconciled with the deposits as per the June 30, 19x1, bank statement as follows:

Deposits per bank statement		$15,000
Less:	Deposit in transit at the end of the prior month	700
		$14,300
Add:	Deposit in transit at the end of the current month	500
Cash receipts per the books		$14,800

In many instances, deposits in transit, outstanding checks, service charges, and errors will be the only reconciling items between the book and the bank balances. Omissions from, or errors in, the accounting records of the firm should, or course, be corrected immediately. If errors made by the bank are discovered in the reconciliation process (such as a check charged to the wrong account), they should be called to the attention of the bank for immediate correction.

In the example, several adjusting or correcting entries would be required. These are as follows:

Note Collected By the Bank

Cash..................................	1,000	
Notes receivable.....................		1,000

Error

Cash..................................	45	
Accounts receivable		45*

Bank Service Charges

Service charge expense.................	5	
Cash................................		5

N.S.F. Check

Accounts receivable	40	
Cash................................		40

*The receipt of a payment on account of $572 was erroneously recorded as $527 by the firm. This entry reduces the customer's account in order to reflect the actual amount which was paid and increases cash to the proper amount.

The effect of these three entries will be to adjust the balance per books as of June 30, 19x1, to the "true cash" balance as of that date. This adjustment procedure may be illustrated as follows:

Cash	
4,000	
1,000	5
45	40
5,000	

It should be noted that only those items which are adjustments of the "balance per books" in the bank reconciliation statement will require adjusting or correcting entries. This is because these items have either not been previously recorded on the books of the firm (in the example, the note collected by the bank, the bank charges, and the check which was returned N.S.F.) or have been recorded erroneously (in the example, the receipt of $572 which was recorded by the firm as $527[1]). Items which are included as adjustments of the "balance per the bank statement" do not require adjustment on the firm's books since these items are either transactions which have been already recorded by the firm but not by the bank (in the example, the deposit in transit and the outstanding checks) or errors which were made

---

[1] Transposition errors (i.e., $572 − $527) are always divisible by nine. This fact may be helpful in locating differences, errors, etc.

by the bank (in the example, the check of Carrol's Tavern which was erroneously charged to the account of Carol's Bakery).

The bank reconciliation procedure may be summarized as follows:

Balance per the bank statement—adjust for:

1. Transactions recorded by the firm but not by the bank (deposits in transit, outstanding checks, etc.).
2. Errors made by the bank.

Balance per the books—adjust for:

1. Transactions recorded by the bank but not by the firm (collections made for the firm by the bank, service charges, N.S.F. checks, etc.).
2. Errors made by the firm.

PETTY CASH FUNDS

A basic principle of control over cash is that all cash disbursements should be made by check. This is not practicable, however, in instances where small expenditures are required for items such as postage, freight, carfare, employees' "supper money," etc. In circumstances such as these, it is usually more convenient and cost effective to make payments in currency and/or coin. This can be accomplished and effective control over cash still maintained by the use of an imprest fund called petty cash.

A petty cash fund is established by drawing a check on the regular checking account, cashing it, and placing the proceeds in a fund. The amount of the fund depends upon the extent to which petty cash will be used and how often it will be reimbursed. As a practical matter, it should be large enough to cover petty cash disbursements for a reasonable period of time—for example, a week. A single employee should be placed in charge of the fund and made responsible for its operation.

A major difference between making disbursements from a petty cash fund and from a regular checking account is that disbursements from petty cash funds are recorded in the accounting records not as they are made, but when the fund is reimbursed. At the time each expenditure is made from the fund, a petty cash voucher, such as the one illustrated below, is prepared. If an invoice or other receipt is available in support of the disbursement, it should be attached to the voucher. In any event, the person receiving the cash should always be required to sign the petty cash voucher as evidence of his or her receipt of the disbursement. If this procedure is followed, at any given time the total of the cash on hand in the petty cash fund plus the total of the unreimbursed receipts should be exactly equal to the original amount of the fund.

The fund would be reimbursed on a periodic basis or whenever necessary. In order to obtain reimbursement of the fund, the employee acting as petty cashier would bring the paid petty cash vouchers to the person who is authorized to write checks on the firm's bank account and exchange them for a check equal to the total of the vouchers. At this point, the petty cash vouchers would be separated and summarized according to the appropriate

```
┌─────────────────────────────────────────────────────┐
│                   Petty Cash Voucher #53            │
│                                                     │
│   TO  Vince Brenner          DATE  May 1      19x1  │
│                                                     │
│   EXPLANATION      ACCOUNT           AMOUNT         │
│     Postage          119             $5.00          │
│                                                     │
│   APPROVED                        RECEIVED          │
│   BY     PN                       PAYMENT   V.B.    │
│                                                     │
└─────────────────────────────────────────────────────┘
```

expense category for recording in the firm's accounting records. Before the check is issued, the vouchers would be reviewed in order to ascertain that all the expenditures made were for valid business purposes. After the petty cash vouchers are approved and the fund replenished, the vouchers and the underlying support should be marked as *paid* or otherwise mutilated in order to prevent their reuse, either intentionally or unintentionally.

To illustrate the operation of a petty cash fund, assume that Barney Company establishes a $100 petty cash fund on January 1, 19x1, by cashing a check in the amount of $100 and placing the proceeds in the fund. The entry to record this transaction would be as follows:

> January 1: Petty cash 100
>   Cash   100

Assume further that during the month of January, disbursements from the fund (supported by vouchers) totalled $85. In order to replenish the fund on January 31, the employee responsible for the fund would exchange the vouchers for a check drawn on the regular cash account for $85. This check would be cashed and the $85 proceeds would be used to restore the fund to its original cash balance of $100. This transaction would be recorded by the following entry:

> January 31: Various expenses 85
>   Cash   85

Note that no entry is made to the *petty cash* account after the fund is established (unless the firm wishes to increase or decrease the fund balance). Effective control over petty cash operations is accomplished in two ways: at any time the cash on hand in the fund plus the unreimbursed petty cash vouchers must be equal to the fund balance, and the expense vouchers must be examined and approved upon reimbursement by a person other than the employee who made the disbursement. If considered necessary or desirable, surprise counts of the petty cash fund also may be made in order to insure that the fund is operating according to its intended purposes.

RECEIVABLES

The extension of credit is a significant factor in the operation of many businesses. Most businesses are both grantors of credit (creating receivables) and receivers of credit (creating payables). Receivables are assets representing the claims that a business has against others. While receivables may be generated by various types of transactions, the most common sources of receivables are the sale of merchandise or services on a credit basis. Normally these assets will be realized or converted into cash by the business. Payables are obligations of a firm which arise from past transactions and which are to be discharged at a future date by payment of cash, transfer of other assets, or performance of a service.

Typically claims against a firm originate from transactions such as purchases of merchandise or services on credit, purchases of equipment on credit, and loans from banks. In an economic system such as ours, which is based so extensively on credit, almost all business concerns incur liabilities. The purpose of this chapter is to describe and discuss the procedures which are necessary to establish effective control over receivables and payables, and to illustrate the accounting practices and procedures which are employed with regard to these assets and liabilities.

CLASSIFICATION OF RECEIVABLES AND PAYABLES

Receivables are classified according to the timing of their expected realization (i.e., as current assets if realization is anticipated within a year, or as noncurrent assets if collection is expected subsequent to the current period). Receivables are also classified according to their form. Notes receivable are claims against others which are supported by "formal" or written promises to pay. These may or may not be negotiable instruments, depending on such factors as the terms, form, and content of the note. An example of a note receivable would be the written promise by a borrower to repay a loan with interest, at a stated date. Accounts receivable, on the other hand, are not supported by "formal" or written promises to pay. An example of an account receivable would be the claim of a business against a customer who makes a purchase on account.

Creditors of a business have claims against the assets of the firm. Depending upon the nature of the particular liability, a claim may either be against specific assets or against assets in general. In any case, claims of creditors have a priority over the claims of owners. Thus, in the event of the liquidation of a business, all debts must be satisfied before any payments are made to owners.

Amounts shown in the balance sheet as liabilities may be classified as either current or noncurrent liabilities. A proper distinction between current and noncurrent liabilities is essential because comparison of current assets with current liabilities is an important means of evaluating the short-run liquidity or debt-paying ability of the firm.

Current liabilities are those debts or obligations of a firm that must either be paid in cash or settled by providing goods or services within the operating cycle of the firm or one year, whichever is longer. The operating cycle of a business is the average period of time that elapses between purchase of an inventory item and conversion of the inventory into cash. This cycle includes the initial purchase of the inventory, the sale of the item on credit, and the collection of the receivable. The most common current liabilities include accounts payable, notes payable, and accrued liabilities.

CONTROL OVER RECEIVABLES

At the time an over-the-counter sale is made, it should be recorded by means of a cash register whether it is a cash sale or a charge sale. The controls described in Chapter 7 apply to both charge or credit sales as well as to cash sales. If a sale is made on account, a prenumbered sales ticket should be prepared and signed by the customer making the purchase. As a minimum, this charge ticket should include the following information:

1. The date.
2. The customer's name and account number.
3. A description of the item(s) purchased by the customer.

4. The total amount of the sale.

5. The customer's signature.

Effective control procedures require that the sales slip be prepared in triplicate: one copy would be given to the customer, a second copy would be placed in the cash register, and a third copy would be retained by the salesperson. An invoice dispenser which automatically retains a copy in a locked container is an ideal control device for this purpose.

At the end of each day, or more often if necessary, the charge slips accumulated in the register would be used in the reconciliation of the cash register receipts as previously described in Chapter 7.

The charge slips will serve as the basis for recording credit purchases in customers' accounts. A "control" account, trade accounts receivable for example, would be used to record the total charge sales and the total payments which are received from customers. Individual ledger accounts, referred to as "subsidiary" accounts, would be maintained for each customer. The amount of each charge sale would be recorded individually in the particular customer's account, and the total sales would be recorded in the control account. Bills would be prepared from the individual customers' ledger accounts and mailed out periodically, usually on a monthly basis. As payments are received from customers, the remittances would be recorded individually in the customer's account and in total in the "control" account. Cash receipts, received either by mail or "over-the-counter," would be controlled according to the procedures outlined earlier in this chapter. At any point in time, the balance in the "control" account should be equal[2] to the total of the balances in the individual customers' accounts. Therefore, a periodic reconciliation should be made of the control and the subsidiary accounts.

ACCOUNTS RECEIVABLE

The most common type of receivable is the *account receivable* that arises from the sale of goods or services on a credit basis in the normal operations of the business. *A determination must be made of both the timing of the recognition of the asset and of the measurement of the value of the asset. The timing factor is intertwined with the recognition of revenue—the point at which a sale is made or a service has been performed.* The measurement factor depends on the due date of the receivable, the terms of payment, and the probability of collection.

As credit sales are made, entries are recorded in both the "control" and the "subsidiary" accounts. For purposes of illustration, assume that a department store makes the following sales during the month of June:

---

[2] If a special journal is used, they may be equal only at the end of the period.

```
To Larry Killough .............................  $   100
To Gene Seago ...............................      150
To Pat Kemp .................................      200
To all other charge customers ................   10,000
                                                 $10,450
```

These sales would be recorded in the "control" account, trade accounts receivable, by the following entry:

```
Accounts receivable ..............   10,450
    Sales ........................              10,450
```

At the same time, these sales would also be recorded in the individual customers' accounts, so that at all times the balance in the "control" account (accounts receivable) would be equal to the total of all the balances in the "subsidiary" accounts (individual customers' accounts). Using T-accounts, this process is illustrated as follows:

```
          Control Accounts                         Subsidiary Accounts

       Accounts Receivable         =          Killough              Seago
          100                               100    |              150   |
          150
          200
       10,000                                                           
       ─────────                              Kemp               All Others
Bal.   10,450                               200    |            10,000  |


             Sales
                  |   100
                  |   150
                  |   200
                  | 10,000
                  ─────────
                  | 10,450  Bal.
```

Now assume that the collections received from customers are as follows:

```
From Killough ................................  $   100
From Seago ...................................      100
From other customers .........................    8,000
                                                 $8,200
```

These collections would also be recorded in the control account by the following entry:

```
Cash ............................   8,200
    Accounts receivable..........              8,200
```

At the same time, the collections would also be recorded in the subsidiary accounts, thereby maintaining a balance with the control account. This procedure is illustrated as follows:

Control Accounts			Subsidiary Accounts			
Accounts Receivable		**Killough**		**Seago**		
Bal. 10,450	8,200	100	100	150	100	
2,250		0		50		
		Kemp		**All Others**		
		200		10,000	8,000	
				2,000		

UNCOLLECTIBLE RECEIVABLES

One of the costs of making sales on a credit basis results from the fact that some of the customers who make purchases on account may never pay the amounts which are owed to the firm. This is to be expected and should be considered a normal cost of doing business. Obviously, if a firm were able to identify the particular customers who would ultimately fail to pay their accounts, it would not sell to them on a credit basis. Unfortunately, although credit investigations of varying degrees of effectiveness are made by firms, some bad debts will still result. In fact, if a firm had no bad debts whatsoever, this might be an indication that its credit department was performing unsatisfactorily. If credit standards were set so high as to eliminate *all* those potential customers whose credit rating was judged to be marginal, the revenue lost from refusing credit to these customers would no doubt exceed the potential losses, thus decreasing the firm's net income. From a theoretical viewpoint, the firm should grant credit to its customers up to that point where the marginal revenue from the granting of credit sales is exactly equal to the marginal expense, including the cost of bad debts. Of course this goal is impossible to attain in actual practice, but a firm's credit policy should attempt to approximate this objective to the extent possible and/or practical.

Uncollectible receivables are generally referred to as bad debts. *A bad debt represents a loss of the revenue that was recognized at the time the receivable originated. Therefore, the accounting for a bad debt requires a decrease in the accounts receivable and a related decrease in income for the period.*

Bad debt expense, then, is a normal business expense which should be expected by those firms selling goods or services on a credit basis. The proper determination of income for a period requires that the revenue earned during that period be matched with the expenses which were incurred in generating that revenue. For firms that make sales or render services on a credit basis, this requires that bad debt expense be matched against revenue in the period in which the revenue is earned. Most accountants agree that this is the period in which the sale was originally made, and not the period in which a particular account is determined to be uncollectible. For example, assume that a credit sale made during the month of June is determined to be uncollectible during July, due to the bankruptcy of the customer. This would represent an expense of the month of June (when the sale was made and the revenue recognized) *not* the month of July (when the account was found to be uncollectible).

The basic accounting problem in recording bad debts is determining the timing for recording the decrease in income and the related reduction in receivables. The two alternative procedures for recognition are as follows:

1. Record bad debts in the period that a specific receivable has been identified as uncollectible—referred to as the *direct write-off method*.

2. Record an estimate of the expected uncollectible accounts (on the basis of sales or from outstanding receivables) at the end of the period in which the sales on account were made—referred to as *the allowance method*.

In both methods, the entry to record bad debts is a debit to bad debt expense and a reduction in the receivables. The direct write-off method records the reduction in the receivables with a credit directly to accounts receivable, whereas the allowance method records the decrease in receivables through an increase in a contra account to the receivables, allowance for bad debts.

To illustrate the use of the direct write-off method, assume that a company, which has a balance of $13,000 in accounts receivable, believes that the Woods Corporation is not going to pay its $500 account because Woods is bankrupt. The journal entry to record the bad debt is as follows:

```
Bad debt expense ................................ 500
    Accounts receivable ...........................      500
```

The basic problem with this approach is that the bad debt expense, in all probability, is not matched with the revenue from the sale. Most of the time, a company will not recognize an account receivable as a bad debt in the same period in which the receivable originated. Therfore, if a sale is made in one period and the customer's account is deemed to be worthless in a subsequent period, there will be an improper matching of revenue and expense. Further, this approach does not result in stating receivables at their estimated realizable value on the balance sheet. As a result, *the direct write-off method is not acceptable unless the amount of bad debts either is not material or cannot be reasonably estimated.*

*In the allowance method, bad debt expense must be estimated, because the particular accounts that ultimately will prove to be uncollectible are unknown. Proponents of the allowance method believe that the proper determination of income requires that bad debt expense be matched against revenue in the period in which the revenue is earned. Most accountants agree that this is the period in which the sale originally was made, and not the period in which a particular account is determined to be uncollectible. Similarly, the establishment of an allowance account that is contra to current receivables achieves an estimate of the net realizable value of the accounts receivable at the end of a period. Even though estimates of future events are required in the application of the allowance method, it is argued that it is preferable to approximate the bad debts relating to the current period using the allowance method rather than to ignore the reality of future bad debts as is done with the direct write-off approach.

There are two commonly used approaches for the estimation of bad debts: (1) a percentage of either total sales or credit sales, and (2) a percentage of accounts receivable at the end of the period. In either approach, when the estimate has been made at the end of the period, the entry to record the bad debt is a debit to bad debt expense and a credit to allowance for bad debts. *The allowance account is reported on the balance sheet as a direct deduction from accounts receivable.*

Bad Debts as a Percentage of Sales

The estimate of bad debts in the percentage of sales approach is normally based on an analysis of the firm's past relationship between credit sales and bad debts. The percentage relationship may be adjusted for current circumstances such as changes in credit policies or economic conditions. The analysis may be on the basis of total sales if there is a stable relationship between credit sales and total sales. It should be noted that the approach used is an income statement approach. The primary consideration is to estimate correctly the bad debt expense for the period.

Assume, for purposes of illustration, that the credit experience of a small firm has been as follows:

Year	Credit Sales	Losses From Bad Debts
19x1	$120,000	$2,300
19x2	130,000	2,650
19x3	150,000	3,050
	$400,000	$8,000

For 19x4, it might be reasonable for the firm to estimate that its losses from uncollectible accounts would be similar to its experience in prior years. A percentage which could be used in estimating bad debts would be $8,000 divided by $400,000 or 2 percent of credit sales. In practice, of course, this percentage would be adjusted for any expected changes in general economic conditions, credit policies, etc.

Returning to the example used earlier in the chapter, recall that credit sales for the period were $10,450. Using the percentage of sales method, the estimated bad debts from these sales would be calculated by multiplying $10,450 by 2 percent or $209. This estimated bad debt expense would be recorded in the accounts by the following journal entry:

Bad debt expense.................	209	
Allowance for bad debts............		209

Note that the credit portion of this entry is to an allowance for bad debts account and not to accounts receivable. While the firm's best estimate of its bad debt expense, based on its past experience, indicates that approximately $209 of the receivables arising from sales made during the month of June will not be collectible, it is unable to identify the individual accounts that may not be paid at this time. Since the particular individual(s) whose account(s) may ultimately prove to be uncollectible cannot be identified at this time, a direct credit to accounts receivable is inappropriate since such a procedure would eliminate the equality of the control and the subsidiary accounts. The effect of the entry to record bad debt expense on the control and subsidiary accounts is as follows:

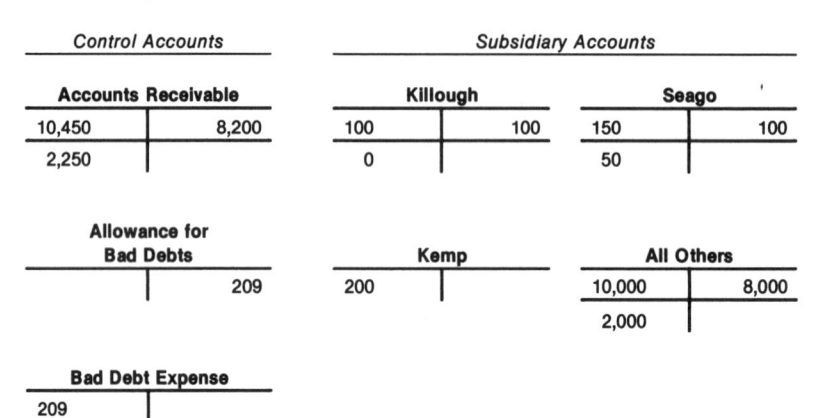

Control Accounts

Accounts Receivable
10,450	8,200
2,250	

Allowance for Bad Debts
	209

Bad Debt Expense
209	

Subsidiary Accounts

Killough
100	100
0	

Kemp
200	

Seago
150	100
50	

All Others
10,000	8,000
2,000	

The allowance for bad debts account has a credit balance after this end-of-period entry. This credit balance is deducted from the asset account, accounts receivable, to produce the proper balance sheet value for this asset.

In the percentage of sales approach, the entry to record bad debt expense at the end of the period is unaffected by any balance existing in the allowance account. The logic for this approach is that the purpose of the entry is to obtain a proper matching between sales and bad debt expense. When uncollectible accounts are written off in the subsequent year, the allowance account is debited, accounts receivable is credited, and the individual accounts in the subsidiary ledger are credited. It is unlikely that the total of the amounts that are written off will be equal to the estimated amount. Any remaining balance (either debit or credit) in the allowance account at the end of the period, but before the current period's adjusting entry is made, represents an underestimate or overestimate of previous periods (assuming that no account originates in the current year is written off in the current year). Recognition of the estimation error is not necessary, unless the amount involved is material.

Bad Debts as a Percentage of Receivables

An alternative to the percentage of sales approach is to base the estimate of uncollectible accounts on the past relationship between receivables and bad debts (again adjusted for any changes in current circumstances). This relationship can be based on either total receivables or on receivables segregated by various age categories. In most circumstances, the use of such aging schedules provides a better predictor of future uncollectible accounts. Under this balance sheet approach, the emphasis is on the measurement of economic resources rather than income determination.

The objective of estimating bad debts on the basis of outstanding receivables is to provide a good estimate of the appropriate balance in the allowance account and, therefore, a reasonably accurate measure of the net realizable value of the accounts receivable in the balance sheet. Consequently, when the estimate of uncollectible accounts is determined at the end of the period, the entry is made to bring the allowance account to the estimated balance. That is, any balance remaining in the allowance account at year-end is taken into account in preparing the journal entry. Another way of viewing this process is that by considering the balance in the allowance account in determining the year-end entry, this approach is corrected automatically for any underestimation or overestimation of bad debts made in previous periods.

The most commonly used method of estimating the uncollectible receivables is to analyze the accounts receivable balance at the end of the period using an aging process to make a judgment as to which accounts ultimately are likely to prove to be uncollectible. *Aging involves the classifying or grouping of accounts according to the period of time that the accounts have been outstanding.* The basic assumption is that, all other factors being equal, the collectibility of receivables decreases as the account remains outstanding. An example of an aging schedule is as follows:

		Number of Days Outstanding			
Account	Balance	0-30	31-60	61-90	91 and Older
Killough	$ 0	$ 0	$ 0	$ 0	$ 0
Seago	50	50	0	0	0
Kemp	200	200	0	0	0
All others	2,000	1,350	400	50	200
	$2,250	$1,600	$400	$50	$200

Based on the experience of the firm, different percentages may be applied to the different classifications of accounts to estimate the amount of uncollectible receivables. For example, the following calculation might be appropriate:

Number of Days Outstanding	Amount	Percentage*	Estimated to be Uncollectible
0-30	$1,600	1%	$ 16
31-60	400	10	40
61-90	50	50	25
91 and older	200	75	150
	$2,250		$231

*The percentage used would be determined by the credit experience of the firm, adjusted as considered necessary for such factors as changes in economic conditions, credit policies, etc.

The older accounts, as well as those which are known to be in financial difficulty, should also be reviewed on an individual basis as an additional test of the amount which is estimated to be uncollectible. Assume that, after this review, the firm decided that the calculation of the amount estimated to be uncollectible using the analysis of receivables by age was appropriate. The balance in the allowance for bad debts account should be increased to $231, the amount estimated to be uncollectible at the end of June. Since this approach is based on the question of how large of an allowance account is needed to reduce the net receivables balance to the amount which is expected to be collected, it is necessary to consider any balance in the allowance account before making the adjusting entry. The allowance account will have a debit or credit balance at the end of the period, prior to the adjustment if the receivables which were actually determined to be uncollectible during the period were not exactly equal to the balance in the allowance account at the beginning of the period. The procedure for writing-off an uncollectible receivable will be discussed in the next section. Assuming that the allowance for bad debts account had a debit balance of $20 prior to this determination, the following journal entry would be required:

Bad debt expense..................... 251
    Allowance for bad debts.............   251

After this entry has been posted to the allowance account, the balance in the account would be $231.

Allowance for Bad Debts	
20	251
	231

Note that when the balance sheet analysis of the receivable balance method is used, the total amount which is estimated to be uncollectible is determined. This amount is then compared to the existing balance in the allowance for bad debts account and the journal entry required to adjust the allowance for bad debts account to the appropriate amount is made.

A difference between the percentage of sales approach and the percentage of receivables approach lies in the handling of any overestimation or underestimation of the previous period (which is evidenced by a credit or debit balance in the allowance account). In the percentage of sales method, any balance in the allowance account is ignored in determining the year-end entry to bad debts expense. This method theoretically provides the appropriate matching of the bad debt expense with the revenues of the period. In the percentage of receivables method, any balance in the allowance account is considered in determining the year-end entry to bad debts expense. This method theoretically provides the appropriate measure of the net realizable value of the receivables. In practice, if the estimation procedures are reasonably accurate, there should not be a significant difference between the two approaches.

Balance Sheet Presentation

In the balance sheet, the allowance for bad debts would appear as an offset to, or deduction from, accounts receivable. For example, the receivables of the firm would be shown as follows:

```
Assets:
    Cash .............................................       $ 5,000
    Accounts receivable ..................    $2,250
    Less:  Allowance for bad debts .........       231         2,019
    Other assets .........................                   10,000
        Total assets .....................                  $17,019
```

Writing-off an Uncollectible Account

When a particular account balance is determined to be uncollectible, an entry is made in the accounts to recognize this fact. Returning to the example used earlier in the chapter, assume that the $50 balance owed by Seago proves to be uncollectible. The following entry would be required:

```
Allowance for bad debts ....................    50
    Accounts receivable ....................          50
```

After this entry has been posted to the accounts, the control[3] account would appear as follows:

---

[3] The effect on the subsidiary accounts would be to reduce the balance in Seago's account from $50 to zero, thus maintaining the equality between the control and the subsidiary accounts.

Accounts Receivable		Allowance for Bad Debts	
2,250	50	50	231
2,200			181

In the balance sheet, the receivables would appear as follows:

Accounts receivable $2,200
Less: Allowance for bad debts 181 $2,019

It is important to note that the entry for the write-off of the uncollectible receivable affects neither expense nor total assets. The net receivable balance (accounts receivable less the allowance for bad debts) remains the same since both accounts receivable and the allowance for bad debts are reduced by the same amount. The expense related to bad debts is recorded when the estimated bad debts are recorded (i.e., when the provision for bad debts is made). The entry to record bad debts expense is normally made during the year-end adjustment process.

Even though a company writes off an account as uncollectible, it will still attempt to collect the balance due. In some instances, it may continue its own efforts to collect the account; in others, it may turn the account over to a collection agency. In any event, if the collection efforts prove to be successful, the company will receive cash; two entries are required in order to record this receipt. The first entry reinstates the balance which has been written off by reversing the original entry made at the time of the write-off. The second entry records the collection of the account balance.

To illustrate the recovery of an account which had previously been written off, we will return to the example used above. Assume now that the $50 balance owed by Seago which was written off as uncollectible is subsequently collected. The collection would be recorded by the following entries:

Accounts receivable 50
    Allowance for bad debts 50
Cash 50
    Accounts receivable 50

Again, note that the first entry simply reverses the previous write-off. The second entry records the collection of the balance.

CURRENT LIABILITIES

Liabilities

Liabilities are probable future sacrifices of economic benefits that arise from present obligations to transfer cash or other assets or to provide services to other entities in the future, due to past transactions or events. In an economic system such as ours, which is based so extensively on credit, almost all business concerns incur liabilities.

Creditors of an enterprise have claims against the assets of the firm. Depending upon the nature of the particular liability, a claim may be either against specific assets or against assets in general. In any case, the claims of creditors have priority over the claims of owners. Thus, in the event of the liquidation of a business, all debts must be satisfied before any payments are made to the owners.

Amounts that are shown in the balance sheet as liabilities are classified as either current or noncurrent liabilities. A proper distinction between current and noncurrent liabilities is essential, because comparison of current assets with current liabilities is an important means of evaluating the short-run liquidity or debt-paying ability of the firm.

Current liabilities are debts or obligations that are reasonably expected to require the use of existing current assets (e.g., cash) the creation of current liabilities, or the provision of goods and services within the company's operating cycle or one year, whichever is longer. Current liabilities include all of those obligations that are due on demand or will be due on demand within one year or the company's operating cycle, whichever is longer. Classification as current liabilities is required even though liquidation may not be expected within that period. Further, long-term obligations may be classified as current liabilities if they are or will be callable by the creditor, because either: (a) the debtor's violation of a provision of the debt agreement at the balance sheet date causes the obligation to be callable, or (b) the violation will make the debt callable if not cured within a specified grace period. These obligations are classified as current liabilities unless: (a) the creditor waives or loses the right to demand repayment for more than one year or beyond the company's operating cycle, whichever is longer, or (b) the obligation will not become callable, because the violation will probably be cured during the grace period.

Current liabilities would include obligations that arose during the operating cycle (e.g., payables incurred in the purchase of inventory), money received in advance for the provision of future services (e.g., rent collected in advance), payables accruing during the operating cycle but not due to be paid as of the date of the balance sheet (e.g., accrued wages), other liabilities that will be paid within the upcoming operating cycle (e.g., payments on serial bonds), and contingent liabilities that must be accrued (e.g., warranty obligations).

Conceptually, current liabilities may be classified into three basic groups: (1) liabilities that are both easily identifiable and definitely determinable in amount, (2) liabilities that are identifiable but have amounts that are dependent upon operating results, and (3) liabilities that are identifiable but are not definitely determinable in amount. The third type requires an estimation of the amount of the liability.

The common current liabilities that are classified into the three types are as follows:

1. Definite amounts:
    a. Accounts payable.
    b. Short-term notes payable.
    c. Dividends payable.
    d. Advances from officers, employees, or stockholders.
    e. Accrued liabilities.
    f. Compensated absences.
2. Amounts dependent upon operations:
    a. Income taxes (subject to verification by the Internal Revenue Service).
    b. Payroll taxes.
    c. Bonus payments.
3. Amounts to be estimated:
    a. Property taxes.
    b. Warranty obligations.
    c. Premiums and coupons.
    d. Refundable deposits made by customers.

Theoretically, liabilities should be accounted for at the present value of the future outlays required to satisfy the obligations. However, in practice, most current liabilities are reported at their maturity amount. This practice is considered to be justified on the basis of materiality, because the difference between the present value and maturity value is minimal due to the limited time period involved (usually less than one year).

Accounts payable normally are classified in the balance sheet in terms of their origin. The major source of accounts payable is debts to trade creditors for goods or services that are purchased on a credit basis. An account payable usually does not involve the payment of interest; in addition, the debtor does not sign a formal written promise to pay.

Entries for accounts payable are recorded in both the control account and the subsidiary accounts in a manner similar to the procedures used to record accounts receivable. As payables are incurred, credit entries are recorded in both the control and the individual subsidiary accounts. As the balances are paid, debit entries are recorded in both the control and subsidiary accounts.

NOTES RECEIVABLE AND PAYABLE

As previously indicated, notes receivable are claims against others which, unlike accounts receivable, are supported by formal or written promises to pay. A typical note is shown below.

> $ _1000 00_   _May 1_ 19x1
>
> _Two months (2)_ after date _I_
> promise(s) to pay to the order of _Willie Davis_
> the sum of $ _1000 00_ with interest at _18_ percent.
>
> _Don Sutton_

The note shown above is an interest-bearing note: Don Sutton (the maker of the note) agrees to pay Willie Davis (the payee) $1,000 (the principal amount of the note) plus interest at 18 percent on July 1, 19x1 (the maturity date). The 18 percent annual interest is the charge that Sutton pays for the use of Davis' funds. Interest, which is an expense for Sutton and income for Davis, is calculated by the following formula:

$$\text{Principal} \times \text{Rate} \times \text{Time} = \text{Interest}$$
$$\$1{,}000 \times .18 \times \tfrac{2}{12} = \$30$$

The maturity value of this note is $1,030 (the principal amount of $1,000 plus interest at $30); this is the amount that Sutton must pay Davis on July 1, 19x1, when the note becomes due and payable (matures).

Note that for ease of calculation, the 18 percent interest rate was expressed as a decimal, .18. Alternatively, a fraction ($\tfrac{18}{100}$) could have been used in the computation. The interest rate stated in a note is usually expressed in terms of an annual or yearly rate. Since the note used in the illustration was for a duration of two months, time was expressed as a fraction of year, $\tfrac{2}{12}$. In some instances, time may be stated in days. If this is the case, a year is usually considered to have 360 days in order to simplify the computation of interest. For example, if the note in the illustration was for a period of thirty days, the calculation of interest would be as follows:

$$\$1{,}000 \times .18 \times \tfrac{30}{360} = \$15$$

To illustrate the accounting for notes receivable, the entries necessary to record the transactions regarding the Sutton-Davis note will be presented in the sections which follow.

Issuance of the Note

On May 1, 19x1, when Sutton borrowed the $1,000 from Davis, the following entry would be made on Davis' books to record the loan:

Notes receivable	1,000	
Cash		1,000

This entry indicates that Davis has exchanged one asset (cash of $1,000) for another asset of equal value (a note receivable of $1,000).[4]

The following entry would be made by Sutton:

    Cash 1,000
        Notes payable   1,000

This entry indicates that Sutton has incurred a liability (a note payable of $1,000) in order to obtain an asset (cash of $1,000).

Accrual of Interest

Interest is the cost of borrowing to the maker of the note or, from the payee's (lender's) viewpoint, the income which is earned. In the example, Davis' earnings during the month of May would be calculated as follows:

$$\$1,000 \times .18 \times \tfrac{1}{12} = \$15$$

If Davis wished to accrue the interest earned during the month of May, (i.e., record it on his books) the following entry would be necessary:

    Interest receivable 15
        Interest earned   15

This entry recognizes the fact that Davis' assets have increased by $15 because of the interest earned during the month of May. This entry would be necessary only if Davis prepares financial statements as of the end of May.

If Sutton wished to record the interest expense incurred during May, the following entry would be required:

    Interest expense 15
        Interest payable   15

This entry recognizes that Sutton has incurred an expense of $15 for the use of the money borrowed from Davis for the month of May. Again, an entry is necessary only if financial statements are prepared as of the end of May.

Payment of the Note

On July 1, 19x1, the maturity date of the note, it becomes due and payable. As previously indicated, the interest for the two-month period was:

$$\$1,000 \times .18 \times \tfrac{2}{12} = \$30$$

The maturity value, (i.e., the total amount that Sutton should pay to Davis), is $1,000 plus $30 or $1,030. Since we have assumed that Davis had

---

[4] In some instances, a note may be taken in settlement of an open account receivable (dr. note receivable, cr. accounts receivable) or at the time of sale (dr. notes receivable, cr. sales). Except for the initial entry, these circumstances do not change the accounting or recording considerations illustrated and discussed.

previously recorded or accrued the $15 of interest earned during the month of May, the entry which would be required on Davis' books in order to record the receipt of the $1,030 from Sutton at the maturity date of the note would be as follows:

```
Cash ............................  1,030
    Notes receivable ................        1,000
    Interest receivable ..............           15
    Interest earned ..................           15
```

Analyzing this entry, the debit to cash of $1,030 records the total proceeds of the note (i.e., its maturity value). This maturity value includes both the principal amount and the total interest earned by Davis during the two-month period that he held the note. The credit to notes receivable removes the note balance from Davis' books since it has been paid at maturity. The credit of $15 to interest receivable eliminates the receivable which had been set up at the end of May when Davis accrued the interest earned for that month. The $15 credit to interest earned is made in order to record the interest income on the note for the month of June.

The entry that would be required on Sutton's books to record the payment by Sutton to Davis would be:

```
Notes payable .....................  1,000
Interest payable ...................     15
Interest expense ..................      15
    Cash ..........................        1,030
```

The debit to notes payable of $1,000 removes the note balance from Sutton's books since it has been paid at maturity. The debit to interest payable of $15 eliminates the payable which had been recorded at the end of May when Sutton accrued the interest expense for the month. The $15 debit to interest expense is made to record the interest expense for June. The credit to cash of $1,030 records the payment of the maturity value of the note (i.e., principal and interest) by Sutton.

Dishonored Note

If Sutton had not paid the note at maturity, the note would be said to be dishonored. Of course, Davis would continue his efforts to collect the amount due him and Sutton would still be liable for his obligation. In the event that the note was not paid at maturity, Davis would make an entry to remove the note from the notes receivable account as follows:

```
Receivable from dishonored note ......  1,030
    Notes receivable ................        1,000
    Interest receivable ..............           15
    Interest earned ..................           15
```

This entry would remove the note from the notes receivable account and place it in a separate receivable classification—receivable from dishonored notes. If Sutton subsequently pays the note, Davis would record the receipt by debiting cash and crediting "receivable from dishonored note." If Davis is unable to collect the $1,030 from Sutton, he would eventually write-off the receivable as an uncollectible account against the allowance for bad debts account.

Notes Issued at a Discount

In some circumstances, the interest on notes is deducted in advance (i.e., at the time the note is issued). The difference between the amount due at maturity and the amount loaned is classified as unearned interest at the date of issuance on the books of the lender. As the note matures, this unearned interest is earned and is reclassified as interest income. For example, assume that on November 1, 19x1, Wynn Company borrows $1,000 from Osteen Company on a three-month note with an 18 percent rate of interest. The entry made on November 1, 19x1, by Osteen Company to record the loan of $955 [$1,000 − ($1,000 × .18 × $3/12$)] would be as follows:

```
Notes receivable.....................  1,000
    Unearned interest..................            45
    Cash...............................           955
```

Wynn Company would record the transaction with the following entry:

```
Cash...............................    955
Discount on notes payable .............  45
    Notes payable.....................         1,000
```

Since interest accrues over time, the $45 which is shown as a discount on notes payable at the date the note is issued is not interest expense at that point in time. The actual net liability to Osteen at the date of the loan is equal to the amount of cash received, or $955. Therefore, a balance sheet prepared at the time of the loan would include discount on notes payable as a contra-liability deducted from notes payable as follows:

```
Notes payable .............................  $1,000
Less:  Discount on notes payable ..............   (45)
                                              $  955
```

At December 31, the following adjusting entry is necessary in order for Osteen to record the interest earned of $30 ($1,000 × .18 × $2/12$) for the months of November and December:

```
Unearned interest .........................   30
    Interest income .........................         30
```

Wynn Company would record its interest expense for the two month period with the following adjusting entry:

  Interest expense 30
    Discount on notes payable   30

At December 31, Wynn Company's liability would appear in its balance sheet as follows:

  Notes payable $1,000
  Less: Discount on notes payable .... (15)
                      $ 985

Note that the original amount of $45 in the discount on notes payable has been reduced by $30 (interest expense for the months of November and December) to $15 (which represents the amount to be charged to interest expense in January).

When the note matures and is paid, the entry to record the receipt is as follows:

  Cash 1,000
  Unearned interest 15
    Notes receivable   1,000
    Interest income   15

The total interest income earned on the note and recorded in the accounts is $45 ($30 in 19x1 and $15 in 19x2). Although a rate of 18 percent was used in determining the original discount on the note, the effective interest rate is actually 18.8 percent since the borrower paid $45 for the use of $955 (not $1,000) for a period of three months.

Wynn Company would make the following entry to record its payment:

  Notes payable 1,000
  Interest expense 15
    Cash   1,000
    Discount on notes payable   15

This entry records the payment of the note at maturity by Wynn and the interest expense for the month of January.

Discounting Notes Receivable Notes receivable are sometimes sold by the payee to a third party in order to obtain funds prior to the maturity date of a note. The process of selling a note in this manner is referred to as discounting a note. The payee endorses the note, delivers it to the purchaser (usually a bank) and receives his or her funds. The payee discounting the note is usually contingently liable on the note (i.e., he or she must pay the note at the maturity if the maker fails to do so).

The calculation of the discount charged by the purchaser is somewhat similar to the calculation of interest:

$$\text{Maturity Value} \times \text{Discount Period} \times \text{Discount Rate} = \text{Discount}$$

As previously indicated, the maturity value is the total amount, both principle and interest, due at the maturity of a note. The discount period is the period of time from the date a note is discounted to the maturity date of the note. The discount rate is the rate charged by the purchaser to discount a note. The amount received by the payee, referred to as the proceeds of the note, is calculated as follows:

$$\text{Maturity Value} - \text{Discount} = \text{Proceeds}.$$

To illustrate the procedures which are involved in discounting a note, we will assume that *before* recording the interest earned for the month of May, Davis sold or discounted the Sutton note on May 31 and was charged a discount rate of 20 percent. The calculation of the amount of the discount and the net proceeds to Davis from the note would be as follows:

$$\$1,000 \times .18 \times 2/12 = \$30 \text{ (interest)}$$
$$\$1,000 + \$30 = \$1,030 \text{ (maturity value)}$$
$$\$1,030 \times .20 \times 1/12 = \$17.17 \text{ (discount)}$$
$$\$1,030 - \$17.17 = \$1,012.83 \text{ (proceeds)}$$

The discounting of the note will be recorded in the accounts by Davis as follows:

Cash..............................	1,012.83	
Interest expense	2.17	
Interest revenue		15.00
Notes receivable discounted		1,000.00

The debit of $1,012.83 to cash records the proceeds received from the sale of the note. The charge to interest expense of $2.17 was calculated as follows:

Principal...............................		$1,000.00
Interest earning during May		15.00
Book value of the note at the date of sale		$1,015.00
Principal...............................	$1,000.00	
Total interest for the note to maturity	30.00	
Maturity value of the note	$1,030.00	
Discount	17.17	
Net proceeds...........................		1,012.83
Interest expense		$ 2.17

As the above calculation indicates, interest expense represents the difference between the cash proceeds and the total of the: (1) face or principal amount of the note, and (2) interest earned up to the date the note was discounted.[5] The credit to interest receivable removes the interest which had been previously accrued at the end of May from the accounts. It should be noted that the credit in the entry is to notes receivable *discounted*, rather than to notes receivable. The credit to notes receivable discounted indicates that Davis is contingently liable for the note (i.e., in the event that Sutton fails to pay the note at maturity, Davis must pay it). On Davis' balance sheet the notes receivable would appear as follows:

Cash		$10,000
Notes receivable	$1,000	
Less: Notes receivable discounted	1,000	0
Other assets		50,000
Total assets		$60,000

Offsetting the notes receivable discounted account against the notes receivable account discloses the contingent liability of Davis with regard to the Sutton note. An alternative to this presentation would be to disclose the contingent liability by means of a footnote to the balance sheet. Such a footnote might be worded as follows: "Davis is contingently liable for notes receivable discounted in the amount of $1,000."

If Sutton pays the note at its maturity, Davis would be notified of this payment and the following entry would be made on Davis' books:

Notes receivable discounted	1,000	
Notes receivable		1,000

By removing both the notes receivable discounted and the notes receivable balances from the accounts, the effect of this entry is to recognize the fact that the contingent liability for the note no longer exists.

If Sutton fails to pay the note at maturity, Davis' *contingent* liability becomes a *real* liability that he must now pay. He would recognize this fact by the same entry as that which was made above:

Notes receivable discounted	1,000	
Notes receivable		1,000

---

[5] Had the discount rate been 10 percent, the entry would have been as follows:

Cash	1,021.42	
Notes receivable discounted		1,000.00
Interest revenue		21.42

In this instance, the credit of $21.42 to interest income represents the excess of the proceeds over the principal amount of the note including the interest of $15.00 earned in May.

It should be noted that both the contingent liability and the notes receivable balance are removed from the books at the maturity date of the note whether or not it is paid by the maker. If it is paid, that is all that is required—no further action on the part of Davis is necessary. If it is not paid, Davis must pay the full amount due (principal plus interest, or full maturity value) to the holder of the note. This payment would be recorded as follows:

Receivable from dishonored note	1,030	
Cash		1,030

Davis would then attempt to recover the $1,030 from Sutton.

STATEMENT PRESENTATION OF RECEIVABLES

Receivables are classified first according to their form: notes receivable and accounts receivable. Generally, those which are expected to be converted into cash within a year are classified as current assets while those which will be realized in subsequent periods are included in a noncurrent category. Any interest receivable from interest-bearing notes will also be classified according to the timing of its expected collection. The income from interest appears on the income statement, usually as an addition to net income from operations, as follows:

Davis Company
Income Statement
For the Year Ended December 31, 19x1

Sales	$100,000
Cost of sales	60,000
Gross profit on sales	$ 40,000
Expenses	25,000
Income from operations	$ 15,000
Other income:	
Interest income	100
Net income	$ 15,100

If there are receivables from sources other than normal operations, such as from officers, employees, affiliated companies, etc., these would be shown as separate items rather than included as a part of regular accounts or notes receivable in the balance sheet.

According to *FASB Statement No. 105*, "Disclosure of Information about Financial Instruments with Off-Balance-Sheet Risk and Financial Instruments with Concentrations of Credit Risk," disclosures pertaining to significant concentrations of credit risk for a company's accounts receivable are required. Such concentrations of credit risk may exist if a number of the company's customers are engaged in similar activities, are located in the same geographical area, and have similar economic characteristics. Such a circumstance may cause their ability to pay their debts to be affected similarly by changes in economic or other conditions (e.g., government regulations).

PAYROLL ACCOUNTING

An employer incurs certain liabilities to the federal and state governments for taxes related to its payroll—both for the taxes levied on the business itself and for taxes withheld from the earnings of its employees. The employer may also deduct from employees' salaries and wages amounts withheld for such items as union dues, insurance premiums, pension plans, and investment plans.

An employer incurs a number of liabilities relating to state and federal payroll taxes. These include the following taxes:

1. Federal old-age, survivors, disability, and hospital insurance (Social Security).
2. Federal unemployment insurance.
3. State unemployment insurance.
4. Income taxes withheld.

Social Security Taxes. The Federal Insurance Contributions Act (FICA) imposes equal taxes on both employers and employees. This act provides for old age, disability, hospitalization, and survivors' benefits for qualified employees and members of their families. The tax rate is applied to the employee's gross wages up to a designated maximum. Both the rate and the maximum earnings to which the tax is applied have been increased frequently over the years. The rate for 1993 for social security is 6.2 percent of the initial $57,600 of salaries and wages paid to each employee. The rate for 1993 for Medicare is 1.45 percent of the initial $135,000 of salaries and wages paid to each employee. The employee's share of this tax is withheld from the wage payment, and employers periodically remit the amounts withheld together with the amounts matched by the employer.

Federal Unemployment Tax. The Federal Unemployment Tax Act (FUTA) provides for a system of unemployment insurance with joint participation of the federal and state governments. Employers are also required to pay state and federal unemployment taxes for their employees. No tax is levied on the employee. Under current provisions, the federal rate is currently 6.2 percent of the initial $7,000 in salaries and wages paid to each employee during the year. However, the employer is allowed a 5.4 percent credit against the federal unemployment tax for paying on time and for state unemployment tax payments, bringing the rate down to 0.8 percent.

State Unemployment Tax. The provisions of the unemployment programs of the various states differ in certain respects. All states levy a payroll tax on employers and a few states levy a tax on employees as well. The basic rate in most states is 2.7 percent of the first $9,000 in salaries and wages paid to each employee.

Income Tax Withholding. Employers of one or more persons are required to withhold income taxes from their employees and remit these withholdings to the federal government. A number of states and cities also levy income taxes which are required to be withheld by the employer from the earnings of the employees. The amounts to be withheld by the employer may be computed by formulas provided by the law or from tax withholding tables made available by the government. The federal income tax withheld and the FICA taxes (both employer's and employee's shares) are remitted to the federal government at regular intervals.

Recording the Payroll. To illustrate the accounting for wages and salaries and the related taxes, assume that the gross salaries of a small business total $10,000 for the month of January. Assume that the FICA rate is 6.2 percent for the employer and employee, and that the state unemployment tax is 2.7 percent of gross salaries. The rate for Medicare is 1.45 percent. The federal unemployment tax (net of the credit for state unemployment taxes) is .8 percent, and federal income taxes withheld for the month total $710. The employer's taxes would be computed as follows:

FICA (.062 × $10,000)	$ 620
Medicare (.0145 × $10,000)	145
State unemployment (.027 × $10,000)	270
FUTA (.008 × $10,000)	80
Total employer's taxes	$1,115

The cash paid to employees would be:

Salaries earned		$10,000
Withholding:		
FICA	$620	
Medicare	145	
Income taxes	710	1,475
Net amount paid to employees		$ 8,525

The journal entries to record the payroll and the employer's payroll taxes follow:

Payroll tax expense	$1,115	
FICA taxes payable		$ 620
Medicare payable		145
State unemployment taxes payable		270
Federal unemployment taxes payable		80
Salaries expense	10,000	
FICA taxes payable		620
Medicare payable		145
Income taxes payable		710
Cash		8,525

The liabilities recorded in the above entries are eliminated when the employer remits the taxes to the appropriate governmental units.

SUMMARY

The proper recording and controlling of cash receipts and disbursements is a concern common to all firms. Certain basic control procedures must be followed to eliminate the probability that cash will be lost or misappropriated. Control procedures applicable to the receipt of cash include preparing a complete record immediately upon the receipt of cash, depositing the cash intact in the company's bank on a daily basis, and involving more than one employee in the handling and recording of cash transactions. In addition, employees involved in handling cash receipts should not also be authorized to make cash disbursements. Cash disbursement control measures include using pre-numbered checks to make payments for all items not paid for from petty cash, supporting each disbursement with an invoice or voucher, and having an employee that does not make cash disbursements reconcile the bank statement at frequent intervals.

Receivables are assets representing the claims that a business has against others. The two principal forms of receivables are accounts receivable and notes receivable. Accounts receivable generally arise from a company's normal course of trade or business and are normally not supported by formal written promises to pay. Notes receivable, on the other hand, are claims that are supported by formal written promises to pay.

Liabilities are claims against the business by its creditors. As such, they represent obligations which must be discharged at some future date. Current liabilities are those obligations which must be discharged within the operating cycle of the firm or one year, whichever is longer. The two major types of current liabilities are accounts payable that arise from transactions with trade creditors and short-term notes payable. A note payable is supported by a written promise to pay and requires the accrual and payment of interest.

Accounting for receivables requires the use of both a control account and individual subsidiary accounts. At the end of a period, the total of the subsidiary balances should equal the balance in the control account. In addition, bad debt expense must be estimated for each period to match this cost of selling on a credit basis with the appropriate revenues. Two common methods of estimating the bad debt expense (often used in combination) are: (1) the use of a percentage based on the firm's past credit sales, and (2) the analysis of the receivables balance at the end of the period. An allowance for bad debts account is used to record and report the resulting offset to accounts receivable.

Accounting procedures for notes receivable include recording the initial issuance of the note at either face or discounted value, accruing the interest income earned on the note, and recording the collection of the principal and interest. In addition, firms may wish to sell notes receivable to a third party to obtain funds prior to the maturity dates of the notes. This process is referred to as discounting the notes. Generally the firm discounting the note is contingently liable if the maker fails to pay it at maturity.

Receivables are classified on the balance sheet as accounts receivable or notes receivable and according to their status as current or noncurrent assets. Current receivables are those that are expected to be converted into cash within a year.

KEY DEFINITIONS

Accounts receivable—receivables not supported by formal or written promises to pay.

Accrued interest expense—interest that has been incurred on a note payable but not paid.

Aging of accounts receivable—the process of classifying accounts according to the period of time that the accounts have been outstanding.

Allowance for bad debts—a contra account to accounts receivable that reflects the portion of the total dollar amount of accounts receivable that is expected to be uncollectible.

Bad debt expense—the expense that occurs from customers' failure to pay debts to the firm.

Balance per bank statement—this balance is the amount in the cash account of the business according to the bank's records.

Balance per books—this amount is the balance in the cash account according to the firm's records.

Bank reconciliation—an analysis made to identify and account for all items which cause differences between the cash balance as shown on the bank statement and the cash balance as it appears in the firm's accounting records.

Cash—consists of currency, coins, checks, and certain other forms of negotiable paper.

Cash disbursement—an outlay of cash made by the firm.

Cash over and short—an account which is credited for any cash overages and debited for any cash shortages. The net balance in this account at the end of a period is treated as miscellaneous revenue or expense.

Cash receipt—an inflow of cash into the firm.

Cash transaction—an accounting transaction that involves either a cash receipt or a cash disbursement.

Charge sales—sales in which the firm provides a customer with goods or services in exchange for the customer's promise to pay at a later date.

Contingent liability—an amount which may become a liability at some future date, depending on the occurrence of some future event. For example, the payee who discounts a note is contingently liable if the maker of the note fails to pay it at maturity.

Contra account—an account which is offset against or deducted from another account in the financial statements.

"Control" account—used to record the total charge sales and the total payments which are received from customers.

Credit memorandum—this memorandum is an addition which is made by the bank to a depositor's account. The addition arises from a transaction other than a normal deposit.

Current liability—current debts of a firm which must be paid within the operating cycle of the firm or one year, whichever is longer.

Debit memorandum—this memorandum is a deduction which is made by the bank from a depositor's account. The deduction arises from a transaction other than the normal payment of a check by the bank.

Deposit in transit—this deposit is a receipt which has been included in the cash balance per books and deposited in the bank, but not yet processed by the bank and credited to the depositor's account.

Discount (D)—the charge made by the purchaser of a note prior to its maturity (MV x DR x DP = D).

Discount period (DP)—the period from the date a note is discounted until its maturity.

Discount rate (DR)—the rate charged to discount a note. This percentage is expressed in an annual rate and is used to calculate a discount.

Discounting—the sale of a note by the payee prior to its maturity date.

Discounted note—on discounted notes payable, the interest is deducted from the maturity value of the note at the time the note is issued.

Dishonored notes receivable—notes which are not paid at their maturity.

Effective interest rate—the actual rate of interest that the issuing corporation pays on the bond as evidenced by the relationship between the periodic interest payment and the issue price of the bonds.

Interest expense (I)—the cost to the borrower of borrowing funds (P x R x T = I).

Interest income—the income to the lender from the lending of funds (P x R x T = I).

Interest receivable—interest earned but not yet received.

Liability—an obligation which arises from a past transaction and which is to be discharged at a future date by the transfer of assets or the performance of services.

Maker—the borrower of funds on a note receivable.

Maturity date—the date a note becomes due and payable.

Maturity value (MV)—the value of a note at its maturity (i.e., principal plus interest).

Note payable—represents a written promise to pay a definite amount of money on demand or at some specified future date to the holder of the note.

Note receivable—a receivable supported by a formal or written promise to pay.

Outstanding check—this is a check which has been issued by the business but not yet presented to the bank for payment.

Over-the-counter sales—these sales are consummated by the immediate payment of cash for the goods or services purchased.

Payee—the lender of funds on a note receivable.

Petty cash fund—a fund established to make cash disbursements for small expenditures.

Petty cash voucher—this voucher is an authorization to disburse cash from the petty cash fund and is usually retained as a receipt for the expenditure.

Principal (P)—the face amount of a note receivable.

Proceeds—the net amount received by a payee selling or discounting a note prior to its maturity. Maturity value less discount equals proceeds.

Rate (R)—the percentage usually expressed as an annual rate used to calculate interest.

Receivable—an asset representing the claim that a firm has against others.

Receivable from dishonored note—this receivable is equal to the maturity value of a note arising from the failure of the maker to pay it at maturity.

Time (T)—the period usually expressed in years or a fraction thereof used to calculate interest. It is normal to assume a 360-day year when calculating simple interest.

True cash—the amount of cash that is actually available to the entity. One format for the bank reconciliation statement adjusts both the book and bank balances to true cash.

QUESTIONS

1. Why is control over cash transactions considered to be more important than control over the other assets of a business?

2. List a few basic principles in connection with cash control. You may wish to organize your discussion along the line of the normal cash flow.

3. What are the principal advantages of maintaining a separation of duties involving cash transactions?

4. In order to establish control over the cash receipts from over the counter sales, a small firm installs a cash register with each sales clerk responsible for ringing up his or her own sales. Discuss.

5. List some procedures other than separation of duties which may be employed in order to establish effective control over cash disbursements.

6. What is the purpose of a bank reconciliation statement?

7. What are the necessary adjustments in the bank reconciliation statement to the balance per the bank statement? To the balance per the books?

8. The petty cash account has a debit balance of $300. At the end of the accounting period there is $35 in the petty cash fund along with petty cash vouchers totaling $265. Should the fund be replenished as of the last day of the period? Discuss.

9. What are some of the steps necessary to achieve effective control over cash disbursements?

10. Compare and contrast accounts receivable and notes receivable.

11. Distinguish between current and long-term liabilities.

12. Why is control over receivables important? How can control be achieved?

13. Explain how the control account, accounts receivable, is related to the individual subsidiary ledger accounts. What could make the two be out of balance?

14. Theoretically, when should a firm cease to grant credit to its customers?

15. Another method for handling bad debt expense—called the direct write-off method—is to wait until the account is known to be uncollectible. The journal entry then is a debit to bad debt expense and a credit to accounts receivable. Compare and contrast this with the allowance method. Which method is theoretically correct? Why?

16. What accounting principle does the allowance method rest upon?

17. What are the two methods for estimating bad debts?

18. Could an allowance method be used with notes receivable? Would it be feasible?

19. What is the entry to increase Allowance for Bad Debts? To decrease it?

20. Suppose an account is written off as uncollectible, but later the customer remits payment. What would the entry be?

21. Calculate the interest on a $10,000, 6-month note, with interest at 6 percent.

22. What adjusting entries may be required with regard to notes receivable at the end of the period?

23. Smith Co. borrowed $5,000 from the bank and signed a 60-day, 6 percent note dated June 1. (1) What is the face amount of the note? (2) What is the amount of interest on the note? (3) What is the maturity value of the note?

24. What is the nature of the notes receivable discounted account?

25. Why is an entry on the books of the payee necessary whether or not a discounted note is paid by the maker at maturity?

26. Explain how the proceeds from the discounting of a note receivable are calculated.

EXERCISES

27. State whether the following bank reconciliation items would need an adjusting or correcting entry on the *depositor's* books:

   a. Checks totaling $1,850 were issued by the depositor but not paid by the bank.
   b. A $1,000 note was collected for the depositor by the bank and was deposited in his account. Notice was sent to the depositor with the bank statement.
   c. The last day's receipts ($1,750) for the month were not recorded as a deposit by the bank until the following month.
   d. The depositor issued a check for $180 but entered it in his records as $810.
   e. The bank paid a check for $150 but entered it as $510 on their records.
   f. The bank charged a bad check that it received in a deposit back against the depositor's account. Notice to the depositor was made by the bank with the bank statement.
   g. The bank charged $21 for service charges and notified the depositor with the bank statement.
   h. The bank had erroneously charged a check, drawn by another depositor with a similar name, to the depositor's account.

28. Prepare the journal entries that are necessary to adjust the cash account on the depositor's books, based on the information included in Exercise 27 above.

29. The following information is taken from the books and records of the Terp Company.

Balance per the cash account (before adjustment)...	$2,860
Outstanding checks............................	820
Deposit in transit..............................	208
Bank service charges..........................	18
Cash on hand—unrecorded on the books and not yet deposited in the bank.................	180
Balance per the bank statement.................	unavailable

Required:

Prepare a bank reconciliation showing the "true" cash balance.

30. Prepare, in general journal form, the entries that Terp Company should make to adjust its cash balance as a result of the bank reconciliation in Exercise 29 above.

31. Test the accuracy of Willard Company's cash receipts records for August given the following information:

Total cash receipts as shown in the firm's records were $14,910.
Payment of $1,110 was received on August 31 but the deposit was not yet recorded by the bank.
Total deposits included in the August bank statement were $14,700.
Deposit in transit at end of July was $900.

32. The Gibbons Company reconciles its one bank account on a monthly basis. The company follows the procedure of reconciling the balance as reported on the bank statement and the balance per books *to a corrected balance.* The corrected balance appears on the balance sheet.

The facts stated in items 1 through 10 below are involved in a reconciliation for the month of December. Decide which of the five answer choices best indicates how each fact should be handled in the December 31 bank reconciliation.

Answer choices for items 1 through 9:

(1) An addition to the balance per books.
(2) A deduction from the balance per books.
(3) An addition to the balance per bank.
(4) A deduction from the balance per bank.
(5) Should not appear in the reconciliation.

1. A deposit of $100 made on December 31 did not appear in the December bank statement.................... (3)
2. A deposit of $130 made on November 30 was recorded by the bank on December 1.......................... (5)
3. Three checks totalling $180 drawn in December did not clear the bank................................... (4)
4. A check from customer Kay for $75 was returned by the bank marked N.S.F.............................. (2)
5. The bank statement was accompanied by a credit memo dated December 30 for the proceeds of a note ($198) which Gibbons Company had left with the bank for collection.. (1)
6. Gibbons Company discovered that a December check recorded in the check register as $150 was actually drawn for $105. This check was cleared by the bank in December... (1)
7. Two checks totalling $120 drawn in November had cleared the bank in December......................... (5)
8. Accompanying the December bank statement was a cancelled check for $60 of Gibson Company............... ( )
9. The bookkeeper of Gibbons Company had recorded a $90 check received from customer Fay on December 29 as $190... (2)
10. Which of the facts disclosed in items 1 through 9 above require adjusting entries on the books of the Gibbons Company?

(1) 1, 3, 8   (2) 6, 8, 9
(3) 1, 2, 3, 7   (4) 4, 5, 6, 9
(5) Some other group

33. Show in general journal form all entries that should be made to reflect the operation of the Eljon Corporation's petty cash fund.

May 10 The company established a petty cash fund of $225.
    12 Paid miscellaneous office expenses amounting to $52.
    14 Paid $15 to messengers for cab fares.
    19 Paid telephone bill of $63.
    25 Paid $21 in postage.
    30 The petty cash fund was reimbursed for the first time.
    31 Eljon Corporation increased its petty cash fund to $300.

8 | Cash, Receivables, and Current Liabilities 8-45

34. Determine the "true cash" balance after the following adjustments or corrections have been made to the Cash account. The cash balance per books was $3,650. (Use a T-account to do this.)

   a. A deposit in transit at the end of the period was $350.
   b. Check #501 for $89 was still outstanding at the end of the period.
   c. An account receivable of $110 was collected by the bank.
   d. The service charge for the period was $47.
   e. Check #101 for $680 which had been outstanding for 10 years was cancelled.
   f. The bank paid $20 more on Check #509 than was written on the face of the check.
   g. Check #513 was incorrectly entered in the books by the bookkeeper for $315 instead of $513.
   h. A stop payment was placed on Check #507 for $265.

35. By reviewing their past credit experience, Brown Company estimated that its losses from uncollectible accounts would be three percent of credit sales for 19x1. Sales for 19x1 amounted to $360,000, of which $100,000 were in cash. Make the entry recording bad debt expense for the year in the books of the Brown Company.

36. Based on an aging of receivables, Blue Company estimated doubtful accounts to be a total of $5,000. Give the adjusting entry for bad debts under each of the following independent situations:

   a. The Allowance for Bad Debts has a zero balance.
   b. The Allowance for Bad Debts has a debit balance of $400.
   c. The Allowance for Bad Debts has a credit balance of $700.

37. Bobby Mitchell's 6%, 60-day note for $600 (principal amount) was discounted by the Washington Deadskunks to the Second National Bank after it was held for 30 days. The Deadskunks received $603.96 as proceeds from the sale.

   Required:

   1. Calculate the discount rate on the sale.
   2. Prepare the journal entry to record the sale of the note on the books of the Washington Deadskunks.
   3. Prepare the entry necessary if Mitchell fails to pay the note at maturity.

38. On February 1, 19x1, Alex Grammas borrowed $700 from Vic Wertz and signed a note in evidence of the loan. Grammas agreed to pay Wertz $700 plus 10 percent interest on August 31, 19x1. Wertz's accounting period ends June 30. Make all entries related to the note on the books of Wertz (assume Grammas does not default on payment).

39. Dallas Company discounted three separate notes receivable at a bank on August 1, 19x1. Each note is in the amount of $1,000. The bank charged a discount rate of 10 percent. Compute the proceeds of each note from the following data.

	Date Note Received	Interest Rate	Life of Note
1.	July 1	8%	3 months
2.	June 1	6%	6 months
3.	July 15	9%	1 month

40. Give the journal entries to record the following transactions:

Mar. 15 Accepted a $2,000, 3-month, 10% note from Bob Hanson in settlement of a past due account.
Apr. 15 Discounted the Hanson note at the bank at a discount rate of 12%.
June 15 Received notice from the bank that the Hanson note was in default. Paid the bank the maturity value of the note.
July 15 Received a check from Hanson for the maturity value of the note plus 10% interest on the maturity value of the note for the 30-day period subsequent to maturity.

41. Determine the maturity value of the following notes receivable held by Staubach Company.

a. $1,000 principal, 4 percent interest, matures in 6 months.
b. $ 800 principal, 7 percent interest, matures in 60 days.
c. $ 600 principal, 3 percent interest, matures in 100 days.
d. $ 500 principal, 5 percent interest, matures in 1 month.
e. $ 900 principal, 6 percent interest, matures in 3 months.
f. $ 200 principal, 7 percent interest, matures in 30 days.
g. $ 400 principal, 4 percent interest, matures in 10 days.

42. The Dorsett Company borrowed $500 from the Pearson Company and issued a note at an 8 percent rate of interest. The interest was deducted in advance and the note was issued on October 1, 19x1 and matures February 1, 19x2. Make the necessary journal entries on Pearson Company's books for the date of issuance, December 31, 19x1, and the maturity date.

43. Prepare the necessary journal entries in Henderson's books for the following events.

a. On March 1, Sam Donaldson agreed to pay David Henderson $2,000 plus 7 percent interest on August 1.
b. Henderson accrued interest earned on June 30 for the months of March, April, May, and June.
c. Donaldson did not pay the note at maturity.

44. Prepare the necessary journal entries in Martin's books for the following events.

   a. Mike Mason purchased merchandise on credit from Martin's Retail Outlet for $150.
   b. Mason's account proves to be uncollectible. (Assume an allowance for bad debts account already exists.)
   c. Mason's account was subsequently collected.

45. Determine the interest on each of the following notes:

	Face Amount	Interest Rate	Days to Maturity
a.	$1,000	6%	60
b.	$5,000	8%	90
c.	$4,000	4%	180
d.	$2,500	5%	36

46. On December 1, King, Inc. issued a 90-day, 6 percent note for $3,000 to Miller Co. to replace an account payable. Give the journal entries necessary to record the following on the books of King, Inc.

   a. Issuance of the note by King, Inc.
   b. Adjusting entry on December 31.
   c. Payment of the note at maturity.

47. Assume that Richardson Company borrows $1,500 on a 6-month note bearing a 9 percent rate of discount. Three months later, the company closes its books. In the next accounting period, the note matures and is paid by Richardson Company. Prepare the necessary journal entries for Richardson Company related to this note.

48. Thompson Co. issues a 180-day, non-interest-bearing note for $10,000 to First National Bank on May 1. The bank discounts the note at 8 percent. Give the necessary journal entries for Thompson Co. to record the issuance of the note and the payment of the note at maturity.

49. On May 1, 19x1, the Bucks Company borrowed $600 on a 120-day note payable bearing an interest rate of 7 percent. This note was used to purchase equipment costing $1,000; the balance of which was paid in cash. On June 15, the company borrowed $800 on a non-interest-bearing 90-day note with a discount rate of 7 percent. The proceeds from the note were used entirely to pay for office supplies. The Bucks Company closes its year on June 30.

Required:

Give journal entries to record the issuance of the loans, adjusting entries on June 30, 19x1, and entries to record their payments when due.

PROBLEMS

50. Red, Inc.'s bank statement for the month ending June 30 shows a balance of $231. The cash account as of the close of business on June 30 indicates a credit balance or overdraft of $123. In reconciling the balances, the auditor discovers the following:

> Receipts on June 30 of $1,860 were not deposited until July 1.
> Checks outstanding on June 30 were $2,215.
> The bank has charged the depositor $10 for service charges.
> A check payable to S.S. Dohr for $56 was entered in Red's cash payments journal in error as $65.

Required:

Prepare a bank reconciliation.

51. The following refers to Ginger's Floral Shop:

a. Prepare a bank reconciliation showing the "true" cash balance for July 31 given the following information:

1. Balance per bank statement at July 31, $4,610.
2. Balance per books at July 31, $3,900.
3. Deposits in transit not recorded by banks, $445.
4. Bank error, check drawn by the Ginger Bread Shop debited to account of Ginger's Floral Shop, $20.
5. Note collected by bank, $1,025.
6. Debit memorandum for bank charges, $10.
7. N.S.F. check returned by bank, $35.
8. Accountants credited cash account for $175 rather than the correct figure of $100 in recording check #55.
9. Outstanding checks of $120 on July 31.

b. Prepare the adjusting or correcting entries required.

52. You have been engaged to audit the Able Company. In the course of your examination, you gather the following information:

a. Balance per cash account, July 31, 19x1, $2,750.
b. Bank service charges for the month included as a debit memo with the bank statement, $22.
c. Outstanding checks at June 30, $195.
d. Deposits received on July 31 and sent to bank but not yet recorded by bank, $216.
e. Checks written in month of June and returned with July statement, $135.
f. Checks written in July but not returned with July 31 bank statement, $535.

Required:

Compute the balance reported on July 31, 19x1 bank statement.

53. In connection with an examination of the cash account you are given the following worksheet:

Bank Reconciliation
December 31, 19x1

Balance per books at December 31, 19x1.............		$17,174.86
Add: Collections received on the last day of December and charged to "cash in bank" on books but not deposited..........		2,662.25
Debit memo for customer's check returned unpaid (check is on hand but no entry has been made on the books).......		200.00
Debit memo for bank service charge for December............................		5.50
		$20,142.61
Less: Checks drawn but not paid by bank (see detailed list below)....................	$2,267.75	
Credit memo for proceeds of a note receivable which had been left at the bank for collection but which has not been recorded as collected.................	400.00	
Check for an account payable entered on books as $240.90 but drawn and paid by bank as $419.....................	178.10	2,945.85
Computed balance...............................		$17,196.76
Unlocated difference.............................		200.00
Balance per bank................................		$16,996.76

Checks Drawn but Not Paid by Bank

No.	Amount
573.............................	$ 67.27
724.............................	9.90
903.............................	456.67
907.............................	305.50
911.............................	482.75
913.............................	550.00
914.............................	366.76
916.............................	10.00
917.............................	218.90
	$2,267.75

Required:

1. Prepare a corrected reconciliation.
2. Prepare journal entries for items which should be adjusted prior to closing the books.

(AICPA adapted)

54. The Backward Company decided to create a petty cash fund because of the increase in small cash disbursements such as supplies and postage. The following transactions took place in the month of May.

Postage.............................	$13
Delivery costs......................	9
Supplies	25
Tapes for recorder..................	3

The petty cash fund was established at $300 on May 1. It was replenished on May 30 and then increased by $50 on May 31.

Required:

Prepare all journal entries related to the petty cash fund for the month of May.

55. The Medich Company's petty cash fund for the first month of operations was as follows:

a. $1,000 was placed in the fund on April 1.
b. Petty cash record for April:

	April 1-15	April 16-30
Postage...........................	$ 50	$ 60
Supplies	400	600
Miscellaneous expenses............	90	70
Total...........................	$540	$730

c. On April 16 the fund was replenished.
d. On April 30 the fund was replenished and decreased by $100.

Required:

Prepare all entries.

56. The Ellis Company's bank reconciliation at March 31 was as follows:

Balance per bank statement...................	$7,000
Deposits outstanding.......................	400
Checks outstanding.........................	(75)
	$7,325
Balance per books..........................	$7,332
Unrecorded service charge..................	(7)
	$7,325

April data are as follows:

	Bank	Books
Checks recorded.........................	$5,750	$5,900
Deposits recorded.......................	5,050	5,500
Service charges recorded................	6	7
Collection by bank.....................	410	0
N.S.F. check returned..................	25	0
Balances April 30......................	6,679	6,925

Required:

1. What are the amounts of the unrecorded deposits and outstanding checks at April 30?
2. Prepare a bank reconciliation for April.
3. Prepare the needed entries at April 30.

57. The balance reported on the bank statement of Harrah Corporation on April 30, 19x1 was $65,978.40. The bookkeeper found the following by comparing the bank and the book balances:

   a. Checks totaling $10,798.50 had not cleared the bank.
   b. A check was recorded in the books at $730 when the correct amount was $370. The check was for the purchase of office supplies.
   c. No entry was made in the books for an N.S.F. check of $210.
   d. The bank had not recorded a deposit of $2,432.
   e. $3 was charged for printing checks.

Required:

1. Determine the balance per books before any corrections or adjustments are made.
2. Prepare a bank reconciliation and any necessary journal entries.

58. Prepare a bank reconciliation for the May Company for September 30, 19x1.

   a. Book cash balance on September 30 was $230.80.
   b. On August 31 outstanding checks totaled $1,394.80. By September 30, only two of these checks had not cleared. Because of the amount of time it had been outstanding, one of the checks for $100 had a stop payment put on it. The other outstanding check was for $57.10.
   c. Checks drawn and still outstanding in September amount to $1,733.48 (assume this figure is correct).
   d. A check was written for $472, but was recorded as $652. It is among the outstanding checks at the end of September.
   e. The September service charge of $6.80 has not been recorded by the company.
   f. Receipts of $236.30 were deposited by mail on September 30.

g. The bank statement showed the collection of a note by the bank in the amount of $406.
h. Included in the checks accompanying the September bank statement was a check drawn by Moy Company but charged to May Company for $114.32.

59. Use the following data concerning King Company to prepare a bank reconciliation statement.

Balance per bank...................................	$10,500
Balance per books..................................	9,250
Deposit in transit...................................	1,015
Refund of cash for damaged material (not deposited)........	35
Outstanding checks.................................	175
Bank service charge................................	3
N.S.F. check received by bank from the Goodman Company (a customer).............................	62
Interest collected by the bank for King Company on a note receivable................................	1,111
$400 deposit from King Company recorded as $410 by bookkeeper.	

Hint: Watch for cash overage or shortage.

60. On December 31, 19x1, the accounting records of the Cavilier Sales Company showed a cash balance of $6,600. A review of its bank reconciliation as of that date disclosed that a deposit of $7,200 was in transit and that checks of $6,350 were outstanding. Cavilier's books showed cash receipts of $108,700 and cash disbursements of $115,250 during the year. The company's bank paid checks totaling $121,000 during 19x1. A deposit of $9,000 was in transit at the beginning of the year.

Required:

Reconstruct the December 31, 19x0 bank reconcilation of the Cavilier Sales Company.

61. The Patrick Company had poor internal control over its cash transactions. Information about its cash position at November 30, 19x1 was as follows:

The cash books showed a balance of $18,901.62, which included undeposited receipts. A credit of $100 on the bank's records did not appear on the books of the company. The balance per bank statement was $15,550. Outstanding checks were: No. 62 for $116.25, No. 183 for $150, No. 284 for $253.25, No. 8621 for $190.71, No. 8623 for $206.80, and No. 8632 for $145.28.

The cashier embezzled all undeposited receipts in excess of $3,794.41 and prepared the following reconciliation:

Balance, per books, November 30, 19x1..		$18,901.62
Add: Outstanding checks:		
8621.........................	$190.71	
8623.........................	206.80	
8632.........................	145.28	442.79
		$19,344.41
Less: Undeposited receipts............		3,794.41
Balance per bank, November 30, 19x1...		$15,550.00
Deduct: Unrecorded credit...........		100.00
True cash, November 30, 19x1..........		$15,450.00

Required:

1. Prepare a supporting schedule showing how much the cashier embezzled.
2. How did he attempt to conceal his theft?
3. Taking only the information given, name two specific features of internal control which were apparently missing.

(AICPA adapted)

62. When aging their accounts receivable, the Wingfoot Company drew up the following schedule:

Accounts Receivable Balance	Number of Days Outstanding			
	0-30	31-60	61-90	91 and older
$5,250	$3,450	$900	$650	$250
	Estimated % Uncollectible			
	1%	5%	15%	50%

Required:

Prepare a table calculating the estimated bad debt expense for the period and make the appropriate journal entry on the books of the Wingfoot Company, assuming that there is a credit balance of $100 in the Allowance for Bad Debts before adjustment.

63. During 19x1, Squeeze, Inc. had $800,000 of sales on credit. Also, during 19x1 the company wrote off $14,000 of accounts receivable as definitely uncollectible and collected $700 from individuals whose accounts had been written off during previous years. The company estimates its bad debts each year to be 2% of credit sales. On January 1, 19x1, the accounts receivable balance was $60,000. Collections on account for 19x1 totaled $775,000 and customers returned goods for credit in the amount of $20,000. The company offers no cash discounts. On December 31, 19x1, after all adjustments and accruals, accounts receivable net of the allowance for uncollectible accounts amounted to $45,400.

Required:

1. Prepare journal entries for *all* transactions during 19x1 involving accounts receivable and the related allowance account.
2. The balance in the allowance account at:

    a. January 1, 19x1.
    b. December 31, 19x1 (after all adjustments).

64. Charlie Tuna, owner of Tuna's Fish Wholesalers, has instructed his accountant, Jack D. Ripper, to make sure the Allowance for Bad Debts account is at least 10 percent of total accounts receivable at the end of each calendar year. The January 1, 19x1, balance in Allowance for Bad Debts is $10,000.

During 19x1, the following transactions took place:

Jan. 13   Notice was received that I.M. Acrook, who owed the company $4,000, was in bankruptcy and no payment could be expected.

May 13   Wheel & Deal, Inc. paid $14,000 applicable to its account which totaled $20,000. Its treasurer was last seen boarding a steamer for South America (with all the company's funds), so no other payments would be forthcoming.

July 10   Received a check for $2,000 from A. Lincoln whose account had been written off as uncollectible in 19x0.

Oct. 13   H.E. Asucker, a customer, notified Charlie that his partner had absconded with all the company funds. Asucker stated that their business had folded and he was unable to pay Charlie the $8,000 he owed him.

Dec. 31   The balance of accounts receivable, as of the close of today's business, was $200,000.

Required:

Prepare general journal entries to record the above transactions.

65. On January 1, 19x1, H.E. Asucker made a loan of $1,000 to S.H. Esacrook. Asucker accepted a one (1)-year, 6 percent note as evidence of this transaction. On July 1, 19x1, Asucker, in need of funds, sold (discounted) Esacrook's note to the Piggy Bank. Piggy charged a discount rate of 10 percent. On January 1, 19x2, Piggy notified Asucker that the note had not been paid by Esacrook. Asucker paid the note.

Required:

Prepare journal entries for H.E. Asucker to record all of the above information.

66. The Marrion Company purchases and sells merchandise on account. The following transactions occurred in 19x1.

Apr.	1	Sold $2,000 worth of merchandise to Jack Palmer on account.
May	17	Purchased $275 of merchandise from the Colonial Company on account.
June	1	Jack Palmer signed a 12 percent two-month note in payment on his account.
	15	Paid for merchandise purchased from Colonial Company.
July	15	Discounted Palmer's note at the Republic Bank. The discount rate was 18 percent.
Aug.	1	Palmer dishonors his note. Marrion Company pays the bank the required amount.

Required:

Prepare journal entries to record the above transactions on the books of Marrion Company.

67. Listed below are selected transactions of Eastern Company for a six-month period ending March 31, 19x1. Eastern's accounting period ends on December 31.

Oct.	1	Sold merchandise on account to Ed Jackson for $1,600. The terms of the sale were n/30.
Nov.	1	Loaned $4,000 to Roger Herman on a three-month, 10 percent note.
	5	Accepted a $1,600, 90-day, 10 percent note from Ed Jackson in settlement of his past due account.
Dec.	5	Discounted the Jackson note at 12 percent at the bank.
	15	Sold merchandise on account to Bill Martin for $400; the terms of the sale were n/30.
	31	Determined by aging of accounts receivable that a $6,500 credit balance in the allowance for bad debts is required. There was a $300 debit balance in the allowance account prior to an adjusting entry.
	31	Made an adjusting entry to record the accrued interest on the note receivable from Roger Herman.
Jan.	24	Determined that the account receivable from Bill Martin was uncollectible, and it was then written off.

Feb. 5 Received notice from the bank that the Jackson note was in default. Paid the bank the maturity value of the note plus a $10 protest fee.

Mar. 5 Collected from Jackson the maturity value of the dishonored note plus 10 percent interest on that amount since the date of default and the protest fee.

20 Full payment of $400 was received from Bill Martin on an account previously written off.

Required:

Prepare general journal entries to record the transactions and adjustments listed above.

68. Calculate the proceeds and the interest expense from discounting the notes described below.

a. A two-month, 8 percent, $1,500 note discounted one month before maturity at a 10 percent discount rate. One month of interest income had been recorded.

b. A four-month, 9 percent, $2,500 note discounted two months before maturity at a 12 percent discount rate. Two months of interest income had been recorded.

Refer to the Annual Report included in the front of the text.

69. Did the cash balance increase or decrease in the most recent year?

70. Where does the company receive most of its cash from?

71. What are the major cash out flows of the company?

72. What were the total collections from accounts and notes receivable during the most recent year, assuming that all sales were made on account?

73. Comparing the two years presented, what was the increase in current liabilities?

74. By how much did the allowance for bad debts change?

75. What is included in short-term borrowings in the current year?

Chapter 9 presents information relating to the determination and presentation of bonds payable and investments in corporate securities and the use of consolidated financial statements. Studying this chapter should enable you to:

1. Describe the various classes of bonds.
2. Explain the concepts of bond discount and bond premium and how they are handled for accounting purposes.
3. Record the early retirement of bonds, including either a gain or loss if applicable.
4. Identify the elements of cost of stocks and bonds purchased as investments.
5. Discuss the methods of accounting for long-term and temporary investments subsequent to acquisition.
6. Describe the criterion used to determine when to prepare consolidated financial statements.
7. Illustrate the procedures and necessary worksheet adjustments for preparing consolidated financial statements.
8. Differentiate between the purchase and pooling of interests methods in accounting for business combinations.

9

Long-Term Liabilities Investments, and Consolidated Financial Statements

INTRODUCTION *Long-term debt includes all obligations that exist because of a past transaction or event and that are not expected to be repaid within a year of the balance sheet date or during the current operating cycle of the business, whichever is longer.* These long-term obligations may vary considerably with regard to the nature of the debt and the conditions and covenants attached to it. Examples of long-term debt include bonds payable, mortgage notes, long-term notes, lease obligations, pension obligations, and deferred income tax liabilities. This chapter focuses on those forms of long-term debt that are issued under formal agreements or contracts, such as bonds.

When a corporation desires to raise additional capital for long-term purposes, it has several alternatives. It may borrow funds by issuing bonds, or it may obtain funds by issuing additional stock to shareholders. Each source of funds has its particular advantages and disadvantages to the issuing corporation. A bondholder is a creditor of a corporation while a stockholder is an owner. As creditors, bondholders normally do not participate in the management of the firm. Therefore, by issuing bonds, a corporation does not spread or dilute control of management over a larger number of owners. Interest expense is deductible for federal income tax purposes while dividends are not a tax deduction.

The interest expense on a bond is a fixed obligation to the borrower. If the interest is not paid on the dates specified by the contract, legal action may be brought by the bondholders. Dividends on stock, on the other hand, are declared at the discretion of the board of directors of the issuing corporation.

BOND OBLIGATIONS

Bonds are issued as a means of borrowing money for long-term purposes. The desired funds are obtained by issuing a number of bonds with a certain denomination (usually $1,000). Normally, a corporation sells all of its bonds to an investment firm, referred to as an underwriter. The underwriter then resells the bonds to investors. For accounting purposes, only the amount received from the underwriter is relevant to the issuing firm. Individual bonds are sold to investors with a promise to pay a definite sum of money to the holder at a fixed future date and periodic interest payments at a stated rate throughout the life of the liability. Since bonds usually do not name individual lenders, they may be bought and sold by investors until their maturity.

When funds are borrowed by issuing bonds, interest payments, and the timing of the repayment of the principal of the debt to bondholders are obligations which are fixed in amount and must be paid at specified dates regardless of the amount of income earned by the firm. If the rate of earnings on invested funds exceeds the interest rate on the bonds, it is usually to the owners' advantage for the firm to issue bonds. However, if the expected rate of earnings is less than the interest rate, it would not be to the advantage of the owners to borrow funds. Furthermore, interest payments must be made when due regardless of whether or not sufficient income is earned. If interest payments are not made, the bondholders may bring action in order to foreclose against the assets of the corporation in the settlement of their claims. Bondholders are creditors and their claims for interest and the repayment of principal have priority over the claims of owners. Therefore, the feasibility of obtaining funds by issuing bonds depends upon factors such as the expected rate of interest and the stability of the earnings of the firm.

Bond interest payments are a deductible expense in the computation of taxable income, while dividends paid to owners are not deductible for tax purposes. Because of the magnitude of corporate income taxes, the effect of taxes is often an important factor in determining the source which will be used by the business to obtain its long-term funds.

Approval of the board of directors and stockholders of the corporation is normally required prior to issuance of bonds. In addition, the firm issuing bonds selects a trustee to represent the bondholders. The trustee acts to protect the bondholders' interests, and takes legal action if the pledged responsibilities of the corporation are not satisfied.

CLASSES OF BONDS

Bonds may be either secured by specific assets or unsecured. Unsecured bonds are referred to as debenture bonds. Debenture bonds have as "security" the general credit standing of the issuing corporation. Therefore, debenture bonds are usually issued succesfully only by companies with a favorable financial position.

A secured bond gives the bondholder a prior claim against specific assets in the event that the issuing corporation is unable to make the required interest or principal payments as they become due. Secured bonds differ as to the type of assets pledged. Real estate mortgage bonds are secured by a mortgage on specific land or buildings. Equipment trust bonds are secured by mortgages on tangible personal property such as equipment. Collateral trust bonds are secured by stocks and bonds of other companies owned by the corporation issuing the bonds.

A bond issue that matures on a single date is referred to as a term bond. Bonds that mature on several different dates and are retired in installments over a period of time are called serial bonds. Bonds that may be retired before maturity at the option of the issuing corporation are referred to as callable bonds. Bonds which may be exchanged for a specified amount of stock at the option of the bondholder are termed convertible bonds.

Bonds may also differ as to the method of interest payment. Registered bonds require that the bondholders' names be registered with the issuing corporation. The corporation issuing bonds is required to maintain a record of the current owners; periodic interest payments are mailed directly to the registered owners. Other bonds, called coupon bonds, have interest coupons attached which call for the payment of the required amount of interest on specified dates. A bond coupon is similar to a note payable to the holder at the date specified on the coupon. At each interest date, the appropriate coupon may be detached by the bondholder and presented at a bank for payment.

Despite the wide variety of bonds offered, it should be noted that the value of bonds to the investor depends to a significant degree on the financial condition and long-term earning prospects of the issuing corporation. While the various optional provisions that may be included in a bond issue may affect the issue price of the bonds, it would be difficult for a company in poor financial condition to issue bonds regardless of the provisions.

Issuance of Bonds

When a corporation issues bonds, it is obligated to pay the principal or face amount of the bonds at a specified maturity date and to make periodic interest payments as well. The interest rate specified on the bonds is referred to as the coupon rate. The interest rate which investors are willing to accept on a bond at the time of its issue depends upon factors such as the market evaluation of the quality of the bond issue as evidenced by the financial strength of the business, the firm's earnings prospects and the particular provisions of the bond issue. This rate is referred to as the market or effective interest rate.

The price of a bond is a function of the relationship between its coupon rate (the amount specified on the bond indenture) and the prevailing market interest rate for bonds of similar investment quality. *The bond will sell at an amount more or less than the principal amount so as to provide the effective yield demanded by the investors at the time that the bond is issued.* It is unlikely that the coupon rate will be exactly the same as the market (effective) rate, because the bond contract must be finalized some time prior to the actual sale of the bonds and because it is difficult, if not impossible, to predict precisely the actual rate of interest that investors will require for a particular bond issue. By allowing the price of the bond to vary from the face amount in this manner, the bond may be issued without amending the coupon rate specified in the bond contract.

If the effective interest rate exceeds the coupon rate, the issue price of the bonds will fall below the face amount of the bonds. When the issue price is less than face value, the difference is referred to as a discount. For example, if Pearson Co. offers bonds with an interest rate of 7 percent when the market rate is 8 percent for similar bonds, the selling price of the bonds will be less than their face value. Since annual interest payments on each $1,000 of bonds will be $70 (.07 × $1,000), the issue price of the bonds will fall to the point where the interest received will yield an effective rate of 8 percent. Similarly, if the coupon rate exceeds the market interest rate for comparable bonds at the time of the issue, the price of the bonds will exceed the face amount. That is, the bonds will be issued at a premium. The bonds will sell at their face amount only when the coupon rate is exactly equal to the market rate.[1]

An investor may purchase bonds at the time of their initial issuance or may purchase the bonds from another bondholder subsequent to their original issuance. The market price of a bond will vary during its life as the general level of interest rates changes or as the perceived risk that is associated with the issuing company changes. In the examples that follow, we will assume that the investor acquires the bonds at the time of their initial sale by the issuing company. However, the investor's accounting procedures for bonds that are acquired on or after their initial issuance are identical.

Bonds Issued at Face Value

If the coupon rate offered on bonds is identical to the market rate, the bonds will be issued at their face value. To illustrate, assume that Dascher Co. had authorization to issue $100,000 of twenty-five year, 18 percent debenture bonds on January 1, 19x1, with interest payable semiannually on June 30 and December 31. If $50,000 of the bonds are issued at face value on January 1, 19x1, the entry for the issuance would be:

---

[1] The procedures for computing the selling price for a bond are presented in Appendix A to this chapter.

Cash	50,000	
Bonds payable		50,000

No journal entry is made for the authorization of the bonds. The balance sheet, however, should disclose all of the pertinent facts with respect to the bond issue. For example, a balance sheet for Dascher Co. on January 1, 19x1, would include the following information:

Long-term liabilities:
    18% debenture bonds payable,
        due on December 31, 19x25.................... $50,000

After the bonds are issued, Dascher Co. must make semiannual interest payments of $4,500 on each June 30 and December 31 that the bonds remain outstanding ($50,000 × $^{18}/_{100}$ × $^{1}/_{2}$). The entry to record each payment would be as follows:

Interest expense	4,500	
Cash		4,500

If the accounting period used by the firm ends between interest dates, an adjusting entry must be made to accrue the interest expense from the last interest date to the end of the period. For example, if the accounting period of Dascher Co. ended on September 30, the following adjusting entry would be necessary in order to record the accrued interest expense of $2,250 ($50,000 × $^{18}/_{100}$ × $^{3}/_{12}$) from June 30 to September 30.

Interest expense	2,250	
Interest payable		2,250

Interest expense will be closed to the income summary account, and interest payable will remain as a liability until the next regular semiannual interest payment. The entry to record the interest payment on December 31 would be:

Interest expense	2,250	
Interest payable	2,250	
Cash		4,500

Issuance Between Interest Dates

Once authorized, bonds may be issued at any time. Bonds are often issued at a time between the interest dates. Since the corporation will pay the full semiannual interest on all bonds outstanding at an interest date, the bondholder is usually required to purchase the interest that has accrued from the previous interest date to the date of sale. This interest paid by the bondholder is returned as part of the first interest payment after issuance. To illustrate, asume that the Dascher Co. bonds from the previous example were issued at face value plus accrued interest on March 1, 19x1. The issue price would be $50,000 plus two months' interest of $1,500 ($50,000 × $18/100$ × $2/12$). The entry to record the issuance is:

Cash	51,500	
Bonds payable		50,000
Interest payable		1,500

On the first semiannual interest payment date, June 30, which occurs four months after issuance, a full six months' interest ($4,500) will be paid. Of this amount, $1,500 is a return to the investor of accrued interest paid at the time of the purchase of the bonds and the remaining $3,000 represents the interest expense for the four months since the issuance. Therefore, the entry for the interest payment on June 30, 19x1, would be as follows:

Interest payable	1,500	
Interest expense	3,000	
Cash		4,500

Issuance of Bonds at a Discount

The issuer records the bonds at their principal amount in a long-term liability account, with any premium or discount recorded in separate premium on bonds payable or discount on bonds payable accounts.

When the coupon rate on a bond issue is less than the prevailing market interest rate for similar bonds, the bonds will sell at a discount. For example, assume the prevailing market interest rate exceeds 18 percent when Dascher Co. offers $50,000 face value of 18 percent, twenty-five year debenture bonds. As a result, assume that the $50,000 of Dascher Co. bonds are issued at a price of $47,500 on January 1, 19x1. The $2,500 excess of the face value over the issue price represents a discount. Normally bonds are carried in the accounts at face value with the discount recorded in a separate contra account. The issuance of the bonds would be recorded by the following entry:

Cash	47,500	
Discount on bonds payable	2,500	
Bonds payable		50,000

Although the issuing corporation receives less than the face amount of the issue when bonds are sold at a discount, the entire face amount must be repaid at maturity. Therefore, the total cost of borrowing includes the discount as well as the interest payments. To illustrate, the total interest cost to Dascher Co. for the bonds issued at a discount is computed as follows:

Amount to be repaid at maturity	$ 50,000
Amount received at issuance	47,500
Excess of cash to be paid over cash received (discount)	$ 2,500
Cash interest payments ($9,000 annually for 25 years)	225,000
Total interest cost	$227,500

The average yearly interest expense over the period until the maturity of the bonds is $9,100 ($227,500 ÷ 25). Therefore, in order to reflect the total interest cost of the bonds, bond discount should be allocated to expense over the twenty-five year life of the bonds as additional interest expense. The process of transferring a portion of bond discount to interest expense during each period is referred to as amortization. One common method of amortizing discount is to transfer or write off equal amounts at each interest payment date. This process is referred to as straight-line amortization.[2] In the illustration above, application of the straight-line method would yield amortization of $100 (1/25 × $2,500) each year, or $50 on each semiannual interest date. The following entry would be made at each interest payment date.

```
Interest expense .....................   4,550
     Discount on bonds payable .........            50
     Cash ..............................         4,500
```

Because of the amortization of the discount, total interest expense recorded over the life of the bond issue will be equal to the cash interest payments plus the bond discount. Further, amortization reduces the balance in the discount of bonds payable account to zero at the maturity date of the bonds.

Unamortized discount on bonds payable should be classified as a deduction from the related bonds payable account. To illustrate, the Dascher Co. bonds in the preceding example were issued at a discount of $2,500 on January 1, 19x1. After two years, on December 31, 19x2, a total of $200 ($2,500 × 2/25) of the original discount would have been amortized, and the balance sheet would include the following amount in the long-term liabilities section.

```
Long-term liabilities:
   18% debenture bonds payable,
      due on December 31, 19x25 ...............  $50,000
   Less:  Unamortized discount
          on bonds payable.................      2,300    $47,700
```

If the accounting period of the firm falls between interest dates, amortization of bond discount must be included in the adjusting entry which is made for the accrual of interest expense. For example, if the accounting period of Dascher Co. ends on September 30, the following adjusting entry would be required in order to record the interest expense for the period from June 30 (the last regular interest payment date) to September 30.

---

[2] The interest method of discount amortization is discussed in Appendix A to this chapter.

Interest expense	2,275	
Discount on bonds payable		25
Interest payable		2,250

The interest payable of $2,250 ($50,000 × $^{18}/_{100}$ × $^{3}/_{12}$) and the discount amortization of $25 ($^{1}/_{4}$ × $100) is the interest expense for the three-month period since the last interest payment was made.

Issuance of Bonds at a Premium

If the coupon rate on a bond issue exceeds the prevailing market interest rate for comparable bonds, the bonds will sell at an amount above their face value. The excess of the issue price over the face value is referred to as premium. For example, assume that $50,000 of Brenner Co. twenty-five year, 18 percent debenture bonds are issued on January 1, 19x1, when the market rate is less than 18 percent. As a result, assume that the bonds are sold for $55,000. The entry to record the issuance of the bonds would be:

Cash	55,000	
Bonds payable		50,000
Premium on bonds payable		5,000

When a premium is received on the issuance of bonds, the total cost of borrowing funds is equal to the cash interest payments made reduced by the amount of the premium. The total interest cost for Brenner Co. over the life of the bonds is calculated as follows:

Amount received at issuance	$ 55,000
Amount to be repaid at maturity	50,000
Excess of cash received over cash paid (premium)	$5,000)
Cash interest payments ($9,000 × 25)	225,000
Total interest cost	$220,000

The average yearly interest cost over the life of the bond issue is $8,800 ($220,000 ÷ 25). Consequently, in order to reflect the actual interest cost of the bond issue, the premium should be periodically written off or amortized as a reduction of the interest cost over the life of the issue. The procedures for the amortization of premium are similar to those used for bonds issued at a discount. In the Brenner Co. example, application of the straight-line method would result in premium amortization of $200 ($^{1}/_{25}$ × $5,000) each year and, therefore, $100 on each semiannual interest date. The entry to record each semiannual interest payment and premium amortization would be as follows:

Interest expense	4,400	
Premium on bonds payable	100	
Cash		4,500

The unamortized balance in the premium account would be reported as an addition to bonds payable on the balance sheet.

As indicated with respect to bond discount, if the firm's accounting period falls between interest payment dates, an adjusting entry is required in order to record the accrued interest expense and amortization of premium for the period since the last interest date.

Convertible Bonds

In certain circumstances, a company may issue bonds which are convertible at a specific rate into the common stock of the corporation at the option of the bondholder. This provision may be attached to a bond in order to enhance the marketability of the bond issue. Usually, these convertible bonds may be sold at a higher price and lower yield rate than nonconvertible bonds. The bondholder initially has the rights of a creditor, but later may convert the bonds to stock and become a stockholder and share in the earnings of the business.

The primary accounting problem associated with the issuance of convertible debt is the valuation of the liability at the date of issuance. There are two treatments that have been proposed for this valuation issue: (1) a portion of the proceeds from the sale of the debt occurs because of the conversion privilege, and that amount should be credited to paid-in capital; or (2) convertible debt should be treated solely as debt with none of the proceeds allocated to paid-in capital, because of the inseparability of the debt and the conversion option and the consequent lack of an objective value for the conversion option.

The Accounting Principles Board took the latter view in the issuance of *APB Opinion No. 14*, "Accounting for Convertible Debt and Debt Issued With Stock Purchase Warrants." This pronouncement provided that no portion of the proceeds should be accounted for as attributable to the conversion feature. Any premium or discount on issuance should be amortized over the period from issuance until the maturity date, because it is impossible to predict when (and if) such bonds will be converted.

The entries to record the issuance of convertible bonds are similar to those which were discussed previously. At the date of the conversion, the carrying value of the bond (face value plus any premium or less any discount) is normally transferred to the stockholder equity accounts which are associated with the new shares of stock issued in the conversion. To illustrate, assume that a corporation had issued a $1,000, ten year convertible bond for $1,100 on January 1, 19x1. The bond is convertible into twenty shares of $10 par value common stock at the option of the holder. Further assume that the holder converted the bond into common stock on December 31, 19x5. At the time of the conversion, there is unamortized premium of $50. The entry to record the conversion would be as follows:

Bonds payable................................	1,000	
Premium......................................	50	
Common stock		200
Additional paid-in capital		850

RETIREMENT OF BONDS

Bonds may be retired by the issuing corporation at maturity or before the maturity date either by redeeming callable bonds or by repurchasing bonds in the open market. If bonds are retired at the maturity, any premium or discount will have been completely amortized and the entry to record the retirement of the bonds would be a debit to bonds payable and a credit to cash for an amount equal to the face or maturity value of the bonds.

Callable bonds may be redeemed at the option of the issuing corporation within a specified period and at a stated price referred to as the call price. The call price is usually an amount which is in excess of face value, with the excess referred to as call premium. In the absence of a call provision, the issuing corporation may retire its bonds by purchasing them in the open market at the prevailing market price.

If bonds are repurchased by the issuing corporation at a price less than their book value (i.e., maturity value less discount or plus premium), the corporation realizes a gain on the retirement of the bonds. The carrying value of the bonds is equal to the face value plus any unamortized premium or less any unamortized discount. Similarly, if the purchase price is greater than the carrying value, a loss is incurred on the retirement of the debt.[3]

To illustrate a redemption prior to maturity, assume that the Carpenter Co. has a $50,000 bond issue outstanding with $2,000 of unamortized premium. Further assume that the corporation has the option of calling the bonds at 105 (i.e., 105% of the face value) and that the company exercises its call provision. The entry to record the redemption of the bonds for $52,500 ($50,000 × 1.05) would be as follows:

Bonds payable.......................	50,000	
Premium on bonds payable	2,000	
Loss on redemption	500	
Cash...........................		52,500

If the bonds do not include a call provision, the corporation could purchase the bonds in the open market. For example, assume that Carpenter Co. purchased one-fifth of the $50,000 face value bonds outstanding for $9,800. The carrying value of the bonds purchased is $10,400 (face value plus one-fifth of the unamortized premium), while the purchase price is

---

[3] According to FASB *Statement No. 4*, "Reporting Gains and Losses From Extinguishment of Debt" (1975), gains or losses from retirement of bonds should be aggregated and, if material in amount, classified in the income statement as an extraordinary item (net of the related income tax effect).

$9,800. Therefore, the company would realize a $600 gain on the retirement. The entry to record the retirement of the bonds would be as follows:

```
Bonds payable ..........................    10,000
Premium on bonds payable ...............       400
    Gain on retirement ......................             600
    Cash....................................           9,800
```

BOND SINKING FUND

In order to offer additional security to the investor, a provision may be included in the bond indenture which requires the issuing corporation to set aside funds for repayment of the bond at maturity by periodic accumulations over the life of the issue. These funds may be accumulated by periodically depositing cash in a bond sinking fund. The cash deposited in the fund is usually invested in income producing assets. Therefore, the total deposits made by the issuing corporation over the life of the bond issue are normally less than the total maturity value of the bonds. At maturity, the securities in the fund are sold and the proceeds are used to retire the bonds.

Cash and securities included in a sinking fund are not available for the retirement of current liabilities; they are normally shown as a single total and included under the caption of investments. Similarly, earnings on the sinking fund assets are shown as a separate item in the income statement.

RESTRICTION ON DIVIDENDS

Another means of increasing the security of the bondholder is a provision whereby dividend payments by the issuing company will be restricted during the life of the bond issue. The actual restriction on dividends may vary. For example, a restriction may limit the payment of dividends during a given year to the excess of net income over the sinking fund requirements for the period. There are various methods for disclosing this restriction in the financial statements. Such a restriction could be shown by a footnote or parenthetically in the balance sheet. Alternatively, the restriction could be indicated by appropriating retained earnings each year. To illustrate, assume that the sinking fund requirement for the year is $20,000 and that net income is $35,000. If dividends are limited to the excess of net income over the sinking fund requirement, an appropriation of retained earnings could be made with the following entry:

```
Retained earnings ...................    20,000
    Appropriation for bonded debt .....            20,000
```

BALANCE SHEET PRESENTATION

The presentation of long-term liabilities in the balance sheet should disclose all information which is relevant to the debt including the maturity dates, interest rates, conversion privileges, etc. In addition, if a liability is secured by specific assets, or restricts the payment of dividends, such information should also be disclosed in the financial statements. To illustrate, the long-term liabilities section of the balance sheet might appear as follows:

Long-term liabilities:		
Twenty-five year, 16 percent mortgage bonds due on December 31, 19x9	$100,000	
Less: Unamortized discount	4,000	$ 96,000
Twenty year, 18 percent debenture bonds, convertible into fifteen shares of common stock, due on December 31, 19x4	$ 50,000	
Add: Unamortized premium	1,000	51,000
Total long-term liabilities		$147,000

INVESTMENTS IN CORPORATE SECURITIES

For financial reporting purposes, the investments of a firm in both debt or equity securities of other entities are classified as either short-term investments (also referred to as temporary investments or marketable securities) or long-term investments. The distinction between the short-term and long-term classifications is based both upon the intent of management in making the investment and the nature of the investment.

Short-term investments normally represent the conversion of otherwise idle cash balances (such as those that result from seasonal excesses of cash) to productive use (earning interest or dividends) on a short-term basis. To be classified as a short-term investment, a security must meet two basic criteria. First, *the security must be readily salable and the volume of trading of the security should be such that the sale does not affect the market price materially.* Second, *there should be an intention on the part of the firm to sell the securities if the need for cash arises within the current operating cycle or one year, whichever is longer.*

Marketable securities include *equity securities* (such as preferred and common stock) and *debt securities* (such as corporate and government bonds, treasury bills, and commercial paper). *Investments that do not meet the criteria for temporary investments are classified in the balance sheet as a noncurrent asset.* These investments are classified as long-term investments if they are readily salable or as other assets if they are not readily salable. Firms acquire long-term investments for a variety of purposes, such as to achieve control over another entity through stock purchases or for setting aside funds for uses beyond the current operating cycle (e.g., future plant expansion).

Marketable securities also can be classified as either marketable equity securities or other marketable securities. Marketable equity securities consist of the following:

1. Common stock (as long as its sale is not restricted by either a governmental or contractual requirement, unless the requirement terminates within one year).

2. Preferred stock (as long as it need not be redeemed by the issuer or cannot be redeemed at the option of the investor).

3. Rights to acquire or dispose of ownership shares at fixed or determinable prices (examples include warrants, rights, call options, and put options).

The distinction between equity and non-equity marketable securities is important, because the accounting requirements differ for each classification of securities. The FASB, in its *Statement of Financial Accounting Standards No. 12*, "Accounting for Certain Marketable Securities," requires that short-term investments in marketable equity securities be accounted for using the lower-of-cost-or-market basis.[4] Because *Statement No. 12* does not apply to non-equity securities, temporary investments in such securities can technically be accounted for on the cost basis. However, since the issuance of *Statement No. 12*, a number of companies have adopted the lower-of-cost-or-market basis for temporary investments in non-equity marketable securities.

INVESTMENTS IN BONDS

Bonds may be purchased as a long-term investment or as a temporary investment. The purpose for acquiring bonds must be determined on the basis of management's intention. Bonds held as temporary investments are classified as current assets, and bonds acquired for long-term purposes are reported as noncurrent assets. The primary difference in the accounting for bonds classified as temporary versus long-term is in the treatment of the premium or discount on the purchase. Companies making long-term investments in bonds must amortize the difference between the cost of the investment and its maturity value over the life of the bonds. This parallels the treatment used for the issuance of bonds discussed earlier in the chapter. Companies acquiring bonds for temporary purposes, however, are not required to amortize premium or discount. Instead, a short-term investment in bonds is normally carried in the investor's accounts at the acquisition cost, and any gain or loss is recognized in the period the investment is sold. The logic for not amortizing premium or discount is that since it is a temporary investment, the company does not expect to hold the bond until it matures. The following discussion deals with the accounting treatment for long-term investments in bonds.

---

[4] Certain industries that have specialized practices with regard to marketable securities (such as investment companies and securities dealers) are exempted from the provisions of *FASB Statement No. 12*.

The cost of a bond includes the quoted price of the bond plus brokerage commissions, transfer taxes, etc. When bonds are purchased between interest dates, the purchase price of the bonds usually includes payment for the interest which has accrued since the previous interest payment date. To illustrate, assume that on June 1, 19x0, Edwards Co. purchases $10,000 face value of 12 percent bonds of the Bell Co. at 111½ plus accrued interest. The bonds pay interest on June 30 and December 31 and mature on December 31, 19x9. The entry to record the purchase would be:

Investment in bonds	11,150	
Bond interest receivable	500	
Cash		11,650

The debit to the investment in bonds account records the cost of the bond—the face value of $10,000 × 111.5 percent or $11,150. This indicates that the bonds were purchased at a premium. Note that this premium is not recorded in a separate account, but instead is included as a part of the investment in bonds account. The debit to bond interest receivable records the fact that Edwards Co. purchased five months accrued interest along with the bonds ($10,000 × .12 × 5/12 = $500). The credit to cash is for the total amount paid by Edwards.

Amortization of Premium

On June 30, 19x0, Edwards Co. will receive its first interest payment which will be recorded as follows:

Cash	600	
Bond interest receivable		500
Investment in bonds		10
Interest income		90

This entry records the receipt of the $600 interest payment ($10,000 × .12 × 6/12 = $600). Of this amount, $500 is the return of the accrued interest that was purchased when the bonds were acquired. Recall that the bonds were purchased at a premium of $1,150 ($11,150 purchase − $10,000 face value). This premium is amortized as a reduction of interest income over the life of the bonds (June 1, 19x0 to December 31, 19x9 = 115 months). The amortization is $10 per month ($1,150 ÷ 115 months). Since Edwards Co. had held the bonds for one month (June 1 to June 30) when the first interest payment was received, $10 of the purchase premium was amortized at that time. Note that the amortization is recorded by a credit to the bond investment account. The income for June is $90, one month's interest of $100 ($10,000 × .12 × 1/12 = $100) minus $10 amortization of premium.

On December 31, 19x0, Edwards Co. will receive its second interest payment of $600. The entry to record the receipt of this interest and the amortization of premium is:

```
Cash ..........................    600
    Investment in bonds ...........          60
    Interest income ...............         540
```

Again, the debit to cash records the receipt of six months' interest ($10,000 × .12 × 6/12 = $600). The credit to the bond investment account is for six months amortization of premium ($1,150 ÷ 115 months = $10 per month × 6 months' = $60). The interest income is the receipt of $600 less the $60 amortization. The total interest income recognized over the life of the bonds will be equal to the total cash interest received minus the amount of the premium.

At December 31, 19x0, the bond investment account would appear in the balance sheet as follows:

```
Investment in bonds ...................  $11,080
```

This represents the original cost of the bonds, $11,150 less $70 for seven months' amortization of premium.[5] The investment in bonds account will decrease each period by the amount of the premium amortized and, therefore, at maturity will be equal to the face amount of the bonds.

Amortization of Discount

When bonds are purchased at less than their face value, the discount is not shown separately, but as a part of the investment in bonds account. Discount is amortized as an increase in the interest income earned over the life of the bonds. The interest income recognized on bonds that were acquired at a discount and held to maturity is equal to the total of the cash interest payments received plus the amount of the purchase discount. The carrying value of the investment will increase each period by the amount of the discount amortized and at maturity will equal the face amount of the bonds.

Sale of Bonds

If bonds are sold prior to maturity, accrued interest from the last interest payment date to the date of sale should be recorded. Any difference between this accrued interest plus the carrying value of the bond investment account and the net cash proceeds of the sale represents a gain or loss on the sale and is recorded as such. For example, assume that the bonds used in the above illustration were sold on January 1, 19x1, for $12,000. The entry to record the sale would be as follows:

```
Cash .........................  12,000
    Investment in bonds ...........      11,080
    Gain on the sale of bonds .........         920
```

---

[5] Premium or discount on bonds held as long-term investments is amortized over the life of the bonds. If bonds are held as a temporary investment, no amortization is required.

Alternatively, had the selling price on January 1, 19x1, been $11,000, the entry would have been:

```
Cash..................................  11,000
Loss on sale of bonds.....................      80
    Investment in bonds ....................           11,080
```

INVESTMENTS IN STOCK

Investments in stock are the temporary or long-term conversion of cash into productive use by the purchase of securities. Such investments are found among the assets of almost all businesses. In general, investments are classified as either temporary or long-term depending on the nature of the security and the intention of the investor firm.

It should be noted that when stock is purchased as an investment, the seller of the stock receives the money paid. Most investment transactions in stock are between two individual investors, one who already owned the stock and who then sells it to the new investor who purchases it. The corporation whose stock is traded in the transaction becomes involved directly only if the shares exchanged are a part of a new issue of securities it sold to raise funds.

Temporary Investments

Temporary investments, usually referred to as marketable securities, normally arise from seasonal excesses of cash and represent its conversion to productive use (earning interest or dividends) on a short-term basis. In order to be classified as a temporary investment, a security must be readily salable and the volume of trading of the security should be such that the sale does not materially affect the market price. In addition, there is general agreement that there should be an intention on the part of the investor firm to sell the securities in the short run as the need for cash arises.

Control Over Investments

The effective control over marketable securities includes the physical safeguarding of the certificates. This usually means that the securities should be kept in a safe if they are retained by the firm, and access to the certificates controlled. In many instances, the firm will leave its investments in the custody of its broker. The authority to purchase and sell is usually vested in the board of directors of the firm or in a specifically designated investments committee. In either case, requiring written authorization in order to either acquire or dispose of investments is another important control feature. Finally, the accounting records themselves are important in establishing control over investments. The periodic reconciliation of the accounting records to the securities on hand or in the custody of the broker and the reconciliation of the recorded income to the income which should have been earned (as detemined by calculation and reference to sources such as *Standard & Poor's Dividend Record*) help to provide effective control over investments.

Accounting for Acquisition of Temporary Investments

The basis for recording temporary investments in the accounts is the cost of the investment. Cost includes all outlays which are required to acquire the investment including the quoted price of the security, brokerage commissions, transfer taxes, etc. To illustrate the accounting for the acquisition of marketable securities, assume that Jones Company purchased one hundred shares of the stock of IBM Corporation at a price of $200 per share on January 1, 19x1. The entry to record this purchase would be as follows:

    Investment in stock................ 20,000
        Cash..........................   20,000

When a temporary investment is sold, the difference between the selling price and the cost of the investment is recorded as a gain or loss of the period in which the sale took place.

Valuation of Temporary Investments

Temporary investments are classified as either debt securities (government and corporate bonds) or equity securities (preferred and common stock). Prior to 1976, there was considerable diversity in the accounting for temporary investments. However, a significant degree of uniformity in practice resulted from the issuance of FASB *Statement No. 12* which was concerned with the accounting for certain marketable securities. This statement requires that marketable equity securities be accounted for at the lower of aggregate cost or market value. Other marketable securities may be valued either at cost or at lower of cost or market.

If a company owns more than a single kind of marketable equity security, the lower of cost or market procedure is applied to the securities as a group. The market value is determined by the quoted market price at the date of the balance sheet. In applying this method, the *total cost* of the group (often referred to as the portfolio) of securities is compared to the *total current market value* of the securities, and the *lower* of these two amounts is reported as the balance sheet valuation. A decline in value of the aggregate marketable equity securities is recorded as a debit to an unrealized loss account and a credit to a valuation allowance account. The unrealized loss is included in the income statement and the valuation allowance account is deducted from the original cost of the marketable securities in the balance sheet. The loss from decline in value is referred to as an *unrealized* loss to differentiate it from a loss which is realized upon the sale of the securities. The aggregate requirement means that the comparison of cost and market value is made for the entire portfolio of current marketable equity securities held at the end of the period. *The cost and market value of any particular security are not considered on an individual basis.*

The balance in the valuation allowance account must be adjusted at the end of every period so that the portfolio of marketable equity securities will be reflected in the balance sheet at the *lower* of cost or current market value. Thus, if there are further declines in market value, the adjusting entry will recognize an additional unrealized loss. On the other hand, if the excess of aggregate cost over market value decreases (or is eliminated) in a subsequent period, a gain on recovery is recognized to the extent of previously recognized unrealized losses. The entry to record a recovery in value is a debit to the valuation allowance account and a credit to an unrealized gain account which is included in the income statement. The limitation on unrealized gains to the extent of unrealized losses previously recognized requires that the valuation allowance account must either have a credit or a zero balance. For income tax purposes, the lower of cost or market method is not acceptable, and taxable gain or loss is determined in the period of sale as the difference between original cost and the selling price.

To illustrate the use of the lower of cost or market method, assume that during 19x1 Carol Company acquires 100 shares of IBM stock for $20,000 and 100 shares of AT&T stock for $10,000. On December 31, 19x1, the company determined the carrying amount of its portfolio to be:

	Cost	Market
IBM stock	$20,000	$19,000
AT&T stock	10,000	10,500
	$30,000	$29,500

The following entry would be required in order to record the unrealized loss (i.e., $30,000 − $29,500):

Unrealized loss on marketable equity securities	500	
Allowance for decline in value		500

The $500 loss would be reported in the 19x1 income statement, and the allowance account would be deducted from marketable securities at cost in the December 31, 19x1, balance sheet.

An increase in aggregate market value in a subsequent period reduces or eliminates the allowance account. For example, assume that Carol Company had no transactions relating to marketable securities during 19x2, and that the aggregate market value of the securities held at December 31, 19x2, was $29,750. The adjustment to the valuation allowance account at December 31, 19x2, would be recorded as follows:

Allowance for decline in value	250	
Unrealized gain on marketable equity securities		250

The gain of $250 ($29,750 − $29,500) would be included in the income statement for 19x2. If the aggregate market value had increased to $30,000 or more, the amount of the unrealized gain would be limited to $500 (the amount required to eliminate the allowance account). If the market value of the temporary investments in marketable equity securities had decreased below $29,500 during 19x2, an unrealized loss account would have been debited and the allowance account credited in order to increase the balance in the allowance for decline in value account to the aggregate difference between the original cost and the current market value of the securities.

Because the allowance for decline in value is based on a comparison of the total portfolio cost and its market value, there is no effect upon the gain or loss recognized when an investment is sold. When a specific temporary investment in marketable equity securities is sold, the total difference between the net proceeds of the sale and the original cost is recorded as a realized gain or loss. For example, assume that Carol Company sold the 100 shares of IBM stock on June 30, 19x3, for $20,600 (net of commissions). This sale would be recorded as follows:

Cash...	20,600	
Investment in stock........................		20,000
Gain on sale of marketable equity securities....		600

Note that the entry made at the time of sale makes no adjustment for previously recorded unrealized gains or losses or for the allowance account. These accounts are adjusted at the end of the period when the aggregate cost and market values of the securities held are compared.

Long-Term Investments in Stock

Investments in stocks which are not held as temporary investments are classified as long-term assets. While companies make investments in the securities of other corporations (investee companies) for a variety of reasons, *the primary purpose is normally to increase the income of the investor company (the company making the investment).* This effect on income may be either direct, through the income that is generated by the investments (in the form of dividends or interest) and appreciation in the market value of the securities, or indirect, by creating positive operational relationships with other businesses. The indirect effect on the income of the investor company results from obtaining a degree of influence or control over the management of another company, such as a major supplier, a customer, or a competitor. Establishing this type of relationship through the ownership of common stock often improves the operational efficiency or financial strength of the investor company. Such investments are recorded at their cost as of the date of acquisition. This cost includes the purchase price of the shares plus all brokerage fees, transfer costs, and excise taxes paid by the purchaser.

The method of accounting for long-term investments in stock subsequent to acquisition is primarily a function of the type of stock purchased (common or preferred) and the percentage of the investee corporation's outstanding common stock that is held by the investor. When the investor holds either preferred stock or less than 50 percent of the common stock of another corporation, there are *three basic accounting methods* that may be applicable in accounting for the investment subsequent to its acquisition: *(1) the lower-of-cost-or-market method (or simply the cost method for non-marketable equity securities), (2) the equity method, and (3) the market value method.*

The characteristics of the particular investment dictate which method should be used. *The lower-of-cost-or-market method generally is used whenever the amount of the investment held by the investor is insufficient to exercise significant influence over the investee. When the investor company owns an amount of voting stock that allows significant influence over the management of the investee, the equity method is used to reflect the changes in the underlying net assets of the investee company. The market value method, which reflects both increases and decreases in the current market value of investments, currently is applied only in the case of investments in specialized businesses such as mutual funds and insurance companies.*

When a company acquires more than 50 percent of the common stock of a corporation (referred to as a controlling interest), consolidated statements that reflect the investor and investee as a single economic entity normally are prepared. The details involved in the preparation of such statements are presented and discussed in the next chapter. However, whether or not consolidated statements are prepared, the investment must still be accounted for in the investor corporation's books. Depending upon the particular circumstances of the investment, there are three methods which may be used in accounting for long-term investments in stock: (1) *the cost method*—the investment is valued at the original acquisition cost, (2) *the lower-of-cost-or-market method*—similar to the cost method except the investments are reflected in the balance sheet at the lower of the aggregate cost or market value of the securities, and (3) *the equity method*—the investment is valued so as to reflect changes in the underlying net assets of the investee corporation.

The cost method is based on the fact that the two corporations are separate legal entities. Therefore, the carrying value of the investment included in the accounts of the investor remains at the original cost. Any changes in the underlying net assets of the investee corporation which may have occurred as a result of its operations are ignored under this method. The logic underlying the lower-of-cost-or-market method is similar to that of the cost method—that is, since both the investor and investee are viewed as separate entities, dividends are recorded as income when received and a gain or loss on the investment is not recognized until the time of disposition. The difference in the methods is that in the lower-of-cost-or-market method a year-end adjustment is used to reflect the investment at the lower of aggregate cost or aggregate market value. The equity method, on the other hand, is intended to reflect the economic relationship which exists between the two companies. This method recognizes that an investment in stock which allows the investor company to exercise significant control or influence over the operations of the investee company should be accounted for in such a way that changes in the underlying net assets of the investee company are reflected in the accounts of the investor company.

While an investment of less than 50 percent of the voting stock does not represent legal control, it is possible for such an investment to provide "significant influence." Ability to exercise such influence may be evidenced by such factors as representation on the board of directors, participation in policy-making processes, material intercompany transactions, interchange of managerial personnel, and technological dependency. Another important consideration in the determination of significant influence is the percentage ownership held by the investor relative to the ownership percentage of any other investors with substantial ownership interest.

The choice between the methods was, for all practical purposes, optional prior to the issuance of *Opinion No. 18* of the Accounting Principles Board in 1971. However, the board stated in this opinion that the equity method should be used if the investment in stock enables the investor company to exercise significant influence over the operating and financial policies of an investee. The board assumed that, in the absence of evidence to the contrary, ownership of 20 percent or more of the voting stock of an investee represented evidence of the ability of the investor company to exercise significant influence over the activities of the investee firm. Thus, the cost method or the lower of cost or market method would normally be used for an investment of less than 20 percent of the voting common stock and the equity method would be used for an investment of 20 percent or more of the voting stock of an investee. Most investments in preferred stocks (regardless of the percentage ownership) would also be accounted for by either the cost method or lower of cost or market method because preferred stock does not normally have voting rights. For investments of less than 20 percent of the common stock or investments in preferred stock, the lower of cost or market method must be used to account for investments in marketable equity securities. Generally, a security is classified as "marketable" if there is a currently available sales price in the securities market. The cost method is appropriate for investments in nonmarketable securities which are not required to be accounted for under the equity method. In summary, long-term investments in stock are accounted for as follows:

Investment	Method
Ownership of 20 percent or more of the common stock	Equity
Ownership of less than 20 percent of the common stock and ownership of preferred stock in the form of marketable equity securities	Lower-of-Cost-or-Market
Ownership of less than 20 percent of the common stock and ownership of preferred stock in the form of non-marketable securities	Cost

Noncurrent marketable equity securities are accounted for at the lower of aggregate cost or aggregate market as of the date of the balance sheet.[6] The application of this approach to long-term investments is similar to the accounting for current marketable equity securities, which were discussed previously in the chapter.

As in the case of the current marketable securities, all noncurrent marketable equity securities are grouped in a separate portfolio for purposes of comparing the aggregate cost and aggregate market value. *However, if the aggregate cost exceeds the aggregate market value of the securities, the unrealized loss or the unrealized recovery in the value of the noncurrent equity securities is not included in the net income for the period.* Instead, a valuation allowance account is established as a contra-asset account in the investments section of the balance sheet, and the unrealized loss account is shown as a contra-owners' equity account in the stockholders' equity section of the balance sheet. Thus, if the aggregate cost of noncurrent marketable equity securities exceeds aggregate market value, *the difference is treated as a reduction in the noncurrent investments and as an equal reduction in the equity section of the balance sheet.* Conversely, if aggregate market value equals or exceeds aggregate cost, both the allowance account and the unrealized loss have a balance of zero. The logic behind not recognizing the unrealized losses or recoveries in the income statement is that temporary price fluctuations often are not reflected in the ultimate realized value of the long-term investment, because it is not the intent of management to sell the securities in the short run.

Losses may be reflected in the income statement only when noncurrent securities are sold, a decline in value of a specific noncurrent security is considered to be other than temporary, or the classification of an investment is changed between noncurrent and current. Gains may be recognized only when the securities are sold.

To illustrate the use of the lower of cost or market method, assume that Winston Company made the following long-term investments in marketable equity securities during 19x1:

1. Purchased 100 shares of IBM common stock at a price of $20,000 including commissions.

2. Purchased 100 shares of AT&T common stock at a price of $10,000 including commissions.

On December 31, 19x1, Winston Company determined the following information regarding its investments:

---

[6] In applying the requirements of *FASB Statement No. 12*, all marketable equity securities are considered to be noncurrent in a nonclassified balance sheet. The accumulated changes in this valuation allowance are reported as a separate amount.

Investment	Cost	Market Value	Difference
IBM Stock	$20,000	$19,000	($1,000)
AT&T Stock	10,000	10,500	500
	$30,000	$29,500	($500)

As is the case with the application of the lower of cost or market rule to temporary investments in marketable equity securities, when market value is less than cost, this difference is recorded in an allowance account which is offset against the investment account on the balance sheet. However, unlike temporary investments, this decrease is not reflected as an "unrealized loss" in the income statement. Rather, a separate allowance account with a debit balance is used and this account is shown as a deduction from stockholders' equity in the balance sheet. The following journal entry would be required at December 31, 19x1:

Allowance for net unrealized loss on long-term investments	500	
Allowance for decline in value of long-term investments		500

If the market value of the Winston Company portfolio of long-term investments in marketable equity securities increases in a subsequent period, the above entry would be reversed to the extent of the increase or to bring the allowance accounts to zero, whichever is less. That is, if market value should exceed cost in a future period, the allowance accounts are eliminated.

According to *FASB Statement No 12, the required disclosures in the financial statements or in the accompanying notes for long-term investments in marketable equity securities are as follows:*

1. The aggregate cost and market value of the portfolio for each balance sheet presented.

2. The gross unrealized gains and gross unrealized losses as of the latest balance sheet date.

3. For each period an income statement is presented:
   a. Net realized gain or loss included in net income.
   b. The basis on which cost was computed to determine the gain or loss.
   c. The change in the valuation allowance included in the equity section of the balance sheet during the period.

4. Significant net realized and net unrealized gains or losses occurring after the balance sheet date.

Cost Method. Under the cost method, the investment account is carried at the original cost of the investment. Any increases or decreases in the net assets of the investee company resulting from earnings or losses do not affect the investor company's investment account. Dividends received by the investor company are recorded as dividend income.

Equity Method. Under the equity method, the investment is initially recorded at its original cost. After acquisition, the investment account is adjusted for any increases or decreases in the net assets of the investee company which have occurred since the stock was acquired. Net income of the investee results in an increase in its net assets. Therefore, the investor company increases the carrying value of its investment and recognizes investment income to the extent of its share (determined by the percentage of the investee's stock owned by the investor company) of the net income of the investee. For example, assume that an investor firm owned 20 percent of the outstanding voting stock of an investee. If the investee reported earnings of $50,000, the investor would increase the carrying value of its investment by $10,000 and simultaneously recognize investment income of $10,000. Similarly, a net loss incurred by the investee company would result in a reduction of the investment account and the recognition of a loss on investments by the investor firm. Since dividends also reduce the net assets of the investee, any dividend distributions made to the investor are recorded by a decrease in the investment account balance. The effect of the equity method is to value the investment at the original cost plus the investor's share of the undistributed retained earnings (net income less dividends) of the investee company since its acquisition of the stock.

To illustrate the difference between the cost and the equity methods, assume that Stolle Company purchases 1,000 of the 5,000 outstanding shares of Most Company stock on January 1, 19x1, at a cost of $10 per share. During 19x1, Most Company reports net income of $20,000 and pays dividends of $10,000, and during 19x2 Most Company reports a net loss of $5,000 and pays no dividends. The journal entries of Stolle Company under both the cost and the equity methods are shown below.

These entries have the following effect on the financial statements of Stolle Company as of the end of 19x2.

	Cost Method	Equity Method
Investment in Most Company— December 31, 19x2	$10,000	$11,000
Income statement:		
19x1	2,000	4,000
19x2	0	(1,000)

Under the cost method, Stolle Company would report its investment in Most Company at December 31, 19x2, at its original cost of $10,000. Under the equity method, the investment would be carried at $11,000. The $1,000

Event	Cost Method	Equity Method
January 1, 19x1 Acquisition of 1,000 shares of the common stock of Most Company	Investment in Most Company .... 10,000 Cash 10,000	Investment in Most Company .... 10,000 Cash 10,000
December 31, 19x1 Net income of $20,000 reported by Most Company	No Entry	Investment in Most Company .... 4,000 Investment income ...... 4,000 To record Stolle Company's $4,000 share (20% × $20,000) of Most Company's net income.
June 30, 19x2 Stolle Company received dividends of $2,000 (20% of $10,000 dividend paid by Most Company)	Cash .... 2,000 Dividends income 2,000	Cash .... 2,000 Investment in Most Company 2,000
December 31, 19x2 Net loss of $5,000 reported by Most Company	No Entry	Investment loss .... 1,000 Investment in Most Company .... 1,000 To record Stolle Company's $1,000 share (20% × $5,000) of Most Company's $5,000 net loss.

increase in the investment account under the equity method reflects Stolle Company's share (20%) of the $5,000 increase in the net assets of Most Company since the time the Most Company stock was acquired by Stolle.

Under the cost method, the investor recognizes income only to the extent of assets received from the investee (i.e., dividends). The equity method, on the other hand, recognizes income to the extent of the investor's share of the net income of the investee company, whether or not dividends were received.

When the long-term investment is in the form of marketable equity securities and the use of the equity method is not appropriate, the lower of cost or market method must be used. The application of this method to the aggregate long-term equity securities is basically similar to the procedures used for short-term investments which were discussed previously. The major difference is that the changes in the valuation allowance account for the noncurrent investment in marketable equity securities is recorded as a contra account (reduction) in stockholders' equity rather than as an unrealized loss or gain to be reported in the income statement.

DISCLOSURES ON FAIR VALUE

Disclosures about the fair value of investments in stocks and bonds is required by *FASB Statement No. 107*, "Disclosures about Fair Value of Financial Instruments." An exception to this requirement is for investments in stock accounted for under the equity method.

In the example for temporary investments in stock, the total cost and market value at December 31, 19x1, for the company's portfolio were $30,000 and $29,500, respectively. The market value is presented on the balance sheet because the market value is less than cost. If the market value of the company's portfolio exceeds cost at December 31, 19x3, the cost amount is presented on the balance sheet, but the market value must still be disclosed. The same requirements apply to long-term investments in stock.

The market value for both temporary and long-term investments in bonds must be disclosed. Therefore, the market value for the investment in bonds carried at $11,080 on the December 31, 19x0, balance sheet must be presented.

In May 1993, the FASB issued *Statement No. 115*, "Accounting for Certain Investments in Debt and Equity Securities," that requires the use of fair (market) value for investments in debt and equity securities, except for investments in debt securities that are to be held until maturity. A discussion of *Statement No. 115* is presented in Appendix B to this chapter.

CONSOLIDATED FINANCIAL STATEMENTS

In many instances, investments in stock are made to secure ownership of a controlling interest in the voting stock of another company. A firm owning a majority of the voting stock of another company is usually referred to as a *parent company*, and the company whose stock is owned is called the *subsidiary company*. A parent company and one or more of its related subsidiary companies are usually referred to as *affiliated companies*. Since a parent and its subsidiary are separate legal entities, separate financial statements are prepared for the stockholders and creditors of each company.

The relationship between a parent and its subsidiary is disclosed in the parent company's financial statements in the investment in stock account. However, parent company statements do not reflect the complete economic effect of the parent's ownership of the subsidiary. Therefore, it is often useful to prepare financial statements based on the financial position and operating results of the combined affiliated companies as if they were a single economic entity. The combined financial statements of two or more affiliated companies are called *consolidated statements*. Consolidated statements provide the stockholders and creditors of the parent company with an overall view of the combined financial position and operating activities of the parent company and its subsidiaries.

There are a variety of economic, legal, and tax advantages which encourage large organizations to operate through a group of affiliated corporations, rather than a single legal entity. For example, the financial statements, which are reproduced in the beginning of this text, are consolidated financial statements.

A basic criterion used in deciding whether or not to prepare consolidated statements is that the subsidiary company must be under the continuing control of the parent. There is no general agreement among accountants as to the percentage ownership which gives the parent company sufficient control to influence the activities of a subsidiary. In many cases, however, ownership of a majority of the voting stock of a subsidiary is considered to be adequate evidence of the ability to control a subsidiary for the purpose of deciding whether or not to prepare consolidated statements.

From a legal standpoint, a subsidiary company is a separate entity. Accordingly, the subsidiary maintains its own accounting records and prepares separate financial statements. However, since the parent owns a majority of the voting stock of its subsidiary, the parent and subsidiary companies are a business entity under common control. Therefore, individual financial statements of the parent and subsidiary do not provide a comprehensive view of the financial position of the affiliated companies as a single economic unit. Consolidated financial statements, which ignore the legal distinction between the parent and its subsidiary, serve this purpose by reflecting the financial position and results of operations of the affiliated companies as a single economic entity.

Consolidated Balance Sheet at Date of Acquisition

In preparing a consolidated balance sheet, the accounts which are included in the individual parent and subsidiary company records are combined. In the process of this combination, however, certain adjustments must be made to avoid duplication or double-counting in determining the balances to be used. For example, the investment account of the parent company reflects its equity in the net assets of the subsidiary. Including both the parent company's investment account and the net assets of the subsidiary in a consolidated statement would result in double-counting the net assets of the subsidiary. Therefore, the parent's investment account should not be included in the consolidated statements. Since the stockholder's equity of the subsidiary is represented by the investment account, it should also be excluded from the consolidated financial statement. The investment of the parent company is referred to as the reciprocal of the stockholders' equity of the subsidiary. Therefore, these accounts and any other reciprocal accounts which may exist as a result of transactions between the parent and its subsidiaries must be eliminated in combining the accounts of the parent and subsidiary companies.

Separate financial records are not maintained for the consolidated entity. The amounts reported in consolidated financial statements are determined using a worksheet and combining the amounts of like items from the financial statements of the affiliated companies. Entries included on the consolidation worksheet are made for the sole purpose of preparing consolidated financial statements. Consequently, consolidating adjustments and eliminations are not posted to the books of either the parent or its subsidiary.

Preparation of consolidated balance sheets under varying circumstances is illustrated by the following examples. First, let us consider the process of consolidating two balance sheets at the time a parent company initially acquired the stock of a subsidiary company.

Complete Ownership Acquired at Book Value. Assume that the parent company, P, acquired 100 percent of the common stock of a subsidiary company, S, at a price of $20,000 on December 31, 19x1. Separate balance sheets of P Company and S Company immediately following the acquisition are presented in Illustration 1.

Illustration 1
P Company and S Company
Balance Sheets
At December 31, 19x1

	P Company	S Company
Cash	$ 10,000	$ 5,000
Accounts receivable	10,000	5,000
Fixed assets	60,000	20,000
Investment in S Company	20,000	0
Total assets	$100,000	$30,000
Accounts payable	$ 10,000	$10,000
Capital stock	60,000	15,000
Retained earnings	30,000	5,000
Total liabilities and equities	$100,000	$30,000

P Company paid an amount equal to the stockholders' equity (common stock and retained earnings) of the subsidiary for 100 percent ownership of S. This indicates that the acquisition was made at the book value of the subsidiary's net assets. Since no transactions have occurred between the companies, the only adjustment required is to eliminate the investment account of the parent against the stockholders' equity accounts of the subsidiary, as shown in Illustration 2.

As previously indicated, the elimination entry is made on a worksheet which is used in order to facilitate the preparation of the consolidated balance sheet. No entries are made in the accounting records of either the parent or the subsidiary.

Complete Ownership Acquired at More Than Net Asset Value. In most cases, when the parent acquires stock in a subsidiary, the cost of the investment will differ from the recorded value of the net assets (assets less liabilities) of the subsidiary. From a consolidated standpoint, the purchase of

Illustration 2
P Company and S Company
Consolidated Worksheet
At December 31, 19x1

	P Company	S Company	Eliminations Dr.	Eliminations Cr.	Consolidation
Cash	$ 10,000	$ 5,000			$ 15,000
Accounts receivable	10,000	5,000			15,000
Fixed assets	60,000	20,000			80,000
Investment in S Company	20,000			$20,000[a]	
Total assets	$100,000	$30,000			$110,000
Accounts payable	$ 10,000	$10,000			$ 20,000
Capital stock	60,000	15,000	$15,000[a]		60,000
Retained earnings	30,000	5,000	5,000[a]		30,000
Total liabilities and equity	$100,000	$30,000			$110,000

[a] Elimination of the investment account against book value of the subsidiary's stock.

subsidiary stock may be regarded as similar to the purchase of the subsidiary's net assets (i.e., its assets less liabilities). Consequently, subsidiary assets should be recorded at an amount equal to the price paid by the parent for its 100 percent interest in the subsidiary. To adjust the carrying values of subsidiary assets to reflect the price paid by the parent for the stock, information concerning the fair values of the subsidiary assets at the time of acquisition must be obtained.

The amount paid by the parent company for the subsidiary's stock may differ from the net asset value of the subsidiary for two primary reasons. First, subsidiary assets may have a fair market value which differs from their recorded book value. This may occur because the accounting methods used for recording assets are normally not intended to reflect the fair value of the assets of the firm. Thus, if the parent company pays an amount which is in excess of book value, this excess may exist because the net assets of the subsidiary are undervalued (that is, the book value of the assets determined on the basis of proper account methods is less than their fair market value). Also, the excess may be due to the existence of unrecorded intangible assets of the subsidiary or from anticipated advantages which are expected because of the affiliation. If the assets of the subsidiary are undervalued, any specific tangible or intangible assets with fair market values in excess of recorded book values should be restated at fair market value in the consolidation worksheet. Thus, identifiable assets will be reported in the consolidated balance sheet at an amount equal to their fair market values at the date of acquisition. If the cost of the subsidiary stock still exceeds the amount assigned to the net assets of the subsidiary in the consolidation worksheet, this excess is assigned to an intangible asset, goodwill or "excess of cost over book value." Therefore, the total excess of the cost of the subsidiary stock over the book value of the subsidiary's net assets is included among consolidated assets—either as increases in the value of specific assets or alternatively as goodwill. Again, it is important to note that these adjustments are made only in the consolidation worksheet.

To illustrate, assume the same facts as in the previous illustration except that P Company acquired all of the stock of S Company at a cost of $25,000. Thus, the cost of investment ($25,000) exceeds the stockholders' equity of the subsidiary ($20,000) by $5,000. Apparently the management of P Company believes that the fair value of specific assets of S Company is greater than their recorded book value or that there are advantages of affiliation, such as future earnings prospects, which justify payment of $5,000 in excess of book value for S Company's net assets. In this illustration, assume that the excess of cost over book value existed because the fair market value of S Company's land exceeded its recorded book value by $5,000. Therefore, this excess would be assigned to land (which is summarized in fixed assets in this example) in the consolidation worksheet. The consolidation worksheet would be as shown in Illustration 3. The eliminating entries on the consolidation worksheet would be:

(a)	Fixed assets—S Company	5,000	
	Investment in S Company		5,000
(b)	Capital stock—S Company	15,000	
	Retained earnings—S Company	5,000	
	Investment in S Company		20,000

Again, it is important to note that these entries would not appear in the accounts of either P Company or S Company. These are worksheet entries that would be used to facilitate the consolidation of the financial reports of the parent and subsidiary company.

If the excess cannot be assigned to any specific assets (that is, the recorded book values of the subsidiary assets are equal to their fair values at acquisition), the $5,000 excess would have been reported in the consolidated balance sheet as goodwill or "excess of cost over book value." This is a new account which is introduced in the consolidated worksheet—it does not appear in the accounts of either P Company or S Company.

Illustration 3
P Company and S Company
Consolidated Worksheet
At December 31, 19x1

	P Company	S Company	Eliminations Dr.	Eliminations Cr.	Consolidation
Cash	$ 5,000	$ 5,000			$ 10,000
Accounts receivable	10,000	5,000			15,000
Fixed assets	60,000	20,000	$ 5,000 (a)		85,000
Investment in S Company	25,000			{ $ 5,000 (a) $20,000 (b)	
Total assets	$100,000	$30,000			$110,000
Accounts payable	$ 10,000	$10,000			$ 20,000
Capital stock	60,000	15,000	$15,000 (b)		60,000
Retained earnings	30,000	5,000	5,000 (b)		30,000
Total liabilities and equity	$100,000	$30,000			$110,000

(a) Adjustment for undervaluation of subsidiary's assets.
(b) Elimination of the investment account against the book value of the subsidiary's stock.

Complete Ownership Acquired for Less Than Net Asset Value. If the cost of the stock acquired by the parent company is less than book value, a similar problem exists. When specific overvalued assets can be identified, the excess would be reflected on the balance sheet by reducing the value of specific assets of the subsidiary. Thus, subsidiary assets would be reported at their fair values in the consolidated balance sheet. When specific assets which are overvalued cannot be identified, the excess is used to reduce noncurrent assets. If the allocation reduces the noncurrent assets to zero, the remainder of the excess is credited to an account referred to as "excess of book value of subsidiary interest over cost." This account is shown as a reduction of assets on the consolidated balance sheet. For example, assume P Company purchased 100 percent of the stock of S Company at a price of $18,000 on December 31, 19x1. At that date, the stockholders' equity of S Company was $20,000, consisting of $15,000 capital stock and $5,000 retained earnings. Eliminating entries on the consolidation worksheet would be as follows:

(a)	Investment in S Company	2,000	
	Specific assets of S Company		2,000
(b)	Capital stock—S Company	15,000	
	Retained earnings—S Company.............	5,000	
	Investment in S Company (from P's books)		20,000

Less Than Complete Ownership. A parent company may obtain control of a subsidiary by acquiring less than 100 percent of the capital stock of the subsidiary. When a parent owns less than 100 percent of the stock, the remainder of the stock held by stockholders outside the affiliated companies is classified as a *minority interest* in the consolidated balance sheet. The existence of a minority interest does not affect the amounts at which the assets and liabilities of the affiliated companies will ultimately appear on the consolidated balance sheet. However, only a portion of the equity in the net assets of the subsidiary company is owned by the parent since a portion of the owners' equity is held by minority stockholders. Equity held by minority stockholders, or minority interest, may be considered a part of the stockholders' equity of the consolidated entity.

To illustrate, assume that P Company acquired only 90 percent of the capital stock of the subsidiary at a cost of $18,000. The remaining 10 percent of the subsidiary's stock represents the minority interest in S Company. The only change required in the elimination entries is that only 90 percent of the capital stock and retained earnings of S Company is eliminated. The remaining 10 percent of S Company stockholders' equity represents the minority interest in the subsidiary and is classified as such in the consolidated balance sheet. The consolidated worksheet used to prepare the consolidated balance sheet is shown in Illustration 4.

The initial consolidation entry (a) eliminated 90 percent of the capital stock and retained earnings of S Company against the investment account of the parent. The remaining 10 percent of the stockholders' equity of S Company was then reclassified as a minority interest in entry (b).

It should be noted that, in this example, the parent company paid an amount which was equal to book value for its interest in the subsidiary. Therefore, the investment account was exactly equal to 90 percent of the stockholders' equity of S Company at acquisition. The existence of a minority interest, however, would not affect the procedures which are required when the investment is acquired at either more or less than book value. Any difference between the cost of the investment and the amount representing the parent company's interest in the stockholders' equity of the subsidiary increases consolidated assets if cost exceeds book value and reduces consolidated assets if cost is less than book value.

Illustration 4
P Company and S Company
Consolidation Worksheet
At December 31, 19x1

	P Company	S Company	Eliminations Dr.	Eliminations Cr.	Consolidation
Cash	$ 12,000	$ 5,000			$ 17,000
Accounts receivable	10,000	5,000			15,000
Fixed assets	60,000	20,000			80,000
Investment in S Company	18,000			$18,000 (a)	
Total assets	$100,000	$30,000			$112,000
Accounts payable	$ 10,000	$10,000			$ 20,000
Capital stock	60,000	15,000	$ 1,500 (b) $13,500 (a)		60,000
Retained earnings	30,000	5,000	500 (b) 4,500 (a)		30,000
Minority interest	0	0		2,000 (b)	2,000
Total liabilities and equity	$100,000	$30,000			$112,000

(a) Elimination of investment against 90 percent of the subsidiary's stockholders' equity.
(b) Adjustment to reclassify 10 percent of the subsidiary's stockholders' equity as minority interest.

Consolidated Balance Sheet After the Date of Acquisition

Net assets of a subsidiary change subsequent to the date of affiliation as a result of the difference between the net income earned and the dividends paid by the subsidiary since the date the parent acquired its interest in the subsidiary. If the parent company carries its investment using the equity method, the parent's share of such changes in the net assets of a subsidiary is reflected in the investment account. This occurs because the parent company increases the investment account and records investment income for its share of subsidiary earnings and reduces the investment account for any dividends which it receives from the subsidiary. Similarly, a loss incurred by the subsidiary is recorded by the parent as a decrease in the investment account and a corresponding decrease in the parent company's earnings. At any time subsequent to the date of affiliation, the change in the parent's investment account for each year must be equal to the parent company's share (that is, the parent company's percentage ownership of the voting stock of its subsidiary) of the change in the retained earnings of the subsidiary company. The eliminations which are required in order to prepare a consolidated balance sheet are basically the same as those which were required at the date of acquisition except that the amount eliminated from the investment account of the parent and the stockholders' equity of the subsidiary will change each year. Since the two entries which are made in the elimination of the parent's investment account against the stockholders' equity of the subsidiary will change by the same amount, the original difference between the cost of the investment and the book value of the subsidiary will be the same for each period.

To illustrate the procedures required for the preparation of a worksheet for a consolidated balance sheet, assume that P Company purchases 90 percent of the outstanding stock of S Company on December 31, 19x1, at a price of $21,000. At that time, S Company had capital stock of $15,000 and retained earnings of $5,000. Therefore, the cost of the investment exceeded the book value of the subsidiary stock by $3,000 (the book value of the net assets purchased was 90% × $20,000 or $18,000). It was determined that this excess of cost over book value was attributed to the excess of the market value of land owned by the subsidiary over the book value of the land. Further, assume that the subsidiary company had net income of $20,000 and paid dividends totalling $10,000 during 19x2. The effect of these transactions is to increase the retained earnings of the subsidiary by $10,000, from $5,000 to $15,000 (retained earnings on December 31, 19x1, of $5,000 plus 19x2 net income of $20,000 minus 19x2 dividends of $10,000). Similarly, net income and dividends paid by the subsidiary will cause a net increase of $9,000 in the parent company's investment account (90% of $20,000 net income minus 90% of the $10,000 dividends). The remaining 10 percent of the increase in the subsidiary's retained earnings represents an increase in the equity of the minority stockholders and would be classified as such. The worksheet (see Illustration 5) for consolidation illustrates the procedures which are required in preparing a consolidated balance sheet (see Illustration 6) one year after the date of acquisition of the subsidiary.

OTHER RECIPROCAL ACCOUNTS

In preparing a consolidated balance sheet, the investment account of the parent company must be eliminated against the stockholders' equity accounts of its subsidiary. If any transactions occurred between the parent and subsidiary companies, there might be additional reciprocal accounts which would also be eliminated in the consolidation worksheet in order to avoid the double-counting of assets and liabilities.

One of the most common of these additional reciprocal accounts involves intercompany receivables and payables. If one affiliated company borrows from another, the debtor firm incurs a liability (payable) equal to an asset (receivable) of the creditor company. From a consolidated standpoint, the payable does not represent an amount owed to an entity outside the affiliated group, nor does the related asset represent a receivable from an outside group. Therefore, in the consolidation worksheet, both the reciprocal asset and liability should be eliminated.

Illustration 5
P Company and S Company
Consolidation Worksheet
At December 31, 19x2

	P Company	S Company	Eliminations Dr.	Eliminations Cr.	Consolidation
Cash	$ 10,000	$ 7,000			$ 17,000
Accounts receivable	10,000	6,000			16,000
Fixed assets	70,000	20,000	$ 3,000 (a)		93,000
Investment in S Company	30,000			$ 3,000 (a) $27,000 (b)	
Total assets	$120,000	$33,000			$126,000
Accounts payable	$ 15,000	$ 3,000			$ 18,000
Capital stock	60,000	15,000	$ 1,500 (c) $13,500 (b)		60,000
Retained earnings	45,000	15,000	1,500 (c) 13,500 (b)		45,000
Minority interest	0	0		3,000 (c)	3,000
Total liabilities and equity	$120,000	$33,000			$126,000

(a) Adjustment for undervaluation of subsidiary's assets.
(b) Elimination of investment against 90 percent of the subsidiary's stockholders' equity.
(c) Adjustment to reclassify 10 percent of the subsidiary's stockholders' equity as minority interest.

To illustrate this point, assume that the parent company owes the subsidiary company $5,000 as of December 31, 19x2. The following entry would be made on the consolidation worksheet in order to eliminate the reciprocal accounts:

Accounts payable—P Company	5,000	
Accounts receivable—S Company		5,000

POOLING OF INTERESTS

In the discussion of consolidated statements included in the preceding section of this chapter, it was assumed that the parent company purchased the stock of the subsidiary with cash or other assets. The consolidated statements were prepared on the premise that the purchase of stock represented a purchase of the underlying net assets of the subsidiary. Therefore, in the consolidated statements, the cost of the acquisition was allocated to the individual assets of the subsidiary with any excess reported as "excess of cost over book value."

Illustration 6
P Company and S Company
Consolidated Balance Sheet
At December 31, 19x2

Current assets:		
Cash	$17,000	
Accounts receivable	16,000	
Total current assets		$ 33,000
Fixed assets		93,000
Total assets		$126,000
Liabilities:		
Accounts payable		$ 18,000
Minority interest in S Company		3,000
Stockholders' equity:		
Capital stock	$60,000	
Retained earnings	45,000	105,000
Total liabilities and equities		$126,000

A subsidiary may also be acquired by the exchange of the parent's stock for the stock of the subsidiary. Under certain circumstances, this combination may be accounted for as a *pooling of interests*. Because the stockholders of the subsidiary become stockholders of the parent company, one group has not acquired the interests of the other. Rather, both have "pooled" their interests in a combined entity. A pooling of interests unites the ownership interests of two or more firms by the exchange of stock. A purchase transaction is not recognized because the combination is accomplished without disbursing the assets of either company. A key feature of a pooling is that the former ownership interests continue and the basis of accounting remains the same.

Since no purchase is recognized and basically the same ownership interests continue, there is no justification for revaluing assets in a pooling of interests. All assets and liabilities of the companies are carried forward to the consolidated statements at their recorded book value. The parent company records the acquisition by debiting the investment account for the par value of the stock issued. Since assets and liabilities are combined at their recorded amounts, there is no excess of cost over book value to be accounted for in the consolidated statements. In addition, retained earnings of the subsidiary at acquisition may be combined with the parent's retained earnings in determining consolidated retained earnings.

To illustrate, assume that P Company issued 1,000 shares of its $50 par value stock in exchange for all of the stock of S Company. Assume that S Company has 6,000 shares of $10 par value stock outstanding. The parent company records the acquisition at the par value of the stock issued as follows:

Investment in S Company	100,000	
Capital stock		50,000
Capital in excess of par		10,000
Retained earnings		40,000

This entry records the investment at the net asset amount of S Company, credits the capital stock account for the par value of the shares issued, credits capital in excess of par for the difference in the par value of the shares issued by P ($50,000) and the par value of S's stock ($60,000) and credits retained earnings for the amount of S's retained earnings.

Under the pooling of interests method, the fair values of the subsidiary's assets are not considered to be relevant for purposes of consolidation. Therefore, the entry required on the worksheet eliminates the investment account of the parent company against the capital stock and retained earnings of the subsidiary. The consolidation worksheet at the date of acquisition is shown in Illustration 7. If the par value of the stock issued exceeds

Illustration 7
P Company and S Company
Consolidation Worksheet
At January 1, 19x2

	P Company	S Company	Eliminations Dr.	Eliminations Cr.	Consolidation
Other assets	$250,000	$120,000			$370,000
Investment in S Company	100,000	0		$100,000 [a]	0
Total	$350,000	$120,000			$370,000
Liabilities	$ 30,000	$ 20,000			$ 50,000
Capital stock:					
P Company ($50 par value)	150,000	0			150,000
S Company ($10 par value)	0	60,000	$60,000 [a]		0
Capital in excess of par value	60,000	0			60,000
Retained earnings	110,000	40,000	40,000 [a]		110,000
Total	$350,000	$120,000			$370,000

[a] Elimination of the investment account against an equal amount of stockholders' equity.

the par value of the shares acquired, the difference may be charged or debited to capital in excess of par value. If capital in excess is insufficient to absorb the difference, the remainder may be charged against retained earnings.

Note that the parent and subsidiary retained earnings accounts are combined under the pooling method. Consolidated retained earnings may be less than the sum of the retained earnings balances if the par value of the stock issued by the parent is more than the par value of the shares acquired and if there is insufficient capital in excess of par value to absorb this difference.

Prior to 1970, accountants often considered the purchase and pooling of interests method to be acceptable alternatives for accounting for any given business combination. The pooling of interests method was popular because in circumstances where the fair value of the subsidiary assets exceeds the recorded book values, the pooling treatment results in higher future net income and earnings per share to be reported than does the purchase method. In addition, pooling normally causes higher retained earnings than the purchase method. The Accounting Principles Board, however, attempted to resolve this problem by issuing *Opinion No. 16*. With respect to the purchase versus pooling issue, the board concluded that ". . . the purchase method and the pooling of interests method are both acceptable in accounting for business combinations, although not as alternatives in accounting for the same business combinations." The board specified the conditions under which each of the two methods is applicable to a business combination.[7]

USEFULNESS OF CONSOLIDATED STATEMENTS

In a situation where one corporation owns a majority of the voting stock of one or more other corporations, financial statements which are prepared for the separate legal corporate entities may not provide the most useful information to management, stockholders, and potential investors of the parent company. Instead, these users are interested in the financial position and results of operations of the combined entity (i.e., the parent company and all other companies under the control of the parent).

On the other hand, minority stockholders of a subsidiary company ordinarily have little use for consolidated financial statements. Since minority stockholders are primarily concerned with their ownership in the subsidiary company, separate financial statements of the subsidiary are usually more useful to them. Similarly, creditors of either the parent or a subsidiary are primarily concerned with their individual legal claims. Therefore, separate financial statements based on the individual entities concerned are of primary interest to these creditors.

---

[7] Discussion of the specific criteria for purchase vs. pooling is beyond the scope of this text.

CONSOLIDATED INCOME STATEMENT

A consolidated income statement is prepared by combining the revenues and expenses of the parent and subsidiary companies. If the parent company owns 100 percent of the subsidiary stock and there have been no transactions between the parent and its subsidiary, consolidation is simply a combination of revenues and expenses resulting from the parent and subsidiary companies' operations. The only adjustment necessary is that which is required in order to eliminate the investment income of the parent company (the parent company's share of the subsidiary's net income). This amount must be eliminated in order to avoid duplication or double-counting of earnings in the consolidated income statement.

As in the case of the consolidated balance sheet, elimination of reciprocal accounts may be necessary in order to avoid duplication or double-counting of revenues and expenses resulting from transactions which have occurred between the parent and its subsidiary. For example, interest expense of one company and interest income of the other resulting from an intercompany loan are eliminated because they do not change the net assets of the total entity from a consolidated viewpoint.

MINORITY INTEREST

If the parent owns less than 100 percent of the subsidiary stock, an additional adjustment is required in the consolidated worksheet in order to allocate the net income of the subsidiary between the parent company and the minority stockholders of the subsidiary. This division of the consolidated income is based on the percentage of the subsidiary stock owned by the parent company and the minority stockholders.

To illustrate the consolidation procedure for the income statement, again assume that P Company purchased 90 percent of the stock of S Company on December 31, 19x2. The 19x2 income statement for P Company is presented in Illustration 8. Also, assume that the parent rents a building to its subsidiary at a rental of $5,000 per year. The procedures which are necessary in order to prepare a consolidated income statement are illustrated in the consolidated worksheet in Illustration 9. It should be noted that the worksheet has a self-balancing format. That is, the net income figures have been included along with the expenses so that the revenues are equal to income plus expenses.

Elimination (a) removes the duplication or double-counting effect of the intercompany building rental. This entry has no effect on consolidated net income since it simply offsets rent revenue of P Company against an equal amount of rent expense of S Company. Elimination (b) cancels the investment income which P Company records as its share of the net income of S Company under the equity method. This entry corrects the double-counting of S Company's net income. Elimination (c) allocates 10 percent of S Company's net income to the minority stockholders of the subsidiary company.

Illustration 8
P Company and S Company
Income Statements
For the Year Ended December 31, 19x2

	P Company	S Company
Revenues:		
Sales	$195,000	$100,000
Rent revenue	5,000	0
Investment income	18,000	0
Total revenues	$218,000	$100,000
Expenses:		
Cost of goods sold	$150,000	$ 70,000
Other expenses	20,000	10,000
Total expenses	$170,000	$ 80,000
Net income	$ 48,000	$ 20,000

The amounts in the consolidation column of the worksheet are used in order to prepare the consolidated income statement in Illustration 10. Notice that the minority interest in net income is treated as a reduction of net income of the consolidated entity to arrive at consolidated net income.

PROFIT ON INTERCOMPANY SALES

An additional problem occurs if the assets which were transferred in intercompany sales were sold at a price which differed from the cost to the selling affiliate. If these assets were not resold by the end of the period, the gain or loss on the sale between the affiliates must be eliminated in the consolidation process. To illustrate this point, assume that the following transactions take place between a parent company (P) and its subsidiary (S):

1. P purchases two ten-speed bicycles for $100.

2. P sells the two bicycles to S for $120 on account.

3. S sells one of the bicycles to an outsider for $80 in cash.

Illustration 9
P Company and S Company
Consolidation Worksheet
At December 31, 19x2

	P Company	S Company	Eliminations Dr.	Eliminations Cr.	Consolidation
Sales	$195,000	$100,000			$295,000
Rent revenue	5,000	0	5,000 [a]		
Investment income	18,000	0	18,000 [b]		
Total revenues	$218,000	$100,000			$295,000
Cost of goods sold	$150,000	$ 70,000			$220,000
Other expenses	20,000	10,000		$ 5,000 [a]	25,000
Net income:					
P Company	48,000				48,000
S Company		20,000		{ $ 2,000 [c] 18,000 [b]	
Minority interest in net income			2,000 [c]		2,000
Total expenses and net income	$218,000	$100,000			$295,000

[a] Elimination of intercompany rent revenue and rent expense.
[b] Elimination of investment income against 90 percent of subsidiary net income.
[c] Adjustment to reclassify 10 percent of the subsidiary's net income as minority interest.

Illustration 10
P Company and Subsidiary
Consolidated Income Statement
For the Year 19x2

Sales	$295,000
Cost of goods sold	220,000
Gross profit	$ 75,000
Other expenses	25,000
Combined net income	$ 50,000
Less minority interest in net income	2,000
Consolidated net income	$ 48,000

These entries would be recorded on the books of P Company and S Company as follows:

P Company Books			S Company Books		
1. Inventory	100		No entry		
Cash		100			
2. Accounts receivable	120		Inventories	120	
Sales		120	Accounts payable		120
Cost of goods sold	100				
Inventories		100			
3. No entry			Cash	80	
			Sales		80
			Cost of goods sold	60	
			Inventories		60

As a result of these transactions, there is a receivable of $120 from S Company on P Company's books and a payable of $120 to P Company on S Company's books. Also, P Company's books show sales of $120 (to S) and a related cost of goods sold of $100, while S Company's books show the cost of the bicycle sold to the outsider as $60. The unsold bicycle is carried in S Company's inventory at a cost of $60.

The problem, in terms of preparing consolidated financial statements, is that the intercompany receivables and payables and the effects of the intercompany sales must be eliminated. Also, the cost of the bicycle remaining in S Company's inventory must be reduced from $60 to $50 (the cost to P) and the $10 profit on the "sale" of this bicycle by P Company to S Company must be eliminated from the net income of P Company. The worksheet entries required to accomplish these objectives are as follows:

Accounts payable	120	
Accounts receivable		120
Sales	120	
Cost of goods sold		120
Cost of goods sold	10	
Inventories		10

The first entry eliminates the intercompany receivables and payables. The second entry eliminates the intercompany sale and the related cost of goods sold, while the final entry corrects the cost of goods sold (and therefore net income) by eliminating the intercompany profit in the ending inventory.

SUMMARY

To raise additional funds for long-term purposes, a firm may borrow by issuing bonds. Bonds require the firm to pay a definite amount (the face value) at a specified date (the maturity date) and may be traded by the investors until that date. In addition, the firm agrees to make periodic interest payments at a stated rate throughout the life of the liability. Bonds may either be secured by specific assets or, in the case of debenture bonds, by only the general credit rating of the issuing corporation.

Since bonds may be traded by investors, the actual selling price received by the issuing corporation may vary from face value. If the selling price is less than the face value of the bond, it is said to be selling at a discount and if the selling price is greater than face value, at a premium. This discount or premium is amortized over the life of the bond and results in either an increase or a decrease in the interest expense incurred on the bond issue.

Bonds may be retired prior to maturity, either by redeeming callable bonds or by repurchasing bonds on the open market. In either case, it may be necessary for the firm to recognize either a gain or loss on the early retirement of the debt, depending on the repurchase price. A firm may be required to provide investors with a degree of security, either by periodically setting aside funds in a sinking fund or by making an appropriation of retained earnings.

Companies often make temporary investments in marketable securities to obtain productive use of seasonal excesses of cash. Temporary investments are considered current assets and include both stocks and bonds that are readily salable. Because of this liquidity, careful control should be exercised over the investment documents. Marketable securities are typically valued at cost, but FASB *Statement No. 12* requires that marketable equity securities be valued in the aggregate at the lower of cost or market for financial reporting purposes.

Corporations often make long-term investments in the stocks and bonds of other corporations. Since bonds may be purchased for an amount greater or lesser than face value, the acquiring company will amortize the resulting bond premium or discount. This amortization is recorded as an adjustment to the interest income earned on the bond. When bonds are purchased or sold between interest dates, the firm must calculate the amount of interest receivable being purchased or sold. In the case of a sale, the firm may also recognize a resulting gain or loss.

Investments in the securities of other corporations are recorded at the purchaser's cost. If there is no significant relationship between the investor and investee corporations, this acquisition cost will remain as the carrying value of the investment. However, if the investor company may exercise significant control or influence over the investee company (e.g., as evidenced by an ownership of 20% or more of its voting stock) subsequent increases and decreases in the net assets of the investee must be reflected in the carrying value of the investment on the investor's books.

If two firms are associated in such a manner that one owns a controlling interest in the other, the firms are referred to as affiliated companies. Since these firms remain separate legal entities, separate financial statements are prepared for each company. However, if the subsidiary company is under the continuing control of the parent company, it may be desirable to prepare consolidated financial statements. When a consolidated balance sheet is prepared at the date of acquisition (unless the purchase price equals the book value of the subsidiary's stock), the subsidiary's assets must be adjusted prior to being combined with the value of the parent's assets. In addition, elimination entries must be made on the worksheet for the parent's investment account and the subsidiary's owners' equity accounts to avoid duplication of information. The elimination entries are varied slightly if the parent company acquires less than complete ownership of the subsidiary. In addition, such a situation will require adjustments to the entries recording changes in the net assets of the subsidiary after acquisition. Regardless of the percentage of ownership by the parent, certain elimination entries may be required on the consolidation worksheet if the affiliated companies engage in business transactions with each other.

A business combination may also be affected by one company exchanging its stock for the stock of another corporation. The former ownership interests continue and the basis for accounting remains the same. Such a situation is referred to as a pooling of interests and requires appropriate worksheet elimination entries prior to final preparation of consolidated statements.

KEY DEFINITIONS

Affiliated companies—a parent company and one or more related subsidiary companies are said to be affiliated.

Amortization of premium or discount—the process of allocating a portion of the discount or premium on bonds payable (investment in bonds) to interest expense (revenue).

Bond—an issuance of debt used as a means of borrowing money for long-term purposes.

Bond discount—the amount by which the face value of a bond payable exceeds the issue price. A discount occurs when the coupon rate on the bonds is less than the market interest rate at the time the bonds are issued.

Bond premium—the amount by which the issue price of a bond payable exceeds the face value. A premium occurs when the coupon rate of interest on a bond is higher than the market interest rate at the time of issuance.

Bond sinking fund—accumulated by the issuing corporation specifically for the repayment of bonds at maturity. A sinking fund may be created voluntarily or required by provisions of the bond issue.

Callable bonds—may be repurchased at the option of the issuing corporation within a specified period at a specified price.

Consolidated statements—consolidated financial statements present the combined assets, equities, and results of operations of affiliated corporations.

Consolidation worksheet—consolidation working papers are used in the preparation of consolidated statements for two or more companies. The consolidating adjustments and eliminations are never posted to the books of the individual companies involved, only to the worksheet.

Convertible bonds—may be exchanged for a specified amount of capital stock at the option of the bondholder.

Cost method—used for an investment in the stock of another company in which the investment account is carried at the original cost and income is recognized when dividends are received.

Coupon bonds—interest coupons attached which call for the payment of a specified amount of interest on the interest dates.

Coupon rate—the interest rate specified on the bond is the coupon rate. Periodic interest payments equal the coupon interest rate multiplied by the face amount of the bond.

Debenture bonds—not secured by any specific assets of the corporation. Their security is dependent upon the general credit standing of the issuing corporation.

Equity method—used for an investment in the stock of another company in which the investment account is adjusted for changes in the net assets of the investee, and income is recognized by the investor company as the investee earns profits or incurs losses.

Long-term investment in stock—this involves the acquisition of stock of other corporations as long-term, income-producing investments. Such purchases are often made for the purpose of obtaining a controlling interest in a company or for some other continuing business advantage.

Maturity value—constitutes the amount that the holder of a note is entitled to receive at the due date. This amount includes the principal plus any accrued interest.

Minority interest—shares held by stockholders of a subsidiary company when the parent acquires less than 100 percent of the subsidiary stock are referred to as a minority interest.

Mortgage—a conditional conveyance or transfer of property to a creditor as security for a loan.

Parent company—a firm owning a majority of the voting stock of another company is called a parent company.

Pooling of interests—a method used for recording a business acquisition where the assets and liabilities of the combining companies are combined at their existing book values.

Purchase—the purchase method for recording a business acquisition is the use of the cost to the acquiring corporation in valuing the assets of the subsidiary.

Registered bonds—have the name of the owner registered with the issuing corporation. Periodic interest payments are mailed directly to the registered owner.

Retirement of bonds—the process of redeeming bonds or repurchasing bonds in the open market.

Secured bond—secured by prior claim against specific assets of the business in the event that the issuing corporation is unable to make the required interest or principal payments.

Serial bonds—bonds which mature on several different dates.

Subsidiary company—a firm which has a majority of its voting stock owned by a parent company.

Temporary investments—a security that is readily salable, and the volume of trading of the security should be such that the sale does not materially affect the market price. In addition, there should be an intention on the part of the investor firm to sell the security in the short run as the need for cash arises.

Term bonds—a bond issue that matures on a single date.

QUESTIONS

1. Define each of the following terms related to the issue of bonds: (a) debenture, (b) secured, (c) callable, (d) convertible, (e) serial bonds.

2. How are interest payments made to the holders of (a) coupon bonds, and (b) registered bonds?

3. How can bonds be sold when the market interest rate for comparable bonds is higher than the stated contract rate on the bond certificate?

4. How does a discount on the issuance of bonds affect the total cost of borrowing to the issuing corporation?

5. What is the effect of a premium on the interest expense of the company issuing bonds? Explain.

6. What is the effect of a discount on the interest expense of the company issuing bonds? Explain.

7. Give the journal entries required for the amortization of (a) Discount on Bonds Payable and (b) Premium on Bonds Payable.

8. How should Discount on Bonds Payable and Premium on Bonds Payable be classified and presented on the balance sheet?

9. If bonds are issued at a time between interest payment dates, why does the issuing company receive an amount of cash equal to the issue price of the bonds plus the accrued interest?

10. Differentiate between long-term (permanent) and short-term (temporary) investments in stocks.

11. Explain the essential characteristics of the cost method.

12. Explain the essential characteristics of the equity method.

13. Under what circumstances would each of the following methods of accounting for long-term investment in stocks be used: (a) cost method? (b) equity method?

14. Define: (a) parent company, (b) subsidiary company, and (c) affiliated companies.

15. Describe the essential condition for the preparation of consolidated financial statements.

16. A consolidated balance sheet prepared for a parent company that owns less than 100 percent of the common stock of the subsidiary shows an item called "minority interest." What is the nature of this balance sheet account, and where does it appear on the consolidated balance sheet?

17. How is the difference between the cost of the subsidiary stock and the book value of the stock at the date of acquisition reported on the consolidated balance sheet?

18. Explain why intercompany debts and receivables should be eliminated in preparing consolidated balance sheets.

19. Why is the investment account of the parent company eliminated in preparing a consolidated balance sheet?

20. What types of users of financial statements are primarily interested in consolidated financial statements?

21. If the parent owns less than 100 percent of the subsidiary stock, the consolidated income statement shows an item called "minority interest in subsidiary income." What does this item represent?

22. Where are the entries recorded for the eliminations that are made in the process of preparing consolidated statements?

EXERCISES

23. Stengel Company has authorization to issue $200,000 of 10-year, 7 percent bonds on January 1, 19x1, with semiannual interest payments on June 30 and December 31. Stengel Company issues $100,000 of the bonds on January 1 at face value. Another $100,000 of bonds are issued on August 1, 19x1, at face value plus accrued interest. Assume Stengel Company's accounting period ends March 31.

    Required:

    Give the firm's journal entries with respect to the bonds for 19x1.

24. Terry Tractors, Inc., has outstanding a $100,000, 10-year bond issue which was sold on January 1, 19x0, at a price of $110,000. The following liability, shown below, appeared on the balance sheet on December 31, 19x4.

Bonds payable..................	$100,000	
Premium.....................	5,000	$105,000

    Make the entry necessary to record the retirement of the bonds in each of the following two situations:

    a. The firm calls the bonds at 106 on January 1, 19x5.
    b. Terry Tractors, Inc., purchases half of the outstanding bonds in the open market for $51,000 on January 1, 19x5.

25. Boyer, Inc., issued 100, $1,000, 20-year convertible bonds at a price of $1,020 each on January 1, 19x1. Each of the bonds is convertible into 20 shares of $20 par value common stock. On December 31, 19x7, 50 of these bonds were converted into common stock. Make the journal entry necessary to record the conversion on the books of Boyer, Inc.

26. The Trail Blazers Company issued a $70,000, 7 percent, 15-year debenture bond on July 1, 19x1, at a price of $68,000. Interest is to be paid on December 31 and June 30 of each year.

Required:

1. Record the journal entries with respect to the bond up to and including December 31, 19x1.
2. What is the total interest cost to the Trail Blazers Company for this bond issue?
3. Assuming the Trail Blazers Company has only this bond issue in long-term debt outstanding, prepare the long-term liabilities section of the balance sheet as of December 31, 19x1.

27. Ames Company had the following transactions relating to marketable securities during the last three months of 19x1.

Sept. 1 Purchased 100 shares of Burden Company common stock for $27 per share plus commission of $100.
Nov. 1 Received a $1 per share dividend on the Burden Company stock.
Dec. 1 Sold 50 shares of Burden Company stock at $32 per share net of commissions.

Required:

1. Prepare the journal entries necessary to record the above transactions.
2. Determine the cost basis for marketable securities at December 31, 19x1.

28. On January 1, 19x1, Lang Company acquired 25 percent of the outstanding shares of stock of Brenner Company at a cost of $250,000. On that date, Brenner Company had common stock of $750,000 and retained earnings of $250,000. Brenner Company reported net income of $100,000 during 19x1, and paid a cash dividend of $20,000. Make the necessary journal entries on Lang's books during 19x1 using the equity method.

29. Assume that Lang Company (Exercise 28) acquired only 19 percent of the shares of Brenner Company at a cost of $100,000. Prepare the necessary journal entries on Lang's books during 19x1 using the cost method.

30. On December 31, 19x1, P Company acquired a controlling interest in S Company. The balance sheets prior to acquisition were as follows:

	P Company	S Company
Current assets.	$100,000	$ 50,000
Fixed assets (net).	300,000	70,000
	$400,000	$120,000
Liabilities	$ 40,000	$ 20,000
Common stock.	300,000	80,000
Retained earnings.	60,000	20,000
	$400,000	$120,000

Prepare a consolidation worksheet at the date of acquisition assuming that P Company paid $100,000 cash for all the outstanding common stock of S Company.

31. Prepare a consolidation worksheet at the date of acquisition assuming that P Company (of Exercise 30) paid $90,000 cash for 90 percent of the outstanding common stock of S Company.

32. On December 31, 19x1, the account balances of a parent and its subsidiary included the following amounts:

	Parent	Subsidiary
Notes receivable.	$ 10,000	$ 20,000
Notes payable.	30,000	15,000
Sales	500,000	100,000
Purchases	300,000	70,000

All of the subsidiary sales were made to the parent company. All of the goods purchased from the subsidiary were sold by the parent company during the year. The parent company owed the subsidiary $10,000 as of December 31, 19x1.

a. What amounts of notes receivable and notes payable should be reported on the consolidated balance sheet?
b. What amount of sales and purchases should be reported on the consolidated income statement?

33. Walton, Inc. is a 100 percent owned subsidiary of Portland Company. The following transactions occurred in 19x1.

a. Portland Company purchased two basketballs for $10.
b. Portland Company sold the two basketballs to Walton, Inc. for $12 on account.
c. Walton, Inc. sold one of the basketballs to an outsider for $8.

Required:

1. Prepare journal entries on the books of Portland Company and Walton, Inc., to reflect the above information.
2. Prepare the necessary elimination entries for consolidation.

34. Armor Company purchased a $1,000 face value, 5-year, 8 percent bond on April 1, 19x1, for $1,020 including accrued interest. Interest on the bond is paid semiannually on June 30 and December 31. Prepare the journal entries required on the books of Armor Company on April 1, June 30, and December 31, 19x1.

35. Prepare the following *worksheet* entries which would appear on the consolidation worksheet of the Samson and Golieth Company as of December 31, 19x1. Do not prepare a consolidation worksheet.

   a. The Samson Company had purchased 90 percent of the common stock of the Golieth Company, for $38,000, on January 1, 19x1, when the stockholders' equity portion of Golieth Company's balance sheet appeared as follows:

Capital stock	$30,000
Retained earnings	10,000
	$40,000

   The management of the Samson Company believes that the fair value of specific assets of Golieth Company is greater than their recorded assets.

   b. During the year, Samson sold Golieth two chariots (the company's stock-in-trade) on account for a total of $2,000. Prior to this sale, Samson had purchased the chariots for $800 each. Neither of these chariots were sold by Golieth during the remainder of the year.

   c. Golieth rented a building to Samson during the year at a rental of $300 per month.

36. On December 31, 19x1, the Brewer Company issued 2,000 shares of its $10 par value stock in exchange for all of the stock of the White Sox Company. White Sox Company has 3,000 shares of $5 par value stock outstanding. Below are their balance sheets prior to acquisition:

	Brewer Company	White Sox Company
Cash	$ 30,000	$ 12,000
Accounts receivable	75,000	36,000
Fixed assets	110,000	78,000
	$215,000	$126,000

	Brewer Company	White Sox Company
Liabilities	$100,000	$ 45,000
Common stock	65,000	15,000
Capital in excess of par value	35,000	0
Retained earnings	15,000	66,000
	$215,000	$126,000

Required:

Prepare a consolidation worksheet at the date of acquisition assuming the pooling of interests method is used.

PROBLEMS

37. Kubek Company is authorized to issue $50,000 of 10-year, 8 percent bonds with semiannual interest payments on June 30 and December 31. Record the journal entries necessary on January 1 and June 30, 19x1, on the books of Kubek Company in each of the following independent cases.

    a. The bonds are issued at a price of $45,000 on January 1, 19x1. Interest is paid on June 30 and December 31.
    b. The bonds are issued at a price of $53,000 on January 1, 19x1. Interest is paid on June 30 and December 31.

38. Dean Co. issued $100,000 of 6 percent, 20-year debenture bonds on January 1, 19x1. Interest is payable semiannually on June 30 and December 31. The following information is given on the bonds at December 31, 19x1:

    Carrying value of bonds $103,800
    Interest expense for the year 5,800

    a. Were the bonds issued at a premium or discount?
    b. What was the amount of premium or discount on the issuance of the bonds?
    c. How much of the discount or premium was amortized during the year?

9 | Long-Term Liabilities, Investments, and Consolidated Financial Statements   9-53

39. On January 1, 19x1, the stockholders of Howard Company authorized the issuance of $8,000 (par value) of 3-year bonds paying interest (8 percent) semiannually on June 30 and December 31. The bonds were sold on April 1, 19x1, for $8,330 plus accrued interest. On April 1, 19x2, Howard Company retired half of the issue at 102 (plus accrued interest).

Required:

Prepare all general journal entries for:

1. Issuance of the bonds.
2. Interest payment on June 30, 19x1.
3. Interest payment on December 31, 19x1.
4. Retirement of portion of issue on April 1, 19x2.
5. Interest payment on June 30, 19x2.

40. On October 1, 19x1, the Badger Company issued $10,000 (face value) of 3 percent bonds which will mature on September 30, 19x3. On December 31, 19x1, the company's accountant made the following adjusting journal entry relative to the bonds (Badger Company's accounting period is the calendar year):

Interest expense............................	90	
Interest payable...........................		75
Discount on bonds payable..................		15

Required:

Give the journal entry made to record the sale of the bonds on October 1, 19x1. Assume that interest is payable annually on September 30.

41. The following data related to long-term liabilities appeared on the books of Summer Co. on December 31, 19x1 (after the payment of interest on December 31, 19x1).

Bonds payable—6 percent, 20-year debenture bonds due on December 31, 19x25, $100,000 authorized interest payable semiannually on June 30 and December 31...............	$100,000	
Discount on bonds payable..............	3,000	$97,000

On January 1, 19x2, half of the bonds were purchased and retired at 102 percent of face value. Prepare the necessary journal entries to record the semiannual interest payment on December 31, 19x1, and the retirement of $50,000 of bonds on January 1, 19x2.

42. Cavalier Corporation issued a $10,000, 5-year, 6 percent convertible bond for $9,280 on September 1, 19x1. Interest is to be paid semiannually on March 1 and September 1 each year. The bond is convertible into 10 shares of $20 par value common stock for each $1,000 of the bond issue.

Required:

Make the required journal entries to record the:

1. Issuance of the bond.
2. Accrual of interest on December 31, 19x1, the end of the fiscal year.
3. Payment of interest on March 1, 19x2.
4. Conversion of $5,000 worth of bonds payable into common stock on November 30, 19x4.
5. Payment of interest on September 1, 19x5.
6. Payment on the remainder of the bond principle and interest on the due date.

43. The Knick Company decided to issue a 5-year, $20,000 bond on January 2, 19x1, at a price and interest rate which has not yet been determined. Interest payments are to be made annually on December 31.

Required:

Prepare a table showing the cash interest payments, amortization of premium or discount, interest expense, and carrying value of the bond (as shown on the end-of-year balance sheet) over the bond's life using each of the following assumptions:

1. The bond was issued at 6 percent interest for $19,520.
2. The bond was issued at 8 percent interest for $20,360.

44. Jason Company issued $100,000 of 6 percent, 10-year debenture bonds at face value plus accrued interest on April 1, 19x1. Interest is payable semiannually on January 1 and July 1.

Required:

Prepare the journal entries necessary to record the issuance of the bonds and to record interest expense for the first interest date subsequent to issuance.

9 | Long-Term Liabilities, Investments, and Consolidated Financial Statements 9-55

45. Dorey Co. issued $500,000 of 20-year, 8 percent bonds on April 1, 19x1, with interest payable on June 30 and December 31. The bonds were callable after January 1, 19x8 at 105 percent of face value and mature on December 31, 19x20. The fiscal year of the company ends on September 30. Give the necessary journal entries for the following transactions:

19x1

Apr. 1 Issued the bonds for $529,750 including accrued interest.
June 30 Paid interest.
Sept. 30 Recorded adjusting entry for accrued interest.
Dec. 31 Paid interest.

19x8

Jan. 1 Called the bonds.

46. Hawk Company issued $150,000, 10-year, 8 percent convertible bonds for $155,392 including four months accrued interest on April 30, 19x0. Interest is to be paid semiannually on June 30 and December 31. The bonds are convertible into 5 shares of $50 par value common stock for each $1,000 of the bond issue. (Any premium or discount on the bonds should be amortized over 116 months, the remaining life of the bonds.)

Required:

Make the required journal entries to record the

1. Issuance of bonds.
2. Accrual of interest on September 30, 19x0, the end of the fiscal year.
3. Payment of interest on December 31, 19x0.
4. Conversion of a portion of the bonds into 375 shares of common stock on August 31, 19x2.
5. Payment of interest on June 30, 19x3.
6. Payment on the remainder of the bond principal and interest on the due date—December 31, 19x9.

47. The transactions of Sandy Company relating to marketable securities during 19x1 are listed below.

Jan. 10 Purchased 500 shares of Smith Corporation common stock at a price of $21 per share plus a $200 commission.
Feb. 5 Purchased 100 shares of Dade Corporation common stock at a price of $40 per share plus an $80 commission.
Mar. 1 Received a cash dividend of $1 per share on Smith Corporation common stock.
Apr. 16 Purchased 200 shares of Consolidated Company common stock at $80 per share plus $120 commission.
June 1 Received a cash dividend of $2 per share on Dade Corporation common stock.
Aug. 20 Sold 100 shares of Dade Corporation stock at $42 per share, net of sales commissions.
Sept. 1 Received a $1 per share dividend on Consolidated Company common stock.

Required:

1. Prepare the journal entries necessary to record the above transactions.
2. Prepare the necessary adjusting entry at December 31, 19x1, assuming that the aggregate market value of the portfolio is $11,000.

48. Handy Company had the following transactions relating to marketable securities during 19x1:

Jan. 20 Purchased 100 shares of Bear Corporation common stock at $50 per share plus a $105 commission.
Apr. 16 Purchased 400 shares of River Corporation common stock at $10 per share plus a commission of $95.
May 1 Received a cash dividend of $1 per share on Bear Corporation common stock.
June 5 Purchased 100 shares of Gunner Corporation common stock at $75 per share plus a $160 commission.
Aug. 11 Received a cash dividend of $2 per share on River Corporation common stock.
Nov. 1 Sold 100 shares of Bear Corporation common stock at $55 per share, net of commissions.
Dec. 1 Received a $1 per share dividend on Gunner Corporation common stock.

Required:

1. Prepare the journal entries to record the above transactions.
2. Prepare the necessary adjusting entry at December 31, 19x1, assuming that the aggregate market value of the portfolio is $9,600.

49. The balance sheets of Stevens Corporation and Thomas Corporation reflected the following on December 31, 19x1:

	Stevens Corporation	*Thomas Corporation*
Current assets..........................	$100,000	$ 30,000
Other assets...........................	500,000	100,000
Investment in Thomas.................	120,000	0
	$720,000	$130,000

	Stevens Corporation	*Thomas Corporation*
Current liabilities.....................	$100,000	$ 10,000
Common stock.......................	500,000	100,000
Retained earnings....................	120,000	20,000
	$720,000	$130,000

Stevens Corporation purchased 100 percent of the capital stock of Thomas Corporation on January 1, 19x1, for $111,000. The stockholders' equity of Thomas Corporation on that date included common stock of $100,000 and retained earnings of $11,000. Stevens Corporation had an account payable of $10,000 to Thomas Corporation at December 31, 19x1.

Required:

Prepare the December 31, 19x1, consolidated balance sheet.

50. The balances presented below were taken from the books of the Burns Co. and its subsidiary, the Gentry Co., as of December 31, 19x2. Burns Co. purchased 90 percent of the stock of Gentry Co. for $110,000 on December 31, 19x1. At the date of acquisition, Gentry Co. had common stock of $100,000 and retained earnings of $10,000. The difference between cost and book value was attributed to land owned by Gentry Co. Burns Co. uses the equity method for accounting for its investment in Gentry Co.

	Burns Co.	Gentry Co.
Cash	$ 20,000	$ 20,000
Accounts receivable	40,000	20,000
Inventories	60,000	25,000
Land	80,000	25,000
Buildings and equipment (net)	281,000	60,000
Investment in Gentry Co.	119,000	0
	$600,000	$150,000
Accounts payable	$120,000	$ 30,000
Capital stock	400,000	100,000
Retained earnings	80,000	20,000
	$600,000	$150,000

At the end of the year, Gentry Co. owed Burns Co. $10,000 on open account.

Required:

1. Prepare a worksheet for a consolidated balance sheet as of the end of 19x2.
2. Prepare a consolidated balance sheet in good form for the two companies.

51. Condensed balance sheet information of P Company and S Company at the end of 19x1 is shown below:

	P Company	S Company
Current assets	$300,000	$ 50,000
Other assets	500,000	100,000
	$800,000	$150,000
Liabilities	$100,000	$ 30,000
Capital stock ($100 par value)	500,000	100,000
Retained earnings	200,000	20,000
	$800,000	$150,000

Each of the cases described below involves a situation in which P Company acquires a controlling interest in the stock of S Company on December 31, 19x1.

Required:

Prepare a consolidated balance sheet at the date of acquisition for each of the following cases:

1. P Company purchased all of the outstanding shares of S Company for $140,000. There was evidence that the buildings and equipment of S Company were worth more than their book value.
2. P Company purchases all the outstanding shares of S Company for $110,000.
3. P Company purchases 80 percent of the outstanding shares of S Company for $105,000. The management of P Company paid more than book value because of anticipated advantages of affiliation.

52. On January 1, 19x1, Ace Co. purchased a 90 percent interest in Deuce Co. Income statement data for 19x1 are shown below:

	Ace Co.	Deuce Co.
Sales	$500,000	$ 88,000
Rental income	0	12,000
Interest income	1,000	0
Investment income	9,000	0
Total income	$510,000	$100,000
Cost of goods sold	$300,000	$ 55,000
Operating expenses (including rent)	180,000	30,000
Interest expense	10,000	5,000
Total expenses	$490,000	$ 90,000
Net income	$ 20,000	$ 10,000

Intercompany items were as follows:

a. Deuce Co. rented a building to Ace Co. for $1,000 a month during 19x1.
b. Deuce Co. paid Ace Co. $1,000 interest on intercompany notes during the year.
c. Ace Co. sold goods to Deuce Co. for $50,000 during the year. All the goods were resold by Deuce Co. to outsiders by the end of the year.

Required:

1. Prepare working papers for a consolidated income statement for 19x1.
2. Did the parent company use the cost method or equity method for accounting for its investment in the subsidiary?
3. If you had not been told that Ace Co. owned 90 percent of Deuce Co., how could you have determined this fact from the income statement data?

53. On January 1, 19x1, the Strock Co. acquired 90 percent of the common stock of the Bristow Co. for $145,000. The stockholders' equity of Bristow Co. on that date was as follows:

Common stock	$120,000
Retained earnings	30,000
	$150,000

During 19x1, the Bristow Co. earned $20,000 of net income and paid cash dividends of $12,000. The Strock Co. reported net income of $50,000 (including investment income) and paid dividends of $20,000. The Strock Co. uses the equity method for accounting for its investment in Bristow. The stockholders' equity of the Strock Co. on December 31, 19x1, was as follows:

Common stock	$400,000
Retained earnings	180,000
	$580,000

Required:

Determine the amounts at which the following items would be shown in the December 31, 19x1, consolidated statements.

a. Difference between cost and book value of subsidiary stock.
b. Consolidated net income.
c. Consolidated retained earnings.
d. Minority interest.

54. Income statement data for 19x1 for King Co. and its 100 percent owned subsidiary, Queen Co., are shown below.

	King Co.	Queen Co.
Sales	$200,000	$100,000
Investment income	20,000	0
	$220,000	$100,000
Cost of goods sold	$100,000	$ 60,000
Operating expenses	80,000	20,000
	$180,000	$ 80,000
Net income	$ 40,000	$ 20,000

During 19x1, Queen Co. sold all of its goods to King Co. An intercompany profit of $5,000 was recorded by Queen Co. on the sale of goods held in King Co.'s inventory at the end of 19x1.

Required:

Prepare the worksheet to develop a consolidated income statement at the end of 19x1.

55. Separate balance sheets for the Cat Company and Mouse Company for the years ended December 31, 19x1 and 19x2 are presented below:

	December 31, 19x1		December 31, 19x2	
	Cat Co.	Mouse Co.	Cat Co.	Mouse Co.
Cash	$ 24,000	$10,000	$ 20,000	$14,000
Accounts receivable	20,000	10,000	20,000	12,000
Fixed assets	120,000	40,000	140,000	44,000
Investment in Mouse Co.	36,000		60,000	
Total Assets	$200,000	$60,000	$240,000	$70,000
Accounts payable	$ 20,000	$20,000	$ 30,000	$ 6,000
Capital stock	120,000	30,000	120,000	30,000
Retained earnings	60,000	10,000	90,000	34,000
Total Liabilities and Equities	$200,000	$60,000	$240,000	$70,000

Cat Company had acquired a 100 percent interest in Mouse Company on December 31, 19x1. The difference in the cost of the company versus its book value is due to a difference between the book value and market value of fixed assets. During 19x2, Mouse Company earned $35,000 in net income and paid out $11,000 in cash dividends. As of December 31, 19x2, Cat Company owes Mouse Company $5,000 and Mouse Company owes Cat Company $3,000.

Required:

1. Prepare a consolidation worksheet for December 31, 19x1 and 19x2.
2. Does the Cat Company use the cost or equity method to record its investment in the Mouse Company?

56. Below is the adjusted trial balance for the Indian Company and Tiger Company for the year ended December 31, 19x1.

	Indian Company	Tiger Company
Cash	$ 10,000	$ 8,000
Accounts receivable	23,000	21,000
Accrued interest receivable	600	1,200
Accrued rent receivable	1,200	0
Fixed assets	168,100	123,600
Investment in Tiger Company	72,900	0
Accounts payable	(9,500)	(6,600)
Rent payable	0	(1,200)
Long-term debt	(126,000)	(65,000)
Capital stock	(84,000)	(41,500)
Retained earnings	(18,000)	(26,000)
Sales	(205,000)	(150,000)
Cost of goods sold	133,250	97,500
Other expenses	60,000	39,000
Rent revenue	(14,400)	0
Investment revenue	(12,150)	0

The Indian Company had purchased a 90 percent interest in the Tiger Company on December 31, 19x0 when Tiger Company had the following balances in its stockholders' equity accounts.

Capital stock	$41,500
Retained earnings	26,000
	$67,500

The Indian Company uses the equity method to record its investment in the subsidiary.

During 19x1, Tiger Company rented a building from Indian Company for $1,200 a month. Rent is paid on the first day of each month.

Required:

Prepare consolidation income statement worksheets and consolidation balance sheet worksheets for the Indian and Tiger Companies as of December 31, 19x1. Don't forget to add net income earned during the year to retained earnings for each company.

57. Jijo Co. purchased 80 percent of the outstanding stock of Eli Co. for $175,000 on January 1, 19x1. Balance sheet data for the two corporations immediately after the transaction are presented below.

	Jijo Co.	Eli Co.
Cash	$ 10,000	$ 5,000
Accounts receivable	30,000	15,000
Inventories	60,000	30,000
Fixed assets (net)	300,000	170,000
Investment in Eli Co	175,000	0
	$575,000	$220,000

Assume that the difference between the cost of the investment and the book value of the subsidiary was attributed to advantages of affiliation.

Required:

Prepare a consolidated balance sheet for Jijo Co. and Eli Co. at January 1, 19x1.

58. Below are given the trial balances of Moore Company and its 90 percent owned subsidiary, Parker Company, as of December 31, 19x1:

	Moore Company		Parker Company	
Cash	$ 31,000		$ 12,750	
Accounts receivable	24,000		12,400	
Advances to Parker Company	10,000			
Investment in Parker Company	76,500			
Inventory	26,000		28,100	
Other assets	80,840		50,000	
Accounts payable		$ 31,960		$ 8,250
Advances from Moore Company				10,000
Capital stock		200,000		60,000
Retained earnings		16,380		25,000
	$248,340	$248,340	$103,250	$103,250

Additional data:

The advances are non-interest bearing. At the time of acquisition, Parker Company's equity section was as follows:

Capital stock	$60,000
Retained earnings	15,000

Required:

1. Elimination entries.
2. Consolidated balance sheet.

59. Below is shown the condensed balance sheets of the A's and Angel Companies at the end of 19x1, before the acquisition of the stock of Angel Company.

	A's Company	Angel Company
Current assets	$100,000	$ 25,000
Other assets	400,000	75,000
Total Assets	$500,000	$100,000

	A's Company	Angel Company
Liabilities	$ 50,000	$ 10,000
Capital stock ($50 par value)	150,000	35,000
Retained earnings	300,000	55,000
Total Liabilities and Equities	$500,000	$100,000

Required:

Prepare a consolidated balance sheet for the year 19x1, under each of the following unrelated assumptions. A's Company has acquired a controlling interest in the stock of Angel Company in each case.

1. A's Company purchased all of the outstanding shares of Angel Company for $80,000 in cash. An appraisal of land held by Angel Company determined the land to be worth less than its book value.
2. A's Company purchased all the outstanding shares of Angel Company for $100,000. They paid more for the shares than book value because the value of several assets had increased over their book value.
3. A's Company purchased 90 percent of the outstanding shares of Angel Company for $79,000. A's Company paid less than book value because the product manufactured by Angel Company was outdated.

60. On January 1, 19x1, Royals Company purchased an 80 percent interest in Twins Company. Their income statements for the year ended December 31, 19x1 are shown below.

	Royals Company	Twins Company
Sales	$250,000	$28,000
Rental income	18,000	3,000
Interest income	1,500	500
Investment income	6,720	0
Total Revenues	$276,220	$31,500
Cost of goods sold	$100,000	$14,000
Operating expenses	50,500	7,900
Interest expense	300	1,200
Total Expenses	$150,800	$23,100
Net Income	$125,420	$ 8,400

Additional data:

a. Royals Company rented a building from Twins Company for $250 a month during 19x1.
b. Royals Company sold $13,000 worth of goods to Twins Company and all these goods were later resold.
c. Royals Company paid $280 interest to Twins Company during the year and Twins Company paid $1,000 interest to Royals Company.

Required:

Prepare working papers for a consolidated income statement for 19x1.

61. On January 1, 19x2, the Ranger Company purchased 80 percent of the common stock of the Blue Jay Company for $310,000. The stockholders' equity of Blue Jay Company on that date was:

Common stock	$100,000
Retained earnings	260,000
	$360,000

The Ranger Company decided to use the equity method to account for its investment in Blue Jay Company. During 19x2, the Blue Jay Company earned $50,000 in net income and paid $30,000 in dividends. The Ranger Company reported $150,000 in net income (excluding investment income) and paid dividends of $90,000.

Required:

1. What amount would be shown on the consolidated balance sheet as "Excess of cost over book value of subsidiary," assuming the fair value of the assets of Blue Jay Company was $10,000 above the book value?
2. What is the amount of the consolidated net income as of December 31, 19x2?
3. What is the amount of Ranger Company's investment in Blue Jay Company which must be eliminated at year-end using the equity method?
4. What is the minority interest on December 31, 19x2 to be disclosed in the consolidated balance sheet?

62. Below are the income statements for Dodger and Red Companies. Red owns 100 percent of Dodger.

	Red Company	Dodger Company
Sales	$56,000	$25,000
Investment income	6,000	0
	$62,000	$25,000
Cost of goods sold	$29,000	$18,000
Operating expenses	6,000	1,000
	$35,000	$19,000
Net Income	$27,000	$ 6,000

During 19x1, Red Company sold $15,000 of its goods to Dodger Company at a mark-up of 30 percent (cost to Red Company being $15,000). At the end of the year, Dodger Company still had $3,900 (cost plus mark-up) in its ending inventory.

Required:

Prepare the worksheet to develop a consolidated income statement on December 31, 19x1.

Refer to the Annual Report included in the front of the text.

63. Does the company have any long-term bonds outstanding?
64. How much is interest expense in the current year?
65. In the last three years, has more money been received from issuing long-term debt or been paid to retire long-term debt?
66. What are the total liabilities due in more than one year at the end of the most recent year?
67. Are current liabilities greater than long-term liabilities at the end of the most recent year?
68. Is total debt greater or less than stockholders' equity?
69. Have acquisitions been accounted for under the purchase or pooling of interests method?

Appendix A

Interest and Present Value Concepts

INTRODUCTION

The principles used in discounting cash flows due at certain future points in time by the use of compound interest concepts are discussed in this Appendix. These concepts have a broad application in business decisions. For example, most business entities often make decisions to: (1) borrow funds in the current period in return for a promise to pay cash or other resources in future periods, and (2) invest resources at the current time with the expectation of receiving benefits at various future times. For both of these types of decisions, the timing of the various cash inflows and outflows has a significant effect on the desirability of the various possible investment and borrowing alternatives. Timing of the cash flows is important because of the following principle: *an amount of cash to be received in the future is not equivalent to the same amount of cash held at the present time*. This statement is true because money has a time value—it can be invested to earn a return (i.e., interest or dividends). For this reason, in both borrowing and investing decisions, consideration must be given to the time values of the various cash inflows and outflows.

In order to understand the implications of such decisions, the accountant must be able to determine the *present value* of future cash flows. Although there are a number of important applications of present value concepts in the financial accounting area, this appendix is limited to the application of these concepts to long-term liabilities.

INTEREST

Interest represents the amount received by the lender and paid by the borrower for the use of money for a given period of time. Thus, upon payment of a debt, interest is the excess of the cash repaid over the amount originally borrowed (referred to as the *principal*). Interest is normally stated as a rate for a one year period.

Simple interest is the amount of interest that is computed on the principal *only*, for a given period of time. Simple interest is computed as follows:

$$\begin{aligned} \text{Interest} &= \text{Principal} \times \text{Rate} \times \text{Time} \\ \text{Interest} &= P \times I \times T \end{aligned} \qquad (1)$$

To illustrate, interest on $1,000 for six months at an annual interest rate of 10 percent is:

$$\$50 = \$1{,}000 \times .10 \times {}^6\!/_{12}$$

Compound interest is interest that is computed for a period of time both on the principal and on the interest which has been earned but not paid. That is, interest is compounded when the interest earned in each period is added to the principal amount and both principal and interest earn interest in all subsequent periods. To illustrate, assume that $1,000 is deposited in a bank which pays interest at 10 percent annually. If the interest was withdrawn each year (simple interest), the depositor would collect $100 in interest each year (or $300 in interest over a three-year period):

$$\begin{aligned} \text{Interest per year} &= \$1{,}000 \times .10 \times 1 = \$100 \\ \text{Total interest for 3 years} &= \$100 \times 3 = \$300 \end{aligned}$$

However, if the interest at the end of each period is added to the principal sum (compound interest), the amount earned over the three-year period is computed as follows:

Original investment............................		$1,000
Balance at the end of year:	1. $1,000 + (.10 × $1,000 × 1)	1,100
	2. $1,100 + (.10 × $1,100 × 1)	1,210
	3. $1,210 + (.10 × $1,210 × 1)	1,331

Compound interest for the three-year period is $331 ($1,331 − $1,000), the difference between the balance at the end of the three-year period and the original investment. This amount exceeds simple interest because interest was earned each year both on the principal and on the interest earned in previous years.

Since compounding occurs when interest is earned on previously accumulated interest, a formula can be developed for computing the compound amount at which the principal sum will increase over a given time period. To develop this formula, consider the compound interest on one dollar invested at an interest rate of I percent. The amount accumulated at the end of the first year would be [$1 + (1 × I)] or (1 + I). If this amount is allowed to accumulate and earn interest for the second year, the amount accumulated is (1 + I)(1 + I) which is equal to (1 + I).² Similarly, the amount at the end of T periods is (1 + I)^T. Consequently, the amount (A) that a principal amount (P) will accumulate over a time period (T) at an interest rate (I) is expressed as:

$$A = P(1 + I)^T \qquad (2)$$

For example, if $1,000 is invested for three years at 10 percent interest per year, the amount accumulated at the end of three years is computed as follows:

$$A = \$1,000 (1 + .10)^3$$
$$A = \$1,000 (1.331)$$
$$A = \$1,331$$

This computation of the sum for a single principal amount and the compound interest at a specified future time may be illustrated as follows:

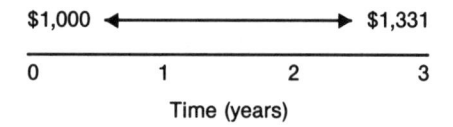

```
$1,000 ◄─────────────► $1,331
───────┼───────┼───────┼───────
   0       1       2       3
         Time (years)
```

PRESENT VALUES OF A FUTURE SUM

The present value of a given amount at a specified future time is the sum that would have to be invested at the present time in order to equal that future value at a given rate of compound interest. For example, it was determined that $1,000 invested at 10 percent compound interest would accumulate to a total of $1,331 in three years. Therefore, $1,000 is the *present value* of $1,331 three years from the present time (given a 10% rate of interest). That is, if you could earn 10 percent on a bank deposit, you would be indifferent between receiving $1,000 now (which could be deposited to accumulate to $1,331 in 3 years) or $1,331 three years from now, all other factors being equal.

The present value of a future amount is determined by computing the amount that a principal sum will accumulate to over a specified period of time. Consequently, by dividing equation (2) by (1 + I)^T, we obtain the formula for computing the present value of a future amount (A):

$$P = \frac{A}{(1 + I)^T} \qquad (3)$$

For example, the present value of $1,331 three years from now would be computed as follows:

$$P = \frac{\$1,331}{(1 + .10)^3}$$
$$P = \$1,000$$

Because of the number and variety of decisions which are based on the present value of future cash flows, tables have been developed from the formula which give the present value of $1 for various interest rates and for various periods of time. These values may be multiplied by any future amount to determine its present value. The factors for the present value of $1 are listed in Table A-1.

To illustrate the use of this table, let us compute the present value of $1,331 to be received three years from now at a compound interest rate of 10 percent. The value from the table for three years at 10 percent is .7513. This is the present value of $1. Accordingly, the present value of $1,331 is computed as 1,331 × .7513 = $999.80 (this amount is not exactly equal to $1,000 because of the rounding error in the present value factor included in the table). The computation of the present value of a simple payment due in the future may be illustrated as follows:

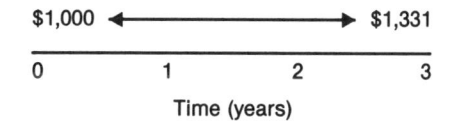

```
$1,000 ◄─────────────► $1,331
   ├──────┼──────┼──────┤
   0      1      2      3
            Time (years)
```

COMPOUND INTEREST AND PRESENT VALUE ON A SERIES OF EQUAL PAYMENTS

Business decisions involving a series of cash flows to be paid or received periodically are more common than decisions involving the accumulation of a single principal sum. It is possible to determine the present value of a series of payments (or receipts) by computing the present value of each payment or receipt and adding these values to obtain the present value for the entire series. However, if all the payments are equal, formulas or tables may be used to compute the present value of a series of payments. Such a series of equal periodic payments is normally referred to as an *annuity*. If the payments are made at the end of each period, the annuity is referred to as an *ordinary annuity*.

The accumulated amount (future value) of an ordinary annuity is the sum of the periodic payments and the compound interest on these payments. For example, the future value of an annuity of $1,000 per year (at the end of each year) for three years at 10 percent interest could be determined as follows:

The initial payment accumulates
at 10% for 2 years to $1,210
The second payment accumulates
at 10% for 1 year to 1,100
The third payment is due at the end of the third year 1,000
Amount of an ordinary annuity
of $1,000 for 3 years at 10% $3,310

The computation of the future value of a series of payments may be expressed as follows:

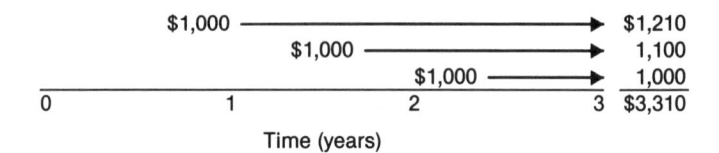

```
$1,000  ─────────────────────────▶  $1,210
         $1,000  ──────────────▶    1,100
                  $1,000  ─────▶    1,000
0          1         2         3    $3,310
              Time (years)
```

The present value of an ordinary annuity is the amount which, if invested at the present time at a compound rate of interest, would provide for a series of equal withdrawals at the end of a certain number of periods. The present value of an ordinary annuity may be computed as the present values of each of the individual payments. For example, the present value of an ordinary annuity of $1,000 per year for three years at 10 percent could be computed as follows (see Table A-1):

Present value of $1,000 in 1 year .... .9091 × $1,000 = $ 909.10
Present value of $1,000 in 2 years .... .8264 × $1,000 =   826.40
Present value of $1,000 in 3 years .... .7513 × $1,000 =   751.30
Present value of an annuity of
$1,000 for 3 periods at 10% $2,486.80

This computation indicates that if $2,486.80 is invested at an interest rate of 10 percent, it would be possible to withdraw $1,000 at the end of each year for three years.

The formula for the present value of an ordinary annuity of $R per period for T periods at I rate of interest may be stated:

$$P = R \left[\frac{1 - \frac{1}{(1 + I)^T}}{I} \right]$$

Table A-2 gives the present value of an ordinary annuity of $1 per period for various periods at varying rates of interest. By multiplying the appropriate value from the table by the dollar amount of the periodic payment, the present value of the payments may be calculated. For example, the present value of three annual cash payments of $1,000 made at the end of the next three years at a 10 percent interest rate would be computed as follows:

$$1{,}000 \times 2.4869 = \$2{,}486.90^1$$

This amount may be interpreted as the present cash payment which would be exactly equivalent to the three future installments of $1,000 if money earns 10 percent compounded annually. The computation of the present value of a series of future payments may be illustrated as follows:

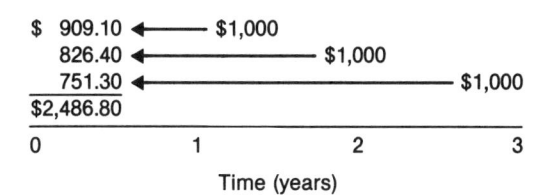

```
$  909.10 ←——— $1,000
   826.40 ←——————— $1,000
   751.30 ←——————————— $1,000
$2,486.80
─────────────────────────────────
0          1          2          3
                Time (years)
```

APPLICATION OF PRESENT VALUE CONCEPTS TO BONDS PAYABLE

A bond is a contract between an issuing company and the purchaser of the bond. There are two types of payments that a company will have to make to bondholders. One payment is a lump-sum payment made at the end of the life of the bond, which is the return of the *face value* or *maturity value* of the bond. The other payment is for interest, which will be made at specific intervals in fixed amounts over the life of the bond. Interest is usually paid semiannually by the issuing company. Bond contracts will state the *coupon* or *nominal rate* of interest on an annual basis.

To calculate the selling price of a bond (the amount the firm will receive upon issuance of the bond), consider a company that has sold a $1,000 face value bond with a nominal rate of interest of 8 percent. The bond will mature in five years and the interest is payable June 30 and December 31 of each year. The company has made two promises to the purchaser of the bond:

Promise 1: To pay $1,000 at the end of five years.
Promise 2: To pay $40 semiannually for five years.

The price that any investor would pay for a bond would depend upon the *effective rate*[2] of interest on the date that the investor decided to buy the bond. The effective rate will be dependent upon many factors such as the prime interest rate in money markets, the risks involved in buying the bond of that specific company, and the provisions of the bond that may make it more attractive for investment purposes. In general, the effective rate will be determined by supply and demand in the bond market.

---

[1] Difference of $.10 due to rounding in tables.
[2] The effective rate is also referred to as the market rate or the yield.

There are three possible general cases that illustrate the potential selling price of the bond. These three cases are dependent upon the earnings expectations of buyers of bonds in the market place. In the prior example, where the nominal rate is 8 percent, the three possible cases are:

1. The effective (market) rate of interest is equal to 8 percent.
2. The effective (market) rate of interest is below 8 percent.
3. The effective (market) rate of interest is greater than 8 percent.

If the market is demanding an 8 percent return on bonds of like kind, and the company enters the market with an 8 percent coupon rate on its bond, the bond should sell at its face value of $1,000. The buyer is demanding 8 percent and the seller is paying 8 percent; therefore, the bond would sell at *par*.

If the market is demanding a return that is less than 8 percent and the company enters the market with an 8 percent coupon rate on its bond, the company is paying a greater return than is demanded in the market, Therefore, the bond will sell for a price in excess of $1,000. This excess is referred to as a *premium*. The investors will buy the bond at a price greater than $1,000 because the coupon rate exceeds the rate demanded by the market.

If the market is demanding a return that is greater than 8 percent and the company enters the market with an 8 percent coupon rate on its bond, the company is paying less than the return demanded by the market. Therefore, the bond will sell for less than $1,000. The difference between $1,000 and the selling price will be a *discount* on the bond.

To calculate the selling price of the bond, assume that the market rate of interest was either 8 percent, 6 percent, or 10 percent. Note that the bond contract provides for a lump-sum payment at maturity and semiannual interest payments over the life of the bond. Thus, in order to find the current value, or selling price, of the bond, it is necessary to determine the present value of the lump-sum payment at maturity and the present value of the periodic interest payments (an ordinary annuity). Illustration A-1 presents the calculations which are necessary to determine the selling price of the $1,000 bond at the three market rates of interest assumed above.

Even though the selling price of the bond will vary according to the three different market rate assumptions, it is important to remember that the bond is a fixed contract that will pay a return of $40 to the bondholder semiannually and $1,000 at its maturity date. These amounts are paid regardless of the initial selling price of the bond.

Illustration A-1
*Selling Price of a Bond With
8 Percent Coupon Rate, Five-Year Life,
and Semiannual Payments*

Present Value Factors for
Ten Periods at 4 Percent
Semiannual Interest

	Table 1	Table 2	Totals

8 percent coupon, 8 percent
market, bond sells at par:
Promise #1 = $1,000 − lump sum....... .6756   = $ 675.60
Promise #2 = $ 40 − annuity.........   8.1109 =   324.44
                           Selling price (rounded)   = $1,000.00

8 percent coupon, 6 percent
market, bond sells at premium:
Promise #1 = $1,000 − lump sum....... .7441   = $ 744.10
Promise #2 = $ 40 − annuity.........   8.5302 =   341.21
                           Selling price (rounded)   = $1,085.31

8 percent coupon, 10 percent
market, bond sells at discount:
Promise #1 = $1,000 − lump sum....... .6139   = $ 613.90
Promise #2 = $ 40 − annuity.........   7.7217 =   308.87
                           Selling price (rounded)   = $ 922.77

ACCOUNTING FOR PREMIUM OR DISCOUNT ON BONDS— THE INTEREST METHOD

The following example will be used to illustrate the accounting treatment of a bond issue sold at a premium or discount using the interest method. Assume that on July 1, 19x1, a company sold a $1,000,000 bond issue with a nominal interest rate of 8 percent and a maturity date of July 1, 19x6. Interest will be paid on June 30 and December 31. The company's fiscal year ends on December 31.

The calculations necessary in order to compute the initial selling price of the bond are the same as the calculations in Illustration A-1, except that the entire issue, $1,000,000, is under consideration. If the market rate of interest demanded is 8 percent, the bonds will sell for $1,000,000. If the market rate of interest is 6 percent, the bonds will sell at a premium. The selling price will be ($1,000,000 × .7441) + ($40,000 × 8.5302) = $1,085,308. If the market rate of interest demanded is 10 percent, the bonds will sell at a discount. The selling price will be ($1,000,000 × .6139) + ($40,000 × 7.7217) = $922,768.

The face value of the bonds is paid to bondholders at the maturity date regardless of the original price of the bonds. The premium or discount on a bond is paid or received, respectively, to adjust the interest that will be paid on the bond to the return on the investment demanded by the market (market rate of interest) given the type of bond and the risk involved as perceived by investors.

There are two acceptable methods for amortizing bond premium or discount. One technique for amortization, the straight-line method, was discussed in the chapter. A second technique, referred to as the interest method, has been suggested by the Accounting Principles Board.[3] This method of amortization results in recognizing a constant rate of interest on the bond liability over the life of the bond. The interest expense for each period is computed by multiplying a constant rate of interest by the beginning liability for that period. The interest method is described in this Appendix.

Bonds Sold at a Premium

If the market rate of interest in the prior example is 6 percent, the bonds will sell at a premium of $85,308 ($1,085,308 − $1,000,000). The interest method will yield a different interest expense for each interest period. To determine the interest expense, the carrying value of the liability (face value plus unamortized premium or minus unamortized discount) is multiplied by the semiannual effective rate of interest. Thus, the interest expense will be a constant percentage (equal to the effective semiannual interest rate on the issuance of the bonds) of 6 percent per year or 3 percent on the outstanding liability at the beginning of each semiannual interest period. The following journal entries would be made in 19x1 under the interest method:

June 30, 19x1	Cash..................	$1,085,308.00	
	Bond premium........		$ 85,308.00
	Bonds payable........		1,000,000.00
December 31, 19x1	Interest expense.........	32,559.24	
	Bond premium..........	7,440.76	
	Cash................		40,000.00

(Interest expense = $1,085,308.00 × .03 = $32,559.24)

At the end of 19x1, the balance sheet presentation of the liability will include both the bonds payable and bond premium accounts. The bond premium account is rounded in the example.

Bonds payable....................	$1,000,000	
Add: Bond premium..............	77,867	
Total bonds payable............		$1,077,867

---

[3] *APB Opinion No. 21* (New York: AICPA, 1972).

Bonds Sold at a Discount

When bonds are issued at a premium, use of the *interest* method will cause the *interest* expense to decrease over the life of the bond because both the premium account and the carrying value of the liability will decrease over the life of the bonds. The bond premium amortization will increase because the cash payment to bondholders remains constant and the interest expense decreases each period. The total interest expense and premium amortization schedule is given in Illustration A-2.

If the market rate of interest demanded by investors is 10 percent, the bonds in the prior example will sell at a discount because the face rate of interest is 8 percent. The discount will be the difference between the maturity value of $1,000,000 and the selling price of $922,768, or $77,232.

The concepts underlying the *interest* method for bond discount are the same as those discussed in the prior section on bonds sold at a premium. The journal entries for 19x1 for bonds sold at a discount are:

Illustration A-2
Interest Expense and Premium Amortization Schedule

Date	Debit to Interest Expense*	Debit to Bond Premium	Credit to Cash	Bond Premium Balance	Total Liability
July 1, 19x1	0	0	0	$85,308.00	$1,085,308.00
December 31, 19x1	$32,559.24	$ 7,440.76	$ 40,000	77,867.24	1,077,867.24
July 1, 19x2	32,336.02	7,663.98	40,000	70,203.26	1,070,203.26
December 31, 19x2	32,106.10	7,893.90	40,000	62,309.36	1,062,309.36
July 1, 19x3	31,869.28	8,130.72	40,000	54,178.64	1,054,178.64
December 31, 19x3	31,625.36	8,374.64	40,000	45,804.00	1,045,804.00
July 1, 19x4	31,374.12	8,625.88	40,000	37,178.12	1,037,178.12
December 31, 19x4	31,115.34	8,884.66	40,000	28,293.46	1,028,293.46
July 1, 19x5	30,848.80	9,151.20	40,000	19,142.26	1,019,142.26
December 31, 19x5	30,574.27	9,425.73	40,000	9,716.53	1,009,716.53
July 1, 19x6	30,291.47*	9,716.53	40,000	0	1,000,000.00
		$85,308.00	$400,000		

*To determine interest expense, the total liability at the beginning of the period was multiplied by the semiannual market interest rate of 3 percent. Any rounding errors are included in the July 1, 19x6, debit to interest expense.

June 30, 19x1	Cash	$922,768.00	
	Bond discount	$ 77,232.00	
	Bonds payable		$1,000,000.00
December 31, 19x1	Interest expense	46,138.40	
	Bond discount		6,138.40
	Cash		40,000.00

(Interest expense = $922,768 × .05 = $46,138.40)

At the end of 19x1, the balance sheet presentation of the liability will include both the bonds payable and the bond discount account. The bond discount account is rounded in the example.

Bonds payable	$1,000,000	
Less: Bond discount	71,094	
Total bonds payable		$928,906

In the case of bonds sold at a discount, using the interest method, interest expense increases over the life of the bond because discount decreases and the carrying value of the bonds increases. The total interest expense and discount amortization schedule is given in Illustration A-3.

Illustration A-3
Interest Expense and Discount Amortization Schedule

Date	Debit to Interest Expense*	Credit to Bond Discount	Credit to Cash	Discount	Total Liability
July 1, 19x1	0	0	0	$77,232.00	$ 922,768.00
December 31, 19x1	$46,138.40	$ 6,138.40	$ 40,000	71,093.60	928,906.40
July 1, 19x2	46,445.32	6,445.32	40,000	64,648.28	935,351.72
December 31, 19x2	46,767.59	6,767.59	40,000	57,880.69	942,119.31
July 1, 19x3	47,105.97	7,105.97	40,000	50,774.72	949,225.28
December 31, 19x3	47,461.26	7,461.26	40,000	43,313.46	956,686.54
July 1, 19x4	47,834.33	7,834.33	40,000	35,479.13	964,520.87
December 31, 19x4	48,226.04	8,226.04	40,000	27,253.09	972,746.91
July 1, 19x5	48,637.35	8,637.35	40,000	18,615.74	981,384.26
December 31, 19x5	49,069.21	9,069.21	40,000	9,546.53	990,453.47
July 1, 19x6	49,522.53*	9,546.53	40,000	0	1,000,000.00
	$77,232.00	$400,000			

*To determine interest expense, the total liability at the beginning of the period was multiplied by the semiannual market interest rate—in this case, 5 percent. Any rounding errors are included in the July 1, 19x6, debit to interest expense.

Table A-1
Present Value of $1.00

Periods (n)	1%	1½%	2%	2½%	3%	3½%	4%	4½%	5%	6%	7%	8%	10%
1	0.9901	0.9852	0.9804	0.9756	0.9709	0.9662	0.9615	0.9569	0.9524	0.9434	0.9346	0.9259	0.9091
2	0.9803	0.9707	0.9612	0.9518	0.9426	0.9335	0.9246	0.9157	0.9070	0.8900	0.8734	0.8573	0.8264
3	0.9706	0.9563	0.9423	0.9286	0.9151	0.9019	0.8890	0.8763	0.8638	0.8396	0.8163	0.7938	0.7513
4	0.9610	0.9422	0.9238	0.9060	0.8885	0.8714	0.8548	0.8386	0.8227	0.7921	0.7629	0.7350	0.6830
5	0.9515	0.9283	0.9057	0.8839	0.8626	0.8420	0.8219	0.8025	0.7835	0.7473	0.7130	0.6806	0.6209
6	0.9420	0.9145	0.8880	0.8623	0.8375	0.8135	0.7903	0.7679	0.7462	0.7050	0.6663	0.6302	0.5645
7	0.9327	0.9010	0.8706	0.8413	0.8131	0.7860	0.7599	0.7348	0.7107	0.6651	0.6227	0.5835	0.5132
8	0.9235	0.8877	0.8535	0.8207	0.7894	0.7594	0.7307	0.7032	0.6768	0.6274	0.5820	0.5403	0.4665
9	0.9143	0.8746	0.8368	0.8007	0.7664	0.7337	0.7026	0.6729	0.6446	0.5919	0.5439	0.5002	0.4241
10	0.9053	0.8617	0.8203	0.7812	0.7441	0.7089	0.6756	0.6439	0.6139	0.5584	0.5083	0.4632	0.3855
11	0.8963	0.8489	0.8043	0.7621	0.7224	0.6849	0.6496	0.6162	0.5847	0.5268	0.4751	0.4289	0.3505
12	0.8874	0.8364	0.7885	0.7436	0.7014	0.6618	0.6246	0.5897	0.5568	0.4970	0.4440	0.3971	0.3186
13	0.8787	0.8240	0.7730	0.7254	0.6810	0.6394	0.6006	0.5643	0.5303	0.4688	0.4150	0.3677	0.2897
14	0.8700	0.8118	0.7579	0.7077	0.6611	0.6178	0.5775	0.5400	0.5051	0.4423	0.3878	0.3405	0.2633
15	0.8613	0.7999	0.7430	0.6905	0.6419	0.5969	0.5553	0.5167	0.4810	0.4173	0.3624	0.3153	0.2394
16	0.8528	0.7880	0.7284	0.6736	0.6232	0.5767	0.5339	0.4945	0.4581	0.3936	0.3387	0.2919	0.2176
17	0.8444	0.7764	0.7142	0.6572	0.6050	0.5572	0.5134	0.4732	0.4363	0.3714	0.3166	0.2703	0.1978
18	0.8360	0.7649	0.7002	0.6412	0.5874	0.5384	0.4936	0.4528	0.4155	0.3503	0.2959	0.2502	0.1799
19	0.8277	0.7536	0.6864	0.6255	0.5703	0.5202	0.4746	0.4333	0.3957	0.3305	0.2765	0.2317	0.1635
20	0.8195	0.7425	0.6730	0.6103	0.5537	0.5026	0.4564	0.4146	0.3769	0.3118	0.2584	0.2145	0.1486
21	0.8114	0.7315	0.6598	0.5954	0.5375	0.4856	0.4388	0.3968	0.3589	0.2942	0.2415	0.1987	0.1351
22	0.8034	0.7207	0.6468	0.5809	0.5219	0.4692	0.4220	0.3797	0.3418	0.2775	0.2257	0.1839	0.1228
23	0.7954	0.7100	0.6342	0.5667	0.5067	0.4533	0.4057	0.3634	0.3256	0.2618	0.2109	0.1703	0.1117
24	0.7876	0.6995	0.6217	0.5529	0.4919	0.4380	0.3901	0.3477	0.3101	0.2470	0.1971	0.1577	0.1015
25	0.7798	0.6892	0.6095	0.5394	0.4776	0.4231	0.3751	0.3327	0.2953	0.2330	0.1842	0.1460	0.0923
26	0.7720	0.6790	0.5976	0.5262	0.4637	0.4088	0.3607	0.3184	0.2812	0.2198	0.1722	0.1352	0.0839
27	0.7644	0.6690	0.5859	0.5134	0.4502	0.3950	0.3468	0.3047	0.2678	0.2074	0.1609	0.1252	0.0763
28	0.7568	0.6591	0.5744	0.5009	0.4371	0.3817	0.3335	0.2916	0.2551	0.1956	0.1504	0.1159	0.0693
29	0.7493	0.6494	0.5631	0.4887	0.4243	0.3687	0.3207	0.2790	0.2429	0.1846	0.1406	0.1073	0.0630
30	0.7419	0.6398	0.5521	0.4767	0.4120	0.3563	0.3083	0.2670	0.2314	0.1741	0.1314	0.0994	0.0573
40	0.6717	0.5513	0.4529	0.3724	0.3066	0.2526	0.2083	0.1719	0.1420	0.0972	0.0668	0.0460	0.0221
50	0.6080	0.4750	0.3715	0.2909	0.2281	0.1791	0.1407	0.1107	0.0872	0.0543	0.0339	0.0213	0.0085

Table A-1 Continued
Present Value of $1.00

12%	14%	15%	16%	18%	20%	22%	24%	25%	26%	28%	30%	40%	50
0.893	0.877	0.870	0.862	0.847	0.833	0.820	0.806	0.800	0.794	0.781	0.769	0.714	0.667
0.797	0.769	0.756	0.743	0.718	0.694	0.672	0.650	0.640	0.630	0.610	0.592	0.510	0.444
0.712	0.675	0.658	0.641	0.609	0.579	0.551	0.524	0.512	0.500	0.477	0.455	0.364	0.296
0.636	0.592	0.572	0.552	0.516	0.482	0.451	0.423	0.410	0.397	0.373	0.350	0.260	0.198
0.567	0.519	0.497	0.476	0.437	0.402	0.370	0.341	0.328	0.315	0.291	0.269	0.186	0.132
0.507	0.456	0.432	0.410	0.370	0.335	0.303	0.275	0.262	0.250	0.227	0.207	0.133	0.088
0.452	0.400	0.376	0.354	0.314	0.279	0.249	0.222	0.210	0.198	0.178	0.159	0.095	0.059
0.404	0.351	0.327	0.305	0.266	0.233	0.204	0.179	0.168	0.157	0.139	0.123	0.068	0.039
0.361	0.308	0.284	0.263	0.225	0.194	0.167	0.144	0.134	0.125	0.108	0.094	0.048	0.026
0.322	0.270	0.247	0.227	0.191	0.162	0.137	0.116	0.107	0.099	0.085	0.073	0.035	0.017
0.287	0.237	0.215	0.195	0.162	0.135	0.112	0.094	0.086	0.079	0.066	0.056	0.025	0.012
0.257	0.208	0.187	0.168	0.137	0.112	0.092	0.076	0.069	0.062	0.052	0.043	0.018	0.008
0.229	0.182	0.163	0.145	0.116	0.093	0.075	0.061	0.055	0.050	0.040	0.033	0.013	0.005
0.205	0.160	0.141	0.125	0.099	0.078	0.062	0.049	0.044	0.039	0.032	0.025	0.009	0.003
0.183	0.140	0.123	0.108	0.084	0.065	0.051	0.040	0.035	0.031	0.025	0.020	0.006	0.002
0.163	0.123	0.107	0.093	0.071	0.054	0.042	0.032	0.028	0.025	0.019	0.015	0.005	0.002
0.146	0.108	0.093	0.080	0.060	0.045	0.034	0.026	0.023	0.020	0.015	0.012	0.003	0.001
0.130	0.095	0.081	0.069	0.051	0.038	0.028	0.021	0.018	0.016	0.012	0.009	0.002	0.001
0.116	0.083	0.070	0.060	0.043	0.031	0.023	0.017	0.014	0.012	0.009	0.007	0.002	
0.104	0.073	0.061	0.051	0.037	0.026	0.019	0.014	0.012	0.010	0.007	0.005	0.001	
0.093	0.064	0.053	0.044	0.031	0.022	0.015	0.011	0.009	0.008	0.006	0.004	0.001	
0.083	0.056	0.046	0.038	0.026	0.018	0.013	0.009	0.007	0.006	0.004	0.003	0.001	
0.074	0.049	0.040	0.033	0.022	0.015	0.010	0.007	0.006	0.005	0.003	0.002		
0.066	0.043	0.035	0.028	0.019	0.013	0.008	0.006	0.005	0.004	0.003	0.002		
0.059	0.038	0.030	0.024	0.016	0.010	0.007	0.005	0.004	0.003	0.002	0.001		
0.053	0.033	0.026	0.021	0.014	0.009	0.006	0.004	0.003	0.002	0.002	0.001		
0.047	0.029	0.023	0.018	0.011	0.007	0.005	0.003	0.002	0.002	0.001	0.001		
0.042	0.026	0.020	0.016	0.010	0.006	0.004	0.002	0.002	0.002	0.001	0.001		
0.037	0.022	0.017	0.014	0.008	0.005	0.003	0.002	0.002	0.001	0.001	0.001		
0.033	0.020	0.015	0.012	0.007	0.004	0.003	0.002	0.001	0.001	0.001			
0.011	0.005	0.004	0.003	0.001	0.001								
0.003	0.001	0.001	0.001										

Table A-2
Present Value of Annuity of $1.00 Per Period

Periods (n)	1%	1½%	2%	2½%	3%	3½%	4%	4½%	5%	6%	7%
1...	0.9901	0.9852	0.9804	0.9756	0.9709	0.9662	0.9615	0.9569	0.9524	0.9434	0.9346
2...	1.9704	1.9559	1.9416	1.9274	1.9135	1.8997	1.8861	1.8727	1.8594	1.8334	1.8080
3...	2.9410	2.9122	2.8839	2.8560	2.8286	2.8016	2.7751	2.7490	2.7232	2.6730	2.6243
4...	3.9020	3.8544	3.8077	3.7620	3.7171	3.6731	3.6299	3.5875	3.5460	3.4651	3.3872
5...	4.8534	4.7826	4.7135	4.6458	4.5797	4.5151	4.4518	4.3900	4.3295	4.2124	4.1002
6...	5.7955	5.6972	5.6014	5.5081	5.4172	5.3286	5.2421	5.1579	5.0757	4.9173	4.7665
7...	6.7282	6.5982	6.4720	6.3494	6.2303	6.1145	6.0021	5.8927	5.7864	5.5824	5.3893
8...	7.6517	7.4859	7.3255	7.1701	7.0197	6.8740	6.7327	6.5959	6.4632	6.2098	5.9713
9...	8.5660	8.3605	8.1622	7.9709	7.7861	7.6077	7.4353	7.2688	7.1078	6.8017	6.5152
10...	9.4713	9.2222	8.9826	8.7521	8.5302	8.3166	8.1109	7.9127	7.7217	7.3601	7.0236
11...	10.3676	10.0711	9.7868	9.5142	9.2526	9.0016	8.7605	8.5289	8.3064	7.8869	7.4987
12...	11.2551	10.9075	10.5753	10.2578	9.9540	9.6633	9.3851	9.1186	8.8633	8.3838	7.9427
13...	12.1337	11.7315	11.3484	10.9832	10.6350	10.3027	9.9856	9.6829	9.3936	8.8527	8.3577
14...	13.0037	12.5434	12.1062	11.6909	11.2961	10.9205	10.5631	10.2228	9.8986	9.2950	8.7455
15...	13.8651	13.3432	12.8493	12.3814	11.9379	11.5174	11.1184	10.7395	10.3797	9.7122	9.1079
16...	14.7179	14.1313	13.5777	13.0550	12.5611	12.0941	11.6523	11.2340	10.8378	10.1059	9.4466
17...	15.5623	14.9076	14.2919	13.7122	13.1661	12.6513	12.1657	11.7072	11.2741	10.4773	9.7632
18...	16.3983	15.6726	14.9920	14.3534	13.7535	13.1897	12.6593	12.1600	11.6896	10.8276	10.0591
19...	17.2260	16.4262	15.6785	14.9789	14.3238	13.7098	13.1339	12.5933	12.0853	11.1581	10.3356
20...	18.0456	17.1686	16.3514	15.5892	14.8775	14.2124	13.5903	13.0079	12.4622	11.4699	10.5940
21...	18.8570	17.9001	17.0112	16.1845	15.4150	14.6980	14.0292	13.4047	12.8212	11.7640	10.8355
22...	19.6604	18.6208	17.6580	16.7654	15.9369	15.1671	14.4511	13.7844	13.1630	12.0416	11.0612
23...	20.4558	19.3309	18.2922	17.3321	16.4436	15.6204	14.8568	14.1478	13.4886	12.3034	11.2722
24...	21.2434	20.0304	18.9139	17.8850	16.9355	16.0584	15.2470	14.4955	13.7986	12.5504	11.4693
25...	22.0232	20.7196	19.5235	18.4244	17.4131	16.4815	15.6221	14.8282	14.0939	12.7834	11.6536
26...	22.7952	21.3986	20.1210	18.9506	17.8768	16.8904	15.9828	15.1466	14.3752	13.0032	11.8258
27...	23.5596	22.0676	20.7069	19.4640	18.3270	17.2854	16.3296	15.4513	14.6430	13.2105	11.9867
28...	24.3164	22.7267	21.2813	19.9649	18.7641	17.6670	16.6631	15.7429	14.8981	13.4062	12.1371
29...	25.0658	23.3761	21.8444	20.4535	19.1885	18.0358	18.9837	16.0219	15.1411	13.5907	12.2777
30...	25.8077	24.0158	22.3965	20.9303	19.6004	18.3920	17.2920	16.2889	15.3725	13.7648	12.4090
40...	32.8347	29.9158	27.3555	25.1028	23.1148	21.3551	19.7928	18.4016	17.1591	15.0463	13.3317
50...	39.1961	34.9997	31.4236	28.3623	25.7298	23.4556	21.4822	19.7620	18.2559	15.7619	13.8007

Table A-2 Continued
Present Value of Annuity of $1.00 Per Period

8%	10%	12%	14%	15%	16%	18%	20%	22%	24%	25%	26%	28%	30%	40%	50%
0.9259	0.9091	0.893	0.877	0.870	0.862	0.847	0.833	0.820	0.806	0.800	0.794	0.781	0.769	0.714	0.667
1.7833	1.7355	1.690	1.647	1.626	1.605	1.566	1.528	1.492	1.457	1.440	1.424	1.392	1.361	1.224	1.111
2.5771	2.4869	2.402	2.322	2.283	2.246	2.174	2.106	2.042	1.981	1.952	1.923	1.868	1.816	1.589	1.407
3.3121	3.1699	3.037	2.914	2.855	2.798	2.690	2.589	2.494	2.404	2.362	2.320	2.241	2.166	1.849	1.605
3.9927	3.7908	3.605	3.433	3.352	3.274	3.127	2.991	2.864	2.745	2.689	2.635	2.532	2.436	2.035	1.737
4.6229	4.3553	4.111	3.889	3.784	3.685	3.498	3.326	3.167	3.020	2.951	2.885	2.759	2.643	2.168	1.824
5.2064	4.8684	4.564	4.288	4.160	4.039	3.812	3.605	3.416	3.242	3.161	3.083	2.937	2.802	2.263	1.883
5.7466	5.3349	4.968	4.639	4.487	4.344	4.078	3.837	3.619	3.421	3.329	3.241	3.076	2.925	2.331	1.922
6.2469	5.7590	5.328	4.946	4.772	4.607	4.303	4.031	3.786	3.566	3.463	3.366	3.184	3.019	2.379	1.948
6.7101	6.1446	5.650	5.216	5.019	4.833	4.494	4.192	3.923	3.682	3.571	3.465	3.269	3.092	2.414	1.965
7.1390	6.4951	5.988	5.453	5.234	5.029	4.656	4.327	4.035	3.776	3.656	3.544	3.335	3.147	2.438	1.977
7.5361	6.8137	6.194	5.660	5.421	5.197	4.793	4.439	4.127	3.851	3.725	3.606	3.387	3.190	2.456	1.985
7.9038	7.1034	6.424	5.842	5.583	5.342	4.910	4.533	4.203	3.912	3.780	3.656	3.427	3.223	2.468	1.990
8.2442	7.3667	6.628	6.002	5.724	5.468	5.008	4.611	4.265	3.962	3.824	3.695	3.459	3.249	2.477	1.993
8.5595	7.6061	6.811	6.142	5.847	5.575	5.092	4.675	4.315	4.001	3.859	3.726	3.483	3.268	2.484	1.995
8.8514	7.8237	6.974	6.265	5.954	5.669	5.162	4.730	4.357	4.033	3.887	3.751	3.503	3.283	2.489	1.997
9.1216	8.0216	7.120	6.373	6.047	5.749	5.222	4.775	4.391	4.059	3.910	3.771	3.518	3.295	2.492	1.998
9.3719	8.2014	7.250	6.467	6.128	5.818	5.273	4.812	4.419	4.080	3.928	3.786	3.529	3.304	2.494	1.999
9.6036	8.3649	7.366	6.550	6.198	5.877	5.316	4.844	4.442	4.097	3.942	3.799	3.539	3.311	2.496	1.999
9.8181	8.5136	7.469	6.623	6.259	5.929	5.353	4.870	4.460	4.110	3.954	3.808	3.546	3.316	2.497	1.999
10.0168	8.6487	7.562	6.687	6.312	5.973	5.384	4.891	4.476	4.121	3.963	3.816	3.551	3.320	2.498	2.000
10.2007	8.7715	7.645	6.743	6.359	6.011	5.410	4.909	4.488	4.130	3.970	3.822	3.556	3.323	2.498	2.000
10.3711	8.8832	7.718	6.792	6.399	6.044	5.432	4.925	4.499	4.137	3.976	3.827	3.559	3.325	2.499	2.000
10.5288	8.9847	7.784	6.835	6.434	6.073	5.451	4.937	4.507	4.143	3.981	3.831	3.562	3.327	2.499	2.000
10.6748	9.0770	7.843	6.873	6.464	6.097	5.467	4.948	4.514	4.147	3.985	3.834	3.564	3.329	2.499	2.000
10.8100	9.1609	7.896	6.906	6.491	6.118	5.480	4.956	4.520	4.151	3.988	3.837	3.566	3.330	2.500	2.000
10.9352	9.2372	7.943	6.935	6.514	6.136	5.492	4.964	4.524	4.154	3.990	3.839	3.567	3.331	2.500	2.000
11.0511	9.3066	7.984	6.961	6.534	6.152	5.502	4.970	4.528	4.157	3.992	3.840	3.568	3.331	2.500	2.000
11.1584	9.3696	8.022	6.983	6.551	6.166	5.510	4.975	4.531	4.159	3.994	3.841	3.569	3.332	2.500	2.000
11.2578	9.4269	8.055	7.003	6.566	6.177	5.517	4.979	4.534	4.160	3.995	3.842	3.569	3.332	2.500	2.000
11.9246	9.7791	8.244	7.105	6.642	6.234	5.548	4.997	4.544	4.166	3.999	3.846	3.571	3.333	2.500	2.000
12.2335	9.9148	8.304	7.133	6.661	6.246	5.554	4.999	4.545	4.167	4.000	3.846	3.571	3.333	2.500	2.000

Note: To convert this table to values of an annuity in advance, take one less period and add 1.0000.

EXERCISES— APPENDIX A

1. Determine the amount that $1,000 will accumulate to in three years at an 8 percent annual interest rate.

2. Determine the present value of $1,000 due in five years at each of the following interest rates:

    a. 6 percent
    b. 8 percent
    c. 10 percent

3. An investor wishes to have $5,000 available at the end of five years. State the amount of money that must be invested at the present time if the interest rate is:

    a. 6 percent
    b. 8 percent
    c. 12 percent

4. Determine the present value of an ordinary annuity for a period of five years with annual payments of $2,000, assuming that the interest rate is:

    a. 7 percent
    b. 10 percent
    c. 12 percent

5. What is the maximum amount you would be willing to pay at the present time in order to receive 10 annual payments of $1,000 beginning one year from now? The current interest rate is 10 percent.

6. Hays Company leases a building at an annual rental of $2,000 paid at the end of each year. The company has been given the alternative of paying the remaining 10 years of the lease in advance on January 1, 19x0. Assuming an interest rate of 8 percent, what is the maximum amount that should be paid now for the advance rent?

7. Determine the selling price of the bonds in each of the following situations (assume that the bonds are dated and sold on the same date):

    a. A 10-year, $1,000 face value bond with annual interest of 9 percent (payable annually) sold to yield 8 percent effective interest.
    b. A 10-year, $1,000 face value bond with annual interest of 9 percent (payable annually) sold to yield 10 percent effective interest.
    c. A 10-year, $1,000 face value bond with annual interest of 9 percent (payable annually) sold to yield 9 percent effective interest.

8. Nancy Company issued $10,000 of bonds payable on January 1, 19x1 with an 8 percent coupon interest rate, payable annually on December 31. The bonds mature in 5 years and were sold at a 10 percent effective interest rate.

a. Determine the selling price of the bonds.
b. Prepare a schedule showing the amount of discount to be amortized each year for the life of the bonds, assuming the interest method of amortization.
c. Give the journal entry to record the interest payment on December 31, 19x1.

9. Joyce Company issued $10,000 of bonds payable on January 1, 19x1, with an 8 percent coupon interest rate payable annually on December 31. The bonds mature in five years and were sold at a 7 percent effective interest rate.

Required:

1. Determine the selling price of the bonds.
2. Prepare a schedule showing the premium to be amortized each year for the life of the bonds, assuming the interest method of amortization.
3. Give the journal entry to record the interest payment on December 31, 19x1.

Appendix B

Mark to Market—
FASB Statement No. 115

Mark to Market refers to the practice of adjusting assets and liabilities to the value at which the item would be sold in an "arms length" transaction. Those who support market value argue that the use of historical cost fails to reflect changes in value in the period in which these changes occur. Those who support historical cost argue that market values cannot be easily verifiable and therefore are subject to manipulation by management.

In the early 1970's the Accounting Principles Board considered using market values for certain financial instruments, but could not reach an agreement. Subsequently, the FASB issued its Statement No. 12 in 1975. This pronouncement requires companies to use lower of aggregate cost or market for marketable equity securities. This approach was discussed and illustrated in the chapter.

Proponents of a change to using market values, whether higher or lower than historical cost, are concerned that the use of historical cost allows companies to sell securities that have risen in value so as to report gains on the income statement and to delay the recognition of losses on many of their investment securities (e.g., all investments in bonds). Opponents claim that the needed market values may be difficult and costly to obtain and that changing market values may introduce too much volatility in the income statement as unrealized gains and losses are recognized.

Richard Breeden, head of the Securities and Exchange Commission, has been campaigning vigorously for the use of market values rather than historical cost for investment securities. In testimony before the Committee on Banking, Housing and Urban Affairs of the United States Senate in 1990, Breeden argued that the use of historical cost for valuing investment securities may have been a significant contributor to the collapse of the savings and loan industry. Using market values may have alerted regulators to the liquidity problems far earlier and may have resulted in closings while the losses of these financial institutions were still manageable.

Alan Greenspan, Chairman of the Federal Reserve Board, does not agree. He believes that if banks have to mark their financial instruments to market, the result would be increased volatility in reported earnings. To avoid this occurrence, banks would invest more heavily in short-term bonds, whose market values are less susceptible to large swings than long-term bonds, and avoid municipal bonds, which are often relatively risky, not actively traded, and therefore more likely to have wide swings in value.

After Breeden's testimony, a meeting was held involving representatives of the SEC, the FASB, and the AICPA. The SEC wanted a resolution to this problem by the end of 1991.

Although the SEC has jurisdiction over accounting and financial reporting for those companies that issue securities through national and interstate securities exchanges, it has for the most part ceded this authority to the accounting profession. The FASB has been prodded and circumvented by the SEC in the past. Consequently, the FASB may have felt pressure to meet the expectations of the SEC in its proposal for instituting market value accounting for investment securities.

FASB STATEMENT NO. 115

In May 1993, the FASB issued Statement No. 115, "Accounting for Certain Investments in Debt and Equity Securities," that requires the use of fair (market) value for investments in debt and equity securities, except for investments in debt securities that are to be held until maturity. Under this Statement, which is effective for fiscal years beginning after December 15, 1993, investments in debt and equity securities would be classified into three categories and accounted for as follows:

1. Debt securities that the entity has the positive intent and ability to hold to maturity would be classified as held to maturity and reported at amortized cost.

2. Debt and equity securities that are held for current resale would be classified as trading securities and reported at fair value, with unrealized gains and losses included in earnings.

3. Debt and equity securities not classified as either securities held to maturity or trading securities would be classified as securities available for sale and reported at fair value, with unrealized gains and

losses excluded from earnings and reported as a separate component of shareholders' equity.

Held to Maturity

Investments in debt securities classified as held to maturity are accounted for as illustrated in the section INVESTMENTS IN BONDS in the chapter. The investment remains at historical cost, adjusted for the amortization of any premium or discount.

If a debt security is held to maturity, the cost will be realized. Any interim unrealized gains or losses will reverse. Amortized cost is relevant only if the security is actually held to maturity. At acquisition, the company must establish the intent and ability to hold the security to maturity, regardless of changes in such factors as market interest rates and general liquidity needs.

Trading Securities

Securities that are held for current resale are classified as trading securities. Such securities are held for short periods of time for the purpose of generating profits on short-term differences in price. Unrealized holding gains and losses for trading securities should be included in income. Dividend and interest income should also be included in income.

Assume that Elizabeth Company acquires 100 shares of Avon stock for $60 per share and classifies it as a trading security. If the end-of-year price is $58 per share, the company has a $200 unrealized loss (100 x $2). If the end-of-year price is $63 per share, the company has a $300 unrealized gain (100 x $3). The unrealized loss or gain is reported in the income statement. The journal entry for the case in which the market value increases by $300 is as follows:

```
Investment in stock  . . . . . . . . . . . . . . . . . .   300
    Unrealized gain on
        marketable equity securities  . . . . . . .            300
```

If the stock is sold during the following year for $67 per share, a realized gain of $400 is recognized. The journal entry to record the sale would be as follows:

```
Cash  . . . . . . . . . . . . . . . . . . . . . . . . . . . . .   6,700
    Investment in stock  . . . . . . . . . . . . . . . . . .            6,300
    Gain on sale of marketable
        equity securities  . . . . . . . . . . . . . . . . . .            400
```

The stock was originally purchased for $6,000 and was subsequently sold for $6,700. The $700 gain was recognized in the two years as follows:

```
Unrealized gain (first year)  . . . . . . . . . . . . . . . . . . . . . . .  $ 300
Realized gain (second year)  . . . . . . . . . . . . . . . . . . . . . . .    400
```

Securities Available for Sale

Unlike FASB Statement No. 12, the changes in market value are accounted for on an individual security basis, not on an aggregate basis. No allowance account is needed.

Unrealized gains and losses for securities available for sale are not reported in the income statement. Instead, they are reported as a separate component of stockholders' equity. The reason for this approach is to reduce the volatility in reported earnings.

Using the same example as above, assume this time that the 100 shares of stock at $60 per share are classified as available for sale. If the market value increases by $300 by the end of the year, the credit would be to a separate stockholders' equity account rather than to income. If the stock is sold during the following year for $67 per share, a realized gain of $700 is recognized. The journal entry to record the sale would be as follows:

Cash	6,700	
Unrealized equity gain on marketable equity securities	300	
Investment in stock		6,300
Gain on sale of marketable equity securities		700

The stockholders' equity account, unrealized equity gain on marketable equity securities, is reduced by $300, and the $700 realized gain is reported in the income statement.

Securities available for sale are classified as current or noncurrent according to the usual criteria. The accounting for these securities is not affected by the classification.

EXERCISES—APPENDIX B

1. Amy Company had the following transactions relating to marketable securities during the last three months of 19X1.

Sept. 1   Purchased 100 shares of Heather Company common stock for $27 per share.

Nov. 1   Received a $1 per share dividend on the Heather Company common stock.

Dec. 1   Sold 50 shares of the stock at $32 per share.

Required:

1. Prepare the journal entries necessary to record the above transactions.
2. Assuming the fair value of the stock is $34 per share at year-end, prepare the journal entry necessary to record the change in market value according to *FASB Statement No. 115* assuming:

    a. The investment is classified as a trading security.
    b. The investment is classified as a security available for sale.

3. Assuming the other 50 shares are sold for $35 per share in the following year, prepare the journal entry necessary to record the sale assuming:

    a. The investment is classified as a trading security.
    b. The investment is classified as a security available for sale.

2. The transactions of Cammie Company relating to marketable securities during 19x1 are listed below.

Jan. 10   Purchased 500 shares of Smith Corporation common stock at a price of $42 per share.

Feb. 5   Purchased 100 shares of Dade Corporation common stock at a price of $75 per share.

Mar. 1   Received a cash dividend of $2 per share on Smith Corporation common stock.

Apr. 16   Purchased 200 shares of Consolidated Company common stock at $150 per share.

June 1   Received a cash dividend of $3 per share on Dade Corporation common stock.

Aug. 20   Sold 70 shares of Dade Corporation stock at $80 per share.

Sept. 1   Received a $2 per share dividend on Consolidated Company common stock.

Required:

1. Prepare the journal entries necessary to record the above transactions.

2. Assuming the fair values of the stocks are as follows, prepare the journal entries necessary to record the changes in market value according to *FASB Statement No. 115* assuming the investments are classified as: (a) trading securities, or (b) securities available for sale:

Smith	$ 45
Dade	82
Consolidated	160

3. Assuming the rest of the shares are sold for the following prices in 19x2, prepare the journal entries necessary to record the sales assuming the investments are classified as: (a) trading securities, or (b) securities available for sale:

Smith	$ 47
Dade	83
Consolidated	156

3. Jamie Company had the following transactions relating to marketable securities during 19x1:

Jan.	20	Purchased 100 shares of Bear Corporation common stock at $90 per share.
Apr.	16	Purchased 400 shares of River Corporation common stock at $30 per share.
May	1	Received a cash dividend of $3 per share on Bear Corporation common stock.
June	1	Purchased 100 of Gunner Corporation 6% $1,000 bonds at $950 each. Interest is payable annually on May 31.
Aug.	11	Received a cash dividend of $2 per share on River Corporation common stock.
Nov.	1	Sold 40 shares of Bear Corporation common stock at $99 per share.
Dec.	31	Accrued interest on the Gunner Corporation bonds.

Required:

1. Prepare the journal entries to record the above transactions.
2. Assuming the fair values of the securities are as follows, prepare the journal entries necessary to record the changes in market value according to *FASB Statement No. 115* assuming the investments are classified as: (a) trading securities, or (b) securities available for sale:

Bear	$ 97
River	22
Gunner	940

3. Assuming the rest of the shares are sold for the following prices in 19x2, prepare the journal entries necessary to record the sales assuming the investments are classified as: (a) trading securities, or (b) securities available for sale:

Bear	$ 98
River	23
Gunner	930

Chapter 10 discusses common techniques of analyzing information presented in financial statements. Studying this chapter should enable you to:

1. Distinguish between horizontal and vertical analyses and discuss the type of information that is provided by each.

2. Discuss the concept of ratio analysis and identify the problems that may be inherent in its use.

3. List the most commonly used standards against which a firm may be compared and explain the strengths and limitations associated with the use of these standards.

4. Describe and apply the basic techniques of financial analysis as they are used by common stockholders, long-term creditors, and short-term creditors.

10

Financial Statement Analysis

INTRODUCTION

The financial statements of a business enterprise are intended to provide much of the basic data used for decision-making and, in general, evaluation of performance by various groups such as current owners, potential investors, creditors, government agencies, and in some instances, competitors. Because general-purpose published financial statements are by their very nature issued for a wide variety of users, it is often necessary for particular user groups to extract the information in which they are particularly interested from the statements. For example, owners and potential investors are normally interested in the present earnings and future earnings prospects of a business. Similarly, short-term creditors are primarily concerned with the ability of a firm to meet its short-term obligations as they become due and payable. Consequently, a somewhat detailed analysis and interpretation of financial statements is usually required in order to obtain the information which may be relevant for the specific purposes of a particular user. In this chapter, several selected techniques which are useful in financial analysis will be described and discussed.

COMPARATIVE FINANCIAL STATEMENTS

In general, the usefulness of financial information is increased when it can be compared with related data. Comparison may be internal (i.e., within one firm) or external (i.e., with another firm). External comparisons may be difficult to make in practice since financial statements of firms may not be readily comparable because of the use of different generally acceptable accounting principles. However, some useful information may be obtained by comparison with industry averages, ratios, etc. (such as those compiled by *Moody's* and *Standard and Poor's*) or by direct comparison with the statements of another firm. Obviously, considerable caution must be exercised when making this type of analysis.

The financial statements of a particular firm are most useful when they can be compared with related data from within the current period, information from prior periods, or with budgets or forecasts. Comparative statements are useful in providing a standard which facilitates the analysis and interpretation of changes and trends which have occurred in elements of the financial statements. Generally, published annual reports of corporations provide comparative accounting statements from the previous period and often also include selected historical information for the firm for a longer period of time, such as ten years.

Assume that the income statement of a firm for the year ended December 31, 19x2, disclosed net income of $100,000. This information, in and of itself, provides a user with only a single indicator of the absolute amount of income for the year. If an income statement for 19x1, disclosing net income of $80,000 was also presented, 19x2 net income would become much more meaningful information to the user. The 25 percent increase of 19x2 income over that for 19x1 indicates a significant improvement in performance that could not be determined from the 19x2 statements alone.

BASIC ANALYTICAL PROCEDURES

Comparisons of financial statement data are frequently expressed as percentages or ratios. These comparisons may represent:

1. Percentage increases and decreases in an item in comparative financial statements.

2. Percentage relationships of individual components to an aggregate total in a single financial statement.

3. Ratios of one amount to another in the financial statements.

Application of each of these three methods will be illustrated by the use of the comparative financial statements of Dolbey Company which follow. These comparative statements will also serve as a basis for the analysis presented in the remainder of this chapter.

Horizontal Analysis

Analysis of increases or decreases in a given financial statement item over two or more accounting periods is often referred to as horizontal analysis. Generally, this type of analysis discloses both the dollar and percentage changes for the corresponding items in comparative statements. An example of horizontal analysis is included in the comparative financial statements

Dolbey Company
Comparative Balance Sheet
December 31, 19x2 and 19x1

	19x2 Dollars	19x2 Percent of Total Assets	19x1 Dollars	19x1 Percent of Total Assets	Increase (Decrease) Dollars	Increase (Decrease) Percent
Assets						
Current assets:						
Cash	$ 80,000	5.0	$ 40,000	2.8	$ 40,000	100.0
Net accounts receivable	100,000	6.3	80,000	5.5	20,000	25.0
Inventories	200,000	12.5	160,000	11.1	40,000	25.0
Prepaid expenses	20,000	1.2	8,000	.6	12,000	150.0
Total current assets	$ 400,000	25.0	$ 288,000	20.0	$112,000	38.9
Land, buildings, and equipment (net)	1,200,000	75.0	1,152,000	80.0	48,000	4.2
Total assets	$1,600,000	100.0	$1,440,000	100.0	$160,000	11.1
Liabilities						
Current liabilities:						
Accounts payable	$ 200,000	12.5	$ 130,000	9.0	$ 70,000	53.8
Notes payable	100,000	6.3	60,000	4.2	40,000	66.7
Total current liabilities	$ 300,000	18.8	$ 190,000	13.2	$110,000	57.9
Bonds payable	200,000	12.5	200,000	13.9	0	0
Total liabilities	$ 500,000	31.3	$ 390,000	27.1	$110,000	28.2
Stockholders' Equity						
Common stock ($30 par)	$ 900,000	56.2	$ 900,000	62.5	0	0
Retained earnings	200,000	12.5	150,000	10.4	$ 50,000	33.3
Total liabilities and stockholders' equity	$1,600,000	100.00	$1,440,000	100.0	$160,000	11.1

presented for Dolbey Company. These statements include data with regard to income, retained earnings, and financial position for a two-year period with the dollar and percentage changes for each item listed in the final two columns.

Interpretation of the increases or decreases in individual statement items cannot be completely evaluated without additional information. For example, the comparative balance sheet discloses an increase in inventory during 19x2 of $40,000, to an amount 25 percent greater than in 19x1. This increase may have been required in order to support a higher sales volume as net sales increased by a third during 19x2. Alternatively, this increase could have resulted from a build-up of an obsolete inventory item. Obviously, the point to be made here is that additional information is often useful and sometimes absolutely necessary for meaningful interpretation.

Dolbey Company
Comparative Income Statement
For the Years Ended December 31, 19x2 and 19x1

	19x2 Dollars	19x2 Percent of Sales	19x1 Dollars	19x1 Percent of Sales	Increase (Decrease) Dollars	Increase (Decrease) Percent
Net sales	$2,000,000	100.0	$1,500,000	100.0	$500,000	33.3
Cost of goods sold	1,400,000	70.0	1,080,000	72.0	320,000	29.6
Gross profit on sales	$ 600,000	30.0	$ 420,000	28.0	$180,000	42.9
Operating expenses:						
Selling expenses	$ 300,000	15.0	$ 240,000	16.0	$ 60,000	25.0
Administrative expenses	180,000	9.0	129,000	8.6	51,000	39.5
Total operating expenses	$ 480,000	24.0	$ 369,000	24.6	$111,000	30.1
Operating income	$ 120,000	6.0	$ 51,000	3.4	$ 69,000	135.3
Interest expense	10,000	.5	9,000	.6	1,000	11.1
Income before income taxes	$ 110,000	5.5	$ 42,000	2.8	$ 68,000	161.9
Income taxes	30,000	1.5	12,000	.8	18,000	150.0
Net income	$ 80,000	4.0	$ 30,000	2.0	$ 50,000	166.7

Dolbey Company
Comparative Statement of Retained Earnings
For the Years Ended December 31, 19x2 and 19x1

	19x2	19x1	Increase (Decrease) Dollars	Increase (Decrease) Percent
Retained earnings (January 1)	$150,000	$135,000	$15,000	11.1
Net income	80,000	30,000	50,000	166.7
	$230,000	$165,000	$65,000	39.4
Less: Dividends	30,000	15,000	15,000	100.0
Retained earnings (December 31)	$200,000	$150,000	$50,000	33.3

Data from the 19x0 statements:
- Total assets (December 31, 19x0) $1,160,000
- Stockholders' equity (December 31, 19x0) 1,035,000
- Net receivables (December 31, 19x0) 70,000
- Inventory (December 31, 19x0) 110,000

Percentage changes included in the statements for Dolbey Company were stated in terms of the data for two years. When a comparison is made between statements of two periods, the earlier statement is normally used as a base in computing percentage changes. For statements which include more than two years, there are two methods which may be used in selecting a base year. One alternative is to use the earliest year as a base. If this alternative is selected, each amount on all succeeding statements will be expressed as a percentage of the base year amount. Since this procedure results in a constant base, percentage changes for more than two years can be interpreted as trend values for individual components of the financial statements. A second alternative is to compare each statement with the statement which immediately precedes it. Adoption of this procedure results in a changing base that may make comparisons of percentage changes over a period of several years more difficult.

Vertical Analysis

The percentage relationship of an individual item or component of a single financial statement to an aggregate total in the same statement often discloses significant relationships. These relationships may be useful information for decision-making purposes. For example, in reporting income data, it may be useful to indicate the relationship between sales and other elements of the income statement for a period. This analysis of the elements included in the financial statements of a single period is often referred to as vertical analysis.

Vertical analysis is also illustrated in the financial statements presented for Dolbey Company. In the comparative balance sheet, the total assets balance and the total liabilities and stockholders' equity balance for each year are used as a base. Each item in the statement is then expressed as a percentage of this base. For example, the statements indicate that current assets increased from 20 percent of total assets in 19x1 to 25 percent at the end of 19x2. An analysis of the composition of the current asset balance provides additional details of the changes in various individual categories of current assets.

Vertical analysis may also be employed in presenting a comparative income statement. In the Dolbey Company illustration, each individual item is stated as a percent of net sales for the period.

Common-Size Statements

Horizontal and vertical analyses are frequently useful in disclosing certain relationships and trends in individual elements included in the financial statements. The analysis of these relationships may be facilitated by the use of common-size statements (i.e., statements in which all items are stated in terms of percentages or ratios). Common-size statements may be prepared in order to compare data from the current period with that from one or more past periods for a firm. These statements may also be used to compare data of two or more business firms for the same period or periods, subject to the limitations mentioned previously.

A common-size statement comparing income statement data for Dolbey Company with that of Nutt Company is presented below. The column for Dolbey Company is prepared by using the percentage figures that were included in the comparative income statement previously given. Net sales of each firm are set as a base of 100 percent and each individual item included in the statement is shown as a percentage of net sales. Consequently, use of this statement format provides a comparison of the relationships of the income statement items for the two firms regardless of the absolute dollar amount of sales and expenses of either company. It can be seen, for example, that Dolbey Company obtained $.04 of net income from each dollar of net sales, while Nutt Company netted only $.01 of net income from each sales dollar.

Dolbey Company and Nutt Company
Condensed Common-Size Income Statement
For the Year Ended December 31, 19x2

	Dolbey Company	Nutt Company
Net sales	100.0%	100.0%
Cost of goods sold	70.0	72.5
Gross profit on sales	30.0%	27.5%
Operating expenses:		
Selling expense	15.0%	17.5%
Administrative expense	9.0	7.5
Total operating expenses	24.0%	25.0%
Operating income	6.0%	2.5%
Interest expense	.5	1.0
Income before income taxes	5.5%	1.5%
Income taxes	1.5	.5
Net income	4.0%	1.0%

RATIO ANALYSIS

A ratio is an expression of the relationship of one numerical item to another. Significant interrelationships which may be present in financial statements are often identified and highlighted by the use of ratio analysis. A simple example of such a relationship would be the ratio of cash to current liabilities for Dolbey Company at the end of 19x2. The ratio would be calculated or computed as follows:

$$\text{Ratio of Cash to Current Liabilities} = \frac{\text{Cash}}{\text{Current Liabilities}}$$

$$.27 = \frac{\$80,000}{\$300,000}$$

Ratios may be expressed in several different ways. Generally, ratios are stated in relation to a base of one. For example, for the ratio computed above, it could be stated that the ratio of cash to current liabilities is .27 to 1 (which is sometimes simply stated as .27 with the "to 1" omitted). In any case a ratio is a method used to describe a relationship between two financial statement amounts. The meaningful use of ratio analysis requires that there be a logical relationship between the figures compared, and that this relationship be clearly understood by the user.

Comparison With Standards

The analytical procedures employed in computing percentage changes (horizontal analysis), component percentages (vertical analysis) and ratios convert financial statement items into a form which may be comparable to various standards. It is comparisons made among the relationships derived from the financial statements and selected standards that allow the user to draw meaningful conclusions concerning the firm. Among the most commonly used standards of comparison against which the position of a particular firm may be measured are the following:

1. Past performance of the firm.
2. Financial data of similar or competing firms.
3. Average performance of a number of firms in the industry.

A major deficiency of comparison with the past performance of the firm is that there is no indication of what *should* have occurred given the nature of the firm, the economy of the period, etc. For example, the fact that the net income of a firm increased by 3 percent from the previous year may initially appear to be favorable. However, if there is evidence that net income *should* have increased by 6 percent, the performance for the current year would be regarded as unfavorable.

The weakness of comparisons with past performance of the firm may be overcome somewhat by using the performance of a similar firm or firms or an industry average as an additional standard for comparison. A problem with this approach, however, is that it is often difficult to identify firms which are truly comparable, both because of the nature of the firms themselves and because of the use of alternative "generally accepted accounting principles." In spite of these limitations, a careful analysis of comparative performance, both internal and external, often provides meaningful input for use in decision-making.

ANALYSIS FOR COMMON STOCKHOLDERS

Common stockholders and potential investors purchase securities of a firm in an attempt to earn a return on their investment through increases in the market price of the stock and by dividends. Because each of these factors is influencd by net income, the analysis of financial statements made by, or on behalf of, an investor is focused primarily on the company's record of earnings. Certain of the more important relationships which are of

Rate of Return on Total Assets

interest to the stockholder-investor are discussed in the following sections of this chapter.

The rate of return on total assets provides a measure of management's ability to earn a return on the firm's assets. The income figure used in this computation should be income before the deduction of interest expense, since interest is the return to creditors for the resources that they provide to the firm. Thus, the rate of return on total assets is computed by dividing net income plus interest expense by the average investment in assets during the year.

$$\text{Rate of Return on Total Assets} = \frac{\text{Net Income (after taxes)} + \text{Interest Expense}}{\text{Average Total Assets During the Year}}$$

Although assets are continually acquired and disposed of throughout a period, an average of asset balances at the beginning and end of the period is generally used for this calculation. The calculation for Dolbey Company would be as follows:

	19x2	19x1
Net income	$ 80,000	$ 30,000
Add: Interest expense	10,000	9,000
Net income before interest expense	$ 90,000	$ 39,000
Total assets:		
Beginning of year	$1,440,000	$1,160,000
End of year	1,600,000	1,440,000
Total	$3,040,000	$2,600,000
Average total assets	$1,520,000	$1,300,000
Rate of return on assets	5.9%	3.0%

This ratio indicates that the earnings per dollar of assets invested have almost doubled in 19x2. It appears that the management of Dolbey Company has increased its efficiency in the use of the firm's assets to generate income.

Rate of Return on Common Stockholders' Equity

The rate of return on common stockholders' equity is a measure of a firm's ability to earn a profit for its residual owners, the common stockholders. Because interest paid to creditors and dividends paid to preferred stockholders are normally fixed in amount, the return on common stockholders' equity may not be equal to the return on total assets. If management is able to earn a higher return on assets than the cost (i.e., interest expense) of assets contributed by the creditors, the excess benefits the owners. This is often referred to as using debt as favorable "leverage" in order to increase the owners' rate of return or as "trading on equity." Of course, if the cost of borrowing funds exceeds the return on assets, leverage will be unfavorable and will reduce the rate of return to the residual owners. The rate of return on common stockholders' equity is computed by dividing net income, less preferred dividends, by the average equity of the common stockholders.

$$\text{Rate of Return on Common Stockholders' Equity} = \frac{\text{Net Income (after taxes)} - \text{Preferred Dividends}}{\text{Average Common Stockholders' Equity}}$$

Since Dolbey Company has no preferred stock, the rate of return on common stockholders' equity would be computed as follows:

	19x2	19x1
Net income	$ 80,000	$ 30,000
Common stockholders' equity:		
Beginning of the year	$1,050,000	$1,035,000
End of the year	1,100,000	1,050,000
Total	$2,150,000	$2,085,000
Average common stockholders' equity	$1,075,000	$1,042,500
Rate of return on common stockholders' equity	7.4%	2.9%

The rate of return on the common stockholders' equity is higher than the rate of return on assets for 19x2 because the cost of funds contributed by creditors is less than the rate earned on assets. Thus the company is experiencing favorable "leverage," using borrowed funds to earn a return in excess of their cost.

Earnings Per Share of Common Stock

Since owners of a business invest in shares of stock, they are usually interested in an expression of earnings in terms of a per share amount. If a company has only a single class of common stock outstanding, the earnings per share figure is computed by dividing net income for the period by the average number of common shares outstanding.[1] If the firm has other securities outstanding which have certain characteristics similar to those of common stock (such as convertible bonds), the usefulness of earnings per share data is enhanced if these other securities are also considered in the computation of earnings per share. These securities are often referred to as common stock equivalents. While a discussion of the inclusion of common stock equivalents in the computation of earnings per share is beyond the scope of this text, the basic principle involved is that earnings per share figures are calculated so as to indicate the effects of the conversion of these securities into common stock.

When there is both common and preferred stock outstanding, net income must be reduced by preferred dividend requirements in order to determine net income available to common stockholders.

---

[1] The calculation of earnings per share was discussed in Chapter 7.

$$\text{Earnings Per Share} = \frac{\text{Net Income} - \text{Preferred Dividends}}{\text{Average Number of Common Shares Outstanding}}$$

In the case of Dolbey Company, which has no preferred stock, the earnings per share of common stock would be calculated as follows:

	19x2	19x1
Net income	$80,000	$30,000
Number of common shares outstanding	30,000	30,000
Earnings per share of common stock	$ 2.67	$ 1.00

Earnings per share is a ratio frequently mentioned in the financial press in relation to the earnings performance of business firms. In addition, earnings per share data is reported on the income statement and usually in various other sections of corporate annual reports. Although the concept of earnings per share has received a great deal of attention, particularly in recent years, it should be viewed with some caution. As a minimum, it should be recognized that all of the significant aspects of a firm's performance simply cannot be reduced to a single figure. This point cannot be overemphasized.

Price-Earnings Ratio on Common Stock

Each investor must allocate his or her limited resources among various investment opportunities which are available to him or her. For this reason, the rate of earnings in relation to the current market price of his or her investment often provides a useful basis for comparing alternative investment opportunities. This ratio is commonly referred to as the price-earnings ratio. It is computed by dividing the current market price per share of common stock by earnings per share.

$$\text{Price-Earnings Ratio} = \frac{\text{Market Price Per Share of Common Stock}}{\text{Earnings Per Share}}$$

Assuming that the market price per common share of Dolbey Company at the end of 19x2 was $24 and at the end of 19x1 was $8, price-earnings ratios would be calculated as follows:

	19x2	19x1
Market price per share at the end of the year	$24.00	$8.00
Earnings per share	$ 2.67	$1.00
Price-earnings ratio	9	8

The price-earnings ratio may be interpreted as the value that investors in the stock market place on every dollar of earnings for a particular firm. An investor may compare the price-earnings ratio of a firm to that of other companies in an attempt to estimate whether a firm's stock is overpriced or underpriced.

Debt-to-Equity Ratio

The debt-to-equity ratio measures the proportion of funds supplied to the firm by its stockholders as opposed to funds provided by creditors. It is computed by dividing total debt by stockholders' equity.

$$\text{Debt-to-Equity Ratio} = \frac{\text{Total Debt}}{\text{Stockholders' Equity}}$$

The debt-to-equity ratio provides a measure of the risk incurred by common stockholders. Since debt consists of fixed obligations, the larger the debt-to-equity ratio, the greater is the chance that a firm may face a situation in which it is unable to meet its obligations. At the same time, however, a high debt-to-equity ratio can increase the rate of return on stockholders' equity through the use of favorable financial leverage. This can occur because interest on debt is fixed in amount, regardless of the amount of earnings. Consequently there is no ideal debt-to-equity ratio. Rather, each investor must define a satisfactory debt-to-equity ratio based on his or her desired degree of risk.

For Dolbey Company the debt-to-equity ratios are calculated as follows:

	19x2	19x1
Total debt	$ 500,000	$ 390,000
Stockholders' equity	$1,100,000	$1,050,000
Debt-to-equity ratio	45.5%	37.1%

ANALYSIS FOR LONG-TERM CREDITORS

Bondholders and other long-term creditors, like stockholders and investors, are also concerned with measures of the profitability of a business. In addition, however, long-term creditors are particularly interested in a firm's ability to meet its interest requirements as they become due and payable. A good indicator of a firm's ability to pay interest is the margin between income and interest payments. A common measure of this margin is the ratio of net income available for interest payments to annual interest expense. This ratio, which is referred to as the number of times interest earned, is computed by dividing net income before interest expense and income taxes by the interest requirement for the period. Income taxes are added back to net income because interest charges are an expense which is deducted in computing income taxes. Similarly, interest charges are added back to net income because the ratio provides a measure of the ability of the firm to pay fixed interest charges.

$$\frac{\text{Number of Times}}{\text{Interest Earned}} = \frac{\text{Net Income + Interest Expense + Income Taxes}}{\text{Interest Expense}}$$

The computation for Dolbey Company would be as follows:

	19x2	19x1
Net income	$ 80,000	$30,000
Add back:		
Income taxes	30,000	12,000
Interest expense	10,000	9,000
Amount available for interest requirements	$120,000	$51,000
Number of times interest earned	12.0	5.7

The increase in the ratio from 5.7 times in 19x1 to 12.0 times in 19x2 would appear to be favorable with respect to a long-term creditor of Dolbey Company.

ANALYSIS FOR SHORT-TERM CREDITORS

Short-term creditors are also concerned with the earnings prospects of a firm. Of primary importance to the short-term creditor, however, is a firm's ability to pay its current debt on a timely basis and to meet its current operating needs. This is often referred to as the current position of the firm.

The ability of a firm to pay its current debts as they fall due depends largely upon the relationship between its current assets and its current liabilities. The excess of a firm's current assets over its current liabilities is termed working capital. Adequate working capital enables a firm to meet its current needs and obligations on a timely basis. However, an analysis of the components of working capital and the flow of working capital is necessary in order to determine the adequacy of the working capital position of a specific firm.

Current Ratio

The absolute amount of working capital may be an inadequate measure of a firm's ability to meet its obligations. As an illustration, consider the following data for two companies:

	Reed Company	Frazier Company
Current assets	$20,000	$50,000
Current liabilities	10,000	40,000
Working capital	$10,000	$10,000

In this example, both companies have $10,000 of working capital. However, the current assets of Reed Company could be reduced by 50 percent and still be equal to the current liabilities, while the current assets of Frazier Company could only shrink by 20 percent and remain equal to current liabilities.

Another means of evaluating working capital is to evaluate the relationship between current assets and current liabilities. This ratio is referred to as the current ratio.

$$\text{Current Ratio} = \frac{\text{Current Assets}}{\text{Current Liabilities}}$$

The use of the current ratio for the example given would disclose a ratio of 2 to 1 for Reed Company and 1.25 to 1 for Frazier Company. This clearly indicates the stronger current position of Reed Company.

The current ratio for Dolbey Company is calculated as follows:

	19x2	19x1
Current assets	$400,000	$288,000
Current liabilities	300,000	190,000
Current ratio	1.3	1.5

Although the working capital of Dolbey Company increased from $98,000 in 19x1 to $100,000 in 19x2, current assets per dollar of current liabilities declined from $1.50 to $1.30. This is an unfavorable trend from the viewpoint of short-term creditors because the margin of safety has declined.

A satisfactory current ratio for a particular firm depends, of course, upon the nature of its business. Although short-term creditors generally feel safer as the current ratio increases in amount, this may not be efficient from a business standpoint. For example, a firm with excess cash in relation to its current needs is inefficient since cash is a nonproductive asset. A good measure of the adequacy of a firm's current ratio is often a comparison with the current ratios of similar firms or industry averages.

Acid-Test or Quick Ratio

In analyzing the ability of a firm to meet its obligations, the distribution of current assets is also important. For example, a firm with a large proportion of cash to current assets is better able to meet its current debts than a firm with a larger proportion of inventories. This is because inventories usually require more time for conversion into cash than do other current assets. Assets with a longer conversion period are usually referred to as being less liquid. For this reason, a ratio which excludes the less liquid assets is often used as a supplement to the current ratio. The ratio of the highly current assets—cash, marketable securities, and receivables—to current liabilities is known as the acid-test or quick ratio.

$$\text{Acid-Test Ratio} = \frac{\text{Cash} + \text{Marketable Securities} + \text{Receivables}}{\text{Current Liabilities}}$$

Since Dolbey Company owns no marketable securities, its acid-test ratio would be calculated as follows:

	19x2	19x1
Cash	$ 80,000	$ 40,000
Net accounts receivable	100,000	80,000
Total	$180,000	$120,000
Current liabilities	$300,000	$190,000
Acid-test ratio	.60	.63

In evaluating the acid-test ratio, again the nature of the business must be considered. The .6 acid-test ratio for Dolbey Company in 19x2 may indicate a serious problem as there may not be sufficient liquid assets to meet current liabilities as they become due.

Analysis of Accounts Receivable

It is obvious that the rate at which non-cash current assets may be converted into cash is an important determinant of the firm's ability to meet its current obligations. Because neither the current nor the acid-test ratio considers this movement in current assets, short-term creditors should use additional tests in considering the liquidation of two significant working capital items, receivables, and inventories.

An approximation of the average time which is required by a firm in order to collect its receivables may be determined by first computing the turnover of accounts receivable. Receivables turnover is computed by dividing net credit sales by the average accounts receivable balance. Ideally, a monthly average of receivables should be used, but generally only the balances at the beginning and end-of-the-year are available to the user of the financial statements.

$$\frac{\text{Accounts Receivable}}{\text{Turnover}} = \frac{\text{Net Sales on Account}}{\text{Average Accounts Receivable}}$$

The accounts receivable turnover is an approximation of the number of times accounts receivable were converted into cash during the period. Therefore, the higher the turnover, the more liquid are the firm's receivables.

Accounts receivable turnover of Dolbey Company is computed below. Assume that all sales were made on a credit basis and that only the beginning and end-of-the-year balances of receivables are available.

	19x2	19x1
Net sales on account	$2,000,000	$1,500,000
Net receivables:		
Beginning of year	$ 80,000	$ 70,000
End-of-the-year	100,000	80,000
Total	$ 180,000	$ 150,000
Average	$ 90,000	$ 75,000
Accounts receivable turnover per year	22.2 times	20.0 times

This increase in the receivables turnover for Dolbey Company during 19x2 indicates that the average collection period for receivables has decreased. This could be a result of more successful collection practices or a change in credit policies, or a combination of both factors.

The receivables turnover may be used to determine the average collection period, which can be readily compared with the firm's credit terms. The average number of days to collect receivables is computed by dividing 365 days by the receivables turnover.

$$\text{Average Number of Days to Collect Receivables} = \frac{365 \text{ Days}}{\text{Accounts Receivable Turnover}}$$

If the average number of days required to collect receivables significantly exceeds the credit terms of the firm, this would indicate that the credit department may be ineffective in its credit granting and collecting activities.

The average number of days to collect receivables is calculated for the Dolbey Company as follows:

	19x2	19x1
Receivables turnover	22.2 times	20.0 times
Average number of days to collect receivables	16.4 days	18.3 days

Analysis of Inventories

A procedure similar to that used for evaluating receivables may be employed in evaluating the inventories of a firm. One indication of the liquidity of inventories is obtained by determining the relationship between the cost of goods sold and the average balance of inventories on hand during a period. Cost of goods sold is used because it represents the cost (rather than selling price) of goods that have been sold from the inventories during the period.

Inventory turnover is calculated by dividing cost of goods sold by the average inventory. Again, if possible, monthly figures should be used to determine average inventory. Usually, however, only the beginning and end-of-the-year inventory balances are available.

$$\text{Inventory Turnover} = \frac{\text{Cost of Goods Sold}}{\text{Average Inventory}}$$

A low inventory turnover may indicate management inefficiency in that excess cash has been committed to the investment in inventory. Although inventories are necessary to meet the demands of a firm, there are advantages in maintaining the investment in inventory at the minimum level necessary to service customers, thus minimizing carrying costs, risks of loss, or obsolescence, etc.

Assuming that only the beginning and ending inventories are available, the computation of inventory turnover for Dolbey Company is as follows:

	19x2	19x1
Cost of goods sold	$1,400,000	$1,080,000
Inventory:		
Beginning of the year	$ 160,000	$ 110,000
End-of-the-year	200,000	160,000
Total	$ 360,000	$ 270,000
Average inventory	$ 180,000	$ 135,000
Inventory turnover	7.8 times	8 times

It appears that the trend of the inventory turnover for Dolbey Company is somewhat unfavorable, since inventories were turned over more slowly in 19x2 than in 19x1. Again, the analyst would want to obtain additional information before making a definitive judgment.

INTERPRETATION OF ANALYSES

The user must exercise considerable caution in the use of ratios in order to analyze the financial statements of a business enterprise. Some of the problems inherent in ratio analysis are summarized below:

1. Comparisons of items for different periods or for different companies may not be valid if different accounting practices have been used. For example, one firm may use straight-line depreciation and the FIFO inventory method while a similar company may use accelerated depreciation and LIFO for its inventories.

2. Financial statements represent only one source of financial information concerning a firm and its environment. Consequently, other information not disclosed in financial statements may have an impact on the evaluation of the statements.

3. Most financial statements are not adjusted either for changes in market values or in the general price level. This may seriously affect comparability between firms over time.

4. As ratio analysis has increased in popularity, there has sometimes been a tendency to develop ratios which have little or no significance. A meaningful ratio can be developed only from items which have a logical relationship.

All of the ratios and measurements developed in this chapter need not be used as input in a particular decision. In determining the financial strengths and weaknesses of a particular firm, relevant measurements need to be selected, developed, and interpreted in view of the conditions relating to the business.

SUMMARY

Financial statements provide a variety of external users with essential data regarding a firm's financial position and the results of its operations. However, most users of financial statements must make a detailed analysis and interpretation of the data presented to obtain evaluative information useful in making decisions.

The actual evaluative techniques used by an individual will vary according to personal preference and the nature of the individual's relationship to the reporting firm. Most techniques involve some type of comparison with related data. The data may relate to the firm's past performance, to similar or competing firms, or to an industry average. Comparisons are often expressed in terms of percentage or ratios, although there are certain problems inherent in ratio analysis.

Firms may present a horizontal or vertical analysis of relevant data along with their regular financial statements. A horizontal analysis usually presents both the dollar and percentage changes for corresponding items for two or more accounting periods. Vertical analysis discloses the percentage relationship of an individual item or component of a single financial statement to an aggregate total included in the same statement. Presentation of these analyses may be facilitated by the use of common-size statements in which all items are stated in terms of percentages and ratios.

Since current and potential stockholders are primarily interested in earning an acceptable return on their investments through increases in the market price of the stock and by dividends, their analyses focus on the company's record of earnings. Examples of earnings relationships of interest to the stockholder-investor are the rate of return on total assets, the rate of return on common stockholders' equity, the earnings per share of common stock, and the price-earnings ratio on common stock. The stockholders may also be interested in the debt-to-equity ratio as a measure of the risk incurred by the common stockholders as opposed to the risk incurred by creditors.

In addition to their interest in the profitability of the business, bondholders and other long-term creditors are concerned with the firm's ability to meet its interest requirements as they become payable. A common measure of such ability is the ratio of net income available for interest payments to annual interest expense. This measure is generally referred to as the number of times interest is earned.

Short-term creditors are primarily interested in the firm's ability to pay its current debt on a timely basis and to meet its current operating needs. Although the absolute amount of working capital available to a firm may provide useful information to a creditor, the ratio of current assets to current liabilities (referred to as the current ratio) is generally thought to provide better evaluative data. If only the more liquid current assets are used in ratio, it is referred to as an acid-test ratio. Other evaluation methods used by short-term creditors include the analysis of accounts receivable and the analysis of inventories.

KEY DEFINITIONS

Accounts receivable turnover—an approximation of the number of times accounts receivable were converted into cash during the period. It is defined as net sales on account divided by average accounts receivable.

Acid-test ratio—this ratio is a measure of a firm's ability to pay its current liabilities as they come due with the more liquid current assets. It is usually the ratio of cash, marketable securities, and receivables to total current liabilities.

Average collection period—this is a measure of the average time required by a firm to collect a receivable. Collection period is computed by dividing 365 days by the receivables turnover.

Common-size statements—in common-size financial statements, all items are stated in terms of percentages or ratios.

Current ratio—this ratio measures a firm's ability to pay current liabilities as they come due. It is defined as the ratio of current assets to current liabilities.

Debt-to-equity ratio—measures the proportion of funds supplied by stockholders as opposed to the funds provided by creditors. It is computed by dividing total debt by total stockholders' equity.

Horizontal analysis—the analysis of the increase or decrease in a given financial statement item over two or more accounting periods.

Inventory turnover—gives an indication of the liquidity of inventories. Its computation involves dividing cost of goods sold by the average inventory.

Number of times interest earned—this measure of a firm's ability to pay interest is computed by dividing net income before interest expense and income taxes by the interest expense.

Price-earnings ratio—the current market price of a share of stock divided by the earnings per share.

Rate of return on common stockholders' equity—this measure of the firm's ability to earn a profit for its common stockholders is computed by dividing net income after taxes and preferred dividends by the average common stockholders' equity.

Rate of return on total assets—this measure of the ability of the firm's management to earn a return on the assets without regard to variations in the method of financing is computed by dividing net income plus interest expense by the average investment in assets during the year.

Ratio analysis—the analysis of items in a financial statement expressing the relationship of one numerical item to another.

Vertical analysis—the percentage relationship between an individual item or a component of a single financial statement to an aggregate total in the statement.

QUESTIONS

1. How is the financial statement analysis related to the needs of the various users of financial statements?

2. Distinguish between vertical analysis and horizontal analysis.

3. What are common-size statements?

4. How are each of the following computed?

    a. Rate of Return on Total Assets.
    b. Rate of Return on Common Stockholders' Equity.
    c. Earnings per Share of Common Stock.
    d. Price-Earnings Ratio on Common Stock.
    e. Debt-to-Equity Ratio.
    f. Number of Times Interest Earned.
    g. Current Ratio.
    h. Acid-Test Ratio.
    i. Accounts Receivable Turnover.
    j. Average Number of Days to Collect Receivables.
    k. Inventory Turnover.

5. Each of the ratios (in Question 4 above) are utilized by one user group more than others. Indicate whether each item is utilized most by (1) common shareholders (or investors), (2) long-term creditors, or (3) short-term creditors.

6. What are the most commonly used standards against which to measure the position of a particular firm? What are the weaknesses inherent in these standards?

7. Business corporations usually provide comparative statements in their annual reports. What is a comparative statement? How do they enhance the usefulness of financial information?

8. What will be the effect (increase, decrease, none) on the rate of return on assets of each of the following?

    a. Cash purchase of a new machine.
    b. Increase in the tax rate.
    c. Reduction of accounts payable.
    d. Cash sale of a fully depreciated machine.

9. What is indicated if the average number of days to collect receivables significantly exceeds the credit terms of the firm?

10. What are the principal limitations that should be considered in evaluating ratios?

11. When percentage changes are given in comparative statements for more than two years, there are two methods for selecting the base year. What are they?

12. Which of the methods in Question 11 makes comparison of percentage changes over several years more difficult? Why?

EXERCISES

13. The acid-test ratio at the beginning of 19x0 was 2 to 1 for the Gilly Company.

    Required:

    How would the following transactions affect the acid-test or quick ratio?

    1. Collection of note receivable from Silly Co. The note was due in 19x3.
    2. Collection of accounts receivable.
    3. Sales on account.
    4. Purchase of inventory on account.
    5. Payment of accounts payable.
    6. Collection of an account receivable.
    7. Cash purchase of common stock of ABC Co. as a temporary investment.
    8. Purchase of a new machine on a credit basis, the purchase price payable in 6 months.

14. The following information has been extracted from the financial statements of Cozeb Corp.

Common stock, $5 par	$ 5,000,000
Common stock, $10 par	5,000,000
Preferred stock, $100 par	10,000,000
Net income	3,000,000
Preferred dividends	1,000,000

    Required:

    Compute earnings per share assuming the number of shares outstanding did not change during the year.

15. The December 31, 19x1 financial statement of Flunkart Company included the following data:

Cash	$ 60,000
Accounts receivable	200,000
Marketable securities	100,000
Prepaid expenses	25,000
Accounts payable	200,000
Notes payable (current)	85,000
Inventory	115,000
Bonds payable (due in 5 years)	300,000
Wages payable	15,000

    Required:

    1. What is the current ratio? Acid-test ratio? Working capital?
    2. Comment on the significance of this current ratio.

16. Using the information given, complete the balance sheet below.

   a. The "quick" ratio is 2:1.
   b. Notes payable are long-term liabilities and are four times the dollar amount of the marketable securities.
   c. Accounts receivable are $2,000 and are one-half of the "quick" assets, one-fourth of the current assets, and equal to plant and equipment.
   d. Total stockholders' equity is equal to the working capital and contributed capital is twice the dollar amount of the net accumulation of earnings.

Assets		Liabilities and Stockholders' Equity	
Cash	_____	Accounts payable	_____
Marketable securities	_____	Notes payable	_____
Accounts receivable	_____		
Inventories	_____	Capital stock	_____
Plant and equipment	_____	Retained earnings	_____

17. Consider the following information concerning the 19x1 and 19x2 operations of ABC Co.

	19x1	19x2
Sales	$800,000	$1,000,000
Purchases	400,000	450,000
Beginning inventory	80,000	90,000
Ending inventory	90,000	90,000
Selling expense	40,000	50,000
Administrative expenses	10,000	40,000
Income taxes	100,000	200,000

Required:

Prepare a comparative income statement for the years ending December 31, 19x1 and 19x2. Indicate the changes both in percentages and dollars.

18. Small Company is a manufacturer of widgets. Industrywide averages (expressed in percentages of sales) for the production and sale of widgets are as follows:

Sales	100%
Cost of goods sold	70%
Selling expenses	10%
Administrative expenses	7%

In order to compare its own performance with industrywide standards, the Small Company has computed the following percentages:

Sales	100%
Cost of goods sold	60%
Selling expenses	20%
Administrative expenses	15%

Required:

1. Comment on the performance of Small Company.
2. What are the problems relating to the use of industrywide standards as a basis for evaluating an individual company's performance?

19. The current ratio of Lap Co. on December 31, 19x1 was 2 to 1 ($200,000 to $100,000). In 19x2 the following transactions occurred:

   a. Payment of accounts payable, $125,000.
   b. Collection of accounts receivable, $50,000.
   c. Sales of $200,000, ¾ of which was cash; cost of goods sold was $125,000.
   d. Purchase of goods, all on credit, $150,000.
   e. A loan for $100,000, due in 5 years.
   f. Cash purchase of marketable securities, $10,000.

   Required:

   On the basis of the preceding information, compute the current ratio at December 31, 19x2.

20. The Hawks Company decided to change its credit policy in 19x3, from 2/10, n/30, the policy in effect during 19x2, to 5/10, n/30. Using the information given below, evaluate whether or not this was a beneficial change.

	19x2	19x3
Total sales	$350,000	$400,000
Cash sales	75,000	85,000
Accounts receivable, 12/31/x1	25,000	
Accounts receivable, 12/31/x2	28,000	
Accounts receivable, 12/31/x3	18,000	

21. The ending inventory for each month of 19x1 is listed below for the Expo Company:

1/31	$21,998	7/31	$35,000
2/28	33,000	8/31	40,000
3/31	28,000	9/30	47,000
4/30	29,500	10/31	48,600
5/31	34,200	11/30	47,300
6/30	29,000	12/31	49,100

   During the last half of the year, the company decided to order inventory in larger quantities to take advantage of a quantity discount. The company was able to pass this discount on to its customers in the form of a price decrease. Cost of goods sold for the first half of the year was $224,000 and for the last half of the year was $410,000, reflecting an increase in demand.

   Required:

   Compute inventory turnover for both halves of the year and decide whether this new inventory policy is beneficial.

22. What would Phillie Company's working capital be after the occurrence of *each* of the following consecutive transactions during March? Working capital as of March 1 was ($10,000).

Mar. 2 Sold $15,000 of merchandise. Cost of goods sold was $13,500.
8 Paid $11,000 on accounts payable.
10 Purchased $6,000 of inventory for cash.
15 Collected $3,000 on accounts receivable.
18 Issued a $10,000, 8 percent bond for $12,000.
21 Purchased a building with the proceeds from the bond.
26 Issued 25 shares of $10 par value capital stock for $13.
31 Adjustment for $200 accrued interest payable.
31 Adjustment for $500 accrued rent receivable.

PROBLEMS

23. The comparative income statement for Joe Company and John Company is presented below.

Joe Company and John Company
Comparative Income Statement
For the Year Ending December 31, 19x1

	Joe Company	John Company
Net sales	$500,000	$250,000
Cost of goods sold	350,000	150,000
Gross profit on sales	$150,000	$100,000
Operating expenses:		
Selling expense	$ 50,000	$ 10,000
Administrative expense	10,000	7,000
Total Operating Expenses	$ 60,000	$ 17,000
Operating income	$ 90,000	$ 83,000
Interest expense	30,000	5,000
Income before income taxes	$ 60,000	$ 78,000
Income taxes	20,000	25,000
Net income	$ 40,000	$ 53,000

Required:

Using the above information, prepare a common-size statement comparing income data for Joe Company and John Company.

24. The income statements for 19x2 for Spahn Company and Sain Company are presented below.

Spahn Company
Income Statement
For the Year Ended December 31, 19x2

Sales		$225,000
Cost of goods sold		140,000
Gross profit from sales		$ 85,000
Expenses:		
Selling expense	$18,000	
Administrative expense	20,000	
General expenses	15,000	
Total Expenses		53,000
Income from operations		$ 32,000
Interest expense		2,000
Income before taxes		$ 30,000
Income taxes		7,000
Net Income		$ 23,000

Sain Company
Income Statement
For the Year Ended December 31, 19x2

Sales		$300,000
Cost of goods sold		195,000
Gross profit from sales		$105,000
Expenses:		
Selling expense	$15,000	
Administrative expense	30,000	
General expenses	21,000	
Total Expenses		66,000
Income from operations		$ 39,000
Interest expense		6,000
Income before taxes		$ 33,000
Income taxes		4,000
Net Income		$ 29,000

Required:

Prepare a common-size income statement comparing Spahn Company with Sain Company.

25. The following information was taken from the financial statements of Maker Company on December 31, 19x2.

Cash	$ 75,000
Accounts receivable	125,000
Inventory	100,000
Fixed assets (net)	500,000
	$800,000
Accounts payable	$100,000
Bond payable (due December 31, 19x27)	300,000
Capital stock ($10 par)	300,000
Retained earnings	100,000
	$800,000
Net income	$ 50,000

Required:

Compute the following:

1. Current ratio
2. Working capital
3. Acid-test ratio
4. Earnings per share
5. Debt-to-equity ratio

26. Following is the condensed common-size income statement for Francis Co.:

Francis Company
Condensed Common-Size Income Statement
For the Year Ended December 31, 19x2

Net sales	100.0%
Cost of goods sold	68.0
Gross profit on sales	32.0%
Operating expenses:	
Selling expense	16.0%
Administrative expense	6.0
Total Operating Expense	22.0%
Operating income	10.0%
Interest expense	0.5
Income before income taxes	9.5%
Income taxes	2.0
Net income	7.5%

Net sales for the period were $3,000,000.

Required:

Prepare the income statement for Francis Company.

27. Your examination of the balance sheet for Reswarts Corp. on December 31, 19x1, 19x2, and 19x3 reveals the following information:

	19x1	19x2	19x3
Cash	$ 50,000	$ 75,000	$100,000
Accounts receivable (net)	150,000	100,000	150,000
Inventory	175,000	200,000	225,000
Prepaid expenses	25,000	25,000	40,000
Land	45,000	45,000	45,000
Buildings (net)	170,000	155,000	200,000
Machinery and equipment (net)	70,000	60,000	50,000
Accounts payable	120,000	140,000	130,000
Notes payable	50,000	40,000	50,000
Capital stock	400,000	400,000	400,000
Retained earnings	115,000	80,000	230,000

Required:

Prepare comparative balance sheets for the three years using (1) the first year presented as a base and (2) the previous year as a base. Include both percentage and dollar changes.

28. Given below are the balance sheets for Meyers, Inc., for 19x1 and 19x2.

Meyers, Inc.
Comparative Balance Sheet
December 31, 19x2 and 19x1

	19x2	19x1
ASSETS		
Current assets:		
Cash	$ 20,000	$ 17,000
Accounts receivable (net)	45,000	60,000
Supplies inventory	8,000	6,000
Prepaid expenses	7,000	5,000
Total Current Assets	$ 80,000	$ 88,000
Land	120,000	70,000
Buildings (net)	200,000	100,000
Total Assets	$400,000	$258,000
LIABILITIES		
Current liabilities:		
Accounts payable	$ 10,000	$ 7,000
Taxes payable	9,000	3,000
Total Current Liabilities	$ 19,000	$ 10,000
Bonds payable	115,000	70,000
Total Liabilities	$134,000	$ 80,000
STOCKHOLDERS' EQUITY		
Common stock ($5 par)	$ 50,000	$ 45,000
Additional paid-in capital	125,000	80,000
Retained earnings	91,000	53,000
Total Liabilities and Stockholders' Equity	$400,000	$258,000

10 | Financial Statement Analysis 10-27

Required:

Prepare a horizontal and vertical analysis of the balance sheets of Meyers, Inc. for 19x1 and 19x2.

29. Shown below are partially completed comparative financial statements of Neil Company.

Required:

1. Complete the statements.
2. Compute the following for 19x2:

   a. Rate of Return on Total Assets
   b. Rate of Return on Common Stockholders' Equity
   c. Earnings per Share of Common Stock
   d. Debt-to-Equity Ratio
   e. Number of Times Interest Earned
   f. Working Capital
   g. Current Ratio
   h. Acid-Test Ratio
   i. Inventory Turnover
   j. Average Number of Days to Collect Receivables

Neil Company
Comparative Balance Sheet
December 31, 19x2 and 19x1

	19x2 Dollars	19x2 Percent of Total Assets	19x1 Dollars	19x1 Percent of Total Assets	Increase (Decrease) Dollars	Increase (Decrease) Percent
ASSETS						
Current assets:						
Cash	$ 55,000		$ 50,000			
Net accounts receivable	200,000		175,000			
Inventories	300,000		225,000			
Prepaid expenses	45,000		50,000			
Total Current Assets	$ 600,000		$ 500,000			
Land, buildings and equipment (net)	1,400,000		1,250,000			
Total Assets	$2,000,000		$1,750,000			
LIABILITIES						
Current liabilities:						
Accounts payable	$ 300,000		$ 350,000			
Notes payable	200,000		100,000			
Total Current Liabilities	$ 500,000		$ 450,000			
Bonds payable	500,000		500,000			
Total Liabilities	$1,000,000		$ 950,000			
STOCKHOLDERS' EQUITY						
Common stock ($20 par)	$ 600,000		$ 600,000			
Retained earnings	400,000		200,000			
Total Liabilities and Stockholders' Equity	$2,000,000		$1,750,000			

Neil Company
Comparative Income Statement
For Years Ended December 31, 19x2 and 19x1

	19x2 Dollars	19x2 Percent of Sales	19x1 Dollars	19x1 Percent of Sales	Increase (Decrease) Dollars	Increase (Decrease) Percent
Net sales	$3,000,000		$2,000,000			
Cost of goods sold	2,100,000		1,500,000			
Gross profit on sales	$ 900,000		$ 500,000			
Operating expenses:						
Selling expenses	$ 400,000		$ 200,000			
Administrative expenses	100,000		50,000			
Total Operating Expenses	$ 500,000		$ 250,000			
Operating income	$ 400,000		$ 250,000			
Interest expense	40,000		30,000			
Income before income taxes	$ 360,000		$ 220,000			
Income taxes	90,000		45,000			
Net Income	$ 270,000		$ 175,000			

Neil Company
Comparative Statement of Retained Earnings
For Years Ended 12/31/x2 and x1

	19x2	19x1	Increase (Decrease) Dollars	Increase (Decrease) Percent
Retained earnings, January 1	$200,000	$ 75,000		
Net income	270,000	175,000		
	$470,000	$250,000		
Less: Dividends	70,000	50,000		
Retained earnings, December 31	$400,000	$200,000		

30. Met Wholesale Company has in recent prior years maintained the following relationships among the data on its financial statements:

1.	Gross profit rate on net sales	35%
2.	Net profit rate on net sales	5%
3.	Rate of selling expenses to net sales	25%
4.	Accounts receivable turnover	8 per year
5.	Inventory turnover	6 per year
6.	Times interest earned in 19x4	2
7.	Current ratio	2.5
8.	Rate of return on total assets	3%
9.	Quick-asset composition:	
	Cash	10%
	Marketable securities	30%
	Accounts receivable	60%

The company has a net income of $240,000 for 19x4. The resulting earnings per share was $0.48 per share on common stock. Additional information follows:

a. Capital stock issued (all in 19x2) and outstanding:

   Common, $20 per share par value, issued at 2 percent premium.
   Preferred, 8 percent nonparticipating, $100 per share par value, issued at an 8 percent premium.

b. Long-term debt issued at par value in 19x0 has an interest rate of 5 percent and is due in 19x10. Total debt is $5,408,000.
c. The company owns no depreciable assets.
d. All sales were on account. Assume the ending accounts receivable, fixed assets, and inventory balances are the average for the year.
e. The preferred dividend's obligation for 19x4 totaled $8,000 and was paid on December 31, 19x4. There had been no dividends in arrears for years prior to 19x4.

Required:

1. Prepare an income statement.
2. Prepare a balance sheet for the Met Wholesale Company for the year ending December 31, 19x4 from the ratios and information given above. Ignore taxes. The two statements will only include the accounts divulged in this problem. (Hint: Retained Earnings is a balancing figure in this problem.)

31. Joe Stockholder is contemplating buying stock in one of the following companies, both in the same business. Below is financial data relating to each company:

	Pirate Company	*Cardinal Company*
Sales	$ 6,000	$18,000
Cost of goods sold	3,800	13,884
Depreciation expense	800	1,400
Interest expense	200	800
Other expenses	44	110
Income taxes	480	600
Cash	1,000	4,000
Accounts receivable	3,500	10,000
Inventory	800	1,900
Fixed assets	10,000	38,000
Accumulated depreciation	4,000	14,000
Accounts payable	1,800	4,000
Income taxes payable	480	600
Bonds payable	200	3,600
Common stock ($20 par value)	6,000	36,000
Retained earnings	2,820	(4,300)
Current market value per share	$ 33	$ 5.35

Required:

Compute the ratio that would best give the answer to each of the following questions, then answer the question. Make all necessary assumptions.

1. Which company has the best current position?
2. Which company has the most effective credit department?
3. Which company is doing the best job at keeping the most appropriate inventory level?
4. Which firm has the best ability to make their interest payments?
5. Which firm is earning the best return on the firm's assets?
6. Which stock is the best buy?

32. From the following stockholders' equity portion of the balance sheet and additional information calculate these ratios for the year ended December 31, 19x2:

a. Earnings per share.
b. Rate of return on common stockholders' equity.
c. Price-earnings ratio.

	December 31 19x1	December 31 19x2
Stockholders' Equity:		
6 percent preferred stock, $90 par value, 10,000 shares authorized, 5,000 shares issued and outstanding in 19x1; 6,000 in 19x2 (callable at $110)	$ 450,000	$ 540,000
Common stock, $8 par value, 100,000 shares authorized, 45,000 shares issued and outstanding in 19x1; 54,000 in 19x2	360,000	432,000
Additional paid-in capital:		
Common stock issued	135,000	270,000
Preferred stock issued	105,000	126,000
Total contributed capital	$1,050,000	$1,368,000
Retained earnings	48,000	89,000
Total Stockholders' Equity	$1,098,000	$1,457,000

Additional information:

No dividends were paid during 19x2. Preferred stock has no dividends in arrears from previous years and is nonparticipative. The market price per share of common stock at the end of 19x2 is $13.50.

33. The following are financial statements of ZYX Corporation for 19x1.

ZYX Corporation
Balance Sheet
December 31, 19x1

ASSETS

Current assets:		
Cash	$100,000	
Accounts receivable (net)	200,000	
Prepaid expenses	50,000	
Inventory	110,000	
Total Current Assets		$ 460,000
Fixed assets:		
Land	$ 50,000	
Machinery (net)	100,000	
Building (net)	250,000	
Total Fixed Assets		400,000
Total Assets		$ 860,000

LIABILITIES AND STOCKHOLDERS' EQUITY

Accounts payable	$ 50,000
Wages payable	5,000
Interest payable	2,000
Bonds payable (due December 31, 19x6)	200,000
Capital stock ($2 par value)	400,000
Retained earnings	203,000
Total Liabilities and Stockholders' Equity	$ 860,000

ZYX Corporation
Income Statement
For the Year Ended December 31, 19x1

Sales (net)		$1,000,000
Cost of goods sold:		
Beginning inventory	$ 90,000	
Purchases	600,000	
Goods available for sale	$690,000	
Ending inventory	110,000	
Cost of goods sold		580,000
Gross profit on sales		$ 420,000
Operating expenses:		
Sales salaries expense	$ 75,000	
Depreciation expense	20,000	
Insurance expense	5,000	
Interest expense	10,000	
Total operating expense		110,000
Income before taxes		$ 310,000
Income taxes		100,000
Net Income		$ 210,000

January 1, 19x0 data:

  Common shares outstanding............ 200,000

Required:

Compute the following:

1. Earnings per Share of Common Stock
2. Debt-to-Equity Ratio
3. Number of Times Interest Earned
4. Current Ratio
5. Acid-Test or Quick Ratio
6. Inventory Turnover

34. Orioles Retail Company has maintained the following relationships in recent years among the data on its financial statements:

1.	Gross profit rate on net sales............	30%
2.	Net profit rate on net sales..............	6%
3.	Rate of selling expenses to net sales......	6%
4.	Accounts receivable turnover...........	10 per year
5.	Inventory turnover....................	7 per year
6.	Times interest earned in 19x4...........	4 times
7.	Current ratio.........................	3.2
8.	Rate of return on total assets............	5%
9.	Quick-asset composition:	
	Cash............................	15%
	Marketable securities................	25%
	Accounts receivable.................	60%
10.	Tax rate............................	40%

The company has a net income after taxes of $450,000 for 19x4. The resulting earnings per common share was $2.50. Additional information follows:

a. Capital stock issued (all in 19x2) and outstanding:

Common, $10 per share par value, issued at 10 percent premium.
Preferred, 7 percent nonparticipating, $100 per share par value, issued at a 10 percent premium.

b. Preferred dividends were paid up through 19x3; 19x3 dividends of $4,900 were paid on July 1, 19x4.

c. The only long-term debt, an 8 percent bond payable, was issued at par in 19x0 and is due in 19x10. Total debt is $3,750,000.

d. All sales were on account. Assume that accounts receivable and inventory balances were the same on January 1, 19x4 as they are on December 31, 19x4.

e. Fixed assets have been owned for five years and are depreciated at a rate of 5 percent on their original cost per year.

Required:

1. Prepare an income statement.
2. Prepare a balance sheet for the Orioles Retail Company for the year ending December 31, 19x4. The two statements will only include the accounts divulged in this problem. (Hint: Retained Earnings is a balancing figure.)

Refer to the Annual Report included in the front of the text.

35. Compute the accounts receivable turnover for the most recent year, assuming notes receivable equal zero.

36. Compute the average collection period for the most recent year.

37. Compute the current ratio for the most recent year.

38. Compute the acid-test ratio for the most recent year.

39. Compute the debt-to-equity ratio for the most recent year.

40. Compute the inventory turnover for the most recent year.

41. Compute the number of times interest was earned in the most recent year.

42. Compute the return on total assets in the most recent year.

Chapter 11 illustrates the procedures used in preparing the statement of cash flows. Studying this chapter should enable you to:

1. Understand and give examples of the types of information an analysis of cash flows will provide.
2. Identify the primary sources and uses of cash.
3. Describe the procedures involved in preparing the statement of cash flows.
4. Prepare a statement of cash flows using both the indirect and the direct methods of computing net cash flows from operating activities.

11

The Statement of Cash Flows

INTRODUCTION

An important consideration in the decision process of many users of financial statements is the amount of, and the changes in, the cash available to a business. Comparative balance sheets indicate the cash available at the beginning and the end of a period. These statements do not, however, explain the causes of any changes in cash. While a part of the change in cash may result from the operations of the business, the net income as reported in the income statement may not be accompanied by an equivalent increase in cash. Consequently, the combination of the balance sheet and income statement may not provide an adequate indication of the cash flows which take place during the business cycle. For this reason, a statement which discloses the analysis of the cash flows of a firm is required along with the balance sheet and income statement as a part of a firm's report "package." This statement, the statement of cash flows, is a significant measure of the effectiveness of the financing activities of a firm. This analysis and the information that it provides is considered to be of sufficient importance that it is now included as a formal statement in the published annual reports of firms.

IMPORTANCE OF CASH FLOWS

Investors are interested in receiving dividends, creditors are concerned about receiving periodic interest payments and principal payments, suppliers want to be assured that they will receive payments for merchandise sold, and employees depend on being able to receive paychecks when due. The critical issue for all these groups is cash flow.

Although some information about cash flows can be derived from comparative balance sheets and income statements, neither of these statements provides a complete picture of a company's cash flows. An income statement discloses the results of operations for a period of time, but does not indicate the cash provided by operations or the cash provided by other activities. Comparative balance sheets show net changes in assets, liabilities, and owners' equity, but do not indicate the specific causes of these changes. A third statement is needed—a statement of cash flows.

The statement of cash flows explains the causes of changes in cash and provides a summary of the operating, investing, and financing activities of an enterprise during a period of time. While the basic purpose of this statement is to provide information concerning the cash receipts and payments of a company, the statement also is useful in appraising other factors such as the firm's financing policies, dividend policies, ability to expand productive capacity, and ability to satisfy future debt requirements.

A BRIEF HISTORY

Prior to the 1960s, many firms voluntarily prepared statements of changes in financial position for their annual reports. The statement of changes usually provided information on the sources and uses of working capital (current assets minus current liabilities) during the accounting period. The statement of changes in financial position was not provided to replace the balance sheet or income statement, but was intended to provide information that was not available directly from the other statements.

While the basic objective of the statement of changes in financial position was to summarize the financing and investing activities of the firm, in practice the form and content of these statements varied considerably. The statement was designed to allow users to analyze the flow of funds. Funds were usually defined as working capital, but some companies defined funds as cash.

Due to increasing attention placed on funds-flow analysis, the AICPA published *Accounting Research Study No. 2*, " 'Cash Flow' Analysis and the Funds Statement," in 1961.[1] This study recommended that the funds statement be presented in annual reports. In 1963, *APB Opinion No. 3*, "The Statement of Source and Application of Funds," recommended, but did not require, that a statement of sources and applications of funds be presented as supplementary information in financial reports.[2] Since the issuance of

---

[1] Perry Mason, " 'Cash Flow' Analysis and the Funds Statement," *Accounting Research Study No. 2*, (New York: AICPA, 1961).

[2] *APB Opinion No. 3*, "The Statement of Source and Application of Funds," (New York: AICPA, 1963).

APB Opinion No. 3, there was a substantial increase in the number of firms presenting funds-flow data. However, the nature of the funds statement varied widely in practice, because *APB Opinion No. 3* allowed considerable latitude as to the form, content, and terminology of the statement.

In 1971, the APB issued its *Opinion No. 19*,[3] which required the presentation of funds flow in annual reports. In this *Opinion*, the APB stated that a statement of changes in financial position is essential for financial statement users and must be presented as a basic financial statement for each period for which an income statement is presented.

The objective of the statement of changes in financial position was to provide information on all of the financing and investing activities that occurred during an accounting period. This statement did not replace the income statement or balance sheet. Rather, it was intended to provide information that the other statements did not provide concerning the flow of funds and changes in financial position.

In 1987, the FASB issued *Financial Accounting Standards No. 95, "Statement of Cash Flows,"* requiring a statement of cash flows. This statement should resolve the differences in the definition of funds, the purposes and presentation of the funds flow statement as well as improve the usefulness of the financial statements.

In recent years, many companies switched from defining funds as working capital to defining funds as cash or cash plus cash equivalents (such as treasury bills, commercial paper, and money market funds). The change can be seen from data provided in the 1989 edition of *Accounting Trends & Techniques* for its survey of 600 companies. In 1985, 587 of the 600 companies presented a statement of changes in financial position, and only one company included a statement of cash flows in their annual report. In 1988, only 58 companies presented a statement of changes in financial position and 540 companies included a cash flow statement.

ALL FINANCIAL RESOURCES CONCEPT

Most financing or investing activities involve a net change in cash or working capital—that is, an increase or decrease in cash or another current asset or a current liability. In some cases, however, a significant financial transaction may affect only noncurrent accounts. For example, the issuance of capital stock or long-term debt in exchange for a long-term asset has no effect on either cash or working capital. This type of exchange would be excluded from the statement of cash flows if only cash transactions were included.

---

[3] *APB Opinion No. 19*, "Reporting Changes in Financial Position," (New York: AICPA, 1971), para. 7.

APB Opinion No. 19 broadened the concept underlying the statement of changes in financial position to include all important aspects of an entity's financing and investing activities regardless of whether cash or other elements of working capital are affected directly. In this approach, referred to as the "all financial resources" concept, a material transaction involving changes in noncurrent accounts must be disclosed in the statement of changes in financial position. Of course, including this type of transaction has no effect on the reported increase or decrease in cash or working capital, but it does provide the user with a comprehensive view of the total inflow and outflow of all financial resources during a period. The FASB has continued this practice in FAS 95 by requiring entities to report the effects of investing and financing activities that do not involve the receipt or payment of cash in narrative form or in a supplemental schedule to the cash flow statement.

THE STATEMENT OF CASH FLOWS

The statement of cash flows consists of three major sections: the cash effects of an entity's operations, its investing activities, and its financing activities. Grouping cash flows into these categories enables significant relationships within and among these activities to be analyzed and provides useful information to users of financial statements.

Previously, the statement of changes in financial position (either on a cash or working capital basis) was in the format of a listing of the sources and then the uses of cash or working capital. However, sources can include such dissimilar transactions as the issuance of bonds and the proceeds on the sale of plant and equipment; similarly, uses can include transactions such as the payment of dividends and the repayment of long-term debt. The new format required by FAS 95 should be more useful and understandable.

The three sections of the statement of cash flows are as follows:

1. *Operating activities*—Operating activities include selling, purchasing, and producing goods; providing services; paying suppliers and employees; interest income; etc.

2. *Investing activities*—Investing activities include receipts from loans, acquiring and selling securities (except for cash equivalents), and acquiring and selling plant assets and land.

3. *Financing activities*—Financing activities include proceeds from the issuance of the entity's bonds or stocks, reductions of long-term debt; outlays to pay the maturity value of bonds, outlays to purchase the entity's stock, and the payment of dividends.

In addition, there may be a separate schedule for noncash investing and financing activities (for example, acquiring land by issuing common stock).

In preparing the statement of cash flows, cash flows from operating activities may be reported by either the direct or the indirect method. Using the direct method, cash flows from operations are computed by subtracting cash disbursements from operations directly from cash receipts from operations. Alternatively, the indirect method computes net cash flow from operations by adjusting the net income for noncash items included in the computation of net income for the period. The format for the statement of cash flows under either the direct or indirect method is presented next.

A format for the statement of cash flows is as follows:

Direct Method

Cash flows from operating activities:		
Cash received from customers	$X	
Dividends received	X	
Cash provided by operating activities		$X
Cash paid to suppliers	(X)	
Cash paid to employees	(X)	
Cash paid for interest and taxes	(X)	
Cash paid for operating activities		(X)
Net cash flow from operating activities		$X
Cash flows from investing activities:		
Proceeds from sale of plant assets	$X	
Purchase of plant assets	(X)	
Net cash provided by investing activities		X
Cash flows from financing activities:		
Proceeds from issuance of bonds payable	$X	
Proceeds from issuance of common stock	X	
Payment of cash dividends	(X)	
Net cash provided by financing activities		X
Net increase (decrease) in cash		$X

This format uses the direct method to obtain net cash flow from operating activities.

An alternative format for the statement of cash flows is as follows:

Indirect Method

Cash flows from operating activities:		
Net income		$X
Noncash expenses, revenues, losses,		
and gains included in income:		
Depreciation and amortization		X
Increase in receivables		(X)
Increase in inventories		(X)
Increase in payables		X
Net cash flow from operating activities		$X
Cash flows from investing activities:		
Proceeds from sale of plant assets	$X	
Purchase of plant assets	(X)	
Net cash provided by investing activities		X
Cash flows from financing activities:		
Proceeds from issuance of bonds payable	$X	
Proceeds from issuance of common stock	X	
Payment of cash dividends	(X)	
Net cash provided by financing activities		X
Net increase (decrease) in cash		$X

This format uses the indirect method to obtain net cash flow from operating activities.

Note that the only difference between the direct and the indirect methods is in presentation of net cash flow from operating activities. The remaining two sections of the statement, cash flows from investing activities and cash flows from financing activities, are identical under the direct and indirect methods.

<u>When the direct method is used, a supplemental schedule reconciling net income to net cash flows from operating activities must be provided.</u> The format for this schedule is as follows:

Reconciliation of Net Income
to Net Cash Provided By
Operating Activities

Net income	$X
Adjustments to reconcile net income to	
net cash provided by operating activities:	
Depreciation and amortization	X
Increase in receivables	(X)
Increase in inventories	(X)
Increase in payables	X
Total adjustments	$X
Net cash provided by operating activities	$X

Note that this schedule, the reconciliation of net income to net cash provided by operating activities, is almost identical to the initial section of the cash flow statement using the indirect method. This is because the indirect method normally provides a reconciliation of net income to net cash flows from operating activities for all noncash expenses, revenues, losses, and gains within the statement itself (or in a supplemental schedule). The same amount of net cash from operating activities is reported under the direct and indirect methods.

While the FASB permits the use of either method, it encourages the use of the direct method because it provides more useful information. Both methods will be illustrated in this chapter.

Cash From Operations

The net income of a firm for a particular period has been defined as the excess of its revenues over its related expenses. Revenues generally result in an increase in cash or other current assets. For example, sales usually cause an increase in either cash or accounts receivable. Similarly, most expenses require either that a current outlay of cash be made or that a current liability be incurred.

Direct Method. As the name implies, under the direct method the statement of cash flows may show cash receipts and payments from operations directly. Such a format could appear as follows:

```
Cash flows from operating activities:
   Cash received from customers .....................    $X
   Dividends received ...............................     X
   Cash provided by operating activities ............         $X
   Cash paid to suppliers ...........................    (X)
   Cash paid to employees ...........................    (X)
   Cash paid for interest and taxes .................    (X)
   Cash paid for operating activities ...............         (X)
   Net cash flow from operating activities ..........         $X
```

Cash received by customers is equal to sales on an accrual basis plus the decrease in accounts receivable or minus the increase in accounts receivable. Net sales is adjusted by the change in net accounts receivable to convert sales on an accrual basis to sales on a cash basis. Assume that sales on an accrual basis are $50,000, beginning accounts receivable are $10,000, and ending accounts receivable are $8,000. Then sales on a cash basis are as follows:

```
      Sales on an accrual basis ........................   $50,000
      Add:   Beginning accounts receivable..............    10,000
                                                           $60,000
      Less:  Ending accounts receivable.................     8,000
             Cash received from customers ..............   $52,000
```

The decrease in accounts receivable ($10,000 − $8,000 = $2,000) results in cash received from customers exceeding sales on an accrual basis by $2,000.

Cash paid to suppliers of merchandise is equal to cost of goods sold: (1) plus the increase in inventories or minus the decrease in inventories, and (2) plus the decrease or minus the increase in accounts payable and other short-term liabilities for merchandise. For example, assume that cost of goods sold is $40,000, beginning inventories are $7,000, ending inventories are $9,000, beginning accounts payable for inventories is $6,000, and ending accounts payable for inventories is $5,000. Then cash paid to suppliers is as follows:

Cost of goods sold		$40,000
Add:	Ending inventories	9,000
Cost of goods available		$49,000
Less:	Beginning inventories	7,000
Purchases		$42,000
Add:	Beginning accounts payable	6,000
		$48,000
Less:	Ending accounts payable	5,000
Cash paid to suppliers		$43,000

Cash paid for other expenses is equal to the expense on an accrual basis plus the decrease in the related payable or minus the increase in the related payable. For example, cash paid to employees is equal to salaries on an accrual basis plus the decrease in salaries payable or minus the increase in salaries payable.

The cash impact of any extraordinary gains and losses should be reported separately.

Indirect Method. As indicated above, the reported net income of a firm is not always equal to the net cash flow from operating activities. Not all expenses or revenues result in a corresponding outflow or inflow of cash. Certain types of expenses enter into the determination of net income but do not affect cash. For example, depreciation on plant assets is an expense that reduces income but does not require an outlay of cash during the current period. Therefore, depreciation expense does not affect cash. Consequently, to determine the net cash flow from operating activities, it is necessary to include only those expenses that required an outflow of cash during the period. An important factor in determining net cash flow from operating activities under the indirect method is to add back to (or subtract from) net income all those items that did not result in an outflow (inflow) of cash.

Examples of items that are added to net income include depreciation expense, amortization expense, bond interest expense due to the amortization of a bond discount, and the reduction to interest revenue due to the amortization of a premium on a bond investment. Examples of items that are subtracted from net income include the reduction to interest expense due to the amortization of a bond premium and interest revenue due to the amortization of a discount on a bond investment.

Additional adjustments are required to convert revenues and expenses to cash receipts and disbursements, because income statement data are based on the accrual method of accounting. To determine net cash flow from operating activities under the indirect method, net income must be adjusted for changes in current assets (other than cash) and for changes in current liabilities (other than those which are not related to operations, such as nontrade notes payable and dividends payable).

These additional adjustments essentially convert the funds provided by operations from the accrual to the cash basis. Some of the more common adjustments under the indirect method to net income to obtain net cash flow from operating activities are as follows:

Add	Subtract
Decrease in net accounts receivable	Increase in net accounts receivable
Decrease in inventories and prepaid expenses	Increase in inventories and prepaid expenses
Increases in accounts payable, trade notes payable, and accrued liabilities	Decreases in accounts payable, trade notes payable, and accrued liabilities

A decrease in accounts receivable results in sales on a cash basis exceeding sales on an accrual basis. Therefore, a decrease in accounts receivable is added to net income to obtain net cash flow from operations. Conversely, an increase in accounts receivable would be subtracted from net income to obtain net cash flow from operations.

In a similar fashion, net income is adjusted by the change in accounts payable, short-term notes payable, and accrued liabilities to convert expenses on an accrual basis to expenses on a cash basis. A decrease in these current payables results in expenses on a cash basis being higher than expenses on an accrual basis. Therefore, a decrease to these payables is subtracted from net income to obtain net cash flow from operations. Conversely, an increase in these payables would be added to net income to obtain net cash flow from operations.

The change in inventories is an adjustment to net income in order to convert cost of goods sold to purchases. An increase in inventories means that purchases exceed cost of goods sold; a decrease in inventories means that purchases are less than cost of goods sold. Therefore, an increase in inventories is subtracted from net income to obtain net cash flow from operations and a decrease in inventories is added to net income to obtain net cash flow from operations.

A firm that experiences a net loss during a period still may generate cash from its operations if: (1) the total expenses that did not require the use of cash exceed the amount of the loss, or (2) adjustments for current assets (other than cash and cash equivalents) and current liabilities convert a net loss on an accrual basis to net income on a cash basis. For example, a firm may have a net loss of $10,000 and have included depreciation expense of $15,000 among its expenses.

Additional adjustments may be required in order to obtain net cash flow from operating activities if net income includes extraordinary gains or losses. The disclosure of cash provided by operations is most useful if the effects of extraordinary items, net of tax, are reported separately from the effects of normal items.

The net cash flow from operating activities may begin with the net income or loss from continuing operations. Any items that did not use or provide cash during the period and were included in the net income or loss from continuing operations should be added or deducted. Cash provided or used by extraordinary items, net of tax, should be reported immediately following cash provided or used in operations. Of course, adjustments are necessary for any of these items that did not provide or use cash during the period.

Similarly, other nonoperating gains or losses should be excluded from cash provided by operations. These amounts should be included as a part of the investing or financing activities. For example, if land that had an original cost of $10,000 is sold for $9,000 in cash, a $1,000 loss on the sale of land is included in the net income for the period. The $9,000 received from the sale represents the cash provided and is shown in the statement as a separate item. Therefore, the $1,000 loss should not be included in determining the net cash flow from operating activities. Thus, to determine the net cash flow from operating activities, it is necessary to add back any nonoperating losses and to deduct any nonoperating gains.

Both the indirect and the direct methods will be used in this chapter to compute net cash flow from operating activities.

Preparation of the Statement of Cash Flows

The change in cash (including cash equivalents) during the period must be equal to the change in the noncash accounts during the period, because the accounting equation must always balance. Based on this relationship, the increase or decrease in cash may be explained by examining the changes in the noncash accounts for the period.

The primary sources of information used in preparing the statement of cash flows are comparative balance sheets, the statement of retained earnings, the income statement, and certain supplementary data concerning the transactions affecting specific noncash accounts during the period. The basic data that will be used to present the required steps for the preparation of a statement of cash flows are shown in the financial statements of the Kraton Company presented as follows:

Kraton Company
Income Statement
For the Year Ended December 31, 19x1

Net sales		$1,000
Cost of goods sold		400
Gross margin		$ 600
Operating expenses:		
Depreciation	$100	
Wage expense	100	
Other expenses	200	400
Net income from operations		$ 200
Gain on sale of land		100
Net income		$ 300

Kraton Company
Retained Earnings Statement
For the Year Ended December 31, 19x1

Retained earnings at beginning of year	$250
Add: Net income	300
	$550
Subtract: Cash dividends	100
Retained earnings at end of year	$450

Kraton Company
Comparative Balance Sheet

	December 31 19x1	19x0	Change
Assets:			
Cash	$ 250	$ 100	+ 150
Accounts receivable	350	200	+ 150
Inventories	200	250	− 50
Building	600	400	+ 200
Accumulated depreciation— building	(200)	(100)	+ 100
Land	100	200	− 100
Total assets	$1,300	$1,050	
Liabilities and Stockholders' Equity:			
Accounts payable	$ 300	$ 200	+ 100
Accrued wages payable	50	100	− 50
Bonds payable—long-term	100	200	− 100
Capital stock	400	300	+ 100
Retained earnings	450	250	+ 200
Total liabilities and equities	$1,300	$1,050	

Assume that the following additional information is available:

1. During the year, a building was purchased for $200 and land was purchased at a cost of $100.

2. Land with a cost of $200 was sold at a gain of $100.

3. All capital stock was issued for cash.

4. A long-term bond was retired for $100.

5. A $100 dividend was paid during the year.

6. The other expenses of $200 were paid in cash.

Change in Cash

The change in the cash account is an increase of $150. The cash balance was $100 at the end of 19x0, but increased to $250 at the end of 19x1.

Changes in Noncash Accounts

Once the change in cash has been determined, the next step is to compute the changes in all of the noncash accounts. All changes in the noncash accounts of Kraton Company from December 31, 19x0, to December 31, 19x1, are summarized below:

Kraton Company
Changes in Noncash Accounts

	19x1	19x0	Increase	Decrease
Accounts receivable—net	$350	$200	$150	
Inventories	200	250		$ 50
Buildings	600	400	200	
Accumulated depreciation—buildings	200	100	100	
Land	100	200		100
Accounts payable	300	200	100	
Accrued wages payable	50	100		50
Bonds payable—long-term	100	200		100
Capital stock	400	300	100	
Retained earnings	450	250	200	

(December 31)

Once the amount of these changes has been determined, it is necessary to consider the effect that each change had on cash. If more than one transaction caused the change in a particular account, the effect of each transaction must be analyzed separately. Let us consider the changes in the noncash accounts of Kraton Company.

Retained Earnings. An examination of the comparative balance sheets reveals that retained earnings increased by $200 during 19x1. An analysis of the statement of retained earnings indicates that net income for 19x1 was $300 and that dividends of $100 were declared and paid during the year.

These two transactions account for the net change in retained earnings. The payment of the cash dividend affected cash as follows:

Cash flow from financing activity:
Cash dividend . . . . ($100)

Under the direct method, net cash flow from operating activities is equal to cash receipts from operations minus cash payments from operations. Cash receipts from operations are equal to net sales less the increase in accounts receivables. Cash payments to suppliers are equal to cost of goods sold less the decrease in inventories less the increase in accounts payable. Cash payments to employees are equal to wage expense plus the decrease in accrued wages payable. Cash payments for other expenses are given at $200. Therefore, net cash flow from operating activities using the direct method is as follows:

Cash flows from operating activities:
Cash receipts from operations ($1,000 − $150) $850
Cash paid to suppliers ($400 − $50 − $100) $250
Cash paid to employees ($100 + $50) 150
Cash paid for other expenses 200
Cash paid for other operating activities   600
Net cash flow from operating activities $250

The effect of the net income of the period on cash is included in the calculation of net cash flow from operating activities using the indirect method. As previously indicated, the net income of Kraton Company is not equivalent to net cash flow from operating activities. Depreciation expense that is included in the income statement did not require an outflow of cash. Therefore, it is necessary to add back depreciation expense of $100 to the net income of the period in computing net cash flow from operating activities under the indirect method.

A second adjustment is required to eliminate the nonoperating gain on the sale of land from net income. The $100 gain is included in the proceeds from the sale of land as an investing activity and must be excluded from net cash flow from operating activities.

The increase in accounts receivable of $150 must be subtracted from net income in calculating net cash flow from operating activities. The decrease in inventories of $50 must be added to net income in calculating net cash flow from operating activities. The increase in accounts payable of $100 must be added to net income in calculating net cash flow from operating activities. The decrease in accrued wages payable of $50 must be subtracted from net income in calculating net cash flow from operating activities. Therefore, using the indirect method the net cash flow from operating activities is determined as follows:

Cash flows from operating activities:
Net income $300
Noncash expenses, revenues, losses,
and gains included in income:
Depreciation 100
Nonoperating gain .... (100)
Increase in accounts receivable .... (150)
Decrease in inventories 50
Increase in accounts payable 100
Decrease in accrued wages payable .... (50)
Net cash flow from operating activities $250

Accumulated Depreciation. The $100 increase in accumulated depreciation—buildings resulted from recording the depreciation expense for the year (see the income statement). The amount of depreciation expense is added to net income in determining net cash flow from operating activities under the indirect method and is not considered under the direct method, because it does not result in a decrease in cash.

Buildings. The increase in the buildings account was the result of a single transaction in which a building was acquired at a cost of $200. The effect of this purchase on cash is as follows:

Cash flow from investing activity:
Purchase of building .... ($200)

Land. The comparative balance sheet indicates that the land account decreased by $100 during 19x1. This decrease was a result of the sale of land during the year exceeding the purchase of land during the year. The cash flow from the sale of land is the proceeds received from the sale. The entry to record the sale was as follows:

Cash.. 300
Gain on sale of land 100
Land.. 200

Thus, $300 of cash was provided by the sale. As indicated previously, the $100 gain on the sale must be subtracted from net income in the calculation of net cash flow from operating activities under the indirect method and not considered under the direct method. The effect of the sale on cash is as follows:

Cash flow from investing activity:
Sale of land........................... $300

The purchase of land for $100 affected cash as follows:

Cash flow from investing activity:
Purchase of land .... ($100)

Bonds Payable. Bonds payable decreased by $100 during the year. An analysis of the additional information provided indicates that this decrease resulted from the retirement of the bonds. The effect on cash is as follows:

Cash flow from financing activity:
Retirement of bonds payable............ ($100)

Capital Stock. The increase in the capital stock account resulted from the issuance of additional stock for $100 in cash during the year. This amount would be included in the statement as follows:

Cash flow from financing activity:
Issuance of capital stock............... $100

The Statement of Cash Flows

All information that is necessary to prepare the statement of cash flows now has been analyzed. Kraton Company's statement of cash flows for the year ended December 31, 19x1, is shown below using: (1) the direct method, and (2) the indirect method to obtain net cash flow from operating activities:

(1) Direct Method

Kraton Company
Statement of Cash Flows
For the Year Ended December 31, 19x1

Cash flows from operating activities:		
Cash receipts from operations		$850
Cash paid to suppliers	$250	
Cash paid to employees	150	
Cash paid for other expenses	200	
Cash paid for operating activities		600
Net cash flow from operating activities		$250
Cash flows from investing activities:		
Sale of land......................................	$300	
Acquisition of land................................	(100)	
Acquisition of building	(200)	
Net cash used by investing activities		0
Cash flows from financing activities:		
Sale of capital stock	$100	
Retirement of long-term bonds	(100)	
Payment of dividends	(100)	
Net cash provided by financing activities		(100)
Increase in cash		$150

(2) Indirect Method

Kraton Company
Statement of Cash Flows
For the Year Ended December 31, 19x1

Cash flows from operating activities:		
Net income		$300
Noncash expenses, revenues, losses, and gains included in income:		
Depreciation	100	
Gain on sale of land	(100)	
Increase in accounts receivable	(150)	
Decrease in inventories	50	
Increase in accounts payable	100	
Decrease in accrued wages payable	(50)	
Net cash flow from operating activities		$250
Cash flows from investing activities:		
Sale of land	$300	
Acquisition of land	(100)	
Acquisition of building	(200)	
Net cash used by investing activities		0
Cash flows from financing activities:		
Sale of capital stock	$100	
Retirement of long-term bonds	(100)	
Payment of dividends	(100)	
Net cash provided by financing activities		(100)
Increase in cash		$150

Worksheet Approach

In a relatively uncomplicated situation, such as that of the Kraton Company described above, it is possible to prepare a statement of cash flows by simply sequentially examining the changes in each account. In a more realistic situation, however, a worksheet often is used to facilitate the analysis and preparation of the statement. Although it is not necessary to use a worksheet, its use normally aids in the preparation of the statement when there are a large number of transactions and various complicating factors.

The following is a worksheet for Kraton Company. The direct method is used to obtain net cash flow from operating activities.

Kraton Company
Worksheet for Statement of Cash Flows
For the Year Ended December 31, 19x1

	Balance December 31, 19x0	Adjustments Debit	Adjustments Credit	Balance December 31, 19x1
Debits:				
Cash	$ 100			$ 250
Accounts receivable (net)	200	$ 150 (3)		350
Inventories	250		$ 50 (11)	200
Buildings	400	200 (5)		600
Land	200	100 (8)	200 (6)	100
	$1,150			$1,500
Credits:				
Accumulated depreciation	$ 100		100 (4)	$ 200
Accounts payable	200		100 (12)	300
Accrued wages payable	100	50 (14)		50
Bonds payable	200	100 (7)		100
Capital stock	300		100 (9)	400
Retained earnings	250	100 (1)	1,000 (2)	450
		100 (4)	100 (6)	
		400 (10)		
		100 (13)		
		200 (15)		
	$1,150			$1,500
Statement of cash flows:				
Cash flows from operations:				
Net sales		1,000 (2)		
Increase in accounts receivable			150 (3)	
Cost of goods sold			400 (10)	
Decrease in inventories		50 (11)		
Increase in accounts payable		100 (12)		
Wages expense			100 (13)	
Decrease in accrued wages payable			50 (14)	
Other expenses			200 (15)	
Sale of land		300 (6)		
Purchase of land			100 (8)	
Sale of capital stock		100 (9)		
Purchase of building			200 (5)	
Retirement of bonds payable			100 (7)	
Payment of dividends			100 (1)	
		$3,050	$3,050	

The explanation of the adjustments is as follows:

1. The declaration and payment of a cash dividend ($100) that decreased retained earnings is recorded as a financing activity.

2. Net sales ($1,000) is included in net income and retained earnings and is a component of net cash flow from operating activities.

3. The increase in accounts receivable ($150) is subtracted from net sales in determining cash received from customers.

4. The increase in accumulated depreciation ($100) is due to depreciation expense, which is included as a negative element in net income and retained earnings but is not considered in determining net cash flow from operating activities.

5. The purchase of the building for $200 is recorded as an investing activity.

6. The sale of land for $300 is shown as an investing activity; the $100 gain is included in net income and retained earnings but is not considered in determining net cash flow from operating activities.

7. The retirement of long-term bonds payable ($100) at face value is recorded as a financing activity.

8. The purchase of land for $100 is recorded as an investing activity.

9. The sale of capital stock for cash is recorded as a financing activity.

10. Cost of goods sold is a negative element in net income and retained earnings and is a negative component of net cash flow from operating activities.

11. The decrease in inventories ($50) is an adjustment to cost of goods sold to determine purchases.

12. The increase in accounts payable ($100) is subtracted from purchases in determining cash paid to suppliers.

13. Wage expense is a negative element in net income and retained earnings and is a negative component in net cash flow from operating activities.

14. The decrease in accrued wages payable ($50) is added to wage expense in determining cash paid to employees.

15. Other expenses is a negative element in net income and retained earnings and is a negative component in net cash flow from operating activities.

The following is an alternative worksheet for Kraton Company. The indirect method is used to obtain net cash flow from operating activities.

Kraton Company
Worksheet for Statement of Cash Flows
For the Year Ended December 31, 19x1

	Balance December 31, 19x0	Adjustments Debit	Adjustments Credit	Balance December 31, 19x1
Debits:				
Cash	$ 100			$ 250
Accounts receivable (net)	200	$ 150 (9)		350
Inventories	250		$ 50 (10)	200
Buildings	400	200 (4)		600
Land	200	100 (7)	200 (5)	100
	$1,150			$1,500
Credits:				
Accumulated depreciation	$ 100		100 (3)	$ 200
Accounts payable	200		100 (11)	300
Accrued wages payable	100	50 (12)		50
Bonds payable	200	100 (6)		100
Capital stock	300		100 (8)	400
Retained earnings	250	100 (1)	300 (2)	450
	$1,150			$1,500
Statement of cash flows:				
Cash flows from operations:				
Net income		300 (2)		
Adjustments:				
Depreciation expense		100 (3)		
Gain on sale of land			100 (5)	
Increase in accounts receivable			150 (9)	
Decrease in inventories		50 (10)		
Increase in accounts payable		100 (11)		
Decrease in accrued wages payable			50 (12)	
Sale of land		300 (5)		
Purchase of land			100 (7)	
Sale of capital stock		100 (8)		
Purchase of building			200 (4)	
Retirement of bonds payable			100 (6)	
Payment of dividends			100 (1)	
		$1,650	$1,650	

The explanation of the adjustments is as follows:

1. The declaration and payment of a cash dividend ($100) that decreased retained earnings is recorded as a financing activity.
2. Net income included in the ending retained earnings balance is reported as the initial component of net cash flow from operating activities. This amount will be adjusted below in determining the net cash flow from operating activities.
3. The increase in accumulated depreciation ($100) is added to net income in determining the net cash flow from operating activities, because the depreciation expense did not decrease cash.
4. The purchase of the building for $200 is recorded as an investing activity.
5. The sale of land for $300 is shown as an investing activity; the $100 gain is subtracted from net income in determining net cash flow from operating activities.
6. The retirement of long-term bonds payable ($100) at face value is recorded as a financing activity.
7. The purchase of land for $100 is recorded as an investing activity.
8. The sale of capital stock for cash is recorded as a financing activity.
9. The increase in accounts receivable ($150) is subtracted from net income in determining net cash flow from operating activities.
10. The decrease in inventories ($50) is added to net income in determining net cash flow from operating activities.
11. The increase in accounts payable ($100) is added to net income in determining net cash flow from operating activities.
12. The decrease in accrued wages payable ($50) is subtracted from net income in determining net cash flow from operating activities.

The procedures used in preparing a worksheet are summarized below:

1. The account balances appearing on the previous year's balance sheet are entered in the first column of the worksheet. All accounts with debit balances are listed first, followed by all accounts with credit balances.
2. Adjustments are entered into the adjustment columns to account for all noncash items from the upper section and to list all of the separate increases and decreases to cash in the lower section of the worksheet. The worksheet adjustments are not entered in any journal; their purpose is solely to facilitate the analysis and classification of the data for the statement of cash flows.

3. The account balances appearing on the current year's balance sheet are entered in the last column of the worksheet. These account balances are used as a check to determine whether the change in the balance of each noncash item has been explained completely—that is, whether the beginning balance plus or minus the change equals the ending balance.

Additional Problems in the Analysis of the Statement of Cash Flows

Many of the problems that occur in the preparation of the statement of cash flows were discussed in the preceding sections of this chapter. However, additional problems may arise that require special analysis to determine the effect on cash of a change in an asset (excluding cash and cash equivalents), a liability, or an owners' equity account. Some of these special problems are examined in the following paragraphs.

Uncollectible Accounts. Under the direct method, the total accounts receivable written-off during the period must be deducted from sales. This is in addition to the adjustment for the change in the receivable accounts. Under the indirect method, a change in the balance in the allowance for bad debts account resulting from either a charge to bad debt expense for the current period or a write-off of uncollectible accounts does not require any adjustment in determining the changes to cash. The allowance for bad debt account is a contra account to a current asset, accounts receivable. Therefore, the change in the allowance account is a part of the increase or decrease to net accounts receivable for the period. The debit to bad debt expense represents a deduction from revenues in determining net income. The decrease to net accounts receivable from the credit to the allowance account is added to net income in determining net cash flow from operating activities under the indirect method. Therefore, the bad debt expense is a deduction in net income and the corresponding decrease to net accounts receivable is added to net income so that there is no effect on cash. A write-off of an uncollectible account reduces both the receivable and the related contra account; it does not affect the balance of net accounts receivable. Accordingly, the write-off has no effect on cash.

Dividends. A reduction in retained earnings resulting from the declaration of a cash dividend to be paid during the following period has no effect on cash. The subsequent payment of the dividend does affect cash and would be a financing activity in the period in which the disbursement is made.

Income Tax Expense. If the amount of income tax expense exceeds the income tax payable, resulting in a credit to deferred income taxes, then the difference should be added to net income in arriving at net cash flow from operating activities under the indirect method. Similarly, if the amount of income tax is less than income tax payable, resulting in a debit to deferred income taxes, then the difference should be subtracted from net income in arriving at net cash flow from operating activities under the indirect method. In addition, net cash flow from operating activities must be adjusted for the increase or decrease in income taxes payable. Under the direct method, income tax expense is decreased by a credit to deferred income taxes and increased by a debit to deferred taxes and is then adjusted by the change in income tax payable to determine cash paid for income taxes. The amount of the income tax expense is debited to retained earnings.

Stock Dividends and Conversions. When a corporation declares a stock dividend, a transfer is made from retained earnings to one or more contributed capital accounts. Such a transfer does not affect either total stockholders' equity or assets. Therefore, the resulting changes in the stockholders' equity items would not be included on the statement of cash flows.

Changes of substance in the individual components of owners' equity should be reported in the statement of cash flows even though these changes do not involve either a receipt or disbursement of cash. Accordingly, the conversion of long-term debt or preferred stock to common stock should be reflected in a supplementary schedule to the statement of cash flows.

Significant Noncash Transactions. The statement of cash flows should report all financing and investing activities, including those that do not involve a receipt or disbursement of cash. Among the most common of these transactions are the following:

1. The issuance of noncurrent debt or capital stock for noncurrent assets.
2. The issuance of capital stock to retire noncurrent debt.
3. Refinancing of long-term debt.
4. Conversion of long-term debt or preferred stock to common stock.

To illustrate, assume that a firm issued 50,000 shares of its $5 par value common stock in exchange for land with a fair market value of $380,000. This transaction would have been recorded in the accounts as follows:

Land	380,000	
Common stock		250,000
Additional paid-in capital		130,000

Although this transaction did not affect cash, the transaction should be viewed as being comprised of two parts—the sale of stock for $380,000, and the purchase of a building for the same amount. Thus, the transaction would be reported on the statement of cash flows as follows:

Schedule of noncash investing and financing activities:
   Issuance of common stock to purchase a building........ $380,000

Multiple Changes Affecting Specific Accounts. Frequently, there may be several transactions that cause a net change in a noncurrent account. In these circumstances, it normally is helpful to analyze the individual transactions affecting the account in order to identify the effect on cash.

For example, assume that the following information is available regarding equipment.

	End of Year	Beginning of Year
Equipment	$212,000	$200,000
Accumulated depreciation	55,000	90,000
Depreciation expense	15,000	
Gain on sale of equipment	7,000	

Equipment with a cost of $70,000 and a book value of $20,000 was sold for $27,000 during the year. Equipment was acquired at a cost of $82,000. The individual transactions that caused the changes in the equipment and the accumulated depreciation accounts may be summarized as follows:

	Equipment	Accumulated Depreciation
Beginning of year	$200,000	$90,000
Acquisition of equipment	82,000	
Sale of equipment	(70,000)	(50,000)
Depreciation expense		15,000
End of year	$212,000	$55,000

The journal entries recorded at the time of each event and the resulting effect on cash are summarized below:

```
Sale of equipment:
  Cash ........................................ 27,000
  Accumulated depreciation..................... 50,000
      Equipment................................          70,000
      Gain on sale of equipment ...............           7,000
    Cash inflow of $27,000 as an investing
    activity; the $7,000 gain is subtracted
    from net income in determining net
    cash flow from operations under the
    indirect method and is not considered
    under the direct method.
Acquisition of equipment:
  Equipment.................................... 82,000
      Cash ....................................          82,000
    Cash outflow of $82,000 as an investing
    activity.
Depreciation:
  Depreciation expense ........................ 15,000
      Accumulated depreciation.................          15,000
    Depreciation expense is added to net
    income in determining net cash flow
    from operations under the indirect
    method and is not considered under
    the direct method.
```

SUMMARY

The statement of cash flows is included as one of the major financial statements in annual reports. This statement explains the causes of changes in cash plus highly liquid marketable securities and provides a summary of the investing and financing activities of an enterprise during a period of time. A majority of nonfinancial companies defined funds as cash or as cash plus cash equivalents prior to the issuance in 1987 of the FASB's pronouncement requiring the presentation of a statement of cash flows. Under the "all financial resources" concept, a material transaction involving changes in noncash accounts must be disclosed in the statement of cash flows.

The sections of the statement of cash flows are as follows: (1) cash flows from operating activities, (2) cash flows from investing activities, and (3) cash flows from financing activities. Investing activities include collections on loans, proceeds from the sale of plant assets, and purchases of plant assets; financing activities include proceeds from the issuance of bonds and stock and the payment of cash dividends.

KEY DEFINITIONS

All financial resources—this concept modifies "funds" to include not only those transactions affecting cash or working capital, but also those transactions of significant amount that affect the financing and investing activities of the firm, even though they involve only noncurrent accounts.

Cash concept of funds—this concept defines funds in terms of cash or near-cash, and utilizes the funds statement to point out changes in the cash flow of the firm.

Cash disbursement—any outflow of cash by the firm is a cash disbursement.

Cash flow—any transaction that increases or decreases the cash balance of the firm is a cash flow.

Cash receipt—any transaction that increases the cash account of the firm is a cash receipt.

Direct method—computing net cash flow from operations as the difference between cash receipts from operating activities and cash disbursements from operating activities.

Financing activities—the section of the statement of cash flows which includes proceeds from the issuance of the entity's bonds or stocks, outlays to pay the maturity value of bonds, outlays to purchase the entity's stock, and the payment of dividends.

Funds—according to *APB Opinion No. 19*, funds are either cash, near-cash, or working capital.

Funds from operations—the effect on funds caused by the normal operating activities of the firm.

Indirect method—computing net cash flow from operations by adjusting net income for noncash items included in income.

Investing activities—the section of the statement of cash flows which includes receipts from loans, acquiring and selling securities (except for cash equivalents), and acquiring and selling plant assets and land.

Noncurrent account—an account that is neither a current asset nor a current liability.

Operating activities—the section of the statement of cash flows which includes selling, purchasing, and producing goods; providing services; and paying suppliers, employees, and lenders.

Sources of funds—involves any transaction that has caused funds to flow into a firm (i.e., any transaction that has increased working capital or cash, depending upon the definition of funds).

Statement of cash flows—a statement which explains the causes of changes in cash plus highly liquid marketable securities and provides a summary of the investing and financing activities of an enterprise during a period of time.

Statement of changes in financial position—a statement summarizing the financing and investing activities of the firm and disclosing changes in financial position.

Uses of funds—any transaction that has caused funds to flow from the firm (i.e., any transaction that has decreased working capital or cash).

Working capital—the excess of current assets over current liabilities.

Working capital concept of funds—this concept defines funds in terms of working capital, and utilizes the funds statement to point out changes in the working capital of the firm.

QUESTIONS

1. Why is a statement of cash flows necessary?

2. What is the all-financial-resources concept and why is it important?

3. What are the three major sections of a statement of cash flows?

4. Give examples for each of the three major sections of a statement of cash flows.

5. Explain how income affects cash. Is reported net income always equal to the amount of cash flows from operations? Explain.

6. List items that may be included in the determination of net income but that have no effect on cash.

7. Compare and contrast the direct and indirect methods of preparing the statement of cash flows.

8. What steps are needed in preparing a statement of cash flows?

9. What is the purpose of a worksheet in preparing a statement of cash flows?

10. State how the following are presented on a statement of cash flows.

    a. Dividends paid.
    b. Conversions of bonds to common stock.
    c. Amortization of discount on bonds payable.
    d. Loss on the sale of equipment.

11. Explain how each of the following are treated in a statement of cash flows.

    a. Bad debt expense.
    b. Purchasing land by issuing common stock.
    c. Reclassifying a note payable from long-term to current.
    d. Loss on sale of current marketable equity securities.
    e. Increase in inventories.
    f. Amortization of patents.
    g. Increase in accounts payable.
    h. Conversion of bonds to common stock.

12. What are two types of financial transactions that would be disclosed under the "all-financial-resources" concept that would not be disclosed without this concept?

EXERCISES

13. Consider the following income statement for Wills Company.

Sales		$1,000,000
Cost of goods sold		750,000
Gross margin		$ 250,000
Selling and administrative expenses:		
Salary expense	$50,000	
Depreciation expense	25,000	
Administrative expense	25,000	100,000
Net income		$ 150,000

Additional information:

Decrease in inventories	$9,000
Increase in accounts receivable	5,000
Increase in accounts payable	6,000

Required:

Compute the cash flows from operating activities.

14. Below is the income statement for Lopes Company for the year ending December 31, 19x2.

Lopes Company
Income Statement
For the Year Ended December 31, 19x2

Sales (net)		$500,000
Cost of goods sold:		
Beginning inventory	$ 50,000	
Purchases	300,000	
Goods available for sale	$350,000	
Ending inventory	40,000	
Cost of goods sold		310,000
Gross margin		$190,000
Expenses:		
Wages	$ 35,000	
Depreciation	30,000	
Advertising	15,000	
Administrative	5,000	85,000
Income from operations		$105,000
Gain on sale of equipment		50,000
Net income		$155,000

The following balances were derived from the balance sheet.

	December 31	
	19x2	19x1
Accounts receivable	$100,000	$90,000
Accounts payable	30,000	50,000
Prepaid advertising expense	5,000	3,000
Wages payable	5,000	4,000

Required:

Prepare a schedule showing cash flows from operating activities.

15. Your examination of the financial statements of Russell Company reveals the following data:

	19x2		19x1	
Sales (net)		$100,000		$75,000
Cost of goods sold:				
Beginning inventory	$17,000		$12,000	
Purchases (net)	58,000		55,000	
Goods available	$75,000		$67,000	
Ending inventory	15,000		17,000	
Cost of goods sold		60,000		50,000
Accounts payable		20,000		25,000
Accounts receivable		50,000		45,000

Required:

Compute the following for 19x2:

1. Cash receipts from sales.
2. Cash disbursements for purchases.

16. Consider the following information for the period ending December 31, 19x1, concerning the Cey Company.

  a. Net income for 19x1 was $250,000.
  b. Depreciation expense on its buildings was $25,000. Accumulated depreciation on the buildings is $200,000.
  c. Extraordinary (non-operating) gains and losses included a loss of $50,000 on an uninsured building destroyed by fire.
  d. Dividends paid during the year in cash—$50,000.

Required:

Compute the cash flows from operating activities.

17. Indicate how each of the items presented below would appear in a statement of cash flows.

   1. Declaration of a cash dividend.
   2. Payment of cash dividend after above declaration.
   3. Depreciation expense for the year.
   4. Fully depreciated equipment written off the books.
   5. Amortization of premium on long-term bonds payable.
   6. Semiannual coupon *payments* on bonds mentioned in item (5) above.
   7. Sale of common stock at a discount.
   8. Purchase of treasury stock at a price above the original issue price.
   9. Payment of wages accrued at the end of the prior year.
   10. Sale of fixed assets at a loss.
   11. Discounting the company's own 90-day note at a bank.
   12. Sale of ten-year bonds at a discount.
   13. Three for one (3-1) split of the preferred stock.
   14. Sale of machinery at a price in excess of its book value.
   15. Amortization of goodwill.

18. Wynn, Inc., hired you as an independent accountant to analyze the reasons for their unsatisfactory cash position. The company earned $42,000 during the year (19x1) but their cash balance is lower than ever. Your assistant prepared a worksheet providing you with the following information:

   a. Additional capital stock was sold in 19x1; the proceeds of the sale were $40,000.
   b. Vacant land purchased in 19x0 at a cost of $27,000 was sold in 19x1 for $30,000.
   c. A payment of $22,000 was made in 19x1 on a long-term mortgage.
   d. Equipment costing $89,000 was purchased during the year.
   e. Included in the firm's expenses for 19x1 were depreciation charges of $7,500.
   f. The firm's accounts receivable increased by $4,000 and their accounts payable decreased by $4,500 during the year.

   Required:

   Prepare a statement of cash flows for the year ended December 31, 19x1, which reflects the reasons for the firm's unsatisfactory cash position.

19. Indicate how each of the following items would be presented in a statement of cash flows.

   1. Net income from operations.
   2. Purchase of treasury stock by company.
   3. Sale of bonds payable.
   4. Issuance of bonds payable for land.
   5. Sale of equipment at a gain.
   6. Declaration (but not payment) of cash dividends.

20. From the following information prepare a statement of cash flows for the Sabre Company for 19x1.

   a. Net income for 19x1 was $6,000.
   b. Dividends paid during 19x1 were $1,000.
   c. Captital stock was sold for $2,500.
   d. Depreciation for the year was $1,500.
   e. Long-term bonds of $1,000 were retired at par.
   f. Land was purchased for $3,000.
   g. Land was sold for $6,000, resulting in a gain of $1,000.
   h. A building was purchased for $4,000.

21. Determine the amount of purchase, the cash disbursements for rent expense, and the cash applied to dividends for the Maple Leaf Company for the month of March from the information given below.

Cost of goods sold	$2,579
Increase in prepaid rent	864
Dividends	4,953
Rent expense	970
Increase in inventory	1,240
Decrease in dividends payable	691

22. Condensed financial statements for the Billy Company are as follows:

Billy Company
Balance Sheet

	December 31 19x2	19x1
Cash	$ 7,500	$ 6,000
Accounts receivable	9,000	11,000
Inventories	15,000	12,500
Fixed assets	30,000	25,000
Accumulated depreciation	(12,500)	(10,000)
	$49,000	$44,500
Accounts payable	$18,000	$15,000
Bonds payable	10,000	15,000
Common stock	15,000	10,000
Retained earnings	6,000	4,500
	$49,000	$44,500

Billy Company
Income Statement
For the Year Ending December 31, 19x2

Sales		$35,000
Cost of goods sold		17,000
Gross margin		$18,000
Depreciation	$ 2,500	
Operating expenses	11,000	13,500
Net income		$ 4,500

Required:

Prepare a statement of cash flows for 19x2.

PROBLEMS

23. The condensed financial statements of Buckner Corporation are as follows:

Buckner Corporation
Comparative Balance Sheet
December 31, 19x1 and 19x2

	19x2	19x1
Assets		
Current assets:		
Cash	$ 50,000	$ 35,000
Accounts receivable	100,000	90,000
Inventory	60,000	65,000
Prepaid expenses	10,000	8,000
Total current assets	$220,000	$198,000
Fixed assets:		
Building and equipment (net)	$200,000	$220,000
Land	50,000	50,000
Total assets	$470,000	$468,000
Liabilities and Stockholders' Equity		
Accounts payable	$100,000	$ 80,000
Interest payable	10,000	10,000
Notes payable (current)	50,000	40,000
Capital stock	200,000	200,000
Retained earnings	110,000	138,000
Total liabilities and stockholders' equity	$470,000	$468,000

Buckner Corporation
Income Statement
For the Year Ending December 31, 19x2

Sales		$250,000
Less: Cost of goods sold		184,000
Gross margin		$ 66,000
Operating expenses	$64,000	
Depreciation	20,000	84,000
Net loss		($18,000)

Required:

Prepare a statement of cash flows for 19x2.

24. Below is the income statement for the Rau Company for the year ended December 31, 19x1.

Rau Company
Income Statement
For the Year Ended December 31, 19x1

Sales		$1,000,000
Cost of goods sold:		
Beginning inventory.........................	$ 20,000	
Purchases	500,000	
Goods available for sale....................	$520,000	
Ending inventory...........................	25,000	
Cost of goods sold.......................		495,000
Gross margin...............................		$ 505,000
Operating expenses:		
Salaries	$ 50,000	
Depreciation..............................	20,000	
Bad debts................................	10,000	
Advertising...............................	20,000	
Patent amortization........................	5,000	
Total operating expenses......................		105,000
Operating income...........................		$ 400,000
Gain on sale of equipment....................		50,000
Net Income................................		$ 450,000

Required:

Prepare a schedule computing cash flows from operating activities.

25. Consider the following selected account balances for Messerschmidt, Inc.

	December 31			
	19x2	19x1	*Increase*	*Decrease*
Cash................................	$ 175	$300		$125
Buildings............................	1,000	800	$200	
Accumulated depreciation—				
building...........................	175	150	25	
Land	300	200	100	
Bonds payable—long-term..............	200	100	100	
Capital stock.........................	200	300		100
Retained earnings.....................	300	150	150	
Cash flow (other than depreciation):	$ 100			

Required:

Prepare a statement of cash flows for Messerschmidt, Inc., for the period ending December 31, 19x2, assuming, where it is necessary, that the changes in the accounts are the result of cash transactions.

26. Given below are the balance sheets for Zahn Company for 19x1 and 19x2.

Zahn Company
Comparative Balance Sheet
December 31, 19x1 and 19x2

	19x1	19x2
Cash	$ 100	$ 300
Accounts receivable	400	350
Inventories	300	500
Fixed assets	900	1,000
Less: Accumulated depreciation	(100)	(200)
	$1,600	$1,950
Accounts payable	$ 400	$ 600
Bonds payable (due in 19x7)	400	200
Capital stock	500	700
Retained earnings	300	450
	$1,600	$1,950

Additional information:

The corporation paid a 10 percent stock dividend on January 2, 19x2, when its capital stock was selling at par. Net income for 19x2 was $200. During the year, the company sold a fixed asset with an original cost of $100 (and a book value of $25 at the date of sale) for $50. All other changes in the accounts are the results of transactions typically recorded in such accounts.

Required:

Prepare a statement of cash flows for 19x2.

27. The condensed comparative balance sheet for Marshall Company is presented below.

	December 31	
	19x2	19x1
Assets		
Cash	$ 80,000	$ 65,000
Accounts receivable (net)	100,000	90,000
Inventory	40,000	45,000
Prepaid expenses	12,000	10,000
Fixed assets	173,000	150,000
Accumulated depreciation— fixed assets	(35,000)	(30,000)
Total assets	$370,000	$330,000
Liabilities and Stockholders' Equity		
Accounts payable	$ 80,000	$ 60,000
Bonds payable	150,000	150,000
Capital stock	100,000	100,000
Retained earnings	40,000	20,000
Total liabilities and stockholders' equity	$370,000	$330,000

Supplemental data for 19x2.

    Net income............................ $20,000
    Depreciation expense................... 5,000
    A building was purchased for $23,000 cash.

Required:

Prepare a statement of cash flows for 19x2.

28. Following are financial statements for Brewer, Inc.:

Brewer, Inc.
Comparative Balance Sheet
December 31, 19x2 and 19x1

	19x2	19x1	Increase (Decrease)
Assets			
Current assets:			
Cash	$ 5,000	$ 45,000	$(40,000)
Accounts receivable	100,000	75,000	25,000
Inventories	50,000	45,000	5,000
Prepaid expenses	30,000	35,000	(5,000)
Total current assets	$185,000	$200,000	$(15,000)
Noncurrent assets:			
Land	$100,000	$ 75,000	$ 25,000
Buildings	200,000	175,000	25,000
Accumulated depreciation—			
buildings	(50,000)	(40,000)	(10,000)
Equipment	100,000	75,000	25,000
Accumulated depreciation—			
equipment	(35,000)	(15,000)	(20,000)
Patents	20,000	30,000	(10,000)
Total noncurrent assets	$335,000	$300,000	$ 35,000
Total assets	$520,000	$500,000	$ 20,000
Liabilities and Stockholders' Equity			
Current liabilities:			
Accounts payable	$ 50,000	$ 40,000	$ 10,000
Notes payable	25,000	25,000	0
Accrued expenses	40,000	35,000	5,000
Total current liabilities	$115,000	$100,000	$ 15,000
Long-term liabilities:			
Bonds payable	$100,000	$140,000	$(40,000)
Stockholders' equity:			
Common stock ($100 par value)	$230,000	$200,000	$ 30,000
Additional paid-in capital	40,000	30,000	10,000
Retained earnings	35,000	30,000	5,000
Total stockholders' equity	$305,000	$260,000	$ 45,000
Total liabilities and stockholders' equity	$520,000	$500,000	$ 20,000

Brewer, Inc.
Income Statement
For the Year Ended December 31, 19x2

Sales		$2,000,000
Cost of goods sold		1,500,000
Gross margin		$ 500,000
Operating expenses:		
Depreciation and amortization expense	$ 50,000	
Selling and administrative expense	265,000	
Miscellaneous expense	170,000	
Total operating expenses		485,000
Net income from operations		$ 15,000
Other revenue and expense		
Add: Gain on sale of building		20,000
		$ 35,000
Less: Loss on sale of land	$ 10,000	
Interest expense	15,000	25,000
Net income before income taxes		$ 10,000
Less: Income taxes		5,000
Net income		$ 5,000

Supplementary data:

a. Depreciation and amortization of patents were as follows:

Building	$20,000
Equipment	20,000
Patents	10,000
Total	$50,000

b. A building which cost $50,000 and had accumulated depreciation of $10,000 was sold for $60,000.
c. Common stock with $30,000 par value was sold for $40,000.
d. Land with a cost of $25,000 was sold for $15,000.
e. Land was purchased for $50,000.
f. Bonds of $40,000 were retired.
g. A building was purchased for $75,000.
h. Equipment was acquired for $25,000 cash.

Required:

Prepare a statement of cash flows for 19x2.

29. Below is information pertinent to John Corp. for the period ending December 31, 19x1.

   a. Sales, $50,000.
   b. Cost of goods sold, $20,000.
   c. Expenses, $10,000 (of which $2,000 was depreciation).
   d. Increase in accounts payable, $5,000.
   e. Increase in accounts receivable, $5,000.
   f. Sold land which cost $500 for $1,000 cash.
   g. Purchased a building for $10,000 cash and $10,000 par value common stock.
   h. Cash dividends paid, $5,000.
   i. Retired bond payable of $500.

   Required:

   Prepare a statement of cash flows for 19x1.

30. From the following information, prepare a statement of cash flows for 19x1.

Ferguson Company
Trial Balances
(in thousands)

	December 31, 19x1		December 31, 19x0	
Account	Debit	Credit	Debit	Credit
Cash	$ 178		$ 84	
Accounts receivable	300		240	
Allowance for bad debts		$ 13		$ 10
Merchandise inventory	370		400	
Building and equipment	420		360	
Allowance for depreciation		180		190
Accounts payable		220		210
Mortgage bonds		300		300
Unamortized bond discount	18		21	
Capital stock		357		270
Retained earnings		125		90
Net sales		4,200		4,000
Cost of goods sold	2,300		2,100	
Salaries and wages	1,500		1,400	
Administrative expense	110		100	
Depreciation expense	20		20	
Maintenance expense	10		10	
Interest expense	16		15	
Bad debt expense	20		20	
Loss on equipment sales*	6		0	
Dividends paid†	127		300	
	$5,395	$5,395	$5,070	$5,070

* In 19x1, equipment costing $40,000 and having a net book value of $10,000 was sold for $4,000.
† Dividends paid in 19x1 include a stock dividend of $27,000.

31. The trial balances of Canuck Company revealed the following information.

	December 31	
Debits	*19x1*	*19x2*
Cash	$ 14,000	$ 15,400
Accounts receivable (net)	26,600	33,600
Inventory	72,800	70,000
Prepaid expenses	4,200	5,600
Permanent investments	14,000	0
Buildings	126,000	168,000
Machinery	56,000	86,800
Patents	7,000	5,600
	$320,600	$385,000

Credits		
Accounts payable	$ 16,800	$ 11,200
Notes payable—short-term (nontrade)	12,600	18,200
Accrued wages	4,200	2,800
Accumulated depreciation	56,000	54,600
Notes payable—long-term	42,000	49,000
Common stock	168,000	210,000
Retained earnings	21,000	39,200
	$320,600	$385,000

Additional data:

a. Net income for 19x2 was $33,600.
b. Recorded depreciation on fixed assets was $11,200.
c. Amortization of patents was $1,400.
d. Machinery was purchased for $21,000; one-third was paid in cash; an interest-bearing note was given for the balance.
e. Common stock was issued to purchase machinery costing $35,000.
f. Old machinery which originally cost $25,200 (one-half depreciated) was sold for $9,800; the gain or loss was reported on the income statement.
g. Cash was paid for the building addition—$42,000.
h. Common stock was issued to pay a $7,000 long-term note.
i. Cash was received for the sale of permanent investment—$16,800.
j. Paid cash dividends.
k. Credit sales were $168,000.
l. Collections of accounts receivable were $161,000.

Required:

Prepare a statement of cash flows for 19x2.

32. The trial balances of Islander Company revealed the following information.

	December 31	
	19x1	19x2
Cash	$ 3,200	$ 4,000
Accounts receivable (net)	4,000	7,200
Inventory	8,000	9,600
Permanent investments	1,600	0
Fixed assets	24,000	37,600
	$40,800	$58,400
Accumulated depreciation	$ 4,000	$ 5,600
Accounts payable	2,400	4,000
Notes payable—short-term	3,200	2,400
Notes payable—long-term	8,000	14,400
Common stock	20,000	23,200
Retained earnings	3,200	8,800
	$40,800	$58,400

Additional data:

a. Net income was $11,200.
b. Depreciation was $1,600.
c. Permanent investments were sold at cost.
d. Dividends of $5,600 were paid.
e. Fixed assets were purchased for $4,000 cash.
f. A long-term note payable for $9,600 was given in exchange for fixed assets.
g. Common stock was issued to pay a $3,200 long-term note payable.

Required:

Prepare a statement of cash flows for the year ended December 31, 19x2.

33. Below is the balance sheet for Ranger Company comparing the years 19x1 and 19x2.

	December 31	
	19x2	19x1
Assets		
Cash	$ 25,000	$ 20,000
Accounts receivable (net)	90,000	75,000
Marketable securities	50,000	55,000
Prepaid expenses	15,000	13,000
Buildings	150,000	120,000
Accumulated depreciation—		
buildings	(85,000)	(65,000)
Total assets	$245,000	$218,000
Liabilities and Stockholders' Equity		
Accounts payable	$ 71,000	$ 50,000
Bonds payable	100,000	80,000
Capital stock	50,000	60,000
Retained earnings	24,000	28,000
Total liabilities and stockholders' equity	$245,000	$218,000

Additional information for 19x2:

Net income	$ 6,000
Cash dividends paid	10,000

Required:

Prepare a statement of cash flows for the year ended December 31, 19x2.

34. The 19x1 financial statements for the Alston Company are:

Alston Company
Income Statement
For the Year Ended December 31, 19x1

Net sales		$50,000
Cost of goods sold		30,000
Gross margin		$20,000
Operating expenses:		
Depreciation	$2,000	
Wage expense	7,000	
Other expenses	1,000	10,000
Net income from operations		$10,000
Gain on sale of land		5,000
Net income		$15,000

Alston Company
Retained Earnings Statement
For the Year Ended December 31, 19x1

Retained earnings at beginning of year	$25,000
Add: Net income	15,000
	$40,000
Subtract: Dividends	5,000
Retained earnings at end of year	$35,000

Alston Company
Comparative Balance Sheet

	December 31	
	19x1	19x0
Assets		
Cash	$ 69,000	$ 60,000
Accounts receivable	25,000	20,000
Inventories	15,000	10,000
Building	100,000	100,000
Accumulated depreciation—building	(27,000)	(25,000)
Land	125,000	100,000
Total assets	$307,000	$265,000
Liabilities and Stockholders' Equity		
Accounts payable	$ 35,000	$ 15,000
Accrued wages payable	7,000	5,000
Bonds payable—long-term	130,000	120,000
Capital stock	100,000	100,000
Retained earnings	35,000	25,000
Total equities	$307,000	$265,000

The following information is also available:

a. Land with a cost of $25,000 was sold for $30,000.
b. Additional land was purchased for $50,000.
c. A long-term bond was issued for $10,000.
d. $5,000 cash dividends were paid during the year.

Required:

Prepare a statement of cash flows for the Alston Company for the year ending December 31, 19x1.

35. From the following pre-closing trial balances, prepare an income statement and a statement of cash flows for the year ended December 31, 19x1.

Rockies Incorporated
Trial Balances
(in thousands)
For the Year Ended December 31, 19x1

	December 31, 19x1		December 31, 19x0	
Account	Debit	Credit	Debit	Credit
Cash	$ 373		$ 26	
Accounts receivable	980		589	
Allowance for bad debts		$ 6		$ 3
Inventory	960		612	
Buildings	495		560	
Allowance for depreciation		170		100
Accounts payable		105		86
Bonds payable, due in 19x9		300		300
Unamortized bond premium, due in 19x2		19		20
Mortgage bond payable		0		50
Capital stock		250		280
Retained earnings		948		399
Net sales		3,100		3,297
Cost of goods sold	1,100		1,600	
Salaries expense	850		980	
Depreciation expense	135		135	
Interest expense	5		5	
Bad debt expense	15		16	
Gain on sale of building		25		0
Dividends	10		12	
	$4,923	$4,923	$4,535	$4,535

Additional information:

a. In 19x1, a building with an original cost of $65,000 was sold for $25,000. The building had been fully depreciated.
b. Capital stock was repurchased and retired.

36. The trial balance of Canadiens Company revealed the following information.

	December 31	
	19x1	19x2
Cash	$20,400	$ 20,700
Accounts receivable (net)	7,200	10,200
Inventory	9,600	8,400
Permanent investments	3,600	0
Fixed assets	48,000	55,800
Treasury stock	0	6,900
	$88,800	$102,000
Accumulated depreciation	$28,800	$ 23,400
Accounts payable	11,400	7,200
Bonds payable	6,000	18,000
Common stock	30,000	36,600
Retained earnings	12,600	16,800
	$88,800	$102,000

Additional information:

a. Credit sales were $42,000.
b. Credit purchases were $24,000.
c. Depreciation was $3,000.
d. Cash disbursements for expenses were $10,800.
e. Inventory decreased by $1,200.
f. Fixed assets were sold for $3,600; their original cost was $12,600 and two-thirds of this cost had been depreciated.
g. Fixed assets were purchased for $2,400 cash.
h. Bonds payable were issued for $18,000 to purchase fixed assets.
i. Permanent investments were sold for $5,400 cash.
j. Treasury stock was purchased for $6,900.
k. Bonds payable of $6,000 were retired by issuing common stock.
l. Accounts receivable collections were $39,000.
m. Accounts payable of $28,200 were paid.
n. Unissued common stock was sold for $600.

Required:

Prepare a statement of cash flows for the year ended December 31, 19x2.

Refer to the Annual Report included in the front of the text.

37. Does the company use the direct or the indirect method in preparing its statement of cash flows?

38. What was the cash flow from operating activities in the most recent year?

39. What was the cash flow from investing activities in the most recent year?

40. What was the cash flow from financing activities in the most recent year?

41. In absolute numbers, what was the largest investing activity in the most recent year?

42. In absolute numbers, what was the largest financing activity in the most recent year?

43. What was the largest noncash investing and financing activity?

Chapter 12 presents a general discussion of the federal income tax. Studying this chapter should enable you to:

1. Identify the primary objectives of the federal income tax.

2. Discuss the process of determining an individual and corporate taxpayer's tax liability.

3. Recognize the important differences in the taxation of corporations versus the taxation of individuals.

4. Describe the purpose of interperiod tax allocation and the accounting procedures involved.

5. Illustrate how intraperiod tax allocation is generally accomplished.

12

Income Tax Considerations*

INTRODUCTION

Income taxes are periodic charges levied by federal, state, and city governments on the taxable income of both individuals and business corporations. Taxable income is a statutory concept (i.e., it is defined by law and is equal to gross income minus all allowable deductions). For businesses organized as corporations, income taxes are accounted for as an expense which is deducted in computing the net income for the period. The amount of taxes owed, but not paid, is a liability which is included in the balance sheet. Because income taxes normally represent a significant cost to a business enterprise, an awareness of the tax laws and how they are applied is essential to a complete understanding of accounting information.

Data which are required for the determination of income taxes are usually found in the accounting records. Taxable income, however, may not be the same as the income reported in the income statement even though both are determined from the identical set of accounting records. This difference often occurs because income tax law is not always the same as the basic concepts which are used for financial accounting purposes.

---

* The authors would like to thank Professors Thomas L. Dickens of Clemson University, Steven D. Grossman of Texas A&M University, Bob G. Kilpatrick of Northern Arizona University, Dennis R. Lassila of Texas A&M University, Kenneth R. Orbach of Florida Atlantic University, and Sarah A. Reed of Texas A&M University who have written and revised this chapter in its various editions.

This chapter is devoted to a general discussion of the federal income tax and its implication for the financial reporting process of a business. Although many states and cities also impose income taxes, which may differ in application from the federal income tax, the income tax liability to all governmental units is treated similarly in the accounting records. For this reason, the following discussion is limited to the federal income tax.

THE FEDERAL INCOME TAX

The modern era of federal income taxation originated in 1913 with the adoption of the Sixteenth Amendment to the Constitution. This amendment gives Congress the power to ". . . lay and collect taxes on incomes, from whatever source derived, without apportionment among the several states, and without regard to any census or enumeration." Soon after the Sixteenth Amendment was adopted, Congress enacted the Revenue Act of 1913, which provided for a general yearly income tax. Since that time, Congress has passed numerous income tax statutes amending the various revenue acts so that there has been a continuous development of income tax law in the United States. In 1939, the Internal Revenue Code was enacted. This code was thoroughly revised in 1954 and extensively amended and supplemented by the Tax Reform Act of 1969, the Revenue Act of 1971, the Tax Reduction Act of 1975, the Tax Reform Act of 1976, the Tax Reduction and Simplification Act of 1977, the Revenue Act of 1978, the Economic Recovery Act of 1981, the Tax Equity and Fiscal Responsibility Act of 1982, the Deficit Reduction Act of 1984, and the Tax Reform Act of 1986. Tax law is also supplemented by interpretations of the Internal Revenue Code by both the courts and the Treasury Department. The Treasury Department, operating through a branch known as the Internal Revenue Service, is charged with the enforcement and collection of income taxes.

The original purpose of the income tax was stated as simply to obtain revenues for the use of the federal government. The income tax on individuals under the 1913 Act consisted of a flat 1 percent tax on taxable income in excess of $4,000 for married persons plus a progressive surtax of 1 to 7 percent on income in excess of $20,000. A progressive tax is one in which tax rates increase as taxable income increases.

Since 1916, both the objectives of the income tax and income tax rates have undergone a significant change. The purpose of the federal income tax today includes such diverse objectives as controlling inflation, influencing economic growth, decreasing unemployment, redistributing national income, and encouraging the growth of small businesses. All of these purposes are in addition to the original objective of raising revenue to finance the operations of the government. Similarly, there have been substantial changes in tax rates. The current rates for taxpayers are presented in Illustration 1.

Illustration 1
Current Rates for Taxpayers

Selected Taxable Income Brackets

Tax Rate	Married/Joint	Head of Household	Single	Married/Separate
15%	0—$35,800	0—$28,750	0—$21,450	0—$17,900
28	$35,800—$86,500	$28,750—$74,150	$21,450—$51,900	$17,900—$43,250
31	above $86,500	above $74,150	above $51,900	above $43,250

Standard Deduction

Filing Status

Married/joint	$6,000
Head of household	5,250
Single	3,600
Married/separate	3,000

CLASSES OF TAXPAYERS

Income taxes are levied upon four major types of taxable entities: individuals, corporations, estates, and trusts. Business entities organized as sole proprietorships or partnerships are not taxable entities. Instead, their income is included in the gross income of the individual owner or owners, whether or not it is actually withdrawn from the business and distributed to these owners. A partnership, however, is required to prepare an information return which indicates the items of its gross income, deductions, and credits and how these are allocated to the partners. The partners then report these amounts in their own tax returns.

A corporation is treated as a separate entity for tax purposes and must pay taxes on its taxable income. In addition, individual corporate stockholders must include any dividends received from the corporation as a part of their taxable income. For this reason, it is often argued that the profits of a corporation are taxed twice—once to the corporation when the income is reported and again to its stockholders when dividends are distributed. Under limited circumstances, a corporation meeting certain qualifications may avoid this "double taxation" of corporate income by making an S Corporation election; the shareholders are then taxed on undistributed income on a current basis.[1]

---

[1] These entities are referred to as "S Corporations." Numerous changes in the tax treatment of S Corporations were made in the "Subchapter S Revision Act of 1982." Subchapter S Corporations are now called S Corporations.

An estate is a separate legal entity which is created to take charge of the assets of a deceased person to pay the decedent's debts and distribute any remaining assets to the heirs. A trust is a legal entity which is created when a person by gift or devise transfers assets to a trustee for the benefit of designated persons. The tax rules that apply to estates and trusts will not be discussed in this chapter, as they are beyond the scope of this text.

INDIVIDUAL FEDERAL INCOME TAX

The cash basis of measuring taxable income is used by almost all individuals in preparing their tax returns. Generally, revenue is recognized upon the actual or constructive receipt of cash and expenses are recognized as cash is expended.

Individual income tax rates depend on the status of the taxpayer. There are different tax rate schedules for married taxpayers who file a joint return, married individuals who file separate returns, unmarried taxpayers, and single taxpayers qualifying as "head of household." Generally, "head of household" status applies to certain unmarried or legally separated persons who maintain the principal residence for a relative.

The amount of federal income tax that an individual must pay is generally determined by knowledge of gross income, deductions for adjusted gross income, adjusted gross income, itemized deductions (deductions from adjusted gross income), personal exemptions, tax table income or taxable income, and credits. The relationship of these concepts and the procedures for determining taxable income are summarized in Illustration 2. A more detailed explanation of the items outlined in the determination of taxable income is given in the following paragraphs.

Gross Income. Basically, gross income is defined as all income from whatever source derived, unless expressly excluded by law or by the U.S. Constitution. This includes income from sources such as wages, dividends, interest, partnership income, rents, and numerous other items. Among the more important classes of income which are currently excludable from gross income by law are gifts, life insurance proceeds received at the insured's death, social security benefits (up to certain amounts), inheritances (but not income from trusts and life estates), worker's compensation, and interest on certain state and municipal bonds.

Deductions for Adjusted Gross Income. The deductions for adjusted gross income are business expenses and other expenses connected with earning certain types of revenue. These include ordinary and necessary expenses incurred by the taxpayer in the operation of an unincorporated business or profession, certain business expenses of an employee, losses from the sale or exchange of certain property, net operating losses from other periods carried back or forward, expenses incurred in connection with earning rent or royalty income, payments to an individual retirement arrangement or to a Keogh retirement plan, and periodic payments of alimony made under a court decree.

Illustration 2
*Process of Determining
Tax Liability for Individuals*

Gross Income	Includes income from all sources except those specifically excluded by law or by the U.S. Constitution.
Minus	
Deductions for Adjusted Gross Income	Includes business expenses and certain other expenses.
Equals	
Adjusted Gross Income	
Minus	
Standard or Itemized Deductions	Standard deduction or itemized deductions for certain personal expenses.
Minus	
Personal Exemptions	Deduction for the taxpayer, his or her spouse, and qualified dependents.
Equals	
Taxable Income	Tax Table or Tax Rate Schedule → Tax
	Minus
	Credits
	Equals
	Tax Liability

Deductions From Adjusted Gross Income (Itemized Deductions). Itemized deductions include such items as a limited amount of charitable contributions, mortgage interest payments, certain taxes paid by the taxpayer, a limited amount of medical expenses, a limited amount of casualty and theft losses, and nonbusiness expenses (other than expenses incurred in connection with earning rent or royalty income). These nonbusiness expenses are the necessary expenses incurred in producing income, for the management of income-producing property, or in connection with the determination, collection, or refund of any tax. These include such items as certain legal fees relating to investments, dues to professional organizations, and expenses incurred for the preparation of tax returns.

A taxpayer can either deduct the sum of itemized deductions or take the standard deduction, whichever is greater. The standard deduction permitted for each filing status is presented in Illustration 1.

Taxable income may now be computed. Generally, taxable income equals adjusted gross income reduced by either the standard deduction or itemized deductions and personal exemptions.

Personal Exemption. A taxpayer is allowed a deduction for each personal exemption to which he or she is entitled. The amount of the deduction was $2,300 for 1992. Each year, the amount is indexed for inflation. Personal exemptions may be taken for the following individuals:

1. *The taxpayer.*

2. *The taxpayer's spouse if a joint return is filed.*

3. *The taxpayer's spouse if a joint return is not filed, but only if the spouse has no gross income and is not a dependent of another taxpayer.*

4. *Certain dependents.* A dependent is an individual who meets all five of the following requirements:

    a. *Support.* More than one-half of whose support is provided by the taxpayer.
    b. *Income.* Dependent's gross income is less than the amount of the personal exemption (unless the dependent is the taxpayer's child and is either less than nineteen years old or is a full-time student).
    c. *Relationship.* Must be related to the taxpayer or the principal place of abode is with the taxpayer.
    d. *Joint Return.* The dependent cannot file a joint return with his or her spouse.
    e. *Citizenship.* Must be either a U.S. citizen or national or a resident of the U.S., Canada, or Mexico.

Credits. A credit is an amount by which the tax liability is reduced. At the time of this writing, the most commonly used credits included the earned income credit, credit for the elderly, credit for child and dependent care expenses, and the foreign tax credit.

Withholding and Estimated Tax. Taxpayers are generally required to make payments on their estimated tax liability during the year. This is accomplished by two principal procedures:

1. Employers withhold income tax on compensation to their employees.

2. Individuals who have income not subject to withholding (such as self-employed individuals) or who have income from which not enough is withheld should file a declaration of estimated tax. This estimated tax is generally paid in four equal installments.

In either instance, any difference between the amounts paid and the actual tax liability at the end of the year is settled when the tax return is filed.

Capital Gain and Losses. Prior to the Tax Reform Act of 1986, gains from the sale of certain property defined by the tax law as capital assets were given special treatment for income tax purposes. Capital assets most commonly held by taxpayers include stocks, bonds, personal residences, and land. To qualify for special tax treatment, capital gains had to be long-term. Long-term capital gains or losses result from the sale of capital assets held by the taxpayer for more than six months, and short-term gains or losses result from the sale of those held six months or less. Short-term capital gains did not qualify for special tax treatment and were taxed as ordinary income. Net capital gains are taxed at the same rate as any other income. Capital losses are allowed to the extent of capital gains plus $3,000. Losses may offset gains and other income (up to $3,000) dollar for dollar. Losses that cannot be used in a particular year may be carried over to succeeding years.

Computation of Individual Income Tax—An Illustration. The example included in Illustration 3 details the computation of the income tax for an individual filing a joint return. This individual, who owns a pharmacy organized as a sole proprietorship, is married and has two minor children. In practice, the information would be reported on standard tax forms provided by the federal government.

CORPORATE INCOME TAX

A corporation is a taxable entity which is separate and distinct from its stockholders. In general, the taxable income of a corporation is computed by deducting its ordinary business expenses and special deductions from its gross income. Although a corporation is taxed in generally the same manner as individuals, there are several important differences:

1. The concepts of itemized deductions and personal exemptions are not applicable to corporations.

Illustration 3
*Income Tax Computation for
Married Taxpayer Filing Jointly in 1992*

Adjusted Gross Income and Deductions From Adjusted Gross Income

Sales		$100,000
Less:		
Cost of goods sold	$50,000	
Business expenses	30,000	80,000
Net business income		$ 20,000
Interest on savings accounts		1,000
Rents received	$ 5,000	
Less: Expenses	2,000	
Net rental income		3,000
Net capital gain		4,000
Adjusted gross income		$ 28,000
Itemized deductions:		
Charitable contributions	$ 800	
Interest on home mortgage	2,900	
Property taxes	2,300	6,000
Less: Exemptions (4 × $2,300)		9,200
Taxable income		$ 12,800
Total tax (at 15%)		$ 1,920
Less: Payments on estimated taxes		3,500
Amount of refund		$ 1,580

2. Corporations may ordinarily deduct a percentage of all dividends received on investments in stocks of other taxable domestic corporations.

3. The deduction for charitable contributions is limited to 10 percent of taxable income (before charitable contributions, before the 70% or 80% dividend deduction and before certain other deductions) in any one year.

    The corporate tax rate also differs from the rate applied to individual taxpayers. A corporation pays a tax of 15 percent of the first $50,000 of taxable income, 25 percent of the next $25,000, 34 percent of the next $25,000, 39 percent of the next $235,000, and 34 percent of taxable income in excess of $335,000.

DIFFERENCES BETWEEN ACCOUNTING INCOME AND TAXABLE INCOME

The taxable income of a corporation often differs from the net income reported in its financial statements for a particular period. Taxable income is determined by the statutory provisions of the Internal Revenue Code while accounting income is based on generally accepted accounting principles. The rules and regulations comprising the income tax laws reflect the objectives of income taxation as well as administrative rulings which have been made to implement the law. These provisions are intended to obtain revenue, in an equitable manner, to operate the government and to stimulate and/or regulate the economy. Financial accounting, on the other hand, is concerned with the proper determination and matching of revenues and expenses in order to measure income and provide useful information to decision-makers.

Some differences between taxable income and accounting income occur because of special tax rules that differ from generally accepted accounting principles. Certain items of revenue are reported for financial accounting purposes that are never reported on the income tax return. These are excluded by law from taxable income. For example, interest on state and municipal bonds is included in accounting income but not in taxable income. Similarly, certain expenses may not be treated as deductions for tax purposes. For example, goodwill is amortized as an expense for accounting purposes but it is not subject to amortization under current tax regulations. These items represent permanent differences between taxable and accounting income and are referred to as such. Permanent differences do not give rise to deferred income taxes.

Other differences between taxable income and accounting income are not permanent. These result from temporary differences in the timing of the recognition of revenues and expenses. Temporary differences affect the determination of accounting income in one period and taxable income in another period. They may occur because, in some instances, one method or procedure may be used for tax purposes and a different method or procedure for financial accounting purposes. The underlying reason why different methods are used is because of the differences in the objectives of accounting and taxation from the viewpoint of the reporting entity. The objective of financial accounting is a fair and accurate measurement of income and financial position, while the objective of a business in selecting among allowable tax methods is usually to minimize taxable income and postpone the payment of taxes. Although over a long enough period of time the temporary differences should "wash out" so that total taxable income and total accounting income are the same, the difference during any one year may be significant. Two major classes of temporary differences are as follows:

1. Current accounting income may be greater than current taxable income, thus the taxable income of future periods will exceed future accounting income.

a. Revenues and gains may be included in accounting income before they are included in taxable income. For example, a firm's treatment of installment sales may recognize the entire profit at the time of sale for accounting purposes and use the installment method which recognizes profit as cash is received for tax purposes. Thus, businesses that sell merchandise on the installment basis may recognize revenue for financial accounting purposes at the time of sale but report the income for tax purposes as cash is actually received.

b. Expenses and losses may be recognized for tax purposes before they are recognized for accounting purposes (i.e., deducted from taxable income before they are deducted from accounting income). For example, different depreciation methods may be used for tax and accounting purposes. Tax depreciation is generally calculated using the Modified Accelerated Cost Recovery System (MACRS).[2] A firm could use MACRS for tax purposes and straight-line depreciation for purposes of financial accounting. The accelerated method results in larger depreciation expense than the straight-line method in the earlier years of the life of an asset, and smaller depreciation charges in the later years. Thus, the use of the different methods may result in lower taxable income than accounting income during the early years but have the opposite effect in later years.

2. Current taxable income may be greater than current accounting income, thus future accounting income will exceed future taxable income.

a. Revenues and gains may be included in taxable income before they are included in accounting income. For example, items that are considered to be unearned revenue for accounting purposes (such as cash received in advance) are taxable when the cash is received and reported as revenue for financial accounting purposes when the service is provided.

b. Expenses and losses may be deducted from accounting income before they are deducted from taxable income. For example, a company may estimate its bad debt losses in order to match expenses with the related sales revenue for accounting purposes, but use the direct write-off method for tax purposes.

Interperiod Tax Allocation

When one accounting method is used for tax purposes and a different method for financial accounting, revenues or expenses may be reported on the income statement and the tax return in different periods. These are called temporary differences. Although the same total revenue and expenses (ig-

---

[2] See Chapter 5 for a discussion of MACRS.

noring permanent differences) eventually are reported for both tax and financial accounting purposes, taxable income, and accounting income during any one period may differ significantly. Therefore, as a result of temporary differences, a part of the income tax liability during one year is caused by revenues and expenses reported during some other year for financial accounting purposes. Consequently, if income tax expense reported in the income statement is based on income taxes actually paid, there is a mismatching of revenues and expenses because earnings may be included in the income statement of one period and the related tax expense reported in a different period. Also, there may be a failure to report the total tax that will actually be due on the temporary differences when they reverse.

To avoid the problems discussed above, income taxes (for accounting purposes) are subject to the same accrual, deferral, and estimation concepts that are applied to all other expenses. This is accomplished using comprehensive income tax allocation procedures to calculate income tax expense for financial statement purposes. Tax allocation provides a more accurate measure of long-term earning power and avoids distortions caused by tax regulations.

Under comprehensive income tax allocation, income tax expense is affected by all transactions and events regardless of how significant and/or recurrent they may be. The tax effect of each individual temporary difference is recognized and allocated/deferred. These procedures recognize that events which create temporary differences affect cash flows in both the period of origination and the period of reversal. Since individual items do reverse, the focus is on individual items rather than groups of items.

The liability method is used to determine the amount to be recorded. The liability method records deferred income taxes using the enacted rate that will be in effect when the reversal occurs and additional taxes will be paid (or saved). It is a balance sheet oriented method that reports the total taxes that will be assessed on temporary differences when they reverse. Taxes that were postponed will be paid in the future at future tax rates.

Generally accepted accounting principles requires a comprehensive allocation approach using the liability method. Using this method, the deferred tax liability or asset should reflect the amount of income taxes payable or refundable in future years as a result of the deferred tax consequences of events recognized on the statements of current or past years. The entry to record deferred taxes (assuming a liability) would be in the general format which follows:

Allocation of Income Tax Within a Period

```
Income tax expense .............   XX
    Deferred income taxes[3] .......            XX
    Income taxes payable ........               XX
```

According to Accounting Principles Board *Opinions No. 9* and *30*, the income statement should disclose separate income figures for: (1) income from continuing operations; (2) income from any segment or division of the business which has been, or is to be discontinued or sold—referred to as discontinued operations; and (3) income from unusual, nonrecurring items, referred to as extraordinary items. Income from continuing operations, income or losses from discontinued operations, and extraordinary gains or losses may be included in taxable income and, hence, affect the tax liability for the period. For this reason, it is believed that allocation of the total amount of income taxes for the period among income from continuing operations, discontinued operations, and extraordinary gains or losses provides a more meaningful income statement.

This allocation, referred to as intraperiod tax allocation, is accomplished by deducting from income from continuing operations the taxes related to that amount, showing income from discontinued operations and extraordinary gains net of applicable taxes and losses from discontinued operations and extraordinary losses, reduced by the related tax reductions.

To illustrate, assume that Cobb Company, which uses the same methods for tax purposes and for financial accounting purposes (so that there is no timing difference), determined its tax liability for 19x2 as follows:

```
Revenues ............................   $100,000
Operating expenses .....................     60,000
Operating income before taxes ............  $ 40,000
Income from discontinued operations ......    20,000
Extraordinary gain .....................     30,000
Taxable income ........................   $ 90,000
```

Further, assume that the tax rate is 40 percent. The total tax liability would be $36,000 ($90,000 × 40%). Of this amount, $16,000 ($40,000 × 40%) is applicable to normal operating income; $8,000 ($20,000 × 40%) is due to discontinued operations; and $12,000 ($30,000 × 40%) is applicable to the extraordinary gain. The following statement illustrates the intraperiod tax allocation.

---

[3] To compute the year-end deferred tax amount under *FASB No. 109*, you would: (1) identify all temporary differences, (2) estimate the particular future years in which these temporary differences will result in taxable or deductible amounts, (3) calculate the amount of tax remaining by applying the enacted tax rates to the taxable or deductible amounts for each year, (4) add the amounts of tax for each future year to determine the amount of deferred tax liability or asset at the end of the current year, and (5) reduce this amount by any previously recognized deferred liability or asset.

Cobb Company
Income Statement
For the Year Ended December 31, 19x2

Revenues	$100,000
Operating expenses	60,000
Income from continuing operations before taxes	$ 40,000
Provisions for income taxes	16,000
Income from continuing operations	$ 24,000
Discontinued operations:	
Income from discontinued operations	
(less related taxes of $8,000)	12,000
	$ 36,000
Extraordinary items:	
Extraordinary gain	
(less related taxes of $12,000)	18,000
Net income	$ 54,000

INCOME TAXES AND MANAGEMENT DECISIONS

Because money has a "time value," it is rational for corporate management to defer as long as possible the incurrence and payment of corporate income taxes. Thus, a major consideration in tax planning is the timing of income and deductions. Management will normally attempt to minimize the current tax liability by deferring income or accelerating deductions to the extent possible under the tax laws. Successful tax planning is dependent upon a timely selection of the most advantageous tax alternatives.

While a detailed review of management decision-making regarding corporate income taxes is beyond the scope of this text, the following are major areas of importance in tax planning:

1. Selecting the form of business organization.
2. Acquisition, use, and disposition of fixed assets.
3. Employee compensation.
4. Corporate reorganizations.
5. Financing arrangements.

SUMMARY

Income taxes represent a significant expense of doing business for both corporate and noncorporate business enterprises. The four major classes of taxpayers are individuals, corporations, estates, and trusts. Sole proprietorships and partnerships are not taxable entities, although the income from these enterprises is taxed as income to their owners.

The individual federal income tax is computed by appropriately utilizing the tax tables or the tax rate schedules. Before calculating one's tax liability, an individual should be aware of the amount of gross income, deductions for adjusted gross income, adjusted gross income, itemized deductions, personal exemptions, taxable income, and credits.

Although the general procedure for determining a corporation's income tax is similar to that used by an individual, the treatment of specific items may differ significantly. In addition, the tax rate structure for corporations differs from that for individuals. Since taxable income is determined by tax law while accounting income is based on generally accepted accounting principles, the tax liabilities based on the two amounts may differ. Tax expense in the income statement should be matched against the income reported therein, regardless of when the income is included in taxable income and the tax actually paid. The process of matching tax expense to the appropriate accounting periods is referred to as interperiod tax allocation. This process is used only when the difference in tax liabilities is due to timing. If a difference is permanent, no allocation is appropriate or necessary. An additional allocation of income tax within a period is made on the income statement to income from continuing operations, from discontinued operations, and from extraordinary items. This is referred to as intraperiod tax allocation.

KEY DEFINITIONS

Accounting income—the amount of income determined using generally accepted accounting principles.

Adjusted gross income (for individuals)—gross income less deductions for adjusted gross income.

Capital assets—generally include all property except such items as trade receivables, inventories, copyrights, or compositions in the hands of their creator, and government obligations issued on a discount basis and due within one year without interest. Real or depreciable property used in a trade or business may be treated as capital assets under certain circumstances.

Capital gain or loss—a realized gain or loss incurred from the sale or exchange of a capital asset.

Deductions for adjusted gross income (for individuals)—deductions for gross income in computing adjusted gross income include business and other expenses connected with earning certain types of revenue. These include ordinary and necessary expenses incurred by the taxpayer in the operation of his or her business or profession and certain employee expenses.

Deductions from adjusted gross income (for individuals)—legally allowable deductions that may be classified as either itemized deductions or personal exemptions.

Double taxation—the corporation is taxed on its reported income and stockholders are taxed upon the receipt of dividends from the corporation. This is sometimes referred to as double taxation.

Estate—a separate legal entity created to take charge of the assets of a deceased person, paying the decedent's debts, and distributing the remaining assets to heirs.

Gross income—includes all income from whatever source derived unless expressly excluded by law or the U.S. Constitution.

Head of household—the title of head of household is a tax status that applies to certain unmarried or legally separated persons who maintain a residence for a relative.

Itemized deductions—deductions for certain employee business expenses and for personal expenses and losses such as charitable contributions, taxes, interest, casualty losses, and medical expenses are referred to as itemized deductions.

Interperiod tax allocation—a procedure used to apportion tax expense among periods so that the income tax expense reported for each period is in relation to the tax liability created by accounting income in the current year and all future years.

Intraperiod tax allocation—the allocation of the total amount of income tax expense for a period among income from normal operations, discontinued operations, extraordinary items, and prior-period adjustments.

Long-term capital gains or losses—gains or losses which result from the sale or exchange of capital assets and certain productive assets of a business held by the taxpayer for more than twelve months.

Permanent difference—a difference between taxable income and accounting income which occurs because of tax rules which differ from generally accepted accounting principles and which will not be offset by corresponding differences in future periods.

Personal exemptions—a deduction of $2,150 (for 1991) from adjusted gross income for the taxpayer, his or her spouse, and qualified dependents. There are additional exemptions for the taxpayer and his or her spouse who are over 65 or blind.

Progressive tax—this is a tax in which the tax rates increase as taxable income increases.

Taxable income—generally obtained by reducing adjusted gross income by the sum of: (1) the taxpayer's itemized deductions or standard deduction, and (2) the deduction for personal exemptions.

Temporary differences—these are differences between taxable income and accounting income which occur because an item is included in taxable income in one period and in accounting income in a different period.

Trust—a legal entity which is created when a person transfers assets to a trustee for the benefit of designated persons.

QUESTIONS

1. Explain how the net earnings of the following types of business entities are taxed by the federal government: (a) sole proprietorships, (b) partnerships, and (c) corporations.

2. The earnings of a corporation are subject to a "double tax." Explain.

3. Certain factors may cause the income before taxes in the accounting records to differ from taxable income. These factors may be either permanent differences or temporary differences. Explain.

4. Does a corporation electing partnership treatment for tax purposes (Subchapter S) pay federal income taxes? Discuss.

5. What are the four major classes of taxable entities?

6. What is the objective of using the interperiod tax allocation procedures?

7. Does it make any difference in computing income taxes whether a given deduction is for computing adjusted gross income or an itemized deduction? Explain.

8. How did the Tax Reform Act of 1986 change the treatment of capital gains?

9. What are some of the differences between the tax rules for corporations and those for individuals?

10. What are some of the objectives of the federal income tax?

EXERCISES

11. Indicate the income tax status for each of the items listed below. For each item, state whether it is (a) included in gross income, (b) a deduction from gross income to determine adjusted gross income, (c) an itemized deduction, or (d) none of the above.

    1. Property taxes paid on personal residence.
    2. Interest paid on mortgage on personal residence.
    3. Damages of $500 to personal residence from a storm.
    4. Capital loss on the sale of stock.
    5. Insurance on home.
    6. Sales taxes.
    7. Inheritance received upon death of a relative.
    8. Interest received on municipal bonds.
    9. Share of income from partnership.
    10. Salary received as an employee.
    11. Rental income.
    12. Expenses incurred in earning rental income.
    13. Contributions to church.

12. James and Martha Gentry, filing a joint return, are entitled to one personal exemption each and two additional exemptions for dependent children. James Gentry owns a business organized as a sole proprietorship. Additional information related to their income tax return is as follows:

Revenues	$100,000
Cost of goods sold	60,000
Business expenses	20,000
Life insurance proceeds (death of father)	10,000
Interest on city of Bowro Bonds	500
Rental income	5,000
Allowable itemized deductions	1,800
Salary—Martha Gentry	6,000

The deduction for a personal exemption is $1,950.

Determine the following:

a. Adjusted gross income
b. Taxable income
c. Income tax liability. (Use the tax rates provided in this chapter.)

13. Don Looney had the following capital gains and losses during the year.

Long-term losses	$ 3,000
Long-term gains	12,000
Short-term losses	8,000
Short-term gains	6,000

Determine the tax on Looney's capital gain assuming that the tax rate is 28 percent.

14. The following differences enter into the reconciliation of financial net income and taxable income of A.P. Baxter Corp. for the current year:

a. Tax depreciation exceeds book depreciation by $30,000.
b. Estimated warranty costs of $6,000 applicable to the current year's sales have not been paid. (Not deductible for tax purposes until paid.)
c. Percentage depletion deducted on the tax return exceeds cost depletion by $45,000.
d. Unearned rent revenue of $25,000 was deferred on the books but appropriately included in taxable income.
e. A book expense of $2,000 for life insurance premiums on officers' lives is not allowed as a deduction on the tax return. (**Note:** This is not a temporary difference.)

f. Gross profit of $80,000 was excluded from the taxable income because Baxter had appropriately elected the installment sale method for tax reporting while recognizing all gross profit from installment sales at the the time of the sale for financial reporting.

Required:

Consider each reconciling item independently of all others and explain whether each item would enter into the calculation of income taxes to be allocated. For any which are included in the income tax allocation calculation, explain the effect of the item on the current year's income tax expense and how the amount would be reported on the balance sheet. (Tax allocation calculations are not required.)

15. From the following information, calculate corporate income tax for the Brown Company.

   a. Sales were $990,000; cost of goods sold was 70 percent of sales.
   b. Dividends from domestic corporations totaled $30,000.
   c. Selling and miscellaneous expenses were 10 percent of sales.
   d. Assume that the corporate tax rates are as stated in the chapter.

16. The partial tax return is shown below for Bengal, Inc. for the year.

Operating income before taxes	$ 80,000
Income from discontinued operations	45,000
Extraordinary gain (capital gain)	25,000
Taxable income	$150,000

    Assume that the tax rate is 40 percent. Bengal, Inc. uses the same methods for tax and financial accounting purposes.

    Required:

    Reflect the application of intraperiod income tax allocation procedures as they would be reported on the financial statements.

17. The taxable income for the Saints Corporation for 19x1 was $12,000, $15,000 for 19x2 and $10,000 for 19x3. Due to temporary differences of reporting income for book purposes and tax purposes, the following differences occurred in these three years: 19x1—Book income exceeded income per tax return by $2,000; 19x2—Income per tax return exceeded book income by $3,500; 19x3—Book income exceeded income per tax return by $5,000. Assume that the tax rate is 40 percent.

    Required:

    Prepare journal entries to record the tax accrual and to reflect tax allocation procedures.

18. Mary and Harry Jones have two children and file a joint return. In addition, they provide for the full support of Harry's mother and Mary's father, both over 65. Mary earns a gross salary of $10,000 a year and Harry earns $8,000. Mary received $250 in dividends and Harry received $70. Together they earned $500 interest on their joint savings account and $700 interest on municipal government bonds. On December 1, one of their children died and they received $5,000 in life insurance proceeds.

Required:

1. How many personal exemptions can the Jones' claim? (Each deduction is $1,950.)
2. What is their adjusted gross income (or gross income in this case)?
3. What is their taxable income?
4. How much must they pay in federal income taxes, using the tax rates provided in the chapter.

19. The taxable income for the Patriot Corporation is $150,000 before capital gains and losses are taken into consideration. Determine the company's corporate income tax under each of the following independent assumptions involving capital gains and losses:

a. Long-term capital gains, $10,000; long-term capital losses, $15,000.
b. Long-term capital gains, $12,000; long-term capital losses, $9,000.
c. Long-term capital gains, $13,000; long-term capital losses, $5,000; short-term capital gains, $3,000; short-term capital losses, $6,000.

Assume that the corporate tax rates are as given in the chapter.

PROBLEMS

20. Jim Simmons and his wife are both 63 years old and own a dry cleaning store. His wife has been legally blind since she was in a car accident when she was 55. In reviewing the books of his dry cleaning store, Jim finds that it had revenues of $95,000 and expenses of $80,000. During the year, Jim rented a vacant lot to a friend at an annual rental of $3,000. Jim paid property taxes of $300 on the lot.

Jim and his wife have a $7,000 savings account and earned interest at six percent compounded annually on this amount. On July 30, Jim realized a $1,000 capital gain on stocks purchased January 1 of the *preceding* year, and a $250 capital gain on other securities purchased June 1 of the *present* year. In examining his personal records, Jim found that he had made charitable contributions of $275 and had paid interest on his mortgage of $300. Also, he had paid $300 of property taxes.

Required:

Compute Jim's taxable income for the year assuming he filed a joint return with his wife.

21. In each of the following cases, determine the amount of capital gains to be included in adjusted gross income or the amount of capital loss to be deducted for an individual taxpayer. Assume taxpayer's taxable income from noncapital sources is $100,000.

	A	B	C
Long-term capital gains........	$20,000	$20,000	$15,000
Long-term capital losses........	15,000	15,000	20,000
Short-term capital gains........	4,000	6,000	4,000
Short-term capital losses........	6,000	4,000	6,000

22. An individual taxpayer had the following capital gains and losses during the year.

	Gains	Losses
Short-term....................	$ 6,000	$11,000
Long-term....................	20,000	5,000

Required:

Compute the amount of income tax on the capital gains assuming that the taxpayer has a marginal tax rate of: (a) 15 percent, and (b) 28 percent.

23. The Hall Company uses MACRS for tax purposes and straight-line depreciation for its financial accounting records. Its taxable income and accounting income (before income taxes) for a four-year period are shown below.

	19x1	19x2	19x3	19x4
Taxable income...........	$ 70,000	$100,000	$140,000	$210,000
Accounting income........	100,000	120,000	150,000	200,000

Assume that the corporate tax rate is 40 percent.

Required:

1. Compute the net income after taxes in the financial statement for Hall Company: (a) assuming that interperiod tax allocation procedures are not used, and (b) assuming the tax allocation procedure is used.
2. Determine the balance in the "Deferred Tax Liability" account at the end of 19x4 in 1(b) above.

Refer to the Annual Report included in the front of the text.

24. What is the amount of deferred income taxes at the end of the most recent year?

25. What was the effective tax rate for the most recent year?

26. What was the income tax currently payable for the most recent year?

27. What was the income tax benefit related to the cumulative effect of change in accounting for postretirement benefits?

Appendix

To illustrate inter-period tax allocation, assume that taxable income exceeds accounting income in earlier years. Under interperiod tax allocation, the excess of the tax liability over tax expense would be debited to a deferred income tax account. For example, assume that Marion Company agrees to rent a portion of its office space to Dean Company on a one-time basis for 19x3 and receives its annual rent of $3,600 for the year 19x3 on December 31, 19x2. None of this amount would be included in accounting income for 19x2 since it will not be earned by Dean Company until 19x3. For tax purposes, however, the entire amount would be included in taxable income for 19x2 since prepaid rent is taxed as it is received rather than as it is earned. Assume that the income of Marion Company from all sources other than rentals was $10,000 for 19x1, 19x2, and 19x3. Its taxable income would be $13,600 (accounting income of $10,000 plus the $3,600 rent received) in 19x2 and $10,000 in 19x3. Further assume that the tax rate in all years was 40 percent. The entries to record the tax expense for 19x2 and 19x3 would be as follows:

19x2	Tax expense..........................	4,000	
	Deferred income taxes	1,440	
	Income taxes payable		5,440
19x3	Tax expense..........................	5,440	
	Deferred income taxes		1,440
	Income taxes payable		4,000

The impact of these differences on the financial statements and the income tax return may be summarized as follows:

	19x2	19x3
Financial statements		
Income before taxes	$10,000	$13,600
Income tax expense.........................	4,000	5,440
Deferred income taxes	1,440	0
Income tax returns		
Taxable income	13,600	10,000
Income taxes payable	5,440	4,000

In this example, the temporary difference in recognizing the rental income was eliminated by the end of 19x3.

To illustrate a slightly more complex situation, assume that Ruth Company purchased several light trucks on January 1, 19x1, for $120,000. The firm plans to use the straight-line depreciation method for financial accounting purposes and MACRS depreciation for tax purposes. No salvage value is anticipated and the trucks are assigned a four year useful life for accounting purposes.

For tax purposes, the trucks would be included in the five year MACRS class and depreciated using the 200 percent declining-balance method. Assume further that the income before taxes and depreciation remains constant at $100,000 for the years 19x1 through 19x6, and that the applicable tax rate is 40 percent. Under these circumstances, the depreciation expense on the income statement will be $30,000 ($120,000 ÷ 4) each year, 19x1 through 19x4 and zero for 19x5 and 19x6, since the trucks were assigned a four year life with no salvage value for accounting purposes. The deduction for depreciation on the tax return, on the other hand, would be as follows:

		Annual	Cumulative
19x1:	(2 × 20%) × ($120,000 − 0) × ½ =	$24,000	$ 24,000
19x2:	(2 × 20%) × ($120,000 − $24,000) =	38,400	62,400
19x3:	(2 × 20%) × ($120,000 − $62,400) =	23,040	85,440
19x4:	(2 × 20%) × ($120,000 − $85,440) =	13,824	99,264
19x5:	(2 × 20%) × ($120,000 − $99,264) =	8,294	107,558
19x6:	$120,000 − $107,558 =	$12,442	120,000

Note that only one-half year's depreciation is taken in 19x1, the year of acquisition, because of the half-year convention required under MACRS rules. In 19x6, the remaining undepreciated cost is charged to depreciation, also because of the half-year convention.

The firm's taxable income and actual tax liability are as follows:

	19x1	19x2	19x3	19x4	19x5	19x6	Total
Income before depreciation and taxes	$100,000	$100,000	$100,000	$100,000	$100,000	$100,000	$600,000
Deduction for depreciation	24,000	38,400	23,040	13,824	8,294	12,442	120,000
Taxable income	$ 76,000	$ 61,600	$ 76,960	$ 86,176	$ 91,706	$ 87,558	$480,000
Income tax paid (40%)	$ 30,400	$ 24,640	$ 30,784	$ 34,470	$ 36,682	$ 35,024	$192,000

The following income statement would result if the income tax due the government for the year is considered to be income tax expense and comprehensive income tax allocation procedures are not used.

	19x1	19x2	19x3	19x4	19x5	19x6	Total
Income before depreciation and taxes	$100,000	$100,000	$100,000	$100,000	$100,000	$100,000	$600,000
Depreciation expense	30,000	30,000	30,000	30,000	0	0	120,000
Income before taxes	$ 70,000	$ 70,000	$ 70,000	$ 70,000	$100,000	$100,000	$480,000
Income tax expense (as above)	30,400	24,640	30,784	34,470	36,682	35,024	192,000
Net income	$ 39,600	$ 45,360	$ 39,216	$ 35,530	$ 63,318	$ 64,976	$288,000

It should be noted that even though Ruth Company had identical operating results during each year, the tax expense and the net income figures vary if comprehensive tax allocation is not used.

To correct this improper matching of revenues and expenses, tax expense in the income statement should be calculated using comprehensive tax allocation as indicated below. Future annual temporary differences are determined by comparing the depreciation taken for accounting purposes to the depreciation deduction for income tax purposes. These differences are then multiplied by the tax rate expected to be in effect when the differences are reversed to determine the amount of deferred income taxes, as follows:

Future Timing Differences	19x2	19x3	19x4	19x5	19x6
Accounting depreciation	$ 30,000	$ 30,000	$ 30,000	$ 0	$ 0
Tax depreciation	38,400	23,040	13,824	8,294	12,442
Differences	$ (8,400)	$ 6,960	$ 16,176	$ (8,294)	$(12,442)
× tax rate	.40	.40	.40	.40	.40
Deferred income taxes	$ (3,360)	$ 2,784	$ 6,470	$ (3,318)	$ (4,976)

These amounts are then used to calculate the balance in the deferred income taxes account at the end of each year.

19x1	$(3,360) + $2,784 + $6,470 + $(3,318) + $(4,976)	=	$(2,400)
19x2	$2,784 + $6,470 + $(3,318) + $(4,976)	=	960
19x3	$6,470 + $(3,318) + $(4,976)	=	(1,824)
19x4	$(3,318) + $(4,976)	=	(8,294)
19x5	$(4,976)	=	(4,976)
19x6	0	=	0

The change in the deferred income taxes account is then combined with the amount of the income taxes actually payable to determine the income tax expense for the period.

	Tax Liability	Change in Deferred Taxes (Dr.) Cr.	Tax Expense
19x1	$30,400	$(2,400)	$28,000
19x2	24,640	3,360	28,000
19x3	30,784	(2,784)	28,000
19x4	34,470	(6,470)	28,000
19x5	36,682	3,318	40,000
19x6	35,024	4,976	40,000

The entries to record the tax expense for the year are:

19x1	Income tax expense	28,000	
	Deferred income taxes	2,400	
	Income taxes payable		30,400
19x2	Income tax expense	28,000	
	Income taxes payable		24,640
	Deferred income taxes		3,360
19x3	Income tax expense	28,000	
	Deferred income taxes	2,784	
	Income taxes payable		30,784
19x4	Income tax expense	28,000	
	Deferred income taxes	6,470	
	Income taxes payable		34,470

19x5	Income tax expense	40,000	
	Deferred income taxes		3,318
	Income taxes payable		36,682
19x6	Income tax expense	40,000	
	Deferred income taxes		4,976
	Income taxes payable		35,024

The deferred income taxes account would appear as follows:

Date	Debit	Credit	Balance	
1/ 1/x1			0	
12/31/x1	2,400		2,400	Dr.
12/31/x2		3,360	960	Cr.
12/31/x3	2,784		1,824	Dr.
12/31/x4	6,470		8,294	Dr.
12/31/x5		3,318	4,976	Dr.
12/31/x6		4,976	0	

Using interperiod tax allocation, the following income statements for the six year period would result:

	19x1	19x2	19x3	19x4	19x5	19x6	Total
Income before depreciation and taxes	$100,000	$100,000	$100,000	$100,000	$100,000	$100,000	$600,000
Depreciation expense	30,000	30,000	30,000	30,000	0	0	120,000
Income before taxes	$ 70,000	$ 70,000	$ 70,000	$ 70,000	$100,000	$100,000	$480,000
Income tax expense (40%)	28,000	28,000	28,000	28,000	40,000	40,000	192,000
Net income	$ 42,000	$ 42,000	$ 42,000	$ 42,000	$ 60,000	$ 60,000	$288,000

Thus, under tax allocation procedures, the tax expense in the income statement is logically related to the earnings before taxes. Note that the tax expense over the six-year period is still $192,000 and the total tax liability is also $192,000.

In this example, the difference between accounting income and taxable income is eliminated over the six year period. Therefore, the deferred income taxes account has a zero balance at the end of the six years. In practice, the differences between accounting and taxable income may last for a considerable number of years or even be created indefinitely since the company is continually replacing its assets and seldom, if ever, would all assets be fully depreciated. The balance in the deferred income taxes account may, therefore, become a significant amount. Also, in this example, there was a single temporary difference and the expected tax rate did not change during the six-year period, so the step-by-step calculations illustrated above may appear to be unnecessary. In a real-world situation, however, there would be multiple permanent differences, temporary differences, and the tax rate(s) expected to be in effect when the temporary differences reversed would change, perhaps significantly. Thus, the systematic approach illustrated above would be not only helpful, but necessary.

Chapter 13 discusses issues relating to foreign currency transactions and translating the financial statements of a foreign subsidiary company to the currency of the parent company in the United States. Studying this chapter should enable you to:

1. Learn about exchange rates.

2. Understand the accounting procedures for foreign currency transactions.

3. Describe the procedures involved in translating the financial statements of a foreign branch or subsidiary company to the currency of the U.S. parent company.

4. Understand the reasons for the differences in accounting standards and disclosure requirements among countries.

13

International Accounting*

INTRODUCTION

Many companies buy and sell merchandise in countries all over the world. From an accounting viewpoint, these transactions are more complicated than those within a country because either the importing or exporting company must be involved with a foreign currency. Gains and losses due to changes in the exchange rate of one currency for another often arise. Examples of the geographical markets for the products of several well-known companies are shown below.

American Brands:	Approximately 60 percent of its sales are to Europe.
Avon:	Approximately 62 percent of its sales are to Europe, the Pacific region, and the Western Hemisphere excluding the United States.
IBM:	Approximately 59 percent of its revenues come from Europe, the Middle East, Africa, Asia, and the Western Hemisphere excluding the United States.
Phillips Petroleum:	Approximately 18 percent of its sales are to Norway, the United Kingdom, Africa, and other areas.
Caterpillar:	Approximately 59 percent of its sales are to Europe, Asia, Canada, Latin America, Africa, and the Middle East.

*The authors would like to thank Steven D. Grossman of Texas A&M University who wrote this chapter.

A company that has branches, divisions, or subsidiaries in more than one country is referred to as a multinational corporation. Examples of multinational corporations, in addition to those listed above, include Coca-Cola, Volkswagen, and Nestle. An accounting problem arises for multinational corporations when the results of operations and balance sheets of the foreign branches, divisions, or subsidiaries must be combined with the results of operations and balance sheets of the remainder of the company to obtain consolidated statements for the company as a whole.

In this chapter, we will examine the accounting problems associated with purchases from and sales to companies in other countries—foreign currency transactions—and the problems associated with combining the results of operations and balance sheets of foreign branches, divisions, and subsidiaries with those of the domestic parts of a multinational corporation—foreign currency translation. In addition, efforts to reduce the differences in accounting standards throughout the world will be discussed.

FOREIGN CURRENCY TRANSACTIONS

If a retail department store in Texas purchases inventory items from a manufacturer in Wyoming, both parties will, of course, deal in dollars. But if an American corporation purchases clothing from a British manufacturer, the American corporation may wish to pay for the inventory in dollars while the British manufacturer prefers to receive payment in British pounds. In the same manner, a British corporation that purchases electronic equipment from an American manufacturer normally wishes to pay in British pounds while the American company prefers dollars. Using different currencies complicates and may restrain transactions between countries.

From the perspective of an American company, a foreign currency is a foreign money commodity (such as British pounds) that has prices specified in terms of the U.S. dollar. These prices are referred to as exchange rates and express the relative values of the various currencies.

An exchange rate between two countries may be expressed in terms of the currency of either country. If a unit of foreign currency is expressed in terms of the equivalent domestic currency, the exchange rate is computed directly—for example, an exchange rate of $1.52 (U.S. dollars) per British pound. Conversely, if a unit of domestic currency is expressed in terms of the equivalent foreign currency, the exchange rate is computed indirectly—for example, an exchange rate of 0.6579 British pounds per U.S. dollar. The direct and indirect quotations are inversely related. Both direct and indirect exchange rates are published daily in the "Foreign Exchange" section of the *Wall Street Journal* and other newspapers.

Exchange rates may be either fixed or floating. Fixed or official rates are established by governments and do not fluctuate due to changes in world currency markets. Floating or free rates reflect fluctuating market prices for a currency as a function of supply and demand in world currency markets. When the demand for a particular currency exceeds the supply, the exchange rate (price) rises. Alternatively, if supply exceeds demand, the exchange rate falls. Foreign trade can be especially inhibited if exchange rates are subject to volatile short-run movements.

The supply and demand of a particular currency depends on trade (imports and exports) and investment. If an American company sells its products to foreign customers, these buyers must purchase U.S. dollars to pay for their purchases. If a foreign investor wishes to invest funds in the United States, the investor must first convert its funds to U.S. dollars. Each of these actions increases the demand for U.S. dollars and causes the exchange rate (price) for the U.S. dollar to rise. On the other hand, if an American company purchases merchandise from a foreign supplier, the purchaser must sell U.S. dollars to acquire the needed foreign currency. If an American investor desires to invest in the capital markets of another country, the U.S. investor must convert U.S. dollars to the needed foreign currency. Each of these actions reduces the demand for U.S. dollars and causes the exchange rate for U.S. dollars to fall.

A country that fixes its exchange rate may establish different rates for various types of transactions in order to further governmental policies. Such rates are referred to as multiple exchange rates. For example, a country may establish one rate for imports and a less favorable rate for exports.

The foreign exchange market is an over-the-counter market in which national currencies are exchanged. Buyers and sellers of foreign currencies are brought together by telephone and telegraphic transfers. This market has developed to a considerable extent due to the very large growth in international transactions. American transactions with foreign entities are facilitated by major U.S. banks that provide bank transfer and currency exchange services.

Spot and Forward Exchange Markets

Foreign currency markets may be divided into spot and forward exchange markets. The spot market involves the exchange of currencies for immediate delivery. Spot rates may be either fixed or floating. If the exchange rates are floating, the spot rate may change several times in a single day. The forward exchange market involves the trading of foreign currencies for delivery and payment at some specified future date at an exchange rate which is also specified in advance. An important function of the forward exchange market is to provide protection against the risk of an adverse movement in the spot rate. *The Wall Street Journal* publishes daily quotations of U.S. exchange rates against other currencies for both immediate delivery and for delivery in 30, 90, and 180 days. Examples of foreign exchange rates are presented as follows:

The exchange rate for the British pound was $1.52 on February 5, 1987. About three years later, the exchange rate for the British pound had risen to $1.6775. The British pound had become stronger (more valuable) relative to the U.S. dollar. In terms of the U.S. dollar, the exchange rate had fallen from £.6579 to £.5961. The U.S. dollar became weaker (less valuable) relative to the British pound. American importers had to spend more U.S. dollars to obtain British pounds; British pounds had become more expensive. On the other hand, American exporters received more dollars for each receivable denominated in British pounds. When the exchange rate was £.6579, a receivable for £6,579 brought $10,000; when the exchange rate was £.5961, a receivable for £6,579 brought $11,036.74.

The following table is the foreign exchange rates for selected countries at three different points in time.

Foreign Exchange Rate for Selected Countries
February 5, 1987, May 11, 1990, and May 14, 1993

Country	U.S. Dollar Equivalent			Currency Per U.S. Dollar		
	February 5, 1987	May 11, 1990	May 14, 1993	February 5, 1987	May 11, 1990	May 14, 1993
Argentina (Austral)	.7593	.0002075	N/A	1.317	4820.21	N/A
Belgium (Franc):						
Commercial rate	.02633	.02943	.03017	37.98	33.98	33.14
Britain (Pound)	1.5200	1.6775	1.5390	.6579	.5961	.6498
30-day forward	1.5142	1.6681	1.5352	.6604	.5995	.6514
90-day forward	1.5025	1.6499	1.5282	.6655	.6061	.6544
180-day forward	1.4884	1.6247	1.5183	.6719	.6155	.6586
Canada (Dollar)	.7488	.8503	.7851	1.3355	1.1760	1.2737
30-day forward	.7481	.8467	.7841	1.3367	1.1811	1.2754
90-day forward	.7468	.8398	.7813	1.3391	1.1907	1.2800
180-day forward	.7453	.8313	.7763	1.34217	1.2030	1.2882
China (Yuen)	.2687	.211820	N/A	3.722	4.7210	N/A
France (Franc)	.1635	.18059	.18503	6.1170	5.5375	5.4045
30-day forward	.1632	.18038	.18425	6.1280	5.5438	5.4274
90-day forward	.1625	.18002	.18297	6.1550	5.5550	5.4655
180-day forward	.1614	.17953	.18132	6.1950	5.5700	5.5150
Germany (Mark)	.5447	.6099	.6205	1.8360	1.6395	1.6115
30-day forward	.5456	.6101	.6181	1.8329	1.6391	1.6178
90-day forward	.5476	.6104	.6141	1.8261	1.6383	1.6285
180-day forward	.5503	.6104	.6089	1.8172	1.6382	1.6422
Hong Kong (Dollar)	.1283	.12837	.12938	7.7930	7.7900	7.7290
Italy (Lira)	.0007645	.0008278	.0006760	1308.00	1208.01	1479.38
Japan (Yen)	.006515	.006542	.009027	153.50	152.85	110.78
30-day forward	.006526	.006549	.009026	153.23	152.70	110.79
90-day forward	.006551	.006561	.009027	152.64	152.42	110.78
180-day forward	.006588	.006582	.009027	151.79	151.92	110.78
Mexico (Peso)	.001013	.0003574	N/A	987.00	2798.00	N/A

N/A—not applicable; currency has changed.

Assume that an American company contracted to purchase goods from a British company and to pay 5,000 British pounds on delivery in thirty days. At the time of the agreement, the spot rate was $1.60 for one British pound. The American company expected to purchase 5,000 British pounds in the spot market to pay for the goods. But when the goods arrived, the British pound was selling for $1.6775. Consequently, the cost of the goods was $8,387.50 (5,000 × $1.6775) rather than the expected $8,000 (5,000 × $1.60). The American company had a loss of $387.50 on the transaction [($1.6775 − $1.60) × 5,000].

The American company could have eliminated the risk of an exchange rate loss on the transaction by entering into an agreement in the forward market to purchase 5,000 British pounds to be delivered in thirty days. Such an action, referred to as a hedge, would fix the dollar cost of the British goods at the forward rate. Payment for the 5,000 British pounds would have been due in thirty days. The forward rate is usually very close to the spot rate. Assume that in this case the forward rate at the time of the agreement with the British company was $1.61 for one British pound. The American company could have guaranteed itself the receipt of 5,000 British pounds in thirty days by agreeing to pay $8,050 (5,000 × $1.61) at that time. For only $50 ($8,050 − $8,000), the American company could have eliminated the risk of an adverse change in the exchange rate between the time of the agreement to purchase the British goods and the time of the payment for them.

Speculators attempt to profit in the forward exchange market by anticipating fluctuations in exchange rates. Assume that the spot rate is $1.52 for one British pound and a speculator expects it to increase to $1.60. The speculator could buy British pounds at the spot rate of $1.52 for one British pound, wait for the pound to appreciate (increase in value) against the dollar, and sell the pounds when the exchange rate has increased. If the speculator sells the pounds when the exchange rate is $1.59 per British pound, a profit of seven cents per pound would be obtained. Alternatively, the speculator could purchase British pounds for future delivery in the forward exchange market (for, say, $1.53 per British pound) and subsequently sell them in the spot market after the pound has appreciated (say, to $1.59 per British pound). Of course, if the speculator's judgment proves to be incorrect, a loss would be incurred.

An advantage of the forward market for the speculator is that no money (except a small security deposit in some cases) has to be paid at the time of the purchase of the British pounds. The speculator is required to pay dollars on the date on which the British pounds are delivered. But the dollars may be obtained by selling the British pounds. If the speculator correctly anticipated the movements in the exchange rate between the U.S. dollar and the British pound, the dollars received on the sale of the pounds will be more than sufficient to cover the obligation to purchase the pounds in the forward market. The speculator has great leverage in the forward exchange market; a positive return can be earned with no capital investment.

Import-Export Transactions

When companies located in two different countries, each having its own currency, engage in transactions (purchase-sale) with each other, one company will make or receive payment in the currency of the other company's country. This foreign transaction is denominated (stated) in terms of one of the two currencies. For example, the purchase of goods by an American company from a British company can be denominated in either U.S. dollars or British pounds. A foreign currency transaction is a transaction that is stated in terms of the other country's currency. Therefore, if the purchase of goods by an American company from a British company is denominated in British pounds, the foreign transaction is considered to be a foreign currency transaction by the American company. Alternatively, if the purchase is denominated in U.S. dollars, the foreign transaction is not considered to be a foreign currency transaction by the American company. Note that the transaction may be measured in either currency. The key point is the currency in which the transaction is stated.

A receivable or payable denominated in a foreign currency is measured in the domestic currency by multiplying the amount of the receivable or payable by the spot exchange rate at the time of the transaction. By the date of payment, however, the exchange rate has probably changed. These fluctuations in exchange rates give rise to exchange gains or losses.

Foreign currency transactions for an American company should be translated into U.S. dollars at the spot rate which was in effect at the date of the transaction. Each asset, liability, revenue, and expense account arising from the transaction is translated into dollars. If the balance sheet date occurs between the transaction date and the date of payment, the receivable or payable is adjusted to reflect the spot rate at the balance sheet date. Any exchange gain or loss resulting from this adjustment is included in income rather than being deferred until the time of payment.

There is a direct relationship between the American company's foreign currency transactions and its cash flows in dollars. Consequently, any fluctuations in the exchange rate for the company's foreign currency transactions will probably be realized at the time of payment. Therefore, exchange gains or losses are included in income for the period ending on the balance sheet date.

An exchange gain or loss arising from a purchase or sale should be accounted for as a separate item rather than combined with the purchase or sale. The risk assumed on the receivable or payable is separate and distinct from the sale or purchase. The purchase or sale is recorded at the spot rate in effect at the time of the transaction. If the company decides not to pay for the purchase or sale immediately, the exchange gain or loss reflects what is, in effect, a decision to speculate in the foreign currency market.

Imports Single Time Period

Assume that Amanda Company, which is located in the United States, purchases merchandise from Otto Company, which is located in Germany. At the time of the transaction, the spot exchange rate is $0.5447 per German mark. Amanda Company agrees to pay for the merchandise in thirty days. If the payable is denominated in U.S. dollars, there is a foreign transaction but not a foreign currency transaction for Amanda Company. Consequently, both the inventory or purchase and the related payable is measured and denominated in U.S. dollars. No exchange gain or loss can occur. On the other hand, if the payable is denominated in German marks, Amanda Company is exposed to risk from exchange rate fluctuations. Assuming that the agreed upon invoice price is 10,000 marks, Amanda Company records the transaction as follows:

Inventory (or purchases)	5,447	
Accounts payable (marks)		5,447

The inventory (or purchase) is measured and recorded in U.S. dollars. The dollar amount is computed by multiplying the number of German marks (10,000) by the spot rate ($0.5447). The account payable is denominated in German marks and, therefore, is subject to remeasurement as the exchange rate changes.

If the spot rate is $0.5647 per German mark at the time of payment, Amanda Company records the payment as follows:

Accounts payable (marks)	5,447	
Exchange loss	200	
Cash		5,647

The $200 exchange loss occurs because Amanda Company has to pay $0.5647 for each German mark for a total of $5,647 rather than $0.5447 for each German mark for a total of $5,447. The loss is due to the change in the exchange rate between the date of the transaction and the date of payment.

Although the payment to Otto Company has to be made in German marks, Amanda Company simply credits cash. Amanda Company can notify its bank to send the payment to Germany in marks without actually buying marks and then making the payment itself.

Imports-Multiple Time Periods

Now assume that in the above example the balance sheet date occurs between the time of the purchase transaction and the time of payment. The spot rate on the balance sheet date is $0.5347 per German mark. Amanda Company records the purchase at the time of the transaction as follows:

Inventory (or purchases)	5,447	
Accounts payable (marks)		5,447

On the balance sheet date, the liability should be adjusted to reflect the spot rate at that time. The spot rate has decreased from $0.5447 to $0.5347.

Therefore, the liability is reduced by $0.01 per German mark for a total of $100 [($0.01 × 10,000) or ($0.5447 × 10,000) − ($0.5347 × 10,000)].

Accounts payable (marks)	100	
Exchange gain		100

At the time of payment the spot rate has increased to $0.5647 and an exchange loss occurs. The loss is equal to the difference between the amount required at the time of payment ($5,647) and the recorded amount of the account payable ($5,347).

Accounts payable (marks)	5,347	
Exchange loss	300	
Cash		5,647

Although the actual exchange loss is $200 ($5,647 − $5,447), an exchange gain of $100 is reported in the income statement in the initial accounting period and an exchange loss of $300 is recorded in the second accounting period. No retroactive adjustment is made.

Exports

Assume that Amanda Company sells merchandise to an Italian company for 10,000,000 liras when the spot rate is $0.0007645 for each lira. At the balance sheet date, which is before the time of payment, the spot rate is $0.0008000. At the time of payment, the spot rate is $0.0008645. Amanda records the transaction as follows:

Accounts receivable (liras)	7,645	
Sales		7,645

On the balance sheet date, the account receivable, which is denominated in liras, should be adjusted for the change in the exchange rate. An exchange gain of $355 [($0.0008000 − $0.0007645) × 10,000,000] is recorded as:

Accounts receivable (liras)	355	
Exchange gain		355

The exchange gain occurs because the exchange rate increased and, if the exchange rate remains the same at the time of payment, Amanda Company will be able to obtain more dollars for each lira upon conversion.

On the date that payment is made, the exchange rate has increased to $0.0008645 and an exchange gain of $645 [($0.0008645 − $0.0008000) × 10,000,000] will be recorded.

Cash	8,645	
Accounts receivable (liras)		8,000
Exchange gain		645

The actual exchange gain is $1,000. An exchange gain of $355 is recorded in the income statement of the initial period; an exchange gain of $645 is recorded in the income statement of the second period.

Amanda Company could have avoided the possibility of exchange rate gains or losses by setting its sales price in terms of U.S. dollars. Then, if the exchange rate changed, the Italian company would spend a greater or lesser number of liras to buy the merchandise, but Amanda Company's receipts in terms of U.S. dollars would not have been affected.

Hedging

A company may be able to avoid gains and losses on foreign currency transactions by immediately paying or receiving the amount denominated in a foreign currency or by hedging with forward exchange (futures) contracts.[1] By immediately paying the liability denominated in a foreign currency or receiving the amount due on the receivable denominated in a foreign currency, the possibility of changes in the exchange rate is avoided. Hedging is like betting with a friend on one team playing in the World Series and then betting the same amount on the other team playing in the World Series with another friend. One bet offsets the other; the possibility of losing (or winning) is avoided.

A forward exchange contract is an agreement to exchange currencies at a specified forward rate at a specified future date. Exchange rate gains and losses can be avoided by hedging—buying or selling foreign currency for delivery on the same date that payment denominated in foreign currency is due.

In most cases, the forward exchange rate is not equal to the spot rate. For example, the spot rate on May 11, 1990, for Canada was $0.8503, while the forward rates were $0.8467 for 30 days, $0.8398 for 90 days, and $0.8313 for 180 days. If the forward price is lower (as is the case for Canada), the difference is referred to as a discount. Conversely, if the forward price is higher (as is the case for Japan on May 11, 1990), the difference is called a premium.

A company with payables denominated in a foreign currency may hedge by entering into a forward contract to buy foreign currency at a specified future date. If the exchange rate increases (as it did for Amanda Company from $0.5447 per German mark to $0.5647 per German mark), a loss on a payable denominated in a foreign currency is offset by a gain in the value of the forward exchange contract. For example, Amanda Company could have entered into a forward exchange contract to purchase marks at the 90-day forward exchange rate of $0.5476 per German mark. Such a hedging transaction does not ensure the complete elimination of a loss on the payable in this example, but it does reduce the $200 exchange loss on the payable by the $171 [($0.5647 − $0.5476) × 10,000 marks] exchange gain on the forward contract to a net loss of $29.

---

[1] This section discusses hedging with contracts for foreign currencies. The accounting requirements for this type of hedging is not covered by *FASB Statement No. 80*, "Accounting for Futures Contracts."

Similarly, a forward exchange contract to hedge an account receivable denominated in a foreign currency may be used. A company could enter into a forward contract to sell foreign currency at a specified future date.

FOREIGN CURRENCY TRANSLATION

The translation of foreign currency financial statements is necessary in order to record an investor's share of the income of a foreign investee and to prepare consolidated financial statements for a company with foreign branches or subsidiaries. The translation process should not alter the financial results of the component entities that report their financial information in terms of a foreign currency. Prior to the translation process, the foreign currency financial statements must be adjusted to conform with the accounting principles of the domestic company.

The development of standards for translating foreign currency financial statements has been a significant problem for the Financial Accounting Standards Board (FASB). The last two decades have been marked by the increased involvement of U.S. companies in international operations and by wide fluctuations in exchange rates. The numerous translation methods proposed over the years can yield significantly different financial statement results. Therefore, there has been a great deal of disagreement among accountants and users of financial information concerning the results produced by the various translation methods.

The translation process required by FASB *Statement No. 52*, "Foreign Currency Translation," involves the following for a U.S. parent company:

1. The functional currency of each foreign entity should be identified. A company's functional currency is the currency of the primary economic environment in which the company normally operates. For example, the functional currency for a subsidiary located in London is probably the British pound.

2. Financial statement items for each foreign entity are measured in terms of its functional currency in accordance with U.S. generally accepted accounting principles.

3. Assets and liabilities are translated from the functional currency into the reporting currency (the U.S. dollar for a U.S. parent company) using the current exchange rate in effect at the balance sheet date. Equity accounts are translated using historical rates. Revenues, expenses, gains, and losses are translated at the current exchange rate in effect at the date the items were recorded; however, a weighted average exchange rate for the period may be used.

4. Translation adjustments are included in stockholders' equity rather than in income.

Translation adjustments for functional currencies that are not the reporting currency (U.S. dollars for a U.S. company) result from the process of translating financial statements from an entity's functional currency into the reporting currency. The FASB pronouncement provides that translation adjustments are not to be included in the determination of net income for the period but are to be recorded in a separate component of stockholders' equity. The FASB's rationale for this position is that translation adjustments have no direct effect on the cash flows of a U.S. parent company. The effects of changes in exchange rates are uncertain and are not realized until the disposal of the foreign entity, if then.

Basic Illustration of Translation

Dayspring Corporation has a subsidiary, Lamblight Company, that began its operations at the beginning of 19x1. The functional currency of Lamblight Company is the British pound (£) and the books are maintained in British pounds. The functional currency of Dayspring Corporation is the U.S. dollar. Lamblight Company's balance sheet at the beginning of 19x1 is as follows:

Assets

Cash	£ 76,000
Inventories	55,000
Plant assets	180,000
Total assets	£311,000

Liabilities and Stockholders' Equity

Accounts payable	£ 45,000
Long-term debt	132,000
Common stock	134,000
Total liabilities and stockholders' equity	£311,000

The plant assets have a ten-year life and a zero residual value. Straight-line depreciation is used. Dividends of £10,000 were declared and paid during September. The exchange rates for 19x1 are as follows:

Beginning of the year	$1.50 per pound
September	1.57 per pound
End of the year	1.60 per pound
Weighted average	1.54 per pound

The income statement for Lamblight Company for 19x1 is as follows:

Sales		£445,000
Cost of goods sold		290,000
Gross profit		£155,000
Depreciation expense	£ 18,000	
Other operating expenses	102,000	
Total operating expenses		120,000
Net income		£ 35,000

The balance sheet for Lamblight Company at the end of 19x1 is as follows:

Assets

Cash	£ 15,000
Accounts receivable	114,000
Inventories	55,000
Plant assets, net	162,000
Total assets	£346,000

Liabilities and Stockholders' Equity

Accounts payable	£ 55,000
Long-term debt	132,000
Common stock	134,000
Retained earnings	25,000
Total liabilities and stockholders' equity	£346,000

The income statement of Lamblight Company for 19x1 translated into U.S. dollars is as follows:

Sales	£445,000 × 1.54 =	$685,300
Cost of goods sold	290,000 × 1.54 =	446,600
Gross profit	£155,000	$238,700
Depreciation expense	£ 18,000 × 1.54 =	$ 27,720
Other operating expenses	102,000 × 1.54 =	157,080
Total operating expenses	£120,000	$184,800
Net income	£ 35,000	$ 53,900

All of the income statement accounts are translated at the weighted average exchange rate for the year.

The balance sheet of Lamblight Company at the end of 19x1 translated into U.S. dollars is as follows:

Assets

Cash	£ 15,000 × 1.60 =	$ 24,000
Accounts receivable	114,000 × 1.60 =	182,400
Inventories	55,000 × 1.60 =	88,000
Plant assets, net	162,000 × 1.60 =	259,200
Total assets	£346,000	$553,600

Liabilities and Stockholders' Equity

Accounts payable	£ 55,000 × 1.60 =	$ 88,000
Long-term debt	132,000 × 1.60 =	211,200
Common stock	134,000 × 1.50 =	201,000
Retained earnings	25,000 see schedule	38,200
Translation adjustment	shown below	15,200
Total liabilities and stockholders' equity	£346,000	$553,600

All of the assets and liabilities are translated at the current exchange rate (1.60). The common stock is translated at the historical rate (1.50).

The schedule for computing the translated ending balance of retained earnings is as follows:

Beginning retained earnings.............	—		—
Net income...........................	£ 35,000	see income statement	$ 53,900
Less dividends........................	(10,000) × 1.57 =		(15,700)
Ending retained earnings...............	£ 25,000		$ 38,200

The translated beginning retained earnings is the translated ending retained earnings from the previous year (zero in this example). The translated income amount is taken from the income statement. The dividends are translated using the exchange rate in effect on the date of declaration (1.57).

The translation adjustment of $15,200 shown in the balance sheet is computed as follows:

	Pounds		Dollars
Beginning net asset balance.................	134,000 × 1.50 =		201,000
Increase in net assets:			
Net income............................	35,000		53,900
Decrease in net assets:			
Dividends declared......................	(10,000) × 1.57 =		(15,700)
Ending net asset balance before adjustment......................	159,000		239,200
Adjusted net asset balance..................	159,000 × 1.60 =		254,400
Translation adjustment.....................			15,200

The beginning net asset balance is translated at the historical exchange rate ($1.50). Individual increases and decreases are translated at the appropriate historical rates in effect at the time of occurrence (net income may be translated at a weighted average exchange rate). The ending net asset balance before adjustment does not consider the effect of the end-of-year exchange rate. The adjusted ending net asset balance takes into account exchange rate changes to the end of the year. The resulting translation adjustment (a credit of $15,200 in this example) is combined with the existing translation adjustment in the stockholders' equity section of the balance sheet (no previous translation adjustment exists in this example).

The translation adjustment is a credit in this example. The net asset position (assets minus liabilities) increased by £25,000. In addition, the exchange rate for the British pound rose. The value of the dollar decreased during the year ($1.50 was needed to purchase a British pound at the beginning of the year; $1.60 is required at the end of the year). If, for purposes of explanation in this discussion, Lamblight Company's net asset position is considered to be a receivable denominated in pounds, then the U.S. parent company (Dayspring Corporation) would receive more dollars for each British pound. Hence, there is a translation "gain" to be reported as an equity adjustment.

UNIFORMITY OF ACCOUNTING PRINCIPLES

While investors can now look throughout the world for investment opportunities, financial analysis may be difficult due to differing accounting standards and requirements for disclosure. Differences arise because of varying economic, political, social, educational, legal, and environmental factors. The financial statements of companies located in different countries may be difficult to compare. Differences exist in terminology, accounts in one system do not exist in another, rules concerning revenue and expense recognition are not the same, and levels of disclosure vary considerably.

Accounting standards are not uniform from one country to another. There is no world body with the power to establish accounting and disclosure requirements.

Efforts have been made to standardize or harmonize accounting standards. To standardize accounting standards means to eliminate any differences between them (i.e., to make them uniform). To harmonize accounting standards means to lessen the differences between them.

Increased interest in standardization or harmonization is due to the need of companies to sell stock or obtain credit in foreign markets. Companies that disclose more information on their financial statements may have an advantage with international investors and creditors. Those companies not providing financial information according to standards established by the United States and United Kingdom find themselves at a competitive disadvantage in these financial markets.

Differences in Accounting Standards

Differences among countries, as well as nationalistic pride, hinder efforts at standardization or harmonization. Each country believes that its accounting system is better for itself than any other system.

Some countries have accounting standards that are set primarily by the private sector (the United States and the Netherlands); other countries have accounting standards that are heavily influenced by legal and tax regulations (Germany and Japan). The accounting practices in some countries are heavily influenced by centralized planning and decision-making (Egypt). Some countries permit a wide choice of accounting practices (France, the Netherlands, and South Africa). Some countries permit a wide variety of reserve accounts for bad debts, depreciation, and specific purposes such as overseas market development and research and development (Japan). Other countries are concerned with social accounting (Egypt and France) or inflation (Brazil). Some countries have highly uniform charts of accounts (France); others do not (Germany). Some countries are concerned with secrecy (Switzerland). Some countries are concerned with conservatism (Germany and Switzerland). Other countries have accounting systems that are similar to those of former colonial powers (the accounting systems in Ireland and New Zealand are similar to that of the United Kingdom).

In view of these differences in accounting standards and procedures, standardization is not likely to be achieved. Harmonization, especially within groups of nations, does appear to be a realistic goal, however.

Standard-Setting Bodies

The International Accounting Standards Committee (IASC) was founded in 1973 to formulate accounting standards to be observed throughout the world and to persuade the business communities and governments of all countries to secure acceptance of and compliance with these standards. The founding members of the IASC were Australia, Canada, France, Great Britain, Ireland, Japan, Mexico, the Netherlands, the United States, and Germany. About 105 accounting organizations representing over 78 countries are now members. The representatives to the IASC from the United States are the American Institute of Certified Public Accountants (AICPA) and the Institute of Management Accountants (IMA); the FASB has no official role.

Although the IASC has no enforcement powers and its standards are not universally applied, the organization's pronouncements have contributed to greater harmonization of accounting standards. The IASC's objective, as set forth in its *Statement of Intent* issued in July, 1990, is to remove the many alternative accounting treatments that are currently allowed so that securities commissions throughout the world will adopt the body's standards as benchmarks for generally accepted accounting principles. At the present time, there are some significant differences between IASC standards and those of some major countries. Whether these countries bring their accounting practices in line with those issued by the IASC remains to be seen.

The International Organization of Securities Commissions (IOSCO), which was established over twenty years ago, is now becoming more influential. The organization is composed of securities regulators from approximately fifty countries. The objective of the IOSCO is to improve international and domestic securities regulation by raising the quality of international accounting standards so that securities regulators can consider them for multinational securities offerings.

The European Economic Community (EEC) has made efforts toward increasing the harmonization of accounting standards among its member nations. Differences among the member countries have impeded this effort; however, some success has been achieved.

Other organizations have made contributions to harmonization. The United Nations has made recommendations for financial disclosure on annual reports for multinational corporations; the proposed code of conduct by the Organization for Economic Development and Cooperation for multinational corporations has a section dealing with financial disclosure. Wide differences of opinion exist on these recommendations between the industrialized and developing countries. Neither party had any real enforcement power to ensure compliance with the disclosure standards.

SUMMARY

A company that buys and sells merchandise in foreign countries may have gains and losses due to changes in the exchange rates between currencies. An exchange rate is the price of one currency in terms of another currency.

Exchange rates may be established (fixed) by governments or may fluctuate (float) due to changes in the supply and demand for world currencies. Supply and demand for a particular currency depend on imports, exports, and investment. Exports to a foreign country increase the demand for the domestic currency and cause the exchange rate for the domestic currency to rise; imports by a domestic company increase the demand for the foreign currency and cause the exchange rate for the domestic currency to fall.

A foreign exchange market has both spot exchange rates and forward exchange rates. The spot rate is the rate for immediate delivery of the currency; the forward rate is the rate for delivery of the currency at some specified future date. The forward market may be used to hedge the risk of gains and losses in import and export transactions. Speculators also use the forward exchange market.

In a foreign currency transaction involving exports and imports, the spot exchange rate is used to measure the receivable or payable denominated in a foreign currency at the time of the transaction. The exchange rate at the time of payment is probably not the same as the spot rate at the time of the transaction. The resulting exchange gain or loss is not combined with the purchase or sale but instead is accounted for separately. A company may be able to avoid these gains and losses by immediately paying or receiving the amount denominated in foreign currency or by hedging with forward exchange contracts.

Foreign currency translation is needed to record an investor's share of a foreign investee's income and to include foreign entities in consolidated financial statements. Assets and liabilities are translated from the functional currency into the reporting currency using the current exchange rate in effect at the balance sheet date. Equity accounts are translated using historical rates. Income statement accounts are translated at the current exchange rate in effect at the date the items were recorded or by using a weighted average exchange rate for the period. Translation adjustments are included in stockholders' equity rather than in income.

Comparison of the financial statements of companies located in different countries is difficult due to differences in accounting standards and disclosure requirements. While efforts at standardizing accounting principles have had little success to date, several international organizations have made some impact on harmonizing accounting standards. The International Accounting Standards Committee, the European Economic Community, the United Nations, and the Organization for Economic Development and Cooperation have all made contributions toward this goal.

KEY DEFINITIONS

Exchange gains and losses—Exchange gains and losses result from fluctuations in exchange rates between the time of a transaction and the time payment is made or received.

Exchange rate—An exchange rate is the price of one currency in terms of another currency.

Fixed exchange rate—A fixed exchange rate is established by the government and does not fluctuate due to changes in world currency markets.

Floating exchange rate—A floating exchange rate reflects fluctuating market prices for a currency as a function of supply and demand in world currency markets.

Foreign currency transaction—A foreign currency transaction is a transaction that is stated in terms of the other country's currency.

Foreign currency translation—Foreign currency translation is the conversion of a foreign entity's financial statements from its functional currency to the reporting entity's functional currency.

Foreign exchange market—The foreign exchange market is an over-the-counter market in which national currencies are exchanged.

Forward exchange contract—A forward exchange contract is an agreement to exchange currencies at a specified forward rate at a specified future date.

Forward exchange rate—A forward exchange rate is a specified exchange rate at a specified future date.

Functional currency—The functional currency is the currency of the primary economic environment in which the company normally operates.

Harmonization—Harmonization is the reduction in the differences in accounting standards and disclosure requirements among countries.

Hedging—Hedging is buying or selling foreign currency for delivery on the same date that payment denominated in foreign currency is due.

International Accounting Standards Committee—The International Accounting Standards Committee is an international body that was founded to formulate accounting standards to be observed throughout the world and to persuade the business communities and governments of all countries to secure acceptance of and compliance with these standards.

Multinational corporation—A multinational corporation is a company that has branches, divisions, or subsidiaries in more than one country.

Spot rate—The spot rate is the rate of exchange between two currencies for immediate delivery.

Standardization—Standardization is the elimination of differences in accounting standards and disclosure requirements among countries.

QUESTIONS

1. What is a multinational corporation?

2. Differentiate between an exchange rate computed directly and an exchange rate computed indirectly. Show the difference for the austral for May 11, 1990, and demonstrate the relationship between the two rates.

3. Differentiate among fixed exchange rates, floating exchange rates, and multiple exchange rates.

4. How do American exports affect the demand for the U.S. dollar?

5. How do American imports affect the demand for the U.S dollar?

6. What is the foreign exchange market?

7. Differentiate between the spot and forward exchange markets.

8. Describe how an exchange loss can occur when an American company contracts to purchase goods from an Italian company and then pays for the goods in thirty days.

9. How do speculators try to make a profit in the forward exchange market? What is an important advantage of the forward market for a speculator?

10. Under what circumstances is a foreign transaction considered to be a foreign currency transaction?

11. How are the financial statements affected if the end of the accounting period occurs between the transaction date for a foreign currency transaction and the payment date? Why?

12. Why is an exchange gain or loss arising from a purchase not accounted for as part of the purchase?

13. How may a company avoid exchange gains and losses on foreign currency transactions?

14. Describe how hedging can offset an exchange gain or loss.

15. Why is the translation of foreign currency financial statements necessary?

16. What steps are needed for translating a foreign entity's financial statements by a U.S. company?

17. How do translation adjustments affect the financial statements? Why?

18. Differentiate between standardization and harmonization of accounting principles. Why might these be desirable?

19. What impediments exist in the efforts to harmonize accounting standards?

20. What is the International Accounting Standards Committee? What other organizations have made efforts toward harmonizing accounting standards and disclosure requirements?

EXERCISES

21. For which currencies had the U.S. dollar become stronger between February 5, 1987, and May 11, 1990?

22. For which currencies had the U.S. dollar become weaker between February 5, 1987, and May 11, 1990?

23. Kate Company, located in the United States, purchases merchandise from a company located in Japan. At the time of the transaction, the spot rate is $0.006542 per yen. Payment is due in thirty days. The invoice price is 50,000 yen. The spot rate at the time of payment is $0.006551. Kate Company uses a periodic inventory method. Prepare the necessary journal entries for Kate Company for the purchase and payment.

24. Alex Company, located in the United States, purchases merchandise from a company located in Hong Kong. At the time of the transaction, the spot rate is $0.12837 per Hong Kong dollar. Payment is due in thirty days. The invoice price is 30,000 Hong Kong dollars. The spot rate at the time of payment is $0.12803. Alex Company uses a perpetual inventory method. Prepare the necessary journal entries for Alex Company for the purchase and payment.

25. Kelly Company, located in the United States, sells merchandise to a company located in Canada. At the time of the transaction, the spot rate is $0.8503 per Canadian dollar. Payment is due in thirty days. The invoice price is 20,000 Canadian dollars. The spot rate at the time of payment is $0.8473 per Canadian dollar. Prepare the necessary journal entries for Kelly Company for the sale and receipt of payment.

26. Kelsie Company, located in the United States, sells merchandise to a company located in Belgium. At the time of the transaction, the spot rate is $0.02943 per Belgian franc. Payment is due in thirty days. The invoice price is 60,000 Belgian francs. The spot rate at the time of payment is $0.02997 per Belgian franc. Prepare the necessary journal entries for Kelsie Company for the sale and receipt of payment.

27. Mercy Company, located in the United States, purchases merchandise from a company located in Mexico. At the time of the transaction, the spot rate is $0.0003574 per Mexican peso. Payment is due in thirty days. The invoice price is 300,000 pesos. The spot rate twenty days later on the balance sheet date is $0.0003584 and on the date of payment is $0.0003598. Mercy Company uses a periodic inventory method. Prepare the necessary journal entries for Mercy Company on the transaction date, the balance sheet date, and the payment date.

28. Crystal Company, located in the United States, purchases merchandise from a company located in France. At the time of the transaction, the spot rate is $0.18059 per franc. Payment is due in thirty days. The invoice price is 10,000 francs. The spot rate ten days later on the balance sheet date is $0.18035 and on the date of payment is $0.18040. Crystal Company uses a periodic inventory method. Prepare the necessary journal entries for Crystal Company on the transaction date, the balance sheet date, and the payment date.

29. Anne-Marie Company, located in the United States, sells merchandise to a company located in Germany. At the time of the transaction, the spot rate is $0.6099 per mark. The invoice price is 40,000 marks. The spot rate fifteen days later on the balance sheet date is $0.6103 per mark and on the date of payment is $0.6105 per mark. Prepare the necessary journal entries for Anne-Marie Company on the transaction date, the balance sheet date, and the receipt of payment date.

30. Justin Company, located in the United States, sells merchandise to a company located in England. At the time of the transaction, the spot rate is $1.6775 per pound. The invoice price is 5,000 pounds. The spot rate twenty-five days later on the balance sheet date is $1.6692 per pound and on the date of payment is $1.6684 per pound. Prepare the necessary journal entries for Justin Company on the transaction date, the balance sheet date, and the receipt of payment date.

31. Wenda Company, located in the United States, purchases merchandise from a company located in Hong Kong. At the time of the transaction, the spot rate is $0.1283 per Hong Kong dollar. Payment is due in thirty days. The invoice price is 60,000 Hong Kong dollars. The spot rate at the time of payment is $0.1297. At the time of the transaction, Wenda Company enters into a forward exchange contract to purchase 60,000 Hong Kong dollars at the thirty day forward exchange rate of $0.1285. Compute the exchange gain or loss on the merchandise transaction, the exchange gain or loss on the hedging transaction, and the net exchange gain or loss.

32. Douglas Corporation, located in the United States, has a subsidiary, William Company, that began its operations at the beginning of 19x1. The functional currency of William Company is the Canadian dollar. The functional currency of Douglas Corporation is the U.S. dollar. William Company's balance sheet in Canadian dollars at the beginning of 19x1 is as follows:

Assets
Cash	50,000
Inventories	80,000
Plant assets	170,000
Total assets	300,000

Liabilities and Stockholders' Equity
Long-term debt	200,000
Common stock	100,000
Total liabilities and stockholders' equity	300,000

The exchange rates for 19x1 are as follows:

Beginning of the year	$0.75 per Canadian dollar
End of the year	0.85 per Canadian dollar
Weighted average	0.80 per Canadian dollar

The income statement in Canadian dollars for William Company for 19x1 is as follows:

Sales		700,000
Cost of goods sold	500,000	
Operating expenses (including depreciation expense of 17,000)	147,000	647,000
Net income		53,000

The balance sheet for William Company in Canadian dollars at the end of 19x1 is as follows:

Assets
Cash	30,000
Accounts receivable	110,000
Inventories	100,000
Plant assets, net	153,000
Total assets	393,000

Liabilities and Stockholders' Equity
Accounts payable	40,000
Long-term debt	200,000
Common stock	100,000
Retained earnings	53,000
Total liabilities and stockholders' equity	393,000

Translate the financial statements of William Company into U.S. dollars.

33. Dan Corporation, located in the United States, has a subsidiary, Jeff Company, that began its operations at the beginning of 19x1. The functional currency of Jeff Company is the French franc. The functional currency of Dan Corporation is the U.S. dollar. Comparative balance sheets at the beginning and end of 19x1 for Jeff Company in francs are as follows:

	End of 19x1	Beginning of 19x1
Assets		
Cash	90,000	110,000
Accounts receivable	320,000	
Inventories	350,000	200,000
Plant assets	450,000	500,000
Total assets	1,210,000	810,000
Liabilities and Stockholders' Equity		
Accounts payable	190,000	90,000
Long-term debt	410,000	410,000
Common stock	310,000	310,000
Retained earnings	300,000	
Total liabilities and stockholders' equity	1,210,000	810,000

The income statement in francs for Jeff Company for 19x1 is as follows:

Sales		2,800,000
Cost of goods sold	1,600,000	
Operating expenses (including depreciation expense of 50,000)	700,000	2,300,000
Net income		500,000

Dividends of 200,000 francs were declared and paid during November. The exchange rates for 19x1 are as follows:

Beginning of the year	$0.1806 per franc
November	0.1755 per franc
End of the year	0.1752 per franc
Weighted average	0.1780 per franc

Translate the financial statements of Jeff Company into U.S. dollars.

PROBLEMS

34. The Kathy Company, located in the United States, had the following transactions relating to imports during 19x1:

Feb. 5   Purchased merchandise from a company located in Germany. At the time of the transaction, the spot rate was $0.6103 per mark. The invoice price was 70,000 marks. A periodic inventory method is used.

Apr. 9   Purchased merchandise from a company located in Japan. At the time of the transaction, the spot rate was $0.00655 per yen. The invoice price was 100,000 yen.

May 3   Paid for the merchandise purchased on February 5. The spot rate on this date was $0.6114 per mark.

9   Paid for the merchandise purchased on April 9. The spot rate on this date was $0.00672 per yen.

Required:

Prepare the necessary journal entries to record the above transactions.

35. The Mayda Company, located in the United States, had the following transactions relating to imports during 19x1:

Mar. 4   Purchased merchandise from a company located in England. At the time of the transaction, the spot rate was $1.6805 per pound. The invoice price was 20,000 pounds. A perpetual inventory method is used.

Apr. 1   Purchased merchandise from a company located in Belgium. At the time of the transaction, the spot rate was $0.02995 per franc. The invoice price was 60,000 francs.

4   Paid for the merchandise purchased on March 4. The spot rate on this date was $1.6245 per pound.

May 1   Paid for the merchandise purchased on April 1. The spot rate on this date was $0.03002 per franc.

Required:

Prepare the necessary journal entries to record the above transactions.

36. The Magnolia Company, located in the United States, had the following transactions relating to exports during 19x1:

May	2	Sold merchandise to a company located in China. At the time of the transaction, the spot rate was $0.2121 per yuen. The invoice price was 10,000 yuens.
	29	Sold merchandise to a company located in Italy. At the time of the transaction, the spot rate was $0.00835 per lira. The invoice price was 40,000 liras.
June	2	Received payment for the merchandise sold on May 2. The spot rate on this date was $0.2154 per yuen.
	29	Received payment for the merchandise sold on May 29. The spot rate on this date was $0.00886 per lira.

Required:

Prepare the necessary journal entries to record the above transactions.

37. The Earl Company, located in the United States, had the following transactions relating to exports during 19x1:

June	3	Sold merchandise to a company located in Mexico. At the time of the transaction, the spot rate was $0.00036 per peso. The invoice price was 200,000 pesos.
	19	Sold merchandise to a company located in Argentina. At the time of the transaction, the spot rate was $0.00021 per austral. The invoice price was 500,000 australs.
July	3	Received payment for the merchandise sold on June 3. The spot rate on this date was $0.00026 per peso.
	19	Received payment for the merchandise sold on June 19. The spot rate on this date was $0.00027 per austral.

Required:

Prepare the necessary journal entries to record the above transactions.

38. The Boomer Company, located in the United States, had the following foreign currency transactions during 19x1:

   Mar. 5 Purchased merchandise from a company located in England. At the time of the transaction, the spot rate was $1.6792 per pound. The invoice price was 50,000 pounds. A periodic inventory method is used.
        28 Purchased merchandise from a company located in Japan. At the time of the transaction, the spot rate was $0.006481 per yen. The invoice price was 100,000 yen.
   Apr. 5 Paid for the merchandise purchased on March 5. The spot rate on this date was $1.6753 per pound.
        17 Sold merchandise to a company located in France. At the time of the transaction, the spot rate was $0.18004 per franc. The invoice price was 40,000 francs.
        28 Paid for the merchandise purchased on March 28. The spot rate on this date was $0.006572 per yen.
   May 17 Received payment for the merchandise sold on April 17. The spot rate on this date was $0.18044 per franc.

   Required:

   Prepare the necessary journal entries to record the above transactions.

39. The Aerin Company, located in the United States, had the following foreign currency transactions during 19x1:

   Sept. 2 Purchased merchandise from a company located in Mexico. At the time of the transaction, the spot rate was $0.000362 per peso. The invoice price was 300,000 pesos. A periodic inventory method is used.
         8 Sold merchandise to a company located in Canada. At the time of the transaction, the spot rate was $0.8581 per Canadian dollar. The invoice price was 60,000 Canadian dollars.
        30 Sold merchandise to a company located in Belgium. At the time of the transaction, the spot rate was $0.02955 per Belgian franc. The invoice price was 80,000 francs.
   Oct. 2 Paid for the merchandise purchased on September 2. The spot rate on this date was $0.000384 per peso.
         8 Received payment for the merchandise sold on September 8. The spot rate on this date was $0.8622 per Canadian dollar.
        30 Received payment for the merchandise sold on September 30. The spot rate on this date was $0.02903 per Belgian franc.

   Required:

   Prepare the necessary journal entries to record the above transactions.

40. The Mary Company, located in the United States, closes its accounting period on June 30. The company had the following foreign currency transactions during 19x1:

June 4   Purchased merchandise from a company located in Japan. At the time of the transaction, the spot rate was $0.006522 per yen. The invoice price was 120,000 yen. A periodic inventory method is used.

28   Sold merchandise to a company located in England. At the time of the transaction, the spot rate was $1.6754 per pound. The invoice price was 10,000 pounds.

30   The spot rates on this date were $0.006483 per yen and $1.6772 per pound.

July 3   Paid for the merchandise purchased on June 4. The spot rate on this date was $0.006477 per yen.

28   Received payment for the merchandise sold on June 28. The spot rate on this date was $1.6769 per pound.

Required:

Prepare the necessary journal entries to record the above transactions and any necessary adjusting entries for June 30.

41. The Red Company, located in the United States, closes its accounting period on August 31. The company had the following foreign currency transactions during 19x1:

Aug. 1   Purchased merchandise from a company located in Canada. At the time of the transaction, the spot rate was $0.8524 per Canadian dollar. The invoice price was 20,000 Canadian dollars. A periodic inventory method is used.

19   Purchased merchandise from a company located in England. At the time of the transaction, the spot rate was $1.6599 per pound. The invoice price was 8,000 pounds.

22   Sold merchandise to a company located in Italy. At the time of the transaction, the spot rate was $0.008412 per lira. The invoice price was 120,000 liras.

31   The spot rates on this date were $0.8817 per Canadian dollar, $1.6423 per pound, and $1.008564 per lira.

Sept. 1   Paid for the merchandise purchased on August 1. The spot rate on this date was $0.8726 per Canadian dollar.

19   Paid for the merchandise purchased on August 19. The spot rate on this date was $1.6498 per pound.

22   Received payment for the merchandise sold on August 22. The spot rate on this date was $0.008568 per lira.

Required:

Prepare the necessary journal entries to record the above transactions and any necessary adjusting entries for August 31.

42. The Carole Company, located in the United States, closes its accounting period on April 30 The company had the following foreign currency transactions during 19x1:

Apr. 2	Purchased merchandise from a company located in Hong Kong. At the time of the transaction, the spot rate was $0.12845 per Hong Kong dollar. The invoice price was 30,000 Hong Kong dollars. A periodic inventory method is used.
11	Sold merchandise to a company located in Japan. At the time of the transaction, the spot rate was $0.006421 per yen. The invoice price was 200,000 yen.
21	Sold merchandise to a company located in China. At the time of the transaction, the spot rate was $0.2133 per yuen. The invoice price was 50,000 yuen
30	The spot rates on this date were $0.12991 per Hong Kong dollar, $0.006767 per yen, and $0.2006 per yuen.
May 2	Paid for the merchandise purchased on April 2. The spot rate on this date was $0.12794 per Hong Kong dollar.
11	Received payment for the merchandise sold on May 11. The spot rate on this date was $0.006744 per yen.
21	Received payment for the merchandise sold on April 21. The spot rate on this date was $0.2027 per yuen.

Required:

Prepare the necessary journal entries to record the above transactions and any necessary adjusting entries for April 30.

43. The Renaissance Company, located in the United States, closes its accounting period on October 31. The U.S. dollar equivalent spot exchange rates for four countries on various dates are as follows:

	Date of Purchase or Sale	October 31	Date of Payment
Belgian franc	$0.02947	$0.02875	$0.02898
British pound	1.6783	1.6744	1.6759
French franc	0.18062	0.18069	0.18075
Italian lira	0.00829	0.00808	0.00792

The company uses a periodic inventory method. The following foreign currency transactions occurred during 19x1:

Oct.	6	Sold merchandise to a company located in Belgium for 60,000 francs.
	10	Purchased merchandise from a company located in England for 10,000 pounds.
	23	Sold merchandise to a company located in France for 40,000 francs.
	30	Purchased merchandise from a company located in Italy for 100,000 liras.
Nov.	6	Received payment for the merchandise sold on October 6.
	10	Paid for the merchandise purchased on October 10.
	23	Received payment for the merchandise sold on October 23.
	30	Paid for the merchandise purchased on October 30.

Required:

Prepare the necessary journal entries to record the above transactions and any necessary adjusting entries for October 31.

44. Bollero Company, a subsidiary of Jessica Corporation, began operations at the beginning of 19x1. The functional currency of Bollero Company is the Italian lira; the functional currency of Jessica Corporation is the U.S. dollar. The balance sheet for Bollero Company on January 1, 19x1, showed land for 80,000 liras; buildings for 190,000 liras; machinery for 50,000 liras; long-term debt for 100,000 liras; and common stock for 220,000 liras. A combined statement of income and retained earnings in liras for Bollero Company for 19x1 is as follows:

Sales		600,000
Cost of goods sold	400,000	
Operating expenses (including depreciation expense of 24,000)	110,000	510,000
Net income		90,000
Beginning retained earnings		0
Dividends		25,000
Ending retained earnings		65,000

The balance sheet for Bollero Company in liras on December 31, 19x1, is as follows:

Assets:

Cash	19,000
Accounts receivable	50,000
Inventories	60,000
Land	80,000
Buildings—net	171,000
Machinery—net	45,000
Total assets	425,000

Liabilities and Stockholders' Equity:

Accounts payable	30,000
Long-term debt	100,000
Common stock	230,000
Retained earnings	65,000
Total liabilities and stockholders' equity	425,000

Additional common stock (10,000 liras) was issued in June; dividends were declared and paid in November. The exchange rates for 19x1 are as follows:

Beginning of the year	$0.008152 per lira
June	0.008113 per lira
November	0.008296 per lira
End of the year	0.008344 per lira
Weighted average	0.008301 per lira

Required:

Translate the financial statements of Bollero Company into U.S. dollars.

45. Golda Corporation, located in the United States, has a subsidiary, Nova Company, that began its operations at the beginning of 19x1. The functional currency of Nova Company is the British pound; the functional currency of Golda Corporation is the U.S. dollar. Nova Company had cash of 450,000 pounds and common stock of 450,000 pounds on January 1, 19x1. At the beginning of February, Nova Company purchased land for 160,000 pounds and buildings for 110,000 pounds in exchange for a three-year note payable. Revenue for 19x1 was 710,000 pounds. Operating expenses, including depreciation of 10,000 pounds, were 500,000 pounds. The balance sheet for Nova Company in pounds at the end of 19x1 is as follows:

Assets:
Cash	210,000
Accounts receivable	340,000
Land	200,000
Buildings—net	100,000
Total assets	850,000

Liabilities and Stockholders' Equity:
Accounts payable	20,000
Long-term debt	310,000
Common stock	450,000
Retained earnings	70,000
Total liabilities and stockholders' equity	850,000

Additional land was purchased in March in exchange for a three-year note payable for 40,000 pounds. Dividends of 140,000 pounds were declared and paid in October. The exchange rates for 19x1 are as follows:

Beginning of the year	$1.6801 per pound
February	1.6822 per pound
March	1.6834 per pound
October	1.6809 per pound
End of the year	1.6775 per pound
Weighted average	1.6800 per pound

Required:

Translate the financial statements of Nova Company into U.S. dollars.

Refer to the Annual Report included in the front of the text.

46. In what geographical areas does the company operate?

47. In which geographic area outside of the United States did the company have the most sales in the most recent year?

48. By how much did the currency translation adjustment increase or decrease from the previous year to the current year?

49. What was the reason for the change in the currency translation adjustment?

Chapter 14 discusses the accounting and disclosures relating to pensions, other postretirement benefits, and leases and examines the disclosures included as a part of comprehensive financial reports. Studying this chapter should enable you to:

1. Describe the basic types of postretirement benefits.
2. Explain the basic characteristics of pension plans.
3. Describe the disclosures relating to pension plans.
4. Describe the differences between pension plans and health care plans.
5. Explain the difference between a capital lease and an operating lease.
6. Explain the use of footnotes in financial disclosure.
7. Describe the independent auditor's report and its uses and limitations.
8. Discuss interim financial reporting.
9. Describe the reporting for segments of a business.
10. Explain the purpose and content of management's discussion and analysis.

14

Accounting for Pensions, Postretirement Benefits, and Leases and Analysis of Other Disclosures

INTRODUCTION

In the previous chapters, we have discussed and examined a number of the basic principles involved in the preparation of financial reports. In the first section of this chapter, we will discuss accounting and disclosures relating to pensions, other postretirement benefits and leases. In the second part of this chapter, we will examine several disclosures included as a part of comprehensive financial reports in addition to the basic financial statements discussed in previous chapters. We will review the following types of disclosures:

1. Accounting policy disclosures.
2. Footnote and other information disclosures.
3. Auditor's report.
4. Interim reports.
5. Reporting for segments of a business.
6. Management's discussion and analysis.

PART I: PENSIONS, POSTRETIREMENT BENEFITS, AND LEASES

This section of the chapter discusses three topics relating to long-term commitments. The FASB's pronouncements dealing with pensions and other postretirement benefits are helpful to users of financial statements to understand the magnitude of these previously unrecognized liabilities. The FASB's pronouncement on leases differentiates a lease that is in substance a purchase from a lease that is merely a rental. Different accounting requirements apply to each.

PENSIONS AND OTHER POSTRETIREMENT BENEFITS

Most large companies and many smaller companies promise benefits to their employees after retirement. These benefits to be paid in the future are earned by the employees as they provide services to their companies. The basic types of postretirement benefits are:

1. *Pension benefits*—monthly payments to employees after retirement.
2. *Other postretirement benefits*—medical costs, dental costs, life insurance, and other benefits.

These costs can be quite substantial. For example, pension costs and other postretirement benefit costs totalled over $1 billion in 1992.

Pensions

A pension plan is a contract between a company and its employees in which the company agrees to provide benefits to the employees on their retirement. If the plan requires periodic contributions by the employee, it is called a contributory plan; if the company assumes the full cost of the plan, it is called a noncontributory plan. Pension benefits are usually paid monthly to the employees after retirement.

Pension plans create substantial long-term financial obligations. Almost all major corporations have pension plans. Most of these are noncontributory plans. Most plans allow for retirement before an employee becomes sixty-five years of age. Some plans allow employees who have at least thirty years of services to retire at age fifty-five with no reduction in benefits.

Accounting for a pension plan requires the measurement of both the current and future costs of the plan and the allocation of these costs to the appropriate accounting periods. The cost of a pension plan to a company is a function of many events (e.g., employee turnover and retirement age). The assumptions about these factors are called actuarial assumptions and have a significant impact on the amount of pension cost recognized for accounting purposes.

A pension plan has several characteristics. The company establishes the pension plan and specifies the eligibility requirements, retirement ages, amounts of retirement benefits, the method and amounts of funding, any employee contributions, and the pension plan funding agent (usually a bank or an insurance company). The company periodically transfers cash to the funding agent. These funds are invested to earn income. The funding agent makes payments to those retirees who are entitled to receive benefits.

Benefits may be vested or nonvested. Vested benefits are benefits that the employees have earned and will receive even if they leave the company. An employee must usually work for a company for a specified number of years before the pension benefits become vested.

There are two types of benefit formulas for determining retirement benefits. A defined benefit pension plan specifies the amount of the pension benefits to be received during retirement. The amount of the benefits are based on such factors as level of compensation and years of employment. A defined contribution plan specifies the amount of the periodic contributions, but the amount of the benefits are not defined.

For accounting purposes, a defined contribution plan presents far fewer problems than does a defined benefit plan. In a defined contribution plan, the pension cost for a period is equal to the amount that the company must contribute for that period. In a defined benefit plan, the pension cost is based on many estimates and assumptions. Consequently, the accounting is much more complicated.

Under a defined benefit pension plan, the pension cost for a period is a function of the following components:

1. *Service cost*—the present value of the benefits earned by employees for the current period of service.

2. *Interest cost*—a cost to reflect the increase in the pension obligation due to the passage of time.

3. *Return on plan assets*—earnings on the pension fund are used to satisfy the pension obligation and therefore reduce the pension cost.

4. *Net amortization*—an allocation over several periods of costs associated with changes in the pension obligation (e.g., amendments to the pension plan to increase benefits).

The accounting requirements, which are detailed in *FASB Statement No. 87*, "Employers' Accounting for Pensions," are very complex and a detailed discussion of them is beyond the scope of this text.

The amounts that are funded each period are not necessarily equal to the amounts charged to pension cost. If contributions are less than pension cost, a pension liability is recorded.

Pension cost	X	
Cash		X
Pension liability		X

If contributions exceed pension cost, a prepaid pension cost is recorded.

Pension cost	X	
Prepaid pension cost	X	
Cash		X

At the end of each period, a reconciliation between the funded status of a company's pension plans and the prepaid pension cost or pension liability recognized on the balance sheet must be disclosed. The funded status of the plan is the difference between the company's obligation for all future retirement benefits to be paid—called the projected benefit obligation—and the fair value of the assets of the pension plan. If the obligation exceeds the fair value of plan assets, the plan is underfunded; if the fair value of plan assets exceeds the obligation, the plan is overfunded.

The funded status of the plan does not necessarily equal the prepaid pension cost or pension liability recognized on the balance sheet, because there are unrecognized pension elements. For example, if pension benefits are increased due to a plan amendment, the increase in the obligation—called a prior service cost—is not recognized immediately, but instead is allocated to pension cost over time (part of the net amortization component of pension cost). To illustrate the reconciliation, assume the projected benefit obligation is $100, the fair value of the plan assets is $60, and there is a prior service cost of $25. Then the unfunded obligation is $40 ($100 − $60), but the pension liability recognized on the balance sheet is $15 ($40 − $25).

Projected benefit obligation	($100)
Fair value of plan assets	60
Unfunded obligation	($ 40)
Unrecognized prior service cost	25
Pension liability on balance sheet	($ 15)

Illustration 1 presents an example of a footnote disclosing pension cost and the reconciliation between the funded status of the plan and the prepaid pension cost recognized on the balance sheet.

Other Postretirement Benefits

Spending for health care is high and is increasing. The cost for health care benefits is exceeding the cost of retirement benefits. Although this section concentrates on health care benefits, other postretirement benefits also include life insurance, housing subsidies, and legal services.

The cost of private insurance to cover health care benefits continues to rise. Reasons for this increase include the following:

1. There are more older people living in the U.S. and people are living longer.
2. Increased prices for medical services.
3. Cost shifting of medical charges due to limitations on prices for patients covered by Medicare and Medicaid and to providing services for uninsured people.
4. Significant improvements in medical technology.
5. High utilization of medical services.
6. Such reactions to the wave of medical malpractice suits as performing unnecessary operations and requesting high-priced medical tests at hospitals.

Although the portion of large companies that offer health care benefits to retirees remained steady at 72 percent between 1991 and 1992, the portion of small and medium-sized companies offering benefits declined to 37 percent. The primary reason for these cutbacks is steeply rising medical costs.

Illustration 1
Example of Pensions Footnote

1991 Annual Report
Eagle-Picher Industries, Inc.

L. Retirement Plans

Employees of the Company and its subsidiaries are covered by various pension and profit sharing retirement plans. The cost of providing retirement benefits was $2,015,000 in 1991, $1,310,000 in 1990 and $2,110,000 in 1989. During 1990, the Company settled three separate pension plans in connection with the divestiture of certain operations. The gain from these settlements amounted to approximately $350,000.

The plan benefits for salaried employees are primarily based on employees' highest five consecutive years earnings during the last ten years of employment. Hourly plan benefits are based on a dollar unit multiplied by the number of service years.

Net periodic pension expense for the Company's defined benefit plans included the following components:

	(In thousands of dollars)		
	1991	1990	1989
Service cost—benefits earned during the period	$ 3,329	$ 3,573	$ 3,265
Interest cost on projected benefit obligation	11,533	10,795	10,186
Actual (gain) loss on plan assets	(29,360)	4,902	(26,264)
Net amortization and deferral	15,763	(18,580)	13,951
Net periodic pension expense	$ 1,265	$ 690	$ 1,138

The plans' assets consist primarily of listed equity securities and publicly traded notes and bonds. The actual return (loss) on assets was 18.8% in 1991, (3.1%) in 1990 and 18.4% in 1989.

The following table sets forth the plans' funded status and amounts recognized in the Company's Consolidated Balance Sheet at November 30:

	(In thousands of dollars)	
	1991	1990
Actuarial present value of benefit obligations:		
Vested benefit obligation	$(120,643)	$(104,802)
Accumulated benefit obligation	$(126,307)	$(112,119)
Projected benefit obligation	$(145,137)	$(124,507)
Plan assets at fair value	166,418	146,300
Projected benefit obligation less than plan assets	21,281	21,793
Unrecognized net gain	(4,309)	(3,759)
Unrecognized prior service cost	4,492	5,033
Unrecognized net asset at November 30	(13,926)	(15,111)
Prepaid pension cost recognized in consolidated balance sheet	$ 7,538	$ 7,956

The discount rate and weighted average rate of increase in future compensation levels used in determining the actuarial present value of the projected benefit obligation were 8.5% and 6.2%, and 9.0% and 6.0%, respectively, at November 30, 1991 and 1990, respectively. The expected long-term rate of return on assets was 9.0% and 8.0% during 1991 and 1990, respectively.

The Company's funding policy is to fund amounts on an actuarial basis to provide for current and future benefits in accordance with the funding guidelines of ERISA.

Prior to the issuance of *FASB Statement No. 106*, "Employers' Accounting for Postretirement Benefits Other than Pensions," most companies were accounting for postretirement benefits on a pay-as-you-go basis. The cost recognized for the period was equal to the cash outlay for insurance premiums or claims paid. This practice resulted in a significant understatement of the financial effects of the promises to provide these benefits.

A postretirement benefit plan is a deferred compensation arrangement in which a company promises to provide future benefits to employees in exchange for current services. *FASB Statement No. 106* requires the cost of providing these benefits to be recognized over the employees' service periods.

The requirements for accounting for other postretirement benefits are basically the same as or similar to those for accounting for pensions. Differences in accounting result from differences between the two types of plans.

Health care benefits are generally paid without limitation, have great variability, and are paid as needed. On the other hand, pension benefits are better defined and are usually paid monthly without regard to need. Health care benefits are payable to not only the retiree but also the retiree's spouse and dependents; pension benefits are usually payable to the retiree only. While pension plans are generally funded, other postretirement benefit plans generally are not.

Pension benefits usually increase the longer an employee works for the company. For example, an employee may receive a specified percentage of average annual pay for each year of service. But the amount of health care benefits received may have nothing to do with years of service. Once the employee has worked for a long enough period to meet the plan's eligibility requirements, the employee is entitled to receive full benefits whether or not he/she works for a longer period of time.

Illustration 2 presents an example of a footnote disclosing postretirement benefit cost and the reconciliation between the funded status of the plan and the liability (accrued postretirement benefit cost) recognized on the balance sheet. The obligation for future postretirement benefits to be paid is called the accumulated postretirement benefit obligation. There is no return on assets for the plan for health care benefits, because that plan is not funded. On the other hand, the plan for life insurance benefits is partially funded; consequently, there is a return on assets included in postretirement benefit cost.

LEASES

A lease is a contract between the owner of an asset (the lessor) and the user of the asset (the lessee). The contract gives the lessee the right to use the asset for a specified period of time in return for stipulated rental payments. A lease may be a simple, short-term rental (such as the use of an Alamo rental car for two days) or a longer, more complex agreement (such as a K-Mart store leasing its retail premises). Acquiring the use of assets through lease agreements has grown considerably. Commonly leased assets include airplanes, computers, railroad equipment, and warehouses.

Illustration 2
Example of Postretirement Benefits Footnote

1991 Annual Report
Phillips Petroleum Company

Other Postretirement Plans

Company plans provide certain health care and life insurance benefits for substantially all retired U.S. employees. The health care plan is contributory while the life insurance plan is noncontributory. Retirees covered by the health care plan essentially pay their own way, except those persons who retired prior to March 1986 and early retirees not yet eligible for Medicare. The company's policy is to fund the health care plan in amounts determined at the company's discretion and the life insurance plan based on actuarial determinations.

Net postretirement benefit cost for 1991 was as follows:

	Millions of Dollars	
	Health	Life
Service cost	$1	1
Interest cost	7	4
Return on assets		
Actual	—	(4)
Deferred gains	—	1
	$8	2

The following table presents the funded status of the plans and a reconciliation with accrued postretirement benefit cost at the beginning and end of 1991:

The health care cost trend rate is assumed to decrease gradually from 10 percent in 1991 and 1992 to 6 percent in 2003 and thereafter. Increasing the assumed health care cost trend rate by one percentage point in each year would increase the APBO at January 1 and December 31, 1991, by $9 and $12 million, respectively, and the aggregate of the service and interest cost components by $1 million.

The primary accounting issue is whether the lease is merely a rental or the lease gives rise to property rights to the lessee. Does the least contract represent in substance a financing arrangement for the purchase of the asset and thereby transfers many of the benefits and risks of ownership to the lessee? If so, then the lease should be treated as an acquisition; the asset and the obligation should be recognized by the lessee on the balance sheet. If not, the lease should be treated as a rental; the asset should continue to be recognized by the lessor.

In *FASB Statement No. 13*, "Accounting for Leases," the criteria for treating a lease as in substance a purchase of the asset were stated. If any one of the following conditions are met at the inception of the lease, the lessee should record the transaction as a capital lease (in substance an acquisition of the asset); otherwise, the lessee should record the transaction as an operating lease (a rental of the asset):

1. The lease transfers ownership by the end of the lease term.
2. The lease contains a bargain purchase option (i.e., the lessee has the option to purchase the asset at a sufficiently low price compared to its expected fair value when the option becomes exercisable).
3. The least term is at least 75 percent of the asset's estimated economic life.
4. The present value of the minimum lease payments at the beginning of the lease is at least 90 percent of the fair value of the asset at that time.

The lessee usually wants to classify a lease as an operating lease. No liability is recognized on its balance sheet. There is not any negative impact on working capital, the current ratio, the acid-test ratio, or the debt-to-equity ratio.

To illustrate the basic accounting differences between a lease that is treated as an acquisition (a capital lease) and a lease that is treated as a rental (an operating lease), assume that on January 1, 19x1 a company leases a machine for three years at an annual rental of $20,000. Each payment is due at the end of the year. The estimated useful life of the machine is five years and its estimated salvage value is zero. The lessee can borrow money at an interest rate of 10 percent.

The first three criteria for capitalizing the lease are not met—there is no transfer of ownership or bargain purchase option and the lease term is only 60 percent of the asset's five-year life. The classification depends on the fourth criterion (the 90% test). The present value of the minimum lease payments is $49,738.[1] If the fair value of the asset is below $55,264.44, the transaction is a capital lease; otherwise, it is an operating lease.

---

[1] The present value factor for an annuity of three payments at a 10 percent interest rate is 2.4869. The present value of the three $20,000 payments is $20,000 x 2.4869 = $49,738.

The journal entries for the lessee for 19x1 if the lease is considered to be an acquisition are as follows:

Jan.	1	Capitalized lease	49,738	
		Liability for capitalized lease		49,738
Dec.	31	Interest expense	4,974	
		Liability for capitalized lease	15,026	
		Cash		20,000
		Depreciation expense	16,579	
		Accumulated depreciation		16,579

Interest expense (rounded to the nearest dollar) is computed by multiplying the lease liability balance at the beginning of the period by 10 percent. Therefore, $4,974 is equal to $49,738 multiplied by 10 percent.

In addition, the lessee must record depreciation on the machine. Assume that the lessee records depreciation (rounded to the nearest dollar) over the three-year term of the lease. Each year the amount of straight-line depreciation is $49,738 ÷ 3 = $16,579 (rounded to the nearest dollar).

If instead the lease is treated as a rental, the journal entry at the end of the year is as follows:

Rent expense	20,000	
Cash		20,000

There is no journal entry to record at the beginning of the year.

The differences on the income statement for 19x1 between recording the transaction as a capital lease or as an operating lease are as follows;

	Lease considered to be	
	An Acquisition	A Rental
Interest expense	$ 4,974	–
Depreciation expense	16,579	–
Rent expense	–	$ 20,000

The total charges are equal over the three-year term of the lease; however, the charges are higher in the earlier years and lower in the later one for a capital lease. Therefore, capitalizing a lease rather than considering the transaction to be a rental results in lower income in the early years as well as a higher debt-to-equity ratio due to recognizing the liability for the payments to be made.

A lessee must disclose its required lease payments for each of the five succeeding years for both capital leases and operating leases. An example of a note to the financial statements by a lessee is presented in Illustration 3.

> **Illustration 3**
> *Example of Leases Footnote*
>
> **1991 Annual Report**
> *PPG Industries, Inc.*
>
> **8. Lease Arrangements and Rent Expense**
>
> We use assets leased under arrangements that qualify as capital leases. The amortization of these leases is included in depreciation expense in the Statement of Earnings. Leases that do not qualify as capital leases are classified as operating leases. Rental expense for all operating leases was $58.5 million in 1991, $57.4 million in 1990 and $55.1 million in 1989.
>
> The following schedule shows minimum lease commitments outstanding at Dec. 31, 1991, for capital leases and for operating leases that have initial or remaining lease terms in excess of one year.
>
> | *(Millions)* | Capital Leases | Operating Leases |
> |---|---|---|
> | Year ending December 31 | | |
> | 1992 | $ 8.5 | $23.2 |
> | 1993 | 6.1 | 18.4 |
> | 1994 | 4.7 | 15.8 |
> | 1995 | 2.9 | 13.3 |
> | 1996 | 2.9 | 9.7 |
> | After 1996 | 44.7 | 23.1 |
> | Total minimum lease payments | 69.8 | $103.5 |
> | Less estimated executory costs | (.5) | |
> | Net minimum lease payments | 69.3 | |
> | Less amount representing interest | (24.8) | |
> | **Present value of net minimum lease payments** | $44.5 | |

PART II: ANALYSIS OF OTHER DISCLOSURES

Management of each organization has considerable flexibility in selecting from alternative generally accepted accounting methods. The accounting methods selected by a firm can significantly affect the determination of financial position, changes in financial position, and results of operations. A hypothetical example of the effects of alternative accounting methods is provided in Illustration 4. In this example, earnings per share could range from $1 to $1.95, depending on accounting methods, given one set of underlying economic circumstances. Therefore, the usefulness of the financial data will be enhanced if disclosure includes information regarding the methods used by the firm. When financial statements are supplemented by such information, the financial data of different firms can be adjusted for differing accounting alternatives to make them comparable.

Illustration 4
Effects of Alternative Generally Accepted Accounting Principles (with identical economics events)

	A Company	B Company
Sales revenues—net	$10,000,000	$10,000,000
Expenses:		
Cost of goods sold[1]	$ 6,000,000	$ 5,600,000
Depreciation[2]	400,000	300,000
Pension and post retirement costs[3]	200,000	50,000
Salaries and bonuses[4]	400,000	200,000
Miscellaneous expense	2,000,000	2,000,000
Total expenses	$ 9,000,000	$ 8,150,000
Income before taxes	$ 1,000,000	$ 1,850,000
Income tax expense	500,000	875,000
Net income	$ 500,000	$ 975,000
Earnings per share (500,000 shares outstanding)	$1.00	$1.95

[1] A Company uses the last-in, first-out method for pricing inventories. B Company uses the first-in, first-out method.
[2] A Company uses accelerated depreciation for book and tax purposes. B Company uses the straight-line method for financial accounting and accelerated depreciation for tax purposes.
[3] A Company accrues post retirement health costs while B Company does not.
[4] A Company pays incentive bonuses to officers in cash. B Company grants stock options to officers.

Those accounting principles and methods of applying the principles selected by management are referred to as the *accounting policies* of the entity. *Accounting Principles Board No. Opinion 22*, "Disclosures of Accounting Policies" requires that a "description of all significant accounting policies of the reporting entity should be included as an integral part of the financial statements." Such disclosure should describe the accounting principles followed by the reporting entity and the method of applying those principles that materially affect the determination of financial position and results of operations. In general, the disclosure should identify principles and describe methods peculiar to the industry or other unusual or innovative applications of accounting principles. Accounting policy disclosure would include such items as the basis of consolidation, depreciation methods, amortization of intangibles, inventory cost-flow assumptions, income realization on long term contracts, and recognition of revenue from franchising or leasing operations. The opinion did not require a specific format for accounting policy disclosures, but it did recommend that the disclosures could appear in a separate "summary of significant policies" preceding the notes to the financial statements or as the initial note. In recent years, most large business enterprises have included in their annual reports a separate summary of their significant accounting policies.

FOOTNOTE DISCLOSURE

The information used in financial analysis is basically derived from the financial statements. Normally, however, the statements alone cannot provide all the information needed to understand the subtleties impounded in the financial position and results of operations. Consequently, *footnotes* are an important means of disclosing additional quantitative and qualitative information required for a proper interpretation of the statements. These footnotes are considered an integral part of the financial statements. Although footnote disclosures tend to be detailed and lengthy, they generally represent a vital input to the analysis process. Some of the more important topics covered by footnotes are the following:

1. Significant accounting policies.
2. Changes in accounting principles and retroactive adjustments
3. Contingent assets and liabilities.
4. Description of liabilities astounding and credit agreements.
5. Information regarding stockholders' equity.
6. Long-term commitments.
7. Subsequent events.
8. Other useful disclosures.

These subjects are discussed and illustrated in the following paragraphs.

Significant Accounting Policies

As indicated previously, *APB Opinion No. 22* requires that the accounting principles followed and methods of applying those principles be described within the financial statements, preferably as the initial footnote or as a separate summary preceding the norms to the financial statements. Frequent disclosures concern the consolidation basis, depreciation methods, inter period tax allocation, inventory cost flow assumptions, translation of foreign currencies, and revenue recognition. Illustration 5 shows the accounting policies footnote from a recent annual report.

Illustration 5
Example of Accounting Policies Footnote

1991 Annual Report
Tektronix, Inc.

NOTES TO CONSOLIDATED FINANCIAL STATEMENTS

ACCOUNTING POLICIES

PRINCIPLES OF CONSOLIDATION
The consolidated financial statements include the accounts of Tektronix, Inc. and its wholly owned subsidiaries (the Company). All material intercompany transactions and balances have been eliminated.

CASH AND CASH EQUIVALENTS
Cash and cash equivalents include cash deposits in banks and investments with a maturity of three months or less at the time of purchase.

INVESTMENTS
Investments in joint venture companies, where the Company holds fifty percent or less of their share capital, are stated at the Company's equity in their net assets. Investments in other companies are accounted for on the cost or equity basis depending on the Company's share in their common stock. Investments are included in other long-term assets. All material intercompany income has been eliminated. Goodwill and other intangibles are amortized over a minimal time frame, generally 5 years, to reflect conservative accounting and the general nature of the technology business.

FOREIGN CURRENCIES
Earnings of non-U.S. affiliates are translated into United States dollars at average rates of exchange. Most non-U.S. sales operations' assets and liabilities are translated into dollars at current rates of exchange with changes in exchange rates reflected in the currency adjustment to shareholders' equity. Non-U.S. manufacturing operations, and sales operations in highly inflationary economies, translate monetary assets and liabilities into dollars at current rates of exchange and include the gains and losses in non-operating income, while other assets and liabilities are carried at their historic values. Transaction gains and losses, other than certain hedging transactions, are included in earnings.

INVENTORIES
Inventories are stated at the lower of cost or market. Cost is determined on the last-in, first-out basis (LIFO) for most United States inventories, and on the first-in, first-out basis (FIFO) for all other inventories.

PROPERTY, PLANT AND EQUIPMENT
Property, plant and equipment are stated at their original cost when acquired. Depreciation for financial accounting purposes is generally provided by accelerated methods over the estimated useful lives of the related assets ranging from 10 to 48 years for buildings and 3 to 10 years for equipment. Leasehold improvements are amortized on a straight-line basis over the estimated useful life or the lease term, whichever is less.

REVENUE RECOGNITION
Revenue from product and component sales is recognized at the time of shipment. Service revenue is recognized over the contractual period or as services are provided.

RESEARCH AND DEVELOPMENT EXPENSE
Expenditures for research, development and engineering of products and manufacturing processes are expensed as incurred.

INCOME TAXES
Investment tax credits and foreign tax credits reduce income taxes in the year utilized. Depreciation and amortization for tax reporting is provided over the shortest allowable lives. Tektronix, Inc. and its U.S. subsidiaries file a consolidated federal income tax return. Each U.S. subsidiary records its own tax provision and makes payments to the parent company for taxes due or receives payments for tax benefits utilized.

RECLASSIFICATION
Certain items have been reclassified to conform with the current year's presentation with no effect on previously reported earnings.

PER SHARE AMOUNTS
The earnings per share amounts are based on the weighted average number of shares outstanding during the fiscal year.

FISCAL YEAR
The Company's fiscal year is the 52 or 53 weeks ending the last Saturday in May. Fiscal years 1991, 1990, and 1989 were each 52-week years.

Changes in Accounting Principle

APB Opinion No. 20, "Accounting Changes," concluded that a change in accounting may significantly affect the financial statements, and therefore disclosures should be made to facilitate financial analysis. For most changes in principle, footnotes to the financial statements generally disclose the nature of and justification for the change as well as the effect of the change on net income and the related earnings per share. Footnotes are also frequently used to disclose the effect on income of a change in estimate. The excerpts from actual annual reports, shown in Illustration 6, show both types of footnotes.

Illustration 6
Example of Accounting Changes Footnote

1991 Annual Report
Zenith Electronics Corporation and Crown Central Petroleum Corporation

CHANGE IN PRINCIPLE:

ZENITH ELECTRONICS CORPORATION
Note 2—Accounting change:
As of December 31, 1991, the company changed its inventory costing method for its remaining electronic components and finished goods inventories from LIFO to FIFO. The company believes that the FIFO method is preferable as it will prevent the inventories from potentially being valued in excess of replacement cost, provide a more appropriate and consistent matching of costs against revenues and improve comparability with other electronics manufacturing companies.

The effect of the change in accounting principle was to reduce the net loss reported for 1991 by $1.5 million, or $.05 per share. The change has been applied to prior years by retroactively restating the financial statements. The effect of this restatement was to increase retained earnings as of January 1, 1989 by $4.3 million. The restatement decreased 1990 net income by $1.9 million, or $.07 per share, and increased 1989 net income by $2.0 million, or $.08 per share.

CHANGE IN ESTIMATE:

CROWN CENTRAL PETROLEUM CORPORATION

NOTES TO CONSOLIDATED FINANCIAL STATEMENTS

Note M. Change in Accounting Estimate
In the second quarter of 1987, the Company increased the estimated remaining useful lives of its refinery units based upon available technology and anticipated severity of service. Remaining asset lives which averaged nine years were increased to an average of twenty years. The change in accounting estimate increased the Company's 1988 net income approximately $2,601,000, or $.36 per primary share, ($.26 per fully diluted share). The change in accounting estimate increased 1987 net income by approximately $1,799,000, or $.25 per primary share, ($.18 per fully diluted share).

Contingencies

A contingency involves circumstances shrouded in a considerable degree of uncertainty that may result in gains or losses through potential effects on asset or liability balances. Contingent liabilities arise from current or prospective litigation against the company, guarantees or indebtedness, and tax reassessments. Contingent assets may arise from loss carry forwards, claims for tax refunds, and patent infringement suits against other parties. The usual means of disclosing contingencies is in the footnotes to the financial statements. An example of a footnote disclosure of a contingent liability is shown in Illustration 7.

> **Illustration 7**
> *Example of Contingencies Footnote*
>
> **1991 Annual Report**
> NACCO Industries, Inc. and Subsidiaries
>
> ---
>
> **NOTES TO CONSOLIDATED FINANCIAL STATEMENTS—CONTINUED**
> NACCO Industries, Inc. and Subsidiaries (Tabular Dollars in Thousands, Except Per Share Data)
>
> **NOTE K — CONTINGENCIES**
>
> NACCO and certain subsidiaries are named as defendants to various legal proceedings and claims, which are incidental to their ordinary course of business. Management believes that it has meritorious defenses and will vigorously defend itself in these actions. Although the ultimate disposition of these proceedings is not presently determinable, management does not believe that such proceedings would have a material adverse effect upon the financial condition of the Company.
>
> Hyster-Yale is subject to recourse or repurchase obligations under various financing arrangements for company-owned retail dealerships and certain independently owned retail dealerships at December 31, 1991. Also, certain dealer loans are guaranteed by Hyster and Yale. When Hyster or Yale is the guarantor of the principal amount financed, a security interest is usually maintained in certain assets of parties for whom Hyster or Yale is guaranteeing debt. Total amounts subject to recourse or repurchase obligation at December 31, 1991, were $79.7 million. Losses anticipated under the terms of the recourse or repurchase obligations are not significant and have been provided for in the allowance for doubtful accounts.
>
> Hyster-Yale enters into foreign exchange contracts generally with maturities of 12 months or less. These contracts are with major international financial institutions and, accordingly, the risk of loss from nonperformance by the banks is minimal.

Description of Liabilities Outstanding— Credit Agreements

Typically, footnotes are used to disclose supplementary information regarding the nature of current liabilities, long-term debt, and loan commitments for future loans or extensions of existing loans. In addition, footnote disclosure is often used to describe imputed interest on long-term payables not bearing interest or bearing an interest rate lower than the prevailing rate.

Information Regarding Stockholder's Equity

Companies present some information in the body of the balance sheet regarding the nature of equity securities. However, additional disclosure is usually presented in footnote form. The need for disclosure in connection with the capital structure of a corporation is stated *APB Opinion No. 15,* "Earnings Per Share" as follows:

> ". . . financial statements should include a description in summary form, sufficient to explain the pertinent rights and privileges of the various securities outstanding. Examples of information which should be disclosed are dividend and liquidation preferences, participation rights, call prices and dates, conversion or exercise prices or rates and pertinent dates, sinking fund requirements, unusual voting rights, etc."

This disclosure should also include a description of stock options or purchase plans outstanding. In addition, it is important to disclose the nature of any restrictions such as the amount of retained earnings available for cash dividends.

Long-Term Commitments

Many businesses make various types of commitments for future performance. Such commitments include long-term lease agreements and pension and retirement plans. Some of these events are typically not reflected in their entirety in the accounts, but they are sufficiently important so that disclosures should be made in the notes to financial statements. Certain disclosures are required for pension plans and for long-term leases. Illustration 8 provides a typical footnote disclosure relating to operating type leases.

Illustration 8
Example of Long-Term Commitments Footnote

1991 Annual Report
M.S. Hanna Company and Consolidated Subsidiaries

Lease Commitments

The Company leases manufacturing facilities, warehouses, transportation equipment and data processing and other office equipment. Several manufacturing facilities are leased under industrial development type loan arrangements. Certain of the Company's leases have options to renew, and there are no significant contingent rentals in any of the leases. Rental expense for all operating leases amounted to $15,369,000 in 1991, $13,515,000 in 1990 and $11,809,000 in 1989.

At December 31, 1991, future minimum lease commitments for noncancelable operating leases amounted to the following (in thousands):

1992	$10,618
1993	8,679
1994	5,788
1995	3,602
1996	2,682
Thereafter	8,901
	$40,270

Subsequent Events

Events or transactions that occur subsequent to the end of the accounting period but prior to the issuance of financial statements and which have a material effect on the financial statements should be disclosed in the statements. Examples of subsequent events that may require disclosure are business combinations pending or affected, litigation settlements, issues of bonds or capital stock, and catastrophic loss of plant or inventories. A footnote disclosing a subsequent event is presented in Illustration 9.

Illustration 9
Example of Subsequent Events Footnote

1991 Annual Report
FL Industries Holdings, Inc.

Subsequent Events

On January 2, 1992, the Corporation acquired FL Industries Holdings, Inc. (FLIH), operating as American Electric, for consideration of $436.8 million. This consideration consisted of $89.6 million (1,564,434 shares) of newly issued common stock, $17.1 million in cash and $330.1 million to retire certain long-term debt of FLIH. A revolving credit facility was established and used to finance part of the purchase price. Additional funds were provided by the January 1992 sale and partial lease-back of the Corporation's principal executive office facility.

This acquisition will be accounted for using the purchase method of accounting. The following table presents, on a pro forma basis, a condensed consolidated balance sheet at December 31, 1991, giving effect to the acquisition as if it had occurred on that date.

In thousands (Unaudited)	Pro forma December 31, 1991
Current assets	$ 455,000
Net property, plant and equipment	315,000
Intangible assets – net	325,000
Other assets	30,000
	$1,125,000
Current liabilities	235,000
Long-term debt	410,000
Other long-term liabilities	25,000
Shareholders' equity	455,000
	$1,125,000

The Corporation's consolidated statement of earnings will not include the revenues and expenses of FLIH until the year 1992. The following pro forma results, however, were developed assuming FLIH had been acquired on January 1, 1991:

In thousands (except per share data) (Unaudited)	Pro forma Year ended December 31, 1991
Net sales	$1,023,000
Net earnings	$ 28,000[1]
Net earnings per share	$ 1.51[1]

[1] Net earnings were significantly impacted by $17 million ($.89 per share) of charges taken by FLIH to restructure operations and provide for claims related to businesses sold.

This unaudited pro forma sales and earnings information is not necessarily indicative of the combined results that would have occurred had the acquisition taken place on January 1, 1991, nor are they necessarily indicative of results that may occur in the future.

In connection with the acquisition, the Corporation expects to incur charges with respect to the integration of its businesses. Additionally, the Corporation intends to evaluate the businesses acquired in order to determine whether the future divestiture of any such businesses would be desirable.

On December 19, 1991, the Corporation entered into a $450 million five-year revolving term credit facility, part of which was used to finance the acquisition of FLIH. This credit facility includes covenants, among which are limitations on the amount of future indebtedness and the maintenance of certain financial ratios. Dividends are permitted to continue at the current rate or to be increased, provided that the dividend payout does not exceed 50 percent of earnings.

In January 1992, the Corporation completed the sale of $125 million of 12-year debt securities through a public offering. The net proceeds from the sale of these securities was used to reduce bank debt incurred to finance the acquisition. As a result of this $125 million financing and the voluntary reduction of an additional $25 million, the credit facility was reduced to $300 million.

Other Useful Disclosure

Footnote disclosure is often used to provide any other information relevant to the understanding and interpretation of the financial statement data. Examples of such information relate to foreign operations, product lines, sales backlogs and inventory profits.

THE AUDITOR'S REPORT AS AN INFORMATION DISCLOSURE

Financial statements are representations of the management of an entity to interested parties. Although management has a responsibility to disclose sufficient information to ensure that financial statements are not misleading, an independent auditor may evaluate these statements to express an opinion to third parties about the fairness of presentation of the statements. This independent audit provides confidence to readers of the financial statements about the quality of information provided to them. Consequently, the report prepared by the auditor may serve as an important input to the financial reporting process. However, readers must understand the meaning of the auditor's opinion and the implications of the opinion for financial statement analysis.

The *auditor's report* is written after the auditor has undertaken an extensive and objective study of the accounting process and the financial statements prepared by management. Auditors indicate in a report to the stockholders the scope of their examination and then express an opinion regarding the fairness of the financial statements. The standard format of a report that indicates no qualification as to the fairness of the financial statements is presented in Illustration 10. This report is referred to as an *unqualified (clean) opinion* because the auditor has not qualified his or her opinion in any way.

Scope of the Audit

In the second paragraph (referred to as the scope paragraph), the statement "We conducted our audits in accordance with generally accepted auditing standards" relates to both general standards and standards of field work. Conformance to general standards implies that the examination was performed by adequately trained, proficient auditors who maintained an independent mental attitude and who exercised due professional care. Conformance to field standards implies that the work was properly planned, that assistants were adequately supervised, and that a sufficient study and evaluation of the internal control (of the business) was made. The audit includes an examination of evidence supporting reported dollar amounts and assessing accounting principles used and significant estimates made by management. The audit must have a sufficient basis upon which to form an opinion concerning the financial statements.

The Opinion

The opinion paragraph of the auditor's report requires the auditor to express an opinion on the financial statements; or if he or she cannot express an opinion, to clearly indicate so and state all the reasons. The four reporting standards are listed below:

> **Illustration 10**
> *Independent Auditor's Report*
>
> [Date]
>
> **INDEPENDENT AUDITOR'S REPORT**
>
> We have audited the accompanying balance sheets of X Company as of December 31, 19x2 and 19x1, and the related statements of income, retained earnings, and cash flows for the years then ended. These financial statements are the responsibility of the Company's management. Our responsibility is to express an opinion on these financial statements based on our audits.
>
> We conducted our audits in accordance with generally accepted auditing standards. Those standards require that we plan and perform the audit to obtain reasonable assurance about whether the financial statements are free of material misstatement. An audit includes examining, on a test basis, evidence supporting the amounts and disclosures in the financial statements. An audit also includes assessing the accounting principles used and significant estimates made by management, as well as evaluating the overall financial statement presentation. We believe that our audits provide a reasonable basis for our opinion.
>
> In our opinion, the financial statements referred to above present fairly, in all material respects, the financial position of X Company as of [at] December 31, 19x2 and 19x1, and the results of its operations and its cash flows for the years then ended in conformity with generally accepted accounting principles.
>
> [Signature]

1. The report shall state whether the financial statements are presented in accordance with generally accepted principles of accounting.

2. The report shall state whether such principles have been consistently observed in the current period in relation to the preceding period.

3. Informative disclosures in the financial statements are to be regarded as reasonably adequate unless otherwise stated in the report.

4. The report shall either contain an expression of opinion regarding the financial statements, taken as a whole, or an assertion to the effect that an opinion cannot be expressed. When an overall opinion cannot be expressed, the reasons therefore should be stated. In all cases where an auditor's name is associated with financial statements, the report should contain a clear-cut indication of the character of the auditor's examination, if any, and the degree of responsibility he or she is taking.

Thus, if an auditor's examination is made in accordance with generally accepted auditing standards, and if the financial statements are fairly presented in conformity with generally accepted accounting principles, applied on a consistent basis, and include all necessary disclosures, the auditor will issue a "clean" (unqualified) opinion. In all other circumstances, the auditor must give either a qualified opinion, an adverse opinion, or disclaim an opinion.

In a *qualified opinion*, the auditor expresses certain reservations in his or her report concerning the scope of his or her examination and/or the financial statements. When the auditor's reservations are more serious, an adverse opinion or a disclaimer of opinion is given. In an adverse opinion, the auditor indicates that the financial statements do not present fairly the financial position and results of operations of the company. A disclaimer of opinion indicates that the auditor is unable to express an opinion. The inability to express an opinion usually occurs because of limitations in the scope of the audit.

The five major types of conditions that require the auditors to express an opinion other than unqualified opinion are as follows:

1. The scope of the auditor's examination is limited by:
    a. Conditions that prevent the application of auditing procedures considered necessary in the circumstances.
    b. Restrictions imposed by the client.
2. The financial statements do not present fairly the financial position or results of operations because of:
    a. Lack of conformity with generally accepted accounting principles or standards.
    b. Inadequate disclosure.
3. Accounting principles are not consistently applied in the financial statements.
4. Uncertainties exist concerning the future resolution of material matters whose effects cannot be reasonably estimated.
5. There is doubt about the entity's ability to continue operations as a going concern.

The auditor's report shown in Illustration 11 shows a qualified opinion based on litigation and going concern problems.

It should be apparent that information very relevant to the process of financial analysis may be revealed in the auditor's report. Consequently, the user of financial statements should carefully examine the auditor's opinion in relation to the other financial data in the annual report.

INTERIM REPORTING

Interim financial reports, usually issued on a quarterly basis, are designed to provide more timely information than annual reports. Interim financial information may include data on financial position, results of operations, and cash flows, and it may take the form of either complete financial statements

Illustration 11
Example of Qualified Opinion

1991 Annual Report
USG Corporation

REPORT OF INDEPENDENT PUBLIC ACCOUNTANTS

To the Stockholders and Board
of Directors of USG Corporation:

We have audited the accompanying consolidated balance sheet of USG Corporation (a Delaware corporation) and subsidiaries as of December 31, 1991 and 1990 and the related consolidated statements of earnings and cash flows for each of the three years in the period ended December 31, 1991. These financial statements are the responsibility of the Corporation's management. Our responsibility is to express an opinion on these financial statements based on our audits.

We conducted our audits in accordance with generally accepted auditing standards. Those standards require that we plan and perform the audit to obtain reasonable assurance about whether the financial statements are free of material misstatement. An audit includes examining, on a test basis, evidence supporting the amounts and disclosures in the financial statements. An audit also includes assessing the accounting principles used and significant estimates made by management, as well as evaluating the overall financial statement presentation. We believe that our audits provide a reasonable basis for our opinion.

In our opinion, the financial statements referred to above present fairly, in all material respects, the financial position of USG Corporation and subsidiaries as of December 31, 1991 and 1990, and the results of their operations and their cash flows for each of the three years in the period ended December 31, 1991, in conformity with generally accepted accounting principles.

The accompanying consolidated financial statements have been prepared assuming that the Corporation will continue as a going concern. The Corporation is in default of various of its loan agreements and does not expect to fund its debt service requirements in 1992 without restructuring its debt. Management's plan to restructure its debt is discussed in the financial restructuring footnote to the consolidated financial statements. As discussed in the litigation footnote, U.S. Gypsum is funding certain asbestos property damage defense costs until resolution of its coverage litigation against its insurance companies. In view of the current financial circumstances of the Corporation and the limited insurance funding currently available for property damage cases, management is unable to determine whether an adverse outcome in the asbestos litigation will have a material adverse effect on the financial condition of the Corporation. These conditions raise substantial doubt about the Corporation's ability to continue as a going concern. The consolidated financial statements do not include any adjustments relating to this uncertainty.

ARTHUR ANDERSEN & CO.

Chicago, Illinois
February 11, 1992

or summarized financial data. The publication of interim reports is required by companies listed on both the New York Stock Exchange and the American Stock Exchange. The Securities and Exchange Commission also requires all listed companies to file quarterly reports on Form 10-Q. An example of a quarterly report is presented in Illustration 12.

Because the ultimate results of operations cannot be known with certainty until the business is finally liquidated, many problems are incurred when allocating costs and revenues to relatively short time periods. Consequently, interim reports are subject to even more significant limitations than annual reports. Given the problems inherent in determining interim financial results, it is important that the user fully understand the limitations of such data. Despite these limitations, however, interim financial results are very important.

The two most significant measurement issues created by interim reporting are the estimation of annually determined items and the seasonality of operating activities. Typically, the determination of income for a year includes several items that are not directly measurable until the end of the year. For example, with graduated tax rates, the income tax expense is a function of the total taxable income for the year. Also, if inventory levels are decreased during the interim reporting period, the cost of goods sold under the LIFO inventory method depends upon whether or not the inventory levels will be increased by the end of the year. These types of problems generally cause interim computations to be even more subjective than the annual figures. As a result of such problems, information available at the year end may be substantially modified from previously reported interim data.

Another problem that affects interim computations is that many companies experience seasonal variations in their operating activities. For example, book publishers sell most of their books at certain times of the year. Such seasonality creates a problem in the allocation of operating costs that may be incurred at a different rate than the revenues. For example, even if sales are highly seasonal, such costs as property taxes, insurance, and executive salaries may be incurred relatively evenly throughout the year. A similar problem exists with the allocation of fixed costs (that is, depreciation) among interim periods.

The Accounting Principles Board attempted to establish consistent guidelines for interim financial reporting by issuing *APB Opinion No. 28* in 1973. The APB's objectives were to develop accounting principles and disclosure requirements that are appropriate for interim statements, and to specify minimum guidelines for information to be reported by publicly held companies.

The same principles and practices followed in the annual period should generally be followed in the interim periods. However, the Board also concluded that certain modifications in accounting principles or practices followed for annual periods are necessary at interim dates.

Illustration 12
Example of a Quarterly Report

June 30, 1991
Form 10 Q
Carter Wallace, Inc.

PART I - FINANCIAL INFORMATION
CARTER-WALLACE, INC. AND SUBSIDIARIES
CONDENSED CONSOLIDATED STATEMENTS OF EARNINGS
(Unaudited)

	Three Months Ended June 30,	
	1991	1990
Revenues:		
Net sales	$170,710,000	$153,401,000
Other revenues	2,243,000	2,180,000
	172,953,000	155,581,000
Cost and expenses:		
Cost of goods sold	52,824,000	48,642,000
Advertising, marketing & other selling expenses	64,138,000	56,717,000
Research & development expenses	13,238,000	11,480,000
General, administrative & other expenses	18,621,000	16,154,000
Interest expense	1,024,000	1,052,000
	149,845,000	134,045,000
Earnings before taxes on income	23,108,000	21,536,000
Provision for taxes on income	7,395,000	7,107,000
Net earnings	$ 15,713,000	$ 14,429,000
Net earnings per average share of common stock outstanding	$1.03	$ .94
Cash dividends per share	$ .23	$ .20½
Average shares of common stock outstanding	15,260,000	15,353,000

Illustration 12 Continued:

CARTER-WALLACE, INC. AND SUBSIDIARIES
CONDENSED CONSOLIDATED BALANCE SHEETS

	June 30, 1991 (Unaudited)	March 31, 1991
Assets		
Current Assets:		
Cash and cash equivalents	$ 20,257,000	$ 20,028,000
Short-term investments	23,029,000	9,925,000
Accounts and other receivables, less allowances of $6,284,000 at June 30, 1991 and $6,542,000 at March 31, 1991	120,125,000	135,943,000
Inventories:		
Finished goods	61,303,000	55,238,000
Work in process	17,256,000	16,938,000
Raw materials and supplies	27,562,000	28,085,000
	106,121,000	100,261,000
Prepaid expenses, deferred taxes and other current assets	25,267,000	23,566,000
Total Current Assets	294,799,000	289,723,000
Property, plant and equipment, at cost	231,985,000	231,656,000
Less: accumulated depreciation and amortization	97,411,000	95,311,000
	134,574,000	136,345,000
Intangible assets	120,030,000	122,881,000
Other assets	12,992,000	13,407,000
	$562,395,000	$562,356,000
Liabilities and Stockholders' Equity		
Current Liabilities:		
Accounts payable	$ 28,495,000	$ 30,549,000
Accrued expenses	90,062,000	94,748,000
Notes payable	10,655,000	12,431,000
Total Current Liabilities	129,212,000	137,728,000
Long-Term Liabilities:		
Long-term debt	16,207,000	16,576,000
Deferred compensation	7,229,000	6,758,000
Other long-term liabilities	18,742,000	18,696,000
Total Long-Term Liabilities	42,178,000	42,030,000
Stockholders' Equity:		
Common stock	11,341,000	11,325,000
Class B common stock	4,394,000	4,410,000
Capital in excess of par value	11,328,000	11,328,000
Retained earnings	386,916,000	374,713,000
Less: Equity adjustment from foreign currency translation	4,032,000	236,000
Treasury stock, at cost	18,942,000	18,942,000
Total Stockholders' Equity	391,005,000	382,598,000
Total Liabilities and Stockholders' Equity	$562,395,000	$562,356,000

Revenues should be recognized as earned during an interim period on the same basis as recognized for the full year. Any significant seasonal variations in the activities of the business should be disclosed in the interim report. Costs associated directly with, or allocated to, products should be recognized from those products as revenue is earned. The gross profit method for estimating inventories is allowable for interim reports. All other nonproduct costs and expenses should be charged to income as incurred or be allocated to interim periods based on an estimate of time expired or activities associated with the periods. Businesses incurring costs or expenses subject to seasonal variations should disclose the seasonal nature of their activities in their interim financial statements.

Income tax provisions should be determined at the end of each interim period based on an estimate of the effective tax rate to be applied for the full fiscal year. To illustrate, assume that a company has pretax income of $60,000 in the first quarter of the year and pretax income of $100,000 in the second quarter. The income tax expense for the first quarter is $10,000. If the effective tax rate for the fiscal year is now estimated to be 34 percent, then income tax expense for the second quarter is computed as follows:

Pretax income for the first and second quarters	$160,000
Estimated tax rate	.34
Income tax expense for first and second quarters	$ 54,400
Income tax expense for first quarter	10,000
Income tax expense for second quarter	$ 44,400

There is no retroactive correction for incorrectly estimating the effective tax rate for the fiscal year in any quarter. Therefore, in the above example, there is no retroactive correction for estimating the effective tax rate for the fiscal year as 16.67 percent in the first quarter and then 34 percent in the second quarter.

Typically, interim reports include summarized financial data that have considerably less detail than are included in annual financial reports. Information required in interim financial reports includes sales, provision for income taxes, extraordinary items, cumulative effect of a change in accounting principle, net income, earnings per share, and the seasonal nature of revenues or expenses. The *Opinion* also encouraged publicly-traded companies to include balance sheets and cash-flow data. When analyzed with the proper caution, it appears that the information contained in interim reports can be used to improve the user decision-making process.

REPORTING FOR SEGMENTS OF A BUSINESS

In the 1960's, conglomerates were formed. These are companies that operate in several lines of business. For example, Tenneco has operations in pipelines, heavy and farm equipment manufacturing, ship building, and agricultural products. The purpose of the diversification is to hedge against downturns in any one area of business activity. Such diversified companies are required to disclose financial information concerning the activities of individual segments of the business. The term *segment* generally is used to describe a component of an entity whose activities relate to a separate major class of customer or product. Individual segments of a diversified company may be uniquely affected by economic conditions and have different rates of profitability, degrees of risk, and opportunities for growth. Therefore, segment financial data can help financial analysts and other users of financial statements learn about and make informed decisions regarding such companies. Some of the more important specific uses of segmented data include the following:

1. To provide information regarding the nature of the businesses a company is involved in and the relative size of the various segments.
2. To use the sales and contributions toward profit as an input to the evaluation and projection of corporate earnings.
3. To appraise the ability of management in making acquisitions.
4. To make credit decisions by using information concerning the sources and use of funds by the various segments.

Problems in Providing Segment Data

There are several potential problems in providing financial data for diversified companies on a segment basis. The three main problems that occur in developing financial data on a segment basis are: (1) allocation of common costs to two or more segments, (2) pricing transactions between segments, and (3) determining segments to be used for reporting purposes. Each problem must be addressed if meaningful information is to be reported.

Disadvantages to the Reporting Company

Concern has been expressed by corporate management that disclosure of segment financial information may cause difficulties harmful to the reporting company. The disadvantages cited often include confidential information that would be revealed to competitors, technical problems inherent in the preparation of the data that might result in misleading information users, and, the cost of providing the data that could be significant.

Determining Reportable Industry Segments

In recognition of the perceived importance of segment information, the FASB in 1976 issued *Statement No. 14*, which requires a diversified company to disclose certain information concerning its operations in different industries, its foreign operations, its export sales, and its major customers. The information to be reported for each significant industry segment includes revenue, operating profit or loss, and identifiable assets.

FASB Statement No. 14 requires disclosure of financial activities for the company's operations in different industries. In general, separate disclosure must be made for each industry segment that is a significant component of the company providing products or services to unaffiliated customers.

FASB Statement No. 14 does not provide detailed rules and procedures that must be followed in defining industry segments because of the inherent differences among businesses by the nature of their operations. Factors that may be useful in identifying industry segments include the nature of the product in its relation to similar products, the extent that a product shares production facilities and labor forces with other products, and the similarity of geographic marketing areas and methods among products.

Since the *Statement* does not require that any single factor be used, the final definition of industry segments is based to a considerable extent on management's judgment. As a result, it is possible that two different companies that are manufacturing the same product could group the product into different industry segments.

Once the products and services have been grouped into industry segments, the segments that are reportable must be selected. A test is made on an annual basis to determine a company's reportable segments. In order to be classified as a reportable segment, the segment must satisfy at least one of the following tests.

1. Industry revenue of the segment is at least 10 percent of total company revenue.
2. Operating profit or loss of the segment is 10 percent or more of the greater of:
   a. The total of all the company's industry segments that had operating profits.
   b. The total of all the company's industry segments that had operating losses.
3. Identifiable assets of the segment are 10 percent or more of the company's combined industry segments' identifiable assets.

In addition, the *Statement* provides two overall tests to be made:

1. Combined revenue from sales to unaffiliated customers of all reportable segments should amount to at least 75 percent of combined revenues from unaffiliated customers. Additional industry segments should be reported until this test is met.
2. However, more than ten segments need not be reported. Segments may be reexamined and possibly combined to avoid an excessive number of reportable segments.

When a company has only one reportable segment (a "dominant" segment) and that segment comprises more than 90 percent of the related combined revenue, then only a description of the dominant industry is needed.

As an illustration of the application of these tests, assume that a company has the following data available:

Segment	Revenue	Operating Profit (loss)	Identifiable Assets
A	$ 700	$ 75	$ 250
B	400	30	190
C	90	15	130
D	80	(10)	50
	$1,270	$110	$ 620

All sales are to unaffiliated companies.

Revenue test. Total revenue equals 1,270. Reportable segments are A and B. Segments C and D do not meet the test because neither has revenue of at least $127 ($1,270 × .10).

Operating profit or loss test. Operating profits total $120 ($75 + $30 + $15), which exceeds the total of the operating loss ($10). Therefore, the test is based on the operating profit of $120. Reportable segments are A, B, and C; each has an operating profit of at least $12 ($120 × .10). Segment D does not meet the test, because the absolute value of its operating loss is less than $12.

Identifiable assets test. Total identifiable assets are $620. Reportable segments are A, B, and C. Segment D does not meet the test, because its identifiable assets are less than $62 ($620 × .10).

The reportable segments are A, B, and C as long as their combined revenues from sales to unaffiliated companies equal at least 75 percent of total sales to unaffiliated companies. Sales to unaffiliated companies for Segments A, B, and C total $1,190 ($700 + $400 + $90). Total sales to unaffiliated companies total $1,270. The 75 percent test is met.

Foreign Operations and Export Sales

When revenues from foreign countries are at least 10 percent of total revenues or identifiable assets in foreign countries are at least 10 percent of total identifiable assets, such information should be disclosed. If a company derives at least 10 percent of its revenue from export sales, that information should be disclosed.

Usefulness of Segment Data

Diversified companies present special problems in financial analysis and decision-making. Since these companies may have varying degrees of profitability, uses, and growth potential for individual components, the analyst needs financial information regarding the components to make meaningful decisions. Despite the potential usefulness of segment information, however, the analyst must use extreme caution in assessments and evaluations of the data. An example of segment reporting is presented in Illustration 13.

MANAGEMENT'S DISCUSSION AND ANALYSIS

An important element of disclosure in financial reporting is management's discussion and analysis. The purpose of this analytical disclosure is to assist investors and creditors in identifying underlying trends in a company's operations in order to enhance predictions of future financial performance.

Illustration 13
Example of Segment Reporting

1991 Annual Report
Dana Corporation

BUSINESS SEGMENTS Dana operates principally in three business segments: Vehicular, Industrial and Financial Services. The Vehicular segment consists primarily of the manufacturing and marketing of axles, frames, transmissions, universal joints, clutches and engine parts (such as pistons, piston rings, filters and gaskets). The Industrial segment manufactures and markets various products, including products manufactured and marketed for off-highway motor vehicles. The Financial Services segment consists of Diamond Financial Holdings, Inc., a wholly-owned financial subsidiary which includes leasing companies, a savings and loan company and real estate development and management companies.

BUSINESS SEGMENTS
Year Ended December 31, 1991

$ in thousands	Vehicular	Industrial	Financial Services	Consolidated
Sales to customers	$3,466,031	$ 918,627	$ 13,552	$4,398,210
Financial services revenue			167,585	167,585
Total revenue	$3,466,031	$ 918,627	$ 181,137	$4,565,795
Operating income (loss)	$ 156,965	$ 10,440	$ (17,248)	$ 150,157
Other income				25,265
Other expense				(216,367)
Income (loss) before income taxes				$ (40,945)
Assets identified to segments	$1,388,728	$ 518,245	$1,325,757	$3,232,730
Corporate assets				946,591
Total assets				$4,179,321
Depreciation	$ 108,303	$ 35,289	$ 39,040	
Capital expenditures	$ 116,912	$ 31,039	$ 1,871	

Year Ended December 31, 1990

Sales to customers	$3,804,625	$1,142,892	$ 4,344	$4,951,861
Financial services revenue			257,065	257,065
Total revenue	$3,804,625	$1,142,892	$ 261,409	$5,208,926
Operating income (loss)	$ 308,818	$ 72,895	$ (45,588)	$ 336,125
Other income				16,545
Other expense				(210,429)
Income before income taxes				$ 142,241
Assets identified to segments	$1,411,143	$ 595,323	$1,423,458	$3,429,924
Corporate assets				1,083,269
Total assets				$4,513,193
Depreciation	$ 99,184	$ 38,405	$ 40,127	
Capital expenditures	$ 175,118	$ 47,921	$ 1,486	

Year Ended December 31, 1989

Sales to customers	$3,747,343	$1,109,982	$ 7,803	$4,865,128
Financial services revenue			239,688	239,688
Total revenue	$3,747,343	$1,109,982	$ 247,491	$5,104,816
Operating income	$ 318,806	$ 69,870	$ 6,926	$ 395,602
Other income				49,228
Other expense				(220,227)
Income before income taxes				$ 224,603
Assets identified to segments	$1,359,341	$ 575,386	$2,258,947	$4,193,674
Corporate assets				1,031,763
Total assets				$5,225,437
Depreciation	$ 85,885	$ 37,698	$ 33,806	
Capital expenditures	$ 170,442	$ 54,085	$ 8,541	

Illustration 13 Continued:

Interarea transfers between countries are transferred at the prevailing market price. Financial services revenue includes lease financing income, financial services fees and interest. Other income includes dividends and interest. Other expense includes interest and corporate expenses. Corporate assets include cash, marketable securities, accounts receivable and investments (excluding such assets as can be identified to Financial Services).

The "Other International" geographic area comprises primarily Brazil and Canada, neither of which exceeds 10% of the consolidated amounts. Export sales from the United States to customers outside the United States amounted to $407,576,000 in 1991, $353,874,000 in 1990 and $360,257,000 in 1989. Total export sales (including sales to Dana's international subsidiaries which are eliminated for financial statement presentation) were $500,005,000, $446,173,000 and $457,950,000 in 1991, 1990 and 1989, respectively.

Worldwide sales to Ford Motor Company and subsidiaries amounted to $676,936,000 in 1991 (15% of consolidated sales), $810,694,000 in 1990 (16%), and $718,619,000 in 1989 (15%) and were primarily from the Vehicular segment. No other customer accounted for more than 10% of consolidated sales.

GEOGRAPHIC AREAS
Year Ended December 31, 1991

$ in thousands	United States	Europe	Other International	Adjustments and Eliminations	Total
Sales to customers	$3,192,732	$587,348	$618,130		$4,398,210
Financial services revenue	152,572	7,067	7,946		167,585
Interarea transfers	92,479	2,484	62,104	$(157,067)	
	$3,437,783	$596,899	$688,180	$(157,067)	$4,565,795
Operating income	$ 129,929	$ 11,282	$ 8,946		$ 150,157
Other income	25,265				25,265
Other expense	(187,200)	(10,707)	(18,460)		(216,367)
Income (loss) before income taxes	$ (32,006)	$ 575	$ (9,514)		$ (40,945)
Assets identified	$2,541,801	$274,198	$416,731		$3,232,730
Corporate assets	613,113	104,445	229,033		946,591
Total assets	$3,154,914	$378,643	$645,764		$4,179,321

Year Ended December 31, 1990

Sales to customers	$3,519,421	$678,401	$754,039		$4,951,861
Financial services revenue	246,152	3,623	7,290		257,065
Interarea transfers	92,299	2,718	78,252	$(173,269)	
	$3,857,872	$684,742	$839,581	$(173,269)	$5,208,926
Operating income	$ 197,898	$ 42,890	$ 95,337		$ 336,125
Other income	16,545				16,545
Other expense	(185,682)	(9,635)	(15,112)		(210,429)
Income before income taxes	$ 28,761	$ 33,255	$ 80,225		$ 142,241
Assets identified	$2,725,776	$291,915	$412,233		$3,429,924
Corporate assets	789,164	123,981	170,124		1,083,269
Total assets	$3,514,940	$415,896	$582,357		$4,513,193

Year Ended December 31, 1989

Sales to customers	$3,598,545	$568,974	$697,609		$4,865,128
Financial services revenue	234,772	776	4,140		239,688
Interarea transfers	97,693	2,918	77,035	$(177,646)	
	$3,931,010	$572,668	$778,784	$(177,646)	$5,104,816
Operating income	$ 247,672	$ 37,450	$110,480		$ 395,602
Other income	49,228				49,228
Other expense	(207,190)	(3,626)	(9,411)		(220,227)
Income before income taxes	$ 89,710	$ 33,824	$101,069		$ 224,603
Assets identified	$3,642,670	$224,998	$326,006		$4,193,674
Corporate assets	794,244	80,398	157,121		1,031,763
Total assets	$4,436,914	$305,396	$483,127		$5,225,437

In *FASB Statement of Financial Concepts No. 1*, the FASB addressed the importance of management explanations and interpretations.

> Financial reporting should include explanations and interpretations to help users understand financial information provided. . . . [T]he usefulness of financial information as an aid to investors, creditors, and others in forming expectations about a business enterprise may be enhanced by management's explanations of the information. Management knows more about the enterprise and its affairs than investors, creditors, or other "outsiders" and can often increase the usefulness of financial information by identifying certain transactions, other events, and circumstances that affect the enterprise and explaining their financial impact on it. . . . Moreover, financial reporting often provides information that depends on, or is affected by, management's estimates and judgment. Investors, creditors, and others are aided in evaluating estimates and judgmental information by explanations of underlying assumptions or methods used, including disclosure of significant uncertainties about principal underlying assumptions or estimates.[2]

Management's discussion and analysis has been required by the SEC since 1974. The content of the information to be contained in Form 10-K was restructured in 1980. Additional guidance was provided by the SEC in 1989. Management's discussion and analysis should include information on the following items:

1. Short-term and long-term liquidity.
2. Capital resources.
3. Results of operations.
4. Favorable and unfavorable trends, demands, commitments, events, or uncertainties.
5. The causes for material changes in line items.

An example of each of these is presented in Illustrations 14 through 18.

---

[2] *FASB Statement of Financial Accounting Concepts No. 1*, "Objectives of Financial Reporting by Business Enterprises" (Stamford, CT: FASB, 1978), para. 54.

Illustration 14
*Example of Management Discussion
and Analysis of Liquidity*

1991 Annual Report
Dana Corporation and Consolidated Subsidiaries

MANAGEMENT'S DISCUSSION
AND ANALYSIS OF RESULTS

LIQUIDITY AND CAPITAL RESOURCES

Total additions to property, plant, and equipment were $150 million in 1991 compared to $229 million in 1990. These additions included completion of new facilities in France and Brazil and reflect adjustments due to the current business downturn. 1992 capital expenditures are budgeted at $122 million, the majority of which was uncommitted at December 31, 1991.

Consolidated domestic and international short-term borrowings averaged $667 million during 1991 at an average interest rate of 7.3% as compared to $782 million at 8.8% during 1990. Dana funds its corporate short-term debt through the issuance of commercial paper and bank borrowings. To cover short-term working capital requirements, Dana has $350 million of credit facilities in place to back-up commercial paper issuance and $708 million in uncommitted lines available for borrowings with banks. At December 31, 1991 Dana's domestic and international short-term borrowings were $217 million, down from $272 million at year end 1990. Dana's financial subsidiary, Diamond Financial Holdings, Inc. (DFHI), funds short-term debt through bank borrowings. DFHI has bank lines totalling $115 million and at December 31, 1991, $115 million was borrowed against these lines. DFHI's subsidiary, Dana Credit Corporation (DCC), funds domestic and international short-term debt through commercial paper and bank borrowings. DCC has commercial paper back-up lines amounting to $250 million and uncommitted bank borrowing lines of $232 million. During 1991, through a securities lending agreement, DCC borrowed $181 million (face amount) of U.S. Treasury Notes from a syndicate of bank investors. Concurrent with the borrowing, DCC sold such securities at their then current market rate. These payments, net of premium amortization, result in an effective interest cost of 7.4%. Under the terms of the securities lending agreement, DCC is obligated to pay the coupon rate of interest and applicable lending fee to the bank investors. DCC is required to return comparable U.S. Treasury Notes to the bank investors prior to May 15, 1992 to satisfy its securities lending obligation. At December 31, 1991 DCC and its subsidiaries had a short-term debt position of $275 million, down from $385 million at December 31, 1990. In total, short-term debt decreased during the year from $767 million to $607 million. A portion of this decrease was due to refinancing with medium-term and long-term debt.

Dana's long-term debt increased $55 million to $1.54 billion in 1991. Medium-term notes which matured were replaced with term notes with similar maturities. During 1991, DCC obtained financing as part of a lease securitization facility. Under the facility, an interest in certain lease receivables is transferred to a third-party investor as support for the financing received. The facility provides for borrowings up to $100 million on a revolving basis through 1995 at committed pricing based on the commercial paper composite interest rate. At DCC's option, the securitized borrowings can be repaid at any time.

Dana anticipates that net cash flows from operating activities along with available short-term and medium-term financing capabilities are sufficient to meet its needs for 1992.

Dana has reviewed the legal proceedings to which the Company and its subsidiaries were parties as of December 31, 1991 (including, among others, those involving product liability claims and alleged violations of the federal "Superfund" and other environmental laws) and has concluded that any liabilities that may result from these proceedings are not reasonably likely to have a material effect on the Company's liquidity, financial condition or results of operations.

Dana is required to adopt the provisions of SFAS No. 106 by 1993. Preliminary estimates of the transition obligation's effect on income upon adoption of SFAS No. 106 range from as low as $300 million to as high as $450 million, and annual expense is estimated to increase by an amount as low as $18 million to as high as $50 million after tax. See "Health Care and Life Insurance Benefits" on page 24 for additional information regarding SFAS No. 106.

Illustration 15
*Example of Management Discussion
and Analysis of Capital Resources*

1991 Annual Report
AMP Incorporated

CAPITAL RESOURCES

In recent years, capital spending has focused more upon the acquisition of machinery and equipment intended to increase efficiency, productivity and the quality of manufacturing and support activities. Floor space has remained nearly constant at approximately 9 million square feet since 1985, during which period sales grew 89%. The Company's facilities are maintained in excellent condition and are capable of supporting perhaps as much as a 20% increase in sales volume without requiring significant expansion.

Capital spending in 1992 will continue to focus on the strategy employed since 1985, with 85% of the budget devoted either to replacement or upgrading of machinery and equipment and tooling of new product programs. A net increase in floor space is not contemplated. The Company leases about 15% of its floor space.

In December 1991 the Company acquired the net assets of National Applied Science, Inc. of Portland, Oregon, in a stock-for-stock transaction. The business will continue as a subsidiary, Precision Interconnect Corporation, which manufactures high performance specialty cables and cable assemblies.

During the period 1989-1991, the Company repurchased more than 1.9 million shares of its outstanding common stock at a cost of $83.5 million. The Company plans to continue repurchasing its outstanding stock from time-to-time, depending upon current market conditions and the absence of a higher priority for the use of its cash resources.

Illustration 16
*Example of Management Discussion
and Analysis of Results of Operations*

1991 Annual Report
Monsanto Company

REVIEW OF CONSOLIDATED RESULTS OF OPERATIONS

MONSANTO OPERATING RESULTS WERE REASONABLY STRONG

In 1991, Monsanto's operating performance was reasonably strong considering the depressed economic climate in several of Monsanto's major markets. Strong performance by most of Monsanto's key products and a continued focus on strategic strengths were the hallmarks in 1991. Monsanto's performance is now far less dependent on economic conditions than in the early 1980s due to the change in the business portfolio mix.

RESTRUCTURING AFFECTS 1991 FINANCIAL RESULTS

In October 1990 and June 1991, the Board of Directors approved restructuring steps to strengthen the Agricultural Products, Chemicals and Fisher Controls units and the corporate staff for the future. Net income for 1991 declined 46 percent because of the $325 million, $2.54 per share, after-tax restructuring charge. This charge, principally affecting the Chemicals unit, was recorded for the shutdown and consolidation of various facilities, reductions in employment, and the sale of certain businesses that are not consistent with Monsanto's long-term strategic goals. Earnings per share were 45 percent lower in 1991.

NET SALES WERE SECOND-BEST IN HISTORY

Despite the decision to dispose of various non-strategic businesses, the lack of economic recovery in the United States and a slowdown in the European economy, net sales for 1991 were down only slightly from that of the prior year and still were the second-best in Monsanto's history. Modest sales volume growth in continuing businesses was more than offset by the lack of sales for businesses divested or planned for divestment. Average selling prices were marginally lower than those in 1990. Net sales in markets outside the United States represented 42 percent of Monsanto's total net sales in 1991.

Net sales for Pharmaceuticals, Agricultural Products and NutraSweet increased, while net sales for Fisher Controls were about the same as in the prior year. Net sales for Chemicals declined. Pharmaceuticals net sales growth was led by the *Calan* family of calcium channel blockers, up 9 percent; *Cytotec* ulcer preventive drug, up 35 percent; and *Canderel* tabletop sweetener, which is made with *NutraSweet* brand sweetener, up 11 percent. Net sales for Agricultural Products grew as weather conditions improved in most key markets. In addition, 1991 strategic price reductions in certain countries for *Roundup* glyphosate-based herbicide generated higher sales volume. Glyphosate sales volume increased 17 percent worldwide. NutraSweet's sales volume increased 5 percent, while selling prices decreased. Fisher Controls experienced lower 1991 sales volume; however, this decline was compensated for by higher average selling prices. Chemicals net sales for 1991 were lower as a result of discontinued product lines and lower demand caused by the depressed North American automotive industry, the delayed U.S. economic recovery and a slowdown in the European economy.

OPERATING RESULTS MIXED

Operating income declined 37 percent in 1991. However, excluding the $446 million pretax restructuring charge, operating income would have increased about 12 percent. Operating results in 1991 were helped by lower raw material costs and improved sales volume and mix from continuing products. The effect of Chemicals lower manufacturing capacity utilization reduced earnings when compared with 1990.

Agricultural Products and Pharmaceuticals operating income increased in 1991, while operating results declined for Chemicals, Fisher Controls and NutraSweet. Agricultural Products operating income benefited from higher sales volume, lower manufacturing costs and cost savings from restructuring actions implemented in late 1990. Operating income for Pharmaceuticals increased in 1991, primarily because of strong volume growth in key products, higher average selling prices and gains from the divestiture of non-strategic product rights. The profit improvement was partially offset by the December 1990 divestiture of several consumer products to a third party under a prior agreement. Chemicals incurred an operating loss compared with operating income in 1990, because of its restructuring expense. Operating results for Chemicals were helped by lower petrochemical-based raw material costs and hurt by the effect of lower sales volume, lower selling prices, and lower manufacturing capacity utilization. NutraSweet operating income benefited from higher sales volume, but was adversely affected by lower selling prices.

Illustration 16 Continued:

REVIEW OF CONSOLIDATED RESULTS OF OPERATIONS *(continued)*

Fisher Controls reported its second-best year; however, operating income was down because of recessionary pressures on volume and a shift in product mix.

Marketing expenses decreased 6 percent in 1991, because of lower advertising and promotional expenses. Administrative expenses increased in 1991, in part because of higher 1991 incentive compensation.

"Other income (expense) — net" in 1991 decreased, principally because the prior year included higher gains from divestitures.

PRINCIPAL FINANCIAL TARGET REMAINS 20 PERCENT RETURN ON SHAREOWNERS' EQUITY

Management's principal financial target is to reach and sustain a 20 percent return on shareowners' equity (ROE). Although the 1991 restructuring charge resulted in ROE declining to 7.6 percent in 1991 from 13.6 percent in 1990, management believes the target is appropriate.

PRODUCT DEVELOPMENT AND COMMERCIALIZATION ARE TOP PRIORITY

New product development and commercialization continue to be the most important strategic priority for Monsanto. Research and development expenditures were $627 million in 1991, 7 percent of net sales, a level that reflects management's strong, long-term commitment to research and development. A major investment continues to be the discovery and development of pharmaceutical and agricultural products. Research in existing product technology and new applications also continues across all business units. University collaborations and product licensing are an integral part of Monsanto's research program. The result is that Monsanto has many potential products in the research and development pipeline, several of which should be commercialized over the next few years.

PRIOR YEAR REVIEW

Net income in 1990 declined 20 percent and earnings per share decreased 16 percent compared with that of 1989. The decline in net income was caused by dramatically higher costs for petrochemical-based raw materials during the latter part of the year, extreme weather conditions in key world agricultural markets and, to a lesser extent, depressed automotive and construction industries in North America. However, Pharmaceuticals, Fisher Controls and NutraSweet had record performances in 1990. Although benefiting from Monsanto's treasury stock purchase program, ROE was lower than that of 1989.

Net sales in 1990 of $9 billion, up 4 percent from 1989, were the highest in Monsanto's history. Sales volume increased 2 percent. The selling price increase was entirely due to the effect of translating non-U.S. dollar denominated sales into a generally weaker U.S. dollar. Net sales in markets outside the United States continued to be significant, 42 percent of Monsanto's 1990 total net sales.

Monsanto's worldwide sales growth was led by Pharmaceuticals. Net sales of the *Calan* family of calcium channel blockers grew 28 percent, and net sales of *Cytotec* ulcer preventive drug grew 52 percent. Fisher Controls net sales increased with higher selling prices and sales volume. Sales volume of NutraSweet increased, while average selling prices decreased. Sales volumes of Agricultural Products were hurt by adverse weather conditions. In addition, selling price reductions for *Roundup* glyphosate-based herbicide were implemented, principally in Europe. Despite the effect of adverse weather conditions, worldwide sales volume of *Roundup* was slightly above that of 1989. Chemicals net sales were about level with the prior year. Chemicals benefited from continued strong European business, but was hurt by lower demand caused by the depressed North American automotive and construction industries.

Operating income declined 16 percent in 1990. Operating results were helped by improvements in sales volume and mix. However, higher raw material and other manufacturing costs, the effect of lower manufacturing capacity utilization and a 10 percent increase in marketing expenses reduced earnings compared with those of 1989. The higher marketing expenses were concentrated on NutraSweet's *Simplesse* all natural fat substitute and *Simple Pleasures* frozen dairy dessert and on Pharmaceuticals product launches.

Agricultural Products operating income declined, as the modest sales volume growth in glyphosate herbicides did not compensate for the reduction in selling prices for those products. In addition, Agricultural Products operating income was hurt by the effect of low use of new manufacturing capacity and higher raw material costs. Chemicals operating income was hurt by increased costs of petroleum-

Illustration 16 Continued:

based raw materials, lower sales volume and the effect of lower manufacturing capacity utilization. Pharmaceuticals operating income improved primarily as a result of continued sales volume growth. Fisher Controls operating income surged 48 percent as a result of selling price improvements, strong customer demand and improved production turnaround of booked orders. NutraSweet operating income increased slightly, as the benefit of higher sales volume was reduced by costs associated with new product introductions and lower average selling prices.

"Other income (expense) — net" decreased in 1990, due primarily to higher 1990 currency losses and higher losses from affiliated companies in which Monsanto does not have management control. Gains from divestitures in 1990 were comparable to those of the prior year. A $45 million pretax gain — $31 million aftertax, or $0.24 per share — was realized on the sale of certain assets of a Monsanto joint venture in Japan, the principal divestiture in 1990.

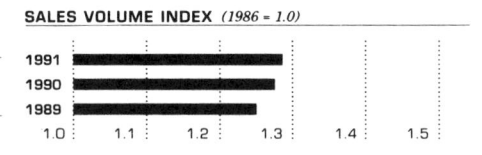

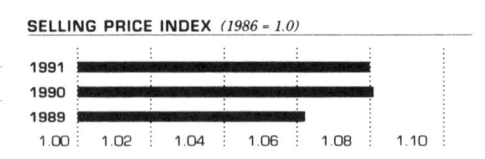

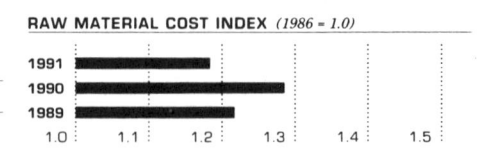

ANALYSIS OF CHANGE IN EARNINGS PER SHARE — BETTER (WORSE)

	1991 vs. 1990	1990 vs. 1989
Sales-Related Factors:		
Selling prices	$ (0.19)	$ 0.72[1]
Sales volume and mix	0.43	0.77
Total Sales-Related Factors	0.24	1.49
Cost-Related Factors:		
Raw material costs	0.98	(0.57)
Manufacturing capacity utilization	(0.26)	(0.38)
Other manufacturing costs	(0.02)	(0.74)
Marketing, administrative and technological expenses	(0.24)	(0.70)
Total Cost-Related Factors	0.46	(2.39)
Other Factors:		
Restructuring — net	(2.54)	
Divestitures	(0.18)	0.11
Total Other Factors	(2.72)	0.11
Operating Income	(2.02)	(0.79)
Interest expense	0.05	0.02
Interest income	0.06	(0.02)
Other income (expense) — net	(0.25)	(0.17)
Change in income taxes	0.22	(0.03)
Change in shares outstanding	0.04	0.21
Change in Earnings per Share	$ (1.90)	$ (0.78)

[1] *Increase was entirely due to the effect of translating non-U.S. dollar denominated sales into a generally weaker U.S. dollar.*

SALES VOLUME INDEX *(1986 = 1.0)*

1991
1990
1989
1.0   1.1   1.2   1.3   1.4   1.5

SELLING PRICE INDEX *(1986 = 1.0)*

1991
1990
1989
1.00   1.02   1.04   1.06   1.08   1.10

RAW MATERIAL COST INDEX *(1986 = 1.0)*

1991
1990
1989
1.0   1.1   1.2   1.3   1.4   1.5

Illustration 17
*Example of Management Discussion
and Analysis of Trends*

1991 Annual Report of
Ameritech Corporation

Regulatory Environment

The regulatory climate faced by the Ameritech Bell companies continues to improve. In recent years, decisions by both state and federal regulatory bodies have enhanced the incentives to invest in the local exchange networks and improved the ability of the Ameritech Bell companies to compete. In various regulatory jurisdictions in the Ameritech region, significant reforms are paving the way for a dynamic communications industry which offers opportunities for lasting growth.

At the FCC and in two of the Ameritech states, traditional rate-of-return regulation is no longer in effect. The FCC process caps prices but also provides for sharing of productivity gains. For 1991, earnings in excess of 12.25 percent will result in reductions to the price ceilings on interstate services on a 50/50 basis. In Wisconsin incentive regulation has been implemented which does not involve sharing. This is a trial plan which lasts through 1993. In Michigan new legislation that became effective on January 1, 1992, eliminated traditional rate-of-return regulation. Based on this legislation, all new intrastate services in Michigan and many existing services are not subject to either price or earnings regulation. Basic local exchange services in Michigan continue to be subject to price, but not earnings, regulation.

In addition, the Ameritech Bell companies continue to implement measured service. Mandatory measured service is in place for most business customers. In addition, two states have mandatory measured service for residential customers. Illinois Bell implemented statewide measured service in 1990, and Wisconsin Bell implemented a mandatory pay-per-call plan in 1991. In 1992, Michigan Bell will implement measured service for residential call volumes over a specified allowance. These measured service plans allow the companies to achieve revenue growth corresponding to usage increases.

Finally, price restructuring and other regulatory changes have begun that will allow the Ameritech Bell companies to effectively compete as local exchange competition becomes more widespread. The pricing changes are reducing many of the subsidies that, if left intact, would unfairly burden Ameritech Bell prices. For example, the Illinois Commerce Commission has taken a number of steps which have laid the groundwork for a truly competitive local exchange industry in that state. These changes have included not only the implementation of measured service described above, but also the restructuring of most local exchange and toll prices to be more reflective of costs, including geographic de-averaging. In addition, Illinois Bell has the freedom to offer market-based contract prices for competitive services. These changes set the stage for Illinois Bell to offer new forms of interconnection with competing access providers in downtown Chicago. Illinois Bell will continue to work with the Illinois Commerce Commission to make the further changes that will be required to enable additional forms of interconnection and competition.

Similar changes have begun in the other Ameritech states as well. For example, the new Michigan telecommunications legislation allows Michigan Bell to adjust prices to meet market conditions without prior regulatory approval. Additionally, each of the Ameritech Bell companies has pricing flexibility for certain competitive services. In the area of price restructuring, the Ameritech Bell companies continue to reduce the prices for intraLATA long-distance in order to better align those prices with costs.

Taken together, these changes represent significant progress towards the pricing and regulatory changes that will provide the platform for a dynamic and competitive local exchange industry. With these changes, and others in the future, the Ameritech Bell companies will be positioned to profitably offer the telecommunication services their customers want at competitive prices.

Illustration 18
*Example of Management Discussion and
Analysis of Causes for Material Changes*

1991 Annual Report of
Avery Dennison Corporation

Management's Discussion and Analysis of Results of Operations and Financial Condition

On October 16, 1990, a subsidiary of Avery International Corporation merged into Dennison Manufacturing Company in a transaction accounted for as a pooling of interests. Consequently, the financial information addressed in the discussion and analysis below is combined Avery and Dennison operations for the years 1989 and 1990. During the fourth quarter of 1990, in connection with the merger, the Company began a restructuring program to integrate and realign certain Avery and Dennison operations; consolidate administrative functions; and divest several non-core businesses.

Results of Operations

Sales decreased 2 percent in 1991 after increasing 4 percent in 1990. Excluding the impact of divestitures, discontinued products and changes in foreign currency, sales increased 3 percent in 1991 when compared to 1990. Excluding the impact of changes in foreign currency, sales increased 1 percent in 1990 when compared to 1989.

The gross profit margin for 1991 was 31.3 percent as compared to 31.2 percent for 1990 and 32.4 percent for 1989. In 1991, the slight improvement in gross margin was the result of the improved profitability in the office products businesses, primarily due to the restructuring of the Dennison brand businesses as well as the discontinuation of unprofitable product lines, and the effects of the reduction of certain inventories accounted for on a LIFO basis as discussed in Note 2 to the Consolidated Financial Statements. This was mostly offset by the continued slow economies in the United States, United Kingdom and France, the continued slowdown in the European automotive industry, and the start-up of two new manufacturing plants in Europe. In 1990 the lower gross profit margin, as compared to 1989, was due primarily to the difficult economic environment plus unsatisfactory operating performances in our European materials businesses and in the Dennison stationery products and data systems operations in the United States.

Marketing, general and administrative expense as a percent of sales was 25.7 percent in 1991 compared with 25.2 percent in 1990 and 23.7 percent in 1989. In 1991, the increase was due to the decline in sales and was partially offset by savings related to the restructuring activities. The increase during 1990 as compared to 1989 was due primarily to higher operating expense in the Dennison stationery and data systems businesses, and the negative impact of the bankruptcies of three large customers of the European specialty tape business.

The Company recorded a pretax charge of $85.2 million in the fourth quarter of 1990 to cover restructuring and other integration-related expenses. The Company also incurred $13.8 million in expenses, primarily during the third quarter of 1990, to cover the direct costs of the merger.

During 1989, the Company entered into a settlement agreement with Minnesota Mining and Manufacturing Company in connection with a patent infringement lawsuit. As a result of payments received under this settlement agreement, the Company recognized approximately $17 million as a reduction of marketing, general and administrative expense. The income

Net Income as a Percent of Sales
1987	1988	1989	1990	1991
3.2%	5.1%	4.6%	0.2%	2.5%

Average Total Asset Turnover
1987	1988	1989	1990	1991
1.44	1.44	1.50	1.42	1.44

Average Working Capital, Excluding Short-Term Debt, as a Percent of Sales
1987	1988	1989	1990^A	1991^A
21.1%	20.0%	18.5%	19.5%	16.9%

^A Excludes the net impact of the 1990 restructuring costs.

Illustration 18 Continued:

from the settlement was offset by charges of $14.2 million to cost of products sold and marketing, general and administrative expenses. These costs related primarily to the disposition of certain inventories and property, plant and equipment and to provisions for various environmental exposures.

As a result of the above, operating profit as a percent of sales for 1991 was 5.6 percent as compared with 2.1 percent in 1990 and 8.7 percent in 1989. Interest expense was 1.5 percent of sales in 1991 and 1990 compared with 1.4 percent in 1989. Interest expense was lower in 1991 as compared to 1990 due primarily to a reduction of debt and lower interest rates. Interest expense increased in 1990 compared to 1989 due to borrowings for capital expenditures and working capital requirements, in excess of cash provided by operations.

As a result of these factors, income before taxes as a percent of sales was 4.1 percent in 1991, compared with 0.6 percent in 1990 and 7.3 percent in 1989. The effective tax rate for 1991 was 39.9 percent, compared with 62.2 percent in 1990 and 36.8 percent in 1989. The high tax rate in 1990 was attributable primarily to the merger-related costs, previously discussed, which decreased income before taxes, but were capitalized for tax purposes.

Net income as a percent of sales was 2.5 percent in 1991 compared with 0.2 percent in 1990 and 4.6 percent in 1989. The results in 1990 were negatively impacted by the merger and restructuring costs discussed above.

Net income per share increased to $1.02 per share in 1991 from $.10 in 1990. Net income per share in 1989 was $1.84. The return on average shareholders' equity was 7.7 percent in 1991, compared with 0.7 percent in 1990 and 14.7 percent in 1989. The return on average total capital in 1991, 1990 and 1989 was 6.7 percent, 1.5 percent, and 12.0 percent, respectively.

Overall sales for the pressure-sensitive adhesives and materials businesses increased in both 1991 and 1990. During 1991, the roll materials and films businesses in the United States and the decorative films business achieved improved sales. This increase was partially offset by decreased sales at the specialty tape businesses in both the United States and Europe, due primarily to the slow economy and market pressures. During 1990, strong demand for self-adhesive materials contributed to sales growth in the roll materials and films businesses in the United States and Europe. Partially offsetting this increase, the specialty tape business in Europe was negatively impacted by the bankruptcies of three large diaper-tape customers. Additionally, a slowdown in the automotive businesses in the United States and Europe negatively impacted sales. In 1991 profitability for the segment was down slightly from 1990. Internationally, profitability at the Company's roll materials, specialty tapes, and automotive businesses was negatively affected by the continuing European recession, increased competition, and start-up costs of a new roll materials manufacturing plant in Luxembourg and a new automotive films converting plant in Germany. Partially offsetting these results, the roll materials and films businesses in the United States and the decorative films business reported improved results over last year. In 1990, segment profits were also down as a result of the factors impacting 1990 sales described above.

The office products business segment reported a slight decrease in sales in 1991 compared to 1990, due principally to divestitures and discontinued products, while profitability improved. Sales from continuing Dennison office products businesses increased. Profitability increased due to restructuring programs as well as to the discontinuation of unprofitable product lines. Avery and K&M brand products reported strong sales growth in the United States, as well as a gain in combined profitability during 1991. In the United Kingdom and France, sales and profitability of Avery and Dennison products declined due to weak economies in those countries. Sales for 1990 increased when compared to 1989 while profitability decreased. Sales of Avery- and K&M-brand office products increased in 1990 when compared to 1989 and sales from the Dennison stationery products businesses in France were also up significantly. Offsetting these increases, the Dennison stationery products business in the United States reported lower sales in 1990. Profitability declined sharply in the domestic Dennison stationery products business during 1990 owing to lower sales volume and continued competitive pressure on margins.

During 1991, the product identification and control systems businesses reported decreased sales. Excluding the impact of divestitures, discontinued products and changes in foreign currency, sales actually increased slightly when compared to 1990. Profitability was flat after adjusting for restructuring costs incurred in 1990 and the effects of the reduction of certain inventories accounted for on a LIFO basis in 1991. The U.S. industrial label businesses, which market both Avery- and Therimage-brand products, reported flat sales and decreased profitability due primarily to the continued slow U.S. economy. The international converting businesses reported increased sales and profitability compared to 1990. The tag, ticket and imprinting systems businesses were affected by the continued recession in the apparel and retail markets resulting in decreased sales and profitability in the Company's Soabar systems business in 1991. In 1990, the product identification and control systems businesses reported flat sales compared to 1989. Higher sales in the industrial label businesses in Europe in 1990 were offset by lower sales of the Soabar systems and Dennison data systems operations in the United States. Segment profits declined in 1990 due to restructuring charges as well as to lower volume in the Dennison data systems and fastener businesses. Also, a slowdown in the domestic retail department store market negatively impacted the Soabar businesses.

Financial Condition

Average working capital, excluding short-term debt, as a percent of sales was 16.9 percent in 1991, compared with 19.5 percent in 1990 and 18.5 percent in 1989. The 1991 and 1990 percentages exclude the net impact of the restructuring costs. The average number of days sales in receivables was 59 in 1991, compared with 62 in 1990 and 60 in 1989. The average inventory turnover rate was 6.4 in 1991, compared with 5.4 in 1990 and 5.5 in 1989.

SUMMARY

A pension plan is a contract between a company and its employees to provide benefits on their retirement. The plan may specify the amount of benefits to be received or the contributions to be made. Accounting for a pension plan requires that the current and future costs of the provided benefits be measured and allocated to the appropriate accounting periods.

A postretirement benefit plan, like a pension plan, is a deferred compensation arrangement in which future benefits are promised in exchange for current services provided. The largest component of these postretirement benefits is health care benefits.

A lease that is in substance a purchase should be recognized as an asset by a lessee. The liability for the payments on the lease should also be recognized. If the lease arrangement is not in substance a purchase, it should be accounted for as a rental with no recognition of the asset or liability.

Footnotes are an integral part of the financial statements. They provide information that is essential for developing an understanding of the information presented in the statements. The footnotes contain information on specific accounting methods or policies adopted by the company, details regarding account information, and information regarding commitments and contingencies. The auditors report indicates the scope of the auditors' investigation and their opinion regarding whether the financial statements are a fair presentation of the results of operations and the financial position of the company. Management's discussion and analysis aids users to form expectations about a company.

Interim financial reports provide information on a more timely basis than annual reports. Generally, the same principles and practices followed for the issuance of annual reports should also be used for interim reports.

Segmental reporting helps users of financial statements to make more informed decisions regarding diversified companies. Segment information provided includes revenues, operating profit or loss, and identifiable assets.

KEY DEFINITIONS

Accounting policies—the particular accounting methods adopted by a company in preparing its financial statements.

Accumulated postretirement benefit obligation—the obligation for future postretirement benefits to be paid.

Auditors report—the auditor's letter that indicates the scope of his or her audit and his or her opinion regarding the fair presentation of the financial statements.

Capital lease—a lease that is in substance a purchase of an asset; both the asset and liability are recognized on the financial statements.

Defined benefit pension plan—a plan that specifies the amount of pension benefits to be received during retirement.

Defined contribution pension plan—a plan that specifies the amount of the periodic contribution, but not the amount of benefits to be received.

Interest cost—a cost to reflect the increase in the pension or postretirement benefit obligation due to the passage of time.

Interim reports—the quarterly financial reports that are issued during the time period between the annual reports.

Lease—a contract between the owner of an asset (the lessor) and the user of the asset (the lessee).

Operating lease—a lease that is not in substance a purchase of an asset; the transaction is recorded as a rental.

Prior service cost—the increase in the pension obligation due to a plan amendment.

Projected benefit obligation—the company's obligation for all future pension benefits to be paid on retirement.

Qualified opinion—an audit opinion that has reservations regarding scope of the audit, uncertainties or going concern.

Return on plan assets—earnings on the pension or postretirement benefit fund used to satisfy the obligation.

Segment information—information presented in the footnotes to the financial statements regarding specific product lines and/or customers.

Service cost—the present value of the benefits earned by employees for the current period of service.

Vested benefits—benefits that employees have earned and will receive even if they leave the company.

QUESTIONS

1. What are actuarial assumptions?

2. What are the characteristics of a pension plan?

3. Differentiate between accounting for a defined benefit pension plan and a defined contribution pension plan.

4. If pension cost for the period does not equal the contribution made to the pension fund, to what account(s) is the difference recognized in a defined benefit plan?

5. What is the funded status of a pension or postretirement benefit plan?

6. What are the differences between pension plans and postretirement benefit plans?

7. How has the issuance of *FASB Statement No. 106* changed the accounting requirements for postretirement benefits?

8. If a company rents a chain saw for two days, would this be considered a capital lease or an operating lease? Explain.

9. What are the criteria for determining whether a lease is a capital lease or an operating lease?

10. Why might a company want to classify a lease as an operating lease rather than a capital lease?

11. What are the differences on the financial statements between classifying a lease as a capital lease or an operating lease?

12. What disclosures and reports, besides financial statements, are large businesses (such as large publicly held corporations) required to prepare or publish?

13. Describe the accounting policies section of footnotes found in financial statements.

14. Why are accounting policies required to be disclosed?

15. What kind of information should be included in the footnotes to the financial statements?

16. List some topics commonly covered in the footnotes to the financial statements.

17. Is the management of a firm responsible for preparing the auditor's report on that firm's financial statements?

18. What kinds of opinions may an auditor express in an auditor's report regarding the fairness of a firm's financial statements?

19. Of what use is the auditor's report to the financial statement user?

20. How does an interim financial report differ from the annual financial report?

21. Why do the major stock exchanges require corporations listed on those exchanges to publish interim financial statements?

22. What limitations exist to the preparation and use of interim financial statements?

23. Define the term business segment.

24. Of what benefit is it to a financial statement user to be provided with financial reports that separately report business segment activities for diversified businesses?

25. Providing financial data for segments of a business is more complex than providing data for the whole business. List some additional accounting problems associated with segment reporting.

EXERCISES

26. The following information is available for Andujar Company's defined benefit pension plan:

Amortization of prior service cost	$ 3,000
Contribution to pension fund	13,000
Interest cost	11,000
Return on plan assets	7,000
Service cost	8,000

Required:

1. Compute pension cost.
2. Prepare the journal entry to record pension cost.

27. The following information is available for Bagwell Incorporated's defined benefit pension plan:

    Fair value of plan asses $43,000
    Projected benefit obligation 68,000
    Unrecognized prior service cost 22,000

Required:

Compute the prepaid pension cost or pension liability recognized on the balance sheet.

28. On January 1, 19x1, Swindell Company leases a machine for four years at an annual rental of $10,000. Each payment is due at the end of the year. The company can borrow money at a rate of 8 percent. The present value of the four payments is $33,121. The machine has a six-year life and no salvage value.

Required:

1. Prepare the journal entries for 19x1 assuming the transaction is considered a capital lease.
2. Prepare the journal entries for 19x1 assuming the transaction is considered an operating lease.

29. Drabek Company has the following information available for the first two quarters of 19x1:

	First	Second
Sales	$44,000	$74,000
Cost of goods sold	25,000	43,000
Selling and general expenses	12,000	13,000
Estimated tax rate	15%	20%

Required:

Prepare an income statement for the first quarter and for the second quarter.

30. Caminiti Company has the following information available concerning its business segments:

Segment	Revenue	Operating Profit (loss)	Identifiable Assets
Food	$ 78,000	$ 5,000	$ 50,000
Hardware	16,000	(3,000)	4,000
Motels	81,000	22,000	27,000
Tires	13,000	1,000	9,000
Watches	92,000	29,000	8,000

Required:

Determine which segments should be classified as reportable segments.

Refer to the Annual Report included in the front of the text.

31. What is the service cost component of pension expense for the most recent year?

32. What is the interest cost component of pension expense for the most recent year?

33. What is the funded status of the pension plan for the most recent year?

34. What is the postretirement benefit expense for the most recent year?

35. What is the postretirement benefit liability at the end of the most recent year?

36. What are the future minimum commitments for capital leases?

37. What is the present value of the future minimum commitments for capital leases?

38. What are the future minimum commitments for operating leases?

39. From Management's Analysis–Results of Operations:

    a. By how much did net sales increase or decrease in the most recent year?
    b. International sales represented what percentage of total sales in the most recent year?
    c. Why did cost of sales as a percentage of net sales increase or decrease in the most recent year?
    d. Why did interest expense increase or decrease in the most recent year?

40. From Management's Analysis–Financial Condition:

    a. By how much did inventories increase or decrease in the most recent year and why?
    b. What was capital spending in the most recent year?
    c. By how much did other liabilities increase or decrease in the most recent year and why?
    d. What was the increase or decrease in stockholders' equity in the most recent year?

41. What are PepsiCo's industry segments?

42. Give an example for each of PepsiCo's industry segments.

43. Which segment had the largest operating profit in the most recent year?

44. Outside of the United Sates, in what geographic area are operating profits the largest for the most recent year?

45. In which quarter in the most recent year are net sales the largest?

46. In which quarter in the most recent year is the provision for income taxes the largest?

Index

—A—

Accelerated depreciation, 5-9 to 5-14
Account, 3-1 to 3-4
Accountancy as a profession, 1-25 to 1-26
Accounting as a process of communication, 1-3
Accounting,
 cycle, 3-5
 defined, 1-1
 ethical issues, 3-45 to 3-47
 financial, 1-4
 managerial, 1-4
 opportunities in, 1-25 to 1-26
 standard-setting process, 1-23 to 1-25
Accounting changes,
 in estimate, 7-22
 in principle, 7-21 to 7-22
Accounting equation, 2-9
Accounting errors, 7-20
Accounting for cost of goods sold, 4-2
Accounting for merchandising operations,
 4-2 to 4-7, 4-9 to 4-11
Accounting for oil and gas, 5-29 to 5-30
Accounting for tangible fixed assets, 5-2 to 5-4

Accounting policies, 14-11 to 14-12
Accounting Principles Board (APB), 1-19 to 1-20
Accounting standard-setting process, 1-23 to 1-25
Accounting system, 3-44 to 3-45
Accounting vs. bookkeeping, 1-4
Accounts payable, 2-5, 8-26
Accounts receivable,
 defined, 2-3, 8-15
 subsidiary ledger, 3-38 to 3-43, 8-15 to 8-17
 turnover, 10-14 to 10-15
Accrual basis, 3-12
Accrued expenses, 3-24 to 3-25
Accrued revenues, 3-27
Accumulated depreciation, 3-25 to 3-26
Accumulated postretirement benefit obligation,
 14-6
Acid-test ratio, 10-13 to 10-14
Additional paid-in capital, 7-11 to 7-12
Adjusted gross income, 12-4 to 12-6
Adjusting entries, 3-12 to 3-14, 3-21 to 3-27
Admission of a partner, 6-11 to 6-15
Adverse opinion, 14-20
After-closing trial balance, 3-19 to 3-20
All financial resources concept, 11-3 to 11-4

I-1

Allocation of taxes, 12-10 to 12-13, 12-22 to 12-25
Allowance for bad debts, 8-17 to 8-24
American Accounting Association (AAA), 1-23
American Institute of Certified Public Accountants (AICPA), 1-18 to 1-19
Amortization,
   intangible assets, 5-31 to 5-32
   natural resources, 5-28 to 5-29
   premium or discount on bonds payable, 9-6 to 9-9
   premium or discount on investment in bonds, 9-14 to 9-15, 9-73 to 9-76
Analysis for common stockholders, 10-7 to 10-11
Analysis for long-term creditors, 10-11 to 10-12
Analysis for short-term creditors, 10-12 to 10-16
Analysis of accounts receivable, 10-14 to 10-15
Analysis of inventories, 10-15 to 10-16
Analysis of other disclosures, 14-10 to 14-31
Annuity, 9-69 to 9-71
Appropriation of retained earnings, 7-33 to 7-34, 9-11
Articles of incorporation, 7-4
Assets,
   cash, 2-3
   current, 2-3
   defined, 1-14, 2-1 to 2-2
   fixed, 2-4
   inventories, 2-4
   marketable securities, 2-3
   other, 2-4
   prepaid expenses, 2-4
   receivables, 2-3 to 2-4
Audit trail, 3-47 to 3-48
Auditor's opinion, 14-18 to 14-20
Auditor's report, 3-28, 14-18 to 14-20
Automated accounting systems, forms of, 3-48 to 3-50
Average cost method, inventory, 4-18
Average number of days to collect receivables, 10-15

—B—

Bad debts, 8-17 to 8-24
   as percentage of receivables, 8-21 to 8-23
   as percentage of sales, 8-19 to 8-21
   balance sheet presentation, 8-23
   estimating expense, 8-17 to 8-23
   recovered, 8-24
   write-off, 8-23 to 8-24

Balance sheet, 1-16, 2-1 to 2-2, 2-6 to 2-7
Balance sheet classifications, 2-2 to 2-5
Bank reconciliation statement, 8-6 to 8-11
Basic accounting principles,
   comparability, 1-8
   conservatism, 1-12 to 1-13
   consistency concept, 1-8 to 1-9
   entity assumption, 1-10
   full disclosure concept, 1-13
   going-concern concept, 1-10
   historical cost concept, 1-11
   matching concept, 1-11 1-12
   materiality concept, 1-9
   monetary unit assumption, 1-10
   revenue realization, 1-12
   stable dollar assumption, 1-10 1-11
   time period assumption, 1-11
   underlying assumptions and concepts, 1-10 to 1-13
Basic analytical procedures, for financial analysis, 10-2 to 10-6
Benefits and costs, 1-6
Bonds,
   investments in, 9-13 to 9-16
Bonds payable,
   balance sheet presentation, 9-11 to 9-12
   callable, 9-10
   classes of, 9-3
   convertible, 9-9 to 9-10
   defined, 9-2
   determining price of, 9-71 to 9-73
   discount, 9-6 to 9-8, 9-75 to 9-76
   interest method of amortization, 9-73 to 9-76
   issuance of, 9-3 to 9-10
   issued between interest dates, 9-5 to 9-6
   premium, 9-8 to 9-9, 9-74 to 9-75
   retirement, 9-10 to 9-11
   straight-line method of amortization, 9-7 to 9-9
Bond sinking fund, 9-11
Book value per share of common stock, 7-35 to 7-36
Bookkeeping, 1-4
Buildings, 5-4

—C—

Callable bonds, 9-10
Capital,
   accounts,
      partners, 6-5 to 6-11
   additional paid-in, 7-11 to 7-12
Capital budgeting,

MACRS, 5-12 to 5-14
Capital gains and losses, 12-7
Capital lease, 14-8 to 14-10
Capital stock,
  common, 7-6 to 7-7
  issuance of, 7-11 to 7-13
  nature of, 7-5 to 7-6
  no-par value, 7-13
  par value, 7-10 to 7-13
  preferred, 7-7 to 7-9
  subscriptions, 7-13 to 7-14
Capitalization of interest, 5-18 to 5-19
Cash,
  controlling cash disbursements, 8-5
  controlling cash receipts, 8-2 to 8-5
  defined, 2-3, 8-1
  disbursements, 8-5
  financing activities, 11-4
  from operations, 11-4 to 11-10
    direct method, 11-5 to 11-8
    indirect method, 11-6 to 11-10
  importance of, 8-1
  internal control, 8-1 to 8-2
  investing activities, 11-4
  over and short, 8-5
  petty cash, 8-11 to 8-13
  receipts, 8-2 to 8-5
Cash disbursements,
  control of, 8-5
  journal, 3-41 to 3-42
Cash dividends, 7-25 to 7-26
Cash flow,
  (see Statement of cash flows)
Cash receipts,
  control of, 8-2 to 8-5
  journal, 3-39 to 3-41
Certified Public Accountant (CPA), 1-25
Change in accounting principle, 7-21 to 7-22, 14-14
Change in estimate, 7-22
Chart of accounts, 3-33, 3-35 to 3-36
Checks,
  Not Sufficient Funds (N.S.F.), 8-6 to 8-11
  outstanding, 8-6 to 8-11
Classes of taxpayers, 12-3 to 12-4
Closing entries, 3-15 to 3-19
Committee on accounting procedure, 1-19
Common-size statements, 10-5 to 10-6
Common stock, 7-6 to 7-7
Comparability, 1-8
Comparative financial statements, 3-27 to 3-28, 10-1 to 10-2
Comparison with standards, 10-7

Comprehensive income, 1-15
Computation of individual income tax, 12-7 to 12-8
Computer,
  hardware, 3-49
  software, 3-49 to 3-50
Conceptual framework, 1-4 to 1-9, 1-14 to 1-18
Conservatism, 1-12 to 1-13
Consistency, 1-8 to 1-9
Consolidated statements,
  balance sheet, 9-28 to 9-39
  income statement, 9-40
  minority interest, 9-33, 9-40 to 9-41
  pooling of interests, 9-36 to 9-39
  usefulness of, 9-39
Contingencies, 14-14 to 14-15
Contra account, 3-26
Contributed capital, 7-11 to 7-12
Control accounts, 3-37, 3-39, 3-41, 8-15 to 8-17
Convertible bonds, 9-9 to 9-10
Copyright, 5-31 to 5-32
Corporate income tax, 12-7 to 12-8
Corporate officers, 7-2
Corporation,
  articles of incorporation, 7-4
  capital of, 7-5
  characteristics, 7-1 to 7-4
  defined, 7-1
  formation, 7-4 to 7-5
  income taxes, 12-7 to 12-8
  nature of capital stock, 7-5 to 7-6
  rights of stockholders, 7-6 to 7-9
Cost Accounting Standards Board (CASB), 1-23
Cost flow assumptions,
  average cost, 4-18
  FIFO, 4-19
  LIFO, 4-19 to 4-20
Cost of goods sold, 4-2, 4-4 to 4-5
Cost of merchandise purchased, 4-2 to 4-3
Coupon rate, 9-3 to 9-4
Credit (Cr.), 3-2 to 3-4
Credit memorandum, 8-7
Credits (tax), 12-6 to 12-7
Criteria for capitalizing leases, 14-8
Cumulative preference, 7-7 to 7-8
Current assets, 2-3
Current liabilities, 2-5, 8-24 to 8-26
Current ratio, 10-12 to 10-13

—D—

Dates,
   for dividends, 7-25
Debenture bonds,
Debit (Dr.), 3-2 to 3-4
Debit memorandum, 8-7
Debt-to-equity ratio, 10-11
Debt securities held to maturity, 9-84 to 9-85
Decision usefulness, 1-6 to 1-7
Declaration,
   date of, 7-25
Deductions for adjusted gross income, 12-4
Deductions from adjusted gross income, 12-6
Deferred taxes, 12-10 to 12-11
Defined benefit pension plan, 14-2 to 14-4
Defined contribution pension plan, 14-2 to 14-3
Depletion, 5-27 to 5-30
Depletion base, 5-28
Deposit in transit, 8-6 to 8-11
Depreciation, 5-4 to 5-14
   accelerated methods, 5-9 to 5-14
   adjusting entry, 3-25 to 3-26
   double-declining balance, 5-10 to 5-11
   methods, 5-8 to 5-14
   Modified Accelerated Cost Recovery System
     (MACRS), 5-12 to 5-14
   on assets acquired during a period, 5-17 to 5-18
   salvage value, 5-8 to 5-12
   straight-line, 5-9
   sum-of-the-years'-digits, 5-11 to 5-12
   useful life, 5-7
Determining reportable industry segments,
   14-26 to 14-28
Differences between accounting and taxable
   income, 12-9 to 12-13
   permanent, 12-9
   temporary, 12-9 to 12-10
Differences in accounting standards,
   13-14 to 13-15
Disclosure techniques, 3-28
Disclosures on fair value, 9-26 to 9-27
Discontinued operations, 7-18 to 7-19
Discount,
   on bonds, 9-6 to 9-8, 9-75 to 9-76
   purchase, 4-12 to 4-14
   rate, 8-32
Discounted notes payable, 8-30 to 8-31
Discounting notes receivable, 8-31 to 8-34
Discounts lost account, 4-13 to 4-14
Dishonored note, 8-29 to 8-30
Distributions to owners, 1-15
Dividends, 7-24 to 7-29
   cash, 7-25 to 7-26
   date of declaration, 7-25
   date of payment, 7-25
   date of record, 7-25
   stock, 7-26 to 7-29
Double-declining balance depreciation, 5-10 to 5-1
Double-entry, 2-1 to 2-2
Double taxation, 12-3
Drawing account, 3-7

—E—

Earnings per share, 7-22 to 7-24, 10-9 to 10-10
Elements of financial statements, 1-14 to 1-15
Entity assumption, 1-10
Equity, 1-14, 2-2
Equity method for investment in stocks,
   9-24 to 9-27
Errors,
   correction of, 7-20
Estimates,
   changes in, 7-22
Estimated tax, 12-7
Estimating bad debts,
   percentage of receivables, 8-21 to 8-23
   percentage of sales, 8-19 to 8-21
Ethical issues in accounting, 3-45 to 3-47
Exemptions, 12-6
Exchange rate, 13-2 to 13-6
Expenses, 1-15, 2-7
   recognition, 1-17 to 1-18
Extraordinary items, 7-16 to 7-18

—F—

Face value on bonds payable, 9-4 to 9-5
Federal income tax, 12-2 to 12-3
Federal unemployment tax, 8-35
Feedback value, 1-7
Fidelity, 1-3
Financial accounting,
   compared to managerial, 1-4
   defined, 1-4
   process, 2-8 to 2-20
Financial Accounting Standards Board
   (FASB), 1-20 to 1-22, 1-24
Financial reporting, 1-4 to 1-6
   objectives, 1-4 to 1-6
Financial statement analysis, 10-1 to 10-16
   interpretation of analyses, 10-16

Financial statements, 3-19 to 3-21
Financing activities, 11-4
First-in, first-out (FIFO), 4-19
Fixed assets, 2-4
    (*see* Long-term assets)
F.O.B., 4-15
Footnote disclosure, 14-12, 14-14 to 14-18
    changes in accounting principles, 14-14
    contingencies, 14-14 to 14-15
    description of liabilities, 14-15
    information regarding stockholder's equity, 14-15
    long-term commitments, 14-16
    significant accounting policies, 14-12 to 14-13
    subsequent events, 14-17 to 14-18
Foreign currency, 13-1 to 13-14
Foreign currency transactions, 13-2 to 13-10
Foreign currency translation, 13-10 to 13-14
Formation of a corporation, 7-4 to 7-5
Formation of a partnership, 6-5 to 6-6
Forward exchange and spot markets, 13-3 to 13-6
Freight-in, 4-14 to 4-16
Full disclosure concept, 1-13

—G—

Gains, 1-15
    extraordinary, 7-16 to 7-18
General journal, 3-36 to 3-37
General journal entries, 3-4 to 3-9
General ledger, 3-36 to 3-37
Generally Accepted Accounting Principles, 1-18
Going-concern concept, 1-10
Goodwill, 5-31 to 5-33, 6-13 to 6-14, 6-16
Governmental Accounting Standards Board, 1-21, 1-23
Gross income, 12-4
Gross profit method,
    inventory, 4-23 to 4-24
Gross profit percentage, 4-23 to 4-24

—H—

Harmonize accounting standards, 13-14 to 13-15
Hedging foreign currency, 13-9 to 13-10
Historical cost, 1-11
Horizontal analysis, 10-2 to 10-5

—I—

Import-export transactions, 13-6 to 13-9
Importance of cash flows, 11-1 to 11-2
Income statement, 2-7 to 2-8
Income statement classifications, 2-8
Income summary account, 3-15 to 3-19
Income taxes,
    classes of taxpayers, 12-3 to 12-4
    corporation, 12-7 to 12-8
    credits, 12-6 to 12-7
    defined, 12-1
    federal, 12-2 to 12-3
    individual, 12-4 to 12-7
    interperiod allocation of, 12-10 to 12-12
    intraperiod allocation of, 12-12 to 12-13
    management decisions, 12-13
    sources of differences between accounting and taxable income, 12-9 to 12-10
    withholding, 8-36, 12-7
Individual income tax, 12-4 to 12-7
Influences on accounting principles, 1-18 to 1-23
    Accounting Principles Board, 1-19 to 1-20
    American Accounting Association, 1-23
    American Institute of Certified Public Accountants, 1-18 to 1-19
    Committee on Accounting Procedure, 1-19
    Congress, 1-23
    Cost Accounting Standards Board, 1-23
    Financial Accounting Standards Board, 1-20 to 1-22
    Governmental Accounting Standards Board, 1-21, 1-23
    Institute of Management Accountants, 1-21
    Internal Revenue Service, 1-21
    Securities and Exchange Commission, 1-21
Institute of Management Accountants, 1-21
Intangible assets, 5-31 to 5-33
Intercompany sales, 9-41, 9-43
Intercorporate investments,
    consolidated statements for, 9-27 to 9-43
    equity method, 9-24 to 9-27
    lower-of-cost-or-market method, 9-19 to 9-24
Interest,
    calculation, 9-67 to 9-68
    compounded, 9-67 to 9-68
    costs (fixed assets), 5-18 to 5-19
    number of times earned, 10-11 to 10-12
Interest method of amortization, 9-73 to 9-76
Interim reporting, 14-20, 14-22 to 14-25
Internal accounting control, 3-44 to 3-45
Internal Revenue Service (IRS), 1-21

International Accounting Standards Committee, 13-15
International aspects, 1-24 to 1-25, 13-1 to 13-16
International Organization of Secutities Commissions, 13-15
Interperiod tax allocation, 12-10 to 12-12
Intraperiod tax allocation, 12-12 to 12-13
Inventory,
   accounting objective, 4-7 to 4-8
   basis of accounting, 4-12
   cost flow methods, 4-17 to 4-21
   cost of, 4-8 to 4-9
   defined, 2-4
   discounts, 4-12 to 4-14
   losses, 4-11
   lower-of-cost-or-market, 4-21 to 4-23
   objective of inventory accounting, 4-7 to 4-8
   periodic and perpetual, 4-2, 4-9 to 4-11
   purchase discounts, 4-12 to 4-14
   returns and allowances, 4-15 to 4-16
   turnover ratio, 10-15 to 10-16
Inventory cost flow methods, 4-17 to 4-21
   average cost, 4-18
   differences in methods, 4-21
   FIFO, 4-19
   gross profit method, 4-23 to 4-24
   LIFO, 4-19 to 4-20
   retail method, 4-25
Investing activities, 11-4
Investment in bonds,
   amortization of premium and discount, 9-14 to 9-15
   purchase, 9-13 to 9-14
   sale of bonds, 9-15 to 9-16
Investment in stock, 9-16 to 9-27
   equity method, 9-24 to 9-27
   long-term investments, 9-19 to 9-27
   lower-of-cost-or-market method, 9-19 to 9-24
   temporary investments, 9-16 to 9-19
Investments by owners, 1-15
Issuance of bonds, 9-3 to 9-10
Issuance of par value stock, 7-10 to 7-13
Itemized deductions, 12-5 to 12-6

—J—

Journal,
   cash disbursements, 3-41 to 3-42
   cash receipts, 3-39 to 3-41
   entry, 3-4 to 3-9
   form of special journals, 3-43

   payroll, 3-41 to 3-42
   purchases, 3-42 to 3-43
   sales, 3-39 to 3-40
   special, 3-38 to 3-43
Journal entry,
   defined, 3-4
Journalizing, 3-4 to 3-9

—L—

Land, 5-4
Last-in, first-out (LIFO), 4-19 to 4-20
Leases, 14-6 to 14-10
Ledger, 3-9 to 3-11
Legal capital, 7-10 to 7-11
Liabilities, 2-4 to 2-5
   accounts payable, 2-5
   current, 2-5
   defined, 1-14, 2-2, 8-24
   long-term, 2-5
   notes payable, 2-5
   taxes payable, 2-5
   unearned revenues, 2-5
Liquidation of a partnership, 6-17 to 6-20
Long-term assets,
   acquired during the period, 5-17 to 5-18
   capital expenditures, 5-20 to 5-21
   control over, 5-2
   cost of, 5-2 to 5-4
   costs incurred after acquisition, 5-20 to 5-21
   defined, 2-4
   depreciation methods, 5-8 to 5-14
   disclosure in the financial statements, 5-19 to 5-20
   disposition of, 5-22 to 5-24
   intangible, 5-30 to 5-33
   interest costs, 5-18 to 5-19
   natural resources, 5-27 to 5-30
   recording, 5-14 to 5-20
   revenue expenditures, 5-20 to 5-21
   tangible, 5-2 to 5-30
   trade-ins, 5-24 to 5-27
   types of, 5-2
Long-term commitments, 14-16
Long-term investments,
   bonds, 9-13 to 9-16
   stock, 9-19 to 9-27
Long-term liabilities, 2-5, 9-1 to 9-12
Losses, 1-15
   extraordinary, 7-16 to 7-18
   inventory, 4-11

Lower-of-cost-or-market method,
    inventories, 4-21 to 4-23
    temporary investments, 9-17 to 9-19

—M—

Machinery and equipment, 5-4
Management's discussion and analysis, 14-28, 14-31 to 14-39
Managerial accounting,
    compared to financial, 1-4
    defined, 1-4
Mark to market, 9-83 to 9-86
Marketable securities, 2-3, 9-12 to 9-13, 9-16 to 9-19
Matching concept, 1-11 to 1-12
Materiality, 1-9
Minority interest, 9-33, 9-40 to 9-41
Model of a financial accounting system, 3-33 to 3-48
Modified Accelerated Cost Recovery System (MACRS), 5-12 to 5-14
Monetary unit assumption, 1-10

—N—

Nature of earnings, 7-16
Natural resources, 5-27 to 5-30
Net income, 2-7
Neutrality, 1-8
No-par value stock, 7-13
Notes payable,
    accrual of interest, 8-28
    discounting, 8-31 to 8-34
    issuance, 8-27 to 8-28
    issued at a discount, 8-30 to 8-31
    payment, 8-28 to 8-29
Notes receivable,
    accrual of interest, 8-28
    calculation of interest, 8-28
    defined, 8-26 to 8-27
    discounting, 8-31 to 8-34
    dishonored, 8-29 to 8-30
    issuance, 8-27 to 8-28
    issued at a discount, 8-30 to 8-31
    payment, 8-28 to 8-29
N.S.F. (Not Sufficient Funds) check, 8-6 to 8-11
Number of times interest earned, 10-11 to 10-12

—O—

Objective of financial reporting, 1-4 to 1-6
Objective of inventory accounting, 4-7 to 4-8
Oil and gas accounting, 5-29 to 5-30
Operating activities, 11-4 to 11-10
Operating lease, 14-8 to 14-10
Opinion, 14-18 to 14-20
Opportunities in accounting, 1-25 to 1-26
Organization costs, 5-31 to 5-33, 7-4 to 7-5
Other assets, 2-4
Other postretirement benefits, 14-4, 14-6 to 14-7
Outstanding checks, 8-6 to 8-11
Over-the-counter sales, 8-3
Owners' equity,
    appropriated retained earnings, 7-33 to 7-34, 9-11
    defined, 2-5
    retained earnings, 7-15, 7-32 to 7-35
    statement of capital, 2-19 to 2-20

—P—

Paid-in capital, 7-11 to 7-12
Par value, 7-10 to 7-11
Parent corporation, 9-27 to 9-28
Participating preference, 7-8 to 7-9
Partnership, 6-2 to 6-20
    accounting for, 6-5
    admission of a partner, 6-11 to 6-15
    advantages, 6-4
    agreement, 6-3
    charactertistics, 6-3 to 6-4
    defined, 6-2 to 6-3
    division of earnings, 6-6 to 6-10
    financial statements, 6-10 to 6-11
    formation, 6-5 to 6-6
    liquidation, 6-17 to 6-20
    statement of partners' capital, 6-11
    withdrawal of a partner, 6-15 to 6-17
Patents, 5-31 to 5-33
Payables,
    accounts payable, 8-26
    classification, 8-14
    current, 8-14
    notes receivable and payable, 8-26 to 8-34
Payroll accounting, 8-35 to 8-37
Payroll journal, 3-41 to 3-42
Pension cost, 14-3
Pensions, 14-2 to 14-5
Periodic inventory procedure, 4-2, 4-9 to 4-11

Permanent account, 3-3
Permanent differences, 12-9
Perpetual inventory method, 4-2, 4-9 to 4-11
Personal exemption, 12-6
Petty cash, 8-11 to 8-13
Plant and equipment
 (see Long-term assets)
Pooling of interests method, 9-36 to 9-39
Posting, 3-4, 3-9 to 3-11, 3-14
Postretirement benefits, 14-4, 14-6 to 14-7
Predictive and feedback value, 1-7
Preemptive right, 7-6 to 7-7
Preferred stock, 7-6 to 7-9
Premium on bonds, 9-8 to 9-9, 9-74 to 9-75
Prepaid expenses, 2-4, 3-22 to 3-24
Present value,
 approach, 9-67 to 9-68
 bonds payable, 9-71 to 9-76
 of an annuity, 9-69 to 9-71
 of a future sum, 9-68 to 9-69
 tables, 9-77 to 9-80
Price-earnings ratio, 10-10
Prior period adjustments, 7-19 to 7-20
Prior service cost, 14-4
Profit on intercompany sales, 9-41, 9-43
Projected benefit obligation, 14-3
Proprietorship, 6-1 to 6-2
Proving the control accounts, 3-44
Purchases,
 accounting for, 4-2 to 4-3, 4-9 to 4-16
 discounts, 4-12 to 4-14
 journal, 3-42 to 3-43
 returns and allowances, 4-15 to 4-16

—Q—

Qualified opinion, 14-20
Qualitative characteristics of accounting
 information, 1-6 to 1-9
  benefits and costs, 1-6
  comparability, 1-8
  consistency, 1-8 to 1-9
  decision usefulness, 1-6 to 1-7
  feedback value, 1-7
  materiality, 1-9
  neutrality, 1-8
  predictive value, 1-7
  relevance, 1-7
  reliability, 1-7
  representational faithfulness, 1-8
  timeliness, 1-7

understandability, 1-6
verifiability, 1-7
Quick ratio, 10-13 to 10-14

—R—

Rate of return (RR),
 on stockholders' equity, 10-8 to 10-9
 on total assets, 10-8
Ratio,
 acid test (quick), 10-13 to 10-14
 current, 10-12 to 10-13
 debt-to-equity, 10-11
 price-earnings, 10-10
Ratio analysis, 10-6 to 10-7
Receivables,
 accounting for, 8-15 to 8-17
 classification, 8-14
 control, 8-14 to 8-15
 defined, 2-3 to 2-4
 notes, 8-26 to 8-34
 statement presentation, 8-34 to 8-35
 turnover, 10-14 to 10-15
 uncollectible, 8-17 to 8-24
 (see Bad debts)
Reciprocal accounts, 9-35 to 9-36
Recognition and measurement in financial
 statements of business enterprises, 1-16 to 1-18
Recognition of expenses, 1-17 to 1-18
Reconciling bank statements with cash account
 balances, 8-6 to 8-11
Record,
 date of, 7-25
Recovery (bad debts), 8-24
Registered bonds, 9-3
Relevance, 1-7
Reliability, 1-7
Reporting for segments of a business,
 14-25 to 14-30
Representational faithfulness, 1-8
Research and development, 5-33
Restriction on dividends, 9-11
Retail method, 4-25
Retailing operations,
 accounting for, 4-1 to 4-25
Retained earnings, 7-15, 7-32 to 7-35
 appropriation, 7-33 to 7-34, 9-11
 statement, 7-34 to 7-35
Returns (inventory), 4-14 to 4-16
Revenue realization, 1-12
Revenue recognition, 1-17

Revenues, 1-15, 2-7
Rights of stockholders, 7-6 to 7-9
Role of the accountant, 1-4
Role of financial statements, 1-16 to 1-17

—S—

S Corporations, 12-3
Sales,
    discount, 4-12 to 4-13
    journal, 3-39 to 3-40
    merchandise, 4-3
    returns and allowances, 4-14 to 4-16
Salvage value, 5-8 to 5-12
Scope of the audit, 14-18
Securities,
    available for sale, 9-84 to 9-86
    equity basis, 9-24 to 9-27
    long-term investments in, 9-19 to 9-27
    lower-of-cost-or-market basis, 9-16 to 9-24
    marketable, 2-3, 9-16 to 9-19
Securities and Exchange Commission (SEC), 1-21, 1-24
Segment data, 14-25 to 14-30
Significance, 1-3
Significant accounting policies, 14-12 to 14-13
Social security taxes, 8-35
Sole proprietorship, 6-1 to 6-2
Special journals, 3-37 to 3-43
Spot and forward exchange markets, 13-3 to 13-6
Stable dollar assumption, 1-10 to 1-11
Standardize accounting standards, 13-14 to 13-15
State unemployment tax, 8-35 to 8-36
Statement of capital, 2-19 to 2-20
Statement of cash flows, 1-16, 2-8, 2-18, 11-1 to 11-24
    basic objectives, 11-1 to 11-2
    non-cash transactions, 11-3 to 11-4
    preparation of, 11-10 to 11-12
    worksheet approach, 11-16 to 11-21
Statement of comprehensive income, 1-16
Statement of distributions to owners, 1-16
Statement of earnings, 1-16
Statement of Financial Accounting Concepts (SFAC), 1-5 to 1-9, 1-12, 1-14 to 1-18
Statement of financial position, 1-16
    (see Balance sheet)
Statement of investments by owners, 1-16
Statement of retained earnings, 7-34 to 7-35
Stock dividends, 7-26 to 7-29
Stock issuance costs, 7-10

Stock splits, 7-29
Stock subscribed account, 7-14
Stockholders, 7-6 to 7-9
    information regarding equity, 14-15
Stockholders' equity in the balance sheet, 7-14 to 7-15
Straight-line method,
    amortization of discount and premium, 9-7 to 9-9
    amortization of intangible assets, 5-31 to 5-32
    depreciation, 5-9
Subscriptions to capital stock, 7-13 to 7-14
Subsequent events, 14-17 to 14-18
Subsidiary,
    accounts, 3-37, 8-15 to 8-17
    corporation, 9-27 to 9-28
    ledger, 3-37
Sum-of-the-years'-digits depreciation, 5-11 to 5-12

—T—

T-account, 3-2
Tangible assets, 5-2 to 5-30
Tax allocation,
    (see Income taxes)
Taxable income, 12-1
Temporary accounts, 3-3, 3-15
Temporary differences in income tax allocation, 12-9 to 12-10
Temporary investments, 2-3, 9-16 to 9-19
Time period assumption, 1-11
Timeliness, 1-7
Trade-ins,
    accounting for, 5-24 to 5-27
Trading securities, 9-84 to 9-85
Transaction, 2-9
Transaction analysis, 2-9 to 2-18
Treasury stock,
    acquisition and reissuance of, 7-29 to 7-32
    in statement of financial position, 7-31
Trial balance, 3-11 to 3-12
    after adjustment, 3-14 to 3-15
    after-closing, 3-19 to 3-20
True cash balance, 8-7
Turnover,
    of accounts receivable, 10-14 to 10-15
    of inventory, 10-15 to 10-16

—U—

Uncollectible accounts, 8-17 to 8-24
Understandability, 1-6
Unearned revenue, 2-5, 3-26 to 3-27
Uniformity of accounting principles, 13-14 to 13-15
Unqualified opinion, 14-19 to 14-20
Useful life, 5-7

—V—

Verifiability, 1-7
Vertical analysis, 10-5
Vested and nonvested pension beneftis, 14-2

—W—

Withdrawal of a partner, 6-15 to 6-17
Withdrawals, 3-7
Withholding tax, 12-7
Working capital, 10-12
Write-off (bad debts), 8-23 to 8-24